Teaching Beautiful Brilliant Black Girls

DEDICATION

From Dr. Omobolade Delano-Oriaran—*To my Creator, who positions me to always give thanks in everything; my mother, Chief Ebunoluwa Delano, who taught me to advocate for Black Girls and women; my father, Justice Isaac Babatunde Delano, who passed away while I was working on this book; my daughter, brilliant Oluwafeyikemi Delano-Oriaran, who radiates Black Girl excellence; my lifetime partner, Philips Oriaran for your unwavering support; and my family for your endless love. To you all, modupe, ese adupe.*

From Dr. Marguerite W. Penick—*To all the women in my life, those before me, those with me now, and those still to come, especially my wonderful daughters, granddaughters, and the remarkable women of this editorial team.*

From Dr. Shemariah J. Arki—*To my maternal ancestors, the names I know— Grandma Jewel Leitha Casey and Cousin Lessie Casey—and to all the ones I have not had the pleasure of meeting in this lifetime: I am because you are. My work is a voice for the treacherous yet beautiful lives you endured for me. Thank you*

From Dr. Ali Michael—*To Chonika, Keisha, Valerie, Celine, and Gwen. Thank you for welcoming me into a team where I got to witness and bask in Black excellence through the sharing of our lives and research. Our work helped me examine my own role in misreading Black children—and learn how to help other white teachers do the same.*

From Ms. Orinthia Swindell—*To my mother Ms. Edna for setting a wonderful example of what it means to be a Black woman.*

From Dr. Eddie Moore, Jr.—*This book is dedicated to my family (Aniya, Jaxsen, and Laura) for their never-ending support.*

Teaching Beautiful Brilliant Black Girls

Omobolade Delano-Oriaran

Marguerite W. Penick

Shemariah J. Arki

Ali Michael

Orinthia Swindell

Eddie Moore Jr.

FOR INFORMATION:

Corwin
A SAGE Company
2455 Teller Road
Thousand Oaks, California 91320
(800) 233-9936
www.corwin.com

SAGE Publications Ltd.
1 Oliver's Yard
55 City Road
London EC1Y 1SP
United Kingdom

SAGE Publications India Pvt. Ltd.
B 1/I 1 Mohan Cooperative Industrial Area
Mathura Road, New Delhi 110 044
India

SAGE Publications Asia-Pacific Pte. Ltd.
18 Cross Street #10-10/11/12
China Square Central
Singapore 048423

Publisher: Dan Alpert
Senior Content
   Development Editor: Lucas Schleicher
Associate Content
   Development Editor: Mia Rodriguez
Production Editor: Megha Negi
Copy Editor: Cate Huisman
Typesetter: C&M Digitals (P) Ltd.
Proofreader: Eleni Maria Georgiou
Indexer: Integra
Cover Designer: Candice Harman
Cover Design Concept: Omobolade Delano-Oriaran
                and Marguerite W. Penick
Marketing Manager: Sharon Pendergast and
                Maura Sullivan

Library of Congress Cataloging-in-Publication Data

Names: Delano-Oriaran, Omobolade, author.
Title: Teaching beautiful brilliant black girls / Omobolade (Bola) Delano-Oriaran [and five others].
Description: Thousand Oaks, California : Corwin, [2021] | Includes bibliographical references and index.
Identifiers: LCCN 2020054401 | ISBN 9781544376998 (paperback) | ISBN 9781544394404 (epub) | ISBN 9781544394411 (epub) | ISBN 9781544394428 (pdf)
Subjects: LCSH: African American girls—Education. | African American girls—Social conditions. | Culturally relevant pedagogy—United States. | Gifted education—United States.
Classification: LCC LC2717 .D45 2021 | DDC 371.829/96073—dc23
LC record available at https://lccn.loc.gov/2020054401

This book is printed on acid-free paper.

SUSTAINABLE
FORESTRY
INITIATIVE
Certified Chain of Custody
Promoting Sustainable Forestry
www.sfiprogram.org
SFI-01268

21 22 23 24 25 10 9 8 7 6 5 4 3 2 1

Contents

RESPECTING

Note From the Publisher

The authors have provided access to video content made available to you through QR codes. To read a QR code, you must have a smartphone or tablet with a camera. We recommend that you download a QR code reader app that is made specifically for your phone or tablet brand. You may also access the videos at **https://resources.corwin.com/TBBBG**

Foreword

Bettina L. Love

University of Georgia

Loving, affirming, respecting, centering, connecting, uplifting, and understanding Black girls is more than just a teaching approach or a "best practice" method for your teaching tool kit; it is a form of liberation for humanity to reach toward unconditional love and loving "blackness as an act of political resistance" (hooks, 1990, p. 20). When we love and affirm Black girls, we love and affirm all humanity. This freedom is not just for Black girls, but for educators to be fully human in the classroom. The Black feminists of the Combahee River Collective said it best: "If Black women were free, it would mean that everyone else would have to be free since our freedom would necessitate the destruction of all the systems of oppression" (1974). Black girls walking into schools filled with teachers who love them, who see them as brilliant learners, and who possess a wealth of knowledge that uplifts the school, the community, and society means freedom for everyone.

A teacher, especially a White woman teacher, who approaches life with the idea that Black girls are essential to her own life and freedom, will teach with a love for humanity that will liberate all students. This type of life practice requires a roadmap to reflect one's own ideas, views, and actions to become a teacher committed to radical intersectional justice. *Teaching Brilliant and Beautiful Black Girls* is that roadmap.

When I was asked to write the foreword for this book, I did not hesitate, because I believe in this book as an educator who teaches future teachers, and as a Black feminist. The authors were asked by mothers, aunties, sisters, and teachers from various backgrounds in their respective communities to assemble a collection of work that spoke to the brilliance of their daughters—and they delivered.

White women make up over 80 percent of the teaching force, so the way in which white women understand and know Black girls is critical to the educational outcomes of Black girls. It is time we have an honest and loving conversation with white women about the harm they have caused and how they can begin their journey toward redemption and using their privilege for the freedom of others. *Teaching Brilliant and Beautiful Black Girls* is broken down into three meaningful and thoughtful categories: understanding, respecting, and connecting. Each section is a daring invitation to unlearn what white supremacy tells us about Black girls and pedagogically act on the contemporary and herstorical contributions, legacies, herstories, and intersectional identities of Black girls. This book will deepen your understanding not only of the beauty and brilliance of Black girls, but also of how to build a classroom on creativity and joy through a Black feminist pedagogical lens.

There is so much thoughtful and loving information packed within the pages of this book—each chapter will push you and expand your thinking for action. It is a primer for teaching Black girl liberation. I hope that as you read this book, you reflect on why we need a book like this, why it was created, and what you will do to ensure that the premise of this book becomes a reality, not only in your classroom, but in your everyday life.

Bettina L. Love
Atlanta, Georgia

Libation

Teaching Beautiful Brilliant Black Girls

LIBATION: Lessons From the Front Porch: A Libation From the Elders

We offer a libation as a prayer of thanksgiving to the Creator for the blessing of the ancestors from Africa the continent and the African diaspora;

We offer a libation to honor our sister ancestors, dead and gone, and we invite them to look upon us and be renewed from the unknowing of their given names, from the dust to which they have returned, and by the legacy of the sacredness of their humanity;

We offer a libation in the name of every girl child born, of every hue, kissed with the love of divine light and "fearfully and wonderfully" made;

We offer a libation to honor our great grandmothers, our grandmothers, our mothers, our aunts, our sisters, daughters, granddaughters, sisterfriends, and daughterfriends;

We offer a libation for the women who have been part of the freedom struggle along with Harriet Tubman, Sojourner Truth, Ida B. Wells, Fannie Lou Hamer, Septima Clark, Rosa Parks, Kathryn Jackson, Althea Gibson, Angela Davis, and Nina Simone, who taught us we were young, gifted, and Black;

We offer a libation for the girls and women whose names were never known or recorded, for women known as domestics with dreams that made their daughters' dreams come true, and women whose labor helped build a nation from the textile industry all the way to banking;

We offer a libation for the women whose lives were destroyed by the hatred of a gun, a lynching tree, a jail cell, and systems that closed down their well-being;

We offer a libation of gratitude to all the Black women who understood our beauty, our voices, our sass, our stories, our intelligence, our smiles, our sadness, our struggles, and our joy;

We offer a libation in celebration of the Black women who built schools, raised children, fought for the right to vote, started businesses, and marched to get laws changed and people treated with dignity and respect;

We offer a libation to Black women who have been prayer warriors, preachers, scholars, activists, community organizers, entrepreneurs, teachers, dancers, lawyers, nurses, doctors, artists, writers, musicians, singers, and women making herstory as we speak;

We offer a libation for women who understand what Toni Morrison meant when she imagined home as a space that is "both snug and wide open . . . where a woman never has to feel like prey," and where she never has to fear the silencing of her voice;

We offer a libation to those who envisioned this book, to those who supported its journey to publication, and to every reader who will learn through these pages that she has worth, that the gifts she brings to this world have meaning, and that her voice is part of a legacy of love;

We offer a libation to ourselves as the inheritors of the majestic power of storytelling;

And we offer a libation for the grace of living as elders on the front porch that attaches us to an endowed space called home, and we know we are fierce and highly favored.

Marilyn S. Mobley, PhD; Patricia M. Stewart, PhD

Acknowledgments

Thank you to all of the Beautiful Brilliant Black Girls and Black women who continue to create change in the world and their communities. It is indeed a blessing to be part of this sistahood. **To our ancestresses, foremothers, and sheroes,** who without them, we would not be; thank you.

To sista scholars, our sincere appreciation and respect; for you entrust us with your lived experiences of radical transformation. To the brotha scholars, our mutual love and respect to you for honoring the lived experiences of Beautiful Brilliant Black Girls. We see you. To the coconspirators who contributed to this book, thank you. Our work is not done . . .

Designing our cover page was indeed an intentional, critical, deliberative process amongst ourselves, as we consciously explored multiple ways to honor, respect, and reflect Beautiful Brilliant Black Girls. Our gratitude to the Beautiful Brilliant Black Girls on our cover page: Oluwafeyikemi Delano-Oriaran, Miracle Goolsby, Aniya Moore, Aisha Olaoye, Halima Olaoye, Sinclair Robins, and their families. We are thankful to our sista artists, Ebony Cox (who took the Moore and Robins photos) and Janet Feranmi Wyse (who took the Delano-Oriaran photo), for skillfully reflecting the beauty and brilliance in Black Girls on our cover page. Thank you to Ama Kwabia for her generative, evocative, and beautiful artwork included within these pages.

Our publication has a companion online site that highlights voices to reflect Beautiful Brilliant Black Girls' experiences. We thank KaLa Keaton for her incredible and detailed work of editing our video collections. Her motivation, thoughtfulness, and willingness to say "yes" are powerful gifts; we thank her for sharing them with us.

To our coconspirators who contributed to this book, thank you. Our work is not done . . .

We thank all the Corwin staff, especially Dan Alpert and Lucas Schleicher, for their commitment to producing books that represent authentic lived experiences of Black and African American Girls.

About the Editors

Dr. Omobolade (aka Bola) Delano-Oriaran

Dr. Delano-Oriaran continues to dedicate her life to advocating for racial and all forms (social, economic, political, educational) of justice for Black, Indigenous, and People of Color (BIPOC). Her mission is to authentically engage with schools, communities, organizations, and businesses to achieve critical transformation with the goal of eliminating manifestations of racism—individual, institutional, systemic, and structural— and intersecting forms of oppression. As a teacher educator, she challenges educators to adopt inclusive, diverse, equitable, and liberatory approaches that are culturally responsible, relevant, and sustaining.

Dr. Delano-Oriaran is an Associate Professor in the Teacher Education Department at St. Norbert College in De Pere, WI, where she serves as director of the Global Student Teaching Program and Bridge Pre-College Program. She earned her undergraduate and master's degrees in public administration at the historically Black Savannah State University in Georgia, and her Ph.D. in comparative and international education with a minor in woman and development from Pennsylvania State University.

An avid researcher and writer, Dr. Delano-Oriaran has published in journals and books and is the lead editor of two volumes on service-learning. She founded and co-founded several award-winning programs, including African Heritage, Inc., Umoja program for transracial families, and the African Heritage Emerging Student Leaders Institute. She is the recipient of numerous awards for social justice and community change, including 2020 Ethics in Action, Sister Joel Read Civic Engagement Practitioner, Appleton's Toward Community Unity in Diversity, St. Norbert College Scholarship, the Wisconsin State Human Relations Association's Outstanding Human Relations Educator, and St. Norbert College's Bishop Morneau Community Service.

Dr. Marguerite W. Penick

Marguerite W. Penick received her PhD from the University of Iowa in curriculum and instruction. Prior to attending graduate school, she worked as a high school teacher in an urban school in Kansas City, Kansas. Dr. Penick is a professor of leadership, literacy and social foundations in the College of Education and Human Services at the University of Wisconsin Oshkosh. Her work centers on issues of power, privilege, and oppression in relationship to issues of curriculum, with a special emphasis on the incorporation of quality literature in K–12 classrooms. Dr. Penick currently serves as a lead editor for the online journal, *Understanding and Dismantling Privilege*. She appears in the movie "Mirrors of Privilege: Making Whiteness Visible" by the World Trust Organization. Her work includes a joint article on creating safe spaces for discussing white privilege with preservice teachers, and she is a coeditor of *Everyday White People Confronting Racial and Social Injustice: 15 Stories* (Stylus Publishing, 2015), *The Guide for White Women Who Teach Black Boys* (Corwin, 2017), and *The Diversity Consultant Cookbook* (Stylus Publishing, 2019).

Dr. Shemariah J. Arki

Shemariah J. Arki identifies as an educator, an activist, and an organizer. Currently serving as a professor in the Department of Pan-African Studies and as the interim director of the Center for Pan-African Culture, both at Kent State University, she is an intersectional feminist scholar with expert knowledge and skills to develop, implement, facilitate, and evaluate curricula that promote institutional equity, communication, and access for traditionally marginalized students and families. Dr. Arki received a graduate certificate from the Penn Equity Institute for Doctoral Students from the Center for The Study of Race & Equity in Education at the University of Pennsylvania. She has also been a certified federal equal employment opportunity investigator since 2017. Serving as the founder and program director of the Ellipsis Institute for Womxn of Color in the Academy and as an auto/ethnographic researcher and creative nonfiction writer, her work centers cultural epistemologies and the construction of a #BlackCommaFeminist pedagogy. She has authored several academic and creative publications that center the lived experiences of womxn of color in education. As a public intellectual, she consistently ensures that education should be free and compulsory to all through her participation, organizing, and mobilizing of diverse constituents.

A proud Clevelander and mom of Solomon Tafari and Malcom Saadiq, Shemariah enjoys traveling, yoga, and making memories with family and friends.

Dr. Ali Michael

Ali Michael, PhD, works with schools and organizations across the country to help make the research on race, whiteness, and education more accessible and relevant to educators. Ali is the codirector of the Race Institute for K–12 Educators and the author of *Raising Race Questions: Whiteness, Inquiry and Education* (Teachers College Press, 2015), winner of the 2017 Society of Professors of Education Outstanding Book Award. She is coeditor of the bestselling *Everyday White People Confront Racial and Social Injustice: 15 Stories* (Stylus Publishing, 2015) and the bestselling *Guide for White Women who Teach Black Boys* (Corwin, 2017). Ali sits on the editorial board of the journal *Whiteness and Education*. Her article, "What do White Children Need to Know About Race?" coauthored with Dr. Eleonora Bartoli in *Independent Schools Magazine*, won the Association and Media Publishing Gold Award for Best Feature Article in 2014. When she is not writing, speaking, or training, Ali is striving to be an antiracist coparent to two amazing young kids. More information is available at alimichael.org.

Orinthia Swindell

Orinthia Swindell has centered the voices and experiences of youth and families as the focal point of her work as an educator for the past 28 years. She credits her mother for instilling in her the importance and value of education and of being connected to their community. As the youngest of six children growing up in Brooklyn, New York, Ms. Swindell developed a passion for learning and teaching others about social justice, equity, and inclusion work. Much of her work over the years has centered around young children's awareness of race and identity and adult skill development around this as well. As a consultant, Orinthia has facilitated numerous workshops and presentations. She has also presented at national conferences and has been a guest speaker at teacher preparation programs. Most recently Ms. Swindell has shifted her attention towards continuing to develop programming for girls in addition to growing her practice as an herbalist. One of her most esteemed accomplishments is being the mother of two amazing young men.

Dr. Eddie Moore, Jr.

Eddie Moore, Jr., has pursued and achieved success in academia, business, diversity, leadership and community service. In 1996, he started America & MOORE, LLC (http://www.eddiemoorejr.com) to provide comprehensive diversity, privilege, and leadership training/workshops. Dr. Moore is recognized as one of the nation's top speakers/consultants, and he's featured in the film "I'm not Racist. . . . Am I?" Dr. Moore is the founder of and program director for the White Privilege Conference (WPC: http://www.whiteprivilege-conference.com). In 2014 Dr. Moore founded The Privilege Institute (TPI), which engages people in research, education, action, and leadership through workshops, conferences, publications, and strategic partnerships and relationships. He is cofounder of the online journal *Understanding and Dismantling Privilege,* and coeditor of *Everyday White People Confront Racial and Social Injustice: 15 Stories* (Stylus Publishing, 2016), *The Guide for White Women who Teach Black Boys* (Corwin, 2018), and *The Diversity Consultant Cookbook: Preparing for the Challenge* (Stylus Publishing, 2019). Dr. Moore received his PhD from the University of Iowa in education leadership. His PhD research is on Black football players at Division III schools in the Midwest. Twitter: @eddieknowsmoore | Instagram: @eddiemoorejr | In: www.linkedin.com/in/eddiemoorejr

About the Contributors

Adams-Bass, Valerie N., PhD

Valerie N. Adams-Bass is an assistant professor in the Youth and Social Innovation program at the University of Virginia. Dr. Adams-Bass's research centers on Black children and youth. She is most interested in examining how media exposure influences interpersonal interactions and self-concept, and how racial/ethnic socialization is related to identity development and social and academic experiences. Dr. Adams-Bass is a developmental psychologist who regularly trains youth development professionals to use culturally relevant practices when working with Black children and youth.

Adens, Rebekah, MDiv, LMSW

Rebekah Adens currently consults with her organization, Community Matters Now. With over 15 years of experience, Rebekah has cultivated her diversity, equity, and inclusion expertise through heading schools as a vice principal, school social worker, and science teacher. Pedagogically, she focuses on integrating family therapy practices into creating solutions that address the mind as well as unprocessed and hidden emotions in order to bring disparate communities into mindsets and practices that meet the needs of their members. She can be reached at community mattersnow@gmail.com.

Alphonse-Crean, Ivy, MA

Ivy Alphonse-Crean, English faculty member and dean at an independent school in New York City, uses myth, music, knitting, and plants to inspire learning. A budding herbalist (pun intended), classical mezzo-soprano, and proud wife and mother, she enjoys creating safe spaces for honest dialogue. Her goal is to stimulate fresh ideas and shift encrypted thinking that no longer serves community well-being. A committed antiracist, her research interests include the formation of institutional identity, ancestral trauma, and the psychology of self. She can be reached at ialphonseleja@gmail.com.

Anderson, Brittany, PhD

Brittany N. Anderson is an assistant professor in urban education at the University of North Carolina at Charlotte. Brittany is a former elementary educator, and her research focuses on preservice and in-service teacher development in relation to the talent development and talent identification of minoritized youth. Brittany's research also centers on the lived experiences of gifted Black girls and women, with an emphasis on their academic and socioemotional needs. She can be reached at bander64@uncc.edu.

Bartoli, Eleonora, PhD

Eleonora Bartoli is a licensed psychologist and consultant specializing in trauma, resilience building, and social justice. She was the director of a master's in counseling program for over a decade and conducted research on multicultural counseling competence, white racial socialization, and social justice principles in psychotherapy. She currently consults with individuals and communities on restorative and preventive strategies for sustainable and effective activism. She has held an independent clinical practice for the past 15 years, and can be reached at dreleonorabartoli.com.

Battalora, Jacqueline, PhD, JD

Jacqueline Battalora, PhD, JD, is professor of sociology at Saint Xavier University, Chicago. She is the author of *Birth of A White Nation* (Strategic Book Publishing & Rights Agency, 2013) and speaks widely on the social construction of whiteness and how it shapes us today. She has published numerous articles and book chapters and is featured in the documentaries *HAPI: The Role of Economics in the Development of Civilization* and *The American LOWS: The American Legacy of White Supremacy*. Dr. Battalora's forthcoming book is titled *Becoming Human*

Bell, Brittany, EdD

Brittany Bell, EdD, is the assistant dean of students and director of the Diversity and Intercultural Center at Lawrence University. Dr. Bell began at Lawrence in January 2019 after previously being on staff at St. Norbert College as assistant director of multicultural student services and then student success librarian. She earned her bachelor's degree from the University of Wisconsin–Whitewater, a master's from the University of Nebraska at Kearney, and a doctorate from Edgewood College. Her research interest is focused on persistence of students of color; she can be reached at bellb@lawrence.edu.

Bentley-Edwards, Keisha, PhD

Dr. Keisha L. Bentley-Edwards is an assistant professor at Duke University's School of Medicine in the Division of General Internal Medicine, the associate director of research for the Samuel DuBois Cook Center on Social Equity, and a codirector of Duke's Special Populations Core. Her interdisciplinary research focuses on how culture, gender, and racism influence healthy development throughout the lifespan, and it has been funded by the Robert Wood Johnson Foundation and the National Institutes of Health. Dr. Bentley-Edwards can be reached at keisha.bentley.edwards@duke.edu.

Blay, Yaba, PhD

Dr. Yaba Blay is a scholar-activist, public speaker, and cultural consultant whose scholarship, work, and practice centers on the lived experiences of Black women and girls, with a particular focus on identity/body politics and beauty practices. Lauded by *O Magazine* for her social media activism, she has launched several viral campaigns including Locs of Love, #PrettyPeriod, and #ProfessionalBlackGirl, her multiplatform digital community. Dr. Blay earned an MA and PhD in African American studies (with distinction) and a graduate certificate in women's studies from Temple University.

Booker, Ansley, PhD

Ansley Booker earned her BA in biology, MS in pharmacy, and PhD in higher education leadership. She has published and presented extensively on the experiences of African American women and minority students in STEM education and student affairs. Her passion for STEM was highlighted in her 2019 TedTalk at the University of Georgia entitled "Unhidden Figures: Uncovering Our Cultural Biases in STEM" (https://www.youtube.com/watch?v=rn1S7phYDMQ). She can be reached at ansleybkr@gmail.com.

Bottley, Nya

Nya Bottley is a senior at Valley High School in West Des Moines, Iowa. She has earned an academic letter for the past three years with a 3.80 GPA. Nya is a member of the National Honor Society, serves on the Principal's Advisory Council, and takes part in school clubs such as Community of Racial Equity (C.O.R.E.) and Youth Equity Stewardship (YES). She is a sprinter on the Valley track team and earned a varsity letter as a freshman. Nya also served as the 2019–2020 Central Region Regional Teen President (RTP) of Jack and Jill of America Incorporated. Nya can be reached at nya.bottley@gmail.com.

Bowden, Samuella

Samuella Bowden is a nursing major attending Howard University in Washington, DC. Samuella hopes to become a nurse practitioner, because she feels as if it would be beneficial to several communities of colors and the medical field in general to have more Black nurses and doctors. She is interested in social justice issues and working towards equality for all people. She can be reached at samuella.bowden@bison.howard.edu.

Brown, Keith

Presidential Lifetime Achievement Award Winner Keith L. Brown, "Mr. I'm Possible," is principal speaker/trainer for 2020 Enterprises and the I'm Possible Institute, as well as a director of external affairs in the Georgia senate. Once labeled "special ed" and "at risk," Keith is now a frequent speaker at conferences and guest on nationally syndicated radio on topics such as education, social justice, motivation, and more. Named a Social Impact Hero by Thrive Global, Keith is the author of *Talk is Expensive.* He may be reached at www.keithlbrown.com.

Burton, Heather, PhD

Heather E. Burton, PhD, serves as senior director of faculty and institutional diversity at Case Western Reserve University, specializing in racial and gender equity. She is adjunct faculty in the departments of theater, African and African American studies, and social work. She is founder of Crimson Heights Ministries, a not-for-profit organization, and author of *Crimson Heights* (Griffin Scott Press, 2nd ed. 2015) and *I'm Single, So What? A Woman's Journey to Spiritual Contentment* (Griffin Scott Press, 2020). If God uses me to touch one person, then my work is not in vain. heather.burton@case.edu

Calig, Lauren

Lauren Calig, director of multicultural curriculum and codirector of diversity, equity, inclusion, and belonging at Laurel School, holds a graduate certificate in DSJI from the University of Colorado's Matrix Center and an MAT from the University of Pittsburgh. She has published articles in *DiversityIS, Independent School Magazine, Your Child,* and *WellSchooled,* and has presented at The White Privilege Conference, NAIS, and NCGS. She can be reached at lcalig@laurelschool.org.

Cannie, Raedell, PhD

Raedell Cannie is the director of the Network for EdWork at the Technology Access Foundation (TAF) in Seattle, Washington. She works to recruit, retain, and sustain leaders of color in education. Dr. Cannie has over a decade of teaching experience, from elementary through graduate school. Her doctoral dissertation was a self-study on her experiences as a Black girl in the American education system, both as student and educator. She is also the founder of Justice For All Everyday, a nonprofit that amplifies the voices and stories of Black women. She can be reached at drcannie@gmail.com.

Carnesi, Sabrina

Sabrina Carnesi is a National Board Certified Teacher Librarian and library educator from Newport News, Virginia, and she has achieved all but dissertation (ABD) in teaching and learning and curriculum instruction. She has 30-plus years' experience in K–12 classroom and school library science. Her specialized focus grounds her in research and children's literature that allow BIPOC youth the opportunity to experience powerful impacts with text without compromising their identity. She can be reached by email at scarnesi56@gmail.com.

Carr, Kendra, EdD

Kendra Carr currently serves as the chief program officer of Girls Leadership, headquartered in Oakland, California. Dr. Carr has a decade of experience in all-girls education and leadership programming that centers the needs of girls at the margins of society. Her doctoral research explored the ways in which adolescent female-identified youth of color developed a leadership identity, an equity and justice lens, and a commitment to community action. Her research includes a focus on critical race feminist pedagogy and equity in education. She can be reached at kendra@girlsleadership.org.

Chapman, Imani

Imani Romney-Rosa Chapman is one of the cofounders of Romney Associates, Inc. She has more than 25 years of experience organizing, educating, and developing curriculum for social justice. Mrs. Chapman works for an equitable world in which her children and the young people in your lives can live wholly and safely into their full humanity, where race is not a major determinant in health, wealth, legal, and educational outcomes. She is enrolled in the doctoral studies program for interfaith clinical education for pastoral ministry at Hebrew Union College–Jewish Institute of Religion.

Chapman, Sandra, EdD

Sandra K. Chapman is the founder of Chap Equity and deputy director of programs and curriculum at Perception Institute. Dr. Chapman has over 30 years of experience translating academic research into accessible presentations and developing antibias curriculum. Her dissertation, *The Role of Racial-Ethnic Identity and Family Socialization on Student Engagement: Latino Youth in Select New York City Independent Schools*, focused on Latinx students' understanding of their Latinidad in the context of school success. She can be reached at chap@chapequity.com.

Coleman-King, Chonika, PhD

Dr. Chonika Coleman-King is assistant professor of teachers, schools, and society at the University of Florida. Her research interests include antiracist teaching, urban education, experiential learning, and the educational experiences of Black immigrant and Black American youth. Dr. Coleman-King is the author of the book, *The (Re-)Making of a Black American: Tracing the Racial and Ethnic Socialization of Caribbean American Youth*, which documents the interplay between race, class, and immigrant status for Afro-Caribbean immigrant youth. She can be reached at coleking@coe.ufl.edu.

DeBerry, Usherla, MEd

Usherla DeBerry, MEd, is currently at the North Carolina Department of Health and Human Services (NCDHHS) working as a Regional Manager for the Wilson region. She is also one class shy of completing her doctorate degree in organizational leadership. Her doctoral dissertation focus is on how instructional designers, faculty, administrators, and educational institutions will select suitable strategies to enable deaf and hard of hearing learners to use cultural and communications tools in a digital multimedia instruction environment to support accessibility and an inclusive approach. Ms. DeBerry teaches part-time intercultural and organizational communications and general studies courses at Gallaudet that focus on the works of antiracism and social justice. She is an active member of National Black Deaf Advocates and Delta Sigma Theta, Inc.

DiAngelo, Robin, PhD

Robin DiAngelo is affiliate associate professor of education at the University of Washington. In 2011, she coined the term *white fragility* in an academic article that has influenced the international dialogue on race. Her book, *White Fragility: Why It's So Hard for White People to Talk About Racism* (Beacon Press) was released in June of 2018 and debuted on the *New York Times* bestseller list, where it has remained for over 95 weeks, and has been translated into nine languages. Dr. DiAngelo has been a consultant and educator for over 20 years on issues of racial and social justice.

Duncan, Worokya, EdD

Worokya Duncan currently serves as head of upper school and director of equity and engagement at The Cathedral School of St. John the Divine. Dr. Duncan has over 20 years of expertise in curriculum, instruction, equity, inclusion, and cultural literacy. She can be reached at worokyaduncan@duncaned.com and www.duncaned.com.

Gaskin, Ha Lien

Ha Lien Gaskin studies at Chapel Hill High School in North Carolina. She is often found making art and researching a wide variety of topics, from psychiatric sciences to race relations in America. She can be reached at hwgaskin@students .chccs.k12.nc.us.

McDonald, Sakenya

Sakenya McDonald is currently a PhD candidate at Prescott College, where her dissertation examines the impacts of systemic apathy on the educational experiences and outcomes of twice-exceptional girls and women of color. Sakenya has expertise in the field of African religions and philosophies and has explored multiple themes in African spirituality as a response to racialized and gender-specific religious trauma. Sakenya's current research combines her knowledge of African spirituality with educational and critical psychology, and she can be reached at sakenya.mcdonald@prescott.edu.

Gay, Geneva, PhD

Geneva Gay is professor emerita of the College of Education at the University of Washington, Seattle. Her areas of specialization are multicultural education and culturally responsive teaching, with emphasis on the intersections of race, culture, and education. She has published numerous articles and books on these topics, and consults nationally and internationally on the same. She can be reached by email at ggay@uw.edu.

Gibney, Shannon

Shannon Gibney is a writer, educator, and activist, and the author of *Dream Country* (Dutton, 2018) and *See No Color* (Carolrhoda Lab, 2015), novels that both won Minnesota Book Awards. Gibney is on the faculty in the English department at Minneapolis College, where she teaches writing. She coauthored *What God is Honored Here? Writings on Miscarriage and Infant Loss by and for Native Women and Women of Color*, with writer Kao Kalia Yang, in 2019. Gibney is currently at work on her new novel, *Botched* (Dutton, 2022), which takes on identity and possibility in the context of transracial adoption.

Griffin, Ashleigh

Ashleigh Griffin, PhD, currently serves as the vice president of policy, evaluation, and research at the Black Teacher Collaborative (BTC). Dr. Griffin has over a decade of experience using mixed methods research to ensure schools and school systems support and develop the genius of Black children by investigating culturally relevant instructional practices and Black educator recruitment/retention.

Dr. Griffin completed her undergraduate studies in psychology at Georgetown University and received her master's degree and PhD in developmental psychology from Howard University.

Griffin Blake, Donovan, EdD

Donovan Griffin Blake currently serves as a visiting professor in the Department of Teacher Development and Educational Studies at Oakland University and is an experienced K–12 teacher. Dr. Griffin Blake has decades of expertise in teaching and learning and conducted her doctoral dissertation on parental involvement of African American parents of disabled high school students. Her research interests are focused on social justice equity in education for marginalized groups through strategies and developing curricular content. She can be reached at degblake2@yahoo.com.

Hinderlie, Kay

As a recent graduate from University of Maryland, Baltimore County, Kay Hinderlie currently works as a program associate at a women's shelter in Washington, DC. After working at their university's women's center as a student staff, Kay continues to work with different marginalized groups to provide resources and build community. They can be reached at kay.hinderlie@gmail.com

Igwebuike, John, PhD., JD

John G. Igwebuike is an attorney, academician, and advocate of the positive power of effective listening. He is the founder of The Lead Listening Institute (www.leadlisteninginstitute.com), which helps colleges, communities, companies, faith-based organizations, nonprofits, and schools grow into *guanacastes* ("listening trees"). He is also the principal founder of The Lead Listening Society—Lambda Sigma Nu, a college-based society dedicated to the mission of growing leaders who lead by listening. He may be reached at drjohnigwebuike@gmail.com.

Johnson, Andrea

Andrea Haynes Johnson was born and raised in Detroit. Her parents met in college, and both worked in Detroit Public Schools. She was educated in Detroit Public Schools and, like her parents, began her career there. Andrea has a BFA in dance performance, an MAT in English education, and a Certificate of Advanced Study in educational leadership and administration. She is a nationally renowned facilitator of Courageous Conversations and is the executive director of the Courageous Conversation Global Foundation. Andrea can be reached at andrea@ccglobalfoundation.org.

Johnson, Dee

Dee Johnson is an international educational development professional and graduate of the University of Pennsylvania and Middlebury College. Her personal and professional interests include women and gender studies, critical race theory, and human rights and global citizenship education, as well as healing and transformative justice. She boasts over a decade of experience in the private, public, and nonprofit education sectors, is a former UN consultant, and is an advisor to several gender justice organizations. Dee can be reached at rameshdeeann@gmail.com.

Jones, Laura

Laura Jones, a native of Chicago, IL graduated from St. Norbert College where she studied Sociology and earned a Bachelor of Arts degree. After graduation, Laura started her professional career at the Boys and Girls Club of the Fox Valley as a STAR (Scholars on Target to Achieve Results) Coordinator working with Black/African American students to close the opportunity gap. Laura now works with African Heritage Inc. as the Social and Community Outreach Service Director. She is currently working on her Master's in Student Affairs Administration and will be finished May 2021.

Jones, Stevie

Stevie Jones, Jr., retired United States Army tactical communicator, has spent more than 20 years teaching our nation's warriors how to effectively create environments built to succeed and positively impact the communities they serve.

Kaaba, Vashalice

Vashalice Kaaba is a doctoral student in the School of Information at Florida State University. She wrote her master's thesis on the use of African-American vernacular English narration performances in audiobooks. Her research interests are focused on children's literature, critical race theory, antiblackness scholarship, and the racial implications of long-held practices within the literary publishing field. She can be reached at voh09@my.fsu.edu.

Kaler-Jones, Cierra

Cierra Kaler-Jones is a PhD candidate at the University of Maryland–College Park in the Department of Teaching and Learning, Policy and Leadership. She has been cocreating healing-centered, community-based arts programs with Black girls for over 10 years. Her research explores how Black girls use arts-based practices (e.g., movement, music, hair) as mechanisms for identity development and resistance. She can be reached at ckalerjones@gmail.com.

Lake, Dora

Dora Lake is currently a student at Case Western Reserve University at the Jack, Joseph and Morton Mandel School pursuing a dual master's in social work administration and nonprofit management. Her goal after graduation in 2023 is to build a Cleveland-area respite home for single mothers based on a community model she has developed through her thesis work. She can be reached at dml93@case.edu.

Lane, Monique, PhD

Monique Lane is an associate professor and academic chair of the Leadership Department at Saint Mary's College of California. She earned a PhD in urban schooling from UCLA's Graduate School of Education and served as a postdoctoral research fellow at Columbia University's Teachers College. Dr. Lane's combined 10 years of experience as an educator in Los Angeles public high schools is the motivating force behind her commitment to underserved youth. Her research specializations include Black feminist praxis and educational justice for African American girl learners.

Liston, Monique, PhD

Dr. Monique Liston, a Black woman who prioritizes Black Women's leadership, is a warrior scholar. She is the founder and chief strategist at UBUNTU Research and Evaluation.

Monique founded UBUNTU Research and Evaluation to disrupt the daily actions that uphold status quo power relations. Since oppression, anti-Blackness particularly, pervades our society and affects people from birth, Monique is a proud HBCU alumna representing Howard University. In 2018 she obtained her PhD at the University of Wisconsin–Milwaukee in urban education.

Love, Bettina

Dr. Bettina L. Love is an award-winning author and the Athletic Association Endowed Professor at the University of Georgia. Her writing, research, teaching, and activism meet at the intersection of race, education, abolition, and Black joy. Dr. Love is concerned with how educators working with parents and communities can build communal, civically engaged schools rooted in abolitionist teaching, with the goal of intersectional social justice for equitable classrooms that love and affirm Black and Brown children. In 2014, she was invited to the White House Research Conference on Girls to discuss her work focused on the lives of Black girls. For her work in the field of hip-hop education, in 2016, Dr. Love was named the Nasir Jones Hiphop Fellow at the Hutchins Center for African and African American Research at Harvard University. Her books include *We Want to Do More Than Survive: Abolitionist Teaching and the Pursuit of Educational Freedom* (Beacon Press, 2019) and *Hip Hop's Li'l Sistas Speak: Negotiating Hip Hop Identities and Politics in the New South* (Peter Lang, 2012).

McDonald, Sakenya

Sakenya McDonald is currently a PhD candidate at Prescott College, where her dissertation examines the impacts of systemic apathy on the educational experiences and outcomes of twice-exceptional girls and women of color. Sakenya has expertise in the field of African religions and philosophies and has explored multiple themes in African spirituality as a response to racialized and gender-specific religious trauma. Sakenya's current research combines her knowledge of African spirituality with educational and critical psychology, and she can be reached at sakenya.mcdonald@prescott.edu.

McGhee, Ramycia, EdD

Ramycia McGhee serves as a professor of English and literature at Linn Benton Community College in Albany, Oregon. Dr. McGhee has over a decade of experience in teaching developmental writing while serving as a mentor for adjunct faculty. In addition, Dr. McGhee conducted her doctoral dissertation on improving the instructional skills of adjunct faculty through professional development. Her research interests include developmental education, composition theory, and adjunct training and development. She can be reached at mcgheer@linnbenton.edu.

McGuire, Keon, PhD

Dr. Keon M. McGuire is an associate professor of higher and postsecondary education in the Mary Lou Fulton Teachers College at Arizona State University. Drawing from Africana and other interdisciplinary frameworks, Dr. McGuire examines how race, gender, and religion shape minoritized college students' identities and their everyday experiences. In 2019, he was named a National Academy of Education (NAEd)/Spencer Postdoctoral Fellow and ACPA Emerging Scholar. He can be reached at keon.mcguire@asu.edu.

McGuire, T. Donté

T Donté McGuire, MEd, is a research analyst at Higher Ed Insight and a doctoral candidate in the University of Maryland's higher education program; he is also in the women's studies graduate certificate program. He has worked in international education, high school reentry/completion, college access, residence life, and institutional diversity, equity, and inclusion. Donté's scholarship focuses on improving educational access and success for marginalized groups, cross-cultural education and understanding, and inclusive leadership, and he can be reached at tdontemcguire@gmail.com.

McNeal, Victoria

Victoria McNeal is from Milwaukee, Wisconsin. She obtained her bachelor's degree from St. Norbert College. Victoria is currently a graduate student at the University of Wisconsin–Milwaukee studying cultural foundations of community engagement and education. As a professional, Victoria works in the Green Bay Area School District as the volunteer and community partners coordinator.

Miles Nash, Angel, PhD

Angel Miles Nash is an assistant professor of leadership development at Chapman University in the Donna Ford Attallah College of Educational Studies. Her research endeavors center on the emboldening of Black girls and women in K–20 education, the professional intersectional realities of Black women, and the ways that educational leaders support underserved students in STEM education.

Mobley, Marilyn S., PhD

Marilyn S. Mobley, PhD, is professor of English and African American studies at Case Western Reserve University (CWRU). She was the inaugural vice president for diversity, inclusion and equal opportunity at CWRU and the founding director of African American Studies at George Mason University. A Toni Morrison scholar and published author, she is a founding member of the Toni Morrison Society. Her talk at the Paradox of Diversity conference was selected for TEDxCLE 2013. An educator for 45 years, she received the YWCA Woman of Achievement Award in 2019. She is a lay minister at her church.

Moore, Abrielle

Abrielle Moore is the founder and CEO of Onyx Life, a lifestyle brand that aims to empower Black people with culturally relevant and ethical creations. She graduated from Brown University in 2020 with a bachelor of arts in Africana Studies and a bachelor of arts in Economics. During her time as a student, she concentrated her studies on African American history and Black women's studies. She can be reached at abrielle_moore@alumni.brown.edu.

Olabode, Toyin

Toyin Olabode is an honors student at Case Western Reserve University, double majoring in psychology and music. She leads the Case Western Reserve University Psychology Students Organization and The Sisterhood, a group that provides community support for Black women on campus. Within psych, Toyin focuses on childhood anxiety, personality disorders, and music therapy. She's also a singer and lover of music. Although she is studying classical music, gospel and R&B is where her heart lies. She is passionate about Black art, women, and children, seeking to uplift them with every opportunity. Toyin can be reached at moo14@case.edu.

Oling-Sisay, Mary, EdD

Mary Oling-Sisay is the vice provost for academic affairs at Humboldt State University. She has oversight of various academic aspects of the university at the undergraduate and graduate levels. She has experience in both academic and student affairs. She has served in positions ranging from academic dean for a school of education to senior vice president for inclusive excellence. Her doctoral research was on preservice teacher candidates of color. Her research interests are institutional excellence, and inclusive and responsive pedagogy. She can be reached at mary.oling-sisay@humboldt.edu.

Osborne, Judith

Judith Osborne currently serves as a diversity, equity, and inclusion strategist and partner coach and has more than 20 years' experience as a writer, educator, and social justice advocate. She has particular interest and expertise in utilizing film, music, and popular culture to inspire student and teacher equity learning practices in both independent and public learning spaces. She can be reached at jdyosborne@gmail.com

Paige, Cordenia

Cordenia Paige currently teaches fifth grade at an independent school in Washington, DC. Ms. Paige has over 25 years of experience as an educator in predominantly white, independent schools in Washington, DC, and in New York City. She attended a Washington, DC, independent school from second through twelfth grades. Supporting Black students in independent schools has been at the heart of Ms. Paige's vocation. Her key interest is ensuring that every voice in the room is heard. She can be reached at capaige4@gmail.com.

Phelps, Erin

Erin K. Phelps, MA, PhD candidate (pronouns: Erin) is an assistant professor in the Department of Sociology at Pierce College in Washington state. Erin quantitatively researches the experiences queer graduate students of color (QGSOC) face in higher education and processes institutions can utilize to increase reenrollment of QGSOC and all students. Erin's work focuses on Black queer liberation, safety in institutions, and student organizing. Erin seeks every day to hold herself accountable to people who are in the margins and foster community via Black feminist praxis.

Phelps-Ward, Robin, EdD

Robin Phelps-Ward is an assistant professor of higher education and director of the master of arts program in student affairs administration in higher education at Ball State University in Muncie, Indiana. She studies mentoring and mentoring programs for students of color, the role of intersectionality in the examination of identity development and systemic oppression, and pedagogical practices for critical consciousness in the higher education context. Her work can be found in *Gender & Education, The Western Journal of Black Studies,* and *The Journal of Student Affairs Inquiry.*

Phillips-Fein, Jesse, MA

Jesse Phillips-Fein is a dance educator, choreographer, and performer based in Brooklyn, New York. Her creative and pedagogical practices are continual experiments in divesting from whiteness. Her writing on the intersections of dance and race have been published in the *Journal on Dance Education,* the *Palgrave Handbook of Race and the Arts in Education* (Palgrave Macmillan, 2018), *Pedagogies in the Flesh: Case Studies on the Embodiment of Sociocultural Differences in Education* (Palgrave Macmillan, 2018), and *Slingshot.*

Powell, Stephany, EdD

Stephany Powell is a retired vice sergeant and director of law enforcement training and survivor services at the National Center on Sexual Exploitation. She is an adjunct assistant professor of sociology at Los Angeles Trade Technical College. She has written a preventative human trafficking workbook entitled *My Choice, My Body, My Rules* (2018, independently published). Her race and law enforcement expertise were highlighted in the book *And Still I Rise* by Dr. Henry Louis Gates, and she was featured on the Chris Cuomo Show for her human trafficking expertise. Contact her at powell.positivechange@gmail.com.

Pugh, Samantha

Samantha Pugh is currently the chief academic officer at Merrick Academy Queens Public Charter School in Queens, New York. Ms. Pugh has over 20 years of experience in K–12 education and has had success with turning around struggling schools, building on the success of high-achieving schools, and founding new effective schools in both district and charter settings across New York City.

Ragland, Allison (Alice), PhD

Alice Ragland is an Ohio-based social justice educator and writer. Dr. Ragland's work focuses on the intersections between education, activism, and Black liberation. She has many years of experience designing and delivering social justice curricula; providing diversity, equity, and inclusion consulting for a variety of organizations; and facilitating antioppression workshops across the United States. She runs the blog Teach Liberation (teachliberation.com), which features social justice education resources for parents and educators. She can be reached at iteachliberation@gmail.com.

Reyes, Rosalie, MSEd

Rosalie Reyes currently serves as the coordinator of teacher engagement and professional development at Teaching for Change. Her research interests are focused on racial identity development, museum-based education, and exploring race and representation in children's literature. She can be reached at rreyes@teachingforchange.org.

Rhim, Stevanie

Stevanie Rhim, resident of Plainfield New Jersey, is in her first year of college. She is a public speaker and host for several community events. Stevanie has been recognized as a student activist and a leader. As a result of her race relations work, she has been recognized by the Kenilworth and Plainfield Boards of Education in New Jersey; Cory Booker, Senator of New Jersey; and Union County Unsung Heroes, among many others, and has been awarded the Princeton Prize in Race Relations from Princeton University. She hopes to continue fighting for positive change in her community.

Rice, Samaria

As a mother of social justice, activist, and the founder and CEO of the Tamir Rice Foundation, Ms. Samaria Rice proudly serves as an advocate for juvenile rights in Cleveland, Ohio. Since the murder of her 12-year-old son Tamir by Cleveland Police in 2014, Ms. Rice has committed her life to justice and standing on the frontlines for children.

Roach, Enyá

Enyá Roach is a native of the U.S. Virgin Islands. She graduated with her bachelor's degree in psychology from St. Norbert College, De Pere, Wisconsin. She is currently working with the Students on Target to Achieve Results (STAR) Program to close the opportunity gap between Black students and their white peers.

Robins, Sabrina, PhD

Dr. Robins earned a doctorate in American government from Wayne State University. She has expertise in operations and project management, research design and methods, and applied statistics. She also has a heart for what she describes as the "near workforce ready," a term she coined to reflect individuals who are often the ignored and overlooked part of the workforce. Most important, Dr. Robins is a wife and mother of a beautiful and brilliant GenZ daughter on the autism spectrum. In support of her advocacy for workplace diversity and inclusion, Dr. Robins is an advocate for neurodiverse students and adults.

Robins, Sinclair

Sinclair Robins is a neurodiversity advocate and refers to herself as a GenZ aspie. She has appeared on two podcasts to discuss jobs, college, and being autistic. Her advocacy covers four main areas: the need for affordable assessments for autism, removal of the stigma of being autistic, antibullying, and teenage mental health awareness. Sinclair enjoys playing eSports, being a recreational manga artist, watching anime, being a Broadway enthusiast, and owning a Netflix account.

Salaam, Yusef

In 1989, at just 15 years young, Dr. Yusef Salaam was tried and convicted in the Central Park jogger case along with four other Black and Latinx young men. After almost seven years behind bars for a crime he did not commit, Yusef's case was overturned, and he was set free. His life was forever changed by this experience, and since his release he has advocated for criminal justice reform, prison reform, and the abolition of juvenile solitary confinement and capital punishment. Yusef has shared his story and stance on these issues on CNN, MSNBC, REVOLT TV, NPR Atlanta, FOX, and more.

Scott, Darla, PhD

Darla Scott currently serves as an assistant professor in the school psychology program at Bowie State University in Bowie, Maryland. Dr. Scott has over a decade of expertise in instructional design and delivery and conducted her doctoral dissertation on the utilization of culturally responsive pedagogy with African American students. Her research interests are focused on the development of educational equity through inclusive instructional strategies, and she can be reached at dmscott@bowiestate.edu.

Serls, Tangela, PhD

Tangela Serls currently serves as an instructor and the undergraduate director of the Department of Women's and Gender Studies at The University of South Florida, Tampa. She has interdisciplinary research and teaching interests that center the global experiences of Black women and women of color. Dr. Serls has taught a wide variety of English and women's and gender studies classes. Her courses have included subjects such as African American literature, literature by women of color, and Black feminisms. She can be reached at serlst@usf.edu.

Shivers-McGrew, Ariel

Ariel Shivers-McGrew is an advocate for military personnel, millennials, and minorities seeking to elevate their distinctiveness and belonging in the workplace. Ariel is currently serving in the United States Army Reserves and is recognized as the 2019 Woman Veteran of the Year.

She holds a master of arts in clinical mental health counseling and certification in nonprofit management and leadership from the University of San Diego. Learn more at www.tactfuldisruption.co/about

Slesaransky-Poe, Graciela, PhD

Graciela Slesaransky-Poe is professor and founding dean, School of Education, Arcadia University, Pennsylvania. Her work is rooted in her commitment to justice, equity, diversity, and inclusion; and it is personal, professional, and political. She has authored numerous publications, delivered multiple keynote addresses, and received honors and awards, including Arcadia's Cultural Ally; Champion of Social Justice, PEAL (Parent Education & Advocacy Leadership); and the Patricia J. Creegan Excellence Award in Inclusive Education from Pennsylvania's Education for All Coalition. She can be reached at SlesaranskyPoe@arcadia.edu.

Smith, Ellise

Ellise Smith is a current doctoral student at Indiana University studying urban education studies with a concentration in higher education student affairs. Smith created the website Fatness Fiction and a podcast, "+Plus Size Magic Radio," in 2017 to dismantle the negative narratives associated with fat bodies of society. Her research interests focus on body image using critical race theory, sense of belonging, black feminist thought, and intersectionality as the frameworks to unpack the experiences of these identities in and outside of the academy. She can be reached at info@fatnessfiction.com.

Snowden, Erica

Erica Snowden, MEd, is a Lion's Story racial literacy trainer and the director of equity and multicultural education at Friends Central School. Erica, a Detroit native, has over 17 years of educational experience within the Friends Schools network and independent schools. She has spent over a decade working toward dismantling white supremacy and promoting diversity, equity, and inclusion practices within K–12 schools, including work with students, parents, teachers, and administrators. She can be reached at ericasnowden916@gmail.com.

Stanford, Fatima Cody, MD, MPH, MPA, FAAP, FACP, FAHA, FTOS

Dr. Stanford practices and teaches at Massachusetts General Hospital/Harvard Medical School as one of the first fellowship-trained obesity medicine physicians in the world. Dr. Stanford received her BS and MPH from Emory University as a MLK Scholar, her MD from the Medical College of Georgia School of Medicine, and her MPA from the Harvard Kennedy School of Government as a Zuckerman Fellow in the Harvard Center for Public Leadership. She was selected for The Obesity Society Clinician of the Year in 2020. In 2021, she will be awarded the AMA Dr. Edmond and Rima Cabbabe Dedication to the Profession Award, which recognizes a physician who demonstrates active and productive improvement to the profession of medicine through community service, advocacy, leadership, teaching, or philanthropy.

Stewart, Patricia M., PhD

Patricia M. Stewart, PhD, is a former public school teacher, university professor, psychologist, school/clinical counselor, and specialist in religious education. She has served as a senior vice president for social services organizations and is a diversity professional and community consultant for well-being from infancy through adolescence. An active member of the Savannah community as a grandmother, senior league tennis player, visionary thinker, and public policy advocate, she was recognized on her 90th birthday as one of Georgia's Outstanding Citizens.

Swalwell, Katy, PhD

Katy Swalwell currently serves as associate professor of social and cultural studies in the School of Education at Iowa State University. Dr. Swalwell is the director of certificate studies for the Education for Social Justice graduate certificate and has over two decades of experience in antiracist education, with a focus on predominantly white, wealthy schools. She can be reached at www.katyswalwell.com.

Tucker, Samarria

Samarria Tucker is a current high school senior at Raleigh Charter High School. She is dedicated to promoting racial equity and justice in her community. For the past two years, she has been working to educate others on the United States' dark past and how it connects to what is happening now. In today's climate, she has focused her research on police reform, how African Americans have been disproportionately affected by COVID, and how we can elevate ourselves. She hopes to speak out not only on racism but also on issues that are within the black community. She can be reached at sjunae02@gmail.com.

Waite, Shannon, EdD

Shannon R. Waite is a clinical assistant professor of educational leadership in the Graduate School of Education at Fordham University. Her research interests include topics on diversity recruitment and pipeline programs, culturally responsive school leadership, developing critical consciousness in educational leaders, and examining hypersegregation and its connection to the school-to-prison pipeline. Dr. Waite is a mayoral appointee on the Panel for Educational Policy for NYC public schools and a trustee on the Board of Education Retirement System (BERS). She can be reached at swaite4@fordham.edu.

Warren, Veronica, PhD

Veronica Warren currently serves as an associate director of the counseling center at University of Wisconsin, Oshkosh. Dr. Warren has provided her expertise to the neglect, abuse, delinquency, and mental health fields for over two decades, serving children, young adults, and families. Her dissertation is entitled *The Experiences of African American women at a Predominantly White College*. Research interests include the influence of Intersectional experiences of women throughout the lifespan. Dr. Warren can be reached at warrenv@uwosh.edu.

Watson, Terri, PhD

Terri N. Watson is an associate professor in the Department of Leadership and Human Development at The City College of New York. Dr. Watson began her career as a classroom teacher over 25 years ago in a Harlem middle school. Her research examines effective school leadership and is aimed to improve the educational outcomes and life chances of historically excluded and underserved students and families. She may be reached at TWatson@ccny.cuny.edu.

Williams, Ny

Ny Williams is a 17-year-old senior at Raleigh Charter High School, in Raleigh, North Carolina. She enjoys community activism and fighting for those who can no longer fight. She is the Youth Coordinator for NCBORN, whose mission is to dismantle all forms of oppression within the state, normalize the utilization of pronouns, and begin inclusivity of all identities while recognizing the power and importance of diversity. She has a focus of ending the abuses of the prison industrial complex specifically through police brutality. She has committed herself to making a change for the better in all ways.

Williamson, Toni Graves

Toni Graves Williamson is a diversity practitioner and consultant, now serving as director of equity and inclusion at Friends Select School in Philadelphia. She is a principal consultant for The Glasgow Group and the codirector of The Race Institute for K–12 Educators. Toni is a contributing author to *The Guide for White Women Who Teach Black Boys* (Corwin, 2018).She holds a bachelor's degree from Duke University, a master's of education degree from the University of North Carolina at Greensboro, and a master's of education degree from Columbia University.

Black Girls are Beautiful and Brilliant

Omobolade Delano-Oriaran, Marguerite W. Penick, Shemariah J. Arki, Ali Michael, Orinthia Swindell, Eddie Moore Jr.

In 2017, Corwin introduced *The Guide for White Women Who Teach Black Boys* to the world, edited by Drs. Eddie Moore Jr., Ali Michael, and Marguerite W. Penick. Based upon the need for a dedicated focus on Black Boys and the practical application to classrooms and school districts, this publication would become an instant bestseller. In addition to the strength that lies in the specificity of the work, there also remains an intentional acknowledgment of the necessary work to address existing inequities in the American educational system, specifically for Black students. *Teaching Beautiful Brilliant Black Girls* is birthed from four major facts: (1) Black Girls are brilliant, beautiful, confident, divine, unapologetic, resilient, independent, self-sufficient, and bold (Ford, 2013); (2) Black Girls have cyclical harsh experiences in schools; (3) there is a call and need for educational justice and fairness; and (4) we have received responses from numerous educators—white educators who are still crying out for help and who have requested a book with an emphasis on Black Girls. The editors of *The Guide for White Women Who Teach Black Boys* reconvened and invited three additional sista scholars—Drs. Omobolade Delano-Oriaran, Shemariah J. Arki, and Ms. Orinthia Swindell—Black and African American Women—to collaborate and focus on the publication of *Teaching Beautiful Brilliant Black Girls*.

Teaching Beautiful Brilliant Black Girls arrives hot on the heels of the work of scholars such as Dr. Bettina Love (2019) and Dr. Monique Morris (2016a, 2016b), who are advocating for just, liberatory (Snowden, 2019), and equitable education for all Black Children and, in the context of this text, specifically for Black Girls. In her work on abolitionist teaching, Dr. Bettina Love states: "To achieve the goals of abolitionist teachers we must demand the impossible and employ a radical imagination focused on intersectional justice" (2019, p. 12). Love continues to talk about how, in education, Black Lives Matter. For us, as editors concerned about the educational plight and experiences of all Black Children, we also empathically assert that Black Lives Matter, and that Black Children Matter. In the context of our publication, Black Girls Matter, and this is therefore our focus with this publication, *Teaching Beautiful Brilliant Black Girls*.

BLACK GIRLS ARE BEAUTIFUL AND BRILLIANT

All Black Girls are beautiful, brilliant, confident, divine, unapologetic, and bold, and "are not only embracing their unique gifts, but also redefining their world—and ours" (Viera & Williams, 2016, p. 84). "Black beauty is a synthesis of external and internal factors and cannot be defined a priori by physical factors alone" (Bennett, 1980, p. 161). After a thorough search through definitions of Black beauty, we draw upon a description from *Ebony* magazine, a publication designed for African Americans with its inaugural release in 1945: "Black beauty is evolving and cannot be defined with finality . . . Black girls are beautiful just as they are . . . the noses, hair and shapes" gifted to them by their creator/s (Bennett, 1980, p. 160). "Black Girls are beautiful by their own standards, not because they are Black or brown copies of some white models; they are beautiful because they look like themselves" (Bennett, 1980, p. 160). Blackness is beautiful, as it is reflected in a diversity of shades, tones, colors, and hues; and Black Girls are emboldened as they shine from the ebony, cacao Black, caramel, espresso brown, milk chocolate shade to the pecan brown, mocha, and ivory skin tones (8 Different Shades, n.d.; Find Your Shade, n.d.). In summary, to every Black Girl around our global world: You are beautiful, and "Black beauty is in the soul of the Black beholder" (Bennett, 1980, p. 161). And you, Black Girl, are the beholder!

Black Girls come from diverse and rich cultural backgrounds based on gender identity/expression, ethnicity, nationality, language, religion, spirituality, socioeconomic status, body shape, family unit, geographic area, sexual orientation, height, abilities, gifts, and talents. The intersection, combination, and interlocking of these backgrounds results in varying forms and degrees of experiences and lived realities of Black Girls, and influences the identities you may perceive or observe in the classroom—for example, with "the combination of sexism and racism, Black girls face a double whammy socially, educationally, and professionally" (Evans-Winters, 2014, p. 23). One thing we do know for sure is that they are beautiful both internally and externally, and that they are brilliant, as they exude strength, courage, and power (French, Lewis, & Neville, 2013); and so we adopt a strength-based perspective. Hence the title of our book: *Teaching Beautiful Brilliant Black Girls*.

"To be young, gifted, and Black is where it's at," Nina Simone sings in the 1970 ode to her fellow melanated trailblazers. And the High Priestess of Soul couldn't have been more correct; the contributions that [Black Girls] people of color have made to the world are indeed precious, they are indeed significant, and they are more than worthy of recognition (Cubit, 2020, para. 1).

As brilliant and gifted as Black Girls are, however, we do know for certain that they are not thriving to their fullest potential in K–12 schools, as a result of systemic harsh experiences that they continue to endure in schools. One of our contributors, Dr. Brittany Anderson, cited in a previous publication that there "is a missing narrative around high-achieving/GBGs [Gifted Black Girls] and their experiences, as well as their disproportionate underrepresentation in gifted programming, services, and AP courses" (Anderson, 2020, p. 86). We are troubled, for example, that Black Girls are underrepresented in gifted programs. We come to this publication not to mask the harrowing experiences that Black Girls face, but to provide you with an **understanding** of their beauty, talents, and brilliance; to engage you in identifying, examining, and exploring approaches and case studies of **respecting** the identities that Black Girls bring to school cultures, and to give you tools in authentically **connecting** with Black Girls so that they can do more than survive—they can thrive.

SYSTEMIC HARSH AND TRAUMATIC EXPERIENCES OF BLACK GIRLS

In recent years, movements and publications have been intentionally created and disseminated in order to honor and call out the state of Black Girls, with some examples of these movements being Black Girl Magic, Black Girls Rock, Black Girls Code, and Black Girls DIVE. Efforts such as these and the twitter hashtag #BlackGirlsAreMagic by CaShawn Thompson, started in 2013, have brought awareness to the magical beauty, brilliance, strength, and perseverance of Black Girls (Walton & Oyewuwo-Gassikia, 2017). These movements also call attention to how Black Girls are struggling, dying, and experiencing harsh school experiences, as highlighted in publications such as "Black Girls Matter: Pushed Out, Overpoliced, and Underprotected" (Crenshaw et al., 2015b), *Push Out: The Criminalization of Black Girls in Schools* (Morris, 2016b), "Girlhood Interrupted: The Erasure of Black Girls' Childhood" (Epstein et al., 2017), and "The Case for #BlackGirlMagic: Application of a Strengths-Based, Intersectional Practice Framework for Working With Black Women With Depression" (Walton & Oyewuwo-Gassikia, 2017).

Informed by aforementioned scholarship from sista scholars (Fordham, 1993; hooks, 1994; Ladson-Billings, 1995, 1999; Lawrence-Lightfoot, 1994; Williams, 2000) who focus on Black Girls' experiences, including Dr. Monique Morris

(2016a, 2016b), we add to the scholarship on the crisis for Black Girls, and emphatically state that their access to quality and equitable educational opportunities should no longer—and cannot—be ignored. In 1991, the American Association of University Women's report *Shortchanging Girls, Shortchanging America*, brought to the forefront, with disappointment, how schools were supposedly denying girls equitable access to quality education, and to our dismay, minimized and marginalized the experiences of Black Girls.

The school to prison pipeline is very real in the lives of Black Girls and Women, with implicit and explicit discriminatory school practices that are pushing Black Girls out of school into the pipeline. "Black Girls have the fastest growing suspension rates of all students" (Annamma et al., 2016, p. 214), which translates into them being the fastest growing group in the juvenile system (Killen, 2019). In Boston, Black Girls were "eleven times more subjected to discipline than their white counterparts (340 vs. 30 cases respectively)" (Crenshaw et al., 2015b, p. 21). In New York City, during the 2011–2012 school year, "Ninety percent of all the girls subjected to expulsion were Black. No white girls were expelled" (Crenshaw et al., p. 23). These statistics of expulsion, suspension, and extreme discipline of Black Girls, such as those seen in Boston and New York, are replicated across the country. It is not safe for Black Girls to attend school, as their experiences are traumatic, including such things as being singled out for minor and subjective issues in school such as loitering, dress code violations, hair issues, and inappropriate cell phone usage (Epstein et al., 2017; Evans-Winters, 2019; Morris, 2016b); they are also assaulted by so-called "resource officers" who are supposed to protect them. Schools are no longer a safe haven for Black Girls, and it is time for a radical shift in schools.

THEORETICAL FRAMEWORK

The framework for this radical transformational pedagogy—and of this publication—is rooted in the original works of Black scholars, including Mary McLeod Bethune, Anna Julia Cooper, Ida B. Wells, W. E. B. Du Bois, Carter G. Woodson, and many more African American scholars, educators and thought leaders. Many of the authors represented in this book—the majority of whom are African American, Black Women, and some white—advocate for the use of a radical transformational pedagogy. All of the chapters in this book are unapologetically centered in Black Girls' identities and build upon Afrocentric feminist epistemology (Collins, 2002), Black feminist thought (Collins, 1986, 2002), Black feminist pedagogy (Omolade, 1987), critical race feminism (Evans-Winters & Esposito, 2010), intersectional feminism (Crenshaw, 1993), and womanist performative pedagogy (Hardy, 2009), as well as Black Girl literacy and multiple intersectional ways of knowing (Muhammad & Haddix, 2016). Using a Black feminist theoretical lens brings about "a culturally congruent model that accounts for both gender and race and seeks to provide a more in-depth look at the lived experiences of Black women" (Aston et al., 2018, p. 53). Additionally, many authors are informed by culturally relevant pedagogy (Ladson-Billings, 2000), culturally responsive teaching (Gay, 2018), multicultural education (Banks & Banks, 2019; Grant & Sleeter, 2009) and Molefi Kete Asante's (1991) scholarship on Afrocentric education, which are all critical to the theoretical underpinnings of a shift toward radical educational transformation for Black Girls.

EDUCATIONAL JUSTICE FOR BLACK GIRLS: A CALL FOR RADICAL TRANSFORMATIONAL PEDAGOGY

All Black Lives Matter! Black Girls Matter! Justice for Black Girls! Black Girls should not be just surviving in our nation's schools, but they must be thriving. Using this publication as a platform, we irrefutably call for a **radical transformational pedagogy** which centers on, honors, responds to, and is relevant to the identities and lived experiences of Black Girls. It is time for America to do right for—and with—Black Girls, by providing them equitable access to an Afrocentric, culturally engaging, relevant, and responsive education. In retrospect, Asante (1991) identified a revolutionary shift to centricity for Black Children, and this book also joins Dr. Asante in this shift, wherein we call for a radical transformational pedagogy. We choose to own our choice of language by contextualizing radical as "very different from the usual" and "favoring extreme changes in existing views, habits, conditions, or institutions" (Merriam-Webster, n.d.). as reflected in the third definitions, items *a* and *b* of the *Merriam Webster Dictionary*. We demand a radical institutional change from existing habits and institutions that are unjust, unfair, and discriminatory for Black Girls. In this context, we emphatically assert an urgent plea for the critical need for intentional, rapid, institutional, radical transformational pedagogical change for Black Girls NOW! Survival for Black Girls is not just enough; Change is Critical, Change is NOW!

RESPONSE TO WHITE EDUCATORS

> In 2017–18, a higher percentage of private school teachers than traditional public school teachers were white (85 vs. 80 percent, respectively), and both percentages were higher than the percentage of white public charter school teachers (68 percent).
>
> —U.S. Department of Education,
> National Center for Education Statistics, 2019, para. 3)

As a majority of Black Girls encounter a majority of white teachers and women, we focus on white teachers and white educators. *Teaching Beautiful Brilliant Black Girls* focuses on the educational and schooling experiences of Black Girls in the

United States, and how their lived experiences are often not in sync with white teachers' Eurocentric expectations (Hyland, 2005). Our publication is a response to those white educators, and is a response to the approximately 76 percent of teachers in public schools who are female (U.S. Department of Education, National Center for Education Statistics, 2020)! It is a call out to folx who use anti-Black pedagogical practices with Black Girls!

The purpose of this publication is to present Black Girls as beautiful and brilliant critical thinkers, and (1) to recall the harsh experience that Black Girls continue to experience in schools; (2) to engage white educators to own the harsh experiences endured by Black Girls, by positioning these white educators in such a way to disrupt the micro and macro anti-Black, racist, discriminatory practices that are embedded in classroom, school, and district culture; and (3) to provide educators with the knowledge, skills, and dispositions that will result in them understanding, respecting, and connecting with Black Girls. To authentically engage with Black Girls, educators must first take ownership of and personal responsibility for the cyclical harsh experiences that Black Girls continue to encounter in schools, and then work to position themselves in ways that will intentionally engage Black Girls based on the inherent strengths that Black Girls bring to school settings.

We invite readers to join a community of scholars and activists in creating a counternarrative for how predominantly white educators—and society in general—view and engage with Black Girls in the classroom and always. If educators are going to change the narrative, then white educators need to invest themselves into the transformation of doing their own identity development work and become aware of the hidden biases and assumptions that society has embedded into their psyche, both of which will require thinking and talking racially.

The conversations that need to happen, but are not happening, to transform the ways that schooling is currently holding Black Girls back from achieving their genius are going to require educators to talk about race and anti-Blackness. White educators need to work through their learned norms of color-blindness and color-muteness (Welton et al., 2015) while simultaneously challenging the stereotypical notions of Black Girlhood that lead educators to see Black Girls from a deficit perspective (Morris & Perry, 2007).

This publication is essential to preparing willing and knowledgeable educators to intentionally engage Black Girls in their own education as the practice of freedom (hooks, 1994).

A Word About Language

A note about terminologies: The authors recognize the evolving political, social, and cultural construct of the terminology *women* and *men*; however, the editors also understand the power of deconstructing the terminology *man* from *woman*.

According to Ashlee et al. (2017), the use of *womxn* has become prominent in the field of gender studies as "a symbol of resistance to move beyond a monolithic, white-dominate, cisgender, man centered understanding . . . and to generate more inclusive language (p. 102)." Authors in this book may use multiple forms, and the editors embrace this diversity in language choices. The editors, however, will use the terms *woman* and *women* like Dr. Love and many other authors, acknowledging the rights of individuals to choose and own their language. Readers may also encounter *herstory* and *Shero* to center the lived experiences, legacies, and value of Black Girls and Women. Throughout the text, authors may switch between *Black*, *African American*, and *Black American*, and some may or may not capitalize the entirety of the phrase *Black Girls*. In addition, readers will encounter the term *sista* or *sistah scholars*, to acknowledge and revere African American, Black women who have come before, and who come with us, on this journey. It is the intent of the editors to recognize and embrace not only multiple voices, but also the multiple dynamic uses of language that create a beautiful kaleidoscope of intersectional identities and ideas.

> My use of language signals a different relationship to my material than that which currently prevails in social science literature. For example, I often use the pronoun "our" instead of "their" when referring to African-American women, a choice that embeds me in the group I am studying instead of distancing me from it. (Collins, 2003, p. 48)

We have made the choice to capitalize the *B* in *Black* and keep the *w* in *white* lower case. This choice represents our desire to honor and emphasize Blackness, while simultaneously decentering whiteness in the project of Black liberation. We made this choice months before the *New York Times* published an article announcing a similar choice. In their explanation, they said, "We believe this style best conveys elements of shared history and identity, and reflects our goal to be respectful of all the people and communities we cover" (Coleman, 2020). The words *white* and *brown* remain lowercase for the *Times: brown* because it refers to several "different" cultures and groups, *white* because it "doesn't represent a shared culture and history in the way Black does, and also has long been capitalized by hate groups" (Coleman, 2020).

TEACHING BEAUTIFUL BRILLIANT BLACK GIRLS BOOK CONCEPTUAL STRUCTURE

The structure of this book is based on the framework of **Understanding, Respecting, Connecting**. This framework was created by Dr. Eddie Moore Jr. and was the starting point for The White Privilege Conference (WPC), which he founded in 1999. Within this framework, **Understanding** refers to understanding self and individual social, political, and religious cultures, as well as understanding the various and complex organizational, systemic, and institutional cultures that impact us daily. **Respecting** requires readers to respect history and the historical context surrounding issues related to equity, supremacy, privilege, differences, multiple identities, and intersectionality. Only once one has engaged in work in the first two areas should they finally turn to **Connecting**, and learn to connect networks, resources, opportunities, and pedagogy to strengthen relationships and impact communities. We take this opportunity to thank Dr. Eddie Moore Jr. for having the fortitude and dedication to develop this framework.

In engaging readers of this publication to understand Black Girls, respecting Black, beautiful Girls, and connecting with beautiful, and brilliant Black Girls, we present longer detailed chapters with references and activities or recommendations; shorter, narrative personal vignettes and poetry, to rely on the lived experiences of Black Girls and women (Collins, 2003); and reviews of recommended books with Black female protagonists for K–12 classrooms. All of these contributions are centered in the realities, experiences, and intersectional identities of Beautiful, Black Girls. These contributions are under each tenet: Understanding, Respecting, and Connecting. Within each tenet, they are presented within themes, titled as quotations, from some of our sista/sistah foremothers, queen mothers, iyalodes, mothers, scholars, activists, and educators who embody soulful Blackness, strength, courage, perseverance, beauty, and brilliance. Throughout the text editors insert connections, found in tan boxes and italics, to guide readers and make critical connections from one reading to the next. We are humbled that the multiplicity of all the contributions in the *Teaching Beautiful Brilliant Black Girls* publication are authored by a majority of sistas—African American girls and women who unabashedly live and have the daily experiences of Black Girls (Collins, 2003) to write about it, complemented with pieces from brothas—African American men scholars and activists, and then white folx who identify as "allies" or "disruptors" and who are committed to dismantling the racist and discriminatory educational institutions that influence the cyclical harsh school experiences that Black Girls endure in schools and in society.

UNDERSTANDING

The first tenet of the book is dedicated to **Understanding** African American Girls, with the solid conviction that they are Black, beautiful, brilliant, bold, and courageous. Our publication focus is unapologetically rooted in a strength-and-asset perspective about Black Girls. Understanding is built upon centering, affirming, honoring, legitimizing, and embracing the lived realities and experiences of Black Girls. It is rooted in their herstories—past, present, experiences, intersectionality of identities, and ways of knowing and learning. In the Understanding section, we honor the activism and sweat equity of Alicia Garza, Patrisse Cullors, and Opal Tometi; Harriet Tubman, Bettina Love, Maxine Waters, Natasha Cloud, and Ella Baker; as reflected in quotations from them.

Authors set the stage for helping us understand the richness in Blackness, beauty, and brilliance of Black Girls as they are created on the African shores, named Sheba, Nefertiti . . . , fierce, bold, tall, short, thick, thin, many shades of beautiful, dark, brown, Black, and infinitely crowned to believe in themselves. As described by Miah Prescod's piece, Black Girls are daughters of the diaspora, made with brown sugar, honey, and spice, and are living testimony as reflected in our Beautiful Brilliant Black Girl physician. Within this section, readers are privy to meeting such Black Girls as Dr. Fatima Cody Stanford, a Black Girl physician and scientist at Massachusetts General Hospital and Harvard Medical School—Girls who continue to rock and be resilient. In her piece, our Black Super Girl Dr. Cody shares how she perseveres in counter spaces, known as a *village*. As it takes a village for Black Super Girls to be beautiful and brilliant, Delano-Oriaran, Roach, Jones, and McNeal provide the characteristics of such villages that learning spaces can adopt, and Rebekah Adens provides a process for preparing to create these villages, such as building awareness and ensuring that all stakeholders have a shared language.

Contributors are committed to ensuring that Black Girls are exposed to affirming images such as the ones depicted in the review of the book *Hey Black Child*, and we are as much concerned about the narratives, stereotypes, and tropes of Black Women. *Nah*, as majestically spoken by one of our foremothers, Harriet Tubman, is a section in which authors present rich chapters on the origins of stereotypical and denigrating images of these tropes and caricatures of Black Girls. For example, Snowden focuses on "Where Does the Sapphire Caricature Come From?" while in "My Eloquent, Angry, Woman," Burton recommends what educators can do in the classroom to counter these narratives. These denigrating images, as described by Bell and McGee in "Colorism in the Classroom," are dehumanizing, and we assert that they are murdering the spirits (Love, 2016), beauty, and brilliance of our Black Girls.

The section titled "Spirit Murdering," as defined by Dr. Bettina Love (2016), is "a slow death, a death of the spirit, is a death that is built on racism" (p. 2). The authors in this section, such as Swindell in her chapter "Visible Black Girls . . . Powerful Beyond Measure," tragically show how Black Girls, in their brilliance, come to the classroom with the spirit of courage and strength, and powerful beyond measure, and encounter anti-Black pedagogical practices as their voices are slowly silenced, and resultantly their spirits, rhythm and blues are murdered. This death is captured by authors in this section with narratives such as that in Chapter 7, "Visible Black Girls . . . Powerful Beyond Measure" from Swindell (who poignantly shares how her entire life was "sucked out of" her as a result of her harsh K–12 school experiences). Like many authors in this section, Warren, in "Why Does My Darkness Blind You? Abandoning Racist Teaching Practices," offers educators strategies for truly moving to take action and bring to life the spirits murdered. Toni Graves Williamson, in her contribution, shows how to position Black Girls in "Finding My Armor of Self-Love."

"Reclaiming My Time" (Emba, 2017) pays homage to Rep. Maxine Waters (D-Calif.)—but in this context, we assert that Black Girls are reclaiming their time, their futures, their power, and their spirits. With your help and power, Black Girls will be liberated from the invisible and institutional systematic traps and pipeline to prison, foster care, sex trafficking, and a myriad of traumatic practices, including "abusive adoptions," age compression, and adultification. These practices often result in the criminalization of Black Girls by schools and society. Jesse Harper, in "Girls in the School to Prison Pipeline: Implications of History, Policy, and Race," provides examples of this, including disparate discipline and zero-tolerance policies. Stephany Powell, in "Girl Trafficking Misunderstood: Understanding The Commercially Sexually Exploited African American Girl" challenges educators to shift their paradigm, thus overcoming their "lack of understanding of complex trauma and the role that institutional racism plays in the education system, conjoined with adultification [age compression as coined by Morris, 2016]," and miseducation of African American Girls, as explained by Erin K. Phelps and Robin Phelps Ward in "Know Your Body, Sis," and Keisha L. Bentley-Edwards in the chapter "Little Black Girls With Curves." These authors provide suggestions for educators to consider for Black Girls, based on their positionalities as victims of human trafficking, as transracial adoptees, and/or as participants within the foster care system.

"Your Silence is a Knee on My Neck" was the title of Washington Mystics guard player Natasha Cloud's (2020) powerful essay, which called out athletes who decided to stay silent after the May 25, 2020, murder of George Floyd in Minneapolis. Natasha says,

> But you know what crushes me most of all?? It's how the systems of power in this country are built so strong, and with such prejudice, that in order for white supremacy to flourish—people don't even have to actively *be about* white supremacy. They don't have to carry the burden of being openly racist, or waste their energy on being loudly oppressive. It's not like that at all. All they have to do is *be silent*. (Cloud, 2020, para. 9)

This quotation accurately frames the contributions in this section, as we speak to white educators, who compose over 80 percent of the teaching force. As the spirits of Black Girls are crushed and murdered, educators can no longer be silent on how white supremacy, dominance, and privilege permeate as societal hegemonic practices, and are manifested in individual teaching and school and district cultures. First, in "Whiteness Competency: How Not to be BBQ Becky," Battalora addresses the elephant in the room—white women across the United States who are, and continue to be, a source of harassment towards people of African descent. She reminds them of how whiteness is an advantage for white people, and of how it has been infused in all structures and systems throughout society. Battalora invites white educators to ask themselves, "Could I be a BBQ Becky, Permit Patty, Corner Store Caroline, License Plate Linda, Golf Care Gail or San Francisco Karen (Lang, 2020)?" She suggests that for as much as most white women would like to think it impossible, any white person in U.S. society is at risk of being a BBQ Becky because of their common socialization in white supremacy. Battalora also offers exercises for building whiteness competency, which can help dismantle that socialization. Nahliah Webber in "Keisha Resists Karen" challenges educators to see the embodiment of Ms. Karen in themselves and to critically think about the wounds and damage on Black Girls when Karen takes the reins. Ali Michael follows this vignette with a chapter on building racial competence, suggesting that white educators who are not racially competent could become so by developing the habits and discipline of an antiracist practice. This chapter is followed by Debby Irving's vulnerable and honest confession of the "Seven Ways I Failed Brilliant and Beautiful Black Girls." With each personal testimony like this from white women authors, we invite readers to ask, "How does this reflect who I am and what I do?" Could I be, as Ali Michael says she is, blocking authentic relationships with Black Women and Girls because of my own insecurities? These questions may make white educators uncomfortable, as the authors in this chapter posited, but that is the fundamental project of building racial humility or stamina: learning to expand your comfort zone by stepping into your discomfort zone. Lauren Calig's "The Culture Walk" asks educators to consider, "How do you think our Black Girls feel?" As hard as it may be for some white educators, Robin DiAngelo, in the last chapter in this section, states that they must challenge what she coins as "racial defensiveness [white defensiveness?]" and the ignorance that comes along with it.

Black Girls rock, and they excel in many roles. We end the Understanding tenet with three critical pieces. The first is a letter from Sabrina Robins, a mother who in "Dear, Dear, Dear!" asks all members of the village to understand the urgency of this call. Her letter is followed by Cierra Kaler-Jones's chapter on "A Reimagined Pedagogy of Affirmation and Artistic Practices for Black Girls." Like Kaler-Jones, we challenge you to respond to the call for educational justice for Black Girls, and to reimagine a radical transformational pedagogy. The section ends with Brown's piece, "Infinitely Crowned," reminding us of the beauty and brilliance of Black Girls. As you continue into Respecting and Connecting, we challenge you to find a way to follow the knowledge, wisdom, and truth of the authors in this book, and, as Ella Baker said, "Give light and people will find a way."

RESPECTING

The second tenet of the book is **Respecting** African American Girls. This tenet challenges educators to acknowledge, validate, honor, affirm, and respect the intersectional identities that Black Girls bring to their spaces. *Black Girls are beautiful, brilliant, and more.* In this tenet, it means respecting the richness and intersections of gender identity, expression, ethnicity, nationality, language, religion, spirituality, socioeconomic status, body shape, family unit, geographic area, sexual orientation, height, abilities, gifts, talents, and many more identities that Black Girls have. The intersection, combination, and interlocking of these identities results in varying forms, layers, degrees of experiences, and lived realities of Black Girls, and influences the identities that educators may perceive in the classroom. Love (2019) reminds us intersectionality is not new; but, Kimberlé Crenshaw coined the terminology intersectionality (Nash, 2008) and now it has advanced as a critical scholarship field, and is used as a "springboard for numerous education studies in which researchers use intersectionality framework as a theoretical framework" (Haynes et al., 2020, p. 751). We challenge readers to frame the multiple experiences of Black Girls from an intersectionality lens and to make meaning of Black Girls' lived realities and experiences (Crenshaw, 1993; Harrison, 2017). In the Respecting section, we honor the activism and sweat equity of Rosa Clemente, Michelle Obama, Solange, Tarana Burke, Angela Davis, and Gloria Ladson-Billings.

This tenet begins with Rosa Clemente's wisdom of "I'll be bossy and damn proud." In understanding how to respect Black Girls, you also need to respect the past, as it influences the present. In the chapter, "Who Are Black Girls: An Intersectional Herstory of Feminism," Arki utilizes an intersectional feminist lens, as it is rooted in Black feminist thought, to help readers understand that the way Black Women and Girls experience sexism is very different from the way white women experience it, as Black Women do not possess and have the advantage of privilege and protection that whiteness inherently brings. Arki's chapter lays the foundation for helping readers to respect the multiple identities of Black Girls. The contributions from Olabode, Oling-Sisay, and Sandra Chapman explore and describe the value of ethnicity and nationality, along with how they influence the identities and consciousness that Black Girls bring to the classroom. Sandra Chapman's piece on "Latinidad, Blackness, and Queer Identity" is extremely powerful. In this piece, readers are reminded of what Black Girls bring to schools. Sandra Chapman, in "It Should Have Been All of Us, Together, Against the System: Latinidad, Blackness, and Queer Identity," reminds us that Latinx folx have African ancestries. In this piece, they discuss how invisibilizing the intersectionalities of Black Girls comes to play in school, as—sadly—aspects of their Latinidad and Blackness had never even been mentioned in school. Additionally, the pieces by Olabode, Oling-Sisay, and Sandra Chapman all remind readers of the connection that Black Girls have to the motherland—the African continent. McDonald, in "Prismatic Black Girls Reflecting African Spiritualities in Learning Environments," weaves in the importance of connecting Black Girls with what she considers to be African spirituality. This connection helps to affirm another layer of Black Girls' identities.

This section is informed by attorney and first lady of the 44th president of the United States of America, Michelle Obama, who says, "I am desperate for change—now, not in 8 years or 12 years, but right now." To us, we also demand change now! The authors remind educators and readers that Black Girls, despite age level, encounter, face, and fight sexism, discrimination, and other forms of oppressive practices, as it is a lifetime of their lived realities. As much as they are fighting against racial and social injustices, they are also demanding respect. A case in point is the four-year old Afrolatina in Sandra Chapman and Imani Chapman's "Black Girl on the Playground," who was playing in a community playground and encountered racial aggression from two white boys, ages 7 and 10. Race is a social construct that cannot be avoided as Black Girls navigate oppressive racist spaces their entire lifetime. Duncan states, "Who's Going to Sing a Black Girl's Song" as one of our Black Girls cries out in school, "I can't take this anymore ... I wanna punch him." Our Black Girls are demanding respect, and our authors ask that you embrace them and create spaces that respect them. Waite, in "Black Girls' Voices Matter: Empowering the Voices of Black Girls Against Coopting and Colonization," offers strategies for providing such spaces. In this chapter, Waite states the need to create programs that empower Black Girls but warns against creating programs perpetuating white, middle-class, patriarchal ideologies.

Another layer that adds to the richness of the diversity of Black Girls' identities is hair! The power of hair identity is that it is "more than hair ... that's why you should care" (Brown, 2014). In her release of the song "Don't Touch My Hair," Solange Knowles (2016) expressed the power of hair for Black Girls and women—literally as also explained by Watson and Miles in their chapter. Sistah and musical artiste Solange says,

> Don't touch my hair
>
> When it's the feelings I wear
>
> Don't touch my soul
>
> When it's the rhythm I know
>
> Don't touch my crown
>
> They say the vision I've found
>
> (Whaley, 2016, para. 12)

The contributions reflected in the chapters, vignette, and book review speak volumes to the beauty and politics of hair and head expression for Black Girls and Women. The policing of hair in schools, as Watson and Nash explain in "She Wears a Crown," is subjecting Black Girls to punitive disciplinary measures, hostile learning spaces, and harassment that could be in various forms, as readers have their intersectional lens on. The authors provide a context for the need for respecting Black Girls and their hair identities as they explain the CROWN Act of 2019, an act that prohibits hair discrimination in many states, and they also provide some dos and don'ts as they relate to protecting the crowns (hair) that Black Girls bring to schools. "It's More Than Hair" (Brown, 2014)—it is the niqab, hijab, head-wraps, Gele, Dhuku, turbans, doek, duku, tukwi, and many more (Siamonga, 2015). Black Girls continue to experience racial aggressions in schools, and—unfortunately—some teachers, as described in the Griffin-Blake piece, perpetuate these aggressions against our Black Girls. As a Black educator, Griffin-Blake—who has also experienced hair discrimination as her students have—provides resources, activities, and book recommendations, such as *I Am Enough*. In Delano-Oriaran's review of this book, the beauty of Black hair is expressed in eight or more hairstyles, as the girl characters mirror the realities of Black and brown young girls in society. In "Covered Girls," Arki and Phelps provide reasons for why some Black Girls and Women wrap their hair and heads, and the authors share powerful images of the impact of wrapping on younger girls, most especially in the words of rapper-poet-activist Mona Haydar, in her 2017 video: "Covered Up or Not, Don't Ever Take Us for Granted" (Aidi, 2019).

In "We Want to Turn Victims Into Survivors—and Survivors Into Thrivers," we lean on the wisdom and words of Tarana Burke, creator of the #MeToo hashtag. In this section, Black Girls share their firsthand experiences of racial, psychological, and gender aggressions, harassment, violence, and trauma in their schools. In "Mirror, Mirror," Bowden shares the rage Black Girls feel when students gawk or when a teacher calls them by another Black student's name, as well as their struggles with the burden of invisibility, like Shivers-McGrew, who also struggles to be visible and to activate her voice—but thrives. Raglands's "Black Girls Say #MeToo!" centers Black Girls as they continue to be assaulted and called thots and swooties in middle school.

Angela Davis reminds us that "freedom is a constant struggle," as reflected in these chapters and vignettes. Black Girls continue to struggle in public, private, urban, suburban, rural, and independent schools. Chapters in this section highlight how Black Girls—especially when they are the only ones in their learning spaces in schools or in honors or gifted and talented spaces, according to Swalwell, Kaaba, and Bottley in "When She is the Only One: High-Achieving Black Girls in Suburban School"—are tasked with "representing, othering," and resultantly have to perform juggling acts of navigating racialized and gender violence.

In "Liminal and Limitless: Black Girls in Independent Schools," Alphonse-Crean brings multiple perspectives to the table as a Black Girl and now an adult educator with experiences with independent schools, and focuses on how independent schools are eager to recruit Black Girls in efforts to fulfill their diversity commitment; however, what happens when Black Girls arrive at these schools? Alphonse-Crean shares a process coined as how the ivory tower is nothing more than smog, as Black Girls experience it from tolerance to dismissive practices. Are there best practices to combat this smog? Yes! You have to read the chapter! What, then, does work for Black Girls? Check out Paige's vignette, "A Black Woman Who Attended a Predominantly White School Returns to Teach Black Girls in Predominantly White Schools," as—like all the other authors—they provide some strategies in disrupting systematic discriminatory practices.

The end of the Respecting Black Girls section is titled "Dreamkeepers" in respect of Dr. Gloria Ladson-Billings's book *The Dreamkeepers: Successful Teachers of African American Children*. We lean on the legacy, knowledge, and scholarship of Dr. Ladson-Billings, who has invested her life's work in African American and Black students. We know it takes a village to raise and educate Black Girls; and in this village, there is a community of effective teachers, as demonstrated in Penick's chapter, "Mrs. Ruby Middleton Forsythe and the Power of Sankofa." Mrs. Ruby is the epitome of effective teachers, and readers gain insight into how she embraced a village that thrived on Black excellence and positioned Black Children to keep their dreams and attain success in full-fledged careers of becoming vice president, medical doctors, educators, and lots more.

CONNECTING

The **Connecting** tenet is about holding a space for good teaching and providing teachers and educators with strategies and resources that will support Black Girls both inside the classroom and beyond. This section offers pedagogical strategies for educators to authentically engage and connect with Black Girls in the classroom. A lack of authentic connection could result in cultural mismatch, incompatibility, discontinuity or desynchronization (Ladson-Billings, 1995), thus affecting the cognitive, social, and emotional engagement with Black girls. All teachers and educators can connect with Black Girls through using pedagogical approaches that are culturally relevant, responsive, and relationally symbiotic to the myriad of identities that Black Girls bring into the learning environment. The point of the Connecting tenet is to share pedagogical practices, which are a bridge to engaging teachers in connecting with Black Girls so that they can also see what we see—Black Girls thrive, Black Girl excellence. In the Connecting section, we honor the activism and sweat equity of Zora Neale Hurston, Marley Dias, Audre Lorde, Madam C. J. Walker, Kobe Bryant, and Nana Yaa Asantewaa.

We begin this next section with paying respect to Zora Neale Hurston, as—in her words—the Black Girl is "Such As I Am, A Precious Gift!" We engage educators to approach the pedagogies they use with the mindset that Black girls got it goin' on, according to Raedell and Gay in "Black Girls Got it Goin' On, Yet Their Best

Can Be Better." The authors provide readers with examples of Black Girls who got it goin' on in their beauty and brilliance as well as provide specific examples for Black Girls to use in embracing their beauty and brilliance. In order to engage Black Girls to demonstrate their beauty and brilliance, in "Educators, Don't Be Kryptonite," Pugh shares a few tips that educators can make use of, including listening to Black Girls on how they learn best. Scott and Griffin, in "Learning to Listen to Her: Psychological Verve With Black Girls," argue that Black Girls are responsive to learning well with highly creative and spontaneous activities, also known as vervistic learning practices. They provide exercises that support teachers in applying verve in the classroom. The following pieces provide responsive practices in engaging Black Girls who identify as LGBTQIAA2S+.

We can't help but dedicate this section to Marley Dias, who at the age of 12 in 2015 established the #1000BlackGirlBooks campaign, because she was sick of the books she was given in school, as they did not—in our words—represent her Blackness, beautiful and brilliant. In this section, Delano-Oriaran, in "Selecting and Using BACE (Blackcentric, Authentic, and Culturally Engaging) Books: She Looks Like Me," develops an at-a-glance, detailed set of criteria to guide readers in selecting books that mirror Black Girls, are engaging, and depict Black Girls in protagonist roles. In "Hair Representation Matters: Selecting Children's Books for Black Girls," Kaler-Jones and Reyes craft questions to guide readers in assessing books from a critical lens, and highlight pedagogical strategies that educators can use in honoring and celebrating the beauty of hair for Black Girls. Carnesi, in "Teaching Reading to Brilliant and Beautiful Black Girls: Building a Strong Culture of Engagement," diverts from picture books to young adult books, but also shares reading strategies for encouraging voice and agency for Black Girls. Yes, this section is all about books—book reviews for Black Girls!

"I Am Deliberate and Afraid of Nothing," a quote from Audre Lorde, is the title of the next section. Liston begins by focusing on Black Girl priming—a process of internalizing self-hate as a result of multiple factors. However, Liston also shares classroom actions by which to disrupt this process of self-hate, which is learned as a result of societal images of stereotypes and tropes. Snowden also explores these pervasive stereotypes in "Respect Black Girls: Prioritize, Embrace, and Value," and offers three skills that educators can acquire in countering the narratives of these tropes in positioning Black Girls to thrive and hone their Black Girl Magic in the classroom. Like Snowden, who discusses classroom approaches on embracing Black Girls, El Mekki identifies classroom approaches with a focus on Black Muslim Girls. Arki, in positioning Black Girls to thrive, shares teaching activities in "#StudentAsSignMaker: Curating Classrooms For Identity Development" that center Black Girls to see themselves in authentic and critical ways, and challenge them to counter the narrative of how the world may see them. "Beautiful, Brilliant, Black, and Deaf" by Usherla DeBerry is a catching narrative that provides a glimpse into the multiple layers of discrimination Black Girls face. DeBerry offers eight strategies for engaging and supporting beautiful, brilliant Black Deaf Girls in the classroom. In "I Wish You Believed in Magic," Robins presents an appeal to educators to believe in the Black Girl Magic of beauty and brilliance. Here, she shares a heartbreaking account of when she first received the diagnosis news that her talented, gifted, beautiful, and brilliant Black daughter was diagnosed with autism. Her gut-wrenching narrative shows how the world saw one of our Black, beautiful, and brilliant Girls, and how this view transitioned into a threat of losing her Black Girl Magic. In "Black Girl Magic: Beauty, Brilliance, and Coming to Voice in the Classroom," Serls challenges educators to revive the Black Girl Magic again, and even recommends "tidbits" for teachers. As this section ends, we remind you to be deliberate and afraid of nothing!

We begin the next section with Madam C. J. Walker's "Perseverance is my motto" quote. Lane and Carr, in "Black Girls Constructing Activist Identities in a School-Based Leadership Program," provide a snapshot of pedagogical practices that adversely affect our beautiful, brilliant Black Girls, but also offer strategies for transformative practice that nurtures Black Girls' power. Spaces for Black Girls to thrive? Consider digital spaces, as shared by Greene Wade in "Developing an Ethics of Engaging Black Girls in Digital Spaces."

We celebrate Kobe Bryant as we lean on his wisdom to "Be Thankful That You've Been Given That Gift, Because [Black] Girls Are Amazing." This section is a celebration of fathers and men who believe in the magic of Black Girls, and who know that Black Girls are the owners of the future, as stated by Yusef Salaam, father of seven amazing Black, beautiful, and brilliant Girls. Debunking the stereotypes and negative narratives about Black fathers, we also include a book review of *Juneteenth for Mazie*, in which Delano-Oriaran highlights how the author Floyd Cooper masterfully shares stories of delayed freedom, Juneteenth, and the Emancipation Proclamation. In this book, as readers browse through the pages, they will be drawn to the relationship between a father and a daughter. The powerful presence, nature, and love of Black fatherhood is magnetic as it is demonstrated with the protagonist-daughter, Mazie. Additionally, we share love letters from Igwebuike, El-Mekki, Jones, and one of our coeditors, Eddie Moore Jr. We end this section with Dr. Moore's words to Black Girls: Be bold, be positive, be strong, be beautiful, be brilliant, be Black, and be you!

As our introduction closes and the chapters and vignettes begin, we are led by the words of Nana Yaa Asantewaa, queen mother of the Ashanti Empire, who said, "We Will Fight Till The Last of us Falls in the Battlefield," and that is our truth. Join in this journey with us as we fight and dismantle the oppressive institutions that are in the spaces of beautiful, brilliant, Black Girls. We intentionally highlight the works of beautiful, brilliant Black Women who value mothering, and will fight like Samaria Rice, mother of Tamir Rice, who was murdered at the hands of a police officer. In "Motherwork as Pedagogy," Arki seeks to transform the radical love of Black mothers into a pedagogy for white teachers to embrace for beautiful, brilliant Black Girls. As in the previous sections, we share love letters from mothers to their beautiful, Black and brilliant daughters, and we close with Snowden. Black Girls are wonderfully made, resilient, feminists, the backbones of our people, and this is the time to shine!

REFERENCES

Aidi, L. (2019, February 6). Muslim women resist: How Mona Haydar counters difference through rap. *Sacred Matters Magazine.* https://sacredmattersmagazine.com/muslim-women-resist-how-mona-haydar-counters-difference-through-rap/

American Association of University Women. (1991). *Shortchanging girls, shortchanging America: A nationwide poll to assess self-esteem, educational experiences, interest in math and science, and career aspirations of girls and boys ages 9–15.* Greenberg-Lake, The Analysis Group. https://eric.ed.gov/?id=ED340657

Anderson, B. N. (2020). "See me, see us": Understanding the intersections and continued marginalization of adolescent gifted Black girls in U.S. classrooms. *Gifted Child Today.* https://journals.sagepub.com/doi/10.1177/1076217519898216

Anderson, B. N., & Martin, J. A. (2018). What K–12 teachers need to know about teaching gifted Black girls battling perfectionism and stereotype threat. *Gifted Child Today, 41*(3), 117–124. https://doi.org/10.1177/1076217518768339

Annamma, S. A., Anyon, Y., Joseph, N. M., Farrar, J., Greer, E., Downing, B., & Simmons, J. (2016). Black girls and school discipline: The complexities of being overrepresented and understudied. *Urban Education, 54*(2), 211–242.

Asante, M. K. (1991). The Afrocentric idea in education. *The Journal of Negro Education, 60*(2), 170–180.

Ashlee, A. A., Zamora, B., & Karikari, S. N. (2017). We are woke: A collaborative critical autoethnography of three "womxn" of color graduate students in higher education. *International Journal of Multicultural Education, 19*(1), 89–104.

Aston, C., Graves, Jr., S. L., McGoey, K., Lovelace, T., & Townsend, T. (2018). Promoting sisterhood: The impact of a culturally focused program to address verbally aggressive behaviors in Black girls. *Psychology in the Schools, 55*(1), 50–62.

Banks, J. A., & Banks, C. A. M. (Eds.). (2019). *Multicultural education: Issues and perspectives.* John Wiley & Sons.

Bennett, L., Jr. (1980, November). *Ebony. What is black beauty: An appraisal of the grandeur of Black womanhood provides new and startling answers.* https://books.google.com/books?id=6VkRHt0MLy4C&pg=PA160&lpg=PA160&dq=defining+black+beauty&source=bl&ots=tVo74xBnvQ&sig=ACfU3U0sYSsCLIWibijRgRGP7XtDRvSBpw&hl=en&sa=X&ved=2ahUKEwih_87GtrzqAhXYXM0KHS5WDAQ4ChDoATAGegQIChAB#v=onepage&q=defining%20black%20beauty&f=false

Brown, N. (2014). "It's more than hair … that's why you should care": The politics of appearance for Black women state legislators. *Politics, Groups, and Identities, 2*(3), 295–312, https://doi.org/10.1080/21565503.2014.925816

Cloud, N. (2020, May 30). Your silence is a knee on my neck. *The Players' Tribune.* https://www.theplayerstribune.com/en-us/articles/natasha-cloud-your-silence-is-a-knee-on-my-neck-george-floyd

Coleman, N. (2020, July 5). Why we're capitalizing Black. *New York Times.* https://www.nytimes.com/2020/07/05/insider/capitalized-black.html

Collins, P. H. (1986). Learning from the outsider within: The sociological significance of Black feminist thought. *Social Problems, 33*(6), s14–s32.

Collins, P. H. (2002). *Black feminist thought: Knowledge, consciousness, and the politics of empowerment.* Routledge.

Collins, P. H. (2003). Toward an Afrocentric feminist epistemology. In Y. S. Lincoln & N. K Denzin (Eds.), *Turning points in qualitative research: Tying knots in a handkerchief* (pp. 47–72). Altamira.

Crenshaw, K. (1993). Mapping the margins: Intersectionality, identity politics, and violence against women of color. *Stanford Law Review, 43*, 1241–1299.

Crenshaw, K., Ocen, P., & Nanda, J. (2015a). Black girls matter. *Ms. Magazine, 25*(2), 26–29.

Crenshaw, K. W., Ocen, P., & Nanda, J. (2015b). *Black girls matter: Pushed out, over-policed, and underprotected.* African American Policy Forum and the Center for Intersectionality and Social Policy Studies. http://static1.squarespace.com/static/53f20d90e4b0b80451158d8c/t/54dcc1ece4b001c03e323448/1423753708557/AAPF_BlackGirlsMatterReport.pdf

Cubit, B. (2020, February 28). To be young, gifted, and black: 30 women of color who are breaking barriers and shaking sh*t up. *Popsugar.* https://www.popsugar.com/celebrity/inspiring-young-black-women-to-know-in-2020-47131349#opening-slide

8 different shades of brown skin, which tone do you have? (n.d.). *ThatSista.com.* https://www.thatsister.com/different-shades-of-brown-skin-which-do-you-have

Emba, C. (2017, August 1). "Reclaiming my time" is bigger than Maxine Waters. *Washington Post*, p. 1.

Epstein, R., Blake, J., & González, T. (2017). *Girlhood interrupted: The erasure of black girls' childhood.* Center on Poverty and Inequality, Georgetown Law. Available at SSRN 3000695.

Evans-Winters, V. E. (2014). Are Black girls not gifted? Race, gender, and resilience. *Interdisciplinary Journal of Teaching and Learning, 4*(1), 22–30.

Evans-Winters, V. E. (2019). Response to Black girls & education research: When racialized gender bias and resistance collide. *Education Week.* https://blogs.edweek.org/teachers/classroom_qa_with_larry_ferlazzo/2019/02/response_what_does_it_mean_to_be_young_black_and_female_in_america.html

Evans-Winters, V. E., & Esposito, J. (2010). Other people's daughters: Critical race feminism and Black girls' education. *Educational Foundations, 24*, 11–24.

Find your shade. (n.d.) *The Lip Bar.* https://thelipbar.com/pages/shadefinder

Ford, D. Y. (2013). *Ford female achievement model of excellence (F2 AME).* http://www.drdonnayford.com/#!black-females/c1zop

Fordham, S. (1993). "Those loud Black girls": (Black) women, silence, and gender "passing" in the academy. *Anthropology & Education Quarterly, 24*(1), 3–32.

French, B. H., Lewis, J., & Neville, H. A. (2013). Naming and reclaiming: An interdisciplinary analysis of Black girls' and women's resistance strategies. *Journal of African American Studies, 17*(1), 1–6. https://doi-org.snc.idm.oclc.org/10.1007/s12111-012-9215-4

Gay, G. (2018). *Culturally responsive teaching: Theory, research, and practice.* Teachers College Press.

Grant, C. A., & Sleeter, C. E. (2009). *Five approaches for multicultural teaching plans for race, class, gender and disability.* Jossey-Bass.

Hardy, K. (2009). *Womanist performative pedagogy* [Unpublished doctoral dissertation]. University of North Carolina at Chapel Hill.

Harrison, L. (2017). Redefining intersectionality theory through the lens of African American young adolescent girls' racialized experiences. *Youth & Society, 49*(8), 1023–1039.

Haynes, C., Joseph, N. M., Patton, L. D., Stewart, S., & Allen, E. L. (2020). Toward an understanding of intersectionality methodology: A 30-year literature synthesis of Black women's experiences in higher education. *Review of Educational Research, 90*(6), 751–787.

hooks, b. (1994). *Teaching to transgress: Education as the practice of freedom.* Routledge.

Hyland, N. E. (2005). Being a good teacher of Black students? White teachers and unintentional racism. The Ontario Institute for Studies in Education of the University of Toronto. *Curriculum Inquiry 35*(4), 429–459.

Killen, E. (2019, April 17). The increased criminalization of African American girls. *Georgetown Journal on Poverty Law & Policy.* https://www.law.georgetown.edu/poverty-journal/blog/the-increased-criminalization-of-african-american-girls/#_ftn12

Knowles, S. (2016). Don't touch my hair. On *A seat at the table* [Audio recording]. Columbia Records.

Ladson-Billings, G. (1995). Toward a theory of culturally relevant pedagogy. *American Educational Research Journal, 32*(3), 465–491.

Ladson-Billings, G. (1999). Preparing teachers for diverse student populations: A critical race theory perspective. *Review of Research in Education, 24*, 211–247.

Ladson-Billings, G. (2000). Culturally relevant pedagogy in African-centered schools: Possibilities for progressive educational reform. In D. S. Pollard & C. S. Ajirotutu (Eds.), *African-Centered Schooling in Theory and Practice* (pp. 187–198). Praeger.

Lang, C. (2020, July 6). How the "Karen meme" confronts the violent history of white womanhood. *Time Magazine.* https://time.com/5857023/karen-meme-history-meaning/

Lawrence-Lightfoot, S. (1994). *I've known rivers: Lives of loss and liberation.* Basic Books.

Love, B. L. (2016). Anti-Black state violence, classroom edition: The spirit murdering of Black children. *Journal of Curriculum and Pedagogy, 13*(1), 22–25.

Love, B. L. (2019). *We want to do more than survive: Abolitionist teaching and the pursuit of educational freedom.* Beacon Press.

Merriam-Webster. (n.d.). Retrieved December 13, 2020, from https://www.merriam-webster.com/dictionary/radical

Moore, E., Jr., Michael, A., & Penick-Parks, M. W. (2017). *The guide for white women who teach Black boys.* Corwin.

Morris, E. W., & Perry, B. L. (2017). Girls behaving badly? Race, gender, and subjective evaluation in the discipline of African American girls. *Sociology of Education 90*(2). 127–148. https://doi.org/10.1177/0038040717694876

Morris, M. W. (2016a). Protecting Black girls. *Educational Leadership, 74*(3), 49–53.

Morris, M. W. (2016b). *Pushout: The criminalization of Black girls in schools.* The New Press.

Muhammad, G. E., & Haddix, M. (2016). Centering Black girls' literacies: A review of literature on the multiple ways of knowing of Black girls. *English Education*, *48*(4), 299–336.

Nash, J. C. (2008). Re-thinking intersectionality. *Feminist Review*, *89*(1), 1–15.

Omolade, B. (1987). A Black feminist pedagogy. *Women's Studies Quarterly*, *15*(3/4), 32–39.

Siamonga, E. (2015, March 12). African women and the significance of a head-wrap (Dhuku). *The Patriot: Celebrating Being Zimbabwean*. https://www.thepatriot.co.zw/old_posts/african-women-and-the-significance-of-a-head-wrap-dhuku/

Snowden, K. (2019, July 10). Equity vs. equality vs. liberation: First steps toward inclusive classroom discussions. *Duke TIP's Teachers Workshop*. https://blogs.tip.duke.edu/teachersworkshop/equity-vs-equality-vs-liberation-first-steps-toward-inclusive-classroom-discussions-with-gifted-youth/

U.S. Department of Education, National Center for Education Statistics. (2019). *Teacher characteristics and trends*. https://nces.ed.gov/fastfacts/display.asp?id=28

U.S. Department of Education, National Center for Education Statistics. (2020, May). *Characteristics of public school teachers*. https://nces.ed.gov/programs/coe/indicator_clr.asp

Viera, B., Lewis, T., & Williams, L. (2016). Black girl magic. *Essence*, *46*(10), 84–95.

Walton, Q. L., & Oyewuwo-Gassikia, O. B. (2017). The case for #BlackGirlMagic: Application of a strengths-based, intersectional practice framework for working with black women with depression. *Affilia*, *32*(4), 461–475.

Welton, A. D., Diem, S., & Holme, J. J. (2015). Color conscious, cultural blindness: Suburban school districts and demographic change. Education and Urban Society, *47*(6), 695–722.

Whaley, N. (2016, October 6). Solange's "don't touch my hair" is an anthem reclaiming Black autonomy. *Huffington Post*. https://www.huffpost.com/entry/solanges-dont-touch-my-hair-is-an-anthem-reclaiming_b_57f67383e4b030884674abca

Williams, P. H. (2000). *Black feminist thought: Knowledge, consciousness, and the politics of empowerment*. Routledge.

UNDERSTANDING

PART I

"BLACK PEOPLE I LOVE YOU, I LOVE US, OUR LIVES MATTER."

—Alicia Garza, #BlackLivesMatter

—Alicia Garza, Patrisse Cullors, Opal Tometi

This book is about taking Alicia Garza's words of love for herself and all Black people and amplifying them for Black girls, Black women, and the teachers who teach them. We want teachers to understand why self-love matters so deeply for Black girls, and how they, as teachers, can take part in it. This first chapter, "Black 'Girls' are Different, not Deficient" by Geneva Gay and Raedell Cannie, helps frame what it means to be a Black girl, in all her beauty and brilliance.

Black "Girls" Are Different, Not Deficient

Geneva Gay, Raedell Cannie

As I (Raedell) got ready for my daily dog walking, I dressed in old but warm winter clothes, and didn't give it a second thought. But then I paused—I was about to wear a head bonnet out in public!—something I was taught (seemingly by osmosis) never to do. But, then another thought entered my consciousness. Why should my beautiful handmade satin bonnet with bright yellows, bold blues, ravishing reds, and pretty purples, which I got on my maiden voyage "home" to Africa (the continent), only be worn in the confines of my house, where no one but me could witness the beauty, brilliance, and magic of the Black "girl" who made it? That's nonsense! But it is also symptomatic of how many Black "girls" are socialized to be so as not to be seen, or to always be as "pretty" as possible in public. The message is to keep your genuine self hidden, or to be small enough to be unnoticed, or to be perpetually filtered through other people's notions of acceptability, or to minimize intrusive questions about the actions and artifices of our Black presence and presentation. I receive pointed questions and commentaries such as, "What is that on your head? It's beautiful but it's so different." Reactions such as these remind us (Black "girls") that, according to some other people's standards, our normal is not quite normal enough, and they chip away at our desire to *be* without wondering if it is okay to do so. Yet, we prevail and even go beyond!

Cannie's reflections here are indicative of the need for alternative conceptions of Black "girls'" identities and behaviors that are different from those of U.S. mainstream society. We offer some of these in this chapter with a focus on their "girlness," beauty, and brilliance.

CONTEXTUAL PARAMETERS

Despite the assumptions of some that Black girls (especially in PreK–12 schools) are only a bundle of pathologies and problems, with largely undesirable attitudes and attributes (see Carter Andrews et al., 2019, for a research review), quite the contrary is true. Admittedly, some Black girls do have social, emotional, and academic challenges, but no more so than other youth. Nor should these define their essence. Instead, Black girls are *beautiful and brilliant,* constructive and productive, intelligent and inventive, and they have long heritages of thriving in the midst of opposition, not merely surviving or enduring. They overcome, create, and innovate! As Morgan Parker (2017), explained, "We're [African American females] infinite.... We ... 'contain multitudes.' Contradictions, colors, varieties, inventions. We are growth embodied. We are shape-shifting." Misconceptions about Black females are due in large part to "othering" in which standards other than their own cultural and experiential criteria are used to assess their being.

Some different contextual parameters are needed to understand and appreciate Black "girls'" beauty and brilliance, because most generally held notions denigrate Black womanhood and girlhood normalcy. When acknowledged positively, they tend to focus on "the special" and "the exceptional," such as African American females who overcome dire circumstances and become high achievers—that is, their *exceptionality.* Such individuals and their accomplishments deserve praise and accolades. But we turn the gaze instead on the greater number of *regula*r Black females, and operate on the premise that there is much unrecognized and unappreciated brilliance and beauty among these average, everyday individuals. Because of our focus on the beauty and brilliance of unseen, unacknowledged, and unknown average individuals, we endorse Janelle Harris's (2015, n. p.) advice to Black "girls" to

> find heroes in the everyday women around you. There's not one thing wrong with looking up to the Beyonces and the Nikkis and the Rihannas of the celebrity world, but there are heroes in good, everyday women, the mothers and grandmothers and aunties and teachers and ministers and neighbors who, if you are willing to listen, could teach you life lessons about turning a little into a lot, keeping lights on, being self-assured, and navigating relationships.

RECONCEPTUALIZING BLACK BEAUTY AND BRILLIANCE

We consider "beauty" as more psychological than physiological, and "brilliance" as more about ingenuity than intellectual or academic competence per se. So when we challenge commonly held boundaries of beauty and brilliance, we are not trying to make Black girlhood and womanhood "normal." We are boldly claiming that they already are, and the rest of the world needs to catch up!

The mother wit or folk wisdom embedded in the sayings that "beauty is as beauty does," "it's more about how you carry yourself than how you look" (translation: personas of self-respect and self-dignity!), and "necessity prompts invention" are apropos here. So the actual physical appearance of Black girls is inconsequential in our conception of beauty, and while intellect may be a contributing factor, it is not sufficient for them to be deemed "brilliant." Instead, Black girls' beauty is their strength of will, and their brilliance is their resourcefulness. For us *wokeness*, astuteness, intuitiveness, perceptivity, "making a way out of no way," and "keep on keeping on in spite of *it* all" are better indicators of brilliance.

In this context, *it* means various forms of race- and gender-based oppressions, insults, and denigrations that many Black girls routinely experience in U.S. schools and society. These encounters demand that they continually "stay woke" to ensure socioemotional self-protection and creative thriving. This type of brilliance is apparent in everyday being, such as the quick, instantaneous, apparently effortless, yet imaginative (and unrehearsed) retorts to conversational challenges and invitations; giving the appearance of saying or doing one thing while actually meaning the opposite; and persisting in challenges and opposition with innovation instead of mere endurance.

BLACK "GIRL-NESS" SIGNIFIES CULTURAL CONNECTION

For African American females, "girl" has no age limitations. It is not so much a designation of chronological age (or a phase within the life cycle) as it is a signal of affinity, allegiance, and kindredness. Consequently, "Black girls" exist across the age spectrum, from young babies to the eldest of elders. African American females have reconstructed "girl" to make it serve purposes that it initially was not intended to do, such as to attribute a sense of gentility to a group of women whom the worlds beyond their own boundaries often consider undesirable, unpleasant, and unworthy.

As African American women, we are intimately familiar with how this conception of "girl" is used among *us* as a counternarrative to insults and denial of maturity. So, we often hear and say things like, "Girl, let me tell you . . . ;" Giirrll, did you see that . . . ;" Giirrll, have you heard . . . ;" Girl, stop it . . . ;" Girl, you know you wrong !" or simply, "Girl, what's up!" Thus, it is an informal greeting, a prelude to sharing confidential information, a commentary, a code—but always a signaled connection among African American females that transcends personal familiarity. (Virtual strangers or new acquaintances often refer to each other as "girl" in their interactions.) Given these parameters, "Black girls" in the subsequent discussion come in all ages and stations and statuses in life, and the term is used interchangeably with Black females and women.

LEGACY AND INNOVATION

We assert that Black girls' beauty and brilliance are composed of both inheritance and invention. That is, some of the constituent components of these attributes are communal, while others are individual; some are historical and others are contemporary; some are cultural and ethnic, but others are more personal; some are self-inspired, and others are responses to imposition. Our focus here is the legacy of beauty and brilliance that helps African American females thrive in an often unsupportive and hostile larger world, both past and present. We connect the importance of legacy in characterizing and cultivating Black girls' brilliance, beauty, and thriving with Khalil Gibran's (1926) idea that "Remembrance is a form of meeting" and Maya Angelou's views that "You can't know where you are going until you know where you have been"; and each of us has "the right and possibility to invent ourselves. If a person does not invent herself, she will be invented" (Lagace, 2020, n. p.).

Although this is not intended to be a historical lesson on diasporic Black females' thriving, African American cultural and heritage museums and documentary films in the United States (such as the Northwest African American Museum and the National Museum of African American History and Culture) and other countries are valuable resources for embodying some of these ancestral legacies. Rather, we want to acknowledge the fact that contemporary Black girls in the United States are not alone in the journey toward living gracefully in challenging circumstances (such as perpetually racist and sexist societies and world). Their foremothers went there before them and left knowledge, experiences, and skills worthy of claiming and perpetuating. This is their legacy; it encompasses and radiates both beauty (as strength, style, and finesse) and brilliance (as ingenuity, imagination, and innovation). It is their birthright and their mandate.

Just as their foremothers and foresisters developed imaginative ways of surviving and thriving—of being beautiful and brilliant—so must their contemporary and future daughters, granddaughters, sisters, nieces, and cousins. Again, in explaining these skills we shift the gaze from exceptionality to regularity, and recommend that the profiles of their beauty and brilliance include examples from both publicly known and privately unknown Black "girls." The "publicly known" are highly visible or famous ones who are easily recognizable, whereas the "privately unknown" are not; they are family, close friends, neighbors, and community members who simply are. They do not do anything that is extraordinary beyond refusing to concede to the pathological scripts constructed and disseminated by others about the unworthiness of Black females. Embedded in their strength of character and ethic of being *Black* is beauty and brilliance that anchor their thriving. They often do not have the accumulation of material possessions, but their dignity of being is uncontestable.

By including these "regular folks" in characterizations of Black girls' beauty and brilliance, we respond to a need to honor and praise Black females now and then for their perseverance, innovation, dignity, and grace despite limited material resources, and in the face of pervasive obstacles. We associate these attributes with Khalil Gibran's contention that "out of suffering have emerged strongest souls; the most massive characters are seared with scars" (1912/2013). We also agree with Lerone Bennett Jr. who, in answer to the question "What is Black beauty?" posed in 1980, said,

> Black beauty is a synthesis of external and internal factors and cannot be defined a priori by physical factors alone. . . . The concept of Black beauty in form is linked to beauty of spirit . . . Black beauty is what black beauty does. . . . Black beauty is not purely an ornamental concept . . . it is . . . a functional category. It is for something. It is for use. For love, for life. . . . Black beauty is joy . . . It is the way the sister laughs, the way she calls a bluff, the patented, wholehearted, whole-bodied way she moves. . . . [It is] the whole of the ineffable, indescribable, indecipherable sauciness of a Sister in full flight, a Sister who loves, gives, works, shares, and endures. (p. 161)

Furthermore, "No one standard applies to all," because "there are many mansions in the house of Black beauty," and "Black beauty cannot, should not, and must not be appraised by alien standards" (Bennett 1980, pp. 159, 161). *These realities were so vivid in presence and magnitude during my trip to Accra, Ghana, that I (Raedell) wondered how anyone could fail to see them. But then I admitted to myself (a member of this community though hundreds of years physically removed) that it was jarring at first to witness so many varieties of Black womanhood in one place just being themselves, without having been called together by some special occasion. My eyes did many double takes as I observed tall, short, thin, thick, narrow-nosed, broad-nosed Black "girls" in so many shades of beautiful dark brown and black everywhere—a virtual mecca of Black girlhood. This was a vision to behold even though it was largely only physical, but on some profound level this was **me**, too. Imagine what a deeper knowing would reveal about the cultivation and manifestation of Black girls' beauty and brilliance "back then and there, now and here, and next and everywhere." I saw myself and simultaneously was shamed at being surprised about the canvas of beauty surrounding me, yet proud to be a part of it, even symbolically and vicariously.* We offer these accolades, reflections, and realities (and others throughout this chapter) as "mirrors and windows" for more Black girls to see and relish, unapologetically, their own and each other's beauty and brilliance, individually and collectively, locally and globally.

Cannie's experiences of and reflections about going to the African continent for the first time are indicative of the origins of Black girls' beauty and brilliance. For her "going to Africa" was a symbolic "going home," or returning to an essential source of self. Initially, the specific country (Ghana) of her destination was inconsequential. The fictive kinfolks she encountered there signified the beginnings of the legacies of her own and other Black "girls'" beauty and brilliance. For Cannie, the experience was both a window and a mirror—an opportunity to simultaneously look outward and inward through different filters of her Blackness. It is reminiscent of Maya Angelou's hope for an ancestral reconciliation with and appreciation for Ghanaian women's beauty (the window), and her greater self-acceptance (the mirror) as told in *All God's Children Need Traveling Shoes* (1986), the fifth installation in her seven-part autobiographical series.

Throughout the course of their existence in the United States, Black females (young, old, and age indeterminate) have had to be ingenious in order to live with dignity in the midst of being perpetually scorned, demeaned, denigrated, and devalued in numerable ways. As Tressie McMillan Cottom explained,

> Even just the day-to-day reality of negotiating with gatekeepers for your well-being requires a certain type of competence, a certain way of presentation, a certain way of engaging the social norms in the dominant society. Any minority group in a majority society must display a very high standard of competence to overcome the negative stereotypes and perceptions about them. (Leviton 2020, p. 6)

Herein lies the impetus for much of Black girls' brilliance!

Two compelling portrayals of these individual and communal competencies and uplifts are Maya Angelou's (1994) poems "Still I Rise" and "Phenomenal Woman." Although she speaks in the first person ("I"), the messages are about proud, self-accepting Black women collectively rather than being exclusively personal accolades. "Still I Rise" is about resistance and resilience with "Black style" in the midst of perpetual racism and sexism. In "Phenomenal Woman" Angelou writes about the sources and personas of Black females' strength, confidence, ingenuity, creativity, and finesse. These attributes are often mystifying to others but are intentionally self-cultivated as necessary protections against psychoemotional assaults from outsider individuals and institutions. According to Angelou this inner mystery is personified by the power of one's presence and grace of her style, not by physical features. These ideas epitomize our conceptions of Black girls' inner beauty and outward brilliance.

EDUCATIONAL IMPLICATIONS

As educators. a question we frequently encounter is this: Should our colleagues (especially if they are not Black and/or female) assist in the further beautification and brilliance of Black girls during their schools years (PreK through higher education)? If so, how can this be done? These questions are less challenging when it comes to conventional notions that equate brilliance and thriving with intellectual prowess. On one level the answer is a no-brainer: Of course educators should aid and assist in the further intellectual development of Black girls. But, what about our conceptualization that associates brilliance, beauty, and thriving more with socioemotional well-being; with ingenuity, recovery and renewal in the midst of oppressive environments that surround Black females in the United States on a daily basis; and with the capability to resist their negative effects without compromising or conceding their own human dignity, self-respect, and ethnic, racial, and cultural kindredness? These needs are especially compelling given that socioemotional well-being is now often treated as an add-on or appendix to "regular" teaching and curriculum in most classrooms. These approaches automatically place being responsive to Black girls' needs in the educational margins (if not ignoring them entirely), and thereby compromise both their beauty and brilliance.

We hope all educators realize that the quality education all students deserve and have the right to is much more comprehensive than intellectual or academic—personal, social, moral, political, and cultural development are also crucial. In fact they may be prerequisites to high-quality intellectual development and sociopolitical functionality. As such they are consistent with long-standing, basic psychological and sociological principles of human growth and development. We extend these ideas to our conceptions of the beauty, brilliance, and thriving of Black girls. They cannot cultivate and maximize their intellectual potentialities unless they are psychologically healthy.

Schools and teachers can and should contribute significantly to these accomplishments. The process can begin with joining us in reconceptualizing what these concepts mean; teaching these reconstructions to Black girls (and other students as well); and providing examples of individuals who exemplify them, as well as practice opportunities to develop the associated skills. Since Black girls are present in all levels of education, these interventions are applicable across the entire educational spectrum (both formal and informal), obviously with developmentally appropriate adaptations.

Because Black girls' beauty, brilliance, and thriving are ultimately communal and cultural affairs, we suggest educators use both publicly known (popular and/or famous) individuals and privately unknown local folks to help characterize and document these attributes. Literary examples are valuable teaching resources for these purposes because of the potency of the images and information they convey. Another viable learning resource and technique is personal stories (or portraitures) because of the value in knowing people "from the inside out" (for example, see Cannie, 2018). Furthermore, Black females look upon each other through eyes of shared experiences and memories, and recognize beauty and brilliance that outsiders don't see, can't see, or won't see. Black girls also may begin to be more conscious and appreciative of their own beauty and brilliance by studying others. Sometimes other people can be mirrors and windows of and into ourselves!

In these interactions Black females may not always endorse what we see and hear in each other, but we can (and do) give kudos for its imagination, finesse, and wit. For example, we may say a sista is "bitchy" or "being ugly" (i.e., unkind, uncaring, uncooperative), but then declare the behavior, attitude, or assessment "ain't right but she sho' is good at it." Or, on witnessing another sista (or Black girl) "in flight" (a form of Black aesthetics and/or highly effective performance; in-the-moment repartee) retelling overcoming some kind of challenging obstacles or describing some accomplishment, we might say, "Giirrl quit!," or "Giirrl, you know you wrong!" What we really mean is keep going in the telling as well as the action being told, and that the teller is really *very* right for taking action!

We offer the two following specific teaching possibilities as illustrative of how our conceptions of Black girls' beauty and brilliance can be acknowledged and enhanced in "regular" instructional programs and practices. Their content and methods evoke some elements of both.

1. TOPIC: BLACK FEMALE BODY BEAUTIFICATION

- Focus: Collect and analyze descriptive information and applied illustrations of different types of beautifying techniques in different contexts and time periods. (Remember that Black girls' beauty is more psychological than physiological.)

- Curriculum location: Multiple subjects

- Content aspects that fit with different subjects:

    a. Arts (Black females' aesthetics, cosmetics, hairstyling, communicative repartee and related motivations and feelings, etc.)

    b. History (Black styles across time and circumstances in fashions, music, self-presentation, resistance to oppression and denigration, etc.)

    c. Literary studies (how Black beauty is embedded in and conveyed through poetry, fiction, biographies and autobiographies, documentaries, political commentaries, and music; audio and visual symbols of various "faces" or types of Black beauty, etc.)

    d. Math and science (chemical elements in Black female beautifying processes, finances of body adornment, Black beauty retail industries)

    e. Sociology and psychology (Black female finesse and style, acts of kindredness and "community" among Black females, counternarratives of Black girls' identity development, cultural connections, resilience and coping strategies, socioemotional effects of asset-based conceptions of beauty and brilliance)

2. TOPIC: CAPTURING AND CONVEYING "UNSEEN" BLACK BRILLIANCE

- This could be part of language, literacy and literature studies, social sciences, and humanities instruction from upper elementary through college-level teaching and learning.

- Focus on the ingenuity, imagination, and creativity of "regular folks" (i.e., relatives, neighbors, teachers, agemates, personal friends, local community leaders, etc.) in everyday living.

- Collect personal stories from these "regular folks" (i.e., "storytellers") that exemplify different aspects and/or types of brilliance as described earlier.

- Encourage (even expect!) students to use imaginative techniques in analyzing and presenting the stories they collected, such as creating videos; writing poetry and graphic novels; composing and performing spoken word, songs, and sociodramas; compiling photos and other collage-type essays, etc.

- Have students talk back to the storytellers (interactive dialogues) about the effects of this learning experience for them, and have them share some examples of their own brilliance through written letters, radio talk-show formats, digital conversations, gift giving, hosting celebratory gatherings between students and the storytellers (i.e., the researchers and the researched), et cetera.

Learning experiences such as these give teachers and students opportunities to witness Black girls' beauty and brilliance up close and personal within authentic cultural contexts. What better way to know, embrace, and embellish what Black girls genuinely are now, and their future potential to become.

Many of the chapters and vignettes in this section speak to the essence of who Black girls are, what they bring to the world, and how they are infinitely and wonderfully made. Drs. Geneva Gay and Raedell Cannie began by delving into the idea that many of the white standards to which Black girls are held fall outside of the inherent beauty and brilliance that Black girls embody. This beauty and brilliance is part of all Black girls' legacy and is passed down by their ancestral foremothers. Whether they are presidents, vice presidents, scientists, engineers, educators, physicians, chemists, technologists, herbalists, or mathematicians, Black girls possess magic distinctly their own. In the next vignette, transformational school leader Samantha Pugh demonstrates Black Girl Magic. Clear about who she is, why she teaches, and how to appreciate the magic that Black girls bring into her classrooms, she also shares the painful reality of how she gained that clarity—through years of neglect and invisibility in school—as a Black girl.

Vignette: Black Girl Got Magic

Samantha Pugh

I remember the first time that I heard the term *Black Girl Magic.* This beautiful term or hashtag (depending on what generation you claim) describes the awesomeness and celebrates the accomplishments of Black women. For this Generation Xer, when I say it and when I hear it, it makes me feel warm and fuzzy inside because this concept attempts to define what is so hard to describe in Black women in general—our essence, style, and spirit—which is so hard to capture in words. When I envision it, I have quick illustrious visions of a Black fairy godmother (she resembles Marla Gibbs) waving her magic wand and sprinkling gold fairy dust made up of the blood, sweat, tears, joy, strength, perseverance, resilience, intelligence, and just plain dopeness of my ancestors, over my sleeping deep chocolate body, every night while I sleep. I can see the gold dust particles in the air surrounding me almost like a forcefield that any Marvel superhero may have. Mysterious but magical, I walk through life with this forcefield, ready to take on its challenges, ready to take on the world, ready to pass everyone this dose of supernatural phenomena of Blackness each and every day—prayerfully making the world a better place to exist.

As a Black woman who is an educator and Queen Mother warrior (term I gave myself, jokingly to describe how relentless I can be for educating Black children), my one goal in life and career is to make sure that all children feel, see, and own that magic—their magic, their super power. There is no greater feeling than to watch and witness children each and every day display that magic, and it is an even better feeling to watch them discover and flaunt their magic. I have seen lives transform when children discover this magic, capture it, and spread it. Over the last 20 years, I've seen the discovery of this magic give a voice to the voiceless, hope to the hopeless, and dreams to the dreamless. I see it in classrooms, on playgrounds, and in hallways through learning and laughter, but far too often through tears and pain. My Black Girl Magic is that I have the power to see that magic (even when they don't and the people around them don't), nurture it, honor it, protect it, reinforce it, and celebrate it. Therefore, my work is to create, advocate, and sustain the conditions where Black children come alive and thrive.

Schools didn't do that for me. Schools, in fact, created conditions that put my magic in a chokehold. Years of systemic racism, classicism, sexism, and educational indifference had my magic screaming for air each and every day in the halls of the "top" schools I attended. For so many years, I walked around with an invisible cloak of shame and failure—I couldn't breathe. I remember sitting in the back of my high school math class for a whole semester, and the teacher never walked past me or

(Continued)

(Continued)

talked to me and never even knew my name. He actually sat all the boys in the front of the class and picked the same five boys to call on, to help, and to talk to. For the first time in my life, I failed a class. No one cared, no one asked why, no one offered help or solutions or any hope that I could recover from this. Therefore, failing and indifference became my way of coping and surviving.

In the following vignette, Dr. Fatima Cody Stanford speaks to her journey of receiving support from key individuals during her school experience, the impact this had on her sense of self and her ability to pursue her dreams. Stanford outlines how, as a Black Girl, she always felt seen, acknowledged, and challenged by the educators in her life, allowing her to remain focused on her studies.

As a practicing physician, Stanford touches on the impact COVID-19 has had on Black Girls and the Black community overall, as well as the plight of Black Girls outside of the school setting - all of which impacts their experiences of education. She illustrates the visceral experience of being raised by a village. This concept is expanded upon in the subsequent chapter by Dr. Delano-Oriaran, and mentoring consultants Enyá Roach, Laura Jones & Victoria McNeal. Dr. Delano-Oriaran and her co-authors focus on creating counter spaces for Black Super Girls to excel and thrive. As such spaces exist within Black communities, authors outline ways in which characteristics of these spaces can be recreated in schools and educational environments to meet the needs of the beautiful and brilliant Black Girls who matriculate there. White educators must envision Black girls as intelligent, beautiful and brilliant, thereby creating spaces for Black Girls to dream and reach their highest potential.

Vignette: It Takes a Village: Black Girl Physician, Black Girl Scientist

Fatima Cody Stanford

It takes a village to raise a child. From sixth to twelfth grade, in the Atlanta public school system, my innocent, brown face had been exposed to Black professionals who would soon become the village I needed to thrive and help me define my own diverse voice in a world crowded with a privilege I wasn't born with: White.

Taken into the womb of strong Black women who were my teachers who never discouraged me, I felt empowered to be taught by people who looked like me, by people who made me feel I could accomplish anything, even by white teachers who took their time to listen to my perspective. This was only the beginning of my premeditated success in becoming a physician and scientist.

My eighth-grade white teacher challenged me to write and do research on the mitochondrial Eve—the matrilineal most recent common ancestor (MRCA) for all living humans—and what I found astounded me, that her Black skin, her Black heritage, her Black being, derived from the oldest of ancestors in human history. At only 14 years of age, I had already completed research in biochemistry and appreciated the fact that it was an opportunity given to me.

By ninth grade, Mrs. Respess taught me literature and poetry, an academic field my people struggled and fought for, and we needed to pass down orally to be recognized as literate, for there's no good that can come from an educated Negro, they've said. Mrs. Respess saw potential and opportunity in my deep, brown eyes, knowing that each opportunity I received was a chance for a Black woman to become great. She taught me to never question my value or worth, for without the strength of Black women, this country would fall and collapse on the pillars Black women have built beneath it to keep it sturdy.

I built a strong relationship with my Black counselor, Mrs. Dorothy Swann, a woman I took a great interest in spending much time with, thinking of scholarships as opposed to going to the cafeteria for lunch like everyone else. Mrs. Swann would always say, "I know what you like, and I'll have it ready."

It wasn't long before I received $1.9 million in college scholarship offers from over 45 colleges and universities. In fact, it seemed inevitable. Mrs. Swann's belief in me pushed me to continue to believe in myself, to never place a limit on my potential. Mrs. Swann never told me what colleges I wouldn't be able to attend; rather, she opened up more opportunities for success that I never would have found on my own. Mrs. Swann made me feel equipped and able.

The long haul through middle and high school brought me to the focal point of my first, ultimate achievement: valedictorian. Though I was praised, my experience had been unique, for I wasn't just a valedictorian to everyone, but a Black woman to the world.

What does it mean to be a Black woman? To our White counterparts, being a Black woman means being a threat, but to others, those who share in such a beautiful uniqueness that the world continues to fail to see, being a Black woman means being independent, for we as Black women stand alone. We learned through struggle and the shackles society puts on us that we cannot trust or rely on anyone but ourselves, yet we are the best contributors to this world.

COVID-19 brings trauma to our Black girls in schools and has disproportionately affected Black people and their communities. In a classroom of children, the Black

(Continued)

(Continued)

girl in the classroom has already seen and faced traumas that her colleagues have not or will not ever face themselves. She has lost family members. She must negotiate her need to stay and excel in school. She needs to be given the care and attention that blessed or privileged others are receiving yet don't need. How do we negotiate such losses when Black girls' financial resources are already compromised?

These daughters of COVID Black communities are caring for their siblings, for at 12 years old, I, too, was taking care of my entire family, potty training my cousins, the youngest of whom today are merely 24 and 26 years of age. A Black girl is commonly forced to become a parent well before she has been a child.

So, why are Black women independent, and strong, and fierce, and a threat to the world?

Because we step up and show up. Because we are mature at such a young age that we take on responsibilities of adults while our friends run across playgrounds. Because we hide our trauma, for we won't dare to be seen as vulnerable human beings who actually have a *right* to feel. Because we are already seen as less. Because we have grace and dignity, yet the world continues to perpetuate us as *angry*. Because the world doesn't give a damn about how many degrees we have or promotions we get at work. Or how about the fact that a university would call itself *diverse* but only have two to five Black professors?

We must learn to put our names on the papers of the work we profess, to make sure we are formally credited from the beginning, for if we don't, the world will attack our *intelligence* and stamp it with *ignorance*.

And they wonder why we wear our armor, yet they say we're the ones carrying the sword.

CHAPTER 2

Black, Beautiful, and Brilliant

It Takes a Village: Counter Safe Spaces for Black Super Girls

Omobolade (Bola) Delano-Oriaran, Enyá Roach, Laura Jones, Victoria McNeal

Black Beautiful Brilliant Super Girls . . . accountants, activists, actresses, advocates, alderwomen, ambitious, architects, assertive, astronauts, athletes, attorneys, authors, beauticians, biologists, bold, business CEOs, charismatic, chemists, chefs, colonels, comedians, computer scientists, construction workers, counselors, courageous, creative, culinary artists, curvy, dedicated, dermatologists, detectives, disc jockeys, doctors, ecologists, electricians, elite, engineers, entrepreneurs, fashion designers, film directors, financial advisors, firefighters, flight attendants, gracious, graphic designers, illustrators, influencers, inventors, judges, lawyers, leaders, legislators, mamas, medical doctors, mentors, models, mothers, mountain climbers, MUAs (makeup artists), music producers, news anchors, nurses, owners, pilots, poets, policymakers, powerful, presidents, principals, producers, professors, sassy, scientists, senators, sergeants, sistas, sistahs, soccer players, stockbrokers, social workers, surgeons, teachers, therapists, thought-provoking, tremendous, valedictorians, veterinarians, vice presidents, video game designers, vocal . . . Black Girls are our ancestors' wildest dreams.

Raylynn Thompson, a Black Girl from Oklahoma, was told that "Black girls can't be Valedictorians" (Santi, 2019, para 1). By maintaining a 4.7 GPA and taking college courses, she excelled and became her high school valedictorian in

May 2019. Raylynn was accepted into over 60 colleges with scholarships totaling over $1 million and is currently at Alcorn State, an historically Black university (Santi, 2019).

Kheris Rogers from Los Angeles was bullied all through her elementary school years for having "dark" skin. In the first grade, she remembers asking to stay in the bathtub longer "hoping it would make her skin lighter" (Clifford, 2018, para 1). Her grandmother started using the phrase "Flexin' In My Complexion" as a positive affirmation to inspire and empower her. That affirmation worked, and at age 10 Kheris decided to put the message on shirts. In 2017, she and her sister launched a t-shirt business called Flexin' In My Complexion, and by 2018 they had $110,000 in sales revenue (Clifford, 2018).

At the age of 15, Marsai Martin made an impressive name for herself in Hollywood, California. Manifesting her dream of becoming a legend, she has been named one of the youngest executive producers in Hollywood history, listed on *Forbes'* 30 under 30, and she owns her own production company. Her message to young people that have big dreams at her age is to "take one step at a time, feel comfortable in the space that you are in" (McCarthy, 2020, paras. 10–11).

Naomi Walder, a young gun-control activist, shared in an interview with Brut media why it is crucial to elevate the voices of young Black Girls. She states that when one watches the news, it is easy to see how often the media glorifies white privileged kids as the center of movements, yet there are Black and Brown Girls that have been saying the same thing and receive no attention. For this reason, Naomi continues to fight for Black Girls and herself as a Black Girl, just as she did at the March for Our Lives ("Young Gun Control Activist," 2020).

These Black Girls and many more exist and are Brilliant, exhibiting Black Girl Magic and Black Girl Excellence, and showing how Black Girls Thrive. Against all odds of racism, sexism, classism, Islamophobia, homophobia, and other porous institutional ills in society and our schools, Black Girls continue to defy the odds. But in spite of such defiance, many are still in the midst of emotional, physical, and verbal assault within school systems across America. These beautiful, brilliant Black Girls are your students; they are Aniya, Enyá, Feyikemi, Halima, Kamala, Kheris, Laura, Marsai, Monique, Takeetria, Victoria, Harriet, Rosa, and Sojourner. They are us! These Black Girls were, and are, raised in village counter-spaces that nurture, educate, support, and believe in them, and against all odds they excel, and still rise (Angelou, 2013).

We assert that all Black Super Girls should be in counter-spaces where they are understood, affirmed, honored, nurtured, educated, engaged, valued, and respected. This chapter will focus on the characteristics of these counter-spaces and offer Blackcentric, Afrocentric, culturally sustaining strategies to engage teachers and school districts in initiating, building, nurturing, and supporting village spaces where Black Super Girls excel, thrive, and succeed. Firstly, we explain Super Girls and the need for capitalizing Girls; second, we expand on the concept of the African village and its application to learning spaces; and, finally, we share the characteristics of village spaces that we assert position Black Super Girls to thrive.

BLACK SUPER GIRLS AND THE AFRICAN VILLAGE

In today's educational system, there is an immense number of stereotypes of Black Girls and women in society. One of those stereotypes is that Black Girls and women have built-in strength and are unaffected by the pain [or sadness] they are forced to bear. The strength, yet pain, of Black Girls led Nia Nunn (2018) to identify Black Girls as Super Girls. Nunn asserts that:

> the 'Super' element describes multiple identities, as well as trials and tribulations relevant to the need to defend, protect, and save oneself and others, like that of a super[s]hero . . . the capital 'G' emphasizes self-defined feminine power in Black girlhood. Super-Girl presents a new phenomenon about balancing both strength and sadness due to regular social battles. Super-Girl's strength describes a self-defined feminine power that fosters resilience and on-going decision making in the face of gendered racism. Super-Girl's sadness defines historically rooted pain, sorrow, and sometimes debilitating current conditions and experiences as a result of gendered racism. (p. 241)

Using Nunn's work, we also capitalize *G* in our references to Black Girls to reflect the balance and imbalances of their lived experiences and their power, resilience, and racialized experiences in educational settings.

The popular saying, "It takes a village to raise a child," is an old African proverb. The original concept of this proverb originates from the Yoruba and Igbo tribes and ethnic groups of Nigeria (West Africa), which acknowledges and legitimizes the value of the culture of collaboration and cooperation for raising children (Tibbett, 2008, as cited in Cara, 2012). The concept of the village is rooted in Black, African, and African American ancestry, past and present, and corresponding traditions, values, experiences, and belief systems. The village concept fosters Black pride, Black excellence, community, unity, collective work, high expectations, shared belief systems, togetherness, humility, mutual respect, and dignity. In a 2012 article, Cara elaborates on the concept of "it takes a village to raise a child" and applies it to the classroom setting with an emphasis on collaboration. We assert that this village is transferable and extends from the classroom, through the entire school, into the school district, and on to the wider community; thus our position that it takes a village to edu[cate] and raise—or eduraise—Black Girls. The village setting model positions Black Girls to be Super Girls, brilliant, beautiful, sassy, full of life and spirit, bold, and audacious. The next sections of this chapter will focus on the characteristics of the village.

VILLAGE SPACES WHERE
BLACK SUPER GIRLS CAN THRIVE

SAFE COUNTER-SPACES

Safe counter-spaces are same-race peer settings, affinity groups, or networks (Carter, 2007), and we believe they are transferable. These spaces are areas where Black Super Girls have the freedom and confidence to express themselves, with the goal of not merely surviving, assimilating, or coping, but feeling a sense of ownership (Davis, 1999). For Black Super Girls, these spaces are free of physical, emotional, and/or psychological trauma or stress.

These counter-spaces are affirming and uplifting environments where Black Girls are visible; places where they are valued, respected, and see a reflection of their authentic selves. Seeing themselves enhances their educational experiences, which allows them to thrive and feel safe in their communities, school districts, schools, and classrooms. They are confident when they are in these spaces, and they look forward to going to these spaces. In a five-week writing institute designed for Black Girls, participants had an opportunity to work with two of the program's Black female leaders (Muhammad, 2012). The students researched Black authors who looked like them, and the facilitators created a curriculum where the girls could see themselves in literature via the lives of these Black authors. Creating such a space ensured that the Black Girls would thrive. One of the participants, Iris, spoke:

> of how the writing institute provided a safe space where she could openly express ideas without judgment or worry about political correctness. Engaging in writing to adhere to someone else's standards or expectations has the potential to silence the voices of Black adolescent girls. (Muhammad, 2012, p. 209)

We share the following strategies based on our own research and practice with, on, and for Black Super Girls that allows them to grow into who they are destined to be.

1. Validate and give voice to Black Super Girls. Create same-gender and same-race opportunities that provide leadership roles and opportunities to express themselves.

2. Create an environment where joy and laughter can flourish without judgment, and the usage of slang and Ebonics is allowed for students who choose to express themselves in this manner.

3. Provide independent, same-race, self-contained physical settings for Black Super Girls to self-segregate with peers that look like them. Also called

"identity-affirming counter-spaces," these spaces "allow Black students to specifically affirm the racial and/or ethnic aspects of their identity..., and (are) a positive coping strategy for some students as a response to experiencing what they perceive as racism in the school environment." (Carter, 2007, p. 543)

4. Fill this space with affirming, positive, and diverse images of Black females (Nunn, 2018); books and magazines that feature black people and girls; and comfortable furniture.

5. Employ multiple opportunities to demonstrate "appreciation for knowledge and abilities that often go unrecognized in the classroom" (Woodard et al., 2017, p. 222).

6. Be coconspirators. The adults, educators, mentors, and other school personnel that are in contact with Black Girls must demonstrate the qualities of coconspirators and advocate for Black Girls. Black Lives Matter cofounder Alicia Garza asserted that such advocacy is about action and conspiring (Move to End Violence, 2016). We emphatically state that educators need to initiate, create, and advocate for critical institutional change that engages Black Super Girls to be successful, even when it gets uncomfortable. Using the equity literacy framework (Gorski, 2016), coconspirators should act and respond to biases and inequities on behalf of Black Super Girls. These coconspirators must also challenge and redress institutional and systematic discriminatory practices (such as racialized tracking, disproportionate rates of suspension, expulsion, and push outs (dropouts), hair discrimination, and zero-tolerance policies), even when it feels uncomfortable to do so as white educators. In order for educators to be coconspirators, they must engage in comprehensive, ongoing, and transformational educational professional development workshops about race. According to Delano-Oriaran and Meidl (2013),

> It is critical for White teachers to examine what it means to be White within American society and to examine the manner in which this intersects with the personal and professional identities they present to CLD [culturally and linguistically diverse] students within the school environment. (p. 21)

TRUST

Establishing trust with students is one of the first actions one must perform to develop an authentic relationship with Black Super Girls. Do not second-guess them; rather, validate the experiences that they bring into the learning environment, as unfortunately they are not seen as experts of their lives but are perceived as societal problems (Edwards et al., 2016). Trust is a two-sided, reciprocal relationship with mutual investment in the relationship, and it requires humility and connection. In a real-life scenario, a teacher was working with a student so that she could raise her grades and pass every class. The teacher collaborated with the student to develop a plan for improving the grades. They mutually agreed that the student would receive a reward if the student passed her classes. Based on this level of mutual trust, the student exceeded the expectation and improved her grades. Such trust, according to authors such as Goddard et al. (2001), leads to higher student achievement.

LISTEN TO BLACK SUPER GIRLS

Listening to Black Girls is critical to all stakeholders' success, especially Black Super Girls. Young Black Girls have their voices, capabilities, *and* autonomy ignored because of the negative stereotypes that mark them *in addition* to their age. In communication with Black Girls, if you get a response, do not automatically assume that they are "defiant" or challenging authority; instead, please *listen*. Black Girls "have embraced a loud and tough persona in order to be heard and not overlooked in classrooms and school buildings that tend to ignore them and marginalize them as students" (Evans-Winters & Esposito, 2010, p. 12).

DO NOT CONFUSE BLACK SUPER GIRLS' SILENCE WITH DISENGAGEMENT

Listening to our Black Girls' silence is just as important as listening to their voices. Have you ever experienced a group of students being silent even when you wanted them to verbally participate? Did you interpret that silence as a lack of attention, interest, or knowledge? Some cultural groups use silence as a sign of protection or power in classrooms (Schultz, 2010).

Take, for example, the experiences of Margaret and Zakiya, two African American middle schoolers from a study conducted by Schultz (2010). These young Black Girls demonstrated silence as a form of protection as they navigated through a majority-white school. Margaret, the highest achieving African American student in her grade, used silence to hold onto her academic identity. She was exiled from her white peers, because they did not understand her nor feel any sort of empathy towards her being the only one that looked like her in many if not all of her classes. On the other hand, she was disconnected from her Black peers, because she felt that the only way to achieve academic success was to disassociate herself from the negative stereotypes that many staff members in her school held about Black youth. Margaret intentionally chose silence as a form of protection in a predominantly white school; she could do well in school while practically being invisible. Black Girls, according to Evans-Winters and Esposito (2010), use silence for getting ahead in class (p. 13).

In the case of Zakiya, another Black female youth in Schultz's study, her silence was used to protect her secrets. She chose silence to "protect her family and community life that did not seem well understood by her teachers and many of her peers. Her silence helped her to maintain her integrity in a school that often felt alienating" (Schultz, 2010, p. 2844). Zakiya had very demanding responsibilities to take on once her school day was out. Even though she herself was the child, she had her mother, her neighbors, younger children, and even older relatives depending on her. Her teachers and peers in her middle-class predominantly white school knew very little about her, including her goals and aspirations, because she hid them through her silence, the same silence that allowed her to protect herself from any possible judgments that they may have had.

HIGH EXPECTATIONS

One of the coauthors cited a scenario with Kenyatta (pseudonym), a student who stated that she failed the class because the teacher didn't expect her to complete the missing work. What if the teacher expected her to complete her work? Our Black Girls need educators that have high expectations of them. In "Seeing, Hearing, and Talking Race: Lessons for white Teachers from Four Teachers of Color," Gregory Michie speaks with educators on having expectations for students of color. Drawing on his own teaching experience, Michie recalls, "Too often, I had let my students' tough circumstances reduce my expectations, consciously or not, to more 'realistic' ones—an all-too-common response of well-meaning 'progressive' teachers" (Michie, 2007, p. 8).

How often have you thought that taking it easy on the student was the right thing to do all the time? It's not, as you just lowered your expectations of them and denied them access to equitable opportunity to be successful. This is deemed as a discriminatory practice; there has to be a balance of understanding and expectations. Michie later addresses that having sad feelings for students and not allowing them to learn is what Gloria Ladson-Billings (2002) calls "permission to fail" (as cited in Michie, 2007, p. 8). When Black Girls aren't challenged when needed, they don't thrive. Instead, make it your goal to engage them to enhance their skills and strengthen their ability to be strong willed.

INFUSE A CULTURALLY RELEVANT, RESPONSIVE, AND SUSTAINING BLACK SUPER GIRL CENTERED CURRICULUM AND PEDAGOGY

The adoption of curricula and cocurricular pedagogies that center Black Girls and their experiences, identities, values, histories, and much more is rooted in the works of Ladson-Billings (2014), Gay (2002), and Alim and Paris (2017). All of these approaches are aimed at helping students achieve academic success. This section of the chapter is not a comprehensive interpretation of these approaches, and we encourage educators to engage in in-depth research on them. These pedagogical approaches and more are key to critically engaging Black Girls academically, socially, emotionally, and politically. In using these curricular approaches, educators should depict Black Girls in dominant, active, lead, affirming and positive roles on a consistent basis that lasts beyond the so-called single group heritage months (i.e., February as Black History month and March as Women's month), as doing so is critical to the achievement and engagement of Black Girls. Some strategies for consideration include the following:

1. Work on dismantling biases that you may have about Black Super Girls.

2. Intentionally track, recruit, and retain Black Girls for academic areas or opportunities in which they are underrepresented (STEM fields, advanced mathematics, gifted programs) (Ford, 2014).

3. Provide instructional opportunities for Black Girls, and let them inform you of "who they are and what they want to know" (Nyachae, 2016, p. 801).

4. Listen to Black Girls' perspectives on what they want to see in the curriculum, and infuse their ideas into the curriculum.

5. Legitimize the languages and dialects that Black Girls bring into your learning space; for example, the use of words such as *y'all* and *finna* (Woodard et al., 2017).

6. Use the Black Girls' Literacies Framework, an approach that empowers Black Girls to "draw on their critical literacies by reading and writing about their individual and collective experiences" (Sealey-Ruiz, 2016, p. 295). This approach utilizes a giving voice so that Black Girls are more apt to trust you. Acknowledge the value of social media and use it to engage Black Girls, as they are using it to change their self-narratives. We encourage you to seek additional resources on using digital literacies, critical media literacies, Black Girls' Literacies Collectives, Dark Girls, and Digital Literacies Collaborative with Black Girls, as scholars show that such approaches are transformative for Black Girls (McArthur, 2016).

7. Use textbooks and instructional materials that reflect Black Girls and are authored by Black/African American experts in the field.

8. Intentionally expose Black Girls to courses that are stereotypically considered challenging and are unavailable to Black Girls. These include STEM subjects and AP courses.

9. Teach using Black Girls' cultural frames of references, which Gay (2002) considers to be cultural scaffolding.

10. Self-reflect on a consistent basis to determine whether your curriculum affirms Black Girls, or if it instead marginalizes, devalues, or makes them feel invisible.

CREATE OR SEEK PROGRAMS JUST FOR BLACK GIRLS

These programs are rooted in the past and present stories, legacies, and experiences of Black people. Programs of this nature are designed and created so Black Girls literally have counter-spaces to enter and be themselves. These formal, structured programs honor the intersections of race (Black) and gender (Girl), coupled with various identities that Black Girls identify with, including gender expression, socioeconomic status, family unit, religion, sexual orientation, language, abilities, nationality, and many more. The following are strategies for such programs:

- Collaboratively develop a contract where students and their mentor/facilitator/leader sign a contract and then read it in unison. In signing the contract, "the girls spoke more freely and comfortably from that point forward and maintained the privacy of their sisters' experiences" (Edwards et al., 2016, p. 431).

- Create opportunities to share meals with each other. For example, in Chicago, three African American women created the Black Girls Break Bread organization, a school district–approved program. This program brings Black "women and girls together to share a meal . . . have important conversations they may not be able to openly have in predominantly white spaces [and] . . . feel valued and connect [with] other Black students they might have never met" (Parrella-Aureli, 2019, paras. 5–6).

- Initiate, nurture, and sustain a relationship with your community at large, especially organizations that are led by Blacks and African Americans. These groups represent families of your students and are experts on their lived Black experiences, which may reflect the frames of references that Black Girls bring to the classroom. For example, the African Heritage, Inc. (AHI) in Wisconsin is an organization that one of this chapter's authors cofounded (and of which all of the authors are members). AHI continues to support school districts by providing year round programming and conferences for teachers and students, as well as acting as a support system for families and school districts.

CONNECT BLACK SUPER GIRLS WITH RESOURCES

Educators must be comfortable being the bridge that connects students with various trusted adults and resources, spread positivity, celebrate success, and position Black Girls to feel more connected in a school setting. Schools should familiarize themselves with opportunities that will benefit students inside and outside of learning environments. Seek out Black Greek lettered sororities, also considered the "Divine Nine," which have undergraduate and graduate chapters. Such organizations, including the Delta Sigma Theta Sorority Inc., Alpha Kappa Alpha Sorority Inc., Zeta Phi Beta, and Sigma Gamma Rho offer mentoring opportunities for young Black Girls. For example, the Deltas offer the Dr. Betty Shabazz Delta Academy for girls ages 11–14, and the Delta GEMS for girls ages 14–18 (Delta Sigma Theta Sorority Inc., 2020).

Furthermore, gifted programs, colleges, TRIO, college-bound programs, and the community at large are just a few additional resources that can authentically engage Black Super Girls; filling the classroom with college brochures, especially those from HBCUs, is a start. In addition, having magazines accessible to students, especially publications representing Black excellence, is another great asset to have visible in the classroom. *Ebony*, *Essence*, and *Vibe* are some Black-owned and centered magazines that feature information about the Black community, and there are many more. Making these various resources available to students can position them to start preparing for a future planned for them by them.

This chapter was developed for educators to understand that Black Girls do thrive and excel given the right learning counter "safe" space, one that is rooted in the African proverb, "It takes a village to raise a child." As authors, we extend the proverb to say it takes a village to eduraise Black Super Girls, and in this chapter, we have highlighted some strategies to use in reaching this goal. Our plea to you is to embrace these strategies and thus enter that village and join us in creating or enhancing village counter "safe" spaces where Back Super Girls can thrive.

In the following vignette, we hear the powerful voice of high school student Miah Prescod, who already knows the myriad of ways that the world misunderstands Black women and a way to counter the dominant narrative.

Vignette: Ode to the Black Woman

Miah Prescod, High School Student

Don't tell me Black women aren't beautiful
for our skin is the color of this earth.
　We are divine beings wrapped
in every shade of pure brown skin.

Don't tell me Black women aren't beautiful
because our hair is too much for you to handle.
Box braids, wigs, havana twists, afros, cornrows,
we can do it all and more.
We are forever crowned in kinks, coils, and curls.

Don't tell me Black women aren't beautiful
because of the stretch marks that decorate our thighs,
because you can't stand the thickness in them,
　because these thighs move mountains
because our thighs makes lightning thunder every time we walk into a room,

Don't tell me Black women aren't beautiful
for it is still these luscious lips and hips
that you want,
every dip and curve of this damn body
you crave for.

Don't tell me my women aren't beautiful
for our eyes have seen and felt it all,
every heartache,
every sorrow,
every pain,
every moment you have deprived us of watching our sons grow up.

Don't tell me Black women aren't beautiful
because of the way we walk,
with our heads held high,
with dignity and pride in our steps,
something that you'll never know.
We walk with a backbone,
and with those who've come before us.
We walk for those who shall come after us.

Don't tell me Black women aren't beautiful
because of the way we talk,
in only a language a black woman can understand
and code switching is a skill
reserved for the elite.

Don't tell me Black women aren't beautiful
because you are jealous the sun favors us more than you
because the sun makes us glow in ways you've only imagined.

Don't tell me Black women aren't beautiful
because we aren't afraid to hold back our tongues
because we refuse to tolerate your nonsense
Did you expect us to be mute?
To be complacent with everything wrong in this world?

Don't tell me Black women aren't beautiful
for we are a living testimony
of all the bullshit we have been through—
still going through.

(Continued)

(Continued)

Don't tell me Black women aren't beautiful
for it's still us you search for in every woman that you seek.
Our image is forever engraved into your mind,
a constant reminder of the kind of woman
you so desperately ache for but can never have.

Don't tell me Black women aren't beautiful
for it is you who can't face your own insecurities.
After all, I guess that's why you strive to be us,
wasting thousands of dollars on stuff that comes natural to us.

Don't tell me Black women aren't beautiful
for we are daughters of the diaspora,
made with brown sugar, honey, island spice, and African gold.
It is royal blood that flows through these veins.
Who else you know can birth whole nations, kings, and queens?

Don't tell me Black women aren't beautiful
for beauty is something you are clearly blind to.
We are the definition of perfection, not just our bodies,
but our hearts and minds too.
Even a blind man can tell you,
a black woman is beautiful,
a divine creation from God himself.

Don't tell me Black women aren't beautiful
for it is you who must bow down
before us
or did you not realize
you were standing in the presence of goddesses?

CHAPTER 3

A Systemic Response to Creating a School Where Black Girls Can Thrive

Rebekah Adens

The following chapter is a must-read for school leaders. Rebekah Adens, a nationally recognized trainer of school administrators, skillfully lays out a framework for systemic change that leaders can use to transform their systems—through constant engagement over time—toward schools where Black girls can thrive. Adens demonstrates that school systems cannot serve Black girls without facing the porous ills of racism, sexism, and many other oppressive institutional factors that are inherent in the U.S. education system.

INTRODUCTION

The frank reality is that as a dark skinned, kinky haired, bright, very loud and assertive Black girl, I have rarely attended and never worked at a school where I was able to thrive. Today there are precious few spaces that value those characteristics in Black women. Schools, like many institutions, lack spaces of revolutionary love of Black femaleness. My early alienation in educational spaces set me on a path to define these spaces for myself. In elementary and middle school, my parents sent me to an Afrocentric school so that I could learn and love my culture. Looking back I can recognize their focus on the whole child; it was clear they understood they were building in me the components that I would need to confront the hurdles specific to Black children. I recall being purposefully affirmed in my color, body type, national origin, and speech patterns. Public speaking and executing a task with pride were skills that were greatly prized. Celebrations were focused on African culture and African American holidays and people of significance, for example. This school was not perfect—there was a subtle preference for peers with lighter skin and longer hair both in male and teacher attention. Yet, my time in that school still served as the last time I would experience that level of affirmation and safety in an educational space, home. Knowing that these spaces could exist was essential in my refusal to accept what followed.

My future, my mother thought, needed to be more concretized. In her mind, white prep schools were the only option, and I was shipped off to the least alienating white prep school she could find. I recall the culture shock of switching from an Afrocentric school to an all-white, Quaker preparatory school in sixth grade. In my Afrocentric school, I was told that Black people were active participants, creators, and owners of history; that we contributed essential components to this country and the world. In the all-white school, there was a head-spinning silence that left me assuming Black people accomplished and contributed little to the world, resulting in my searching for value in my people, myself, and my education for years. Worst, when that silence was interrupted, it was to view Black people only through the trauma of slavery for a few classes in American history. How I came to see my potential had suddenly and drastically shrunk. The emotional toll of racism and sexism is often underappreciated—the emotional exhaustion and time that is spent trying to survive, push back, recover, and heal is lost energy that interrupts the growth and educational process. What I hope to portray for white educators, and people who educate Black girls, is the growth-stunting obstacles of oppression that Black girls have to climb just to walk into the building. These obstacles are largely invisible, minimized, or ignored and, thus, rarely removed.

I responded to these unseen obstacles in ways that were logical if one knew to look for oppression disillusionment. Viewed through gender and racial color-blindness, the narrative about me was that I suddenly wasn't living up to my potential, without a sense of what triggered the change. White educators recognized my intelligence but simply couldn't put a finger on why I was suddenly alienated from education and learning. I wish I could have explained, but I wasn't aware of the obstacles myself. It took excessive study just to find the language to explain it today. It is critical that educators build the lens that reveals these structures and begin the process of removing these structures (internally, systemically) so that Black children can express the fullness of their potential.

I have watched white educators struggle to bring together a combined sense of self-awareness, social justice practices, and educational excellence in a manner that reaches all students and, most especially, Black girls. While their efforts are laudable, they continue to fall short because they are looking to diagnose the problem in their students and not in themselves, not in the systems they inhabit, embrace, and create. The alienation begins not in the student but in the people in the environment, in the systems of hierarchy and control. Because racism and sexism in the educational industrial complex is inherent, that means there are also revolutionary spaces of resistance in all aspects that white educators inhabit.

In a transparent acknowledgement of my educational privilege, I will concede that I have thrived educationally, but it was largely *in spite* of the educational systems I have attended, not because of them. It needs to be said—and said quickly—Black girls and children are not thriving as a group. And it's not because there's something wrong with them, their single mothers, their culture, or their home environment. It's because of racism, classism, and many other expressions of oppression inherent in an education system steeped in an unjust sociopolitical structure. I grieve what is lost in the children who face the violence of oppression instead of space to become fully realized contributors to themselves and their families and communities. We must recognize that social injustice isn't just a space outside of the school building but is intimately woven inside of the building as well. Until the threads of oppression are untangled and mitigated, we will continue to create physiologically dangerous spaces for Black girls and all children of color. The effect goes beyond a failure of cultivating the academic genius of Black people; these structures kill it.

This chapter outlines six entry-level practices for disrupting inequity so that Black girls can thrive. These components are a reflection of common structures one should expect to see in schools that are working to disrupt inequity, but they are not intended to be exhaustive. I have shared this framework with school leaders across the country, and many of them have expanded on the framework in innovative and expansive ways. As it is written here, this list appears linear, but it is a continuous cycle of considerations that should be reconsidered regularly, and should support and expand your ability to reveal unjust artifacts over time. This system of searching and reflecting must be an ongoing cycle because white supremacist culture—"the system"—is the default, and without careful and consistent attention your efforts will be co-opted. Treating these practices as a one-and-done checklist will make you vulnerable to a return to the status quo. Check listing will reify your current systems and institute long-lasting harm to those populations you seek to impact. I recommend, instead, that you come back to these steps regularly to support the overall development of systemwide antiracist mindsets and practices.

PRACTICE 1. INTERPERSONAL WORK—BUILDING AWARENESS: EVALUATING THE BIAS INSIDE

All humans have bias as a function of the way our brains work. However, in the United States, white people disproportionately have, and use, their power to create and propagate their own supremacy in hiring, promotion, curriculum, discipline, culture, expulsion, inclusion, and so on—it's systemized. These systems run in perpetuity and prevent the fulfillment of the majority of educational missions that seek to disrupt inequity. If you are a leader of a school that educates minoritized students, then to disrupt and undo the sociopolitical experience of those children is the only way to fulfill your educational mission. The opportunity gap persists because and only because of social inequity. The system perpetuates the gap; neither is undone without the other. This means that every person in your system must recognize and eradicate their unresolved (racial and class) bias while simultaneously building their sociopolitical awareness.

Without healing and self-actualization, the sickness of bias will infect all those who participate in the system. This means that educators who are responsible for the education of oppressed or minoritized communities must be experts in the sociopolitical systems that are producing the achievement or opportunity gap in the first place. This is the first and most important job.

It takes time. There must be structured time to reflect and absorb this work individually and as a team. It cannot be done during summer training hours and left until the next summer. If it isn't built into something like a four- to six-week initial process, then the stage is set for co-option. It is likely necessary for the homogenous teams or teams with a sole minority (who is not responsible for teaching and explaining) to partner with a local expert to provide checks, challenges, and connections to the topic of bias. How will you know when an appropriate level of awareness has been reached? Racism and social inequity have a head start of centuries and unlimited resources. The work is never done. Instead of asking when you will be finished, envision a horizon just out of reach. Find ways to determine whether you have made real headway toward the horizon. Regularly ask yourself the following questions:

- Do you know what privileges you hold?

- Can you state and notice ways that your privilege hurts you?

- Can white people on your faculty fully discuss the ways that white supremacy has harmed their students and harmed themselves as individuals?

- Can you, as a leader, openly and publicly, own your participation in racism/ oppression?

- Can you name aspects of your humanity that you have lost in order to benefit from the oppression of others?

When leaders are truly in touch with engagement around these questions in an ongoing way, space is made for antiracist education to manifest.

Building Awareness Questions

1. Do leaders have a deep knowledge of the systems that are perpetuated against their school's vulnerable population with a keen awareness of antiblackness?

2. Are they aware of bias, privilege, implicit bias, racism, antiracism, and other social systems that affect Black girls and others?

3. Are they aware of and able to speak to their own privileges and the ways these may be enacted in their own roles? Are they able to openly own their implicit bias?

4. Can they receive and take feedback from members of the community when these biases present themselves?

5. Is your team able to system-check for bias perceptions, decisions, and thoughts openly and without knee-jerk rejections?

Quick Resources

Bonilla-Silva, Eduardo. (2017). *Racism Without Racists: Color-Blind Racism and the Persistence of Racial Inequity in the United States.* Rowman & Littlefield.

Kendi, I. X. (2019). *How to be an Antiracist.* One World.

Hard Conversations: Introduction to Racism (online seminar). (n.d.) https://www.pattidigh.com/racism/

National SEED Project. nationalseedproject.org

National Equity Project (sessions and books). www.nationalequityproject.org

PRACTICE 2. CREATING THE VISION

Designing schools where Black Girls can thrive requires a vision statement—a description of where you want the organization to go and how you intend to get there. Your vision will guide your work, righting it toward the horizon over time. Vision statements have different content and structure dependent on the organization. They range from simple statements of intention to complex statements with outcomes and tracked goals. Baseline vision statements should begin by acknowledging bias in the organization and establishing a commitment to address it. They should acknowledge the system being addressed (i.e., racism) and resist vague or euphemistic language (e.g., *urban* or *diverse*). This emergent process with the whole community is key in creating a lasting, effective commitment to the work that follows.

Of utmost importance, this process cannot take place in secret. It must have full community involvement. This involvement requires thoughtful assessment of the state of community relationships and careful processing of a nonhierar-chical structure of community process. Leadership should be able to make pub-lic the need for equity work to the school community (staff, parents, community partners, students, etc.). Often the public aspect is met with resistance, as public statements invite criticism, scrutiny, and questions that systems naturally want to avoid. Public statements are required to ensure that minoritized groups know that the space is attempting to be safer while allowing for blind spots in the sys-temic response to be made visible. They also create the potential space for those groups to speak up when leadership violates this commitment. Public statements are the result of the work of the leader, the team, and the community expressing an understanding of the social systems that shape their students' lives.

Quick Resource

Jackson, Baily, & Hardiman, Rita. (2013). *Continuum on Becoming an Anti-Racist Multicultural Organization.* Adapted from the original concept by Baily Jackson and Rita Hardiman, further developed by Andrea Avazian and Ronice Branding, and further adapted by Melia LaCor. https://www.aesa.us/conferences/2013_ac_presentations/Continuum_AntiRacist.pdf

PRACTICE 3. ESTABLISHING SHARED LANGUAGE

As educators, we know language frames our perceptions, and perception influ-ences our actions. It is important that the community uses language that projects and propagates an antiracist vision. In general, our society thrives on an uncritical mainstream understanding of social systems. We are often comfortable relying solely on our gut to explain complex realities. Asked to define racism, most people will generally share a sense of what they think it might be while struggling to correctly explain an antiracist conception of racism and oppression. Educators cannot undo a system they do not understand. Educators cannot help a student fight back against a system they do not see. Educators cannot join nor support a student in their self-actualization within a system of injustice that countermands that actualization.

Entry into shared language can be professional development that engages your teachers in the process of study and group creation of the definitions of *oppression* and *racism*. Specifically, the shared creation of what these words mean to partici-pants can be a process whereby group dynamics are strengthened, trust is built through healthy conflict, and deep incorporation of the meaning and implication of the words in the experience of students and self can take place. Misconceptions and disagreements will bring many mindsets, beliefs, and perceptions, likely buried, to the surface. These can then be digested and processed together. The process will move your building toward perceptions and beliefs that create psychologically safe spaces for all students and staff. When educators begin applying these concepts and using them as a lens to view their own pedagogy and student engagement, the process has healing potential.

Depending on your context, this process would benefit greatly from outside groups and individuals who can guide the group using an external lens and expertise in understanding antiracist education. The process requires more than just a dictionary; experts can assist with values that guide the work, ensure the nonhierarchical process, and provide clear boundaries and safety measures with which to maintain a balanced and effective discovery process.

Building this muscle of understanding concepts and seeing them in your systems is a key action of moving toward the horizon. It is not necessary to corroborate the definition of experts, but to come to an agreement as a community.

Common Terms for Exploration

race; racism (internalized, interpersonal, structural, systemic); colorism; ethnicity; privilege; bias; implicit bias; microaggression; antiracism/antiracists; color-blindness; culture of poverty; culturally relevant teaching; classism; homophobia; opportunity gap; ally work

Reflection Questions

- Does your school have a common accepted and agreed-upon definition of the words above, and most importantly the words that describe the experience of the marginalized members of your community?

- Are there shared readings that explain these concepts that the staff has read and can use to reflect on their work with students?

Quick Resources

Bonilla-Silva, Eduardo. (1997, June). Rethinking Racism: Toward a Structural Interpretation. *American Sociological Review, 62*(3), 465–480. http://www.jstor.org/stable/2657316

Sue, Derald Wing. (2010). *Microaggressions and Marginality: Manifestation, Dynamics, and Impact.* John Wiley and Sons.

PRACTICE 4. SHARED SPACE FOR BUILDING AWARENESS: AFFINITY WORK

Affinity work—where groups who share identity markers meet on a variety of topics—is powerful work. These groups provide space for differentiated racial affinity work. They provide minoritized groups with a space for sharing, advocacy, and community involvement. They also can signal a workplace that is intentional about its community's equity involvement. Employment spaces are rarely safe spaces—this is more true when touching on topics and conversations that are likely to bring differences and conflicts to the surface.

There is a real need for those in the minority to explore their experience of the bias in the organization and have spaces where they freely, without retribution, discuss experiences and share stories. For those who have racial privilege, affinity space is where they can express their own learning and understanding (understanding that is—most often—still rudimentary) without subjecting those who are under these oppressive systems to their foibles and fumbles. Careful and correct use of affinity spaces means that vulnerable populations decrease the rate of trauma.

Which groups you choose should be created by community survey but also should answer the needs of the equity vision. For most organizations there should be an antiracist affinity space for white people and at least one group dedicated to people of color. The purpose of the groups should be aligned to the diversity, equity, and inclusion vision, but activities are defined by the members of the group. Topics and activities can range from shared reading and outings to talks, museum visits, and other activities in which antiracism is explored. For large organizations there may be restrictions of topics and activities that can be undertaken in affinity spaces. Ensure that you consult your human resource specialist prior to starting.

PRACTICE 5. WHO'S IN THE BUILDING? HIRING PRACTICES

The way that white supremacy plays out in hiring, retention, and promotion is unlimited and too large of a topic to cover here. There are two small ways you should ensure that your attention and practice protect Black girls in hiring. It is a common experience that Black girls find support in the staff of color in the building—these are people who understand and can empathize with the bias that Black girls confront inside and outside of the school building. They may provide a listening ear or suggestions on how to handle and face their common experiences of racism and oppression. Often these staff members are not found in the teaching staff or leadership, and are unable to ensure—through involvement in hiring—that Black girls have examples and through lines to educational excellence within the school building. It should be noted that all staff should have the ability to support

Black girls. The inability of non-Black faculty to do this well is a function of racism and can be addressed.

If your mission is to address communities of color, staff who have proven experience and positive outcomes with this group should be prioritized and promoted over staff who have the right answers, pedigree, and skin color. The skill of building rapport and warm relationships with students has to be included in faculty and staff evaluations, along with other outcomes. If your mission is largely linked to communities of color and your management and concentrations of power are largely white, your system is co-opted from the start. Evaluate and respond to these expressions of white supremacy. Ignore them at the peril of the minorities in your community.

Reflection Question

- Where are the majority of the Black staff located? Why is it this way? Does it reify racial hierarchies?

- Does your school have a commitment to retaining, promoting, and hiring staff of color?

- Does your evaluation process highlight the ability to reach students of color/ Black students with other important metrics?

- Do you double-check your retention data across lines of difference to highlight and prevent social inequity for targeted staff?

- Are the spaces of concentrated power held, in large part, by white people? How does this affect your mission? How does this affect your community? How does this affect minorities in your community? How does it affect Black girls?

Quick Reference

Booker, Chaka. (2020). *Mastering the Hire: 12 Strategies to Improve Your Odds of Finding the Best Hire.* HarperCollins Leadership.

PRACTICE 6. LONGEVITY: A FINAL WORD ON BUILDING CYCLICAL PRACTICES

Frequently, structures that attend to antiracist practices are temporary. Likely it is the pet focus of one or two staff members, and when those staff members leave, the work leaves with them. Consideration must be given to aligning the work of diversity investigation and implementation with the understanding that diversity, equity, and inclusion are superordinate to the work of educating Black girls.

For minoritized or targeted communities, a great curriculum isn't enough. *Great* almost always isn't defined by the needs of minoritized communities. Instead of assigning a person to this work, assign it to a role or roles. Define the persistent roadblocks and prepare for them. Keep a history of the work and rationale for key decisions so that they can be revisited in the future. Codify your vision both in the mission of the school and in the roles and responsibilities of the leadership. Keep hope, be bold, and be fearless.

Hey Black Child, by U. E. Perkins, illustrated by Bryan Collier

Book Review by Omobolade Delano-Oriaran

Hey Black Child (Perkins, 2017) is an adaptation of a 1975 poem, an ode to Black children, by social worker and playwright Useni Eugene Perkins. Perkins wanted to "inspire and motivate all [B]lack children to achieve their God-given potential regardless of the challenges they face in life" (n. p.). On the front cover, illustrator Bryan Collier magically weaves in bold gold, red, and yellow paint colors to complement the varying shades of blue, which depict love, harmony, togetherness, and peace in some West African countries. These colors breathe life into the book's images of a Black Girl and Boy, their head and shoulders visible to readers. Each page delivers positive affirmations to Black children while providing them characters who share in their Black heritage and persona. In affirming, assertive, and leadership roles, the Black children characters demonstrate brilliance and strength emboldened with words about "what you can do . . . and what you want to be" (n. p.). The book also beautifully illustrates a Black female child as a pianist, astronomer, astronaut, and ballerina, which transmits messages of academic excellence, high expectations, and that the sky is not the limit; it's only the beginning. Useni weaves past and present "layering images from African civilizations, the civil rights movement, and Black Lives Matter into the spreads, connecting the book's triumphs to African Americans' roots and ongoing struggles against racism and oppression" to instill a sense of Black history, more accurately known as American history (Friedman, 2018).

PART II
"NAH"
—Harriet Tubman

The complex experiences of Black girls and womxn cannot be understood without a clear grasp of the stereotypes and biases placed upon them as they navigate society. This section will help readers identify those tropes and understand how they impact Black girls and women in school and the workplace. The first vignette in this section, by independent school administrator Erica Snowden, explores the origin of the Sapphire caricature, one of the most pervasive tropes shaping the misrepresentation of Black women in the United States. Dr. Heather Burton in the next chapter demonstrates how it feels to navigate a minefield of stereotypes and tropes. The next chapter by Dr. Karen Dace focuses on relationships between Black and white women in the academy by explicating the narrow pathways Black girls and women navigate to be labeled the "right kind of Black girl." Widening those pathways requires educators to understand the sociopolitical history of Black girls and womxn while developing the capacity to see their own role in perpetuating what many Black girls and women refer to as respectability politics.

In that spirit, the following chapter by scholars Bell and McGhee looks at colorism, a term that delineates a hierarchy of racism within and amongst people of color, based on skin tone (lightness or darkness) and used as a proxy for proximity to whiteness. While not widely discussed in the classrooms, this concept directly impacts Black girls in schools. Developing an understanding of the history of colorism, its roots in the enslavement of people of African descent in the United States, and the current ways that it continues to manifest in society will help illuminate a key detriment in Black girls' psyches and sense of self. This section ends with a vignette by Abrielle Moore, an undergraduate student who speaks to Black women's tokenization as another trope that narrows the path for Black girls. Laced with details of cognitive dissonance, this heartfelt vignette offers students, educators, administrators, or anyone who works in schools the opportunity to be conscious of the plight of those who are being othered.

Vignette: Where Does the Sapphire Caricature Come From?

Erica Snowden

The first negative and demeaning trope of Black Women began in the 1800s as "sassy mammies." Hattie McDaniel played several of these characters and is well known for her role in *Gone With the Wind*. The sassy mammie could criticize her husband, family, and friends and jokingly chastise the white men on the plantation, but she remained loyal. She was loyal to the racial hierarchy. She actually supported an idea that slavery and segregation were not extremely oppressive. In schools, we sometimes see the older Black secretary or other paraprofessional who talks to the principal in a way that most others cannot. Maybe it is because she has been at the school for 20 years, maybe she has known him the longest, or maybe she knows the family. In any case, onlookers may question the professionalism in this relationship, while others may be happy to see a Black woman in that office. This characterization would not become known as the Sapphire caricature until the early 1900s with the introduction of *Amos 'n' Andy*, a radio show that later became a TV show. *Amos 'n' Andy* was the stereotypical minstrel show, an early take on cultural appropriation, with two white men mimicking and mocking the culture of Black folx. In the 1950s, it aired on television with an all-Black cast, promoting internalized oppression and supporting whiteness as a product of individualism, while Black folx were propagated as a funny race and not as individual actors.

The name Sapphire comes from Sapphire Stevens, the wife of George "Kingfish" Stevens, a stereotypical Black man perpetuated as lazy, unemployed, broke, ignorant, and constantly spewing malapropisms in the *Amos 'n' Andy* show. Sapphire's character would berate him repeatedly, earning herself a reputation as domineering, aggressive, and emasculating towards her husband. The character was also seen as unattractive, which added another layer. Though not yet generalized as the Angry Black Woman trope, the Sapphire caricature caught on and was used in many comedies. Aunt Esther (1972) in *Sanford & Son*, Florida Evans (1974) in *Good Times*, Florence Johnston (1975) in *The Jeffersons*, Pam (1992) in *Martin*, and Rochelle (2005) in *Everybody Hates Chris* all serve as Sapphire caricatures in their roles. In predominantly white schools, where Black girls may be small in number, we often see them trying to fit in by joking with other students. They desperately want to be seen and accepted, so they have the loudest voice, the most dramatic movements, and possibly the harshest jokes. Black girls just want to belong, and instead of seeing them as girls that need some time to adjust to a new environment and maybe learn to code-switch as a means of survival, they are seen as aggressive, loud, and over the top.

It's important to note that no Sapphire is complete without a stereotypical Black male who, in the audience's eyes, is undeserving of respect. This changed with the introduction of blaxploitation films in the 1970s, where the Sapphire caricature merged with the Jezebel caricature, morphing into the Angry Black Woman (ABW) whose focus was less on Black men and more on injustice and actors of injustice. This caricature continues to be perpetuated on TV with shows such as *How to Get Away With Murder, Scandal,* and *Being Mary Jane.* We've seen it in family-friendly shows such as *Family Matters, Saved by the Bell,* and *Moesha.* TV shows such as *The Cosby Show,* with a Black female lead—Claire Huxtable—and *Blackish,* with Tracey Ellis Ross, neither of which plays into the ABW stereotype, are a rarity.

It's not just the fictional TV world where this plays out. There are many well-known public figures, such as Anita Hill, Maxine Waters, and Michelle Obama, who have been accused of being Angry Black Women. More important, there are young girls in schools every day being implicitly and explicitly treated as Angry Black Women, though they aren't necessarily walking around with frowns on their faces. It is common to see Black girls and women crossing the campus with a "resting face." This face is neither happy nor mad or anything in between. It is the natural look of the face when one is not emoting. However, girls are often asked about and accused of being upset because they do not perpetually smile from place to place. The resting face goes against the societal norms that girls should be passive and happy at all times.

We need to create a new norm for Black women and girls, one that does not confine Black girls to a sassy, oversexualized, or angry narrative. As Sonya Renee Taylor (2018) said, "The body is not an apology."

Black girls and women, unleash yourselves to be unapologetically you. Shine and spread your #BlackGirlMagic. The time is now.

CHAPTER 4

My Eloquent, Angry, Black Rage

Heather E. Burton

During a staff meeting at the predominately white institution I work for, my safe space was challenged by the Angry Black Woman trope (Fordham, 1993). A white, female colleague verbally recalled a conversation that occurred between her and a Black female student. As she regurgitated the story, she fixated on the words of the Black student, "I'm tired of talking to white people!" My colleague shared that she responded to the student suggesting the comment meant she was intimidated or uncomfortable with white people. Immediately, because of my own experiences as a Black girl in the classroom as student and teacher, I knew the student's words were not of intimidation or discomfort; they are a warning against a social disconnect based on race. My colleague no longer saw a student, a young person, a scholar, but an angry Black woman who she inadvertently described as enraged, bitter, and irrational. She had no idea the use of the word *angry* to describe a Black woman was more than an interpersonal stereotype, but also a racial microaggression steeped into a socially accepted cultural trope. She did not realize, or did not want to realize, how many times the textbooks, newspapers, and media have mislabeled successful Black women such as tennis champion Serena Williams, former first lady Michelle Obama, and Congresswoman Maxine Waters as angry, perpetuating the angry Black woman trope. (Prasad, 2018)

Everyday nonverbal and verbal cultural norms within the United States Black community reject the cultural norms of white privilege, white supremacy, and whiteness; therefore, Black girls who employ these expressive narratives are labeled as aggressive, overbearing, and disrespectful—hence positioning them as the Angry Black Woman. Therefore, by our very nature of being, the mere existence of Black women and girls is in direct opposition to the dominant power structure, politicizing us, our bodies, and our actions.

Returning to my colleague's statement, her words not only questioned the legitimacy of the student's comments, but also questioned my very own display of this similar sentiment, or what Black, feminist scholar Brittany Cooper describes as "eloquent rage." Despite our many nonsynonymous identity markers (age, education, socioeconomic status), she and I are still viewed the same by this person, and therefore, equally disrespected. Knowing I had to do something, I challenged myself to offer my white colleague a historical overview of the Angry Black Woman trope. For this chapter, I also offer an overview for any white woman educator or administrator who finds herself working with or on behalf of Black girls in the classroom.

ORIGINS OF THE ANGRY BLACK WOMAN: CULTURAL NORMS OR STEREOTYPES?

The original Angry Black Woman was the Sapphire caricature, which:

> portrays Black women as rude, loud, malicious, stubborn, and overbearing . . . she is tart-tongued and emasculating, one hand on a hip and the other pointing and jabbing (or arms akimbo), violently and rhythmically rocking her head, mocking African American men for offenses ranging from being unemployed to sexually pursuing white women. . . . Although African American men are her primary targets, she has venom for anyone who insults or disrespects her. The Sapphire's desire to dominate and her hyper-sensitivity to injustices make her a perpetual complainer, but she does not criticize to improve things; rather, she criticizes because she is unendingly bitter and wishes unhappiness on others. The Sapphire Caricature is a harsh portrayal of African American women, but it is more than that; it is a social control mechanism that is employed to punish Black women who violate the societal norms that encourage them to be passive, servile, non-threatening, and unseen. (Pilgrim, 2008/2012)

The Sapphire character became popular with the *Amos 'n' Andy* radio show in the 1950s, which portrayed Black women as "domineering, aggressive, and emasculating" (Pilgrim, 2008/2012). When the television version of the show emerged, it brought a visual representation of the Angry Black Woman. Are these expressions cultural norms or racial microaggressions? A white teacher in a predominantly Black setting has a responsibility to familiarize herself with cultural norms, just as anyone does who merges into a different culture other than their own.

> There are shared experiences/practices that bind people of a shared culture. . . . These things don't become stereotypes until they are used to

demean . . . stereotypes are typically rooted in surface observations that lack context and are presented/critiqued through an outside lens. (Seales, 2019, p. 71)

There are shared experiences/practices that exist within the culture of Black women, "a totality of traits and characters that are peculiar to a people to the extent that it marks them out from other peoples or societies" (Idang, 2015, p. 98). These traits include the Black woman's dialect, style of dress, music, work, arts, religion, dancing, and so on. "The shared culture of Black women does not suggest that they are a monolith, but rather implies, recognizes and validates the similarities between them unlike other cultural groups or social identities" (Idang, 2015, p. 98).

THE IMPACT

In my experience working with K–12 students and educators, there is a significant disconnect between white women educators and Black girls. Stemming from the misinterpretation of verbal and nonverbal communication from Black girls as in the above example, interpreted behaviors lead the educator to assume, "Why is she so angry? So bent out of shape? So sen-si-tive?" (Jones & Norwood, 2017 p. 2044). When a Black girl pushes against the white societal norms of behavior, she is labeled loud, erratic, uncontrollable, full of attitude, and ultimately, an Angry Black Woman (Jones & Norwood, 2017). When this happens in the teacher–student relationship, educators can find themselves addressing the Angry Black Woman through biased treatment and the use of microaggressions.

Negative images open the door for biased treatment towards Black girls when white teachers are limited to historical and racially insensitive images of Black women. The image of the Angry Black Woman is a danger to the white teacher and the Black girl. The Black girl is seen as sassy, outspoken, short-tempered, having a negative attitude, and violent in her approach to problem solving. Lack of information about this stereotype fosters emotional discourse between the teacher and the student. The student becomes defensive when words such as *angry* are used to describe her, because sometimes, unlike the teacher, she understands the historical context of the current situation. In her ignorance about word choice, the teacher becomes defensive and feels disrespected, because she cannot understand the emotional escalation, laying a path for microaggressions to occur.

In order to counter these images, white teachers must incorporate an intersectional perspective not only into their own personal learning but also into their classroom teaching methods; they must work to transform curriculum *and* their pedagogy. It is important to incorporate an intersectional feminist pedagogy into all aspects of the education system, classroom, textbooks, speakers, and programs to engage in dialogue around cultural norms. Effort must also be put forth by the educator to learn about tropes such as the Angry Black Woman.

In understanding the trope of the Angry Black Woman, one must also understand the reality of the Angry Black Woman. The Black woman may in fact be justified in her anger because she has dealt with centuries of systemic oppression against the intersectionality of her race and her gender (Cooper, 2018, Crenshaw, 1994, Seales, 2019). Understanding the source of the anger, whether perceived or real, can assist in combating the bias of the Angry Black Woman trope and guard against biased treatment. Incorporating diverse perspectives and understanding into the education system will not stop all bias and microaggressions; but it will combat some of the negative biases towards Black girls in the classroom.

TEACHING TO OPPRESS OR EDUCATING TO LIBERATE?

The image of the Black woman has been distorted in the classroom since the inception of chattel slavery. With limited positive images of Black women in textbooks and media, how are white teachers expected to teach Black girls if the formal education system perpetuates Black women stereotypes? In a typical, K–12 education, the curriculum is male centric and oppressive (Swartz, 1993), and teacher pedagogy is often limited to one's often minimal exposure to images of Black women and Black culture. This may not be customary for all formal education; however, as a product of a predominately white school district and in my experience as a diversity consultant for several predominately white districts, this, unfortunately, is the standard.

When I was attending a predominantly white junior and senior high school (3 Black students and 387 white students in my graduating class), I remember a limited number of images that represented Black women, and the majority were negative. If required readings such as *Uncle Tom's Cabin* (Stowe, 1851/1999) feature the promiscuous slave girls, Cassy and Emmeline, the unruly slave, Topsy, and the brave maid, where does the white educator familiarize herself with positive images of Black Women? What is she to do when *The Adventures of Huckleberry Finn* (Twain, 1884/2002) *To Kill a Mockingbird* (Lee, 1960/2006) and other books limit realistic views of the Black woman or never introduce the Black woman? Or the viewing of Alex Haley's *Roots* is the 11th-grade Black history lesson? Once they are out of high school, educators' preservice teaching training is shaped in the practical application of teaching and leaves little room to reverse the Angry Black Woman and other tropes:

> Sometimes the assumption we make about others comes not from what we have been told or what we have seen on television or in books, but rather from what we have not been told. . . . Stereotypes, omissions, and distortions all contribute to the development of prejudice. (Tatum, 1997, pp. 4 & 5)

This type of formal education cultivates a space in which the educator forms biases and preconceived notions towards Black girls, thus resulting in disparate treatment in the classroom. This, arguably, is not intentional on the part of white teachers, but occurs because of the omissions, distortions, and overt invisibility of Black girls in the classroom and the lack of curricular and pedagogical inputs that internally counter the Angry Black Woman trope.

How do educators combat the use of microaggressions and biased treatment when they possess limited or no knowledge of the Angry Black Woman trope? First educators must revisit their formal education to examine its impact on shaping their unconscious bias. Next, educators should seek to understand "cultural norms versus stereotypes" (Seales, 2019, p.71). White teachers of Black girls should make a commitment to understand the Angry Black Woman trope. Where did the trope originate? How does the trope impact the teacher's method of classroom instruction and behavior discipline? How does this trope impact the behavior of the Black girl? Why not reverse the stereotype as a means for understanding how to avoid microaggressions and unbiased treatment?

ACTIVITIES

The following exercises are ways in which white teachers can work to combat bias towards Black girls in the classroom. Activities 1 and 2 are for self-inventory. Activities 3 and 4 are for classroom instruction; both can be done by the individual or as a class.

Activity 1

Self-Assessment Questionnaire (Be Open and Honest)

1. What is the first memory you have of a Black Woman? Was it in a text book? A movie? Or in person?

2. What were your first thoughts towards Black Women—positive and negative? Provide concrete examples

3. Reflecting on books, film, TV, and media, what images of Black Women do you see? Are these positive or negative images?

4. Are you aware of biases or stereotypes that have developed from these images?

Activity 2

Complete the Harvard Implicit Bias Test:

https://implicit.harvard.edu/implicit/

Activity 3

Read two books or watch two movies with historical images from the time before slavery was established in the United States, and compare/contrast these books/movies with two books/movies portraying the period after slavery was abolished. (Use the following questions as a guide for your discussion.)

1.   What images of Black women were portrayed?

2.   Are these familiar images?

3.   Did it change your perspective towards Black women?

4.   Did it provide you with a historical connotation you were unfamiliar with?

Examples

from the preslavery period:

Nzinga African Warrior Queen (Moses, 2016)

Chronicle of the Queens of Egypt (Tyldesly, 2006)

from the postslavery period:

Gone With the Wind (Mitchell, 1936/1999; Selznick & Fleming, 1939)

Imitation of Life (Hurts, 1933/2004; Laemmle & Stahl, 1934)

Activity 4

Identify images of Black Women in books, magazines, et cetera, and display pictures in the classroom. These images will allow the teacher and the student to see that Black women existed in strong positive roles before the stereotypes occurred in early American literature.

CHAPTER 5

The Right Kind of Black Girls

Karen L. Dace

Afriend—I'll call her Theresa—recently shared a conversation she had with someone she thought to be a friend. Theresa is a Black woman pursuing college-level diversity and inclusion administrative positions. In an effort to offer encouragement as Theresa prepared for an upcoming interview, her friend, a white man, explained "You are the right kind of Black woman for diversity jobs." When pressed, Theresa's friend could not, perhaps would not, elaborate. An explanation wasn't necessary. Immediately, Theresa knew her fair or light skin, accompanied by her decision to straighten her naturally kinky hair, made her more appealing to her friend's white sensibilities.

In 2012, I edited *Unlikely Allies in the Academy: Women of Color and White Women in Conversation*, which included narratives of 10 women of Color and 10 white women about obstacles to cross-race alliances. This chapter will share some of the lessons learned during the editing and publication process of that text, as they are helpful in identifying and understanding the exchange described above and the microaggressions Black women and Girls encounter in their relationships and experiences with some white women K–12 instructors.

RACIAL SCRIPTS

Lori Patton Davis and Rachelle Winkle-Wagner (2012, p. 182) explain racial scripts "stem from sources within the environment and are learned and transferred generationally":

Individuals are taught to see race, ascribe particular characteristics to individuals from various racial groups and judge these individuals based upon these observations. Enacted racial scripts are based solely on "salient attributes" or the aspects of one's identity that are most visible (e.g., skin color). . . . Racial scripts are not only dependent on what individuals see and perceive, they are equally grounded in one's lack of consciousness or their purposeful choice to ignore what is visible. (p. 182)

Patton Davis and Winkle-Wagner (2012) offer traditional notions of beauty as an example of racial scripts relevant to this discussion, as they place Black and white women at opposing ends of a continuum of attractiveness. In the media, for example, "White women are represented as the epitome of beauty in magazines, the dutiful mother and wife on television sitcoms, or the object of affection and attraction to men (of any race) in feature films" (p. 182):

The racial script that extends from this attention toward White women is that they are valued and desired above all other women, and in this case Black women, who in many instances have neither been deemed as beautiful nor desirable. (p. 183)

Research reveals, in multiple settings and circumstances, Black men and women with light skin receive preferential treatment and are perceived as less threatening than those with dark skin (Burch, 2015; Maddox, 2004; Mendes et al., 2002). In this chapter, I suggest that racial scripts concerning Black women's beauty, approachability, and temperament can negatively impact relationships between white instructors and Black students. Racial scripts are pervasive, and, as Patton Davis and Winkle-Wagner (2012) explain, "exist *before* the interactions . . . even if these particular scripts are not explicitly referenced in the interaction (p. 183)."

The "external ugliness" of Black skin in racial scripts is accompanied by an innate anger also attributed to Black women and girls. The "angry Black woman" is a well-established stereotype prevalent in depictions of Black womanhood. It is the go-to trope used to explain away and dismiss Black women's opinions, ideas, and expressions. Without being specifically referenced, the image of the angry Black woman is a readily available, ingrained-in-our-psyches, nearly unanimously recognized and accepted way of understanding Black women and girls. Sociologist David Pilgrim (2008/2012) explains that, with roots in the fictional Sapphire caricature, the angry Black woman is viewed as "rude, loud, malicious, stubborn and overbearing" (p. 1). Defining Black women and girls in this manner makes ignoring them and dismissing their feelings, thoughts, and ideas possible. Pilgrim (2008/2012) notes it is "a social control mechanism that is employed to punish [B]lack women who violate the societal norms that encourage them to be passive, servile, non-threatening and unseen" (p. 2).

What happens when an instructor has a room full of students who are not "the right kind of Black girl?" How are their bodies, minds, and experiences interpreted, accepted, or rejected in classrooms? What are the strategies used to silence and render them passive? Could an expulsion rate twice that of white girls be the "go-to" method for dealing with Black Girls? (National Women's Law Center, 2017).

MAKING BLACK BEAUTIFUL

There are two powerful memories from my childhood that contributed to my eventual embrace of my Blackness. First, as a four-year-old attending Sunday school at an African Methodist Episcopal Zion Church on Chicago's South Side, I was fortunate to have Olivette Davis as my nursery/kindergarten Sunday school teacher. As a child, I could not understand the significance of a simple act we engaged in weekly—coloring the drawings accompanying each lesson. Mrs. Davis's words continue to resonate: "Use a nice brown crayon to color that picture of Jesus," she sweetly coaxed. Or, she would insist, "Use this beautiful brown crayon to color that little girl and make her pretty just like you." How powerful her guidance and our compliance turned out for all of Mrs. Davis's Sunday school students.

The second memory is of a book my parents gave me in the 1960s. Originally published in 1963, the very title of *Color Me Brown* instructed children to use rich, brown crayons to shade in the women and men featured on the beige pages of the coloring book.

Both experiences illuminated strategies employed by Black adults to counter dominant messages of white supremacy prevalent at the time with proof that Black people have done and could do great things. Without uttering the words, Black adults in my childhood were letting me know that Black is beautiful. These early lessons helped me resist the messages of Black as less than white that were to come, and with a vengeance.

White school teachers committed to the success of Black girls in their classrooms will acknowledge the multiple and overwhelming images of white beauty as the norm. The white instructor who sees and believes in the beauty of Black skin can change lives, perhaps reduce the pain felt when one is never good enough (Collins, 2009):

> African-American women experience the pain of never being able to live up to prevailing standards of beauty—standards used by White men, White women, Black men, and most painfully one another. Regardless of any individual woman's subjective reality, this is the system of ideas that she encounters. (p. 98)

The National Center for Education Statistics (2017) reports that 80 percent of K–12 instructors are white, and that the percentage of Black educators has decreased from 8 to 7 percent since 2000. When less than 12 percent of K–12 educators are Black, the celebration of Black children, of Black ways of knowing and being, falls upon non-Black teachers. More than any other group, white instructors have the ability to empower or disempower Black children through the way they speak to students, as well as the content of assigned readings, tenor of class discussions, and diversity of course materials. Without appreciation of Black culture, literature, and experiences, along with the capacity to share this information with the entire class, many instructors find themselves ill-equipped to create racially inclusive and equitable classrooms where all students are engaged and have the opportunity to learn. Because white instructors continue to hold the vast majority of teaching positions, awareness and appreciation of Black culture is an imperative.

From Intrusion to Inclusion

In *Feminist Theory: From Margin to Center* (2000), bell hooks discusses the condescending attitudes of White women toward Black and other women of Color in feminist academic circles:

> The condescension they directed at [B]lack women was one of the means they employed to remind us that the women's movement was "theirs"—that we were able to participate because they allowed it. . . . They did not see us as equals. They did not treat us as equals. . . . If we dared to criticize the movement or to assume responsibility for reshaping feminist ideas and introducing new ideas, our voices were tuned out, dismissed, silenced. We could be heard only if our statements echoed the sentiments of the dominant discourse. (pp. 12–13)

This condescension has been extended to the university setting (Dace, 2012, p. 50) and appears to be present in elementary, middle, and high school settings where white women rule and Black women and girls are guests who must present themselves in ways that support and bring comfort to their white hosts. Should the Black student have an idea that runs counter to "the way we do things," questions an established practice, or introduces information based on her own cultural experiences, efforts may be made to remind her of her place. In K–12 settings, as in others, Black women and girls are welcome as long as they toe the line.

Another memory from my youth helps illustrate this point. This time the instructors are two White women, albeit nuns, at the all-Black, all-girls, Catholic high school I attended in the 1970s, Aquinas Dominican. As a member of the speech team in both prose and poetry categories, I read and performed the work of Black artists almost exclusively. Our speech team coaches were two nuns who encouraged our choices. It did not take much time for us to realize that the only Catholic school girls permitted to read or perform the work of Black poets and writers at speech contests were Aquinas Dominican students. We noticed the Black girls at the other Catholic schools performed the work of white writers exclusively. They read poetry by Emily Dickinson and Robert Frost. I did too. I also read Mari Evans, Nikki Giovanni, Haki Madhubuti, Langston Hughes, and Gwendolyn Brooks, Black writers whose words spoke of Black culture, history and experiences. Unfortunately, the other Catholic schools with young Black women on their speech teams did not permit the performance of Black artists' work. They saw the work of Black writers as provocative and controversial. In this way, the young Black women at the other schools were silenced and kept in line by being forced to read the work of white writers. How fortunate we all were that Sisters Denise and Diane believed we should perform work that resonated with our lives, poetry we found meaningful. Had my desire to include Black writers in my program been refused, it is very likely that I would not have joined or remained a member of the team. The inability to perform culturally relevant material may be the reason Black girls from the other Catholic schools never participated beyond their first year of competition.

The exclusion of Black voices, culture, and ways of being—through disallowing curriculum, silencing questions and expressions of discontent, and excluding images reflecting black aesthetics—signals their visitor status to Black children. As many Black women learned as participants in the feminist movement (hooks, 2000), young Black women soon discover the classroom belongs to White women—it is "theirs" and we are merely guests (p.12). Rather than possessing a voice or opinions worthy of hearing, Black girls are silenced when they do not repeat back to White hearers the prescribed messages of white order and comfort with the threat of punishment for disobedience ever present.

Imagine the frustration of a young Black girl, in search of her voice and desperately trying to love herself, being told the work of great Black writers was unacceptable. Should she press the issue by making her dissatisfaction known to her teacher and other school leaders, the young woman might find herself described as rude, pushy, or angry. Too often, we place Black women and girls in boxes that cannot hold them and punish them when they call attention to inequities. As hooks (2000) explains, the message is that K–12 schools belong to someone else, and as Black women, "We are invited guests who must mind our manners by remaining silent or risk being seen as obstacles and 'in the way.'" (Dace, 2012, p. 50).

If white people are going to educate Black children, it is imperative that they resist the temptation to judge and interpret every situation from their own perspectives. Fortunately, there are programs, training, books, and an assortment of extracurricular activities to address a lack of knowledge and experience. My hope is that more white teachers will make the effort to understand and explore Black culture, history, and art, especially those teaching Black students. School was a place where my culture was affirmed as worthy of inclusion, and I grew into Black womanhood. That should be every little Black girl's story.

CHAPTER 6

Colorism in the Classroom

Brittany Bell, Ramycia McGhee

Beginning with a simple internet search of "Black girls and education," the results are overflowing with degrading and dehumanizing descriptions, which alone do not represent or define the beauty and diversity of Black girls and women. Black girls and women are often taught by educators who may not have a deep understanding of the cultural backgrounds of their students (Ladson-Billings, 1995). This chapter explores and homes in on understanding the diversity of Black girls and women in relation to colorism in the United States. Moreover, this chapter centers on disrupting and changing the narrative of Black girls and women and how they are seen, portrayed, and taught in the educational system(s). This chapter will provide white teachers strategies for working with Black girls in the classroom and best practices for assisting, shifting, and cultivating their experiences.

Understanding colorism and its origins provides knowledge for the potential impact it can have in the learning environment. *Colorism* is defined as a custom of discriminating by which those with lighter hues are treated more generously than those of darker hues (Banks, 2000). According to Banks (2000), "Colorism, skin tone discrimination against dark-skinned but not light-skinned blacks, constitutes a form of race-based discrimination (p. 1706)." These variances based on skin tones become hierarchical and create psychological obstacles (McGee et al., 2016). This form of oppression is expressed through a hierarchical treatment of individuals where, typically, favoritism is demonstrated toward those of lighter complexions, and those of darker complexions experience rejection and mistreatment in areas such as income, education, and housing (Jackson-Lowman, 2014, p. 26).

The practice of colorism can be traced to slavery and the racist institution of white superiority that is built into the DNA of the United States, in that it endorses the white standards of beauty (Keith & Monroe, 2006). Colorism also has roots in the European colonial project (Jordan, 1968) and the plantation life of enslaved African Americans (Stevenson, 1996). For example, during slavery, slave masters would often father children with slave women, producing mulatto children. The terms *mulatto, quadroon,* and *octoroon* were developed by white people to distinguish various levels of African ancestry (Williamson, 1980). These children were often of lighter complexion and most of the time were granted better treatment, such as working in the house, that is, they were house slaves rather than field slaves, who were of darker complexion (Graham, 1999). Furthermore, individuals with biological differences in skin color were equalized by law through the "one-drop" rule, although significant differences in hair textures, skin tones, and facial features were recognized (Omi & Winant, 1986). The one-drop rule deemed anyone with a drop of Black blood to be legally "Black" (Sweet, 2005). These biological differences of skin color often created, and still create, conflicts within the Black community and have caused Blacks to internalize the same principles of racism, the idea that light-skinned Blacks are smarter and superior to their dark-skinned counterparts (Hunter, 2016).

It is critical for educators to unpack and understand the dynamics of colorism in schools, because colorism serves as a subsystem of institutionalized racism (Keith & Monroe, 2016). These stereotypical beliefs were transferred from generation to generation among both Blacks and whites. In a system of structural racism, African Americans of all skin tones are subjected to discrimination, because they are members of a particular racial group (Hunter, 2016). Hunter (2007) also states:

> The maintenance of white supremacy (aesthetic, ideological, and material) is predicated on the notion that dark skin represents savagery, irrationality, ugliness, and inferiority. White skin, and, thus, whiteness itself, is defined by the opposite: civility, rationality, beauty, and superiority. (p. 238)

It is important for white teachers to understand colorism and the impact it could potentially have on the education of beautiful Black girls. Even though teachers may learn about multiculturalism (and other race- and ethnicity-related initiatives) during their teacher preparation coursework and student teaching, their education rarely prepares them to face the racial and interracial perceptions about skin color they often bring to the classroom, and such preparation is an integral step in teaching students of color (McGee et al., 2016). It is imperative that educators understand the possible colorism experiences students may have had, even among their peers, so the teachers can offer support and resources to students who are experiencing challenging situations around discrimination based on issues of colorism.

Colorism Narratives

Personal narratives provide perspectives from traditionally marginalized groups, specifically the experiences of Black girls. These narratives do not speak for all Black girls but do provide multiple voices to describe their experience with colorism. These narratives seek to provide a deeper understanding of personal reactions to situations in which colorism was demonstrated, that is, in homes, social settings, and classrooms.

In a study from Baxley (2014), eight Black girls in grades six through eight were interviewed. A student shared a family experience that involved skin complexion differences within her family. The student felt that her light-skinned cousin was often treated better than her dark-brown-skinned cousin, highlighting how colorism that stems from an early age is often found in families, exhibited through commentary or unfair treatment. In another study conducted by McGee et al. (2016), Black high school students were asked if skin color played a role in how they were treated at school. One student responded that her skin tone has raised negative assumptions and educational challenges (Baxley, 2014). In addition (as cited in McGee et al., 2016), 8 of 16 girls with similar stories experienced compounded stress, and they felt their skin tone was linked to negative stereotypes and perceptions (Capodilupo & Kim, 2014; Thompson & Keith, 2001).

Looking at the social arena, a student shared how the media highlight skinny white girls or skinny light-skinned Black girls, but felt like they did not accurately represent her as a Black girl (Baxley, 2014). She asked, "Does that mean I am not beautiful? Or to be beautiful I need to look like them?" The media continue to endorse a white standard of beauty. According to the Associated Press (2019):

> When images from "Ralph Breaks the Internet" came out last year, it appeared Princess Tiana, Disney's first Black princess, had a lighter complexion and sharper features. Anika Noni Rose, who voices Tiana, met with animators and spoke about how important it was that dark-skinned girls see themselves represented. The studio also consulted the civil rights group Color of Change. "They had to spend some real money to actually fix this. They recognized the problem, they listened and they worked to change it," said Color of Change executive director Rashad Robinson. (para. 9)

Moreover, this is a clear indication that representation matters, and if Black girls don't see their particular complexion in movies—particular mainstream movies—they internalize what they perceive beauty to be, and often it doesn't look like them. The need for media companies to be corrected shows that much work, conversation, and education needs to continue in an effort to avoid racism that can unknowingly result in colorism issues.

STRATEGIES FOR WHITE TEACHERS
NAVIGATING COLORISM IN THE CLASSROOM

- White teachers need to examine the personal biases they may have against students with darker skin tones. During a bias assessment, they can write down their assumptions about students with whom they share the same skin tone or are closest to, and those whose skin tones are different from theirs. Teachers can also complete the skin-tone ("Light Skin—Dark Skin") implicit association test (IAT), an online test that measures unconscious bias and helps individuals recognize complexion bias, since it reveals the preference for light-skinned relative to dark-skinned (https://implicit.harvard.edu/implicit/takeatest.html). This reflection is central to dismantling colorism and bias from the onset in the classroom.

- White teachers should become more knowledgeable of colorism manifestations through trainings, workshops, and seminars with consultants and other experts on the topic in order to foster and maintain productive change.

- White teachers should stay current with literature related to skin tone bias/colorism and be comfortable with initiating discussions on racism in the curriculum. Teachers must cultivate opportunities for students to collaborate, challenge, and learn from each other in a safe and inclusive classroom environment (Knight, 2015). For example teachers can facilitate critical conversations with students about colorism by including both current events and age-appropriate works, including *The Skin I'm In* by Sharon Flake (2007), *Genesis Begins Again* by Alicia Williams (2019), and *Sulwe* by Lupita Nyong'o and Vashti Harrison (2019). They can also discuss the structural racism that exists within various Black leaders. In this discussion, teachers can ask students to think about leaders they know in the community or within the media, so students can discuss and identify colorism issues.

- White teachers can advocate for, model, and teach ideologies to combat colorism bias and messages. For example, white educators can redefine self-love and beauty while combating societal negative images and messages. One place to start would be the #BlackGirlMagic movement that was popularized in 2013, which promotes empowerment of Black girls and women.

- Similar to racial equity audits, colorism audits should be done within classrooms. White educators can do a comprehensive investigation based on skin tone, and consider which students are more likely to be chosen for leadership roles, which students are likely to be placed in advanced placement courses, and which students are likely to be formally disciplined within their classroom. For example, in a study conducted by Blake et al. (2017), they found skin tone to be a significant predictor of school suspension risk. Participants that identified as Black with a darker skin tone were almost twice as likely to be suspended as their white peers. Those same findings were not found for Black students with light skin. Considering these factors helps to minimize the inequalities that may exist between the lighter and darker skinned Black students.

CONCLUSION

Although colorism continues to be a prime topic in society, educators have a role in combating colorism in the learning environment, where Black students are often impacted the most. For far too long society has told Black girls they are not pretty enough, smart enough, thin enough, et cetera. In addition, Black girls have had to maneuver another layer of being separated or treated differently because of how dark or light their skin tone is. Colorism is a social problem, and although teachers have a role in combating colorism within classrooms, the issue should also be addressed within administration and at the community level. Teachers are role models, and as such it is important for them to stand against colorism and uplift and celebrate all Black skin tones and promote self-love by affirming the work and beauty of all Black shades.

Activities for White Educators Guiding Discussions

Activity 1

Goal of Activity: To assist students in self reflecting and engaging in dialogue to foster a deeper understanding of the colorism issue.

Directions

Divide students into small groups. Encourage them to sit by someone they don't normally work with. Give students 5-10 minutes to discuss each question as a group, and then have them share out in the larger group, in which they identify common colorism themes and/or experiences.

Group Discussion Questions

1. Why do I have a positive/negative attitude about dark or light skin?

2. How did my attitude about skin color develop throughout my life thus far?

3. Why does my reflection on this issue matter?

4. What's my role in combating colorism?

Activity 2

Always have in your classroom multicultural art materials in colors that include all potential skin tones—crayons, paint, construction paper, markers, clay, et cetera. Encourage your students to explore using these multiple materials whenever they are drawing, painting people, et cetera. Celebrate the varied skin tones in your classroom.

Activity 3

Be certain your classroom includes books about skin tone. Examples:

Katz, K. (2002). *The Colors of Us*. Macmillan.

Manushkin, F. (2015). *Happy in Our Skin*. Candlewick Press.

Tharps, L. L. (2016). *Same Family, Different Colors: Confronting Colorism in America's Diverse Families*. Beacon Press.

(Continued)

(Continued)

Tyler, M., & Csicsko, D. L. (2005). *The Skin You Live In*. Chicago Children's Museum.

Williams, A. (2019). *Genesis Begins Again*. Caitlyn Dlouhy Books.

The Skin I'm In, by Sharon Flake

Grade Level 6–8

Contemporary Realistic Fiction

Book Review by Marguerite W. Penick

The Skin I'm In is one of those classic books that should be in every school. Flake has created a novel that addresses colorism, bullying, poverty, and peer pressure. From the opening taunt of "I don't see pretty, just a whole lotta black (p. 3)" to the final "Welcome back (p. 172)," readers are confronted with uncomfortable but real issues too often faced by Black Girls but rarely confronted or discussed by educators. Through open and honest conversations around the multiple realities for Black Girls presented in *The Skin I'm In*, educators can discuss the current racial climate and issues of power, privilege, and oppression. The discussions may not be easy, but if these topics are buried they only grow and continue to be perpetuated through their silence. Promoting conversations of change is critical, and *The Skin I'm In* is an essential read.

Vignette: The Token Tax

Abrielle Moore

I was the token Black girl in a predominantly white independent school for the final six years of my precollege education. However, my grooming process began well before then. In my younger years, my teachers often praised me for how "well-spoken," "proper," "well-mannered," and "elegant" I was. Perhaps more startlingly, many of my teachers constantly reminded me that I "wasn't like the other students." Initially, I thought my teachers were referring to all of the students. In hindsight, it is clear that they were speaking of me in comparison to other Black students.

Starting around ninth grade, I became hypervisible. My school started putting me in advertising materials, sending me to conferences, and regularly inviting me to schmooze with potential donors (which was more along the lines of uncompensated labor than a privilege). I was granted more opportunities as I proved reliable in serving as another "diverse" face and a model of "appropriate" behavior for other Black girls. These perks were only available if I kept up with the reputation that the school had crafted for me. So, I put an immense amount of pressure on myself to always meet their unspoken (but powerful) standards. I dressed in a "presentable" manner, spoke with extreme precision, got top-notch grades, and remained overinvolved in extracurricular activities. To an outsider, I probably looked like an engaged student. However, I knew the terms of my condition, and if I did not stick to them, I knew they would have found someone else.

It was difficult to connect with my schoolmates—particularly my Black peers—because they viewed me through the persona and reputation that my school bestowed upon me. Many felt I was a sellout. I could not settle into white social circles without assimilating into their styles and interests, and thus compromising my true self-identity. Additionally, many white students believed I was someone with whom they should compete. Tokenism uprooted me from the community I could have formed with black students and did not guarantee my acceptance within other groups. I was often socially isolated and lonely throughout my later schooling years. As a product of my hypervisibility, many people in my community knew who I was, but few truly knew me. This illusion of knowing often masked the isolation I was experiencing. I rarely spoke of these hardships, as my outcries were often perceived as ingratitude. Others made it clear they were eager to take my place. In silencing the pressures and challenges I experienced, tokenism prompted others to view my experiences through rose-colored lenses. They could not see beyond the perks and the persona.

Tokenism has left me with many wounds—only some of which I have begun to heal. For example, I still struggle against measuring my worth by the value I add to institutions. Additionally, I remain guarded in my social interactions because of my negative experiences in school. My experience demonstrates the exploitative nature of tokenism: while an institution treats the token as disposable, the token will indefinitely experience the consequences of her limited condition.

PART III
"SPIRIT MURDERING"
—Bettina Love

The chapters and vignettes in the following section speak to the concept of spirit murder-*ing, which Dr. Bettina Love defines as "a slow death, a death of the spirit, a death that is built on racism and intended to reduce, humiliate, and destroy people of color" (2016, p. 2). As you read about specific and distinct lived experiences of Black girls of hypervis-ibility and invisibility, ask yourself: How does my teaching contribute to my Black girl students' social and emotional well-being? How does my teaching add to (or mitigate) the devastating psychosocial impact that schools can have on Black girls as they move through a system that sees them as peripheral?*

The first chapter, by independent school administrator Orinthia Swindell, explores the impact of this system—and the teachers within it—on introverted Black girls, who are often more susceptible to being victims of misrecognition by people who have internalized the stereotypes and tropes about Black Girls.

A vignette follows by transformational school leader Samantha Pugh, who writes pow-erfully about how school squelched her rhythm and deepened her blues. Pugh's vignette is a motivator to read the following chapter, by Veronica Warren, who shares strategies for how teachers could do better.

Colorism, discrimination based on skin tone, is a big issue in the Black girl community. It is rooted in antiblackness, patriarchy, and capitalism, and schools often reinforce this message through implicit structural bias and unconscious personal bias. Teachers must tune in to these so-called microaggressions that make a macro impact on the developing adolescent brain. Author Veronica Warren is asking you to see Black Girls and treat us like the queens we are.

CHAPTER 7

Visible Black Girls . . . Powerful Beyond Measure

Orinthia Swindell

THE FORMATIVE YEARS

> Learning what our various social identities means is a lifetime journey that begins in toddlerhood.

> —Derman-Sparks & Olsen-Edwards, 2010, p. 12

The realization that there is power in the use of one's voice and in one's presence is something that was modeled for and encouraged within me as a young Black girl growing up in Brooklyn, New York. As the youngest of six children, with two brothers and three sisters, I grew up in an environment where I felt seen, heard, and validated. My relationship with my siblings was one in which I was inspired. As the youngest child, before starting school, I spent a great deal of time with my mother, who was a single parent and a homemaker. Growing up during the early 1970s, I had to wait until I was five years old to attend kindergarten. My days at that time were spent watching a minimal amount of children's programming on television, engaging in imaginative play, reading many books with my mother, and accompanying her on various errands while waiting for my older siblings to return from school in the late afternoon.

I was taught from a very young age that the inner light that exists within me shines at all times. I've carried this belief with me throughout my life as it was instilled in me by my mother. The combination of this belief and the impact of feeling seen, heard, and validated had an immensely positive effect on my sense of self during this time in my life. There wasn't anything I felt I could not do. My family encouraged me to take risks and to use my voice, and it was a constant source of love and support. The purpose of this chapter is to provide educators with insight into the introverted Black girl experience. Although I do not claim to speak for all introverted Black girls and Black womxn, the breadth of my experience existing within each of these intersecting identities has provided me with countless opportunities to connect with others who share in and relate to these experiences.

SCHOOL DAYS. . . . THE BEGINNING YEARS

> Antiracist education also works to undo these systems while working to create new ones built upon the collective vision and knowledge of dark folx. For educators, this work starts in the classroom, school, and school community.
>
> —Bettina Love, 2016, p. 55

During the early years of my education, I remember having Black women as teachers in kindergarten and first grade. They encouraged me to take risks and also helped to shape the avid learner in me. I was a quiet student who enjoyed receiving and processing new information and really wanted my teachers to know I had a solid grasp of the material. I remember being actively involved in classroom activities, and I thoroughly enjoyed interacting with my peers. However, the second, third, and fourth grade years in school brought a shift in my experience as a young Black girl. Reflecting back on this time in my life, I realize that those were the years I was introduced to white women as teachers. Having had Black women as teachers who set the bar and level of expectation higher and higher was something that had been familiar to me up until that point. As Milner (2006) states, "Black teachers can have a meaningful impact on Black students' academic and social success because they often deeply understand Black students' situations and their needs" (p. 93). During those beginning years with white women as my teachers, the support and understanding was pretty much nonexistent.

A pivotal turning point occurred during my fourth-grade year that impacted the way that I saw myself and who I knew myself to be. This disconnect had deep implications for how I would relate to white teachers in the future. I remember accompanying my mother to my parent–teacher conference that year while Ms. Klein talked with her regarding her observations of me as a student. During this meeting Ms. Klein stated, "Orinthia doesn't talk much in class, and I don't know who she is." Hearing that negatively impacted my sense of self, because up until that point, my Black teachers had always been able to see and acknowledge my presence, gifts, skills, and abilities. I was hurt by Ms. Klein's statement. I felt unseen, which then caused me to retreat when I was in the classroom setting. "If students feel recognized and acknowledged as individuals, it is likely to increase their motivation to attend class, prepare, participate . . . rather [than] withdraw or give up-when they encounter setbacks." ("Students Lack," para. 3) Although I maintained my grasp of the material presented in class, as a result of not showing up in Ms. Klein's class the way that she wanted me to, I wasn't allowed to transition with my classmates to the highest-level fifth-grade class the following year.

As a result of Ms. Klein's actions, I was robbed and stripped of my identity as a confident, adventurous, and risk-taking Black girl. My entire life was sucked out of me due to her treatment towards me, her decision to isolate me from my peers, and her inability to see me as a young Black girl who had a thirst for learning and a desire for it to be quenched with as much knowledge as I could obtain. The power that one single white woman's decision had on my future forever changed my life. Upon processing the parent–teacher conference incident as an adult, I am cognizant that as a young Black girl I'd begun to internalize the idea that I needed to be hyperaware of my Black girl body in spaces, as judgment was being placed on my way of being. Morris (2016) speaks to this as it relates to Black girls and Black womxn in society when she states, "They live with this knowledge in their bodies and subconsciously wrestle with every personal critique of how they navigate their environments" (p. 35).

Years later, as a teenager on an outing to Manhattan with my mother, I noticed Ms. Klein and her daughter walking on the opposite side of the street. I pointed this out to my mother and asked if we could cross the street to say hello to them. Although Ms. Klein's comments had deeply hurt me years before, there was still a bit of hope within me that she would finally see me. As we approached her and my mother began to explain who we were, Ms. Klein simply responded by saying, "I remember you but I don't remember her." I was shattered; The trauma from that experience of being in her class came back all at once. I was sucked into this pit called introvertedness and was never to come out of that shell any more, by the power of one single white teacher who did not attempt to see the value and the talent that I demonstrated in class. I connected in that moment to the feelings from many years before. Those feelings of being devalued, marginalized, powerless, and invisible returned and stripped me of my essence. Black Girls continue to be marginalized and experience what some have called the invisibility syndrome paradigm (ISP), a process that Black Girls experience when they struggle internally with not being validated, recognized, acknowledged, and/or valued (Haynes et al., 2016).

Swiss psychologist Carl Jung introduced the concept of introversion to the world in 1921 by using it to describe one of the ways people respond to and interact with the world around them.

"He described introverts as those who prefer small groups rather than large ones. He also stated that introverts enjoy quiet activities such as reading, writing and thinking" (Shulman, 2018, para 1). "Jung suggested the principal distinction between the personalities is the source of the direction of an individual's expression of energy—defining extroversion as the 'outward turning of libido' and introversion as an 'inward turning of libido' (Houston, 2020, para 2). According to the article, "Teaching Introverted Students: A Guide for Educators and Parents" ("Teaching Introverted Students," para 2), some common characteristics of an introverted student may include the following:

- Ability to focus on one task for an extended period of time

- Active listening

- A dislike for small talk and group work

- A preference for spending time alone, particularly after social interactions

- Careful consideration before taking risks

- Creativity

- Preference for deep thought and reflection

It is also important to keep in mind that introversion is a personality trait, not an impediment to learning or something to be fixed ("Teaching Introverted Students," para 2).

IMPLICATIONS FOR THE INTROVERTED BLACK GIRL STUDENT

In the book *Quiet*, author Susan Cain (2013) makes reference to the concept of the extrovert ideal being the standard by which people are measured in society. She states, "We live in a value system that I call the Extrovert Ideal—the omnipresent belief that the ideal self is gregarious, alpha and comfortable in the spotlight. She works well in teams and socializes in groups" (Cain, 2013, p. 4). For some introverted Black girl students, coming up against this ideal can begin to feel like part of the course when attending school and existing in society in general. I came up against this more times than I care to remember from the beginning years of school through my postgraduate degree years. The educational system intrinsically taught me about the white Eurocentric value of individualism within the context of the extrovert ideal. Yet far from being treated as an individual, I often felt as if I were being measured up against one type of "individualism" that expected me to be like everybody else. "We like to think that we value individuality, but all too often we admire one type of individual—the kind that's comfortable putting himself out there" (Cain, 2013, p. 4). As I attempted to fit into educational spaces, the consistent message seemed to be that I needed to conform to an ideal, ultimately, that I as myself was not good enough. As Melissa Harris-Perry points out, "It is emotionally taxing to have to manage this disconnect between self and others' perception" (2013, p. 89). Reflecting back on these experiences, I realized I struggled with a sense of cognitive dissonance as I tried to remain true to myself and tried to measure up to the extrovert ideal as the standard that was reflected back to me.

Author Monique Morris (2016) summarizes this well when highlighting some of the most salient aspects of Black girls' and Black womxn's existence: "They have long understood that their way of engaging with the world—how they talk, how they walk, how they wear their hair, or hold their bodies—is subject to scrutiny, especially by those in positions of relative power" (p. 35). If I'd had language to rationalize the ways I felt throughout my entire school experience as the introverted Black girl, I would have realized that I was constantly grappling with the following two questions subconsciously:

- How does the concept of the ideal self impact the lives of introverted Black girls when intersected with race, gender identity/expression, and class?

- How does the introverted Black girl reconcile showing up the way in which she is most comfortable with the pressure she feels to show up in a way that others expect, when this falls contrary to who she knows herself to be?

These questions or variations on them are important for white women educators to ponder when in the presence of the introverted Black girl student, particularly as they relate to how the introverted Black girl may be experiencing the teacher's pedagogy, classroom environment, and overall school setting.

As I continued my educational journey, my presence as the quiet girl who expressed herself well through written assignments with the occasional verbal share continued. I'd never been fond of the idea that percentages of student grades were determined by the amount of verbal participation that took place in class. I noticed as a student, and years later as an educator, that there were other students like myself who participated and engaged in other ways that presented added value to the classroom and school environment. There was a level of engagement that was occurring that did not seem to be accounted for—and in many ways was overlooked by teachers. For the quiet, introverted Black girl student, this poses the risk of having teachers misunderstand or misinterpret their way of being. By this I mean, teachers would somehow equate my quietness with disengagement, being aloof, or not being able to fully become part of the group. What they failed to recognize was the deeply reflective, thoughtful, creative, friendly, and passionate learner that sat before them on a daily basis, ready for any challenge that they could pose to students.

As an educator, and based on these experiences, it became clear that to continue measuring students through narrowly defined margins on a consistent basis yields the introverted Black girl student with a stack of unclaimed opportunities to be fully embraced and recognized in the classroom setting.

With such an emphasis on verbal participation and a high concentration of group work within the school environment, there wasn't much room for individual think time or acknowledgement of the various ways that processing takes place outside of these two seemingly highly valued and narrow options for participation. Insistence on time for completing projects, as well as for moving through the curricula, made it clear to me as an educator that some teachers do not veer from methods that they experienced as students in school. Author Carol Ann Tomlinson (2014) states:

> Curriculum has often been based on goals that require students to accumulate and retain a variety of facts or to practice skills that are far removed from any meaningful context. Drill and practice worksheets are still a prime educational technology, a legacy of behaviorism rooted firmly in the 1930s. Teachers still run "tight ship" classes. (p. 40)

This does not, however, provide students with avenues for expressing themselves as individual learners, each with a specific set of needs that ought to be met. "Those expectations can be changed, as we act within or against the traditions of which we are a part (Applebee, 1996, p. 17)."

Having had countless experiences as an introverted Black girl student who has gone unseen in the classroom setting by white teachers, I was eventually led to an unconscious belief that people did not see me. As an adult, I entered predominantly white spaces as a student and employee with the belief that I was invisible. I felt like an outsider in these spaces. I continued to encounter white women as teachers and even as supervisors who would at times acknowledge my work ethic yet would also try to change how I was showing up in order to make themselves more comfortable. During these experiences, I subconsciously continued to connect and align with the feelings that I felt as a fourth-grade student. Much like Ms. Klein, these white women did not take the opportunity to get to know me as a person and were quick to place me in a box along with a primary focus on dictating how I should move, talk, and behave. As I enter my 27th year as an educator, I realize that my journey as a student deeply impacted the educator that I've become. My disposition as the quiet observer has afforded me the capacity to be able to connect with and see other Black girls like me deeply. I am able to provide my students with the opportunity to express themselves in ways that come naturally to them, and I am able to account for ways of participating in the life of the classroom setting that fall outside of the margins that were in place during my experience as a student. I like to think of myself as one of what Holloway (2016) identifies as "careful listeners, observers and deep thinkers who have the power to make an impact in the classroom and the world" (p. 3).

I didn't fully understand the degree of intensity associated with traveling throughout my life as the invisible Black girl until I was in my 40s. I remember that moment so clearly and how I was able to trace the origin of this feeling back to my fourth-grade year in Ms. Klein's class. The cognitive dissonance that I'd experienced consisted of fully being aware of all that I bring to the table coupled with other people's expectations that I should be less observant and should speak up more so people will be aware of what I'm thinking, and that there isn't any room for quiet. This isn't something I want other Black girls to experience. I always wondered how it was possible for my family and the Black women teachers in my life to be able to fully see me while the white women teachers in my life did not. This erasure of my presence led to a silencing of my voice. I have often thought about what it would have been like to have those white teachers in my life actually see me and make space for me and other introverted Black girls in a way that allowed us to be ourselves. What would it have been like to have them figure out ways to reach us and set the bar higher and higher instead of breaking us down?

With a plethora of research that explores the manner in which teacher expectations reflect racial biases, Rosen (2016) writes, "When evaluating the same Black student, white teachers expect significantly less academic success than do Black teachers" (p. 1). As an educator, I know that appealing to the whole child is necessary to assist in their growth and development. I believe that forming a relationship with Black girls that allows them to feel seen, heard, and valued is an essential part of the foundation through which white teachers can begin to make a connection with them. This is a major missing piece of the puzzle as it relates to beginning to meet Black girls' needs as students. Although I traveled through much of my life in white classrooms and spaces feeling invisible as the introverted Black girl, I've awakened to fully embracing and reminding myself of the foundation my family built for me as a young Black girl, where I felt seen, heard, and valued. It was through this process that I reconnected with who I know myself to be, and I am able to stand in my power. I also realized the power and importance of finding spaces where others reflect back to me all of that which I know myself to be and bring to this world. Finding my way back to who I know myself to be has impacted my sense of self in countless ways. When I hear people trying to use stereotypical language that is attributed to Black womxn and Black girls to describe my being, I intuitively know that my power, passion, beauty, brilliance, strength and magic is shining brightly. Understanding the value of the introverted Black girl is key for white educators being successful teachers of Black girls. I am constantly in conversation with educators and posing the question: What will it be like for Brilliant and Beautiful Black girls when they are fully seen and accepted for all that they bring?

SUGGESTIONS FOR EDUCATORS

As an educator, I firmly believe curriculum begins once students enter the school building. It's not just what takes place in the classroom setting. With this in mind,

I offer the following as tools for white women teachers when interacting with the introverted Black girl student:

1. Allow Black girls the opportunity to be the authors of their own experiences. Make space for them to be who they are, and find ways to connect with them according to their distinct personalities. It's all about relationships! Upon developing a relationship with a Black girl, do not assume that a one-size-fits-all approach is what's needed. This is of particular importance when interacting with Black girls, as much of their experience in the world has been clouded by the stereotypic images projected onto them.

   To ensure maximum student growth, teachers need to make modifications for students rather than assume students must modify themselves to fit the curriculum. (Tomlinson, (2014) p. 42)

2. Invest time and energy into understanding what it means to have a white identity. This can be done by attending conferences, workshops, webinars, and talks that focus on this. Do your research through reading various books and articles and locating online material that explores white identity, white privilege, white fragility, et cetera. Stay engaged in the work and the conversation!

   As educators, knowing how our identity positions us in a classroom, a school, and the larger community helps ensure that we are not missing opportunities for meaningful connections with our students and their families or inadvertently abusing our power and privilege, especially if we have different backgrounds from our students. (Simmons, 2017)

3. So often educators are impacted by the demands placed on them and those of the classroom setting from sources outside of themselves. Whether its district, state, parent, or administrative demands, teaching to the students who are sitting before you is of great importance. Some educators can fall into the trap of teaching to the center of the room without taking into account the varying needs, learning styles, or personality types present in the room. Taking the opportunity to serve in the role of observer while teaching would benefit not only all of your students but also your personal and professional development.

   The bias against introverted students is embedded in our educational system: years of unrelenting focus on cooperative learning, thinking aloud, and talking-as-learning, with grades for class participation, required public speaking (often now as a disproportionate pedagogical focus displacing more traditional forms of scholarship and substantive mastery), and a pervasive, almost normative, value placed on being social and well liked, particularly in a large-group context. In sum, the classroom focus is now too often on "doing," in sacrifice to "thinking" (Cain & Klein, 2015, p. 2)

4. When assessing Black girl students, preparing classroom materials and talking with colleagues about them, are your views based on tangible ideas or things that you believe to be true? Developing awareness around this may indeed provide insight into how Black girl students are navigating the classroom and school environment.

   Our assumptions about students influence the way we interact with them, which can affect their motivation and, in turn, their learning. ("Students Lack," 2020, para. 5)

5. White teacher assessment:

   The purpose of this assessment is for white teachers to critically think about and analyze the ways in which they use language to describe Black girls and begin to develop an understanding of the correlation between language and their interactions with Black girls.

   - Take a sheet of paper and divide it into three parts. Begin to answer the following:
   - Column 1: What words and comments are used to describe Black girl students' performance/character within the educational setting?
   - Column 2: Make a list of the words you use to describe Black girls (their behavior, appearance, mannerism, learning styles).
   - Column 3: Begin researching language that has been used (and is currently used) to describe Black girls and Black women. What are the stereotypes that exist about them?
   - Look over the words within the three columns. What do you notice?
   - Engage other white teachers in participating in this assessment. What are you noticing?
   - How can you use this information to inform your interactions, relationships, and teaching of Brilliant, Beautiful Black Girls?

     These stereotypes are more than representations, they are representations that shape realities." (Harris-Perry, 2013, p. 89)

Vignette: You Murdered My Rhythm and Blues: Black Girls Still Got Magic

Samantha Pugh

"They want our rhythm but not our blues." This phrase is used to describe the effects of cultural appropriation—*selecting certain aspects of a culture and ignoring their original significance for the purpose of belittling them as a trend.* Everyone wants the beauty that is Blackness—hair, clothes, moves, sassafras, skin color, and brilliance—the rhythm of us. But when it comes to our blues—experiences of oppression and the sadness that comes with the ever-changing social and political landscapes of racist systems—no one wants to touch them and experience them. It is advantage, an entitlement, a birthright of sorts for white folks to be able to choose one over the other—leaving them color-blind and saturated in privilege. This entitlement is perpetuated every day in American institutions—particularly in schools.

In school, what should have been my rhythm quickly became my blues. Schools drained my energy, drowned my voice and my cries, smoldered my inner fire, and almost killed me. Instead of me walking every day through the halls of schools with excitement and joy, my life's struggles with childhood depression and anxiety, my early immersion in a family life of addiction (drug and alcohol), and my witnessing of physical and emotional abuse and low self-esteem ruled my expressed emotions. For many years, not one adult heard the lyrics to my song of life. They didn't see behind the failing grades, the unexcused absences, the lateness, the sleeping in class, my mistrust and disrespect for authority, and my indifference about life. They didn't see that there was a beautiful song waiting to be tapped into.

I went to some of the best schools in New York City. As a result of my test scores, I was heavily recruited and anticipated. They wanted my diversity and my Black brilliance but had no intention of including all of me in the school or classroom cultures. I often heard things like *you are so smart, it's a shame that you are wasting it away; you are bright but that mouth is going to get you killed; you don't deserve to be here; you are wasting a seat that could go to someone who really wants it.*

Even the people who tried to cultivate my rhythm in spite of my blues did damage to me. My high school American history teacher, who captivated me with her love and passion for history as well her sassy but confident presence, despite her small stature, was one of the first to do this. I would attend regularly and on time. I sat in the front waiting for her "history show." Her pedagogy curated a classroom concert marked by her passionate voice and performative teaching style. With her clicking heels walking down the rows of the classroom and her beautifully painted red nails covered with chalk, she'd call on me, smile at me, and pat me on the back. Until she didn't anymore—until my blues interrupted my rhythm and disrupted her music.

This was music that she was used to dancing to every day; the rhythm made her feel comfortable and privileged. When we began to cover the Civil War, I thought it was strange that we didn't talk much about slavery. I asked my teacher if we could, because I was really interested in learning about Black people. She looked at me with disgust (for the first time ever) and said, "You can do that on your own, but my job is to get you to pass the Regents (a New York state proficiency test), and the last time I checked, the Regents doesn't spend time on slavery unless it speaks of the causes of civil wars. So as far as I am concerned, that's all that is

(Continued)

(Continued)

important." She went on to tell me, "You should be honored to be in this school and feel lucky to be in my class, because I'm the best. Ninety-five percent of my students pass the Regents." She wrapped it up by telling me that if I wanted to change the curriculum or the way that she teaches, to encourage my people to vote, and if they don't it is because they are lazy and don't want more out of life. I was stunned, and after that day things changed between us; our rhythm was off because my blues was turned up. My rhythm is influenced more now than ever by James Baldwin's famous quote: "The paradox of education is precisely this—that as one begins to become conscious one begins to examine the society in which he is being educated" (Baldwin, 1963, p. 42). My new music challenged her privilege, and that could not happen.

Despite her rude demeanor and subpar curricular and pedagogical implements, I earned an A in her class. Through the help of a few caring adults (both Black and white), I graduated high school and became the first of over 60 grandchildren in my family to graduate from college. I attended a prestigious HBCU where I learned about the Civil War *and* slavery. I read Emily Dickinson *and* Toni Morrison. Black authors like Baldwin, Ellison, Wright, and Walker continued to help write the lyrics of my rhythm and blues. I learned there, through my experiences in high school, that the beauty of my blackness could not be "cherry picked"—rhythm and blues are not mutually exclusive, and there is pride, beauty, and excellence in that. I also learned that recognizing and acknowledging the blues threatens the privilege of the people who benefit from it, mainly because it is hard to accept that they and their systems of White supremacy cause a great deal of those blues.

CHAPTER 8

Why Does My Darkness Blind You? Abandoning Racist Teaching Practices

Veronica Warren

In my previous research (Warren, 2019) on Black female students at a predominantly white school, a Black female student shared the challenges she had with her white female physical education instructor. This student believed that the teacher did not like her. There were several assignments given during the course. The instructions were sometimes confusing, and when the student sought clarification, she was ignored or met with the response, "There's no questions at this time." When she would turn in the assignment, she was then told, "That's not how you do it." Even with that response, the instructor did not further offer assistance to ensure a quality assignment. The student did not see other students having this same issue and eventually turned to her classmates for support with the assignments.

A white teacher's cultural indifference, lack of respect, and lower expectations of Black students can "cultivate actual negative attitudes toward Black students (Douglas et al., 2008, p. 49). Another Black female student reflected that when preparing an assignment on racial issues, she was told by her white teacher not to come off as angry.

If educators are going to truly move the conversation and take action to best teach beautiful and brilliant Black Girls, there are so many behaviors that white educators must abandon. Black Girls have historically been framed by negativistic and stereotypical narratives, which perpetuate the falsehoods that Black Girls are ill equipped academically, immoral in character, and deficient in beauty (Warren, 2019). Images dominating school literature and social media of Sapphire, Mammy, and Jezebel continue to dehumanize the essence of Black Girls and are used to perpetuate maltreatment (Gibson, 2016). The slanderous use of these images hinders how girls view themselves, and others devalue these girls as a result. Not seeing Black Girls as valuable is dismissive in nature. This dismissal can be detrimental during any time in a Black woman's life, but for Black adolescent Girls this is particularly challenging, because adolescence is when identity is being formed (Warren, 2019). During this transitional stage of development, Black Girls will come to understand they have varying intersectional identities—such as their race, economic class, gender, sexuality, ethnicity, nationality, and age—which will shape their experiences (Crenshaw, 1989; Lewis et al., 2013). Unfortunately, the totality of Black Girls' experiences is relegated to their Blackness. It is the varying hues of Black Girls that blinds you to their brilliance, boldness, and beauty. Blindness is a condition where one's vision is compromised, but actively engaging in supportive activities like those listed below will help educators restore this vision so that they can see Black Girls as assets and not as a threat.

ABANDON THE PHRASE, "I DON'T SEE COLOR"

Research is very clear about the fact that there is no such thing as being color-blind (Kang et al., 2010; Pérez, 2017); however, Black Girls are invisible in social, political, and economic spheres in society. Despite their contributions, they are marginalized, oppressed, and experience discrimination on micro and macro levels. According to the report *Women in the Workplace 2019* (Huang et al., 2019), compared to women of other races and ethnicities, "Black women are the most likely to have their judgment questioned in their area of expertise and be asked to prove their competence" (p. 48), and 18 percent of white women compared to 4 percent of women of color in business organizations have made it into the upper levels of leadership (Huang et al., 2019). The examples listed above serve to highlight how society as a whole is blind to Black Girls' basic needs, desires, and wants, and most important, their strengths.

Educators need to understand that color-blindness is a microinvalidation, a type of a microaggression. It is easy for educators to ascribe to the notion they cannot identify or acknowledge what they have never taken the time to understand, but to do that allows them to continue to invalidate the racial and ethnic experiences, and possibilities, of Black Girls. Color-blindness is an excuse for white people, a commonly used strategy by educators, to appear unbiased, but this approach allows for the concealment of serious inequity issues rooted in racism, which perpetuate discriminatory practices within schools (Joseph et al., 2016). Black Girls suffer harm when teachers' implicit and explicit biases go unchecked, and because of these harmful discriminatory and racist practices, such as this ideology that it is acceptable to be color-blind (Starck et al., 2020), it is critical schools take a systematic approach to education and training in efforts to reduce racial bias. Everyone sees color, because the moment they observe a Black Girl, that girl becomes invisible. The viewer becomes blind to all her basic needs, desires, and wants.

Predominantly white classrooms are not safe spaces for Black Girls (Warren, 2019). When one notices Black Girls congregating together in the lunchroom, hallways, or football stands, it is because they have created a counter space (Carter, 2007). This space becomes a haven for them to express their experiences with racism and provides them affinity groups where they can be understood and supported without judgement (Carter, 2007).

ABANDON FALSE NARRATIVES

"Counternarratives have always existed; however, the dominant culture has always had control over whose knowledge represents science and truth" (Joseph et al., 2016, p. 10). It takes courage to refute stories that are not only false but also damage the very essence of Black Girls. American history taught in our schools is void of the full and rich record of the history of African people. By providing an accurate historical context of the natural wealth of the continent and the sociopolitical context of why it's not viewed that way today, educators can teach through an asset-based approach and center a strength-based learning narrative. When schools selectively choose to begin teaching Black Girls' heritage only from a deficit-based perspective, that is, beginning with slavery, they deliberately minimize Black Girls' greatness and contribute to their inability to take pride in this part of their legacy.

Unfortunately, Black Girls all too often have to counter these narratives themselves. Garcia et al. revealed that the Black Girls viewed "participation as an effective mechanism for combating stereotypes that personally and collectively impact their lives" (2019, p. 10). To create these counternarratives, Black Girls may participate in activities and groups where they do not feel supported, but they prefer to associate with peers of their culture who understand their journey and challenges.

ABANDON THE MYTH OF MERITOCRACY

Black women are identified as the most educated gendered racial group in the United States (National Center for Education Statistics, 2018). Black Girls excel in academics and have a graduation rate higher than that of their Black male counterparts. Black Girls perceive they have to prove themselves academically when in white spaces, as their white peers do not see them as academically astute (Warren, 2019). A student shared during a precollege program I taught, "I was in biology class and my teacher called on me and some kids in the class were acting all shocked because I'm an intelligent young Black woman. After class, the students were like, '[Expletive], I didn't know you people were smart.'" Black Girls thrive academically in supportive environments (Warren, 2019). As mentioned earlier, when teachers hold racial implicit and explicit biases, they further perpetuate the racial disparities regarding achievement and discipline (Starck et al., 2020).

ABANDON THE TERM ALLY

Most people reading this will be familiar with the term *ally*. This term unfortunately has become watered down from its original intent of using one's privilege to show solidarity for marginalized individuals. An ally has simply become a verbal alignment with oppressed people without any corresponding action. Rather, one should strive to be a coconspirator:

> To be a white co-conspirator means to deliberately acknowledge that people of color are criminalized for dismantling white supremacy. It means we [white people] choose to take on the consequences of participating in a criminalized act, and we choose to support and center people of color in the reproductive justice movement. (Knittel, 2018, para. 4)

Coconspirators use their privilege to deliberately dismantle systematic racism. White teachers must be willing to not only educate but take action against social injustices for Black Girls (Warren, 2019). As coconspirators, they must use their leverage to dismantle structures that are detrimental to the success of Blacks, such as unequal punishment and hypersexualized imagery.

CONCLUSION

The racial identity of Black Girls is continually evolving during middle childhood, adolescence, and early adulthood. The way in which teachers engage Black Girls in the classroom will impact their ability to fully achieve, engage, and feel supported. White teachers must abandon [all] biases towards Black Girls. Only when teachers are no longer blinded by Blackness, because they have abandoned all their preconceived notions and seen Blackness as something to behold, will Black Girls be able to say with confidence and sincerity, not out of a response to oppression, "I am brilliant, powerful, and beautiful."

Genesis Begins Again, by Alicia D. Williams

Grades 5–8

Contemporary Realistic Fiction

Book Review by Marguerite W. Penick

Reading this book elicits a multitude of emotions: anger, frustration, disbelief, and dismay. But of all the emotions that arise from reading this book, the one the reader is consistently immersed in is heartbreak. There is heartbreak at every corner. There is the heartbreak of poverty, the heartbreak of a father who can't relate to his daughter, and the heartbreak of a new school. But it is the heartbreak of Genesis's self-hate because of the darkness of her skin and the curl of her hair that makes readers want to take Genesis into their arms and tell her it is society that is to blame, not her, not her skin tone, not her hair. That she is wonderful and strong and smart and deserving. Yes, by the end of the book Genesis has begun to believe in herself, but the heartbreak she has to endure is unspeakable and unimaginable. If readers use this book to create change, then others may not have to endure the heartbreak, but if readers don't take their responsibility seriously, then the cycle of heartbreak will continue for too many of our Black Girls.

Despite the myriad of factors that could derail our educational careers, Black girls thrive. In the next chapter, teacher educator Toni Graves Williamson tells the story of feeling like a slow reader her whole life—despite evidence to the contrary—and how this unconscious categorization affected her personal and professional relationships. It wasn't until she saw mirrors, positive reflections of herself, that she was able to quiet the voice in her head she believed to be true. Williamson's scholarship is a reminder that Black girls thrive in spite of the educational trauma they endure. Often, outward-facing traits such as academic success and performance confidence mask the wounds that they carry, caused by the racial context in which they move.

CHAPTER 9

Finding My Armor of Self-Love

Toni Graves Williamson

"I'm a slow reader."

I don't remember when I started saying this. Perhaps it was in second grade when I told Ms. Wilson that I had read 10 pages of *Charlotte's Web* the night before, and her response was lackluster at the number of pages completed. Maybe it was in the fifth grade when I first started analyzing my scores on end-of-grade standardized testing. Though I was in the 99th percentile overall, my reading comprehension always hovered in the mid 80s. Maybe it was in sixth grade—when all of the neighborhood elementary schools joined together to make one middle school—and somehow it seemed like the students in my class (which was now populated by wealthy White kids) had more time at night to do their homework and read the book of their choice so that their "number of books read" bar on the bulletin board bar graph always grew faster than mine. Wherever it started, it is the narrative that followed me. Through high school. Through college. Through two graduate degrees.

What this meant for me was never feeling quite smart enough. Not as smart as Linnea in college, because I couldn't read through the books as fast as she could. She finished her degree in three years, while it took me every second of the four years that I had. Not as smart as Ruth Ann in graduate school, who would do the reading assignments and summarize them for me when I couldn't get through them so that we could leave for dinner. If I did insist on doing my own reading, she would say, "New York City awaits . . . ." Not as smart as the two heads of school that I worked with earlier in my career, who somehow had time to not only read, but also recommend a slew of reading for everyone all of the time. Reading was always my Achilles' heel. I wasn't able to get through the chapters of a book in a timely fashion, which meant my shelves were full of books that were unfinished.

All too often there was evidence supporting the theories of my own intelligence. When I shared my SAT and ACT scores with my white roommate in college, she asked me, "How did you get in?" My college advisor told me that my first semester grades were "pretty good" (A in drama, A in writing, C in psychology, and C in calculus). Grades that had never been considered "pretty good" in high school were now suddenly acceptable, and I assumed it was because I had been *gifted* this opportunity to attend one of the most prestigious universities in the country. I didn't think I'd earned it. I didn't think I was supposed to be there. They had offered this acceptance to me at this fine institution because they needed to fill their Black folk quota, right?

I do realize just how much the stories that I told myself have had an effect on my self-image, examples of what Young (2011) identifies as *impostor syndrome*. A vivid memory struck me recently from a class that I took as a senior in college. This class only had about 10 folks in it, so class participation played a major role. I was very interested in the topic and had waited a few semesters to finally be let in. I mean who doesn't want to be in a class titled *Politics and the Libido* that began at the height of Bill Clinton's impeachment? I did *all* of the reading—no matter how slowly that went for me—and I would show up for class early. As my classmates filed in before our professor, I helped fill them in with the knowledge of the pages that they had skipped. By the time our professor showed up to class, they were able to raise their hands faster than I and contribute using much bigger words than I could. All along, I knew they were all full of shit. All along, I understood the content and idiosyncrasies about a topic that was much more complex than I had ever imagined. But I *thought* I wasn't as smart as they were because I couldn't get my hand in the air. I got a C in the course. Comments I received from my professor included, "I wish I could have heard your voice more in class." Years later, I can acknowledge the voice in my head that told me I wasn't good enough or that I didn't belong or that I wasn't smart enough to add to the conversation. I see her. And she continued to show up, reminding me of the impostor that I thought I was.

My logical brain has been socialized to believe that how fast someone reads, how quickly they throw their hands in the air to answer questions, or how many big words they say doesn't make them smarter than I. I mean, I am a teacher. This is something that I know intrinsically, but have also seen repeatedly demonstrated in classrooms, and specifically with Black girls (Morris, 2016). However, I have still fallen into stereotypes throughout my schooling and my career: making good grades, being successful at my job, getting accepted into respected universities, teaching myself the tricks to do well on the GRE. This little Black girl from the countryside of North Carolina still has to fight her own negative internal self talk. I am a first-generation college grad. I know that I've been lucky and in the right place at the right time. None of this negates my hard work, visible and invisible labor to get to this point in my life and career. No matter how much work I do to move past the stories that I have worked to unlearn, I am clear on this: I can easily be thrown back into that place.

Recently, I was part of a hiring committee at my school. My colleagues pored over the resumes of potential teachers and critiqued them in a manner I felt to be too harsh. I began dropping hints that we were being unreasonable in some cases. I even said, "You know, I didn't learn to write a proper resume until I was 30." "You all would have overlooked me and my pitiful attempts at writing such an important document." "Even for our top candidates, remember we can't put too much emphasis on the cover letter, there is no guarantee that this person actually did this writing."

I get it—there were a lot of resumes to get through and we didn't have much time. But as their snarkiness rose, so did my defenses. I could see how they were weeding out people who I felt affinity with; perhaps they were told they were slow readers at one point, just like I was. Then, one of my white colleagues made a comment about a candidate that had a traditional African American sounding name. Her comment was about the first sentence of the cover letter: *I am thrilled to apply for this position.* "Well, doesn't this sound ridiculous. 'I am thrilled to apply . . .' Who says that?!"

And then . . . I lost it. I didn't get angry. I got small. I was suddenly back in my place as the second grader who didn't read enough of *Charlotte's Web.* I was that college senior that couldn't get my hand up fast enough in my class. I was that grad student being rushed by her friend to complete her reading assignments. I was that little Black girl from the country who could never get the right big words together to be smart enough. After crying for a while and totally forgetting where I was, I had a conversation with my colleague. The logical part of my brain and the deep feelings of my heart managed to align, and I reminded myself that the negative stories that I repeat in my head about that little Black girl are bullshit (Liston, in press).

Only now—with two graduate degrees and 20 years of professional experience—am I finding words for this experience, thanks in no small part to Julie Lythcott-Haims's memoir, *Real American* (2018). In it, she shares her experience at Stanford University, which started off similar to my undergraduate experience. Low grades in her first semester of college confirmed the narrative we get as Black girls that she had believed—she didn't belong there (Anderson & Coleman-King, in press; Swalwell et al., in press). "I had stolen his spot at Stanford with my Blackness" (Lythcott-Haims, 2018, p. 70) describes an encounter with one of her white classmates in high school. According to Dr. Claude Steele, Julie and I were experiencing stereotype threat. In his book, *Whistling Vivaldi,* Steele (2010) shares the research he discovered from hundreds of experiments that confirm when members of marginalized groups are exposed to the threat of a stereotype, they experience cognitive stress that negatively affects performance. This stress kept my hand from shooting up in class. Perhaps this stress confirmed the stories that I started developing well before I could read Dr. Steele's work.

Seeing myself in Julie's words helped me to alleviate that stress. Surrounding myself with colleagues and friends who, like me, defied stereotypes and found themselves at tables they deserved to sit at—but that were not designed *for* them—helped me feel less alone (Arki, 2016). About her life, Julie says, "I am becoming a Black woman, treated in the world as such and lacking the armor or self-love to withstand that treatment" (Lythcott-Haims, 2018, p. 86). I have found those places for self-love. I am one of the blessed and lucky ones that has learned to do so.

Steele (2010) posits that there is "no single, one-size-fits-all strategy (p. 181)." The research that has been done includes strategies that help to minimize threat. "Students do better when they have strong relationships with their teachers that challenge and support them. They do better when they are part of settings that foster hope and belonging (Steele, 2010, p. 181)." He says, "When the effort to change identity-relevant cues and contingencies in a setting can go no further, helping people understand the safety they do have in a setting is immensely valuable—academically valuable" (p. 184). Steele (2010) refers to the work of psychologist Douglass Massey and his team at the University of Pennsylvania and Princeton University. Their work focused on exploring the concept of stereotype threat of Black and Brown students in a national study of various colleges (big and small, Ivy and non-Ivy, public and private). Of the students they interviewed, those who were worried about their "perception" experienced lower grades throughout the semester. In addition to other predictors of underperformance, the presence of stereotype threat amplified the underperformance. However, they also found that when those students had Black professors, they experienced almost no stereotype threat (pp. 156–159). This explains why the class where I read the most books in high school was taught by Ms. Lea, a Black woman. These studies illuminate the need for hiring practices that prioritize ways of employing teachers in whom all students can see themselves reflected.

My eyes are now open to all of the strong Black folks in my life. Queer and hetero, religious and not, older and younger. They are mirrors—the mirrors that weren't always around me in the predominantly white spaces that I frequented. I love wearing my "Young, Gifted, and Black" sweatshirt to the gym. I love being able to be a mirror for the young Black girls in the PWI (predominantly white institutions) where I work. I love my beautiful Black friend, Rodney, who has done the work to put "doctor" in front of his name. And the #BlackGirlMagic of my friend, Jalene, whose words dance so eloquently in the simplest of notes. I love reminiscing about the intelligence that existed in my grandmother, who didn't know how to read. And my mother whose brilliant mind can see fabric magically take shape. I am motivated by my sister Lervetris's understanding of medicine—she is the one everyone in the family always calls for expert advice. And I love how my smart and brave sister Phyllis followed in our brilliant father's footsteps as a small business owner. Intelligence is all around me. It always has been. My mirrors help remind me that I am a smart little Black girl from the countryside of North Carolina.

And by the way, I read Julie's book from beginning to end in record time.

ACTIVITY

Schools should clarify their institutional goals for hiring. Attention to student population and representation should be a critical step. In order to ensure that hiring committees uphold those institutional goals, all members should go through antibias training each time they are chosen to be part of a search committee. This training should include participating in the Harvard Implicit Bias Test (implicit .harvard.edu) and sharing readings about affirmative action, cultural sensitivity, and implicit bias.

The final vignette in this section is by Sipho Sgwentu, born into a free South Africa in 1992 (two years after the end of apartheid) on its way to electing Nelson Mandela the first Black president. Sipho grew up navigating a multicultural country and international independent school while continuing to face apartheid's legacy as the third child of Black Xhosa parents, who were born, raised, and lived the majority of their adult lives under apartheid. This piece is a testament to the hundreds of minute ways in which apartheid lives on and must be faced—in South Africa and the United States—even after official segregation is declared illegal.

Vignette: Black Student, White Teacher

Sipho Sgwentu

Although it may not seem like a particularly important lesson to teach at educational institutions, I think a very important lesson that white female teachers (including white moms of kids in interracial schools) must be tasked with is to teach their young white male students that there is no universal beauty. Show them that their Black female classmates are beautiful and that the blue-eyed blond girl in their class is not the standard by which beauty should be measured.

Having been raised in predominantly white schools, I have noticed there tends to be a lot of focus on the mental development of a child of color. Significant measures are taken to ensure the child can cope academically and compete with their classmates. In the first six years of school, this approach is fine, however as you grow older you start becoming aware of your "Blackness." This self-recognition may not be brought on by overt racism but rather through the subtleties of conversations and the racially charged undertones of the child's daily life. Indeed, it is in these unspoken moments where the true discomfort of going to a white-dominated school lives. The ability to recognize this crucial moment in a child's life is not something that can be taught through a seminar; educators and parents must make every effort to be certain their students and children are comfortable enough to approach them about the racism in their lives.

When you enter your teen years, you go through the same issues that all teens go through, sweating at weird times, hair in funny places, fluctuation of hormones—you get the whole experience. However, in addition to becoming aware of your "Blackness," you also realize you are living in a white man's world. You become aware that your beauty is not always defined nor desired. Your hair does not blow in the wind; instead it is deep rooted and strong. Your eyes are not a pearly green or blue but a deep Black brown. Your nose is not sleek and pointy, but wide and round. You begin to realize that your beauty does not meet the standards that the world has presented to you. When your schoolmates start making lists of "Who is the Most Beautiful," you never make the list. When you open a magazine you never see yourself. When you think of the word *beautiful* you imagine Hitler's dream of Aryan perfection, a beauty standard that is impossible for you to reach. All of this creates a resentment of self, one that begins to seep into your deepest parts and cement itself in your identity.

As we who don't identify as white strive to balance out the racial injustice of this world, especially in schools, we must remember the historical ways in which Black men and women were oppressed and take note of how those techniques are still used today. The Black man's daily life is very physical. We are beaten, we are shot, we are arrested, we are followed in shopping centers, we are "randomly" selected for searches at airports, and we even have our children taken from us as we walk past. All these occurrences are examples of physical interactions we have with the world around us. Of course, we Black men carry deep psychological scars, but our environment is physically grueling.

On the other hand, the reality of a Black woman is that of a deep and constant psychological attack. In this "man's world," men have objectified women to such a degree that women too often believe their self-worth is based purely on their beauty. This ideology is hammered home through the media. When the white man controls your media and perpetuates a "new" standard of beauty, the result is often the very opposite of what a Black woman looks like. This standard is even highlighted in "Black" magazines, featuring Black women with very white features (fair skin, weaves, long noses, hazel eyes, etc.), all the while subtly demeaning the authentic beauty of the Black woman.

(Continued)

(Continued)

This is psychological warfare, designed to divide the Black population and create a deep self-loathing. This false image creates a generation of Black women that are not proud of their Blackness. These women will marry white men in order to give their children a chance. They do not want their children to go through what they went through. And in a way, this is understandable, as it is sometimes unbearable living in this white man's world; you would do anything to make sure your children do not experience what you went through. However, in the midst of trying to protect their children, some women live vicariously through them, giving them the Caucasian features they always desired, knowing full well the benefits of having them.

This does not have to be that way. I believe that white teachers and parents need to take on the responsibility that all Black teachers and parents bear and have these uncomfortable conversations at home, daily. Teach your son to tell the Black girl in his class that she is beautiful every day until he believes it. Teach your daughters to love the authentic Black look and to appreciate their friends' Afros. Teach your children the depth of oppression, not only the legal kind, but the psychological kind. Teach them the privilege of being white. Teach them that if they want to see justice for all and true equality in this world, then they must take on the burden of their privilege and recognize it as such. Young white people tend to attempt to brush off any form of responsibility, closing the door on the actions of their fathers and labelling it as history. However, we as Black people live that history every day. This is something that white children must also be taught through a constant uncomfortable conversation, for all. Basically, teach your white son to put my sister in his "top ten list," because no matter how small that action is, it has profound resounding effects.

PART IV

"RECLAIMING MY TIME"

—Maxine Waters

The United States is a country founded upon systems that rendered Black women vulnerable in every imaginable way. Black women were then—and continue to be today—among the most vulnerable people in the United States. The following chapters describe how the current education system intersects with other institutions, for example, criminal justice and foster care, to compound the threat to Black girls by not recognizing their vulnerability. When schools require that students have access to particular resources (time, money, people) to be successful, they automatically establish a hierarchy in which the least vulnerable are most successful. Such systems widen the opportunity gaps; the most vulnerable fall through.

In "Girls in the School-to-Prison Pipeline," Dr. Jessie Harper explores the history of the pipeline and how policies in schools and school districts—institutions charged with protecting and nurturing our Black girls—lead to the disproportionate policing, arrest, and imprisonment of Black girls. In the subsequent chapter, entitled "How Dare You be Brilliant," Dr. Mary Oling-Sisay describes in detail the precise vulnerabilities that Black girls face, including a systemic expectation that makes them "less than" to survive in a system that insists on seeing them as such. Further exemplifying the failure of our systems to support vulnerable Black girls and women, the next chapter by Dr. Stephany Powell demonstrates how Black girl bodies get used and abused before the girls have the opportunity to know themselves or understand their sexuality. Powell suggests how teachers can interrupt this pipeline of expectation by adopting a trauma-informed lens when working with Black girls, asking, "What happened to you?" rather than "What's wrong with you?" This chapter on commercial sexual exploitation is followed by a piece from a 20-year veteran foster care professional, Jennifer Stiller, who helps us understand how that system could more effectively support Black girls by honoring their resilience and vulnerability.

CHAPTER 10

Girls in the School-to-Prison Pipeline

Implications of History, Policy, and Race

Jessie Harper

A 6-year old girl was taken to the office after acting out in class. A staff member grabbed her wrists to try to get her to calm down, and the six-year-old kicked the staff member. The young African American girl was handcuffed and arrested on a battery charge *(Binion, 2019)*.

A 15-year-old African American girl who was diagnosed with ADHD and bipolar disorder and was jailed for skipping school. A second charge of resisting arrest was added after she got into a fight with a fellow student *(Breslow, 2015)*.

A 16-year-old girl who was an excellent student was working on a science project before school when she went outside to mix common household chemicals in an eight-ounce plastic water bottle. The experiment produced a little smoke and caused the bottle's top to pop off. There were no injuries, and no damage was caused. The school had the African American teen arrested and charged with a felony *(Winter, 2013)*.

How is it that arresting a 6-year-old could be considered an appropriate response for a temper tantrum? How is it that a 15-year-old with a dual diagnosis of ADHD and bipolar disorder could be jailed for skipping school? Why is an excellent student being charged with a felony for her intellectual curiosity? Unfortunately, these are not isolated incidences. Black girls often receive more severe penalties than their white peers receive for the same behavior. It is not that

Black girls misbehave more, but that they have been disproportionately impacted by harsh discipline practices (Morris et al., 2018). The term *disproportionality* is determined by the 10 percent of the population standard. In other words, a population is disproportionately underrepresented or overrepresented if its proportion in the target classification exceeds its representation in the population by 10 percent of that population (Losen, 2012). Black girls have certainly been overrepresented in harsh discipline practices in schools. According to a report from the U.S. Department of Education (Inniss-Thompson, 2017), during the 2013–2014 school year, Black girls made up only 16 percent of the female student population. However, 28 percent of them were physically restrained, 43 percent were referred to law enforcement (a percentage 2.5 times greater than that for white girls), and 38 percent were arrested (a percentage four times greater than for white girls) (Inniss-Thompson, 2017).

How could this happen? How can we reverse the trend of these harsh discriminatory practices and support the learning experiences and achievement of our Black girls? The purpose of this chapter is to examine what the available scholarship suggests about the reasons for discipline disparities experienced by Black girls in schools. It will also highlight some promising practices for a way forward.

Disparate Discipline

Disparate discipline practices are a result of the growing problem of the criminalization of Black girls by schools, and what some scholars call the school-to-prison pipeline (Fuentes, 2011a, 2011b; Morris et al., 2018; Winn & Behizadeh, 2011) The term *school-to-prison pipeline* typically refers to a disturbing trend in which punitive policies have led to children being funneled out of schools and into the criminal justice system at an alarming rate. This issue is multifaceted and has its roots in racial and social inequality. In fact, how students are punished in school for misbehaving is often determined by race (Losen, 2012; Morris et al., 2018; Smith & Harper, 2015). This pipeline often begins when a student, due to a perceived discipline problem, is branded a troublemaker. After a referral is made for disruptive behavior, the student is suspended or expelled. This results in lost classroom time and causes the student to fall behind in school. School failure is often the result, and if the student subsequently drops out of school, this can lead to juvenile detention and then adult prison (Fuentes 2011a, 2011b; Losen 2012; Pane & Rocco, 2014; Skiba, 2002). Although the conversation about the school-to-prison pipeline has historically centered around young boys of color, boys are by no means the only ones impacted by this punitive cyclical practice. Black girls have become targets of punitive school discipline practices and are the fastest-growing population to experience school suspensions and expulsions (Morris et al., 2018).

ZERO TOLERANCE

The term *zero tolerance* originated with the Drug-Free Schools and Communities Act in 1986, which mandated zero tolerance for any drugs or alcohol on public school grounds. In 1994, the Safe and Gun-Free Schools Act mandated a one-year expulsion for anyone who brought a firearm to school. Zero-tolerance policies contributed to police presence in schools. In April of 1999, Eric Harris and Dylan Klebold, two seniors at Columbine High School in Littleton, Colorado, an affluent, predominantly white suburb near Denver, shot and killed 13 people and injured 24 others (American Civil Liberties Union, 2017; Fuentes, 2011a; Skiba, 2002). After this and other high-profile school shootings, the U.S. Department of Justice started the COPS in Schools program, which expanded on the earlier school-policing initiative. This program makes grants to school districts for school resource officers (American Civil Liberties Union, 2017; Fuentes, 2011a). Policies that were originally intended to protect students from guns and drugs have expanded to include automatic suspensions for students who get in fights with other students, or who are perceived as threatening in other ways to students and/or teachers (Morris et al., 2018). In districts across the country, the presence of police inside public schools has led to rising rates of arrests of students of color for minor violations of disciplinary codes or behaviors that in another era would have landed a student in the principal's office (Fuentes, 2011b).

THE MYTH OF THE SUPERPREDATOR

In the mid-1990s, criminologist John Dilulio coined the term *superpredators* to describe young Black and Brown males (Dilulio, 1995). He and other criminologists advanced the theory that Black and Brown youth in urban settings are violent, have "no conscience, no empathy," and are brutal and without remorse. In 1996, Dilulio and his colleagues wrote *Body Count: Moral Poverty and how to Win America's War on Drugs*, which predicted that youth violence would increase at an alarming rate because of these superpredators (Bennett et al., 1996). However, these criminologists were mistaken, and over the decade after Dilulio and Bennett made these predictions, youth violence declined in urban areas. The superpredator turned out to be a myth.

However, this myth has unfortunately continued to impact the lives of children of color (Fuentes, 2011a). We have seen the results, not only in the way zero-tolerance policies continue to disproportionately impact students of color, but in the fact that the United States has the highest prison population in the world. By the end of 2016, about 2.2 million individuals were held in U.S. prisons and jails (Kaeble & Cowhig, 2018). There are more than 700,000 juvenile arrests per year (Office of Juvenile Justice and Delinquency Prevention, 2018). According to a report from The Sentencing Project (2017), Black children are five times more likely to be detained than white children for similar offenses (Sickmund et al.,

2017). Such racial disparities have led to Black and Brown juveniles being fun-neled into the criminal justice system when court referrals are used for disciplining students in school (Nicholson-Crotty et al., 2009). The increase of school resource officers has also led to the criminalization of students of color when even minor offenses, such as perceived disrespect or student disagreements, have led to student arrests and convictions (American Civil Liberties Union, 2017; Fuentes, 2011b).

"Underachiever," "Insubordinate," "Dangerous," "Hypersexualized"—Myths, Stereotypes, and other Misconceptions

Though there are more men incarcerated than women, the rate of growth of the female prison population has been twice that of the male population for the past 40 years (Kajstura, 2019). Black girls are more likely to be referred to school resource officers or police for disciplinary infractions and are four times more likely to be detained (Inniss-Thompson, 2017). Research suggests that teacher bias rather than students' actual misbehavior contributes to disproportionate discipline practices (Blake et al., 2011; Skiba, 2002, Skiba et al., 1997). According to a 2016 report from Georgetown University's Center on Poverty and Inequality (Blake & Epstein, 2017), adults view Black girls as more adult-like and less innocent than their white counterparts starting at age five. They are often viewed as more dangerous than their peers, hypersexualized, angry, loud, and defiant, and they are punished for more subjective infractions, such as talking back or perceived disrespect (Epstein et al., 2016; Fordham, 1996; Morris, 2007; Morris et al., 2018).

Black girls are often considered less academically able than their white counterparts by educators (Winn & Behizadeh, 2011). Their nonconformity to traditional expectations has also prompted educators to respond harshly to their behaviors (Blake et al., 2011; Morris et al., 2018). When Black girls respond to oppression by speaking out against it or in other ways fighting back, they are cast as social deviants rather than leaders or critical thinkers (Morris et al., 2018). Other factors contributing to teachers' overreliance on referrals to school resource officers and to other harsh discipline practices, include teacher inexperience and lack of skill in classroom behavior management (Blake et al., 2011; Fenning & Rose, 2007; Gregory & Mosely, 2004; Monroe & Obidah 2004).

Promising Practices and a Way Forward

Know Your Own Biases

It is important to acknowledge that teachers, administrators, school resource officers, and others who interact with students do not exist apart from their own social contexts. They are all members of the larger society and not immune to a cultural conditioning process that creates within us biases and prejudices that can negatively impact students of color (Abelson et al., 1998; Banaji et al., 1993; Burkard & Knox, 2004; Sue, 2005). Since most people are exposed to powerful and enduring narratives about Black students, and because these narratives and biases have a harmful impact on these students, it is important for teachers and administrators to consider the views they may personally hold about students of color. An important first step may be for each individual to consider their own personal biases when contemplating their interactions with Black girls. Implicit association tests are helpful in measuring thoughts and feelings that are outside of our awareness but that impact our actions and attitudes. One example is the Harvard Implicit Association Test, which has been successfully used by individuals in a variety of fields including education, social work, and medicine (https://implicit.harvard.edu/implicit/aboutus.html).

As a way forward, Pane and Rocco (2014) suggest engaging in "critical reflection." Critical reflection requires, first, listening to and learning about students' lives and experiences and how they feel about such experiences. These include their experiences both in and out of school. A second step requires reflection on how your students' experiences differ from your own. A third step is to integrate what you learn from your students with your own teaching practice and theories. This will allow you to challenge long-held biases and stereotypes and help you to create a more inclusive learning environment.

RETHINK DISCIPLINE;
REIMAGINE PROFESSIONAL DEVELOPMENT

The National Women's Law Center (NWLC, 2017) outlines other promising practices for educators. Instead of rushing to punishment and labeling students as problems, it is good to take a moment to consider why a student may be misbehaving. This does not mean excusing wrong or even dangerous behavior and it is of course not without its challenges. Instead of branding Black girls as problems, it is helpful to seek ways to provide help to these students for the problems that they may be experiencing and to address the causes for these problems. For these girls, who are often marginalized, it could mean the difference between getting them the help they need and exacerbating their problems.

In addition, it is essential that educators rethink discipline. The word *discipline* is derived from the Latin word for instruction. How should discipline be defined in our schools? For many, discipline has become synonymous with punishment. Reimagining discipline as training and instruction, and as a way to support our Black girls in their academic achievement and future success, is an important step in reversing the effects of the school-to-prison pipeline (NWLC, 2017). There are more effective alternatives to the harsh and exclusionary approaches to discipline that have become a part of our practice and our policies (i.e., referral to school resource officers, suspension, expulsion, detention). Some promising practices include positive behavioral interventions and supports (PBIS) and restorative justice practices.

Since making such significant changes will require training and professional development opportunities, the center (NWLC, 2017) also recommends providing educators with professional learning opportunities that help them to discover and unpack biases that may cause them to misinterpret and/or overreact to the behavior of Black girls. Training that informs educators to recognize and respond to trauma is also essential. Other recommendations include becoming familiar with the discipline statistics and other information about your classroom, school, and district, and continuing to reflect on your own practices as educators and administrators.

COMMIT TO THE BELIEF IN THE POTENTIAL OF ALL STUDENTS

Esteemed educator Christopher Emdin asserts (2016),

> The effectiveness of the teacher can be traced directly back to what that teacher thinks of the student. If the teacher does not value the student, there is no motivation to take risks to engage with the student. . . . How successful the teacher is in the classroom is directly related to how successful the teacher thinks the student can be. Teachers limit themselves and their students when they put caps on what their students can achieve. (p. 207)

Unfortunately, schools have often simultaneously claimed to be color-blind and yet have had lower expectations for Black girls (Winn & Behizadeh, 2011). To the contrary, Black girls are quite resilient when given the opportunity and support they need to succeed. They want to learn, achieve, and succeed academically (Evans-Winters, 2011).

Educators have a profound impact on the lives of the students that they serve. Therefore, it is essential that they aim to be a force for good, to inspire, to treat with respect and equity, and to support our beautiful and brilliant Black girls.

CHAPTER 11

How Dare You be Brilliant

The Precarious Situation for Black Girls

Mary Oling-Sisay

> Whatever affects one directly, affects all indirectly. I can never be what I ought to be until you are what you ought to be. This is the interrelated structure of reality.
>
> —Dr. Martin Luther King Jr.

INTRODUCTION

Black girls are on average stigmatized and described collectively as unsophisticated, defiant, and having bad attitudes (Blake et al., 2011). The stigma extends to K–12 education, where some teachers harshly judge and punish Black girls (Crenshaw et al., 2015). The differential treatment partially contributes to the school-to-prison pipeline. While the school-to-prison pipeline jeopardizes Black boys in the same way it imperils Black girls, there is a paucity of attention to the experience of Black girls.

Despite barriers, minoritized groups view education as a mechanism to attain the freedoms enjoyed by their White counterparts. According to Anderson (1988, p. 2), "Between 1800 and 1835, most of the southern states enacted legislation making it a crime to teach enslaved children to read or write." During slavery, Black women were denied the right to education, and at the same time penalized for their inability to read and write (Adams, 2010). Black women sought innovative mechanisms to access education for themselves and their children. Mary McLeod Bethune, for example, succeeded in education not only herself but for others as well (Berry, 1982). She was a fearless civil and women's rights activist who founded an institution that became the foundation for today's black institutions. Later, as an advisor to President Franklin Delano Roosevelt, she utilized her position to further advocate for equity in education for Black children. There has been considerable progress since the days of slavery; however, the contemporary educational system in the United States still fails Black children. There was a rekindling of hope with the 1954 Brown vs. Board of Education ruling that overturned Plessy vs. Ferguson's separate but equal doctrine. Yet, Black people, regardless of age, gender, or socioeconomic status, are still fighting for equal access to educational opportunities. Equity in educational opportunities is crucial for the nation's future.

Against this backdrop are shifting demographics. By the year 2050, women of color will compose approximately 53 percent of the U.S. population (U.S. Department of Education, Office for Civil Rights, 2016). The Civil Rights Data Collection (U.S. Department of Education, Office for Civil Rights (2016) reports that of the 50.7 million public school students in the United States, 48 percent are White, 28 percent are Hispanic, 16 percent are Black, 5 percent are Asian, and 3 percent represent two or more races.

THE DISCIPLINE CONTINUUM

School discipline data for K–12 schools reveal that the number of Black girls in the discipline system is six times higher than the number of White girls and 67 percent higher than that of boys overall ("A First Look," 2016). Teachers and school officials extensively and routinely scrutinize Black girls' behavior, and expectations of them are exacting (Carter et al., 2014; Chavous & Cogburn, 2007).

BRILLIANT BLACK GIRLS AND GIFTED PROGRAMS

According to the National Center for Education Statistics (Chapman et al., 2012; NCES, 2010), 8.1 percent of girls participated in gifted education programs in public and private K–12 schools in the United States. About 5.2 percent of Black girls were identified by school districts as gifted and talented, compared to 35 percent of White girls. Scholarship on culturally conscious gifted pedagogy indicates that talent continues to be conceptualized from a Eurocentric middle-class model of intelligence and achievement (Ford, 2013a, 2013b). Thus, Black students are underrepresented in gifted programs (Riley et al., 2015). Many states utilize adapted versions of the federal definitions of giftedness. Scholars posit that the definitions lead to misinterpretations that often contribute to the exclusion of some groups (Renzulli, 1978). The 1978 definition is the commonly used version:

> "Gifted and talented" means children, and whenever applicable, youth who are identified at the preschool, elementary, or secondary level as

possessing demonstrated or potential abilities, that give evidence of high performance capability in areas such as intellectual, creative, specific academic, or leadership ability, or in the performing and visual arts and who by reason thereof require services or activities not ordinarily provided by the school. (Gifted and Talented Children's Education Act of 1978)

Black girls may supposedly attend schools in poor districts that do not have the resources to offer gifted programs. To be categorized as high achieving or smart, Black girls have to work twice as much as their white counterparts (Evans-Winters, 2011). In the process, they begin to doubt their abilities (Gilliam, Maupin, Reyes, Accavitti, & Shic, 2016). Several legislations have been passed to change gifted education, but these programs remain inaccessible for most Black girls due to the schools they attend.

INTERSECTIONALITY

Intersectionality provides a theoretical framework to understand overlapping identities and experiences (Crenshaw, 1991). Crenshaw asserts that because "the intersectional experience is greater than the sum of racism and sexism, any analysis that does not take *intersectionality* into account cannot sufficiently address the particular manner in which Black women are subordinated" (1989, p. 140).

The intersectionality of race, gender, class, and perception of the "threat" posed by brilliant Black girls (Morales, 2014) limits their access to gifted programs. They are also often torn between loyalty to their own culture and pressures to fit in with white culture so as to experience the privileges and benefits of such belonging (Squires, 2008). This cultural trading often leads Black girls to adopt stereotypical opinions about Blacks, and conversely, they may develop negative views of themselves, resulting in poor performance regardless of their abilities. Black girls bring to the classroom varied experiences, including those of family dynamics, gender, race, class, and socioeconomic status.

While this identity challenge is detrimental for all ages, brilliant and gifted adolescent Black girls are especially vulnerable, as they are at a critical juncture in their psychosocial development. As a result, some Black girls drop out of gifted programs (Buckley & Carter, 2005). Research on the intersectionality of race, gender, brilliance, and high achieving Black girls is nascent. Evans-Winters and Esposito (2010) posit:

Because feminist epistemologies tend to be concerned with the education of White girls and women, and race-based epistemologies tend to be consumed with the educational barriers negatively effecting Black boys, the educational needs of Black girls have fallen through the cracks. (p. 12).

Tyson (2003) acknowledges the nuances of Black identity formation and the challenge of supporting strong Black girl group identity while at the same time teaching "normative standards of behavior and deportment, such as self-restraint and silence." (p. 335)

In conclusion, Black girls in general experience marginalization and "chilly" classrooms (Morris, 2007). The situation is worse for brilliant, high-achieving Black girls. When they speak up or protest, they risk going against the mold of what is expected of them and are often punished by the teachers (Morales, 2014).

CHAPTER 12

Girl Trafficking Misunderstood

Understanding the Commercially Sexually Exploited African American Girl

Stephany Powell

AFRICAN AMERICAN GIRL—AN INTERSECTIONAL APPROACH

The traditional role of education must be broadened to include trauma literacy. As Bloom (1995) noted in her article "Creating Sanctuary in the School," effective learning environments are two things: safe and secure. Many children today live in environments that are neither safe nor secure places for living, much less learning. In order to create a paradigm shift in the way we view the world and the students we serve, we must have an insatiable desire to find answers to the questions, "What happened to you?" as opposed to "What's wrong with you?" and "How can we help?" (pp. 1–9).

The purpose of this chapter is to help teachers create a paradigm shift in their own teaching and learning experiences to understand students like Julie (mentioned in the next section), without prejudicial judgment. The answers to such questions promote understanding through the intersectional lens of trauma, race, and adultification. Once they have addressed these questions, teachers will clearly understand how these factors contribute to and influence some Black Girls' behavior.

What's Wrong With You?

Julie is a 21-year-old African American female born in South Central Los Angeles. She was an exceptional student and found her public school to be a means of escape from the poverty and abuse she experienced at home. Her teachers always had good things to say about her during her early school years; in fact, these were the only times that she received such praise from adults. When Julie reached 10th grade, it was as though her presence no longer seemed important. No one really noticed Julie's irregular attendance, weight loss, and fatigue, or the word *PayDay* tattooed on her neck. But even if the school had noticed and called her mother, the mother would not have been home due to her drug addiction and overall neglect.

No one knew that Julie had run away from home, because she continued to try to attend school and would often return home from time to time, when her "boyfriend" allowed. What school officials noticed was her disruptive behavior. She began to fight and was subsequently kicked out of school due to her numerous suspensions. Julie was then sent to a continuation school. She did her best in her new school but had trouble concentrating, because the classroom was noisy with people yelling and not doing their work. Many times, she would leave the classroom due to anxiety induced by long-ingrained memories of conflict. When she would leave the classroom or become disruptive, her teachers would become angry and send her to the office. When her mother could be reached, she would only say, "I can't do nothing with that girl." Julie left school the second semester of 10th grade and blended into the environment of South Central Los Angeles, where she was soon forgotten and misunderstood, and became the unknown.

VS.

WHAT HAPPENED TO YOU?

The lack of understanding of complex trauma and the role that institutional racism plays in the education system, conjoined with adultification of African American girls, confirms the notion something is wrong with Julie. However, a closer look into her physical appearance, behavior, and demeanor should spark the question, What happened to you? If her teachers had employed an asset-based approach that included community- and trust-building activities, perhaps they may have learned more about her past. Julie was molested between the ages of 12 and 15 by her mother's numerous boyfriends. Had Julie's teachers asked, "What happened to you?" as opposed to "What's wrong with you?" they would have learned her history of emotional and physical abuse by her mother at an early age. If they had asked about her tattoo, they would have learned she had a pimp who would sell her on the streets at night and take her to school during the day so no one would know. Julie needed a caring adult fully engaged in the process of teaching and learning to ask the right questions to learn about her past as victim of human sex trafficking. Although Julie's story is fictitious, it is a common story told by many Journey Out clients. Journey Out is a Los Angeles–based nonprofit organization dedicated to adult victims of domestic human sex trafficking.

WHAT IS HUMAN TRAFFICKING?

In order to understand the relationship between human trafficking, the federal government's Trafficking Victims Protection Act of 2000 (TVPA) and its subsequent reauthorizations, and commercial sexual exploitation of children (CSEC), human trafficking must first be defined:

a) Sex trafficking in which a commercial sex act is induced by force, fraud, or coercion, or in which the person induced to perform such act has not attained 18 years of age; or

b) The recruitment, harboring, transportation, provision, or obtaining of a person for labor or services, through the use of force, fraud, or coercion for the purpose of subjection to involuntary servitude, peonage, debt bondage, or slavery. ("Human Trafficking Defined," n.d.).

Although there is no legal definition of CSEC, there are criminal provisions within the definition:

> Commercial Sexual Exploitation of Children refers to a range of crimes and activities involving the sexual abuse or exploitation of a child for the financial benefit of any person or in exchange for anything of value (including monetary and non-monetary benefits) given or received by any person. (Office of Juvenile Justice and Delinquency Prevention, n.d.)

All individuals under the age of 18 who trade sex for money are defined as victims of human trafficking. The commercial sexual exploitation of children can also include situations where a child engages in sexual activity in exchange for anything of value. Nonmonetary items include food, shelter, drugs, or protection. Mothers have been known to sell their daughters for sex in order to pay rent or buy food. Understanding the TVPA and the definition of CSEC are important for the purposes of victim identification. Any delay in victim reporting not only hinders safety but delays services to the victim. This also holds true when identifying the pimp/trafficker. Marcus et al. (2014) explained the traditional view of traffickers should be discarded; the TVPA redefined all adults who aid, abet, or benefit from a relationship with an underage sex worker as human traffickers. Based on the understanding of these definitions, school officials should exercise caution when handing over a minor victim to a familial trafficker.

Who Are the Victims?

The public has been subject to a false narrative about human trafficking victims. The antitrafficking movement will often depict an image of an underage white girl with a brown hand or tape over her mouth, indicating that she is not for sale. African American girls are often not identified as victims, because they do not fit the public perception of the human sex trafficking victim. Helen Taylor, director of intervention and outreach for Exodus Cry, pointed out, "America has the perception of the 'good victim,' the white, typically blonde, typically blue-eyed girl that was taken from the street" (as cited in Reese, 2017, p. 5).

Reese (2017) further described the face of the typical victim: "According to the FBI, 40 percent of victims of sex trafficking are African-Americans, with that number being significantly larger in the major metropolitan areas. In Los Angeles County, the African-American victim rate reaches 92 percent" (p. 1). The overrepresentation of underage African American girls is consistent across the country. Researchers believe that African American girls are overrepresented due to poverty and their disconnection from schools and other community support. Butler (2015) explained the high percentage in her research: "African American girls experience both physical and sexual abuse at young ages and witness multiple forms of violence at higher rates than their white peers" (p. 1489). Early victimization and complex trauma are clear risk factors for sex trafficking. Both Butler (2015) and Reese (2017) agree: The overrepresented numbers are due to the intersection of race, class, gender, and other forms of oppression. These factors push people of color and other minoritized populations disproportionately into prostitution and keep them trapped in the commercial sex industry.

Innocence Taken

The adultification of African American girls is another factor leading to the misunderstanding of the sexually exploited African American girl. Adultification of African American girls refers to the perception that they are less innocent and more adult than white girls of the same age. In 2017, Epstein et al. surveyed 325 adults across the United States. Study participants were predominantly white and female; over half of the participants had degrees above a high school diploma. The results suggested that "participants perceived Black Girls as needing less protection and nurturing than white girls, and that Black Girls were perceived to know more about adult topics and perceived to be more knowledgeable about sex than their white peers" (p. 8). What was even more striking about this study was that African American girls were considered less innocent across all childhood age groups, beginning at the age of five.

Epstein et al. (2017) portrayed a perfect example of adultification in their study of an incident that took place in New York:

> A 15-year-old African American girl was perceived to be biologically older. The 15-year-old was arrested by police for using a student Metrocard that is valid only for youth younger than 19. The officers did not believe the girl's claim that she was 15 years old, nor the affirmations of her age that they obtained from each of her parents when reached by phone. Police held the girl in handcuffs until the girl's mother brought her birth certificate to the police station. The girl was treated at a hospital for the damage the handcuffs inflicted on her wrists. (p. 6)

The role of implicit, unconscious, and/or explicit bias prevented the officers from believing the truth of the girl's age even when provided proof. The officers' vision was blinded by adultification; it was inconceivable that someone who appeared to be over 19 was only 15. An example of this can also be seen inside schools and other education-based institutions, where African American students are overdisciplined. One study, conducted by Riddle and Sinclair (2019), showed significant differences in the discipline of African American students and their white counterparts—the result being increased suspension amongst African Americans. The most frequent reason for discipline was the subjective category of defiant behavior. In the case of Julie, there was a reason for her defiant behavior. Julie learned that her defiant behavior enabled her to regain control over her environment, even if it meant suspension. Julie deserved another response to her actions.

RESILIENCE IS THE KEY TO FUTURE SUCCESS

Monique Morris (2016) [believes the success of the African American female student lies within a created safe school environment. This environment must include culturally competent and humble teachers and school leaders, discipline that is structured but not punitive, curriculum that includes images and life situations African American female students can relate to, and authentic teachers who believe in these students' successful future as opposed to dominant narratives of despair and criminalization. The female African American human trafficking victim lives in a world where she feels as though she is on the outside looking in. The inside world is filled with societal judgement and the idea of her being nurtured does not exist. The education system can teach her that she is important and that can prepare her for a viable future. Trauma informed training of teachers can build resilience and empowerment.

Resilience and empowerment are the key to her success, and who better to provide that than a teacher she can trust. The Seven Cs: The Essential Building Block of Resilience ("The 7 C's," n.d.) list the key ingredients needed for youth resilience.

The Seven C's are listed below:

Competence: When we notice what young people are doing right and give them opportunities to develop important skills, they feel competent. We undermine competence when we don't allow young people to recover themselves after a fall.

Confidence: Young people need confidence to be able to navigate the world, think outside the box, and recover from challenges.

Connection: Connections with other people, schools, and communities offer young people the security that allows them to stand on their own and develop creative solutions.

Character: Young people need a clear sense of right and wrong and a commitment to integrity.

Contribution: Young people who contribute to the well-being of others will receive gratitude rather than condemnation. They will learn that contributing feels good and may therefore more easily turn to others and do without shame.

Coping: Young people who possess a variety of healthy coping strategies will be less likely to turn to dangerous quick fixes when stressed.

Control: Young people who understand that benefits and respect are earned through demonstrated responsibility will learn to make wise choices and feel a sense of control.

The Seven C's can be used to promote self-empowerment and boundary setting and to combat stress. The support of trusted adults coupled with a safe environment can assist and sustain the victim of human trafficking for the rest of her life, helping her move from being a victim to being a survivor.

CONCLUSION

> The most disrespected woman in America, is the Black woman. The most unprotected person in American is the Black woman. The most neglected person in American is the Black woman.
>
> —Malcolm X (1962, as quoted in Emba, 2019)

The statements of Malcolm X are still reflected in conversations regarding African American girls in our criminal justice and education systems. African American girls trapped in the web of human trafficking need to be in an environment that promotes understanding without judgement. The intersections of trauma, race, and adultification can contribute to spirit murdering through misunderstanding and implicit bias (Love, 2019). The African American girl who lives with complex trauma learns early on that she does not matter. Not being nurtured, and being treated as if she is older than her years, steals the innocence she deserves. When this goes unaddressed, it drives a behavior that is often misunderstood by her teachers and any other adult that she comes in touch with. A lesson can be learned through the art form of Kintsugi, which reconstructs broken pottery, sealing the pieces together with gold to create an image more beautiful, with all of its cracks and chips, than the original, unbroken piece. It is a part of Zen philosophy—finding the beauty in broken pieces as a part of one's personal history. A closer look at Black Girls in the classroom would reveal a beautiful spirit that was shattered but can be recreated and empowered with gold.

A trauma-informed teacher can restore beauty and promote empowerment by asking the right question, What happened to you? as opposed to What's the matter with you? The role education plays in the healing of the CSEC victim is to promote hope and safety. The first step to changing the paradigm of educators is through disruption.

Vignette: Black Girls Trapped in Our Foster Care System

Jennifer Stiller

There are many factors that come into play when even *one* of our Black daughters enters the foster care system. Please understand that no parents dream of placing their daughter or daughters in foster care. As an advocate for the welfare of Black female children working with our daughters for the past 20 years, I bring some food for your soul and ideas that emerge from my years of experience in my practice. My heart continues to wrench when I interact with another Black Girl entering foster care. These are some key considerations as you engage with Black Girls in foster care.

1. Is she placed with a relative, her siblings, a family that represents her Black identity?

2. What are the reasons that she entered foster care? Is she having regular contact with her birth family and siblings?

3. Has she been able to remain in the school district that she had been in, or is she in a brand new school?

4. Has she moved to many placements and schools?

These are some questions a teacher should be trying to answer to have a grasp on the identities/identity that she presents in class. Does the Black Girl that enters your class seem quiet, sad, or withdrawn? Is she perceived as "angry and explosive"? Is she gifted and talented and hiding her pain behind her success? Is there something in your classroom environment or behavior that is possibly a trigger for her past trauma? Paying attention, close attention to this Black Girl will tell you a lot about her story. What is trauma and how does it impact this Black Girl learning and classroom behavior? If I can stress one thing most, being trauma-informed, is going to help navigate this process and relationship.

In your engagement with Black Girls in the foster care system, I encourage you to consider the following strategies:

- Separating the Black Girl's behavior from who she is as a learner and person will help her to feel visible and safe.

- Keep showing up and being present for her. The key to engaging and making a difference is to learn her story. Be involved with her social worker, foster parent, and relative caregiver, and take the time to understand. Black Girls in foster care often feel invisible, overlooked, and misunderstood. They get labeled by their behavior and then feel defeated. The perceived "aggressive/angry" girls are the ones who get the most response; however, who is really getting to the bottom of the anger and aggression? Is her perceived "loudness" a cry for help? Is her perceived "aggression" her way of having a voice? What is her behavior really trying to tell you? Is this her defense mechanism to keep people from getting close to her? The biggest keys are to show up, learn her story, listen, and continue to show up.

Is she showing up to your class with her hair not done? Is she in a family that does not know how to take care of her hair care needs? This may seem odd, to add hair-care into a discussion on education. However Black hair care is such a big part of a Black Girl's identity and culture. This is a big deal, and maybe you taking notice will make all of the difference. Sometimes it's the little things that make the biggest difference. Advocate for these girls and help them feel visible and known.

The preceding vignette, "Black Girls Trapped in our Foster Care System," asks involved parties to consider whether Black Girls have been placed with a Black family, a family that can support them racially and culturally. This question connects to a preference issued by the National Association of Black Social Workers (NABSW), which in 1972 demanded that Black children be placed with Black families. The NABSW at that time was working from an understanding that many white people, including educators and potential

(Continued)

(Continued)

adoptive families, struggled to grasp: that white people rarely understand the intentional racial socialization that Black families engage in for the protection of their children. The NABSW wrote, "We affirm the inviolable position of Black children in Black families where they belong physically, psychologically, and culturally in order that they receive the total sense of themselves and develop a sound projection of their future" (1972, para. 1). This statement from the NABSW does not dictate adoption policy today, but the sentiment they asserted almost 50 years ago is increasingly understood in adoption circles.

In the same way that adoption professionals need to ask whether a family is able to support a Black child's racial identity, so do educators and administrators need to ask whether white educators will be able to support Black Girls psychologically and emotionally in a way that will help them achieve excellence. The upcoming vignette by April Dinwoodie, entitled, "My Transracial Adoption Experience: Being Seen and Not Seen at All," is instructive not only to white adoptive parents but to white teachers, who may believe that color-blindness will be sufficient for serving Black Girls equitably. As Dinwoodie points out, the fact that her family believed they did not see color could not protect her from the fact that other people did. Nor did it help them meet her needs as a biracial child, which were specific and different from the needs of her white siblings. Dinwoodie's vignette precedes a vignette by Dr. Erin K. Phelps and Robin Phelps-Ward, biological sisters, on the importance of Black Girls understanding their own bodies and taking ownership over their own pleasure.

Vignette: My Transracial Adoption Experience: Being Seen and Not Seen at All

April Dinwoodie

When the adoption agency reached out to let my then prospective white adoptive parents know their desire to adopt a baby girl could soon be a reality, they were filled with joy. When the same adoption agency casually mentioned that it was "possible" I was biracial, they leaned into their well-intended albeit naïve "color-blind" philosophy and did not give differences of race between us much thought. Their only preference had been tied to gender and a wish to add a baby girl to round out their family, creating an even sibling group of two girls and two boys. My parents let the professionals transacting my adoption know they were open to a medically fragile child, as well as a child of a race different from theirs; they told the professionals what they believed in their hearts—that they could love any child independent of any differences the child might possess.

After about eight months of temporary foster care, I was placed in my foster-to-adopt family. As the transactional elements of the adoption process were attended to by professionals and my parents, there was one big thing that received little to no attention—the fact that I was biracial/Black and my prospective adoptive family was not. There was no practical conversation about what my white adoptive parents might need to do to adjust their actions and expand their lives—and in turn the lives of my brothers, sister, and extended family—in service of protecting me physically, psychologically, and emotionally. This needed recognition, education, and subsequent transformation to make room for me to be fully seen simply did not happen. Instead, fueled by love, the hopeful utopian idea that differences of race would not impact any of us was their North Star.

The conventional wisdom of my parents was to think there was no need to address differences of race or the possible challenges that could arise when white families choose to adopt a BIPOC (Black Indigenous Person of Color) child, specifically a Black or Brown child. In the early 1970s, my professional parents, blinded by optimism and willful ignorance, convinced themselves it would be easier, simpler, and better not to address the differences. They chose to focus on love, thinking that would be surely enough. Truth is, neither the professionals nor my parents ever had to navigate differences of race, and certainly not at this level. Not many white folks were practiced at having race-based conversations; therefore, many white folks felt it was easier to not have them. While there was no shortage of love bestowed upon me, there was very much a shortage of being seen for who I was: a Black/biracial child who fundamentally needed different things than my white siblings. These survival skills are essential for children to develop a healthy racial identity and be equipped to navigate predominantly white spaces such as my small New England town as well as a bigger world, both of which were organized by institutional racism.

The only advice the professionals gave to my parents about navigating our transracial adoption experience was to begin using the word *adoption* in their everyday language with me. No other guidance or coaching was offered, not about what it meant to be separated from family of origin and not about what it meant to shift in their lives in order to accommodate me. They were left to their own devices to untangle everything from my hair to how to explore history. The untangling of my hair was at best frustrating and at worst both physically and emotionally painful; with the spirit of not seeing color, there was no exploration of Black history and no weaving of Black culture into our lives. There was also no understanding of how being adopted and of a different race than the majority of those around me would play out in real time.

After I entered the family, my enthusiastic parents quickly learned that while they did not "see color," members of their extended family did. These relatives were not interested in "seeing that" (meaning me, the Black/biracial baby my parents hoped to adopt), and they believed my parents should be careful, because I might kill them in their sleep. Those relatives were quickly exited from our lives, and yet no further action was taken in terms of preparing us for how we as a family and me as a person of color would be seen and treated in the world.

(Continued)

(Continued)

The palpable tension between being seen and not seen at all as a Black/biracial girl in my white family and majority white community began when I started school. As a child, I thought every family had a brown girl like me in it, and I was disappointed almost every day when only one or two of the same brown girls I already knew would show up, and that would be it. I wondered why there were not more brown kids like me in families. Didn't everyone have one? And why wouldn't everyone want one? While my parents did not reset their white personal operating systems to make room for cultural expansion on my behalf, they instilled in me a level of grounding and deep love, and with that a certain level of self-confidence. I absolutely loved my skin color, oftentimes wishing I was darker than I was, and at the same time wanting desperately to see myself mirrored in others around me. Not just once or twice, but many times over. My eyes ached for it. Because there was little to no conversation about differences of race and adoption, I learned early on that there wasn't space for my thoughts, questions, and confusion.

Once it set in that my family structure was unique and that the small handful of Black, Brown and biracial kids including me was it, my personal operating system of vigilance began to further solidify. The combination of having been separated from my mother and family of origin soon after being born with being a Black/biracial girl adopted into a white family and community resulted in my belief that my hard wiring was fundamentally set to notice the nuances of how people treated and responded to me. Early on I was not able to verbalize this noticing and the internalized survival mechanisms that had formed and would continue to form over time.

The two big realities of adoption and differences of race were such a big part of my identity, yet many failed to recognize how they both impacted me and my experiences. Growing up adopted, and being seen as "lucky" to have been so, meant there was no room for the complex feelings of loss related to my family of origin as well as feeling less-than along with feelings of abandonment related to not being kept by the family I was born into. When I was a child, some days were harder to navigate with these realities as a foundation. Some of the most challenging times I can remember took place in school settings, when the family tree exercise or the Punnett Square genetics lesson would come up, and my mind would be foggy with confusion, my body riddled with anxiety, and my heart aching for understanding.

Generally, the transactional elements of the academics were not the issue. It was about feeling like I belonged and balancing a very secret struggle to process and understand my adoption experience. I would sit with internalized questions such as these:

Why are there so few people who look like me at school?

Why am I one of the few kids who is adopted?

Why does my family have to be different from other families?

Are my other parents ever going to try to come back and get me?

I hope they do not make us do the family tree project again this year . . . ugh!

Just like my parents, my often well-meaning teachers would not give my experiences as an adopted kid a second thought and work to create an alternative lesson, or at least acknowledge what the majority of my classmates could do with ease might be fundamentally and emotionally harder for me. I never let on to them what was happening inside; feeling it was too risky, I kept my head down while doing the work as best I could. I think back now and recognize my behaviors and quick-to-cry nature, at times outside of these moments, were where my emotions would finally be given life. Of course, in those moments, it was confusing to those around me, and I was often labeled "dramatic" or a "crybaby."

The other reality that intersected with adoption was being a biracial/Black Girl in a white family, in a small, mostly white New England community. There were several ways being seen and not seen played out around me as a light-skinned girl. The first was not being seen as a person of color and often met with "You're not really Black, April," and more of the "we don't see color" mentality. During the worst of times, I would hear these kinds of statements right before or right after someone dropped a racist joke or slur. During the best of times, people were trying to make me like them. So much of this did not pass the smell test for me. I always knew I was Black, and these actions to erase my color—whether they were well-meaning and convenient or ugly and racist—made for a very complicated existence. Somehow, even with all of this, deep down I loved being Black; as a matter of fact, I wanted to be darker to quell any speck of opportunity for folks to question my Blackness.

Balancing being seen and not being seen at all was the sum of my experience as a Black/biracial girl in a white community, and I had the notion that this somehow made me a novelty. This reality was most pronounced in school, from invasion of my personal space with constant hair touching, to receiving unwanted attention good and bad. I was often balancing liking the attention, as I thought it was an indication that I was liked, that I belonged and people wanted me around. All of this was taking place while I was also trying to mind my actions and movements with precision, as it was already very clear that I would be singled out more often and treated differently than my white peers when rules were broken or infractions made. Then there were the confusing and often triggering lesson plans about history. When they came into rotation, so did the questions in my mind. What makes me brown? Who are my ancestors? Is Black history my history, and do I have a right to know and celebrate it?

The danger in not having my adoption and my family structure along with the differences of race recognized in educational settings meant that school was a hotbed of confusion and emotion for me that often went unrecognized by grown-ups, leaving

(Continued)

(Continued)

me to navigate these complex realities on my own. There were very few soft places for my full identity to land and blossom. I often felt unsafe and as though I could not vocalize what was making me feel that way for fear of not being heard and protected. At times, I enjoyed having the spotlight on me, and I realize now that my personality commanded attention regardless of the color of my skin. Yet I know being Black/ biracial contributed to my being noticed more as well as being held accountable more. It was a daily and delicate balance to strike as I received my education.

Taking the lead in unpacking differences of family structure and race while building whole and healthy identities in children is the foundation of the intricate work that adults must lead. Those charged with the education of children and young people need to commit to the physical, emotional, and psychological protection of children just as they commit to academic rigor, especially for Black and Brown girls. Before educators can act in better service of Black and Brown girls and their families, they must as individuals do the intentional and transformational work of building their own healthy identity related to race and family experience. This requires a mix of exploring our experiences and actions, processing related feelings and emotions, and self-reflection.

Vignette: Know Your Body, Sis

Erin K. Phelps, Robin Phelps Ward

Before we get started we just want to proclaim, we are Black Girls, in Black Girl bodies living Black Girl lives. The thoughts we share are informed by the academy and the years of formalized education at predominantly white institutions (PWIs). But they're also informed by our experiences as low- to middle-class kids living in a white suburb in the 2000s. We are not sexologists or people who research the sexual experience; however, we are sexual beings with a scholarly knowledge of gender and sexuality, and, of course, we are Black Girls talking about Black Girl things. In our time from primary school to now as a sociology doctoral candidate and an assistant professor of higher education and student affairs (respectively), we have some theoretically based insights into why some of us have grown into the sexual beings we are now and how we can help young Black Girls in our classes.

In this essay, we, two Black sisters, will outline how conversations related to sex and sexuality can be shaped to empower young girls, and how their educators can be positively involved in their coming of age sexual experiences.

I (Erin) want to talk about how I learned about sex, sexuality, and the politics of each, and how I am continuing to learn about my body every day. Because so many young girls (of all races) are faced with the choice to give in to whatever they are feeling physically, or to be the chaste beings their religion or society has chosen for them, balancing the politics of those options is an all but impossible task. In a society where hedonism is both praised and scrutinized, many do not know how to have a relationship with their bodies and their sexuality. As a sociologist, I have learned the messages we get as young girls tell us a story of how we should grow into our Black womanhood. The journey through the period from Black Girlhood to Black womanhood is a muddy path wrought with controlling images, stereotypes, character archetypes, misinformation, and assumptions steeped in the dominant Western cultural narrative. This "dominant culture" coupled with the "dominant" or "master" narrative permeates all of our lives, and it is highly detrimental to Black people's lives. For Black Girls, this narrative disallows them to express their full, shifting, and fluid selves and complicates the process of developing identities outside of the hegemonic narratives that exist societally about them.

In my (Erin's) eighth-grade suburban classroom, my teacher shared an impromptu story about a friend who got pregnant when she lost her virginity. All girls in the class at the time were about 14 years old and already had periods and first kisses, but we were extremely concerned. I am not sure if providing worst-case scenario anecdotes was the best tactic. It perpetuated the narrative that if we wanted to engage in intercourse (specifically) we should be ready to care for a child. I was enrolled in Catholic school at the time, so my teacher's approach was to be expected, but still extremely effective when it came to the promotion of abstinence or sexual risk avoidance.

Only after being prompted by a mentor's question did I begin to think about how my eighth-grade teacher's message was coded through the lens of race. The impact of telling a handful of white girls and one Black Girl not to have sex because of the reproductive consequences was greater than I could've imagined at the time. Could I go as far as to say what she said was deeply anti-Black? How helpful is it to say the same thing to all of us, regardless of our identities? Over a decade later, I am still reflecting on how that story influenced many of my subsequent decisions.

My life as a student has been centered on a one-size-fits-all education, as if it were in direct opposition to "student-centered" learning. I found myself struggling more with how to present my thoughts as a Black Girl (even in math) than with the actual content itself; I spent more time coding and decoding language. (I also struggled in AP U.S. history and other social science courses. I could not identify with Manifest Destiny or care about the rise of baseball in the American identity. Both the content and the language were abstract ideas that I had to internalize to be able to "effectively" externalize my thoughts.) The dominant narrative is like a

(Continued)

(Continued)

factory that produces social scripts. The factory can only produce certain colors and sizes of shirts, which perpetuate an idea of what people should wear/be. For Black Girls, all the factories in town make variations of the same shirt; that shirt is usually poorly made, is not fitted, and does nothing for our skin tone. (Just kidding, brown skin looks good in all colors and hues!)

The dearth of Black women educators and educators who are committed to antiracist teaching places Black Girls in a position to be taught the aforementioned through a one-size-fits-all perspective. When the experiences of white kids, namely white boys, are centered, so many students lose. No wonder so many Black Girls fall victim to sexual violence at the hands of men and boys; their education is centered on white boys!

One way we know this one-size education is detrimental to *all* kids is by looking at the failure of noncomprehensive sexual education in K–12 education. In 1988 Michelle Fine argued that sex education in high schools is characterized by "the promotion of a discourse of female sexual victimization; and the explicit privileging of married heterosexuality over other practices of sexuality" (p. 30). One could argue, more than 30 years later, the same is true.

The miseducation of Black Girls via abstinence-only education, or otherwise, places Black Girls in a spot that is prime for victimization. For girls of color, sexual abuse is a starting point through the prison pipeline due to the criminalization of their victimization. According to a 2015 report by the Human Rights Project for Girls, Georgetown Law Center on Poverty and Inequality, and the Ms. Foundation for Women, African American girls constitute 14 percent of the general population nationally but 33.2 percent of girls detained and committed (Saar et al., 2015):

> African-American girls constitute 14 percent of the general population nationally but 33.2 percent of girls detained and committed. Native American girls are also disproportionately involved in the juvenile justice system: they are 1 percent of the general youth population but 3.5 percent of detained and committed girls. (p. 7)

Masculine individuals are socialized to believe it is okay to engage in nonconsensual practices, because the narrative surrounding denying pleasure is not as heavily surveilled and subject to social sanction. What is the masculine equivalent to a Jezebel/being "fast"/being "hot in the pants"? There is not a male equivalent that has a similar sociohistorical connotation. Black Girls are adultified and chastised *to be perceived as* acknowledging their bodies and themselves as sexual beings.

We (Erin and Robin) share the sentiments of Dr. Aria S. Halliday (2017), who with their hip-hop feminism work states, "The need for Black Girlhood studies, for me, is rooted in the desire to articulate sexual agency and empowerment for Black Girls alongside horrifying incidents of sexual abuse and violence, while refusing respectability and compulsory heterosexuality" (p. 66). We feel our job as educators is to teach Black Girls (and those we see as younger versions of ourselves) where they have power and how to use it in pursuit of their own safety and pleasure.

adrienne maree brown's *Pleasure Activism: The Politics of Feeling Good* (2019) tells us to "recognize that pleasure is a measure of freedom; notice what makes you feel good and what you are curious about; [and to] learn ways to increase the amount of feeling good time in your life, to have abundant pleasure." (p. i). Fine (1988) also explained how sex education in high school "suppresses discourse of female sexual desire" (p. 30). As educators of Black Girls, we can counteract the narrative that Black women need others to fulfill their desires; they are enough. That is not to say yearning and searching for another person to fulfill their desires is wrong or bad. Patricia Hill Collins (2004) and Brittney Cooper (2018) discussed the high rates of unmarried Black women compared to women of other races and why empirically and conceptually the highest-educated people in the United States—Black women—are uncoupled. It is our hope that the narrative shifts to center Black Girls and women and how we are able to love ourselves, rather than the narrative of why others fail to love us.

FIGURE 12.1 Teaching Black Girls About Sex in the Classroom

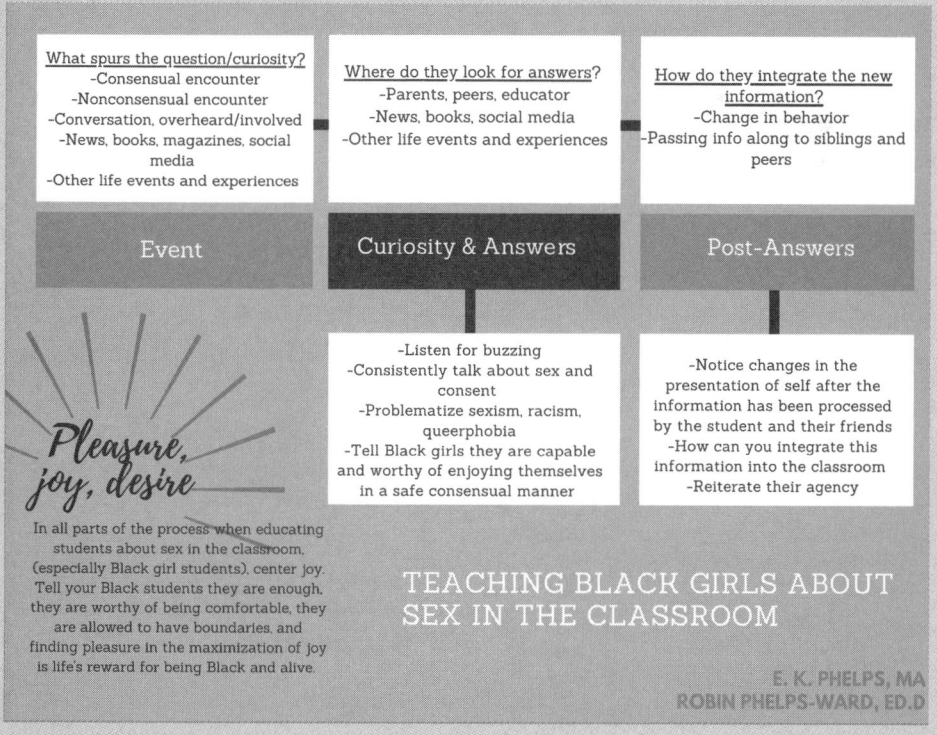

(Continued)

(Continued)

The difficulties accompanying the process of becoming a Black woman are not lost on us as educators. Black Girls, women, and femmes are placed in precarious situations based on their continuously evolving subjugation. Some of these situations include nonconsensual sexual contact. Many of these acts of violence against women and femmes have been highlighted in the media. Tarana Burke's #MeToo movement and the national outing of sexual predators such as Harvey Weinstein, Bill Cosby, R. Kelly, Brent Kavanaugh, and Donald Trump, is another bookmark in the conversation about sexual violence against Black women.

Back to intersectionality (Collins, 2002; Collins & Bilge, 2016; Combahee River Collective, 1977; Crenshaw, 1989). Black Girls get free whenever we understand the conditions we live within as well as the nature of power and control in our society. Understanding how power and control manifests for our students, based on the intersecting social identities they possess, remains a large piece of meeting our students where they are. Meeting students where they are involves getting to know them, understanding what their goals are, and communicating effectively.

Figure 12.1 demonstrates some ways educators can navigate conversations about sex, sexual violence and trauma, autonomy, and consent within the classroom. Figure 12.1 also establishes where pleasure can be discussed and emphasized for their learning about sex and sexual-emotional health. If we are meeting students where they are, the outlined process will be embedded in those interactions. Based on our love for our students, our knowledge, and our skills as pedagogues and educators, we can demonstrate how to both *empower* and educate Black Girls.

Each one, reach one, teach one. This is for the Black Girls just trying to figure this mess out.

Implications for Teachers

1. Talk about consent whenever possible. This does not have to center on sexual encounters. Consent must be obtained when there is any entrance into a person's personal space physically or otherwise.

   a. Reiterate Amanda Seales' (2019) point, "Consent does not have to continue. It is not a blood oath or an unbreakable contract" (p. 16).

   b. Before you touch any students, ask for their permission in *every* situation. Just as people ask infants for consent (rhetorically) before they change their diaper, it is important to reiterate when a person (especially an adult) is touching them, they have a say in what happens to their bodies.

   c. Teach and talk to your students about boundary work. What are your physical boundaries as their educator? What boundaries are embedded in classroom room rules?

d. As your students age, how do you encourage them to set their own boundaries?

e. How do you display respect for other people's boundaries (colleagues, counselors, principals) in front of your students?

2. Encourage, rather than discourage, acknowledging that even the youngest students are sexual beings.

a. Understand that many students have endured sexual violence and trauma even before society at large understands them to be sexual beings.

3. Talk about LGBTQIA2S+ people!

a. Include this with everything from your examples in class to having classes that constantly cover queer issues.

4. Tell your students it is okay to talk about sex and understand sex outside of the guise of procreation.

a. This will, over time, change the public opinion of people with uteruses having the opportunity to practice their own bodily autonomy.

b. This method will also destigmatize people who can't have children, don't want them, and/or want them at certain times in their lives.

c. Hopefully the conversations about sex will aide in the students' discernment of dangerous (sexual) situations.

5. Be careful of speaking in absolutes. There are always exceptions, and we as educators don't know how all people live their lives.

6. Normalize self-touch, self-soothing, and self-care in class.

a. Although autoeroticism and masturbation are tricky topics to handle as educators, we can still support our students' physical exploration and the pleasure that comes from physical exploration. Perhaps a way to destress for the class could look like each of them rubbing their own faces and necks. This can demystify the anxiety around laying your hands on yourself in non-sensual ways and make students more comfortable with giving themselves permission to touch their own bodies for their own physical body's benefit.

7. Build and define your own "decadence practice" or "[give] [yourself] that which is sensual and rich and overflowing. (Taylor, 2020).

a. Sonya Renee Taylor teaches us to indulge in our joy and do the things that "fuel life."

b. How can you as an educator demonstrate doing the things you love just because you love them? What is your students' "reward for being Black and alive"?

(Continued)

(Continued)

8. Celebrate all wins!

    a. "Create more room for joy, wholeness, and aliveness (and less room for oppression, repression, self-denial and unnecessary suffering) in your life" (brown, 2019, p. i).

9. Build a classroom that encourages pleasure as an outcome.

    a. The recently (2017) revised work of Banner and Cannon outlined how to insert pleasure in the classroom. Remember: Pleasure means creating an atmosphere in which students enjoy learning; Pleasure requires letting others' wit shine; Pleasure leads teachers to reveal their own joys and pleasures in learning and teaching; Pleasure means acknowledging the difficulties as well as the joys of learning. Normalize self-reflection.

This second grouping of chapters in this section illuminates the power of Black Girls' agency and voices. The next chapter, "Little Black Girls With Curves" by Dr. Keisha Bentley Edwards, explores the physiological realities of Black Girls. Bentley-Edwards ties together the chapters and vignettes in this section, demonstrating how the misinterpretation of Black Girl physical development leads to many other issues discussed in this section. Her chapter ends with powerful activities for educators to shift their perceptions of Black Girls and use their power to support them, rather than collude in systems that increase their vulnerability. This powerful collection of pieces ends with a vignette from Ellise Antoinette Smith, called "Fat, Black, and Female: The Vignette of a 'Normal' School Girl." Smith, a doctoral candidate and creator/founder of Fatness Fiction, frames her vignette around school stories: first day of school and picture day, celebratory moments that became moments of trauma when she received explicit messages that her body was wrong. Smith implores educators to do better and to stop finding students' bodies "wrong."

CHAPTER 13

Little Black Girls With Curves

Keisha L. Bentley-Edwards

As I was transitioning to third grade, my mother took me to Penney's to shop for a "training bra." After several unsuccessful attempts to find one that fit, she realized my development had progressed so quickly that I had skipped over that rite of passage and fit seamlessly into a small women's bra. My mother was quite horrified. I assumed it was because she thought I was growing up "too soon." Later, she revealed that my growing up made her more weepy and nostalgic, rather than concerned. In reality, she was looking at me with fresh eyes, and understood that the world would not see her newly eight-year-old baby girl, but would instead see a young Black woman. And for that, she was horrified.

Given my experiences in school and the broader community, as well as research showing that my experiences are not unique, her worries were justified. Epstein et al. (2017) found that in comparison to white girls, Black girls were perceived by some as needing less protection, nurturing, support, and comfort. Conversely, they were perceived to be more independent and have greater knowledge of adult issues, including sex. Whereas white girls were perceived in childlike ways from 0 to 19 years old, Black girls' perceived independence and need for support was in the 5- to 9-year-old range. Perceiving Black girls as women has deep roots in American society, with implications for their interactions with teachers and fellow students and their overall life outcomes. In this chapter, I will highlight the myths versus the reality of Black puberty, and how perceiving Black girls as adults informs their learning environment and engagement with teachers.

Black Girls With Curves: Puberty Myths and Realities

"Well, you don't look like an 8 (9, 10, 11) year old," has been spoken to me by too many people to name, including teachers, principals, security guards, and grown men. There is a long-standing belief that Black girls physically mature earlier than girls of other races. Is this true? Yes, with some caveats. The first thing that must be understood about the ways in which girls mature is the distinction between primary and secondary sex characteristics.

You may have learned in biology or sex education that primary sex characteristics are the traits and organs that enable childbearing. For girls, this maturation would be occurring in the uterus, ovaries, and vagina. Most important, this maturation includes menarche, or the activation of the menstrual cycle. On average, African American girls do have an earlier onset of menarche than girls of other races. To be fair, these differences are statistically significant and earth shattering for scientists in the health and medicine fields, but would not ring alarms in our everyday life. The average onset of menstrual cycles has been reported as 11 years and 6 months for Black girls and 12 years and 1 month for White girls (Herman-Giddens, 2001, 2013). Americans in general have been seeing an earlier onset of menarche over the last 20 years, but the Black/White difference in onset has remained fairly constant at roughly six months, not even an entire academic year (Herman-Giddens, 2013; Herman-Giddens et al., 1997). But how can this be? This is not what you may be seeing in your classroom. Which gets us to the real issue—secondary sex characteristics.

Secondary sex characteristics are those we can see and associate with (emerging) womanhood, the development of breasts, the widening of hips, increased height, and voice changes (yes, that happens to girls too), among other things. These changes are actually precursors to primary sexual characteristics, which may be the reason that the two maturation processes are often conflated. Similar to the way they experience the development of primary sex characteristics, Black girls experience the development of secondary sex characteristics earlier than their White counterparts in ways that are huge in the scientific community, but may not have as much meaning to people in their everyday life (Herman-Giddens, 2013). Researchers typically investigate secondary sex characteristics for girls based upon the development of breasts, or thelarche. Biro et al. (2013) found that on average, thelarche occurred at ages eight years and nine months for Black girls, and nine years and seven months for white girls, about a ten-month difference. In terms of the academic environment, we are talking about the difference between developing breasts in the third grade versus the fourth grade. Unless you are a third-grade teacher, which you may be, the differences in secondary sex characteristics between black and white girls should not be so evident. However, Black girls and their bodies are perceived differently.

Regulating Black Girls With Curves

In the sixth grade, my school district started to institute strict dress codes in an attempt to deter the gang-related violence that was a real issue in my Southern California community. These dress codes included a long laundry list of restrictions targeting girls' attire that had nothing to do with violence prevention. When late summer heatwaves occurred, it was a given that the principal's office would be filled with Black and Latinx girls, myself included. In our school that lacked air conditioning, we saw ourselves as dressing appropriately for the weather, and most important, we were not skipping school given the weather conditions. Unfortunately, teachers, assistant principals, counselors, and security guards—basically all of the adults on campus—would be on alert to determine whether our shorts were "three fingers above the knee" and that our belly buttons did not peak out of our shirts. If their subjective assessment of how our clothes fit our 11-year-old bodies was unacceptable, we were sent directly to the office—loudly and with great fanfare. We were humiliated and lost valuable instructional time, because restricting our bodies so as not to distract boys or make adults uncomfortable took priority over our learning. Looking back, the way we were treated by our teachers and school staff was much more scandalous than anything we wore.

Presently, this trend of punitive responses to the fit of Black girls' clothes continues (Epstein et al., 2017; Morris, 2015; NAACP Legal Defense and Educational Fund & National Women's Law Center, 2014; Raby, 2010). Black girls are disciplined at twice the rate of White girls for dress code violations (Epstein et al., 2017), and these violations represent the second highest reason for which Black girls are disciplined overall (Blake et al., 2011). Is it that Black girls somehow dress more provocatively than students of other races? Not necessarily. Dress codes are more strictly enforced for girls than boys, and Black girls receive the strictest enforcement of all students (Barret, 2018; Epstein et al., 2017; Morris & Perry, 2017; Morris, 2015).

When Black girls are not seen as innocent or are sexualized in their appearance and intentions, their clothes are perceived as provocative. For example, the National Education Association reported that when a student asked a (male) administrator at her school why Black girls were disciplined more for dress code violations than White girls, she was told it was "because white girls don't have as much to show" (Barret, 2018, p. 6). This rationale negates what we know about physical development and falls in line with perceptions of the sexual promiscuity and the adultification of Black girls. Perceiving Black girls as women has implications for how teachers engage with them and how they respond in return (Adams-Bass & Bentley-Edwards, 2020; Bentley-Edwards & Adams-Bass, 2013; Epstein et al., 2017).

Misunderstood Self-Advocacy

One semester, I asked my Black Women's psychology class to describe Black teenage girls using one word. I received a wide range of mostly affirming responses:

strong, smart, bad-ass, magnificent. Then a student who did not identify as Black said with great confidence, "Loud." After getting some curious looks, she said, "You can hear Black girls before you see them, and they were always in trouble at school for being too loud." I was intrigued by this response. So, I asked her, "What were they saying?" She returned a blank stare and said she didn't know. She remembered that Black girls at her high school were loud, she remembered that they got in trouble for it, but she had no recollection of what they were saying . . . which gets at the root of my next point. *Sometimes Black girls are loud because they will otherwise go unheard, and even then, they may not be listened to.*

Black families teach their children to instill cultural pride, while also teaching them how to identify racism. This child-rearing approach is used to manage racial stress while equipping Black Girls with the skills needed to stand up for themselves and not let anyone take advantage of them (Adams-Bass & Bentley-Edwards, 2020; Bentley et al., 2009; Bentley-Edwards & Adams-Bass, 2013). However, the assertiveness and self-advocacy that is applauded at home is often interpreted as being loud and disrespectful at school. *The top reason Black girls are disciplined in school is for exhibiting what is perceived by some educators to be "defiant behavior" or "talking back to authority"* (Blake et al., 2011). These subjective assessments of the behaviors and bodies of Black girls are the difference between celebrating "girl power" and providing access to a quality, supportive education.

Morris (2007) conducted a two-year qualitative study that included interviews, observations, surveys, and an analysis of school records in a predominantly Black middle school. His study revealed that the assertiveness of Black girls was beneficial if they also demonstrated high academic aptitude. Even still, their assertiveness also led them to being perceived as disruptive and confrontational and as challenging authority. The researcher observed that class outbursts, even when they were on task, were interpreted as more disruptive for Black girls than for girls of other races or boys overall. In his interviews, the White teachers described Black girls as socially but not academically mature (Morris, 2007). Many of the teachers perceived Black girls as preadults. Black girls were also perceived as controlling and attempting to dominate the class and their classmates (Morris, 2007).

Conclusion and Suggestions

Being perceived as a child is more than being believed to be innocent, it is about receiving the benefit of the doubt, and not being seen as a finished product before entering middle school. The following are three points to consider in your interactions with Black girls.

1. **Don't interpret assertiveness as defiance.** Challenging authority is considered a part of typical adolescent development. However, as noted throughout this chapter, Black girls are not seen as children, or even as teenagers. This may

be why White students (who are seen as children) are less likely to be punished for defiant behavior than Black students—even though defiance occurs at similar rates across race. Because class disruption or "willful defiance" is the top reason that Black girls, and Black children overall, are suspended from school, California saw a steep decline in out-of-class disciplinary actions for Black children once willful defiance suspensions were prohibited by most districts in the state (Losen & Whitaker, 2017).

2. **Pace yourself; really listen.** Are you *listening* to what Black girls are saying, or are you responding to their volume? Can you picture a time when a Black girl confronted you in class? If you met this girl on the street, you might have assumed she was a woman, but she's not; she's your student. Standing face to face with her may feel threatening to you, so your first reaction may have been to eliminate the threat and the stress—sending the girl to the assistant principal's office. But can you recall what the confrontation was about, and what she said?

3. **When in conflict with black girls, be the adult and advocate**. Adolescents self-advocate in childish ways because they are children, and they often do not have the skills to articulate their stance as effectively as adults. Black girls self-advocate when they feel that they cannot rely on the adults around them to do so on their behalf. So, when will you become the advocate who has their best interests in mind? I argue that when Black girls are talking back to teachers or other authority figures, it is up to the adults to recognize they are talking to a child and to acknowledge the power dynamics at play.

The world can be a harsh place for Black girls and women. For teachers, nurturing Black girlhood begins with recognizing them as little girls in the first place.

Vignette: Fat, Black, and Female: The Vignette of a "Normal" School Girl—*Ellise Antoinette Smith*

By the time I reached my 25th first day of school, I thought the anxiety around how my body looks would be a thing of the past. As a 30-year-old doctoral student, I find myself still feeling anxious that my body may draw unwanted attention, unlike the bodies of thinner classmates. I find myself falling into the routine of quickly scanning the classroom to locate a body that resembles mine—a fat, Black female taking up space that I rightfully deserve. However, it has been hard to convince the world that I deserve to exist in this body when the media and society portray my identities as wrong. The aforementioned identities, especially around size, have always drawn negative responses from celebrities praising weight loss and photo-editing programs making all bodies appear perfect, as well as comments from classmates who despise fat bodies.

(Continued)

(Continued)

I first learned my body was incorrect in the same classrooms that I hoped would provide me another identity: intelligence. Watching television growing up, I always saw fat people portrayed as stupid. I decided to change that narrative by obtaining as much education as possible with a twofold mission: to hide behind my education to reduce the ridicule about my size, and to end generational poverty by being the first in my family to move beyond a high school education. However, I learned that K–12 schooling did not prepare students to accept differences.

I vividly remember my seventh-grade picture day and the fear I had of showing up at school. My grandmother picked out the outfit she felt showed off her precious grandchild: a skirt, black tights, and a ruffled shirt. As we walked in a single line to the common area for photos, I remember my teacher asking me to step to the side as she needed to speak with me. All the other students watched, wanting to know what I did wrong. She began pulling at my skirt, telling me that I should have worn pants instead of the skirt, because I was too big of a girl for the outfit my elderly grandmother had selected. At that moment I felt tears rush to my eyes but I refused to cry. I chose not to cry because I did not see a problem with my body, but she reminded me that I was fat. Another one of my classmates who was a heavier kid dropped her head and began pulling on her clothes, stretching them to make herself also disappear.

There were a few students ahead of me, and I decided to get out of line and refuse to take pictures. I refused to be captured in a picture just moments after I was reminded that I did not look perfect in the eyes of my teacher. Once I got home I told my grandmother, and I could tell she was not equipped to explain what I had experienced. Instead, she told me we would find a way to afford bigger clothes. As I reflect, I did not need bigger clothing, I needed my teacher to understand that students come in all sizes. I was robbed of the opportunity to exist as I was, and I wish I had had the language to stand up and flourish in that moment.

Many young students notice differences immediately: race, height, socioeconomic status, and size. Although this is not an exhaustive list of identities, in my experience size was one of those things students would band together and tease someone about. As a young person you could be everything but fat. It gave everyone, including teachers, a pass to talk about, and it was unacceptable. The narrative was always centered on the idea that a fat kid should and could lose weight. There were unsolicited suggestions from teachers to enroll in additional physical education courses and activities, continuous commentary on clothing, and reminders that our clothing should not be "too tight."

However, I began to notice a difference between my experience with teachers and students and that of other girls. As we continued to grow and develop, heavier/curvier/fatter Black girls were told their outfits were inappropriate compared to the thinner white girls. Often, bigger Black girls were sent to the office for disciplinary actions or their parents were required to bring a change of clothes. Following my picture day experience, my grandmother took me to buy clothes. We ended up in the boys section, where I felt defeated. I had to wear clothes that clearly were not made for the gender I identified with. I feared classmates would notice the less feminine clothing, and they did. That is when my sexual orientation was questioned, and perceptions of it were limited to my external appearance.

Even as a doctoral student, I still scan the room to find someone that resembles me. I took a moment to reflect on this lingering fear of standing out due to my size and realized the trauma I was internalizing came from the same educational spaces I was hiding behind. At this point, I was still hearing that fat people were "stupid," "unattractive," "self-loathing," and a plethora of different monikers associated with size.

I encourage teachers to understand the diversity in bodies, sizes, and shapes and the value of fat acceptance in the classroom, especially for Black girls. Our bodies are not an accident and should not be surveilled in comparison to those of our white counterparts. Comments such as the one I heard on picture day are not exclusive to my experience. I have talked to numerous fat Black women who recall first learning to feel ashamed of their bodies because classmates were not corrected and teachers perpetuated similar disgust. I challenge those reading to understand that a fat body is not an error or incorrect body. Society must understand that a child of a particular size should not be shamed if their existence does not align with thinness.

I leave readers with this: In order to connect with the students you teach, you must accept their diversity in all forms. Do not project your ideas on your students, who have an entire world yet to experience. As an adult, you must teach growing youth about diversity, and that includes diversity of size. Create a world for them to flourish in, and remember they are the seeds to a different world if you help water those seeds with acceptance.

PART V
"YOUR SILENCE IS A KNEE ON MY NECK."
—Natasha Cloud

The first chapter in this section is by law professor, historian, and former police officer, Dr. Jacqueline Battalora. Battalora helps readers develop whiteness competency by learning the history of how whiteness was inscribed in and protected by law. Her chapter, which establishes the historical and systemic backdrop to how whiteness functions today, is followed by a vignette from Nahliah Webber, entitled "Keisha Resists Karen." In masterful prose, Webber challenges white educators—teachers, policymakers, administrators, curriculum writers, teacher educators—to consider whether Black girls need closer proximity to whiteness to be academically successful. She poses the question, Is proximity to whiteness part of the problem? Webber's vignette is followed by a chapter by Dr. Ali Michael entitled "Can I Do This if I'm White?" For educators who read Webber's vignette and begin to wonder if they can even teach Black girls, we encourage you to read Michael's piece on the concrete steps you can take to build up the racial humility required to create a classroom where Black girls thrive.

The next chapter was written by dance teacher Jesse Phillips-Fein, who demonstrates how her conscious awareness of individual oppressive practices of whiteness helps her be a more effective and aware teacher. Following the chapter by Phillips-Fein is a vignette by Debby Irving, who spells out the impact of how her whiteness in her teaching impacted Black girls in her classroom, and how she could have done things differently if she knew then what she knows today. This is paired with another vignette by white teacher Kristen Steele, who demonstrates cultural humility in response to feedback from a student. Her accounting of this interaction early in her teaching career help readers imagine how they might navigate those inevitable painful moments when they do not serve their Black girl students in the ways that Black girls deserve.

CHAPTER 14

Whiteness Competency

How Not to Be BBQ Becky

Jacqueline Battalora

On April 29, 2018, the Smith family went to Oakland, California's Lake Merritt to have a family BBQ. As they entered the park, a white woman hurled racial epithets at the Smith family, who were Black, while she held her phone up to her ear. She was heard saying, "Oh no, not more n-words." She called the police to report the family for using a charcoal grill, which is a common practice at Lake Merritt. While on her cell phone, she said to them, "Y'all going to jail." In response to the incident, one of Oakland's city council members said, "I think it is really incumbent on all of us, that when we call the police, it is for emergency purposes" (Fearnow, 2018), suggesting that this call had not been an emergency. The video of the incident circulated around social media, where people raised the question of what would happen in a situation like this if the police arrived agitated, or believed the family to be aggressive? When white women call the police on unarmed Black people doing ordinary things, it is the white callers who remain anonymous and safe, while innocent Black lives are endangered. In this case, though we don't know the woman's name, she will go down in history as "BBQ Becky."

White women across the United States have been a source of harassment toward persons of African descent and a source of unwarranted consumption of law enforcement time and energy, and they have served as rich cultural sources for memes. Incidents involving white women have included a Starbucks manager calling the police on two Black men waiting to meet a colleague, a white woman calling the police on Black people barbequing in a public park, a white female graduate student at Yale calling the police on a Black female graduate student who fell asleep studying, a white woman calling the police on African Americans leaving their Airbnb, and a white woman threatening an African American bird watcher in Central Park saying, "I'm going to call the cops. I'm going to tell them there's an African American man threatening my life," among so many others (Marcius & Annese, 2020). Incidents like these have been met with memes the likes of BBQ Becky, Permit Patty, Corner Store Caroline, License Plate Linda, and Golf Cart Gail.

Each of the incidents is underscored by expectations on the part of white women regarding who belongs in their space and who ought to be responsive to their demands, and that their perspective will be backed by police. What does this disturbing pattern reveal about white women? How might these incidents inform interactions with Black girls? One approach to this phenomenon is to explore U.S. law and policy in relation to white expectations. The presumption of white superiority was built into the institutions of the United States of America from its founding. Take, for example, the Naturalization Act of 1790, passed by the first U.S. Congress. This law required a person be white in order to become a naturalized citizen of the United States. The requirement was in place until 1952, affording more than 150 years of advantage for those considered white. The preference for white people and the structured advantages they received were foundational to immigration and naturalization law and functioned to create a *white equals American* equation. The preference afforded white people was not limited to naturalization or immigration but shaped countless laws, policies, court rulings, practices, and interactions, and was one of the influences shaping a culture of Whiteness.

What is Whiteness?

I use the term *whiteness* to refer to dynamic processes and practices intrinsically linked to a system that positions white people above all others. This understanding is derived from the work of sociologist Ruth Frankenberg (1993), who defines Whiteness as

> a location of structural advantage, of race privilege. Second, it is a "standpoint," a place from which White people look at ourselves, at others, and at society. Third, "Whiteness" refers to a set of cultural practices that are usually unmarked and unnamed. (p. 1)

The workings of Whiteness become clearer through a consideration of history that captures the impact of specific laws, policies, and practices on those seen as white as well as upon those excluded from it. There is no easy way to capture the full breadth of U.S. laws, policies, and practices that have elevated white people over all others, but the Whiteness Chart that follows is a helpful sample. The first column of the chart refers to concrete historical examples of structural advantage for white people across most every decade of U.S. history. Examples of structural advantage include federal and state legislation, the establishment of national institutions, widespread ideology, court rulings, military action, federal policy, and law enforcement practices. The second column identifies how the specific structural advantage from the first column worked to shape how white people view themselves, view others, or view the world. The final column considers how the structured advantage overlapped and intertwined with the range of white viewpoints and, in turn, constituted cultural values presented as objective—or simply American—norms.

The structural advantage for white people, the variety of white viewpoints shaped, and the cultural practices produced are by no means separate and distinct, as the columns make them appear. Rather, they constitute and reaffirm each other in dynamic interaction and fuel the next generation of whiteness. The Whiteness Chart provides only a small portion of the laws, policies, and practices that represent structural advantage for white people within *each decade*. In fact, those noted in the chart can be called grossly insufficient as a reflection of U.S. history. The intent here is not to pretend that the history referenced is in any way complete or even remotely thorough. Rather, the intent is to provide some examples, spread across more than 200 years, that prove sufficient enough incentive to challenge Whiteness and to open pathways toward equity that are rooted in history.

The historical breadth and depth of whiteness has fundamentally and dramatically shaped U.S. culture and society and profoundly impacted the lives of those seen as white and those excluded from it. For various groups excluded from Whiteness, the harm inflicted as a result of law and policy has been extensive (Acuña, 2007; Alexander, 2010; Anderson, 2016; Glenn, 2002; LaDuke, 2005; Marable, 1983). Consider a few examples from the Whiteness Chart, which is presented in its entirety at the end of this chapter:

Whiteness Chart

	WHITE STRUCTURAL ADVANTAGE	WHITE STANDPOINT VT—VIEW THEMSELVES VO—VIEW OTHERS VW—VIEW THE WORLD	AMERICAN NORM
1870	Along the Marias River in Montana, U.S. troops kill almost 200 Blackfeet without provocation.	(VT) White people can commit violence against indigenous people with impunity.	Lives of indigenous people do not matter.
1956	The Federal-Aid Highway Act devotes billions to the construction of a national system of interstate highways, which disproportionately cut through established neighborhoods where Black and brown people reside.	(VW) White neighborhoods/wealth are to be protected.	White economic advantage. The property of white people is valued.

WHITE STRUCTURAL ADVANTAGE		WHITE STANDPOINT VT—VIEW THEMSELVES VO—VIEW OTHERS VW—VIEW THE WORLD	AMERICAN NORM
1994	The Violent Crime Control and Law Enforcement Act is a three-strikes law that rapidly increases penalties for the use of drugs commonly used by people of color (crack) more than it increased penalties for drugs commonly used by white people.	(VO) They get what they deserve. (VO) People of color who commit crimes should be incarcerated.	Blame and punish. Black and brown lives do not matter.

The advantage in economic opportunity for white people is just as clear (Allen, 1997; Battalora, 2013; DiAngelo, 2018; Harris, 1993; Lipsitz, 2006; Roediger, 1999; Rothstein, 2017). Again, consider a few examples from the Whiteness Chart:

Whiteness Chart

WHITE STRUCTURAL ADVANTAGE		WHITE VIEWPOINTS VT—VIEW THEMSELVES VO—VIEW OTHERS VW—VIEW THE WORLD	CULTURAL NORMS
1790	First Congress of the United States of America passes Naturalization Law of 1790; it requires a person to be white in order to be naturalized as a U.S. citizen, conferring advantage upon immigrants seen as white for more than 150 years.	(VW) United States is for white people.	White = American.
1937	U.S. Housing Act is signed into law. It provides federal subsidies for housing construction, requires that developments be white-only, makes few funds available for nonwhite housing, and gives more dollars per house built for whites than for people of color.	(VW) White is preferred. (VT) White people are worthy.	White = good credit risk. White economic advantage.
1964	Civil rights workers Chaney, Schwerner, and Goodman go missing in Mississippi. The fact that two white men are missing sparks outrage, receives national media coverage, and results in the deployment of the National Guard and FBI.	(VT) White people deserve the empathy and resources of the nation.	White lives matter.

Taken as a whole, the Whiteness Chart exposes the following prevailing national practices:

- white = American
- economic advantage for white people through exclusion, expulsion, subjugation, and exploitation of people of Indigenous, African, Latinx, Asian, and Pacific Island descent
- white perspectives and interests define law and policy
- white lives matter

Through the repeated assertion of these practices, the chart helps to highlight that Whiteness has been constructed as domination and exclusion with stubborn consistency throughout U.S. history. The Whiteness Chart reveals that white people have more than two centuries of racial belonging. It highlights that white people's interests, particularly their property and feelings of security, will be protected by law and law enforcement. Finally, the Whiteness Chart reveals a voluminous circulation of messages that white lives are the most valuable.

WHITENESS IS NOT A CHOICE

Whiteness has been imposed on us all. Advantage for white people has been baked into the structures, institutions, and practices of the nation as a matter of law, institutional perspective, and national values (Feagin 2006; Omi & Winant 1994). While the privileges of whiteness are certainly mediated by gender, economics, sexuality, ability, and religion, among others, there are still advantages conferred simply by being white. For example, access to U.S. citizenship through naturalization, which required one be white, conferred advantage to immigrants deemed white for more than 150 years. The Whiteness Chart reveals how structural advantage worked to shape white viewpoints. A useful exercise to do is to consider how each structural advantage also shaped specific expectations on the part of white people. Some expectations that are hard to miss include racial belonging, being positioned above people of color and expecting deference from them, that property held by whites will be protected even above the lives of people of color, and that the views and interests of white people will be reflected in law and enforced by police.

WHITENESS COMPETENCY

Every person in the country has been shaped by Whiteness and is impacted by the advantages it either confers or denies. The ability to identify these workings of Whiteness and their impact personally, structurally, and in dynamic interaction in the present is what I refer to as Whiteness Competency.

Whiteness Competency uses the historical context of whiteness to inform behaviors, feelings, structures, institutions, policies, practices, narratives, and communications today. It is the ability to see structural advantage imposed on white people, the range of vantage points white people hold, the choices that result, and the often unmarked cultural practices advanced by them. Whiteness Competency is a critical disruption of *Whiteness as usual*. For white people, it can prevent BBQ Becky from erupting. BBQ Becky, here, serves to represent feelings of anger, fear, or threat that can arise in the face of inconsistencies between the expectations Whiteness produces and the expression of people of color as fully human, fully free.

Recall that Whiteness produces division and domination on the part of white people in relation to those of African, Asian, Native American, Pacific Island, and Latinx descent. There is the potential of BBQ Becky in each white person precisely because, in a nation where structural advantage is commonplace, white people are inculcated with messages of their racial centrality and significance from the moment of their birth. More recently, these messages have coexisted with narratives of color-blindness and claims of being postracial. Whiteness Competency helps to keep the expectations that Whiteness produces for white people in check. It informs interactions with Black girls by challenging the expectations of deference and subjugation that Whiteness produces. Whiteness Competency is a guide through the terrain of Whiteness. It forges a pathway that rejects division and domination. It is a pathway out of Whiteness and toward greater equity.

Whiteness Chart

WHITE STRUCTURAL ADVANTAGE		WHITE STANDPOINT VT—VIEW THEMSELVES VO—VIEW OTHERS VW—VIEW THE WORLD	CULTURAL NORM
1681	First reference in Colonial North American law to a group of people called "white."*	(VT) White people are superior. (VO) Others are different and inferior.	White people are superior.
U.S. History			
1776	Declaration of Independence signed July 4.		
1787	U.S. Constitution ratified—it protects practice of enslavement of people of African descent (Fugitive Slave Clause; Three-Fifths Clause; prohibition on abolishing slavery before 1808).	(VO) Black people are less than human. (VT) White men deserve liberty and protection of their property.	Black people are not fully human. White people's property is valued above life and liberty of Black people.

(Continued)

(Continued)

WHITE STRUCTURAL ADVANTAGE		WHITE STANDPOINT VT—VIEW THEMSELVES VO—VIEW OTHERS VW—VIEW THE WORLD	CULTURAL NORM
1790	First Congress of the United States of America passes Naturalization Law of 1790; it requires a person to be white in order to be naturalized as a U.S. citizen, conferring advantage upon immigrants seen as white for more than 150 years.	(VW) United States is for white people.	White = American. Zero sum game.
1802	U.S. Military Academy is established at West Point, New York. It admits only white men.	(VT) White men are the protectors of the country.	Patriarchal power is centered among white men.
1820	Missouri Compromise admits a free state and a slave state and permits slavery south of 36°30' north, temporarily reducing national tensions.	(VW) White interests define and resolve conflict.	Dualism.
1830	Andrew Jackson signs the Indian Removal Act, displacing 125,000 Native Americans west of the Mississippi, opening this area for white settlers.	(VW) Land and resources are for white people.	Economic gain for white people via exclusion of others.
1845	Manifest Destiny popularizes a mindset of divine (Christian) sanction for U.S. expansion.	(VT) Taking of land by white people is ordained by God.	White wealth and domination must be pursued and protected.
1850	First session of the California State Assembly passes a law prohibiting Blacks, Mulattos, and American Indians from testifying against whites.	(VO) White people expect deference from Black and Indigenous people.	Law aligns with interests and perspectives of white people.
1854	California Supreme Court rules that Chinese and all other people of color are prohibited from testifying against a white person, in *People v. Hall*.	(VO) White people expect deference from Asian people.	Law benefits white people.
1857	U.S. Supreme Court rules that Mr. Scott, and thereby all African Americans, were not and could not be citizens of the United States despite being born in the nation, in *Dred Scott v. Sanford*.	(VT) White people are deserving.	The rights and privileges of the constitution are for whites only.
1870	Along the Marias River in Montana, U.S. troops kill almost 200 Blackfeet without provocation.	(VT) White people can commit violence against indigenous people with impunity.	Lives of indigenous people do not matter

WHITE STRUCTURAL ADVANTAGE		WHITE STANDPOINT VT—VIEW THEMSELVES VO—VIEW OTHERS VW—VIEW THE WORLD	CULTURAL NORM
1889	Oklahoma land rush begins for whites only.	(VW) Land and resources are for white people.	Economic gain for white people via exclusion of others.
1896	U.S. Supreme Court affirms "separate but equal" doctrine, allowing Jim Crow laws, in *Plessy v. Ferguson*.	(VT) The best is for whites. (VO) Indignities are for people of color.	Comfort is a right of white people.
1907	Indiana is the first of 31 states to pass a eugenics law, requiring sterilization of certain people. This is the first eugenics law passed in the world—more than 25 years before the rise of Hitler.	(VT) WASPs who are not poor/disabled/gay = ideal.	White = ideal race.
1913	The first Alien Land Law passes, making it illegal for those ineligible for naturalization (not white) to own agricultural land or lease it.	(VW) Land and resources are for white people. (VO) People of color are to serve as cheap labor.	People of color are a threat. Economic advantage for white people via exclusion.
1924	Congress passes the National Origins Act, which establishes a quota system limiting immigration from everywhere except northern Europe.	(VT) The United States is for white people.	Nonwhite = not American. White = America.

*See Battalora, J. (2013). *Birth of a white nation: The invention of white people and its relevance today.* Strategic Book Publishing and Rights Agency.

Whiteness Chart

WHITE STRUCTURAL ADVANTAGE		WHITE STANDPOINT VT—VIEW THEMSELVES VO—VIEW OTHERS VW—VIEW THE WORLD	CULTURAL NORM
1937	U.S. Housing Act is signed into law. It provides federal subsidies for housing construction, requires that developments be white-only, makes few funds available for nonwhite housing, and gives more dollars per house built for whites than for people of color.	(VW) White is preferred. (VT) White people are worthy.	White = good credit risk. White economic advantage.

(Continued)

(Continued)

WHITE STRUCTURAL ADVANTAGE		WHITE STANDPOINT VT—VIEW THEMSELVES VO—VIEW OTHERS VW—VIEW THE WORLD	CULTURAL NORM
1949	Federal Housing Administration Board announces FDA will continue to allow restrictive covenants (used to prohibit nonwhites, Jews, and Catholics from purchasing property).	(VT) WASPs have a right to include or exclude.	Domination by exclusion. WASP economic advantage.
1954	Phase 1 of Operation Wetback forces some 1.3 million documented and undocumented Mexican people out of the country while Congress refuses to punish employers hiring undocumented workers.	(VO) Mexican people are laborers, not citizens with rights and privileges.	Mexicans are not white. Mexicans are not American.
1956	The Federal-Aid Highway Act devotes billions to the construction of a national system of interstate highways, which disproportionately cut through established neighborhoods where Black and brown people reside.	(VW) White neighborhoods and wealth are to be protected.	White economic advantage. The property of white people is valued.
1964	Civil rights workers Chaney, Schwerner, and Goodman go missing in Mississippi. The fact that two white men are missing sparks outrage, receives national media coverage, and results in the deployment of the National Guard and FBI.	(VT) White people deserve the empathy and resources of the nation.	White lives matter.
1977	The U.S. Supreme Court approves use of a zoning ordinance that has the effect of ensuring few Black and brown people can reside in the suburb of Arlington Heights, Illinois.	(VT) White people can construct human make-up of neighborhoods.	Economic advantage for white people via exclusion.
1989	In Central Park, New York, a white female jogger is sexually assaulted and beaten into a coma, after which five Black youth are targeted, falsely accused, and imprisoned. It is one of the most publicized crimes of the 1980s.	(VO) Young Black men are seen as violent animals.	White lives matter. Black lives do not matter. Fear Black men.

WHITE STRUCTURAL ADVANTAGE		WHITE STANDPOINT VT—VIEW THEMSELVES VO—VIEW OTHERS VW—VIEW THE WORLD	CULTURAL NORM
1994	The Violent Crime Control and Law Enforcement Act is a three-strikes law that rapidly increases incarceration rates of Black and brown men, mostly for nonviolent offenses. Harsher penalties are given for the use of drugs commonly used by people of color than for the use of drugs commonly used by white people (cocaine).	(VO) People of color who commit crimes should be incarcerated. (VO) They get what they deserve.	Blame and punish. Black and brown lives do not matter.
2002-07	Affirmative action in education is restricted by the U.S. Supreme Court, requiring "strict scrutiny" and a "narrowly tailored" program, via University of Michigan *Bollinger* cases and *Parents Involved in Community Schools v. Seattle School District No. 1.*	(VT) Victims of exclusion via affirmative action.	Continued inclusion of white people is more important than inclusion of people of color who have been historically excluded.
2013	While walking home from a convenience store, high school student Treyvon Martin is fatally shot by neighborhood watch volunteer George Zimmerman, who is acquitted under Florida's "self-protection" laws.	(VO) The presence of a Black man is a threat to white space.	Feelings of safety and security for white people are more important than Black lives.

Whiteness Chart ©2020 Jacqueline Battalora

Activity 1

1. **BBQ Betty**. Quickly research online and review the factual information surrounding the incident that gave rise to the meme "BBQ Betty" or any of the other similar memes.

2. **Expectations.** (If working in a larger group, I recommend dividing the group into four smaller groups for this activity. Each group should be assigned a different set of five or six structural advantages from the Whiteness Chart.)

   Read through each assigned structural advantage from the Whiteness Chart. Reflect upon each one, including the viewpoints it shaped and the cultural practices it produced. Work your way through them one at a time, and try to identify at least two expectations on the part of white people that each structural advantage worked to promote.

Example

2013	While walking home from a convenience store, high school student Trayvon Martin is fatally shot by neighborhood watch volunteer George Zimmerman, who is acquitted under Florida's "self-protection" laws.	(VO) The presence of a Black man is a threat to white space.	Feelings of safety and security for white people are more important than Black lives.

The structural advantage (interpretation of self-protection law as justifying the killing of an unarmed Black high school student walking through a predominantly white neighborhood to a convenience store) works to promote expectations that

- fears of a racial other, held by white people, will be acknowledged and affirmed by the legal system (i.e., my racial perspective is authorized by judges/juries/laws);

- predominantly white spaces need to be protected against people of color, especially Black people;

- white people's feelings, especially concerning safety, are more important than even the life of a person of color.

3. **Default Expectations.** Reflect upon the list of expectations that the five or six structural advantages on the Whiteness Chart produce. Are there logical groupings of expectations that can be reduced into a single expectation by broadening or generalizing? Follow the example below, and see whether it makes sense to shorten your list of expectations. The list created can be titled "default expectations."

Example

From the expectations listed in the example for Activity 2, I can generalize these expectations into one:

- the expectation that the law (law enforcement, courts) will reflect white perspectives and interests

4. **The BBQ Becky Link.** Return to what you learned through your online search in Activity 1. Are any of the expectations identified in Activity 3 present in the behavior of the white woman whose actions gave rise to the meme? List them, and explain how the behavior reveals the expectation noted.

5. **The BBQ Becky Within.** For this activity, you should be paired in groups of two (share partners). Reflect upon the list of expectations that the structural advantages produce, and recall a time and situation when you saw a white person

reflect one or more of these expectations. For one minute, share this memory (do not use names that identify people) with your share partner. Afterward, for one minute, the second person should share their memory. Now, reflect upon a time when your actions/behaviors/thoughts reflected one or more of the expectations noted in your list. For one minute, share this experience with your partner. Then for one minute, it is your partner's turn to share their experience.

> *It is critical to understand that each one of us has been shaped by the deep history of Whiteness, including its current production and manifestation. The expectations that Whiteness produces in white people are not incapable of being challenged, but it takes intentionality and hard work over an extended period of time.*

6. **Whiteness Competency Checklist**. One way to advance Whiteness Competency is to create a tool kit that helps you challenge the very expectations that Whiteness promotes. Return to your narrowed-down list of default expectations from Activity 3, and see whether you can propose a statement that, if reduced to memory and drawn upon frequently, may help stop you from going to the default expectation that Whiteness encourages.

Example

The default expectation that the law (law enforcement, courts) will reflect white perspectives and interests

Checklist

- My interests and perspectives are among many and deserve no more or less weight than those of others.

Build your checklist.

7. **Whiteness Competency Building**. Commit to reading your checklist multiple times throughout each day for a minimum of three weeks. Once you are comfortable that your checklist is an everyday tool that you go to in your head before acting and reacting, Whiteness Competency will be seeded.

8. **Unwhiteness Washing.** Whiteness has shaped every institution within the United States, including its education systems. The workings of whiteness are both subtle and boisterous, fragile and tenacious. It is fair to presume that Whiteness has shaped us and most of what we do in school, from how we decorate the classroom, structure the day, reward and punish students, and cover content to the pedagogy we use and the structure of school itself. Whiteness has ensured seamless racial inequality generation after generation. It must be intentionally and sharply challenged.

- How does the knowledge of whiteness (using the Whiteness Chart) inform you about what is needed to contest whiteness?

- How can you translate this into
  - the way you decorate your room?
  - the way you structure the day?
  - how you approach reward and punishment?
  - the content you teach and how you teach it?
- How does it inform your approach to Black girls in your classroom, Black boys, Black parents, Black colleagues and staff?
- How does it inform your approach to persons of Latinx, Pacific Island, indigenous, or Asian descent?

Vignette: Keisha Resists Karen

Nahliah Webber

Educators and policymakers fret about racial segregation in American schools. Advocates conclude that the system's ills and solutions are to be found in Black children's proximity to white children. The Black and white education journeys, they say, are painfully separate and unequal in childhood. When they are adults, they worry, it's too hard, perhaps too late, for them to overcome America's Black-white gaps.

But, I wonder, is this true?

If we switch our gaze to the experience of Black girls in schools, for example, instead of the white children we believe they should be closer to, we well might see they are not so far from each other after all. That the bridge is shorter than it appears. This connection is not so much a bridging of two spaces as it is an understanding that Black girls experience an alternate reality of white childhood at the hands of their white—usually female—teacher. Ms. Karen we'll call her.

"Do you have a pass…?"

"Are you supposed to be here…?"

"That's not professional.…"

"Hello school security? Keyonna is threating me.…"

Cries

Ms. Karen—white supremacy's duchess of protocol who keeps order over Blackness with vigilant aggression, protected by the sword and shield of white woman fragility—teaches classes filled with Breionnas, Kenyas, and Charmaines about what it means to grow up white.

The ideology of Ms. Karen's childhood obfuscates reality, making what is false appear true and what is connected seem apart. In schools, perpetrators of violence are depicted as saviors and models for ethics and morality, while those surviving their abuse are deemed enemies requiring fixing. Even how Black girls meet Ms. Karen is perverse: While young and (be)coming into their power, Black girls are taught by an adult already raised in the ideology of their deficiency with state-sanctioned authority over their minds and bodies. Maybe this is why little Black girls are perceived as "older" and "grown," because from kindergarten they must overcome a steep learning curve dealing with an adult raised to not see them. Coming from whitewashed schools, blank history books, and watered-down communities, Ms. Karen shares with her class an artificial purity that blinds her to her violence, while Keisha works through the muck of stigma and stereotype to protect herself from the violence of Ms. Karen's childhood.

Ms. Karen will feign infantile weakness when she gets to "Quontierha" or "Akosua" during attendance. With acidic politeness she'll ask for Black girls to weaken their names for her comfort. Kinesha's and Breasia's hair will be written in and out of uniform codes—overregulated and erased until it falls limp, lifeless and "professional." Nzinga's body will be policed and positioned back into Ms. Karen's expectations for obedience. Cowering in the face of a Black womanhood that scares her imagination, Ms. Karen will oversexualize and shame India and Fatima while taking a few swipes at their mothers for good measure. Rashida will be monitored in hallways and demerited to a place where Ms. Karen can call the cops on her for daring to exist loudly.

With Ms. Karen, Black girls are bridged into white children's worlds every day. They experience what white children learn, think, feel, and don't see about them. When Black girls become aware of this distorted reality, they speak out. The Blackness called out of their names demands it. The Blacker they are—that is, the more they rest in the beauty of their Blackness and draw power from it—the more Ms. Karen withers and weaponizes. But with affirmation from Black mothers, grandmothers, and play cousins, Black girls exist outside of violent white childhoods and embody an eloquent language of resistance.

"Oh, Keisha look good, yea?!"

"That's racist!"

"COME ON hair!"

"Wait 'til I tell my mother and she gonna come up to this school!"

Claps

A remix of their mothers' tongues communicates Black girls' beauty, giving them full expression of themselves. History braided down their backs carrying routes to

(Continued)

(Continued)

self-advocacy and freedom. Bejeweled ears ring like tambourines calling in the ancestors to order their rhythmic steps. Hands clapping out the syllables of what Ms. Karen is not about to do.

In school Black girls see the altered reality of white childhood every day and spend their formative years resisting its violence with everything that is Black in them. Perhaps the solutions to the "problems" in education aren't in the distance between Black and white children but in the beauty of the resistance of Black girls.

CHAPTER 15

Can I Do This if I'm White?

How White Educators Can Be the Teachers Black Girl Students Deserve

Ali Michael

It's essential to my life and work now that I talk about race and racism, confront racist policies, and challenge racially disparate outcomes. But I didn't grow up this way. I am white and I grew up in a predominantly white town, where I was taught—through the shared practices around me—to imagine I was acting in a color-blind fashion by staying silent about race and treating everybody the same. When I got to college, I learned that such imagined color-blindness only serves to reinforce racist structures, because it makes it impossible to talk about or challenge those structures. Even with that knowledge, however, I was so uncomfortable talking about race that I imagined I was biologically wired in a way that made such conversations impossible for me. In an African American literature course, when I opened my mouth, I would stutter and stumble, confusing my terms and hesitating out of fear of saying something offensive. I would stop suddenly and let my voice trail off, hoping someone would come to my rescue. I even believed for a time that talking about race and strategizing about racism was something people of color were born able to do. I would never be able to do it—because I'm white.

Time and education and experience would change this for me, of course. But those transitional times gave me clear insight into the difficulty many white people have talking about race. Here, I hope to convince white educators that bridging their discomfort is essential. It's far better to start and stumble and grow than to hide silently in privilege.

159

How do white people get beyond awkward stumbling fear and build the skills necessary for racial competency? We learn with practice. We learn by trying, making mistakes, taking feedback, and keeping at it. This revelation was offered to me in graduate school when my mentor, Dr. Howard Stevenson, a professor of urban education at the University of Pennsylvania, stated directly: Racial proficiency is a skills-based competency—a set of skills one must gain through practice (Stevenson, 2014).

So what are those skills? In an attempt to break down some of the component parts of racial competency—sometimes called racial literacy (Sealey-Ruiz & Greene, 2015; Stevenson, 2014)—I organize my thinking around the racial competency framework for training counselors (Sue &Torino, 2005), which involves four main components: knowledge, self-awareness, skills, and action. Here, I delineate some of the specific knowledge, self-awareness, skills, and action that white educators can engage in to build their racial competency for serving Black girls in school.

Overall, it's important that white educators understand that we cannot teach Black girls well if we cannot even say the word Black; if we don't understand the beauty, power, integrity, and struggle that come together in the history of that term. We cannot teach Black girls if we are unable to recognize that our teaching and their learning happens in the context of a white supremacist society, in which our social power as white people is as profound as their vulnerability as Black girls; in fact, our power and their vulnerability come from the same place. Recognizing and confronting the history and the system that deal these cards is the way for us to stand with, protect, and support Black girl students. We are "blind" to it at their peril.

KNOWLEDGE

Building knowledge about race starts with challenging the narratives white people have been taught and unlearning a mainstream story about fairness and meritocracy. It involves learning the realities of racism and oppression, and acquiring knowledge about people whose racial experiences and dynamics are different from ours. Part of this knowledge building is straightforward—reading articles and books or listening to podcasts that will help one understand history that doesn't reify a traditional narrative but amplifies the stories of people of color that are so rarely told. It is also important for white people to learn about the history of whiteness, and the way that it shapes their lens on the world. Understanding Black girls means nothing if you see them as an aberration from an invisible, unnamed norm shaped by whiteness. Whiteness needs to be understood, not as a neutral objective category, but as a subjective standpoint that impacts how one sees and understands Blackness.

For more knowledge about Black girls, read

- *I'm Still Here: Black Dignity in a World Made for Whiteness*, by Austin Channing Brown

- *Bone Black: Memories of Girlhood*, by bell hooks
- The Combahee River Collective Statement (available at https://combaheeriver collective.weebly.com/the-combahee-river-collective-statement.html)
- *Sister Outsider*, by Audre Lorde
- *Other People's Children*, by Lisa Delpit
- *Emergent Strategy*, by adrienne maree brown
- *Post Traumatic Slave Syndrome*, by Joy DeGruy

For more knowledge about Whiteness, read, watch, or listen to

- *White by Law*, by Ian Haney Lopez
- *White Rage: The Unspoken Truth of Our Racial Divide*, by Carol Anderson
- *Dying of Whiteness*, by Jonathan Metzl
- *Everyday White People Confront Racial and Social Injustice: 15 Stories*, edited by Eddie Moore Jr., Marguerite Penick, and Ali Michael
- *The Guide for White Women Who Teach Black Boys*, edited by Eddie Moore Jr., Ali Michael, and Marguerite Penick
- *Playing in the Dark: Whiteness and the Literary Imagination*, by Toni Morrison
- *White Women, Race Matters*, by Ruth Frankenberg
- "The Souls of White Folks," by W. E. B. Du Bois
- *Up Against Whiteness*, by Stacey Lee
- "Seeing White," a Scene on Radio podcast
- *Race: The Power of an Illusion* (PBS)
- *Waking Up White*, by Debby Irving
- *White Fragility*, by Robin DiAngelo
- *Birth of a White Nation: The Invention of White People and Its Relevance Today*, by Jacqueline Battalora
- *Raising Race Questions: Whiteness and Inquiry in Education*, by Ali Michael
- *Witnessing Whiteness* by Shelly Tochluk

Self Awareness[1]

Developing knowledge of history, the realities of people of color, and the history of whiteness is *key* to racial competence. But many white people learning about racism pursue knowledge development without a visceral sense of their own involvement.

This is why we can have so many book clubs without social transformation.[2] Knowledge, self-awareness, and skills are integrally connected; they cannot be seen as distinct processes. New knowledge about ourselves and the world around us often challenges what we were taught. Most of us were acculturated into false-hoods, and then—for those of us who are white—we grounded our sense of self on those falsehoods. As we learn the true history of the United States and ongoing racial realities and histories, we also learn that much of what we know and have been taught is wrong. This can be profoundly disorienting. As we struggle to under-stand knowledge that challenges our previous assumptions and truths, there is a newer, bigger task: We need to find a new sense of self based in reality. The follow-ing are tasks to engage in for developing a racially conscious self-awareness:

- Negotiate your own personal history with the systemic history you learn.

  Consider how the stories and history you are learning impacted you. When you learn about historical racism, ask, "How was my white family impacted by that particular event?" or "How does this impact me, where I live, the money I have, the resources I have access to, my social networks, the health of those I love?"

- Figure out how you feel.

  Some white people step onto an antiracist path because of work, school, a per-sonal relationship, or a traumatic experience with racism. But more often, white people begin to learn about racism because it is a requirement at their school or work. As a result of this, many white people tend to *think* their way into understanding racism and what to do about it, rather than *feel* their way. This is actually a well-identified component of identity development for white peo-ple (Helms, 1995; Tatum, 2017). Essentially, we may know a lot about racism, but we keep it at an emotional distance. We would respond differently to rac-ist events if we *felt* their impact in our bodies. Instead, white people (myself included) often don't know what to do or say, because we don't have gut-level feelings about what is right or wrong with regard to race. To get in touch with your own feelings about racism, try going deeper into particular news stories and connecting with the stories of people and their families. You can also do this by meditating on something that makes you feel vulnerable and connecting that to the vulnerability of Black girls, or by reading one of the vignettes in this volume and imagining it was written by your child.

- Don't be afraid to cry.

  Racism deserves tears. The history of racism is a history of loss, trauma, anguish, dehumanization, and fear. Learning about it brings out all kinds of emotions. I believe white people need to cry about racism, but not in the way we usually do. We often cry because the conversation becomes too much for us, so we want it to end. Or we want to show we are taking it in, so we cry in a public way that recenters the conversation on us and our sadness. When we do this, it takes the focus away from the pain of people of color, and then those who are actually impacted by racism—physically, economically, emotionally, institutionally—get left out of the conversation. One self-awareness strategy is to create space in your life where you can feel the pain and sadness of racism, without taking the attention away from people of color.

- Journal.

  Journal about what you are learning about racism, how it impacts you, and how it makes you feel. Use your journal to record confusing or challenging racial moments when you don't know what to do or say. Find a white ally to help you process it. Return to it again and again.

- Recognize you are a part of a mainstream group, with behaviors that go along with it.

  If you are white, you are a symbol of a group called white people. The more you engage in common White-Group Level Behaviors, the more your Black girl students will see you as just another white person. When you act in ways that are counter to the mainstream behaviors of the vast majority of white people, you will be seen more as an advocate or coconspirator. Classic examples of White-Group Level Behaviors[3] include consistently questioning the competence of a person of color; negating a person of color's reality (e.g., "I don't think that was racism . . ."); and not noticing when there are only white people (e.g., on a hiring committee or administrative council).

- Learn the terrain of your bias.

  Take an implicit bias test online. Recognize that we all have bias. Don't try to hide it; try to reprogram it and be conscious of it. When you go into class, when you grade, when you discipline, when you meet with parents, remind yourself of what you know about your bias.

- Recognize you may be acting or speaking from a sense of internalized white superiority. We talk a lot about internalized oppression and how it stops people from oppressed groups from speaking up, taking action, or even just taking up space. But we fail to talk about the counterpart to this phenomenon, which is internalized white superiority. This sense of superiority can lead individuals to believe they should always speak up, take action, and take up space, and that they have the right to; in fact it can feel wrong not to. Part of racial proficiency is recognizing this tendency in oneself and undoing it.

SKILLS

The skills component of racial competency involves repetitive motion. Antiracism is a practice. These are the skills to practice over and over again, as one might in a weight-training or meditation practice. As we practice these skills—day in and day out—we make ourselves heartier, more robust, more lithe vessels for resisting racism and taking action.

- Fall and recover.

  They say that ice skaters[4] will never learn to be great if they don't know how to fall and recover, because many of the most challenging tricks require falling hundreds of times before they can be mastered. Antiracism is similar. We have to be able to make mistakes, get feedback on those mistakes, and keep learning. No person who has stayed on an antiracist path more than a few weeks has not made a mistake.

- Solicit and respond to feedback. Give surveys to parents or exit tickets to students to find out how things are going in your class. Plan to meet with the diversity practitioner at your school to find out what you could be doing differently. Listen closely when people say they have something to say. Thank them and develop a plan to address their concerns. Do not allow yourself to be demoralized by strangers on the internet. Take feedback from people who you trust.

- Listen to the voices of Black women in your school and in the lives of your Black girl students. When parents are organizing a panel discussion, or when your students have a poetry night, make it a point to be there to hear their voices.

- Build a network of white "allies."

  White people who are working to be antiracist need support from other white "allies," people who will support you and your learning without shaming you, but who will also not let you off the hook. White allies are different from friends who believe you are too hard on yourself, or who may even look down on your anti-racism goals. White allies might be your friends, but they also help you to process and dismantle your own racism in a supportive and accountable way.

- Support in, dump out.[5]

  Support the people who are closest to the pain. If you need spaces to find support for yourself, do not go to the people who are closer to the pain of racism than you are. "Dump out." In other words, dump your own sadness on people who are less impacted by racism than you are, not people of color who are already traumatized. This is the idea of ring theory—readily available online.

ACTION

There is no change without action. If you are to become an educator who truly supports Black girls, you need to engage.

- Build relationships with accountability partners of color. In my own life, I have people of color who I am accountable to, who will help me remember how to stay on an active antiracist path, and who will help me direct my energies towards what matters. My accountability partners are people I love and trust, who will tell me when I'm doing something racist.

- Lean in proactively to do what you can in your own sphere of influence, no matter how small you think it is.

- Follow people of color leadership *and* don't lead without consulting people of color. Remember that when you take action, it will impact the people of color in your local context even more than it impacts you. Responding to their localized concerns may likely be more crucial than addressing the most pressing forms of racism you perceive.

- Demonstrate gratitude for critical feedback. Work with a white ally to process it, even though it hurts and all you want to do is defend your intention.

- Practice. Use your white allies to begin role-playing responses to racist remarks that you hear from white students, colleagues, friends, or relatives. There is no reason to expect that you will know exactly what to say when these scenarios come up. That's why you need to practice.

- Strategize and enact interventions (both overt and covert) to racist policy.

- Talk to BIPOC student and faculty groups to offer allyship and action.

- Attend events at your school offered by BIPOC folx. Listen to what their concerns are so that your interventions can be locally informed.

- Brainstorm racial issues in your school or workplace, and strategize how you might support antiracist efforts overtly or covertly.

- Establish accountability for your action with BIPOC folx.

- Treat everything you do as a draft. Give up on trying to do the perfect antiracist thing. If anyone knew how to end racism, they would already be doing it. Many white people don't take action because they don't know the perfect thing to do. Treat everything you do as a draft, and be willing to make mistakes. If you didn't start the draft, you wouldn't have anything to revise or get feedback on.

What would a racially competent white person look like?

Being racially competent means that a person has built up the muscle, the resilience, the vast comfort zone, the robust antiracist support network, the familiarity and comfort with the discomfort zone, the self-care habits, and the chutzpah to be able to learn from mistakes and from racially stressful or challenging situations.

Being racially competent means that, under pressure, one doesn't give up, turn silent, flee the scene, or blame others.

Being racially competent means taking action informed by the needs and concerns of people of color in their localized context, with a nuanced understanding of the impact of systemic racism and the impact of one's intervention on people of color.

Racial competency is the combination of knowledge, self-awareness, skills, and action that helps white people be contributing members of a healthy multiracial community.

Even as I offer this framework for competency, it is imperative that teachers recognize that racial competency is not actually a destination. Once a person is truly competent in matters of race and racism, they recognize that there is so much more to learn. Rather than arriving at a point of expertise and completion, the next step beyond competency is humility (Foronda et al., 2016). It is about having the humility to recognize that no matter how much one knows about race and racism, there is always more to learn. It is about realizing that no matter how much you know about whiteness, there will always be things you cannot see. It is about knowing that no matter how many books you read about Black girls, you cannot know how an individual child's Blackness and girlness impact her until you get to know her. A color-conscious awareness (as opposed to color-blind) helps you understand that race and racism have likely impacted her life in profound ways. But it doesn't mean you know everything—or even anything—about *how* it has impacted her, until you meet her and build a true relationship.

NOTES

1. Thank you to Eleonora Bartoli for helping to clarify this point for me, and for sharing her knowledge. For more on Eleonora's work, see her blog at www.eleonorabartoli.com.

2. See Tre Johnson's piece "When Black People Are in Pain, White People Join Book Clubs" (2020).

3. The examples come from the White People Confronting Racism manual.

4. I learned this analogy from Sarah Halley, who leads the White People Confronting Racism work based in Philadelphia.

5. This concept comes from grief counseling, but it was originally applied to anti-racist learning by Colleen Lewis in a workshop we taught together with Nolan Cabrera for USC's Equity Institutes.

CHAPTER 16

Not Knowing and Not Controlling

Learning Alongside Black Girl Students

Jesse Phillips-Fein

INTRODUCTION

Writing this chapter is a contradiction I hope I can sustain, for while it presumes I "know something" that can assist white womyn in teaching Black girls, what I am offering instead are the ideas of "not-knowing" and "not-controlling." To know and to control are difficult desires and habits to give up as a teacher, for aren't we *supposed* to have knowledge to share with our students and to be able to manage our classrooms? I suggest not-knowing and not-controlling as ongoing practices for white womyn teachers to decenter our own perspectives and comfort, so that we can fight alongside Black girl students for their self-expression and freedom.

Another potential contradiction is that in my work as a white dance educator for nearly 20 years (the past 14 at an urban private school), I am aware that some Black girl students have experienced my teaching, or parts of it, as a failure. Sharing these shortcomings is an encouragement to let go of seeking the magic formula by which we can feel like we are in control and know exactly what to do to be the "perfect" white teacher. This is not to excuse racism on the part of white teachers, but rather to engage with the discomfort of our mistakes, as that is what being self-reflective and accountable requires us to do.

Learning to Know and Control: Internalizing Racism

When I reflect on how my socialization as a white girl has affected my relationships with Black girls throughout my life, I see three toxic behaviors: internalized racial superiority, invisibilizing, and exploiting. It's important to emphasize that I was *not* taught these behaviors explicitly. In fact, many aspects of my childhood have made it difficult to acknowledge my own racism: My white parents were committed political activists, they intentionally chose to send me to an integrated school, and I lived in a racially diverse neighborhood—how could *I* be racist?

Yet the dance classes I took at my elementary, middle, and high schools as well as private dance studios were spaces (amongst others) where I implicitly absorbed the biases that underpin my racist behaviors. Dance education in the United States is a realm where white dominance is enacted, as Eurocentric forms such as ballet and modern dance are deemed the foundation of professional dance training and form the core of dance education, and the slim body type and light skin associated with whiteness are prized (Davis and Phillips-Fein, 2018). I internalized the belief that Black dance forms such as jazz and hip-hop were "purely entertainment" and not "art." As the movement vocabulary of Black dance forms is often communally owned and shared, I erroneously thought they were not creative or original. I felt superior—that I was a "real" dancer training in ballet and modern—in contrast to my peers who "only" danced hip-hop. Even though I had the opportunity to learn choreography from Black artists, my training was predominantly monocultural, and I did not learn about the African-derived influences on *all* American dance forms (Dixon-Gottschild, 1996). I had little knowledge of and looked down upon Black dance forms, while also simultaneously feeling envious of the popularity of hip-hop and exploiting Black movement practices to feel cool.

The racist attitudes engendered in me, in part through my dance training, reflect broader antagonisms between white and Black womyn in a racist and patriarchal society. The category of "woman" itself is defined through proximity to whiteness and denied to Black womyn, and furthermore, the "protection" of white womyn and our sexuality is essential to maintaining the imagined purity of whiteness (Shuller, 2017). In contrast, as Aimee Meredith Cox (2015) describes, Black girls are seen as inherently deviant, as a "problem" to be managed, who need to be molded into the respectability and acceptability that is ascribed to white girls. In the field of dance, this deviance is expressed by associating Black girls and Black social dances with sensuality, sexuality, bodily excess, and natural physical ability, rather than the skilled training, refinement, properness and poise associated with ballet (Desmond, 1993). In the dance classroom, the management of Black girls can take many forms, including unjust punishment in disciplinary practices, the suppression of self-expression and artistic choices, the privileging of ballet and modern dance in the curriculum, and the lack of acknowledgement of and appreciation for Black dance forms and aesthetics.

Here is an example of how some of these internalized beliefs have manifested in my own teaching. In an advanced-level elective dance class, a dark-skinned Black girl student arrived tardy. "You're late!" I barked at her. A few minutes later, a white-passing mixed race girl came in late, and I asked calmly, "How are you? Are you okay?" After the words were out of my mouth, I could see my racial and colorist bias in these unequal responses. Later, I told the Black student that I recognized what I did, and I committed to not repeating that behavior. What struck me is that I couldn't picture myself talking to a white or white-passing student the way I had spoken to the Black girl student. My behavior reflected an assumption that Black girls are emotionally tough, an extension of what Christina Sharpe (2016) has articulated as the inhumane notion that Black people don't feel pain, or as Cox (2015) asserts, that Black girls are superhuman in their resiliency. Unless I actively intervene on my own biases, I will treat white girls as if they are soft and innocent, and Black girls as if they are defiant and not trustworthy. I have found participation in a white affinity group with other white teachers a helpful tool for reflecting on, processing, and being accountable for changing these behaviors.

NOT-CONTROLLING AND NOT-KNOWING: FIGHTING ALONGSIDE

A practice of not-controlling and not-knowing facilitates the flourishing of Black girls by affirming exactly who they are, and recognizing the tremendous knowledge they have developed together for navigating a world that despises them. This is knowledge that I simply cannot give them, for it emerges from their own experiences, but I can learn about, celebrate, honor, and fight for what they know they need to survive. I can use my resources as a teacher to protect the zones of freedom and the reservoirs of knowledge that Black girls create for themselves.

In order for me to be able to do this, I had to go through a process of challenging what I had learned in my own dance education. The pedagogical practices of culturally relevant teaching and cultural humility were pivotal for me in realizing this change. *Culturally relevant teaching*, a term coined by Gloria Ladson-Billings, is a pedagogy that enables students to relate the course content to their own cultural backgrounds and lived experiences (McCarthy-Brown, 2017). Cultural humility is a practice of self-evaluation and self-critique grounded in challenging my own internalized racial superiority, and building relationships in order to shift power imbalances (Hook et al., 2013).

When I began teaching, I knew very little about the dance forms that emerge from the Black and Latinx cultures of my students, and when the students didn't meet my aesthetic preferences or standards, I judged them as deficient instead of interrogating my own bias in perceiving their skills. For the past 13 years, I have studied dance traditions from cultures other than my own, with a focus on dance forms from the African Diaspora. This ongoing study is an unlearning of the biases I learned as a young white dancer, both physically and philosophically. I now understand Black dance forms as rooted in practices of liberation within conditions of unfreedom, a mode of surviving, thriving, and enacting alternative possibilities against white dominance and cultural norms (DeFrantz, 2012). Becoming a student myself of African Diasporic dances not only changed my views on dance, it also enabled me to share culturally relevant and resonant information with Black girl students.

However, culturally relevant teaching without a practice of cultural humility can also become a way for me to continue to feel in control and in the know. Becoming more familiar with another culture can have the allure of being a way to extend my reach and expand the spaces and places in which I feel comfortable (Ahmed, 2006). Cultural humility helps me recognize that my commitment to learning about Black culture is for Black students' to be reflected, seen, and heard in the classroom. It's not about me being "down," it's not about me distancing myself from whiteness, and it is certainly not the same as having the lived experience of being Black. As a Black girl student once said to me in a conversation on race, "You can't teach me about Blackness!" A practice of not-knowing and not-controlling challenges me to *stay in the disorientation* that happens when I step outside of whiteness, rather than to approach other cultures as something to consume and make my own (hooks, 1992).

As powerful and essential as it is to have a diverse dance curriculum, there can also be something profoundly painful about learning African Diaspora dances from a white dance teacher, because of the history of cultural rupture during transatlantic slavery, the legacies of blackface minstrelsy and cultural appropriation, and the ways in which Black people have been denied opportunities to represent themselves. Furthermore, as Jane Desmond writes, white people may "dance Black" without paying the social penalty of being Black (Desmond, 1993). Therefore part of my curriculum is explicit conversation about what my identity means in the context of what I am teaching. While students usually assert that it's okay for me to teach dances from cultures that are not my own as long as "you're respectful" and "you do them correctly," I emphasize that these dances will always have different meanings in my body because of my positionality as a white womyn. There is something about these dances I can never know or fully embody, for my performance of them will not be about affirming an ancestral lineage that was violently severed, and is not an expression of my own cultural identity as a resistant act against the marginalizations of colonialism and racism. The dances are tools used by Black people to resist anti-Blackness, and my relationship to resisting anti-Blackness isn't that of being its target, but of being protected from it. My stewardship of the dances is a small contribution to the larger collective who share the responsibility of maintaining the revolutionary power of the dances. In this way, I am participating in and contributing to a broader struggle against white cultural dominance.

To conclude, I want to share an anecdote of this practice in action. For our school's annual dance performance, a fellow white teacher was working with a group of Black girls to perform a repertory piece on Black women identity, choreographed by her former student. The piece had been reperformed several times since the student graduated, and over time it had become an important tradition to Black girls at the school. As the director of the performance, it came to my attention that a conflict had developed between the teacher and one of the students. The teacher wanted to pull the student out of the performance to hold her accountable for missing a few rehearsals. The student confided to me she did not feel comfortable with the teacher, and that's why she had missed rehearsal. I decided she should be allowed to perform the piece (a decision I was ultimately called to defend), because the dance had crucial significance to her as a young Black womyn. She had a right to the piece because the experience it represented was her own, and this need was more important than teaching her a lesson about timeliness and responsibility.

We could call this "allowing" or "making space" or "helping a student find her voice," but all of these frameworks focus on how I hold power and could use it "for" her, instead of recognizing that she is already powerful. Instead of managing or repressing her power, I affirmed it by fighting for her to manifest it on her own terms. This is a learning alongside and with, where I am not the one who knows or controls the process, but rather I follow the lead of Black girls who are already ingeniously building and creating what they need.

Suggested Exercises

1. Write about and then discuss these questions: What were the dynamics of your relationships to Black cultural practices as a young person? If you were not exposed to Black culture, why was this? What did you learn about Black culture, and how did you learn this in the absence of Black people?

2. List at least three ways that knowing and controlling manifest in your teaching practice with Black girls. Imagine what it would feel like to let go of these behaviors, and write about what that feels like in your body. Share with a partner.

3. Write about and/or discuss what cultural familiarity means in the subject you teach. How does (or could) knowledge of Black cultural traditions change the content of your curriculum? What would not-knowing and not-controlling look like in relationship to this content?

Vignette: Confessions of a White Teacher: Seven Ways I Failed Beautiful and Brilliant Black Girls

Debby Irving

As a white woman, I entered teaching unaware of the damage I could inflict on Black girls simply by not understanding how whiteness had shaped my worldview. Without understanding my own inherited patterns of racist beliefs and behaviors, and the gaping blind spots they held in place, I unwittingly reproduced an American white woman problem all too familiar in the Black community: good intentions, devastating impact. Following are seven limitations that undermined my ability to live into my own values and likely caused harm to the Black students and families who encountered me.

1. *Low Expectations for Myself*

Though low expectations for students of color has become a common understanding in the opportunity gap discourse, for me that began with low expectations for myself. My primary expectation was to excel at the job I was hired to do. Missing from my understanding was the reality that I was entering an institution designed to hold in place a racial hierarchy, and that simply doing the job I was hired to do set me up to perpetuate a racial divide born of history and policy I knew nothing about. My goal, to be kind and compassionate and treat all students "equally," is the kiss of death in challenging racism. Had my expectations for myself included vigorously interrogating my limitations, and seeking out mentors who would push me beyond my comfort zone, perhaps I would've had a chance at supporting Black girls in growing their intellectual, social emotional, spiritual selves.

2. *Lack of Black Women Role Models in My Life*

When I look back on my life, I am appalled at the dearth of Black women in it. Segregation through housing, education, employment, and social role has led me again and again to affiliate with women within my race and class. Until the age of 50, my circle of closest friends looked, thought, and lived remarkably like me: suburban, white, heterosexual, female, and upper-middle class. We were liberal-minded and big-hearted do-gooders. Had I been introduced to the work of Janet Helms (2007), a brilliant Black woman scholar, perhaps I would've understood the need to develop my own racial identity, or that I even had one. Lacking this level of awareness and development left me unable to form deep, trusting relationships with the Black women in my communities. Endemic to the vicious cycles born of oppression, not having brilliant Black women in my life kept me from learning about the legacies of Recy Taylor, Maggie Lena Walker, Angela Davis, Diane Nash, Zora Neale Hurston, Sarah Breedlove, bell hooks, and Shirley Chisholm, which would have changed the way I understood the intersection of women and race, and more specifically the role brilliant and beautiful Black women have long played in pushing for a more humane and just society.

3. *Inability to Disrupt the Rosa Parks Myth*

Rosa Parks, the one brilliant and beautiful Black woman on my radar, was there only in a distorted, whitewashed form, her brilliance removed from her Blackness. Dominant white history had taught me that Rosa Parks was a tired old lady, too tired to get up out of her bus seat. As a young mother I took out a library book that perpetuated the feeble old lady myth. I proudly read it to my daughters, patting myself on the back for bringing diversity into my household. I repeated this misstep in the classroom, proudly displaying and reading a dumbed-down version of the Rosa Parks story. How differently I would've understood Black woman brilliance had I been taught about the real Rosa Parks and the sophisticated organizing world she moved in. When I discovered that Rosa Parks was a highly trained activist and a mere 42 years old, I felt engulfed in the humiliation and regret of having perpetuated such fiction. How many young minds did I whitewash through the telling of that story?

4. *Lack of Representation in the Classroom*

I imagine now the ways in which Black women could've been integrated into every piece of the curriculum. Instead, I strove to create a more multicultural school and classroom by hanging images of children and adults from a range of ethnicities on classroom walls. I cringe now to think of the images of children and adults from far-flung countries and cultures who bore little resemblance to the brilliant and beautiful Black U.S. children and families we hoped to attract as part of our diversity initiative. Though meant to familiarize children with their diverse human family, the images more likely reaffirmed feelings of otherness across ethnic and racial lines. My inability to integrate Black scholars, thinkers, scientists, historians, artists, bankers, mathematicians, inventors, entrepreneurs, and activists into this project was mirrored in the classroom library. Even as I developed an understanding that Black students would learn to read better through books that included Black characters, I missed that the books we added fed into Black tropes. Limited to Black as "urban" and Black as basketball, my book choices missed the kind of nuance and complexity that would offer all students windows and mirrors, to the same multidimensionality of Black girls that white characters are afforded.

5. *Lack of Nuance*

My narrow white lens left me with a clunky way of seeing Blackness, a perspective that didn't recognize the myriad additional identities and personality traits that constitute a person's full humanity. The stark contrast to the ways in which I'd long been able to quickly take in a white person's unique mix of identities and personality traits confirms for me just what a limitation this was. A lifetime of exposure to thousands of white girls and women in books, TV shows, movies, and my own life, peppered with sporadic exposure to negatively stereotyped Black girls and women, forged in me a lopsided perception of girls and women across racial lines. The mismatch between my cultural training and my aspirations to set Black girls up for success cannot be overstated.

(Continued)

(Continued)

I understand now how my inability to see Black girls for the multidimensional human beings they were likely caused them to lose bits of themselves in my presence.

6. *Entrapment in White Mythology and Culture*

Not only was I unable to elevate and center Black beauty and brilliance for all students, I was unable to debunk and decenter the proliferation of white myths, stereotypes, and cultural norms that crowded them out. I never recognized Black history month as the weak whitewashing countermeasure that it is. I purported to not see color. I oohed and aahed over the handprint turkeys at Thanksgiving and freely used the term Columbus Day. I saw punctuality as an asset and more relaxed relationships to time as a deficit. I had no skills to support white students in developing a constructive white identity or learning how to be better friends, accomplices, and truth tellers. Deep in my subconscious was a belief that the white way was the right way, and I was a benevolent bridge to it.

7. *Inability to Create Meaningful Family Connections*

I can only imagine the quick assessment parents of Black girls made of me. *Ugh, another year with a clueless white lady teacher,* I imagine them saying. If I could do it again, I would have private conversations with parents of Black girls and say something like this: *I am learning every day that as a white woman I have some serious limitations in teaching your child. I want to assure you that I am committed to doing better. Please know that if you have ideas about how I could better support your child, I will be all ears. I want your child to have a wonderful year in this classroom, and I'd be honored to partner with you to make that happen.*

Exercise

Create a list of the disciplines your students will encounter in your school. For each discipline, find three Black women who exemplify brilliance in that field.

- How might you integrate these women into your classroom?
- What do you think the impact of having these women represented might have on Black girls in your classroom?
- How does teaching all students about Black female brilliance and beauty contribute to the social, emotional, and intellectual well-being of Black girls?
- How does teaching all students about Black female brilliance and beauty contribute to the social, emotional, and intellectual well-being of students who do not identify as Black girls?
- How does teaching all students about Black female brilliance and beauty impact the families of Black girls?
- How does teaching all students about Black female brilliance and beauty impact the families of students who do not identify as Black girls?

Vignette: Humbling Feedback

Kirsten Steele

"Ms. Steele, your classroom is no longer a safe space."

Needless to say, this sentence sent my budding confidence as a brand-new teacher into a nosedive. I had modeled a Socratic seminar after those of my amazing mentor teacher, Jaclyn Novotny. She had this uncanny ability to mediate discussions of tough topics, and I thought I had done pretty well for my first solo class discussion—until two days later.

My student, a fierce young Black woman, was respectful and yet unapologetic as she stood proudly in front of my desk after class. I looked at her, and a million thoughts rushed through my head, the most prominent being, "Oh my God, I'm a failure."

"OK," I replied hesitantly. "Can you explain a bit more about what you mean?"

I would like to tell you that she looked at me with respect and admiration for being willing to listen, but that would be (1) a lie, and (2) a perpetuation of the white savior complex. No, she stood there, head held high, and eloquently shared how one young man in particular had derailed the entire Socratic seminar with his prejudiced, uninformed ideas, cutting other people off and demeaning Black and Latinx voices. I had failed to curtail him, and she was absolutely not going to let me off the hook.

At that moment, I could have gone a couple of routes. I could have told her she was too sensitive. I could have told her that he absolutely had the right to say anything he wanted because he hadn't used a direct slur. I could have dismissed her opinion.

This never even crossed my mind as an option. As a white, middle-class woman, I came to the classroom with scads of privilege. However, my mentor teacher—another white woman—modeled how to create a safe space for students, particularly students with marginalized voices. I had vowed to myself that if a student gave me feedback, even if it felt rude, I would search for the kernel of truth.

This student wasn't being rude. She was stepping out, speaking up for both herself and other voices of color. I admired her courage.

We sat down, and we discussed how to address the issues. She gave her account of other students' comments. I ended up speaking to the young man and his friends; my words fell on deaf ears. I spoke with their parents. I worked to reestablish norms in the class.

In other words, I treated her feedback as valuable, because it was. An administrator might give me good feedback, but the ones who can best tell me about what I am

(Continued)

(Continued)

and am not doing well are the students. The day that I stop listening to what my students need from me—how I can support them and facilitate their success—will be the day I stop teaching. They have their fingertips on the pulse of the world. We would be remiss not to pay attention and use their feedback wisely.

The second half of this section opens with a vignette from Dr. Ali Michael, who shares the ways that her own insecurities can impact the authenticity (or lack thereof) she brings to relationships with Black women. She offers an exercise to support readers to be able to read, see, listen to, and hear the voices of Black women in this very book with an open heart, and to help readers be persons deserving of the solidarity they seek. This vignette is followed by a chapter by Dr. Eleonora Bartoli, who suggests that white women are limited in their impact as antiracists, because they are held back by an investment in white male supremacy. Bartoli offers two powerful exercises for white women to engage in so that they might access their own power as women, which they can use to fight racism. Bartoli's chapter is followed by a vignette by Lauren Calig, demonstrating through her writing and her work what it can look like to be an antiracist white administrator, modeling antiracist leadership with both competence and humility. The section closes with a chapter from Dr. Robin DiAngelo, who explores the ways in which white fragility manifests in relationships between white teachers and Black students and offers suggestions for reversing that dynamic.

Vignette: Is This the Solidarity I Seek?

Ali Michael

In grad school I was on a research team with five Black women and one Chinese international student. I was the only white person. I held that space as sacred, so honored to be a part of that particular conversation—a space that I had rarely been a part of in my life. Most of my life had been full of almost all white spaces. As a collective—and as individuals—my teammates were funny, fierce, brilliant, and stylish; they were quantitative analysts, qualitative researchers, and prolific writers, deeply committed to exposing racism in schools. When I look back, I wonder how I must have appeared to them. I can remember feeling unworthy, making myself small, dull, afraid of saying the wrong thing. I wanted to be worthy of their trust and inclusion, but I was unsure of how to be me without being unwittingly igno- rant; how to be loud without amplifying my mistakes or taking up too much space. I can remember thinking to myself at the time, "I am so much more than this. Why can't I show them who I am?" Over the three years we worked together, clearly some of me came out, because we built real friendships—and in the 10 years since, our relationships have continued to evolve in different ways. I now feel able to say what I think, be wrong, hear their feedback, laugh out loud, be bold, dance in meetings, be me.

But that smallness comes back sometimes, especially when I am presenting to a new group, or entering a new relationship with a Black colleague with whom there is less history, less established trust. I imagine they don't trust me. I fear they don't like me. And I've come to see how I hold myself back from authentic relationships as a result. It's hard to connect, because I feel the need to be liked and trusted before I can be me. This vignette offers reflections and tools for entering relationships with Black women from a place of authenticity and connection.

As I explore this—generally unconscious—phenomenon within myself, I realize there are a few things I need to understand about this dynamic in order to move forward. First, this need I have to be liked and trusted, before I can be me, is backwards. How can someone like and trust me if they don't yet know me? How can someone like and trust me if I am not being my authentic self? Second, my extra sensitivity and caution towards Black women or girls in a lecture hall, or on a research team, can be equated to a fear of Black women or girls. It's not the same as locking my car doors when a Black person passes (our stereotypical image for fear of Blackness), but it is fear nonetheless. For teachers, when we are extra nervous about a parent-teacher conference with a Black parent, when we hesitate to call home because we know a Black parent doesn't give us the benefit of the doubt or because we perceive Black parents to be authoritative disciplinarians, when we hesitate to be rigorous in our grading or our editing, when we feel more on eggshells around Black colleagues than around others, this counts as fear of Blackness too. This walking on eggshells that many white women do with Black women, this assumption that Black women are coming at me from a judgmental place, that they are *not here to play*, is reductive. It's a stereotype that limits the range of what's possible for Black women—and the range of possibilities for how I might interact with individuals who fall into that group. Finally, when I feel at ease with Black women from the beginning, it is because they are willing to offer me the familiar social niceties and white middle-class norms of politeness that make me feel safe. But those same norms that I learned growing up, are part of what keeps white supremacy in place. Those are the very features of the racial contract that say we shouldn't challenge racial hierarchies, we shouldn't challenge the status quo, that women are supposed to smile, to be friendly, to not make anybody uncomfortable.

So how do white women—myself included—be authentic and get past this need to be liked? We are currently sabotaging the possibility of connection and solidarity because we need to be given smiles and the benefit of the doubt before we can be in a relationship—and that is a lot to ask given the history of whiteness.

Is this the solidarity I seek? Do I want to build relationships premised on the expectation—the requirement—that Black women go out of their way to make me

(Continued)

(Continued)

comfortable, to smile at me, to give me the benefit of the doubt *so that* I will listen to their truth? How twisted that seems when I write it out now—that they would have to earn my openness and willingness by smiling at me so that I can hear their anger and pain.

To this end, there is an exercise we can do to explore how people go into "inauthentic mode" when we are experiencing fear or trepidation. This exercise is called the idealized self-image exercise,[1] and it invites readers to work with the blocks we have to bringing our full selves to relationships. If you—the reader—are not white like me, you will still benefit from answering these questions. The blocks that exist inside me are generally a particular biproduct of my race and gender, but even Black men and Black women—not to mention people of all racial backgrounds and gender identities—have an idealized self-image that shapes their relationships to Black women as a group. The exercise involves four basic questions, each of which should be journaled and discussed with a trusted peer. Here are the four questions:

1. What is the idealized self-image that you try to project to the world, particularly with regard to race and racism? What is the idealized self-image you want Black women to see about you? *"My idealized self-image wants Black women to see me as . . ."*

2. What is underneath this idealized image that you are projecting? What fears, doubts, and insecurities are being covered up by it? What are you afraid Black women will see about you? *"Underneath my idealized self-image, I'm really just afraid . . ."*

3. Who are you in your core self? What is good and true about you? What are things you don't have to prove that are part of who you are that lead you to want to be in a clear, right relationship with Black women? *"In my core self . . ."*

4. How does your idealized self-image get in the way of having authentic relationships with Black women? How does your idealized self-image get in the way of realizing the solidarity you seek? *"My idealized self-image gets in the way of having authentic relationships with Black women because . . ."*

I will share my answers to these questions—as an example—and then I encourage you, as a reader, to do the same.

Question 1: My idealized self-image wants Black women to see me as . . .

My idealized self-image wants Black women to see me as unique among white women, perfect in my anti-racism, worthy of their friendship and respect. My idealized self-image needs Black women to know that I am not like other white people, that I have been working to uncover my racism for the last 20 years.

NOTE: Hopefully it is clear from my answers that the idealized self-image is highly problematic, and that when I am interacting from my idealized self, rather than my authentic self, there is no way to build an authentic connection. My idealized self-image is that part of me that needs to be liked, likeable, and trustworthy in order to be in a relationship with somebody. When I'm hiding behind my idealized self-image, I try to put it first, to wield it as a defense, so that people will be more likely to trust me. I end up feeling threatened by people who don't already know and like me. I feel easily hurt when Black women assert that all white people are oppressive. I want people to see the work I've done and how I've made myself "different." This is the fragile, all-or-nothing part of the idealized self-image. When I'm operating from my idealized self-image, I'm not open to feedback that suggests I am imperfect, oppressive, or hurtful. This is ironic, because that is exactly what I need to hear.

Question 2: Underneath my idealized self-image, I'm really just afraid . . .

Underneath my idealized self-image, I'm really just afraid I'm not actually able to be a good friend to Black women. I'm afraid my bias will show up and hurt them. I'm afraid I will look ignorant. I grew up around only white people. I know I have implicit bias. I know it's harder for me to remember Black names and faces than white names and faces. I'm afraid of being seen as a racist. I'm afraid of actually *being* racist or hurting people. I cover up the fact that there's *still* a lot I don't know about Black cultural references.

NOTE: Underneath my idealized self-image is a lot of fear and uncertainty. Much of it is about my fear that I might not be able to form friendships with Black women, or that I will hurt Black women while trying to be in supportive relationships with them. It's also about the shame and embarrassment of looking ignorant or looking racist.

Question 3: In my core self, I am . . .

In my core self, I know I'm deeply committed to racial and social justice, even though I don't always know how to get there. I know I have deep and loving relationships with people who are racially different from me. I am loving and I am authentic. I love to dance, which isn't necessarily a part of my relationships with Black women, but it's something that is core to who I am. I know some things, and there's a lot I don't know.

NOTE: My core self is a place where I have strength and goodness that I don't have to prove to anyone. It's not all or nothing. It's just part of who I am.

Question 4: My idealized self-image gets in the way of having authentic relationships with Black women because . . .

My idealized self-image gets in the way of having authentic relationships with Black women because I get so busy trying to prove my goodness and my smartness

(Continued)

(Continued)

and my anti-racist credentials that I cannot pick up what they're putting down; my hands are too full of my own baggage. I might meet their questions or even their gaze with defensiveness rather than connection and understanding. When I'm operating from my idealized self-image, I take up all the space trying to prove how likeable and trustworthy I am, so that I cannot hear their words or messages enough to be the person they *might* like, they *could* connect with. Even when—especially when—a Black woman is talking to me from a book or the internet, when she doesn't know me and couldn't know me—my unconscious takes up all the space in my brain and heart trying to defend myself about how I'm not like all the other white people, or how she might like me if she knew me, so much so that I don't hear what she says. I block the very connection I seek.

As an editor of this book—a book that is meant to help teachers hear the truth about the experiences of Black girls in school so that they can better teach and support them, I struggle with how to edit the voices of Black authors. I want to make the voices of Black women heard in a way that doesn't eclipse their voices but also allows readers who are non-Black—and especially who are white—to be able to hear them. But what I'm realizing is that there is no particular way Black women can package their voices to be heard by white readers. Fundamentally, the work of writing a book full of Black women's voices that teachers of all racial backgrounds will be able to hear, is the work of helping readers recognize and dismantle their own blocks to listening. I encourage readers of this book to engage in the idealized self-image exercise. Challenge yourself to quiet your idealized self-image. Listen and read from your core self—in relationships that are live as well as relationships that are on the page—so that you can begin to be the person deserving of the solidarity you seek.

NOTE

1. This exercise was designed by Lorraine Marino for the *White People Confronting Racism* workshop series, based on the work of Eva Pierrakos. It was taught to me by Lorraine Marino and Sarah Hally in the context of facilitating the White People Confronting Racism workshops.

CHAPTER 17

Not in Our Name

Fierce Allyship for White Women

Eleonora Bartoli

As a psychologist specializing in multicultural counseling and trauma, I often attend workshops or conferences about diversity issues. Over the years, I have noticed a pattern in conversations about race, which has become a signpost of sort: If a person of color makes a statement that triggers a white woman, I have come to assume the person of color is correct even before fully understanding what they mean. Recently, I attended a diversity workshop where a woman of color (we'll call her Teresa) was describing an experience of being let down by a white female colleague (we'll call her Karen). Karen didn't speak up when a racist comment was made at a faculty meeting they both attended, where Teresa was the only person of color. Since Karen had been consistently vocal about her antiracist views, Teresa was disappointed by Karen's silence and confronted her after the meeting. Initially, Karen did not welcome Teresa's challenge and was adamant that the racist comment was not "bad enough" to warrant making the rest of the faculty uncomfortable, and that pointing it out would have "inappropriately derailed" the focus of the meeting. Because of their friendship and longstanding collaboration, they were able to process the incident again, and eventually Karen understood Teresa's perspective.

Teresa reported this experience to us in the workshop as an example of white women's tendency not to act on their antiracist beliefs when opportunities arise. Quickly, another white woman (we'll call her Sara) contradicted Teresa, saying that she was generalizing her experience without having proof of a larger trend at play. Both Teresa and other participants of color reported additional similar experiences of feeling let down by white women who had supposedly positioned themselves as antiracist allies. Despite this additional data, Sara was not persuaded and said that they could simply "agree to disagree."

As a white, cisgender woman, I often deeply resonate with the reaction of other white women; but I also experience the dissonance that comes when you know you are hearing the truth even if you can't quite fully grasp it. It took me a long time to realize why, for white women truth can be a tricky business. I was born and raised within a country (Italy), family, and time (the 1970s) that espoused deeply sexist beliefs and practices. Unfortunately, such beliefs and practices are not altogether unlike what we are seeing with the #MeToo movement in the United States. That said, while growing up, I was overtly taught that women are unintelligent and "ditzy" in nature (with rare exceptions, carrying mostly negative connotations), and that much of women's value comes from being beautiful in the eyes of men and from their ability to cater to men's needs. These lessons came in overt and covert ways (e.g., who was praised for doing what), and I experienced them both directly and indirectly (as they were acted upon and by other women). For example, regardless of actual success, what men did or were going to do for a living was always valued and considered central to their identity. In contrast, women saw themselves and were most often talked about in terms of beauty, weight, partnership status, and skillfulness in raising children and otherwise taking care of others. So even when I was not explicitly told that I was less intelligent than men (which I was, whether the proof was that women were absent from history books and public life, or whether it was deemed an "obvious" fact), I heard that message clearly both in what I heard others say *and* by the ways in which my opinions and perspectives (as a woman) were repetitively dismissed or ridiculed.

Because of this early socialization, I came to the conclusion that white men, contrary to popular belief, are not knights in shining armor. They might *choose* not to exploit your body, whether by gazing (catcalling being only its most overt form), requesting a specific behavior (female "politeness" includes quietly listening, acting interested, laughing at demeaning jokes, prioritizing men's wishes or needs, and accepting sexual advances), or being physically violent; but at any one moment the (largely unrestricted) prerogative to exploit is there. For many of us as white women, the experience of direct violence is all too real; for others it's vicarious knowledge, but we all learn the rules of engagement. Outright or direct experience of violence is not necessary for us to come to embody the attitudes and behaviors that are welcomed and rewarded both personally and professionally. In this context, white men's choices not to act on their prerogative to dominate women is implicitly considered an act of benevolence, or something to be merited, rather than an expectation, and is viewed often enough even as normative and acceptable behavior (as highlighted by the #MeToo movement).

As white women, we become pros at seeking and deserving white men's benevolence—by making ourselves smaller, less smart, accommodating, flirtatious, nurturing, and so on. This is most easily and safely done if we are able to adequately distort the truth (of our intelligence, our power, our deservedness, our humanity, and not least of all, our safety[1]), because not doing so is dangerous. No matter what, we are always intuitively navigating men, most of whom in both our personal and professional lives are white.

To be sure, white men are *not* intrinsically evil. The boys-will-just-be-boys adage teeters in that direction; it dehumanizes men and serves no one. We are all acculturated into white supremacist culture, according to which cisgender, able-bodied, white, Christian, and heterosexual males are framed as the superior "race" (Liu, 2017). As such, they have automatic access to rights and resources, without having to fight for or demand them. (This includes feeling the right to keep the bodies of others in inferior positions.) Sometimes white supremacist ideology shows up in small ways (e.g., our opinions, as white women, might be seen as less valid than the opinion of a white man), at other times in big ways (e.g., not being paid a financially viable wage, fearing for one's physical safety). Either way, the underlying narrative is always present. Within it, we all play our roles to remain safe (white women) or live up to our potential (white men). Because of the privileges white women are still afforded by being white, we are not as conscious of the ways in which, within white supremacy, we are still second-class citizens. This is why it's all too easy to enlist us in preserving the status quo; as long as we agree to uphold the system, we can maintain a place of relative safety and access, even if it is at the cost of our own freedom and power.

There is no doubt in my mind that my deep love for antiracism came from the balm of hearing the truth—about the manifestations and impact of racism—spoken out loud and unabashedly, *and* hearing it from a place of relative comfort. (As a white person, I resonate with that truth without directly feeling its pain.) But that truth from people of color also scares me, because to fully hear it is to want to do something about it, and that is a direct challenge to white men's privileged social standing. That truth, then, intrinsically threatens my ability to deserve white men's benevolence. And so I find myself putting up resistance to seeing or believing the experience of people of color. Whether consciously or not, self-preservation takes over.

How can we teach the brilliant and beautiful Black girls in our classrooms if we can't hear the truth of their experiences, if fully seeing them feels like a personal threat? Being effective teachers of Black girls hinges on us reclaiming our power, our truths, and our innate fearlessness, traits we forget we have because of the real pressures to conform to sexist and racist beliefs. We must remember that as white women we have survived centuries of oppression and have continued to thrive and love all the while. This means that we are the lived expression of immeasurable strength and wisdom. To get back in touch with our power, our wisdom, and our ability to choose, we must face our fears, heal our wounds, and boost our resilience. These provide the most essential foundation for our teaching practices; cultivating fearlessness is our way out of white supremacy and into true allyship.

How do we do that? I will propose two exercises that will guide you in identifying old wounds and boosting your resilience to the anxiety that comes from entering spaces and conversations that our bodies have been taught to consider inappropriate or off limits. These exercises may bring up memories and feelings requiring deeper work than resilience building. I invite you to see this as an opportunity; if we had chosen a more impersonal line of work, which did not directly challenge white supremacy, we might never have to get in touch with some of our wounds or require healing. However, the work of empowering individuals directly impacted by white supremacy (Black girls), done in a body that has been asked to be a weapon of white supremacy (white women), can't help but require deeper preparation. Personal work is critical to our effectiveness, and it brings with it much lightness and freedom in the rest of our lives. That said, the following exercises should be engaged with full awareness that they may lead you to identify targets of further emotional work.

The first exercise is part of the standard eye movement desensitization and reprocessing (EMDR) assessment, and is called *floatback* (Shapiro, 2018). In trauma treatment, it is used to connect current symptoms to past traumatic experiences, in order to identify a specific target for EMDR treatment. Here, I will invite you to ask yourself questions to determine how past experiences might impede your ability to fully hear the dreams and needs of the Black girls you teach. To begin, think of a few recent times when you were confronted with information that questioned your multicultural competence and to which you had a strong negative reaction (whether the information came to your attention directly from your own students' verbal or nonverbal behaviors, or indirectly from your students' caregivers, a colleague, a friend, or others). Among the scenarios you have identified, choose the one that is still (i.e., *currently*, *not* when it originally happened) the most distressing for you to recall. Then bring to mind the image that represents the worst moment of that experience, again considering how that moment feels right now. You might replay the memory as a video in your mind and pause it at the scene that currently creates the most distress. Then ask yourself, "What is the negative belief about myself that goes with that image?" That usually starts with "I am . . . " and ends with phrases such as "not safe, not good enough, not in control." Now, as you place your awareness on that image and the negative belief that accompanies it, pay attention to the emotions and associated physical sensations that arise from them. Once you have tapped into these, let your mind scan your past (e.g., you may hover your awareness around specific time periods, such as your 20s, your elementary school years) for images of experiences that carry the same feelings and sensations, letting go, as best you can, of any expectations of what might come up. As you float back through your past, make a list of these past experiences, and notice which ones still carry a considerable amount of sting. These are the experiences you want to find avenues for processing more deeply, whether by journaling about them, sharing them with trusted allies, seeking counseling, or doing something else. What you are looking for are avenues to reprocess and heal memories of times when your body learned that it was not okay in some way, because when these memories are triggered by current experiences, they will fuel a defensive reaction *to the current experience*, unbeknownst to us. This is why facing and reprocessing such memories with the appropriate support not only allows you to gain ease and confidence in your daily life, but will also enable you to enter difficult conversations with greater courage and clarity.

The negative belief about yourself that you identified in the first part of this exercise (e.g., "I am not good enough") is likely to be a core fear, learned and rehearsed through any number of past events. For our second exercise, you might choose that fear as your starting point, or a different one specifically related to teaching Black girls or being multiculturally competent (e.g., "I fear I am seen as racist"; "I fear I am callous"). When such fears are triggered, the danger-detection system located at the center of our brains will automatically initiate a defensive response, which prepares us to "fight, flight, or freeze" by temporarily shutting down our abilities to *both* think clearly and empathize—just as we need our ability to think and empathize the most! Once again, freedom from our fears comes through working through them (not by avoiding them using attack or withdrawal strategies). To work through these fears, we borrow another counseling technique, called *exposure,* here applied to an imagined worst-case scenario (Hoyer & Beesdo-Baum, 2014).

First, choose a fear that activates a fair amount of worry. Then, write a short (one- or two-paragraph) script, in the present tense, that plays out the negative outcome of the worry. You should choose a specific scenario to write about based on your fear, using partly real or fully hypothetical events. The script should describe the story of exactly what happens in this worst-case fear-based scenario, from beginning to end, including the worst possible outcome, and should include details about your thoughts, feelings, and other sensory experiences (as relevant). The task is to read the script (preferably out loud) over and over again for at least 20 minutes a day, focusing on the thoughts and feelings that arise from doing it. The idea is to do the exercise for as long as it takes (usually anywhere from a few days to a few weeks) for the script to no longer activate significant anxiety, or for your perspective on your fear to shift in ways that allow you to remain open, present, and empathetic.

Fully welcoming the beauty and brilliance of Black girls is a radical act in a society founded on white supremacist principles and practices. As white women committed to "the work," we are always searching for answers, as new questions continuously arise because the lives of the Black girls we want to partner with are complex and in constant evolution. This is where conquering our fears matters the most. As long as we have human bodies, we have to contend with the fact that they are beautifully designed to protect us from danger. But fear confuses our perceptions, constrains our actions, and can indeed distract us from our purpose. Fearlessness (understood not as the absence of fear, but the courage to act with full awareness of the limits of our safety) opens the doors to our deep capacity for empathy, love, connection, and wisdom; it brings with it the ability to learn as well as immense creativity. Conquering our fears allows us to question the safety granted by white men's benevolence, and to actually choose how we want to present ourselves and how we want to take action. Fierce resistance and allyship starts as an inside job; the answers we need become available to us when we are fully present and open. Your task is to get on the path of fearlessness; the road is fully open from there.

NOTE

1. It takes a fair amount of propaganda and of overriding one's perceptions for white women to believe that white men's violence towards men of color is perpetrated in service of white women's protection.

Vignette: The Culture Walk

Lauren Calig

Here is the problem. A poster with a Black scientist is no big deal to a white person. We see ourselves every day, everywhere, all the time. "White teachers are teaching white, Black, and brown students about the value of whiteness as they have cornered the identity market within educational settings. Whiteness not only shapes and informs acceptable blackness and brownness in the American educational system, but it also begets whiteness" (Hancock & Warren, p. 6).

Walking into white spaces as white people, rarely do we recognize that there is a "white culture" to adhere to. As a white teacher, I must create a place where my Black students can be celebrated, loved, accepted, cared for, welcomed, and valued for who they are and the culture they bring.

Diversity 101 tells us that this is a good place to begin. Let people be observers in their own spaces; create the space for them to lean in.

"I see myself at my school, and I know that I can do/be anything," I wrote on the board. The faculty: one African American/Black woman, one Indian American woman, and 16 white women all gathered not knowing the plan. They read the words on the board: "The Culture Walk." I explained what this meant: "We will be walking through the school observing what we see both as ourselves and as if we were African American/Black girls. We will reconvene to share observations."

Returning to our space after the walk, I asked, "What did you notice? How do you think our Black girls feel? Do you think they feel valued and seen?"

The room was silent; I spoke. "I noticed very few photographs of students. When I did see photographs, those were the few times that I saw Black girls. I saw very few posters of Black women as professionals. I saw a bulletin board in the hallway that said *Dream, Dare, Do,* and there were five photographs—all of white girls." Hands started to go up. They hadn't realized what it looked like before the walk. They hadn't looked, I mean, looked as a Black girl, a Black parent, a Black person.

"I understand this is important," one person said, "But isn't it important for all of our girls to see themselves?"

This statement, this truth that a white colleague was holding was what I was fighting. "When you are a Black adult, and you make the choice of bringing your Black girl to a predominantly white school, founded by white women and run mostly by white women, you need to know that you can trust the school to understand your beautiful, Black girl. You need to know that she is safe."

Beginning the year with *The Culture Walk* prepped our school for an open dialogue about what our school looked like and should look like for those who are not white. While our schools can be progressive, liberal, and welcoming, we now are faced with the recognition that this may only be the case for white students. Once we recognize this, we must make changes.

CHAPTER 18

White Teachers, Black Girls, and White Fragility

Robin DiAngelo

(adapted from *White Fragility: Why It's So Hard for White People to Talk About Racism*)

North America is a society that is deeply separate and unequal by race, and white people are the beneficiaries of that separation and inequality. As a result, those of us who are white are insulated from racial stress at the same time that we have come to feel entitled to and deserving of our advantage. Given how seldom we experience racial discomfort in a society we dominate, we haven't had to build our racial stamina. Socialized into a deeply internalized sense of superiority that we either are unaware of or can never admit to ourselves, we become highly fragile in conversations about race. We consider a challenge to our racial worldviews as a challenge to our very identities as good, moral people. Thus, we perceive any attempt to connect us to the system of racism as an unsettling and unfair moral offense. The smallest amount of racial stress is intolerable—the mere suggestion that being white has meaning often triggers a range of defensive responses. These include emotions such as anger, fear, and guilt and behaviors such as argumentation, silence, and withdrawal from the stress-inducing situation. These responses work to reinstate white equilibrium as they repel the challenge, return our racial comfort, and maintain our dominance within the racial hierarchy. I conceptualize this process as *white fragility* (DiAngelo, 2018). Though white fragility is triggered by discomfort and anxiety, it is born of superiority and entitlement. white fragility is not weakness per se. In fact, it is a powerful means of white racial control and the protection of white advantage.

The most recent data about U.S. teachers show that despite the fact that the public school population is becoming increasingly racially diverse, more than 80 percent of elementary and secondary school teachers are white, and 77 percent are female (Lindsay et al., 2017). Many students, regardless of their own race, will graduate from high school having been taught only by white teachers, most of them white women. The majority of current teacher education students are white, and they are being instructed by a teacher education profession that is 88 percent white (Picower, 2015). This racial homogeneity is compounded by unabated racial segregation in schools and housing, and it may be hypothesized from these statistics that the majority of white people have not lived near or attended school with people of color; have had few if any teachers, friends, family members, or authority figures of color; and do not interact with people of color in any direct or equal way in their lives or in their teacher preparation programs. Yet as evidenced in many studies, while most teacher education students live their lives in racial segregation, they believe that racism is in the past, that segregation "just happens," that they were taught to see everyone the same and therefore they don't see color, and that being white has no particular meaning (Banks et al., 2010). The consequences of these delusions are profound, for they leave white teachers with no ability to think critically about race, no skills for interrupting racism, and no emotional capacity to withstand the discomfort of being challenged racially. Thus white teachers continue to reproduce racial inequality in their teaching, classroom, and school community interactions, and to reinforce the messages of white supremacy for both white children and children of color.

The overwhelming majority of white people in the teaching field, particularly as public schools are increasingly filled with children of color in a country marked by racial inequality, has profound implications for the role white teachers play in reproducing racial inequality. The following example illustrates several dimensions of white fragility as manifested by two white teachers in an interaction with two Black girls.

In my capacity as a former teacher education faculty member and consultant on issues of racial equity, I was asked to provide one-on-one mentoring for a white male teacher (I will call him Mr. Smith), who had made inappropriate racial comments to a Black female student. When the girl's mother complained, the teacher became defensive, and the conflict escalated. The incident ended up in the newspaper, and potential legal action was discussed. I met with Mr. Smith regularly for several weeks to coach him through this conflict. During one of our sessions, Mr. Smith told me about his colleague, a white female teacher, who recently had two Black students at her desk. She prefaced something she said to one of them with, "Girl, . . ." The student was clearly taken aback and asked, "Did you just call me girl?" The other student said it was OK; the teacher called all her students "girl."

In relaying this story to me, Mr. Smith expressed the anger that he and his colleague felt about having to be "so careful" and not being able to "say anything anymore." They perceived my intervention with Mr. Smith as a form of punishment and felt that because of the incident with him, Black students were now "oversensitive" and complaining about racism where it did not exist. For these teachers, the student's reaction to being called "girl" was an example of this oversensitivity. This is a familiar white narrative, and in this instance, it was rationalized based on the following: (1) The teacher called all her students "girl" and so the comment had nothing to do with race, and (2) one of the students didn't have an issue with the comment, so the student who did was overreacting. The white teachers' response illustrates several dynamics of white fragility:

- The teachers never considered that in not understanding the student's reaction, *they* might be lacking in knowledge.

- The teachers did not demonstrate curiosity about the student's perspective or why she might have taken offense.

- The teachers did not demonstrate concern about the student's feelings.

- The teachers did not know their racial history.

- The teachers did not understand that actions or words that may not be problematic for a white person can have a very different impact when used across race.

- The teachers were not able to separate intentions from impact.

- In spite of the fact that Mr. Smith was so lacking in cross-racial skills and understanding that he was involved in a racial violation with potential legal repercussions, he remained confident that he was right and the student who was Black was wrong.

- His colleague, aware that Mr. Smith was in serious trouble regarding a cross-racial incident, still maintained white solidarity with him by validating their shared perspective and invalidating the Black student's.

- The teachers used the student who excused the comment as proof that the other student was wrong; she was the "correct" student, because she denied any racial implications.

- Mr. Smith used the mythological white narrative of Black oversensitivity to justify his own (power) position and invalidate—even punish—any Black student who questioned that position.

- The teachers used this interaction as an opportunity to increase racial divides rather than as an opportunity to bridge them.

Unfortunately, the teachers' responses are all too familiar. Like most of us who are white, these teachers are culturally incompetent. They had an invaluable opportunity to increase their cultural competency, but they used it to maintain their limited worldview rather than expand it. Further, they used it as an opportunity to increase their racial resentment toward Black students who raise racial issues.

Imagine how the interaction could have gone if the teacher had replied, with openness and sincerity, "It seems I offended you. I'm sorry. I use that term a lot. Can you help me understand why it's problematic?" Seeking understanding would not have necessitated agreement; we don't have to agree with or understand someone's offense in order to support and validate them. However, neither I, nor any colleague I know who is involved in antiracist education, had any difficulty understanding why the student reacted as she did. There are at least two reasons why.

First, while the term "girl" may not be offensive to most young white women, it was historically used to demean and infantilize Black women (as "boy" was used in the same way against Black men) and has a different impact when used by white people to describe Black women. While most white people may not know this history, some humility about that lack of knowledge and the ability to focus on impact rather than intent would have made for a very different and much more constructive interaction.

The second reason is an unconscious pattern white people often exhibit when relating to Black people: taking up stereotypical phrases and mannerisms we associate with Black culture. This is a form of cultural appropriation, sometimes termed *performative blackness* (see Jackson, 2019, and Johnson, 2003). For example, while I would not refer to a white woman I respect as "girl," I might unconsciously slip into calling a Black woman this term or some historically demeaning variation such as "gal" or drawn out exaggeration such as "guuurrlllll." Other examples include suddenly speaking with a southern accent, switching my neck, widening my eyes, and putting my hand on my hip while saying something like, "Oh no you didn't!"; fist bumping and offering elaborate handshakes; and making a point of mentioning an appreciation of music by a Black artist. White people don't typically engage in these behaviors when interacting with white people, and whether we are conscious or not of what we are doing, the impact is deeply objectifying.

White teachers can begin to challenge the racial defensiveness, ignorance and certitude that underlies white fragility in the following ways:

- Be willing to withstand the discomfort associated with an honest appraisal and discussion of our internalized superiority and racial privilege. Recognize discomfort as a necessary part of antiracist work, rather than seeing it as something to be avoided.

- Acknowledge ourselves as racial beings with a particular *and necessarily limited* perspective on race; strive for racial humility.

- Work to understand the racial realities of people of color through authentic interaction rather than through the media or through unequal relationships.

- Take action to address our own racism, the racism of other white people, and the racism embedded in our institutions. Insist that racism get on the table, and work to keep it on the table. Center antiracism work by resisting the pull to include every kind of diversity so that nothing is addressed in depth and racism is sidelined.

- Continually challenge our socialization and investments in racism. Recognize that we are the least likely to be able to determine how well we are doing given our investment in a system that serves us. Build accountability partnerships with other white people working against racism and *paid* accountability partnerships with people of color. (Paid accountability partnerships are with colleagues who have agreed to coach you in your antiracist work, and you pay them for their time.)

- Follow the leadership of Black women and girls.

- Educate yourself on the history of race relations in our country. There are myriad resources available and accessible for anyone with enough interest to look them up.

- Break silence on racism with other white people. Bring racism up. Share your struggles and your insights. Name racism when you see it, and continually work to see it.

- Change the question from "*Have I* been shaped by the forces of racism?" to "*How have I* been shaped by those forces?"

We must remember that Black people's mistrust in our schools *is rational*. Our educational institution has not done well by Black children. Black parents are delivering their precious children into an institution with a deep history of harm towards those children. White teachers must earn racial trust, not demand it.

PART VI

"GIVE LIGHT AND PEOPLE WILL FIND THE WAY."

—Ella Baker

The Understanding section closes with a vignette by a mother, Dr. Sabrina Robins, who has a message for Black children and the adults in their lives. Robins's vignette is followed by the empowering work of doctoral candidate Cierra Kaler-Jones, who lays out strategies for teachers to reimagine their pedagogy by placing affirmation, creativity and a critical consciousness into their classrooms to create spaces of supportive positive identity development and relationships. Kaler-Jones offers educators a step-by-step three-principle pedagogy to enhance the environment for Black girls so they can have a space to embrace all their beauty and brilliance in their journey to wholeness. This chapter is one of many in the book that will highlight the realities faced by Black girls in the educational system but also will give specific guidelines to create the radical change called for in this book. Read, listen, love, and reimagine what can be done. Finally, this first part of our book closes with a poem from an educator, motivational speaker, and Black man, Keith L. Brown. Keith's original poem, "Infinitely Crowned," closes the first third of our book, "Understanding," and helps us begin Part 2: "Respecting."

Vignette: Dear, Dear, Dear!

Sabrina Robins

Dear White teacher,

Cut the emotional abuse and neglect. Your privilege and racism is showing. Stop hurting our kids and build a foundation of love they deserve. Children look up to you and want

(Continued)

(Continued)

to learn. Their learning matters. Make the Black kids feel like they matter. See their magic. Stop LYNCHING it.

Dear White secretary,

Learn how to smile. Stop making Black children feel unwelcomed in their school building. DO BETTER.

Dear Black parents,

BELIEVE that your child is magic, and create a space mentally, emotionally, and physically for them to dream, feel supported, and feel that they matter. Listen to them. Advocate for them.

Dear Beautiful Magical Black girls,

A message from my very daughter I now pass unto you:

"Let no one take away your power. Let no one diminish your individuality as a student. Let no one downplay your successes. Do not let anyone take that away from you. Do not let anyone try to diminish who you are as a student. Do not let them diminish who you are as a person."

*I believe in your **magic**. Black girl magic. Black boy joy. You are exceptional, talented, gifted, and so much more.*

Sincerely,
A Loving Black Mother

CHAPTER 19

A Reimagined Pedagogy of Affirmation and Artistic Practices

Cierra Kaler-Jones

REFLECTIONS FROM A DANCE EDUCATOR

As a dance educator I teach and learn with Black girls through artistic practices. As students finish their school day and head to extracurricular programming, I am usually the first person they share their internal reflections with about their experiences from school. When I greet each student and welcome them into my classroom, I ask, "What did you learn in school today?" Interestingly, they often reply with what they did not learn. Their responses include these:

> "Can we have a girl power day? I know there's a lot of girls doing cool things, but we never learn about them at school."

> "Can we learn about Black history? We only ever learn about Martin Luther King Jr."

> "Can we talk about racism? People at school always want to touch my hair, and it makes me uncomfortable."

> "Can we talk about politics? The world is messed up, and I want to figure out how I can fix it."

These thoughtful questions and statements showcase the depth of Black girls' perspectives of the world. In a society where they are often dehumanized and treated harshly, as exemplified by their discussion of the lack of their experiences being present in classrooms, they are still thinking strategically and intentionally about how they can create solutions and resist oppression (Evans-Winters & Girls for Gender Equity, 2017). What does a reimagined pedagogy that affirms and amplifies Black girls' strengths and talents look like?

The answer to the question, coupled with the answers to my students' questions, guides the following pedagogical principles. These pedagogical principles include (1) a pedagogy of love, belonging, and acceptance; (2) a pedagogy of creativity and joy; and (3) a pedagogy of critical consciousness. The following chapter describes each principal and lists strategies to guide how teachers can incorporate these pedagogies in ways that are meaningful and effective.

A PEDAGOGY OF LOVE, BELONGING, AND ACCEPTANCE

In 2017, sisters Mya and Deanna Cook were told if they did not get rid of their braids, they would be removed from cocurricular activities, banned from prom, and given detention. In 2018, Faith Fennidy, an 11-year old Black girl, was sent home, in tears, from her Louisiana Catholic school because administrators deemed her braids did not adhere to school policy. These are just a few examples of how Black girls are punished for showing up authentically and made to feel unwelcome in school.

A 2017 report produced by the Georgetown Law Center on Poverty and Inequality showed that, in general, adults see Black girls as less innocent and more adult-like than their white peers, starting at age 5 and peaking from ages 10 to 14 (Epstein et al., 2017). The authors coined this phenomenon as the *adultification* of Black girls. This adultification leads to increased punishment and policing of Black girls. When Black girls are not accepted for how they show up in school spaces, they can internalize the deficit message that they are inferior. By treating them as more adult-like than their white counterparts, adultification also denies them a sense of childhood (Epstein et al., 2017).

Morris (2007) observed that although Black girls compete for attention and affirmation from their teachers, educators focus less on the academic progress of Black girl students and more on their appearance and how they behave. To counteract the impact of this scrutiny, students are constrained to create space—even for a few moments each day—where they know they are cared for and loved "for who they are, what they are, and what they have to contribute," including their dress and behavior (Robinson & Lewis, 2017, p. 128). The acceptance of how they show up at school is especially important for Black girls, who are often criticized for not adhering to—and not being able to meet—standards of white femininity.

Schools can be sites of oppression for Black girls, which is evidenced through school curriculum, pedagogical practices, and policies that police their bodies and behaviors and suppress their culture (Paris & Alim, 2014; Hines-Datiri & Carter

Andrews, 2017). Bettina Love (2019) said that when Black and Brown students are denied the opportunity to fully express themselves in school, they are being "spirit murdered." It is because of the policing and suppressing of Black girls' identities that culturally responsive and affirming education should be centered in practice, especially for Black girls. Culturally responsive pedagogy asserts that cultural background, the assets and strengths of the learner, and deep relationships should be at the core of teaching (Ladson-Billings, 1995). Building relationships with Black girls by learning more about their lives outside of school and creating classrooms that are healing centered can help Black girls develop a positive sense of identity and feel loved.

Strategies for Building a Pedagogy of Love, Belonging, and Acceptance

- Greet each student at least once a day. Give them an option of greeting (e.g., a hug, a fist bump, a high five, a wave). Build time in the day, such as a ritual or morning circle, where students have the opportunity to share about their lives and their thoughts.

- Transform your physical space into positive, affirming learning areas. Include affirmations and uplifting quotations they can understand in words that are relevant to them.

- Respond to Black girls using positive reinforcement. Be cautious about how you correct them when they answer incorrectly in class. Assure them that mistakes are part of life. Using a Black feminist pedagogy, move away from the racist, sexist, elitist forms of evaluation, such as standardized tests and unsophisticated rubrics, and provide students with grades based on their concepts and ideas, not just their grammar (Omolade, 1987).

- Provide compliments in your daily interactions with Black girls that focus not only on their outward appearance, but home in on their brilliance and talents. Do not punish them for their ways of expressing themselves, including dress and hair.

A PEDAGOGY OF CREATIVITY AND JOY

In 2019, four Black girls were strip-searched for drugs by school officials in Binghamton, New York, because they were perceived as being hyper and giddy. They were punished and violated for expressing childhood joy and playing. Play is essential to development, because it helps with physical, social, and emotional well-being.

In my dance classroom, I try to be aware of when students need a break. They will usually start to fidget, move around, or look out the window. A strategy I use is what I call "five seconds of silly." In five seconds of silly, I announce that for five seconds, they can play, be as silly as they want, and move their bodies. At the end of the five seconds, we clap our hands together, breathe in, and pull in our energy to focus. Joy should not be a reward for good behavior, but rather an essential part of everyday practice.

A large part of play for Black girls involves dancing, making music, and moving their bodies. Historically, understandings of play have used white girls as the standard. Black feminist theory positions Black women as knowers and as experts of their own experiences, so in order for educators to connect with them, they must learn about the ways Black girls express themselves and their intelligence (Collins, 1990). In her definition of *womanism*, Alice Walker (1983) stated, a womanist "loves music. Loves dance." The idea of dance being a part of the definition of womanism, juxtaposed with attempts to control Black women's bodies, denotes a symbolic representation of the freedom and appreciation of movement and music as being an integral piece of how Black girls express themselves in classrooms.

Educators must tap into students' voices while recognizing that sometimes a student's best way of expressing themselves is not how society regards intelligence (i.e., reading, writing, repeating facts), but rather through artistic practices that allow for processing (i.e., dance, song, social media). Further, engaging models of teaching that make Black and Brown girls active participants in the learning process gives "girls a chance to center their experiences, tell stories, dance, sing, write, meditate, and play their knowledge into a curriculum that recognizes and values these expressions as commensurate with the other 'data' they will learn in school" (Morris, 2019, p. 127).

Strategies for Building a Pedagogy of Creativity and Joy

- Infuse choice into your lessons. Ask students what they might be interested in learning about a topic, and support them as they deeply explore their questions or wonderings. For example, could they interview people about the subject or observe a phenomenon? Could they test their hypothesis with an experiment and analyze the data they collect? They are journalists, researchers, investigators, and scientists.

- Incorporate assessments that give students opportunities to show their understanding of content in diverse and creative formats. For example, instead of a test, allow students to demonstrate knowledge by creating a song or rap or by doing a performance or skit. As another example, students can show content knowledge through blogging or creating graphics that exhibit creative, technological skills.

- Give students space to dream during the day. Provide uninterrupted time to think, doodle, or ponder without it being tied to an assignment or assessment.

- Decorate your classroom or hallway with students' work, and let them share their work with peers and the school community.

- Give students an inventory to fill out that shows what type of learner they are (i.e., visual, aural, or kinesthetic). Teach using a combination of videos, hands-on activities, visual aids, student participation, and lecture-based lessons to cater to all types of learners. Black girls' identities are multiple and complex, so the approach to literacy and meaning-making should be also (Muhammad & Womack, 2015).

A PEDAGOGY OF CRITICAL CONSCIOUSNESS

As evidenced by the student questions at the beginning of this chapter, many Black girls want to learn about the world around them. They not only want to engage in conversation about current events, but they want to use their talents to create change. Inspiring Black girls to build a critical consciousness moves learning to an emancipatory and liberatory process. It is about teaching Black girls history and discussing current events in a way that is truthful and authentic. For example, in brief lessons on the civil rights movement, curricula often highlight Rosa Parks as the sole figure of the bus boycotts; however, history shunned other Black girls, such as Claudette Colvin, who boycotted the bus before Rosa Parks. She was not highlighted like Rosa Parks in history because of intersections—her dark skin, her youth, and her pregnancy.

Encouraging a critical consciousness in Black girls is a form of love, because it is a form of truth telling. Empowering curriculum work can be and should be designed to liberate Black girls by welcoming storytelling, creativity, decision-making processing, and critical thinking about personal, school, and general social realities (Nunn, 2018). Encouraging a critical consciousness means allowing Black girls to interrogate, analyze, and come up with their own answers, rather than giving them answers. A pedagogy of critical consciousness recognizes Black girls not only as critical consumers of knowledge but as producers of knowledge.

Strategies for Building A Pedagogy of Critical Consciousness

- Discuss current events in your classroom. Bring in news articles from various sources, so students get multiple perspectives on issues, and encourage students to bring in news stories they are interested in, so they can relate to what they are learning in class. Have brave conversations with students about social justice issues.

(Continued)

(Continued)

- When teaching about Black history, bring in unique examples that highlight Black girls' and women's contributions. Let students conduct their own research about potential "hidden figures" in movements or historical events you are studying. Note that Black herstory/history month should not be relegated to one month; it should be all 12 months, 365 days a year.]

- In your curriculum, use examples that are not only from the United States. Share global perspectives and examples in classroom conversations, and discuss other countries and continents to disrupt the Eurocentric curriculum. Talk about countries from an asset-based perspective, rather than using deficit-based language using words such as *poor* or *developing*.

- Encourage and incite classroom debate and dialogue to deepen critical thinking skills. Create space for students to voice their opinions in constructive ways. Provide opportunities for students to reflect on their values and beliefs in a variety of formats. For example, have them do an individual reflection, a pair and share, a small group discussion, or a large group conversation.

In conclusion, teachers can use this chapter to critically reflect about their own practices to help embrace a pedagogy that affirms and amplifies Black girls' strengths and talents. Together, the three pedagogies: a pedagogy of love, belonging, and acceptance, a pedagogy of creativity and joy, and a pedagogy of critical consciousness, create a classroom environment where Black girls are able to express themselves without fear of ridicule or retaliation. Despite negative stereotypes about Black girls that rob them of the protections of childhood joy, teachers can play an integral role in the positive development of Black Girls.

Vignette: Infinitely Crowned: For Black Girls Everywhere

Keith L. Brown

From the beginning of time, you created paths for others to **follow**—
The world created negative images of you that brought great **sorrow**—
These images were created to make you feel inferior and **bound**—
But the world did not realize you were royalty and **Infinitely Crowned!!!**

Named Sheba, Nandi, Nefertiti, Amina, Makeda and so many **more**—
Black Girls your Brilliance was created on the African **Shores**—
Black Girls you all have the potential to be positively World **Renowned**—
For you come from a royal ancestry and you are **Infinitely Crowned.**

Yes—"Black Girls Rock," and they excel in many **Roles**—
They are fierce and fearless and beloved and **Bold**—
Their excellence is on display in every nation, state, city and **town**—
So walk with your backs straight and heads up, for you are **Infinitely Crowned.**

Don't you fall prey—to a society that defines beauty as the mannequin on **display**—
You're not likely to see images of yourself in those stores, so don't you **dismay**—
Understand you were beautifully and wonderfully made at **birth**—
And the Mannequin is on display but has no value or **worth**—
So don't you dare hold your heads **down**—
And never forget your worth is priceless, for you are **Infinitely Crowned.**

Black Girls you come in all shapes, sizes, shades and **tones**—
You are outstanding originals and cannot be **cloned**—
When you leave the scene, your light has shone and been **shown**—

Show the world your smile—don't allow others to make you **frown**—
For they will never understand you are **Infinitely Crowned.**

From the shores of Africa—you now live in many global **communities**—
Wherever you are—keep soaring towards your **destiny**—
You will proudly Graduate in your Caps and **Gowns**—
Walk across many stages of life while being **Infinitely Crowned.**

Each day you awaken, look in the mirror and say:

I Love Myself!
I Believe in Myself!
I'm Proud of Myself!
I'm a Genius!
For you see, there's a GENE IN US—and that gene is called greatness!!!
That gene is more important than any jeans you will **wear!**
That gene will be more important than how you style your **hair!**
That gene will be more important than your yearly **wage!**
That gene will be more important than the number of "likes" and followers on
your **page!**
That gene will guide your every **decision!**
That gene will cause you to support your Black sisters instead of "hating" on each
other and causing **division!**
That gene will give you purpose and **vision**—

When you open your mouth—out will come a mighty **sound**—
Promising Princesses—Never forget you are **Infinitely Crowned!!!!**

RESPECTING

PART I

"I'LL BE BOSSY AND DAMN PROUD."

—Rosa Clemente

If there was one word we could choose to describe why feminism does not apply in the same way to Black women and white women, it would be intersectionality. *The word emerges throughout this book, because it is central to the work of teaching Black girls. "In the early 20th century, Anna Julia Cooper (1892) wrote about the specific lived experiences of Black women. She and Wells-Barnett were forerunners of contemporary intersectionality. Others—such as Sojourner Truth (1851) and Mary McLeod Bethune—likewise brought attention to the importance of thinking about race and gender simultaneously over 100 years ago" (McKenzie & Richards, 2019, p. 2). Intersectionality is the term that Dr. Kimberlé Crenshaw coined to describe how Black women experience racism and sexism in ways that are distinct from those of Black men and white women.*

Yes, Black women experience sexism; their experience of sexism is wholly different from that of white women, because they do not experience the privilege and protection that whiteness brings. In the same way, feminism is meant to serve all women, but it has historically served white women as the unspoken default in a way that invisibilized, erased, and further marginalized Black women. The chapters and vignettes in this section shed light on the long-term impacts of the suffrage movement for those who identify as Black, beginning with an intersectional herstory by Dr. Shemariah J. Arki in an attempt to rewrite the narrative of American feminism. the chapter is followed by a vignette by one of her undergraduate students, Toyin Olabode, who shares what it took for her to become a proud (Pan)African feminist.

CHAPTER 20

Who Are Black Girls?

An Intersectional Herstory of Feminism

Shemariah J. Arki

This chapter provides a chronological narrative, a people's herstory, if you will, of American feminist praxis by highlighting feminist iterations of Black womxn[1] from 1831 to 2020. The very nature of what it meant to identify as a Black womxn, an enslaved African female in the colonial United States, creates agency and fuels resistance in the persons identified as such. The facts that Black womxn endured deplorable living conditions, broken families, brutal beatings, breeding and rape, suggest a perpetual sense of agency (Collins, 1990). Enslaved African womxn worked sunup to sundown in service to a family—a society that has never proclaimed their humanity (Collins, 1990).

The narratives of the enslaved African womxn, their personal experiences, and their oral histories are the foundational building blocks of Black feminist thought (BFT), the type of feminism described by Guy-Sheftall (1995c). Through these stories, Black womxn of today learn how the intersections of race, class, gender identity/expression, and sexuality affect one's agency, and subsequently, how they must negotiate their own identities. Maria Miller Stewart was the first American woman, therefore the first Black woman, to address a mixed-race crowd (Guy-Sheftall, 1995b). Her speech was delivered at Boston's Franklin Hall before the New England Anti-Slavery Society, preceding the Grimke sisters' well known white antislavery activist speeches by at least five years (Guy-Sheftall, 1995b).

---

[1]The use of *womxn* is inclusive of those who identify as cisgender, gender queer, gender-nonconforming, transgender, and/or femme—people who may use she/her pronouns. *Womxn* is often used by those who identify as part of the intersectional feminist movement and written with the *x* to be intentionally subversive to the Eurocentric and patriarchal dominant narrative.

Steeped in a clear feminist iteration, as early as 1831, Stewart speaks directly to her sisters, who hold a clear place in her heart:

> O, ye, daughters of Africa, awake! Awake! Arise! No longer sleep nor slumber, but distinguish yourselves . . . o, ye, daughters of Africa, what have ye done to immortalize your name beyond the grave? What examples have you set before the rising generation. (Stewart, 1831/1995, p. 27)

Submerged in the sociopolitical context of abolition and religious morality, "Stewart stands at the beginning of an unbroken chain of [B]lack women activists whose commitment to the liberation of Blacks and women defines their life's work" (Guy-Sheftall, 1995b, p. 25).

Frequently, the history of American feminism often begins with stories of Seneca Falls, the first convention that centered womxn's rights. Stories from the late 1800s and early 1900s and stories of Elizabeth Cady Stanton and Susan B. Anthony. Stories that focused on the promotion of equal work contracts, marriage, parenting, and property rights for women. This interpretation of feminism, shaped primarily by the hetero-patriarchal system of the time, is incomplete at best, and at worst, represents first-wave feminism as perpetuating whiteness while neglecting the intersections of identity (Guy-Sheftall, 1995c).

The organizing women at Seneca Falls deliberately and intentionally left Black womxn and their roles in American society out of the movement, and nothing of the time constrained them or held them accountable (Guy-Sheftall, 1995c). Black women were, and still are, invisible to many self-identified, first- and second-wave feminists led by white women, including and perpetuating Eurocentered classroom management and teacher pedagogy (Love, 2019; Morris, 2016). Black women have been on the front lines of both the suffrage and abolition movements since their inception, living, breathing and writing feminism long before the term was coined (Collins, 1990; Guy-Sheftall, 1995c). The definition of feminism that resonates most with those who denounce traditional feminism, or white feminism, is given to us by Beverly Guy-Sheftall, Black feminist scholar, writer, editor, and the Anna Julia Cooper Professor of Women's Studies and English at Spelman College (Guy-Sheftall, 1995c). The definition states:

> I use the term "feminist" to capture the emancipatory vision and acts of resistance among a diverse group of African American women who attempt in their writings to articulate their understandings of the complex nature of [B]lack womanhood, the interlocking nature of the oppressions [B]lack women suffer, and the necessity of sustained struggle in their quest for self-definition, the liberation of [B]lack people, and gender equality. (Guy-Sheftall, 1995c, pp. xiv)

Guy-Sheftall goes on to include in the definition the solidarity many Black women share with other oppressed identities as a result of capitalism, imperialism, and colonization, citing bell hooks in the definition addendum, "theorizing on the part of [B]lack women, including herself, coming from our 'lived experiences' of critical thinking, reflection and analysis" (Guy-Sheftall, 1995c, xiv). In 1851, Black and white women heard the lived reality of Sojourner Truth in her famous "Ain't I a Woman" speech as she tactfully displayed the interlocking oppressions of racism and sexism. While the accuracy of the recitation of Truth's words is still in debate today, her role in contemporary feminism remains clear, serving as "the link for [B]lack women with their activist foremothers" (Guy-Sheftall, 1995c, p. 35). Throughout the antebellum period in America, many Black women used their service in the strength of their vision to become more powerful and less afraid (Lorde, 1984).

Collectively, these courageous and trailblazing educators, activists, and organizers have laid the foundation and opened the way for many Black womxn scholars to contribute to the dominant narrative of American education, classroom management, teaching, learning, and pedagogy. Engaging in a clear focus on what is now named reproductive justice, Margaret Garner escaped her Kentucky plantation while pregnant in 1856. Captured in Cincinnati, Ohio, Garner beheaded her newborn daughter rather than send her back to the plantation (Guy-Sheftall, 1995c; Weisenburger, 1998). Also included in this era, known as first-wave feminism, are several Black womxn—Anna Julia Cooper, Mary Church Terrell, Ida B. Wells-Barnett—who were active participants in liberation, identifying classrooms, conferences, and other spaces of teaching and learning as their preferred arenas.

As the sociopolitical landscape changed, Black womxn remained at the forefront of manifesting change in their own communities. As news of freedom from slavery traveled through the American colonies, the work of two Black womxn in particular helped to transition the movement from center to margin. The work of Amy Jacques Garvey, wife of Pan-Africanist Marcus Garvey, demonstrates this transition with a call for others to participate in a "race first" movement. Understanding her identity as a nationalist, Garvey's feminist iterations include a transnational approach to liberation through a display of her intellectual prowess (Taylor, 1995). The creative fiction and nonfiction writings by Lorraine Hansberry can also be included in this transition of American feminisms (Guy-Sheftall, 1995c). Hansberry was well known for her artistic work, and her play, *A Raisin In The Sun,* was one of the first of its kind to present Black womxn as complex and intersectional, foreshadowing the framework of intersectionality. In her unfinished essay, "Simone de Beauvoir and The Second Sex: An American Commentary," Hansberry (1957) identifies many contemporary feminist issues and delineates why they are different for Black womxn, including the concepts of professional attire, style, and hair styles/head wrapping—many of the issues today's intersectional feminists identify collectively as respectability politics. Garvey, Hansberry, and countless other women of their time took substantial risks in their role as precursors in building the contemporary feminist movement (Guy-Sheftall, 1995c).

BUILDING A CONTEMPORARY FEMINIST MOVEMENT

Guy-Sheftall (1995a) refers to the 1960s and 1970s as the angry decades of civil rights and women's liberation. Rightfully so, the writings of women such as Angela Davis, The Combahee River Collective, bell hooks, and Audre Lorde are well documented and often identified as the foundational theorists of contemporary Black feminist thought. The lived experience of the women, coupled with the frustrations of the civil rights movement, the emergence of the Black Power movement, and other, more-radical organizing overall, contributed to the materialization of a new role for Black womxn in the face of their dynamic identity development (Guy-Sheftall, 1995a). The vision of creating a new world free from oppression provides the centripetal force and momentum needed for these young women activists and their new function on the front lines of the fight for justice.

WE ARE BLACK FIRST

The Black Power movement resonates with many Black womxn in the United States as a celebration of urban Blackness (Christian, 2014; Ransby, 2014). Many previous movements (civil rights, abolition) were outwardly led by men, and therefore, laden with a reflexive patriarchal structure of American society (Ransby, 2014). The womxn of the Black Power movement, as a result of the movement convergence, emerged as thought leaders, orators, and radical revolutionaries (Guy-Sheftall, 1995a; Ransby 2014). These women proudly denounced the respectability politics of the nonviolent civil rights movement by wearing their hair in natural styles, trading their Sunday best for black leather and dashikis, and, most important, using a loud and proud expression of energy and collective Black pride also known as the Assata Chant: "We have a duty to fight for our freedom. We have a duty to win. We must love and support one another. We have nothing to lose but our chains" (Chesimard, 1973, p. 18).

As the Black Power movement took shape, Black womxn became major players on all sides. All societal roles Black womxn possessed (educator, activist, organizer, etc.) were in conjunction with their primary community role of mother and/or othermother—womxn who share in child rearing and other family responsibilities—independent of their biological connection to the family structure (Arki, 2016; Collins, 1990, 1994). This instance of identity convergence and the current sociopolitical context helped to shape the Black Power movement by contributing to the manifestation of the overall message of the Black Panther Party for Self Defense, and to the extension of Black Power that sought to build economic and political power for all oppressed people in the United States and beyond. While nowhere near perfect in its interrogation of white privilege, white supremacy, and whiteness, the Black Power movement helped to curate the space of women activists and intellectuals and bring their voices to the front of the movement as radical revolutionaries, thought leaders, and freedom fighters (Ransby, 2014).

COMBAHEE RIVER COLLECTIVE STATEMENT

The fort located on the Combahee River in South Carolina was the site of Harriet Tubman's victorious rebellion that freed over 750 slaves in 1863 (Guy-Sheftall, 1995d). Expounding on the foundations of African critical theory, Rabaka (2009) posits there is a link between names and the power one possesses; Black feminist author Barbara Smith knew there was a need for a powerful name of this coalition of Black women who would help to usher in a new Black feminist politic (Guy-Sheftall, 1995d). Dissatisfied with the direction of the National Black Feminist Organization, Smith, along with her colleagues Demita Frazier and Beverly Smith, came together to curate a key document that situates the need for an antioppressive identity development framework that would be adapted by radical educators, political organizers, and social theorists (The Combahee River Collective, 1995).

The Combahee River Collective Statement, often referred to as a manifesto of the contemporary Black feminist movement, centers four major topics: (1) the genesis of contemporary black feminisms; (2) what we believe, that is, the specific province of our politics; (3) problems in organizing Black feminists, including a brief history of our collective; and (4) Black feminist issues and practice (The Combahee River Collective, 1995, p. 232). Members of the collective articulate the juxtaposition of identities and roles of Black womxn in the fight for justice, independent of their official affiliation with any organization. It was the movement, the process of building community through life-sharing experiences, that changed their lives and constrained each of them to work towards ending oppression (The Combahee River Collective, 1995). By declaring self-care a revolutionary act, the collective boldly expressed their solidarity with Black men and openly confessed the need for consistent self-work to be done to avoid the pitfalls of practicing feminism, as outlined in the work of Michelle Wallace (1982) in *A Black Feminist's Search for Sisterhood*. By evoking the witnessing and testifying liberation practice as described by many of the writers of the times, the collective recognized the value of multiple modalities to interrupt oppression (Collins, 1990, 1994; Davis, 1995; Ross, 2003; The Combahee River Collective, 1995). Whether through politics, writing, educating, or organizing, the collective remained dedicated and "ready for the lifetime of work and struggle before us" (The Combahee River Collective, 1995, p. 239). This is the legacy of Black girls in the classroom.

INTERSECTIONALITY

The concept of intersectionality is used to refer to the way in which a person's numerous identities (be they cultural, social, or biological) can often overlap and contribute to the social injustices perpetrated against them. This term was first coined by legal scholar Kimberlé Crenshaw during the late 1980s in an effort to explain the discriminatory hiring practices most Black womxn in the workplace encounter. Crenshaw argued that at the intersection of these two identities, Black and female, were individual problems such as racism and sexism—thus creating layers of social inequality (Crenshaw, 1995).

Intersectionality not only confronts the idea of power dynamics in social structures, but it also focuses on how they affect the lives of others. In her TedTalk, The Urgency of Intersectionality, Crenshaw (2016) exemplifies this framework through the case of Emma DeGraffenreid. Emma filed a lawsuit against a company for race and gender discrimination. However, the case was thrown out by the judge due to the fact that the employer indeed hired Black people and women. What was not understood, however, was that Emma was specifically saying that she was discriminated against for being a Black woman. The only Black people who were hired were men, and the only women who were hired were white. This is where we see how important it is to recognize the intersections of identities. The court was only able to acknowledge either gender discrimination or race discrimination, but not both, even though acknowledging that both are at play was the only way to fully understand Emma's claim (Crenshaw, 2016).

Intersectionality forces Black women to wrestle with their identity and its development; it validates lived experience as empirical evidence and affirms that Black women are constantly engaged in this as a double hermeneutic process—interpreting the information that has already been interpreted for them (by media, families, schools, etc.). Based on the multitude of intersecting social identifiers that often leave them at a deficit, Black feminists must work incessantly towards creating a legacy as a survival tactic in their daily interactions.

WHY YOUR FEMINISM MUST BE INTERSECTIONAL

Classrooms today represent multiculturalism in its truest form, including identities that stretch far beyond race and ethnicity. This multitude of identities leads to endless othering (Carlton Parsons, 2008; Fennel & Arnot, 2008). Othering is a concept that has deep roots in American history and is perpetrated daily by those who hold privileged roles (Arki, 2016, 2018). In schools, adults with privileged identities generally hold those roles, but there are also students who are perceived to have power based on their social status or preferred social identifiers. Research has shown that being an other, particularly in education, can be used to help one chart their own educational path and subsequently, a profession (Carlton Parsons, 2008). Despite the systemic, covert attempts to routinely marginalize othered groups from educational success, Black girls have managed to turn negative experiences in the margins into theories, pedagogies, and frameworks that have changed how education is viewed from the perspective of the other, including Kimberlé Crenshaw (2016).

This conscious thought, and the space that has been created as a result, allows one's experiences as the other to be considered empirical data. In her widely cited and revered work, bell hooks (1994) speaks on her othered experiences and contextualizes them on a systemic level by differentiating schooling from education, through sharing her story and citing life, relationships, work, and research that births a sweet spot. This is where hooks (1994) begins to operate in her gift, where her identities merge to form a new, authentic, and even more beautiful bell than before.

CONCLUSION

For Black womxn, a true feminist praxis must be intersectional. By understanding the herstory and experiences of Black girls in the classroom, separate from their role as student or teacher, white women teachers can begin to use their own intersections of identity to curate learning environments that are connected, respected, and valued. By placing their feminist identity at an intersection with race, class, and gender, white teachers are able to do their own introspection about how they actually practice feminism. As a noun, it's an identity. For Black girls and women, feminism must be a verb. For us, Black girls and women, intersectional feminism is a practice.

Crossing Ebenezer Creek, **by Tonya Bolden**

Grade Level 7–12

Historical Fiction

Book Review by Marguerite W. Penick

Mariah and her brother have been liberated from slavery by Lincoln's Emancipation Proclamation and Sherman's Union Army. With no idea of where to go with their new "freedom," they join hundreds of "freed" enslaved Africans who view the Union as their saviors. Throughout *Crossing Ebenezer Creek,* Mariah displays her resilience for survival time and time again, not only caring for those she considers family but consistently fighting for all those in the caravan who have been enslaved and are now free and struggling for freedom. The characters in *Crossing Ebenezer Creek* are scarred by mistreatment and violence yet are full of hope for a future free from it.

Bolden masterfully weaves a little-known horrific historical massacre into the story to show that emancipation did not guarantee freedom from prejudice, and that it may not be wise to trust those who appear to believe in freedom, who may not be as supportive as they appear. Although the characters in this book are fictional, the journey to Ebenezer Creek and the tragedy that happened there is a historical fact. The inclusion of this text into classroom curriculum is critical for students to be able to question what is presented to them as real, and what myths are taught to justify the perpetuation of dominance and superiority.

Vignette: This is What A (Pan)African Feminist Looks Like

Toyin Olabode

I believe that I have always been a feminist. Using the definition that Chimamanda Ngozi Adichie gave in her TedTalk, "We Should All Be Feminists," as a base, a feminist is simply a person who believes in the social, political, and economic equality of the sexes. However, I never consciously identified as a feminist until a couple of years ago. I first learned what a feminist was in 2015. I was introduced to the term in my 10th-grade humanities class using the same TedTalk. A little over a year later came the 2016 election cycle. During that time, many white feminists introduced the "pussyhat," and it took the media by storm. It became a huge buzz-word, especially in my hometown, but personally, I wasn't really into it. I brought this up in my one of my classes, and a classmate, who was white, basically told me that since this whole pussyhat thing was a feminist movement, and I didn't quite agree with it, I was not a feminist.

I now know that that is not true but at the time, I actually believed her, and it tore me up. It was not until I read up on blogs and articles written by other Black women and people of color that I realized that (1) I was not the only one who felt this way, and (2) there was and still is a stark difference between what white feminism is and what Black feminism is. In high school classes, we learn about the civil rights movement and the women's rights/suffrage movement, but the reality is, Black women are largely left out and forgotten in regard to their impact on these movements.

(Continued)

(Continued)

My initial thought as I registered for a (Pan)African Feminisms class was, "Well, I am Nigerian and a feminist, so, why not take it?" Both of these identities contribute to a big part of who I am as a person, so of course, I would love to learn more about each one and how they work together. As I continued to think about it, however, I realized that there might be more to it. For all of my grade school years, K–12, I attended predominantly Black public schools, where I was surrounded by classmates and teachers who looked like me. I was very comfortable in that environment and did not feel as if I had some type of moral responsibility to advocate for hypervisibility for Black women; I already felt seen. That being said, coming to college at a predominantly white institution (PWI) was a huge culture shock. I mentally prepared myself for it being a little different than what I am used to, but I did not think it would be quite like it was.

I was not used to seeing white people in my classes, much less having to interact with them. It was funny, in a way, when I had to do a group project with four white males, and they somewhat shunned me and my ideas when we worked together. Every time we met up to work on the project, I would always walk away wondering if the reason that they were underestimating me was because I was Black or because I was a woman. I did not initially think that it may have been both. It was tough to adjust, and still is, but just being here and having this experience makes me realize that although I felt safe and seen in my all Black schools back home, I now understand that not every space is like that.

This is one reason I chose to take (Pan)African Feminisms. A rap line from one of my favorite shows, *The Get Down,* says, "When you know better, you do better; Each one, teach one, come together." I feel inclined to know more so that I can do better for myself and for other Black women on this campus. Not only do I enjoy discussing basically anything related to Black women, but I know that I have so much more to learn! I want to be able to learn the history behind (Pan)African feminism so that I will be able to articulate my thoughts on certain subjects and share knowledge with other people who may not know as much.

The following chapters and vignettes offer readers the opportunity to sit with the authors in the intersections of identity and to feel—through the lived experiences—how Black girl identity is shaped by a multitude of sociopolitical factors: centering Blackness and girlhood. Mary Oling-Sisay writes about Black girls who are first- or second-generation immigrants from Africa, and how their immigrant identities impact their experiences of both schooling and Blackness. Many teachers who may be afraid to use the word Black are often unaware that Black serves as an inclusive term, which includes all folx of

African descent. This includes those who identify as Caribbean and/or West Indian, an ethnic group often identified in its relationship to Black people in the United States, whose descendants are also the ones who survived the transatlantic slave trade.

The subsequent vignette by Dr. Sandra (Chap) Chapman describes Chap's experience as someone who identifies as Afrolatina and queer, helping readers appreciate how young people in the classroom are constantly negotiating and navigating their own identities. They are often unclear themselves as to what it means to be Black, and are seeking ways to process their experiences of race and sexuality, among other identities, in school. Chap's vignette is followed by Dr. Graciela Slesaransky-Poe's work on creating trans-affirming classrooms and schools for Black trans girls and gender-nonconforming youth. Both of these pieces remind readers that trans-affirming schools are not just for White youth, and that antiracism and Black liberation is not just for cisgender and heteronormative Black students.

CHAPTER 21

Navigating Multiple Identities

The Black Immigrant Girl Experience

Mary Oling-Sisay

> *Wealth, if you use it, comes to an end; learning, if you use it, increases.*
>
> —Swahili proverb

I watched with amazement during tutoring sessions as Akumo "magically" straddled cultures and accents. In one minute, she would speak to the white teachers in a "white" English accent, to her parents slowly with an "African" accent, and to her African American peers in their respective "accents," which were often varied.

This brief observation comes from my work in a New York City public school, where I met Akumo, whose family were new immigrants from an African country. Akumo was an expert in code-switching. She would alternate speech registers depending on who she was engaging with. This hybrid identity is attributed to Black immigrants' complex navigation of both familial and American/peer cultural norms (Cone et al., 2014; Knight & Watson, 2014; Njue & Retish, 2010). This chapter will address themes that are specific to the children of African immigrants, some of which—because of brilliant code-switching like Akumo's—are barely visible to U.S. teachers.

BLACK IMMIGRANT DIVERSITY

The population of foreign-born Black Americans and children born to immigrant parents is diverse and continues to grow (Anderson, 2015). According to Anderson (2015), compared to other Americans, Black immigrants are more likely than U.S.-born Blacks to have a college degree and to be married. Many immigrants from Africa came to the United States through the diversity visa program, which required applicants to have at minimum a high school diploma. They tend to hold U.S. citizenship and be proficient in English. According to the U.S. Census Bureau, by 2060, 17 percent of Black Americans will be immigrants (Johnson, 2020; Vespa et al., 2018), and half of Black immigrants originate from the Caribbean (Johnson, 2020; Anderson & López, 2018). Smaller percentages of Black immigrants can also be traced to South and Central America, Europe, and Asia.

The Black immigrant experience is difficult to pinpoint, because it is influenced by both country of origin and in-country region of origin (Blum, 2015). Between 2000 and 2013, Africans composed the fastest-growing immigrant group and, by 2015, there were 2.1 million African immigrants in the United States (Anderson, 2015).

There is a paucity of scholarly research on the experiences of Black American immigrants in their early and formative stages of schooling. In general, studies tend to focus on high school and college experiences. Foreign-born Black Americans, and Black Americans born in the United States to immigrant parents, are sometimes viewed in similar ways and at other times in dissimilar ways to U.S.-born Black Americans, depending on context (Blum, 2015). Black American immigrant children are constantly negotiating various expectations in a bifurcated manner (Awokoya, 2012; Blum, 2015; Gilbert, 2009).

In comparative studies, Black American immigrants are often aggregated into a broad immigrant group (Mugisha, 2015). Their diversity is manifested by language, socioeconomic status, whether they came to the United States voluntarily or as refugees or seeking asylum, English language ability, and previous educational experiences (Allen et al., 2012; Anderson, 2015). Voluntary immigrants are those who have a choice regarding whether or not to migrate. Refugees/asylees are immigrants who are forced to flee for a variety of reasons that can include government policies, authority, war, or civil strife.

The journey to the United States is frequently characterized by different family members arriving at different time frames. Asylees often spend at least one year in refugee camps, and, in some instances, young girls find themselves separated from their parents in the process (Awokoya, 2012). Voluntary Black immigrants have to save travel funds and complete paperwork. These considerations may result in family members traveling separately from one another. There is further diversity within both groups in that some of the children may be foreign born and are later joined by their American-born siblings.

Scholars of education posit that this diversity impacts how Black immigrants engage with the U.S. education system (Cone et al., 2014). Understanding these nuances is important so that scholarly research does not hypostatize a one-size-fits-all narrative for Black Americans (Mwangi, 2014; Peguero et al., 2015).

BLACK AMERICAN IMMIGRANT GIRLS

It is common for Black American immigrant girls to face pressure to achieve in school and to attain the wishes and dreams of their parents in the United States and their extended family members in their countries of origin. According to Halter and Johnson (2014), many of those Black immigrants who originate from Africa strive for and achieve high academic performance due to the belief that "work is the medicine for poverty." However, their achievement does not come easily due to multiple barriers (Coutinho & Koinis-Mitchell, 2014).

In the academy, legislation, and other sectors of the United States, the words *African immigrants* are used to describe Black immigrant girls regardless of whether they are first- or second-generation immigrants (Awokoya, 2012; Coutinho & Koinis-Mitchell, 2014). This generalization is deleterious, because it is silencing and does not take into account the intersectional identities that include gender, race, ethnicity, nationality, and class.

Black females, in general, are often stereotyped as Jezebels, mammies, Sapphires, and matriarchs (Crenshaw, 1995). For Black immigrant girls, these labels can lead to difficulty with identity development relating to their immigrant identity (Awokoya, 2012; Gilbert, 2009). This identity confusion often results in stigmatization and feelings of self-doubt even for the most brilliant student (Habecker, 2016).

On average, African immigrant girls choose contexts in which to associate or disassociate each of their identities in order to negotiate and to minimize the feelings of stereotyping based on being African or African American (Coutinho & Koinis-Mitchell, 2014; Habecker, 2016). The shuttle diplomacy is exhausting and can be alienating, as their social identity keeps changing. In their quest to manage multiple identities, these girls begin to engage in "cultural straddling" (Awokoya, 2012). They venture into cultural conformity or cultural resistance similar to U.S.-born Black Americans, who also strive to negotiate cultural expectations in order to endure in the U.S. educational system (Coutinho & Koinis-Mitchell, 2014).

These struggles often lead to systems of oppression that are related to their intersectional identities of gender, race, ethnicity, nationality, and class (Awokoya,

2012; Cone et al., 2014; Fries-Britt et al., 2014). The story at the beginning of this chapter is an example of what that can look like in the life of a child. Scholarly research on the educational experiences of immigrants highlight challenges that they experience due to tensions between their sociocultural identities as immigrants in the United States, the ethnocentric nature of cultural norms, and expectations in American schools (Lee, 2005). For example, some Black immigrant girls miss school days because of cultural expectations of communal citizenship that include performing domestic duties such as taking care of siblings (Knight & Watson, 2014). These African cultural expectations are compounded in the United States due to challenges within the immigrant family, such as income loss and lack of familiarity with resources (Njue & Retish, 2010). Black immigrant girls are also expected by their families to be the guardians of their cultures (Lee, 2005). Despite the challenges, the literature reveals that African immigrants perform better academically than other foreign populations and U.S.-born Black Americans. For example, Halter and Johnson (2014, p. 213) note that "Africans composed the most highly educated group in the country, surpassing White Americans, Asians, and Latinos."

Structural racism in the nation's policy making and policy implementation continues to impact Black immigrants negatively (Arthur, 2000). This racism exacerbates the experiences of Black immigrant girls. It is imperative that professional development for teachers and administrators cover ways that professionals can be sensitive to the fact that ethnic and racial teasing and stereotyping has a lasting impact on Black immigrant students. Teachers should, in their classrooms and playgrounds, foster an environment where they and their students can learn about the diversity of cultures that exist in their schools. Allen et al. (2012) aptly assert:

> Educators can work against anti-immigrant discourses by embracing culturally relevant pedagogies and recognizing West African immigrant students as assets in U.S. classrooms and society. Such pedagogies affirm West African immigrant students' knowledge as complementary to American schooling while acknowledging their cultural experiences as varied and diverse. (p. 13)

Professional development should ensure that teachers do not reinforce cultural stereotypes regarding students who do not conform to the cultural identity that is being ascribed to them (Carter, 2005; Obiakor & Grant, 2005). A best practice is for teachers to diversify portrayals of Africa and Africans in the curriculum (Lee, 2019). Uplifting and culturally responsive approaches to enriching the curriculum include utilizing a more multidimensional portrayal of Black immigrant girls. These should include portraying Black immigrant girls' achievements and also leveraging diasporic films and documentaries about the African continent and Black immigrants (Allen et al., 2012).

Vignette: It Should Have Been all of Us, Together, Against the System: Latinidad, Blackness, and Queer Identity

Sandra (Chap) Chapman

I am a native New Yorker, having spent my formative years in the vibrant, culturally rich community of Spanish Harlem, fondly known as El Barrio. If I had to describe myself, I would say the following:

> I identify as an Afrolatina of Dominican and Puerto Rican descent; a lesbian and cisgender female who grew up culturally rich and financially poor; a first-generation immigrant with an advanced degree, who publicly celebrates Catholicism and more privately practices Santeria; someone married to a bisexual Afrolatina Jewish woman and raising three children of different races in New York City; a Democrat and an antibias educator committed to examining anti-Blackness in myself and in my communities while uplifting antiracism work; a person who has ADHD and growing physical disabilities in her 52nd year of life!

What a mouthful! As I considered the experiences that contributed to my identity, I realized that schooling—in the home, community, and at school—substantially affected who I thought I was and how I felt about myself. My first (re)memory of my sexual identity as a lesbian was around age 5, though probably more clarity came at age 10. I didn't grow into my Black racial consciousness until age 40. This should not have been the case given that there were ample moments in my life when my social identities were salient, forming, and in need of affirmation.

One identity that shifted periodically, like the hour hand on a clock, is my racial construct. Ethnically, I knew I was Puerto Rican by age 5, and that the white Catholic nuns who came for coffee and chats with my mom were not Puerto Rican, even though they spoke Spanish fluidly. The nuns made periodic visits to the homes of their parishioners, drinking cafe con leche and eating whatever crackers we could find with the delicious block of government cheese our poor community received. The cultural, linguistic, and ethnic associations related to being Puerto Rican were explicitly communicated in my home, and these visits by these nuns reaffirmed that Spanish was good, Puerto Ricans were good, and even our crackers and cheese were good (and they were)!

Ironically, and sadly, aspects of Latinidad and Blackness were never mentioned in school, despite the fact that 60 percent of the students were first-generation Puerto Ricans (who were racially Black, White, and mixed), and the remaining 40 percent of the student body was African American.

One day, while I was playing with my motley crew of friends, an argument broke out about our fourth-grade teacher, who was a Black Puerto Rican. She lived in the building across from mine in the Johnson Housing Projects, and when I saw her in the neighborhood she would speak Spanish to me and my mother. In school, it was an unnamed rule that she spoke to us all in English. The argument was between the Black and Latinx students, each group wanting to claim our teacher as belonging to us. The Black students racialized her and felt affirmed. The Latinx students heard her Spanish, understood her to be Latina, and felt affirmed. The dispute ended when the bell rang and we rushed to line up. Our inability to get clarity on understanding race and ethnicity was equally disrupted.

Our sense of personal and group identity, two of the most important aspects of racial identity formation, were impacted by mixed messages we received from a school that did not talk about race or skin color and Puerto Rican homes that did not acknowledge Black or African heritage and features. My peers and I fended for ourselves in regard to acquiring knowledge about race, racism, culture, ethnicity, and language variations. School was not a place for discussions about these concepts, and, because of the lack of racial-cultural history, school became the place where racism existed between the light-skinned Latinx students and the Black/African American students. We did not yet recognize that racism was something we each endured in different ways; that it shouldn't have been us against each other—it should have been all of us, together, against a racist system.

Meanwhile, while sorting through what it meant to belong, or not to belong, to a racial-ethnic group (feeling grounded in my Latinidad and disconnected from Blackness), I also had to find ways to process my growing attraction to girls and women in a Catholic home, school, and community. Most of the explicit and negative messages I heard about homosexuality and gender fluidity came from my traditional Latinx home community and the church with which my school was associated. The pressures to conform to heterosexuality and my assigned gender kept me in the closet about my lesbian identity until I was 19, and I'm still navigating my internal and external sense of gender.

Many of these messages were reinforced by people at school. Two boys in second grade were publicly reprimanded when they got into line holding hands. They both looked horrified, and I stared on from the girls line wishing they would rejoin hands.

Sometimes the messages about gender were outright contradictions to what was taught. As faculty in a Catholic school, our teachers likely felt the need to preach openly from a heteronormative stance. "Sandra, you must not always wear your uniform pants to school. Wear your skirt more often." Contradictory messages came in one of the teachers they hired, a white female who presented as more masculine. Her clothing choices, mannerisms, and other forms of gender expression comforted me. I didn't know my fifth-grade teacher's sexuality, and in my child's

(Continued)

(Continued)

mind, the lines between teacher and student were blurred. It didn't stop me from imagining conversations with her.

"Will you help me tell my mom that I can have short hair like you?"

"Were you always this comfortable with your stance and clothing?"

Developing a more complete sense of my intersecting identities has been a 51-year process, because identity formation is a journey, not a destination. As time passes, aspects of the identity statement I presented at the beginning of this chapter may change, while others remain the same. For example, I grew up in poverty, on food stamps and other forms of government assistance; if you could taste the government cheese I mentioned earlier, then you get where my roots are. I am no longer in that financial bracket. I was assigned "girl" at birth and comfortably claimed a female identity for most of my life. Over the past five-plus years, as my internal sense of maleness and external male gender expression have become more visible, I wonder if I would have claimed a more gender-fluid identity if I had been born in 2015 instead of 1968.

I have vivid and fond memories of my elementary school, my classmates, and my teachers, but the silence around race, gender and sexuality, socioeconomic class, and other social identities left me fending for myself to find positive role models and groups with which to bond. There was no mention of the Black transgender people who ignited the gay liberation movement at the Stonewall riots, or of Baker's gay pride flag, which debuted in 1978. I was 10 years old and felt isolated in my growing feelings towards girls. I have come to know many Catholic schools, even religious same-gender schools, that are reexamining their stance and making room for their LGBTQIA+ students, parents, and employees. Imagine a school that partners with children and their families to teach about social identities, social issues, and how to develop a "fight song" through adversity. That is a school my childhood self deserved.

CHAPTER 22

Yes! Black Girls Are Genderqueer[1] and Transgender, too!

Graciela Slesaransky-Poe

My Gen Z mixed Black, White, and Latino, 20-year-old son was 3 when he began to express his gender in ways that defied society's expectations of boyhood. Back then families with children like ours did not have a lot of guidance to navigate what, at that time, felt like very scary and unfamiliar territory. In those days, we lacked the confidence and conviction we now have; we now know that there was no harm in allowing our children to nourish all their gender sides. We did not know that by partnering with their schools (Slesaransky-Poe et al., 2013), learning to navigate the legal system, and surrounding them—and us—with supportive and welcoming communities, our children would not only be OK, but would thrive and grow into well adjusted, self-confident, and healthy young adults.[2]

A lot has changed over these past two decades; much of it is a result of the self-advocacy of Gen Zers themselves, the most diverse generation ever (Levin, 2019). Their consistence, persistence, and insistence communicated that the society's binary categories of gender were too limiting and incongruent with the way they knew themselves to be. Some schools have been responsive to their gender diverse needs, understanding that gender inclusion benefits all. But the work is far from over.

According to the latest GLSEN's School Climate Survey (Kosciw et al., 2018) transgender and gender nonconforming students experience extreme hostile environments in schools: 84 percent of transgender and 70 percent of gender nonconforming middle and high school students reported being bullied in school; over 25 percent faced discrimination in school, 42 percent have been prevented from using their name and pronouns, and 45.6 percent from using the bathroom that aligns with their gender identity. Truong et al. (2020), sharing groundbreaking data on the intersections of gender identity and Blackness, report that Black gender nonconforming and transgender students experience even higher levels of violence and victimization than their non-Black gender nonconforming and trans peers.

ON BLACK TRANSWOMEN'S INVISIBILITY AND VIOLENCE

Historically, lesbian, gay, bisexual, transgender, and queer (LGBTQ) texts seldom mention race or acknowledge whiteness. This omission fosters a sense of invisibility of racial diversity within the LGBTQ communities, which in turn makes it harder for Black and non-Black students and teachers to learn how to support Black gender nonconforming, nonbinary, and trans[3] students. Similarly, research does not specifically address the experiences of Black queer girls and women, making it even more difficult for gender nonconforming and transgender girls to see themselves reflected in the narratives of other Black transwomen and to normalize their experiences.

The very few media images, news, and stories about Black transwomen portray them as targets of violence. Even within the Black Lives Matter movement, Black trans individuals are rendered invisible, equating transness with whiteness, which, in turn, increases stigma and creates more barriers for Black trans girls, and for their families and teachers to accept, affirm, and uplift them. The epidemic of murders of Black trans women prompted the emergence of the Black Trans Lives Matter movement. Trans Black girls and women sit at the intersection of multiple interlocking system of oppression and discrimination (Crenshaw, 1989): racism, cisgenderism, transphobia, and sexism. It is that invisibility that makes Black trans women particularly vulnerable to violence.

Black girls who are parented by Black adults get guidance on how to navigate a hostile, anti-Black racist world. From an early age, parents teach their Black children that there is nothing wrong with them, but that they live in a white supremacist society (Kendi, 2019). They have "the talk" on how to interact with law enforcement and other threatening authority figures. Black girls are taught about self-love and self-respect and how to navigate a white-supremacist, sexist, and misogynistic world from their Black mothers, grandmothers, Black female teachers, and other Black role models in their lives. Genderqueer and transgender Black girls, on the other hand, may not have adults in their lives equipped to prepare them to learn how to be safe in navigating their trans identity (Nealy, 2017). Further, some of their Black caring adults may have unquestioned and unexplored homophobic and transphobic feelings themselves.

Expanding the Scope of the Work

Over the past 15 years, through my work as a pre- and in-service PreK–12 teacher and leader educator, I have had the opportunity to support educators learning about gender diversity. The vast majority of the educators I come in contact with seem transformed by their new understandings of gender diversity, and genuinely interested in engaging in the work of welcoming and supporting their transgender students. They feel responsible for the safety and learning of their own transgender students, but they do not engage in the work of disrupting the ways in which cisgender-binary normativity operates in their schools (Smith & Payne, 2016; Staley & Leonardi, 2019). In some instances, schools' efforts to protect transgender students end up further marginalizing them. Antibullying policies constitute one such example. As Payne and Smith (2013) state, the dominant understanding of LGBTQ students' experiences has been shaped by discourses that reduce the "problem" to bullies who express homophobic and transphobic attitudes. As a result, interventions typically focus on eliminating bullying behaviors and protecting the victim. Within this framework the prevailing cultural hetero and cisgender normativity goes unquestioned.

The current national climate, a moment of increased critical social consciousness, calls for a different approach to supporting Black transgender girls: a more intersectional, collective, visible, and intentional one. As Angela Davis said, "In a racist society, it is not enough to be nonracist, we must be antiracist" (as quoted in Kendi, 2019, p. 429). Respectfully paraphrasing: In a transphobic and sexist society, it's not enough to be nontransphobic and nonsexist, we must be antitransphobic and antisexist.

Becoming an Antiracist, Antitransphobic, and Antisexist Educator

What can educators individually and collectively do to create schools where Black trans girl students feel that they are seen, that they matter, that they belong, that they are uplifted and affirmed? The lack of research and resources on the intersection of Black identity, trans identity, and gender matters; the need to address this void is most important. Creating pro-Black antiracist, antitransphobic, and antisexist interventions will require a "radical [re]orientation of our consciousness" (Kendi, 2019, p. 23).

Most of the work to address the needs of gender nonconforming, nonbinary, and transgender students centers around indicators of safer school climate. These indicators include the presence of supportive student clubs, inclusive curricular resources, inclusive LGBTQ sex education, supportive school personnel, inclusive and supportive school policies (Kosciw et al., 2018), classroom culture, and family and community engagement (Collins & Ehrenhalt, n.d.).

Additionally, Simmons's (2019) antiracist framework could offer synergy to address the intersection of race, gender identity, and expression. Simons recommends five actions to become an antiracist, and I add antitransphobic and antisexist, educator. I have made modifications to include trans and gender identities as well. They are listed in *italics*. Simons's five actions are to

- Engage in vigilant self-awareness

- Acknowledge racism, *transphobia, sexism,* and the ideology of white, *cisgender, and male privilege and* supremacy

- Study and teach representative history

- Talk about race, *gender identity, and gender expression* with students

- When you see racism, *transphobia, or sexism,* do something

This kind of radical work rarely happens, and when it does, it happens individually and in isolation. A community of practice (CoP)—a team of equally motivated individuals engaged in self-reflection, inquiry, and discussion—could be a safe space for learning and support. A CoP formed by a variety of school stakeholders, educators, staff, students, family, and community members that regularly collaborate to improve students' experiences and outcomes of Black genderqueer and transgender students could be instrumental in bringing about necessary change. CoPs could take on the role of collecting data on students' experiences, observing peer and staff interactions and practices in and out of the classroom—including use of names and pronouns, responding to misgendering, and other microaggressions—and demonstrating how educators can endorse and implement racial and gender inclusive practices (Shriberg & Baker, 2019), while accomplishing these five critical actions to end racism, cisgenderism, and sexism in schools.

ADDITIONAL RESOURCES (NOT LISTED UNDER REFERENCES)

TEACHING TOLERANCE (WWW.TOLERANCE.ORG)

Ehrenhalt, J. (2019, January 30). Let's talk about nonbinary. *Teaching Tolerance Magazine.* https://www.tolerance.org/magazine/lets-talk-about-nonbinary

McKenzie, G. B. (2015, May 6). *Seeing all identities of LGBTQ youth of color.* https://www.tolerance.org/magazine/seeing-all-identities-of-lgbtq-youth-of-color

Rupp, L. J. (Host), & Beemyn, G. (Guest). (n.d.). *Queer America: The experiences of trans people* [Audio podcast]. https://www.tolerance.org/podcasts/queer-america/experiences-of-trans-people

NATIONAL CENTER FOR LESBIAN RIGHTS

Orr, A., & Baum, J. (2015). *Schools in transition: A guide for supporting transgender students in K–12 school.* http://www.hrc.org/resources/schools-intransition-a-guide-for-supporting-transgender-students-in-k-12-s

WELCOMING SCHOOLS (WWW.WELCOMINGSCHOOLS.ORG)

Top diverse picture books for a welcoming school that is gender and LGBTQ inclusive. https://www.welcomingschools.org/pages/great-picture-books-diverse-families-bullying-gender-and-lgbtq/

Diverse children's books to support transgender and nonbinary youth and to understand gender. https://www.welcomingschools.org/resources/books/transgender-youth/

Notes

1. I recognize the complicated history of the terms *queer* and *genderqueer.* They are used by mostly younger LGBTQ+ individuals as positive, empowering, or even neutral terms of gender and sexual identity. In this chapter I use *queer* as "an inclusive term to refer to those who fall outside of cisgender or heterosexual identities—not as a pejorative" (Collins & Ehrenhalt, n.d.).

2. To learn more about the experiences of parents raising gender nonconforming children, see Pyne (2016) and Slesaransky-Poe (in press).

3. For the purpose of this chapter, I will use the terms *queer* and *transgender* as inclusive of gender nonconforming, gender nonbinary, and transgender students, acknowledging that not all gender nonconforming and gender nonbinary individuals identify as transgender. To learn about these and other gender-inclusive terms, see Collins & Ehrenhalt (n.d.)

In the following section, doctoral candidate Sakenya MacDonald helps readers understand the value of spirituality in the lives of Black women and girls as a key component of the frameworks (intersectionality, Black feminist thought and [Pan] African feminism) discussed in this section.

MacDonald moves fluidly from illustrating the palpable and generative aspects of spirituality to practical application in the classroom. The classroom suggestions that she presents herself, as an intersectional feminist scholar, are a result of her orientation to spirituality. These include incorporating art and stories into the way we introduce children to STEM. In addition, these are strategies that will work for many children who may not initially connect to the ways that STEM is traditionally presented in today's classrooms. Using the concept of universal design, she suggests that when we design around the needs of a subset of the population (Black girls), we often serve all students—including students outside of that subset—with more effectiveness. As we do with many strategies in this book, when we design for the needs of Black girls, we often create classrooms that more precisely impact all of our students.

Prismatic Black Girls Reflecting African Spiritualities in Learning Environments

Sakenya McDonald

INTRODUCTORY STORY

Educators: This story may be shared with students in your classroom. We encourage you to share. At the end of the story, there are some reflective questions that you may use to facilitate discussion with your students. These questions may be modified, and this activity is recommended for youth between the ages of 8 and 18.

The little girl liked to walk barefoot. The freedom her toes felt as they moved wistfully across grass, dirt, and mud belonged to her and sat full bellied in her soul. The earth never demanded more than she could offer, only requesting from the little girl her natural presence while providing a temple of wonder, beauty, and purification. The earth longed to be her playground and she knew it, she played in it and with it, and her joy became an act of piety. The little girl danced on the earth with no shoes and no socks and felt the energy of the soil radiating beyond her body and into her spirit. She loved the earth and the earth loved her back with the kind of love that was ancient and primal. When others would test that love with a pair of woolen socks or soft-soled shoes, the little girl would giggle, because she couldn't explain to the others that her soul would never be trapped in a pair of socks. Not when the earth was her playground. The little girl knew that the others were foolish with their gestures of civility and tiresome formalities of wearing silk stockings and leather boots.

But she was wise because the earth had made her wise; the earth had shared its secrets with her; and so, she chuckled when others called her wild and untamed. She laughed when the others fretted over her health, begging, "Please child, cover your feet or you'll get sick." The little girl simply continued to grow stronger and bolder, and her giggles and laughter changed to silent prayers to the earth for patience when dealing with those who did not or could not understand her place in the world.

The day the ships arrived bringing foreigners to the village, the little girl was no longer little; she was both a woman and earth. Her back was as straight and strong as a baobab tree, her skin polished like the precious metals of copper and bronze, her hair thick and black like the soil along the Nile. She smelled of herbs and roots and laughed like the ocean tide coming up in waves. Her voice was softer than air but her song roared like thunder. Along her neck were her gifts from the earth, small stones hiding diamonds and quartz and the remains of her deceased brothers and sisters— ivory from the elephant, bones from the zebra, feathers from the crane. She had not hunted or killed; she only took what the earth offered her. And her bounty was full.

The foreigners, like the others in her village, did not understand her, and so they feared her. And they took her. The earth cried out for her as she was silent but not afraid. The earth was her playground and promised her it would follow her wherever she went. And so, she went. The woman sat for days as the seas carried her. The waves lashed about violently. The sea raised its mighty fists and pounded the sides of the boats for days, yet the foreigners did not turn back. The woman watched and waited, the cold wooden ship boards scratching and tearing at the soles of her bare feet. Her belly ached, and her soul no longer felt full but empty and pained for freedom. She smelled death and rot and longed for the days that smelled like rain and growth and life.

Debrief Questions

1. How old do you think the little girl in the story is?

2. What do you think she looks like?

3. Who are the foreigners mentioned in the story? Where did they come from?

4. Where did the foreigners take the little girl?

5. What was her life like in her new land?

6. What do you think the little girl remembered about her homeland? What do you think she missed the most?

Activity: Take a moment and visualize the little girl in your head. Draw a picture or write a paragraph describing what you believe she may have looked like, and share your picture/paragraph with one classmate.

For Black women and girls, spirituality is *culture*. Spirituality is the invisible, nurturing hand of our ancestors reminding us of our dynamic heritage and purpose. If a poll was conducted on the significance that spirituality plays in the lives of Black women and girls, the responses might suggest a unified voice. A voice that Black girls everywhere share with recognized and admired leaders such as Harriet Tubman, Ida B. Wells, Sojourner Truth, Angela Davis, Toni Morrison, Audre Lorde, and, more recently, Michelle Obama. The beauty of African spirituality is represented in the lives and accomplishments of these, and countless other, Black women. My voice is also amongst the thousands of voices, past and present, being lifted and carried by the women who have influenced me, and, in turn, my voice gives depth and dimension to the prismatic voices of the Black girls whom I seek to inspire.

In African spiritual and religious traditions, culture, community, and connection are core values that are tangibly present in all aspects of the African diaspora. For example, spirituality is firmly rooted in appreciation of, and respect for, one's natural environment. In southeast Africa, the Matobo Hills are home to the Matobo National Park, tucked in the southwest corner of Zimbabwe. In 2017, Belinda Ncube published an article about her observations of cultural distinctions regarding the environment and spirituality as evident in the Ndebele tribe. Ncube wrote:

> Environmental consciousness has always been a part of the Ndebele belief system. . . . Ndebele women have also had a spiritual connection to the land. Indeed, the role of women in Ndebele culture is enhanced by a culture that is infused with rituals that are meant to instill respect for the land and environment. (2017, p. 230)

As educators, perhaps you have seen or read about African spiritual rituals or belief systems and felt empowered, emotional, or frustrated. Or maybe you are an educator who recognizes that the educational needs of Black girls are defined not by their aptitude, test scores, and willingness to conform to the dominant social structure but instead by culturally relevant spiritual traditions that are sometimes invisible but still present in their lives.

The word *spirituality* often conjures up varying meanings and emotions. The definition of spirituality relates to "spiritual character or function" and "the quality or condition of being spiritual; attachment to or regard for things of the spirit as opposed to material or worldly interests" (Simpson, n.d.). Riyad Shahjahan (2010) referred to spirituality as "a way of being in the world characterized by connection to one's cultural knowledge and/or other beings" (p. 478). In 1995, Roxana Ng published a study of academics of color working in higher education and noted that regarding spirituality, one participant, "Gregory," defined it "as my possibilities of being in the world, my possibilities of appreciating the being of others in the world" (Ng et al., 1995, p. 487). These concepts are hard to conceptualize in traditional educational settings, yet that does not minimize the fact that for many

Black girls, spirituality is a centralized component informing their growth and development. Therefore, the purpose of this chapter is to focus on African spirituality as a way of identifying ways to better support, nurture, and nourish the academic success of brilliant, beautiful, Black girls.

As if defining spirituality were not challenging enough, defining African spirituality, with all of its intricacies and idiosyncrasies, can best be described as trying to "bottle lightning." The reason for this is due to the fact that the variations of African tribes and societies are extensive, and each possesses its own interpretation of spirituality. A shared theme, however, is one of interconnectivity, that all life is interwoven and connected, and thus, humans are not separate from their environments but, rather, embedded in them. Jacob Olupona, professor of indigenous African religions at Harvard Divinity School and professor of African and African American studies in Harvard's Faculty of Arts and Sciences, explained that African spirituality acknowledges the ways in which our beliefs inform every detail of our human lives (Olupona & Chiorazzi, 2015).

Olupona further stated that the term *religion* is problematic for some Africans, because religion often positions "the divine" outside of the everyday; a force that is outside of us, greater than us, or judgmental towards us (Olupona & Chiorazzi, 2015). This ideology is not representative of African spirituality, which is complementary to a belief system that begins with our oneness with the entire physical and spiritual worlds. In other words, our culture, societies, and environments are different manifestations of spirituality and often inform how Black women and girls view their positions within these structures as opportunities for inspiring socially just and inclusive practices.

My own experience is an example of the role that spirituality plays in the lives of Black girls, especially as they seek to navigate an educational system that was *not* designed for or by them. Their voices have historically been underrepresented, or worse, completely eliminated in the planning and implementation of educational policies. One day, in my first-grade classroom, we were assigned a worksheet to complete. Naturally, I cannot remember what the content of the worksheet was, but I do remember that I finished my worksheet quickly and, as a result, I began to wander around the classroom. I distinctly remember that I wanted to "help" one of my classmates with their worksheet; it was important to me that we all complete the work so that we could do more enjoyable things like painting or coloring. As I drifted through the classroom, my teacher, an older White woman with very intimidating hair and spectacles, demanded that I return to my seat until all the students had completed their assignments. I did not agree with this assessment of what someone else had clearly defined as effective, and so I ignored the advice of my teacher and continued to try and help others. What happened next is an experience that shook me to my core and that I will never forget as being the first time I felt disappointed in the school system.

As I moved through the classroom, the teacher became increasingly aggravated and confrontational. Although I may have been only six or seven years old at the time, I recall feeling confused, frustrated, and ultimately, defiant. A power struggle ensued. The teacher attempted to physically confine me to my desk; this was met with my display of equal, yet opposite, physical power. As the teacher struggled with me, the other students seemed frozen in their chairs, appalled and terrified. The struggle spilled into the hallway and up two flights of hard, concrete stairs; me being dragged the entire way. Once in the principal's office, I completely blacked out and only remember being in my parent's home feeling exhausted.

There has never been a time that I have told this story that has not resulted in me shedding tears. There has never been a time where my Ubuntu, an African spiritual concept ("I am because we are"), was more vilified. At no point in this entire scenario did the teacher ask me what I was doing and why it was important to me. If she had, she would have uncovered the truth that my joy and passion for learning is a spiritual gift, meant to be shared with others, not hoarded or kept isolated. If the teacher wanted to, she could have offered me many alternatives to be a "classroom helper" that would have fulfilled my need to be helpful and courteous without being a distraction to my classmates. Or, she may have uncovered the truth that in my family's culture, we share what we have with others so that the entire community is enriched and empowered. My African DNA is coded to believe that when one is strong, we are all strong, like many cords bound together, and that is a spiritual tradition that still exists in many African tribes and cultures today.

My experience is not an anomaly. Black girls are still significantly disadvantaged and invisible, even in contemporary educational systems (Morris, 2016). This relentless marginalization process starts from the first day a Black girl excitedly gets on the bus to go to school, and it follows her throughout her academic career. Even in contemporary times, Black women feminist scholars are still uncovering *our* truths about educational disparities, the criminalization of Black girls in education, impostor syndrome, and the systemic relegating of Black girls to special education or remedial classroom settings. These disparities are what brings us to *Teaching Beautiful and Brilliant Black Girls*, a book designed intentionally to equip educators with tools to embolden the success of Black girls in the classroom. Understanding the social narrative that spirituality plays in the lives of these young girls is a tool that cannot easily be mapped or contextualized. Our spirituality, like life itself, is highly complex and always evolving. Part of our spirituality manifests in how we view ourselves and how fragile our sense of self can be when inundated by daily onslaughts depicting Black women as what I refer to as "less than" (i.e., less attractive, less educated, less mannered, less approachable, etc.).

For example, I can remember growing up in a conservative religious household and reading Bible passages that confused me. How is it that things that are *dark* are always referred to as evil, unclean, or impure, yet, I *am* dark? These missed signals also spilled into educational settings, especially in classes where language reinforced the idea that dark is always bad, and light is always good. One way that educators can mitigate missed messages in the classroom is to examine language politics in the class. Engaging in critical reflection on terms such as *black sheep, black-listed,* or *dark times* can be enough to show support to Black girls in the classroom. As Rymes (2015) explained, "Patterns in how teachers and students take turns at talk, introduce topics, use multiple languages and language varieties, or tell stories in different ways can illustrate how misunderstandings between different social groups in classrooms evolve—and how they can be overcome" (p. 6).

Another way to reflect how spirituality informs the education process of Black girls is by looking at how they seek to connect to their natural environments, and then nurturing that desire. For example, in the natural sciences, Black girls may display innate knowledge about biology or botany, but that knowledge may be suppressed when it fails to meet scientific rigor. Yet, for years, Black women have been creating complex and sustainable methods for farming, healthcare, and infrastructure in their environments that have been minimized or ignored. In Alice Walker's (1982) remarkable novel, *The Color Purple*, protagonist Shug Avery proclaims, "My first step away from the old white man was trees. Then air. Then birds. Then other people" (p. 178). Walker's narrative describes a woman who steps away from oppression and with her first free step walks into nature; it represents the symbiotic ways in which African spirituality has always communed with nature.

Finally, consider the disparities that exist between Black girls' spiritual approach to science and the typical presentation of scientific principles in STEM-related fields. To illustrate, the relationship between African science and math is ancient (Brandt & Chernoff, 2015). Unless an intentional connection is made between a scientific theory and nature, it can often be challenging for teachers to find ways to make meaning of STEM fields in the lives of Black girls. One option for STEM teachers to consider is implementing universal design into courses and creating multiple avenues for Black girls to identify and synthesize STEM materials. This is not to say that Black girls cannot meet the demands and rigor of learning the most advanced scientific principles and theories, but this *is* to say that when educators are perplexed over creating paths for Black girls to actively engage with STEM, it may be because the initial introduction to STEM fields lacks a spiritual component. For example, in college, I was able to take a math course that introduced math terms, such as fractals, using art and sacred geometry, and I was highly successful in this course, because the material was presented in stories and art. While some might argue that this method can further isolate an already marginalized population by focusing on their "otherness," expert on African ethnomathematics Ron Eglash (1997) would disagree and argues that successful multicultural curricula will recognize disciplinary and cultural diversity.

To conceptualize, as a girl I held (and still hold) a natural affinity for complex pattern recognition. In hindsight, I now realize this natural ability is related to being on the autistic spectrum and not being properly diagnosed as a child, but this skill lends itself to efficiency in a variety of math-related fields, such as cryptology. Additionally, I have always held a fascination with physics and theories related to time and manipulation of time. As a child, however, I cannot recall ever having a math or science teacher who knew how to reach these parts of me. These classes were always a challenge, because the focus was on learning to do things the right way rather than asking questions about why this topic should be important in my life or how these theories fit my cultural belief system. I believe that if a teacher had implemented universal design in a science class, for example, and expanded the discourse to include a conversation on how patterns appear in nature and represent perfect design, I may have pursued a different educational path and became a renowned Black woman code breaker or physicist.

Navigating educational waters is a process that may feel foreign to some young, Black girls. My own experiences with education, and the process of becoming educated, have been fraught with their fair share of challenges and success. My spirituality, the one I was born into and not indoctrinated into, has always been a part of my identity. Charles Long (1997) wrote, "So even if he had no conscious memory of Africa, the image of Africa played an enormous part in the religion of the [B]lack [woman]" (p. 26). In the story at the beginning of the chapter, I am that little girl. I am the one who loves the rain for sustaining our planet as much as I love the spider for its ingenuity and creativity. It is my obligation as a spiritual mother to break barriers and make space for Black girls in education, and to equip educators with pragmatic solutions for facilitating positive, reaffirming educational experiences for Black girls.

Dear Teacher, never forget: *We are all these little girls.*

Pet, by Akwaeke Emezi

Grade Level 7–12

Genre-Defying

Book Review by Marguerite W. Penick

Jam, the trans girl protagonist of *Pet,* has been raised to believe all of the "monsters" who used to exist in Lucille are gone. But when one emerges from her mother's painting, Jam realizes they may still exist, but they are not who she had been taught they were. Instead of fearing the monster she names "Pet," they set off together to protect Jam's best friend and bond as you can only with those you trust with your life.

In the setting, Lucille—never quite defined as a town, city, state, or nation—the angels "tore down those horrible statues of rich men who'd owned people and fought to keep owning people" (p. 2), and built monuments where "the names were of people who died when hurricane[s] hit and the monsters wouldn't evacuate the prisons or send aid" (p. 2). "The people of Lucille would remember the temples that were bombed, the mosque, the acid attacks, the synagogues. Remembering was important" (p. 3).

Pet is not a dystopian story, and it isn't science fiction or fantasy, because at its heart it is really contemporary realistic fiction. It is about what happens when people only see what they want to believe or what they are told to believe. *Pet* is about the monsters who surround us and the angels who watch over us. Winner of the 2019 Stonewall Honor and the 2019 Walter Dean Myers Honor, and a finalist for the 2019 National Book Award, this truly remarkable book challenges society at its best and worst.

PART II

"I AM DESPERATE FOR CHANGE—NOW— NOT IN 8 YEARS OR 12 YEARS, BUT RIGHT NOW."

—Michelle Obama

The following chapter highlights how racial aggressions impact Black Girls. In this chapter, Dr. Sandra "Chap" Chapman and Imani Chapman share how racism and sexism play out on a playground as two boys, ages 7 and 10, impose their privilege and displace a 4-year-old Afrolatina girl. The playground dynamics in a public space demonstrate how children internalize race and gender oppression as early as age 3. We see how the Afrolatina girl at the center of the story is impacted when whiteness and maleness dominate and invade her space. The authors give readers an intersectional lens for looking at playtime. They offer an activity to help readers switch perspectives on how they moderate that time—so that children can respectfully play and enjoy the playground and each other.

CHAPTER 24

Black Girl on the Playground

Sandra Chapman, Imani Chapman

> *Research about the impact of racism on children's identity development exposes the damage it inflicts on both White children and children of color.*
>
> —Derman-Sparks & A. B. C. Task Force, 1989, p. 4

The following story centers a young Afrolatina in a book about Black girls. Moll and Ruiz (2002) state, "The schooling of Latinos should be analyzed not independently, as is usually the case, but rather in relation to the situation of African American children, for they share similar political environments and colonial forms of education" (p. 270). In addition, some Latinx embrace their African roots and consider themselves Afrolatina, and others identify ethnically as Latinx and racially as Black (Diaz-Imbelli, 2013; Tatum, 1997). The example the authors use assumes gender based on stereotypical forms of expression and race based on phenotype and U.S. racial categories.

A brown-skinned Afrolatina, four years old, walked eagerly into a playground in her neighborhood. She climbed on the structure, balanced on beams, and pushed herself on the swing before entering the water sprinkler area. By then, there was an Asian girl her size speaking with an adult, two white boys between ages 7 and 10, and two other white children, siblings, a boy about 5 and his younger sister.

The adult with the Afrolatina girl, one of the chapter's authors, wavered between reading her book and keeping her eye out on the girl's encounters with the other children, because she was aware that 3-year-olds begin to develop attitudes about race and can act on those perspectives. An outsider viewing this scene would likely have observed the children engaged in their own worlds, taking full advantage of the equipment and enjoying their friends and family. Nothing unusual, just kids at play.

To the authors, there were distinct moments that transformed this playground into a space where white male dominance, Black female inferiority, and fear and silence took place. Some may think this is a harsh and unnecessary politicized overlay to put on children at play. There was no physical violence, no derogatory words or racial slurs used, no explicit exclusion from play equipment, and no signs that stated that Asian, Black or Brown people could not be in the area.

Why the racial and gender analysis? Young children are able to categorize others and develop prejudices in favor of the group to which they belong, even going so far as to apply words such as *good* to their in-group and *bad* or *ugly* to their out-group. This is possible because they are able to make sense of low- and high-status groups in society due to their early understanding of discrimination and prejudice (Aboud, 1988). Children between 5 and 10 years of age also demonstrate a heightened awareness of positive and negative stereotypes about race and ethnicity (Aboud, 1988; McKown & Weinstein, 2003), which become more salient for ethnic minorities in heterogeneous communities where a dominant group exists (Umaña-Taylor & Fine, 2004). The authors hope to demonstrate the ways in which young children show early signs of racism, sexism, classism, internalized superiority and inferiority, and colorism in their everyday choices, language, stance towards their group, and disposition with and towards groups they consider the out-group.

The playground had three separate areas where the water streamed from grates on the ground. The Brown girl was playing in one of the streams when the first interaction happened. One of the white adults asked her children to rinse off. The white boy walked up to the Brown girl and snapped, "Move!" to which the Brown girl responded by stepping back. The younger sibling yelled the same directive at the Brown girl. The siblings entered the water stream the Brown girl had just been in, even when there were two unoccupied streams. The Afrolatina was being raised with a color-conscious approach, because a healthy racial-ethnic identity is known to serve as a protector of self-esteem (Gonzalez-Backen & Umaña-Taylor, 2010; Harris-Britt, et al., 2007). However, the girl's natural instinct was to retreat when whiteness and maleness demanded her space. The siblings' adult observed the exchange and her silence served as permission for the siblings. The adult with the Afrolatina debated whether to step in. The situation was over in a matter of minutes.

A second situation occurred 20 minutes later. Once again, the Brown girl played in the stream closest to her adult. The older boys, who were running around squirting each other and accidentally wetting persons near them, needed to refill their water guns. The smaller of the two boys, with his choice of two unoccupied water streams, walked over to the one the Brown girl played in and, without saying a word, proceeded to refill his toy. The Afrolatina stepped back again, but this time her adult intervened, telling the white boy to use one of the empty streams, because the young girl was already using the one he approached. Without hesitating, he scooted to another stream. While this adult intervention did not seem to faze the older white boy, the adult said it for the Brown girl's edification. She modeled for the Afrolatina what to say the next time this happened to her. This type of racial socialization, the preparation for and response to prejudice, is an important component to boosting Black girls' self-esteem while they navigate high-risk environments (Cabrera, 2013). Harris-Britt et al. (2007) claim that "racial socialization might be even more important as a buffer for African American students—in majority White schools" (pp. 6–7).

Each day we are asked to wade through millions of pieces of data, most of which our brains filter out. The lessons that stick are often based on repeated exposure (Staats et al., 2016). This is true, too, of lessons about who we are and who we are in relation to others. Messages about our racial selves are ubiquitous. Buck (2017) captured this messaging in his photo essay. It can also be seen in the representation of protagonists in storybooks, who wins Academy Awards (#oscarsowhite), and the executive and legislative branches of our government. The consistent, dominant messages we receive about those who have come to be called white is one of superiority, and about those who are Black, Indigenous, or People of Color (BIPOC), particularly those who are Black, one of inferiority. The People's Institute for Survival and Beyond (2018) describes racial messaging of internalized racial oppression this way:

> **Internalized Racial Superiority**: The acceptance of and acting out of a superior definition is rooted in the historical designation of one's race. Over many generations, this process of empowerment and access expresses itself as unearned privileges, access to institutional power and invisible advantages based upon race.

> **Internalized Racial Inferiority**: The acceptance of and acting out of an inferior definition of self, given by the oppressor, is rooted in the historical designation of one's race. Over many generations, this process of disempowerment and disenfranchisement expresses itself in self-defeating behaviors. (2018, para 8)

Families raising girls and children of color often begin early to develop survival strategies in their children for a world that was not made for them (Harris-Britt et al., 2007). In education, a term often used is "windows and mirrors" to talk about the narratives we engage (Style, 1996). Windows share perspectives from "others," while mirrors affirm and reflect our own identities. For people with "dominant" identities, schools and media predominantly provide mirrors; conversely, people with identities that have been marginalized are exposed to windows, with an unparalleled focus on those stories by and about cisgender heterosexual white

Christian males in the United States. It is not hard from this position to connect one's worth to the prevalence of or absence of one's own story.

Girls are socialized early not to take up too much space. Messages include "don't block the way," "close your legs," and "keep your voice down." In addition to messages about how to perform femininity, there are particular dictates regarding the intersections of being female and Black. Black girls are socialized to center family, project respectability, preserve safety, and demonstrate unflappable strength. We tell them, "be respectful," "don't talk back," "just walk away," and "we don't have time to cry over spilt milk." When we engage in the multilayered ritual of hair care, we tell them "no pain, no beauty." Meanwhile, white boys are taught about their inherent worth and power, their achievements, and the limitless opportunities they have through an individualistic cultural framework (Hammond, 2015). We tell them, "one day you can be president," and "if you work hard you can achieve anything." No one is telling them to step back, take up less space, be curious about others' experiences, or be mindful of the spaces already occupied by people with marginalized identities.

Given that maleness and whiteness is increasingly seen as capable and authoritative, and Blackness and femaleness is seen as lesser or subservient, the playground scene played out as culturally designed—the young white male commanded, and the young Afrolatina girl obeyed. In a recent blog post, Drake (2018) discussed "The Sidewalk Challenge," the adult version of the vignette described. She described how Black people are regularly asked to cede the space they hold to white people, who often nonverbally move into unwelcome proximity, whether that be in a public café, on the sidewalk, or on the playground. This echoes the research of psychiatrist Dr. Chester M. Pierce, who coined the term *microaggression* in the 1970s (Sue, 2010). The current definition, popularized by Derald Wing Sue, is "brief, everyday exchanges that send denigrating messages to certain individuals because of their group membership" (Sue, 2010, p. 24). These messages underlie each of the quick exchanges between children, and with each additional experience, we have the opportunity to reinforce or undermine this ubiquitous messaging.

White teachers teaching Black girls need to be particularly mindful when young children occupy space together. The development of difference demonstrates that children are susceptible to believing stereotypes about their group, mask fears of differences with avoidance, are beginning to show signs of aggression through insults and name calling, and are aware of racism against their own group (Derman-Sparks, 2012). To interrupt these systems we offer four possible action-oriented solutions.

1. **Moving through racial fragility and ethical learning**

White teachers need to be mindful of the emotional toll that doing this work with a racial lens can take. Chugh and Kern (2016) argue that focusing on ethical learning, "defined as the active engagement in efforts to close the gap between one's self-view and one's actual behavior" (p. 475), rather than ethical perfection, is the key to warding off feelings of self-threat, which is an impediment for many of us when taking action. DiAngelo (2015) says that humility and openness are critical tools for white people moving through the learning process when it comes to race: "Our socialization renders us racially illiterate. When you add a lack of humility to that illiteracy (because we don't know what we don't know), you get the break-down we so often see when trying to engage white people in meaningful conversations about race" (para. 2). The obstacles to doing the work that will best serve all our children can be managed with reasonable expectations and well-paced forward movement.

When engaging in professional settings, interpersonal humility could be demonstrated through the following offerings:

- "This is difficult to take in; I appreciate you letting me know."

- "Thank you for sharing your experience; this is something about which I have a beginning understanding."

- "I understand that we experience social situations differently because of the identities we hold."

- "I appreciate your investing in my growth. I want to be the best teacher I can to all the children, and I know that understanding this will allow me to better understand my students."

- "What do you imagine the outcome could be if I incorporated your perspective?"

2. Making inferiority and superiority transparent

Often when talking about bias in our society, those of us who are marginalized can feel like we are undergoing decade after decade of gaslighting. When white people are able to use the framework of racial inferiority and racial superiority to unpack race for students in racially conscious developmentally appropriate ways, it empowers students to begin to recognize racialized moments and power dynamics and how they want to better engage with their peers. If educators teach only about prejudice or inferiority without teaching about superiority, the work falls to the marginalized to work their way out rather than partnering with peers who see how they can change the dynamics. The kinds of responses listed under Item 1 above can enable white teachers to become aware of internalized superiority and the ways this may impact their views of themselves and white boys, as well as their views of marginalized people, in this case, Black girls. These attitudes also provide great support for classroom practices like wait time, which gives more students opportunities to respond. Typically boys raise their hands first, often not having yet thought through a response, and white students (whose authority and voices are affirmed in dominant U.S. culture) are also among the first to respond to questions or take up space.

3. Incorporating racial socialization in the classroom

Exposure to the effects of racial discrimination and low racial-ethnic identity impacts student engagement, performance, and general health and happiness (Aronson et al., 2002; Harris-Britt et al., 2007; Steele, 2010). Umaña-Taylor et al. (2014) claimed that youth who are in the numeric minority in school rely on their racial-ethnic identity to inform their sense of self and contribute to their overall adjustment. White teachers can capitalize on the immersion stage of Black racial identity development by borrowing from Black parenting practices that instill a sense of racial pride and prepare children for experiences with racism and bias (Harris-Britt et al., 2007). In the classroom, white teachers can adapt these practices for the many hours that Black girls are out of their family's range.

4. Framing for positive outcome

Schools that do not embrace the wealth of knowledge that stem from Black and Latinx families, and are instead sources of explicit and/or implicit negative messages about cultural beliefs, history, and people, are likely to contribute, albeit unintentionally, to young children's low racial-ethnic and academic identities. Framing Black girls with a positive outcome allows white teachers to capitalize on these girls' strong oral-narrative, social, and social-cognitive skills to sustain peer-play situations, pride in their racial-ethnic identity, strong family orientations, and cultural socialization that promotes their self-esteem and protects them from racism (Cabrera, 2013).

Teacher Exercise

Alone or with a small group of teachers, reread the two interactions between the children from the beginning of the chapter. Respond to the following prompts based on what you would do before, during, and after the interactions. Push yourself to use a frame that includes racial-ethnic identity development, an understanding of white male internalized superiority and Black female internalized inferiority, the display of power and privilege in young children's actions, the developmental stages of difference, and the potential for self-threat and white fragility (Derman-Sparks, 2012; Michael, 2015).

Practicing racialized responses prior to an incident occurring allows for positive priming, helping white teachers to access the tools and language they would like to use rather than relying on silence, fear, and anxiety. There are benefits to doing this exercise with a small group of other teachers who also identify as white (Michael, 2015) as well as with a small racially diverse group of teachers who can offer different perspectives.

Before heading to the playground

1. You are the teacher taking kids to the playground. What is your understanding of your racial identity formation as a white teacher?

2. What have you done to prepare your students and yourself for racialized and gendered student interactions?

During playtime

1. Observing the exchange between the children and hearing the white male child say, "Move," how do you respond to him?

2. Observing the exchange between the children and watching the Afrolatina child step back, how do you respond to her?

3. Observing the two white male children squirting water at each other and other people not in their game, how do you respond to them?

After the playground

1. How do you follow up with each child?

2. How do you follow up with the parents of each child?

3. How do you follow up with the class?

Switching perspectives

Imagine now that, rather than being the teacher who witnessed the interaction, you heard about the incident from your teaching partner.

1. What training have you included in your partnership to prepare your partner to teach with a color-conscious approach?

2. What questions would you have for your partner?

3. What part, if any, of your response would you broach with your partner?

The story from Dr. Worokya Duncan in the following vignette is horrifying. Unfortunately, this story is often the story of Black girls in schools. The lived experiences in the following vignette are shared by many of the authors in this text, one too many to be ignored. Read, breathe, and realize how vital it is for educators to allow their Black girls to sing.

Vignette: Who's Going to Sing a Black Girl's Song?

Worokya Duncan

> Dr. Duncan, I can't take this anymore. I hate him, and he hates me and I just want to leave." "Breathe Baby Girl, Breathe." "I don't wanna breathe. I wanna punch him in his face! How dare he talk about my grade or progress to someone other than me?? Why is he talking about a part of my grade that isn't too hot, but ignoring HER grade that's worse than mine!!!! Is it because she's white?? Wait a minute! It's because I'm Black and he thinks he can do whatever he wants to me." "Right now, I just need you to breathe. Come into my office and breathe."

My position as director of inclusion and community engagement is as much focused on the curriculum and institution as it is on the very spirits of the children under my care. It's about 300 kids right now, and out of 300 children, about 18 identify as Black girls, spread across all grades.

Ntozake Shange (1975) hints at a vital question in "For Colored Girls." Who is singing the song of, for, and with Black girls? In independent schools, that question could not be more poignant. There are times I look at my students, and I wonder if I'm doing them a disservice. I wonder if I should be telling their parents that this was not the best possible option for them. I wonder if I should tell them that they are spending money for their girls' lives to be invisible lies written by admissions officials, marketed by advancement officials, and barely remembered by teachers. I wonder if I should tell them that some teachers look at them with scorn and wonder how in the world they got into the building. I wonder if I should tell them that these brilliant, beautiful girls are not always seen as little girls, but as willful and full-grown women, who need to be sidelined or punished or castigated or put to the side—anything but heralded, anything but given praise.

But then I remember why their parents sent them in the first place. I tell the admissions team that you should never believe that the families of Black girls should be grateful for being here. Instead you should understand the risk that a parent is taking whenever they send their child into the world, especially in today's independent schools, especially if the child is a Black girl. When has the world been a safe place for girls? Now add Black to that descriptor. I tell them that just as Warsan Shire (2011) tells us that no parent puts their child in a boat across the water unless what they have at home is worse, that might be the case here.

The schools in New York City are not all bad, but they're not all good either. That is by design. Parents are often given the false choice of an overcrowded

(Continued)

(Continued)

public school (not all, but many) or a charter that does not take into account the strengths or humanity of the children they should serve (not all, but many). Many of these Black girls would not be seen in their public schools, but not because folks were directly trained to ignore them, and not because the system of admission is such that the school seldom has to know who's applying. It is because of what happens when anything is sold wholesale. You lose the individuality of the original. So, parents turn to independent schools, often through organizations, sometimes as typical parents just trying to see what is out there. They hear about the smaller classrooms. Check. They hear about the facilities. Check. They hear about the diversity and are walked around to see that their child will not be the only person that looks like them in the school. Check. But what of belonging? What of being home, and not visiting?

I wish the conversation at the start of this chapter were an anomaly. I wish I could say that happened at another school that did not have my position, or did not tout itself as being inclusive and social-justice facing. That's the very issue though. Little Black girls are paying to be othered by the people who are given the independence and resources to help them become fierce advocates for themselves, while learning to use academic skills in a cross-disciplinary manner. I guess it can be said these girls are learning early what it is to tackle the plight of those who live at the intersectionality of race and gender in America. These girls are bright and vibrant. I know this because I teach them weekly, and I know how they show up. They are proud of their names, and their hair, and their abilities, and even some weaknesses, and are consistently taught that their weakness, as a function of their color, is the most important thing about them. How do you fight that? How does an educator create strategies to fight against their structure of employment?

What Black girls deserve in these spaces is to truly belong. For so long, they've had to wear a mask, a mask that many of the Black women in the spaces also wear. If you are always wearing a mask to protect yourself in these spaces that were not created for you, though it had you in mind where exclusion is concerned, then when can you be fully you? When does the institution get to see the fullness of your contribution? Furthermore, why is the onus often on Black girls to remove the mask instead of on the institutions that made these masks a necessity in the first place?

I live for the day when the armors and masks are laid to the ground, when little Black girls are afforded the opportunity to walk in newness. When their wings are able to be unfurled and celebrated as strength, instead of castigated as opulence and conceit. Who is singing the song for these Black girls? If this is the rainbow, what's at the end for these Black girls?

There is an overwhelming air of ego amongst some who serve these girls. Physics tell us no two things can occupy the same space at the same time. The same is true in this instance. Where there is ego, nothing else can breathe. There is no growth. Until schools are willing and committed to telling the truth of what is not done well, there will be no breath, no life. Currently, there is an overemphasis on the need for schools to be validated because they have "come so far." I tend to believe if you have admitted Black girls to a space that is neither able nor willing to honor them as whole beings that are vital to the growth and development of the school, then you are engaging in a violent act.

To properly serve Black girls, because it is an act of service, we must separate ourselves from popular belief around respectability politics and how they are inequitably applied to the experiences of Black girls:

- Shaming and judgement through comparison must be eliminated, especially when one has not mitigated for all Black girls encounter when they walk into a school building.

- They do not have to learn grit. They live it.

- The term *defiant* should be interrogated, as many adults choose to penalize Black girls who are practicing debate and advocacy skills on which they are graded in other classes and that will be required in their future.

- The idea of better choices or logical consequences must be named as the mechanisms of compliance and conformity, and we must admit that the consequences of nonadherence to this are illogical and biased. It is the thought that one should be grateful for being "exceptional" and should, therefore, ignore the isolation that may be part of that so called exceptionalism. This is violence to children.

It will take every person deciding that affirming unjust conditions through silence is a deliberate act of violence. It will take schools to stop focusing on diversity and start focusing on antiracist and antimisogynistic practices as they relate to Black girls. It will never matter how many Black girls are enrolled or how many Black women are employed if there are no initiatives that directly confront and actively pose a threat to racist and misogynistic structures. Schools have learned to elocute beautifully about race while ignoring racism and how that system affects Black girls in schools.

"An educator in a system of oppression is either a revolutionary or an oppressor."—Lerone Bennett Jr.

Some educators and parents believe that children do not see race. As Duncan's important work demonstrates (in the previous vignette), not only do our teenagers see race, but they think about it, it impacts their lives, and they are craving spaces to talk about and better understand race and how it operates as a social construct. For those readers who keep asking, "What can I do?" the following vignette, written by then–high school senior Stevanie Rhim, serves as a perfect example of stepping up, stepping out, and getting the process started. As a Black student who recognized there was no space to have conversations about race in her predominantly white school, she created one. We can all learn from Conversation Matters and the power of our students. All sessions of Conversation Matters have been posted online; follow the link to view how multiracial students discuss implicit bias: https://www.youtube.com/watch?v=y4eVG07NO9s.

This section closes with a chapter by Dr. Shannon Waite, who introduces a framework for how educators can intervene in their own teaching practice in an attempt to create learning spaces where Black girls thrive.

Vignette: My Black, My Beautiful, My Brilliant

Stevanie Rhim

"You are Black. You are beautiful. You are brilliant." My aunt used to repeat those words to me every time we saw each other. As a child, I never knew that phrase would become my daily affirmation. You don't really know how much the color of your skin defines the way the world perceives you until you are surrounded by people who look nothing like you. It's what makes you stand out from the rest, which can be overwhelming and intimidating. But, keeping my aunt's words in mind, I chose to see my color as an opportunity to stand out in a different way. I decided to work to change the racial status quo at my predominantly white school by providing a platform and safe space for students to confidently use their voices and express their opinions in order to create a better understanding of one another.

Believing that young people are capable of having mature discussions about race and other difficult topics, I decided to create a space for them to show off that ability. *Conversation Matters* is a series of videotaped interracial student panel discussions on complex subjects of interest to young people. One of my original goals was to get more white students involved and feeling comfortable about discussing the uncomfortable. Once the project got off the ground, several white students joined in on these conversations without hesitation. I discovered they really did want to discuss race and had so much to say. They just couldn't figure out a way to take that first step.

Although our country is currently divided, discussing our differences and how we can better understand one another is one of the most important things that we as people can do. We are so much better together than separated. The power of respect and truth is what brings us together. After one faculty member watched our well-known *N*-word episode, she said that we had done what the adults were unable to do, which was to bring awareness to a recurrent problem that causes hurt and pain for our Black students.

Conversation Matters has not only opened a space for students to speak about race and other important topics, but has allowed our voices to be heard and responded to by the entire school community and beyond. The students have proven to adults not only that they can have mature conversations, but that they have the ability to make change in the world; they just need the opportunity and drive to do it.

I am happy to have been able to give them that opportunity, but I could not have done it without the belief in myself that I got from my aunt's words of affirmation. I had to draw strength from them because, although I have had the support of several of my white teachers and administrators, representation matters. With no Black teachers to look up to at school where I spend the majority of my time, I had to learn to be the representative for myself. I had to work to bring about the changes I wanted to see, because I know that the best way to inspire change is to become it. Remember to be the change you want to see in the world.

CHAPTER 25

Black Girls' Voices Matter

Empowering the Voices of Black Girls Against Coopting and Colonization

Shannon R. Waite

INTRODUCTION

In 2020, one can assert that the words *Black* and *girlhood* in the context of schools are antithetical (Crenshaw, 2015; Evans-Winters, 2011; Watson, 2018). Unfortunately, the magic of Black girls is not routinely celebrated in PreK–12 education. In an effort to acknowledge, combat, and change this narrative, some schools and districts have partnered with nonprofits and a number of organizations to mitigate the challenges Black girls experience in schools. The number of empowerment programs designed to uplift, celebrate, and—as the title describes—empower Black girls has increased within the last decade. In schools, these often-well-meaning initiatives push and promote patriarchal, white, middle-class ideologies about what empowerment looks like, as the voices of Black women and girls are often overlooked or left out (Knott-Dawson, 2018; Muhammad, 2011). Any program operating from an uncritical, ahistorical, color-blind perspective further sustains and perpetuates white supremacy and diminishes Black girlhood.

In this chapter, I seek to highlight the unintentional and often unrecognized consequences of the efforts of white educators, as well as educators of color, who have assimilationist and colonized perspectives about the ability, brilliance, beauty, and potential of Black girls. Recognizing there may be a need to empower, and not discipline, Black girls is in and of itself positive, and is a credit to these educators and leaders. However, without examining, exploring, and interrogating why this need even exists, schools and districts are reinforcing dysconscious racist, sexist, and hegemonic structures that harm Black girls (King, 1991). This chapter additionally offers educators practical tools and strategies that will assist them by helping to challenge their internal narratives to help authentically support and teach brilliant and beautiful Black girls.

HISTORICAL CONTEXT: SCHOOLS AS OPPRESSIVE SPACES FOR BLACK GIRLS AND CRITICAL CONSCIOUSNESS

The challenges Black girls face in schools are well documented in articles, books, documentaries, and reports on the subject (Crenshaw et al., 2014; Evans-Winters, 2011, 2017; Morris, 2016, White, 2018). These challenges are intersectional, as they are pernicious and pose a great to harm to Black girls. Black girls are also hypersexualized and are at greater risk than their white counterparts of being brutalized by law enforcement both inside and outside of schools (Crenshaw, 2015; Fantz et al., 2015; Stelloh & Connor, 2015).

In order to authentically empower Black girls, schools must affirm their voices. This empowerment includes embracing their cultural identities as well as the communities from which these Black girls come. Schools must also seek to develop, reinforce, and support their entitlement to self-advocacy and agency. This can only be done through intention and specifically designing a program or initiative to achieve those goals. Empowerment programming for Black girls must be rooted in culturally responsive education and, more specifically, designed to be responsive to and inclusive of the student's community values and cultural identities (Duncan-Andrade & Morrell, 2008; Singleton, 2015). Despite best intentions, these programs often seek to instill white, hegemonic norms and do not affirm Black girls (Muhammad, 2011). In order to prevent this, schools, districts, and organizations must understand the necessity of interrogating their intrapersonal narratives about the brilliance and beauty of Black girls by developing their internal sense of critical consciousness (Freire, 1970; Kinloch, 2018). Developing a critical consciousness will allow them to begin challenging their dominant narratives and, in turn, any racist and/or implicitly biased beliefs about the competence, potential, and/or limitations of Black girls that society has weaponized against them (King, 1991).

TOOLS AND STRATEGIES TO SUPPORT EDUCATORS

In order for educators to begin tackling the aforementioned issues, it is imperative to acknowledge the responsibility of school building leaders to support their educational leaders within the school building. Teachers need the autonomy and support of their principals in order to genuinely engage in this work. Educational leadership does not occur in a vacuum, and effective leadership is done in collaboration (Fahey et al., 2019; Gronn, 2002; Leithwood & Jantzi, 1994). Teachers are able to build community within classrooms; however, in order to improve the collective experiences of Black girls, this work must be done by the school community. Securing support to cultivate and invest in developing the brilliance and beauty of Black girls warrants a collective effort. All faculty, administrators, and staff must believe in and commit to making these types of initiatives a success.

FRAMEWORK FOR DEVELOPING CRITICAL CONSCIOUSNESS

Interrogating the inherent racism and whiteness in the field of education and examining how its presence influences one's personal and professional interactions with Black girls and the communities they come from is a necessity. Educators may begin this work by committing to interrogate *their* implicit bias and internalized racism by utilizing the following framework to develop *their* critical consciousness. Theories such as conscientization or critical consciousness can help to frame the problem, provide a lens through which the problem may be examined, and give educators a means for exploring avenues through which potential solutions may be derived. However, theory absent of the application to practice is not useful to practitioners. I offer the following practical framework educators may use to help them begin thinking about how to apply the theory offered to their praxis. Engaging in the following practices continuously allows practitioners to take stock of their internal beliefs that may dysconsciously impact, affect, or limit their interactions with Black girls and the communities that raise them (King, 1991).

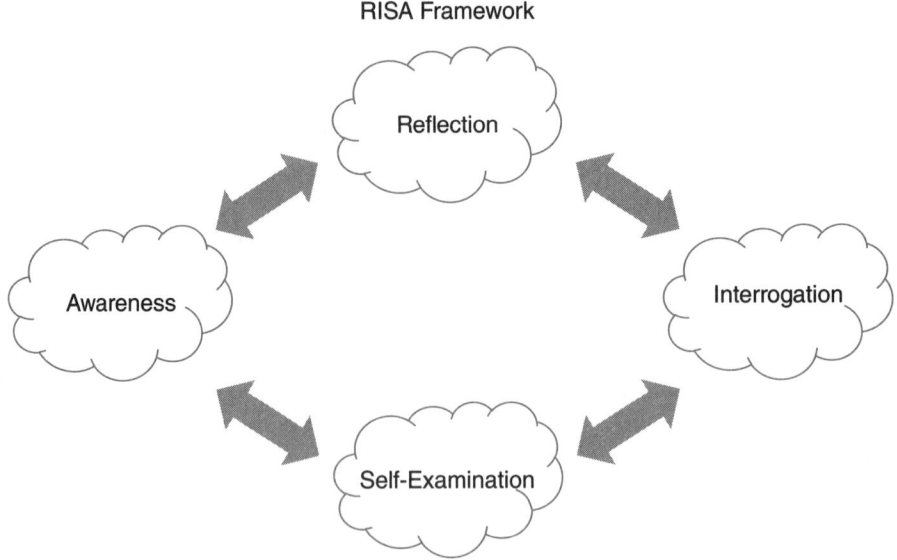

RISA Framework

RISA Framework

1. **R**eflection—allows one to develop strong reflective practices that call for examination of personal core values and beliefs that influence one's professional practices.

2. **I**nterrogation—involves engaging in a deep, introspective, internal examination of *what* norms and narratives are accepted at face value as valid, and concretized as standard.

3. **S**elf-Examination—requires analyzing how one's personal values influence one's professional actions, and authentically exploring whether those actions reinforce and sustain institutionalized racism.

4. **A**wareness—enables the recognition and development of conscientization and the formation of critical consciousness over time, which will allow one to make change.

Educators engaging in these practices in continuous cycles may find themselves on the path towards conscientization and active antiracism.

STRATEGIES TO HELP PREVENT COOPTING AND COLONIZATION

Designing programming and initiatives for Black girls to be protected from being coopted and/or colonized entails including the voices of Black women and girls. The field of education has intensified and amplified the recognition of the significant need for role models, particularly in the scholarship around the importance of role models for students of color (Bristol, 2015; Waite et al., 2018). One implication of this work is to commit both to the initiative *and* to protecting the integrity of the initiative. A strategy to guard empowerment programs against being coopted and colonized is to intentionally seek out the voices and perspectives of Black women *who are invested in the communities the students come from* (Duncan-Andrade & Morrell, 2008; Watson, 2018). These women can help model and develop programming for Black girls that represents the values and norms of the communities these brilliant and beautiful Black girls come from and live in. Not only will it be integral in helping to reinforce that the cultural identities of these women and girls is important, it will ensure that their voices are magnified and also validate their histories, literacies, and heritages (Muhammad, 2018). Finally, educators can utilize these experiences as opportunities for them to learn about the brilliance and beauty of these Black girls *and* their communities (Sealey-Ruiz, 2016).

Another important implication is to be intentional and meticulous in responding to the needs of Black girls by understanding that the Black experience is not a monolith. I cannot emphasize the importance of ensuring that the Black women invited to lead and/or guide this work come from and/or are *authentically* invested in the communities the students come from. This is essential, as another unintended consequence of well-intentioned initiatives is the misguided notion that any woman of color will do; and/or thinking that every Black woman loves, believes in, and seeks to support the evolution of Black girls and children. Identifying a Black woman with assimilationist or colonized perspectives or a Black woman who weaponizes respectability politics can inflict the same harm or perhaps may be even more damaging than a dysconsciously racist white person.

In essence, to ensure that empowerment programs for Black girls are effective and protected against coopting and colonization, schools and districts must

1. **Trust Black women and girls** (Evans-Winters, 2011; Kinloch, 2018; Watson, 2018). Listen to the voices of Black girls, and seek guidance from the Black adults in their communities on how best to develop relationships and cultivate trust with them.

2. **Learn about the history, narratives, and literacies of Black women and girls** (Muhammad, 2018; Sealey-Ruiz, 2016). In order to empower Black girls, teachers must have knowledge about our lived experiences—our stories, from us, and articulated by us.

3. **Learn about critical theories, such as critical race theory (CRT), and reexamine history through a CRT lens** (Ladson-Billings & Tate, 1995). Black girls deserve spaces that are loving and supportive. In order to provide these, all educators must be critical, reflective, and introspective, and this will require that their teachers challenge the deficiency-driven narratives they have been taught about Black girls.

4. **Commit to adopting antiracist practices to debunk myths and false narratives about Black girls** (Evans-Winters, 2015; Kendi, 2019). In order to ensure that Black girls thrive, they must have safe spaces where they are free to be themselves.

5. **Become an ally and then commit to becoming a coconspirator** (Love, 2019). Black girls need support in order to realize their brilliance and beauty. They do not need teachers to speak for them *but to create space for their voices.* And, they need teachers who are invested in meeting them where they are at by utilizing pedagogies that are culturally responsive (Emdin, 2016).

Finally, the list that follows will aid schools and/or districts in identifying programs they might partner with, or help them develop and build their own empowerment programs for brilliant and beautiful Black girls.

Empowerment Programs for Black Girls and Rites Of Passage Programs

Gyrl Wonder: https://www.gyrlwonder.org/

BLACK GIRLS ROCK! https://www.blackgirlsrock.com/

Brown Girls do Ballet: https://www.browngirlsdoballet.com/

Women in Entertainment Empowerment Network: http://www.weenonline.org/

Black Girls Smile: https://www.blackgirlssmile.org/

Black Girls Code: http://www.blackgirlscode.com/

The Brotherhood/Sister Sol: https://brotherhood-sistersol.org/

PART III
"DON'T TOUCH MY HAIR"
—Solange

The first chapter in this section leads readers to cheer and groan simultaneously. Drs. Teri Watson and Angel Miles Nash demonstrate the legal efforts to outlaw anti-Blackness discrimination that targets Black women for their hair texture and styles. While this is both a great legal and social victory, it demonstrates how much work it will take to systematically and legally dismantle anti-Blackness in all of its manifestation (including and beyond hair), in all 50 states, in law and in practice. Educators will learn from this chapter not only the history and importance of the CROWN Act, but also five specific ways they can honor Black girls' hair and five critical Black girls' hair don'ts. Once readers have a solid background on the CROWN Act, the subsequent chapter by Dr. Donovan Griffin-Blake explores the microaggressions found in schools that are centered around Black girl hair. Using a group of Black girls she works with, Griffin-Blake not only shares their real life encounters with teachers, but also shares the action they took together, as a village, to raise awareness and share their voices as a means of education. By situating their lived experience as empirical evidence, we learn, through their actions, strategies to increase respect and awareness of the long and beautiful history of the magic of Black girl hair.

CHAPTER 26

She Wears a Crown

Centering Black Girlhood in Schools

Terri N. Watson, Angel Miles Nash

Bedecked with brilliance,

Decorated with decorum,

Embellished with excellence,

Her crown, we need to protect her crown.

—Angel Miles Nash

In her book, *Pushout: The Criminalization of Black Girls in Schools*, Monique W. Morris (2016) chronicles the miseducation, adultification, and criminalization of Black girls in schools across America. Black girls are disciplined in schools more than all other girls and most boys in every state in the nation, and they are adultified at ages as early as five years old (Epstein et al., 2017; National Women's Law Center, 2017). Many of these punitive actions have led to their arrest and criminalization. The two youngest Black girls to be criminalized were only six years old: one was placed in handcuffs and taken to the police station for having a tantrum at school (Campbell, 2012). The other, who has special needs, was taken by local law enforcement agents to a mental health facility because she was deemed "out of control" (Chavez & Alonso, 2020). In a separate incident, a 16-year-old honor student was arrested and expelled from her Florida high school when her science experiment went awry (Klein, 2013). As a result of the unjust and excessive punishment of Black girls in schools, Black America's commitment to protecting Black girlhood has become a public imperative.

As Black women and professors of educational leadership, we have constructed the following chapter to shine a needed light on the ways schools and the process of schooling have reduced Black girls to mere targets of egregious surveillance and have subjected them to harassment based on their identities, appearances, and unapologetic expressions of existence in manners that follow them into womanhood (Mbilishaka & Apugo, 2020). In this chapter, we pay close attention to the policing of Black girls' hair in schools and the passing of the Create a Respectful and Open Workplace for Natural Hair (CROWN) Act in several locales, including California and New York, our respective home states. We then define whiteness and its challenge to Black girlhood in general and Black hair specifically. Last, we conclude with best practices for educators to honor Black girls' crowns.

THE POLICING OF BLACK GIRLS' HAIR IN SCHOOLS

Recently, several disciplinary incidents targeting Black girls, and their hair, in schools have garnered national attention. For instance, in 2018, in Terrytown, Louisiana, an 11-year old Black girl was tearfully escorted from her Roman Catholic school for wearing braided hair extensions. The transgression was recorded by several of her classmates and soon went viral, prompting outrage across multiple social media platforms (Jacobs & Levin, 2018). Further, in the fall of 2019, school officials in Jackson, Michigan, denied an eight-year-old Black girl the opportunity to take her school picture because the color of her hair extensions was deemed not "of natural tones," as dictated by the school's guidelines (Rivera, 2019). The surveillance of the style, color, and even the natural state of Black girls' hair continues to challenge the notion that schools are places wherein *all* children can learn and feel happy and secure.

The school-based policies—and policing—concerning hair singles out Black girls for how their hair naturally grows and for the distinct and creative manners they fashion their hair in. The troubling results, which include restricting Black girls from participating in school programs and activities, obviate their abilities to flourish academically and socially (O'Brien-Richardson, 2019). Moreover, it is the impetus of legal efforts being enacted across the United States to protect Black girls and women from discrimination based on the appearance of what we affectionately refer to as our *crowns*.

THE CROWN ACT

The CROWN (Create a Respectful and Open Workplace for Natural Hair) Act of 2019, an extension of the Fair Employment and Housing Act and state education codes, is a legislative mandate that protects against discrimination based on natural hair texture and styles. Initially passed into law in the state of California on July 3, 2019, the act went into effect there on January 1, 2020. New York became the second state to pass the act on July 12, 2019 (see SN 6209), followed by New Jersey on December 19, 2019 (see SB 3945). The states of Virginia, Colorado, and Washington have passed the act along with the municipalities of Montgomery County, Maryland, and Cincinnati, Ohio (CROWN Coalition, 2020). Importantly, on December 5, 2019, Congressman Cedric L. Richmond and Congresswomen Barbara Lee, Marcia Fudge, and Ayanna Pressley introduced the CROWN act in the House of Representatives to "prohibit discrimination based on a person's hair texture or hairstyle if that style or texture is commonly associated with a particular race or national origin" (see HR 5309—CROWN Act of 2019). At this time, there are 57 cosponsors for the act (including the 29 original cosponsors), representing 28 U.S. states and territories.

WHITENESS AND BLACK GIRLHOOD IN SCHOOLS

In the chapter "Black Girls, White Privilege, and Schooling," Watson (2018) examined the impact of White privilege on the educational experiences of Black girls. She detailed how America's public schools, by and large, affirm White privilege while purposefully disenfranchising Black girls from their school community based on the hue of their skin. White privilege centers whiteness. The latter is defined as the articulation of a constructed state of privilege based on one's race (Crenshaw et al., 1995; Delgado & Stefancic, 2001). It affects how and the extent to which Black girls are afforded opportunities for educational advancement. Moreover, white educators' perceptions of Black girls and their brilliance are oftentimes (mis)informed by the comparisons they make between Black girls and their proximity to white norms (Morris, 2012; Watson, 2018). Meaning, most educators judge Black girls and their academic prowess (or lack thereof) on how closely they align with whiteness and white ideals of femininity. Both, not surprisingly, are incompatible with Black girlhood.

Based on the norms of whiteness, Black girls are often characterized as too loud, too bold, and too aggressive for the schoolhouse, making them uneducable. Ironically, these very characteristics have been found to sustain Black girls in and out of schools (Watson, 2016). If we are to successfully challenge whiteness in schools, we must let Black girls be who they are. They must be allowed to stand in their own light, and their cultural assets should be considered complements to their respective school communities (Yosso, 2005). Accordingly, if we are to effectively center Black girlhood in schools, we must unpack how whiteness influences, impacts and, in many ways, defines norms and standards in schools (Watson, 2018). Many educators consider academic promise alongside how Black girls act, speak, and look, paying close attention to the way they wear and style their hair. The latter is a false correlation, as the way a Black girl styles her hair has no relationship to her academic aptitude. Nevertheless, Black girls often find themselves stereotyped and stymied by their hair, and hairstyles, in classrooms across the country.

HONORING BLACK GIRLS' CROWNS IN SCHOOLS

If educators are to effectively and affectively support Black girls and their brilliance, they must honor their crowns. Hair, for many Black girls, is a source of joy and creativity. They style and adorn their hair to reflect their moods as well as the current trends and fashions. The following practices and rationale are offered to support and encourage educators to honor Black girlhood and Black hair.

Do's

1. Do feel free to compliment Black girls' hair in genuine ways. Affirmative celebration of creative personal expression promotes self-confidence and self-efficacy.

2. Do ask if the hairstyle is for a special occasion and/or celebration. Understanding students' lives and cultures enhances diversity and feelings of inclusion.

3. Do provide mirrors and windows that highlight multiple examples of Black girlhood. Positive identity development supports students' self-esteem and sense of belonging.

4. Do conduct your own research to understand the culture of Black hair. Investing in understanding students' differences is the cultural responsibility of educators.

5. Do appreciate the diversity in the presentation of Black hair. Black girlhood is not a monolith, and Black girls must be viewed as individuals if they are to self-actualize.

Don'ts

1. Do not touch Black girls' hair. Encroaching on personal space is a safety violation and is often perceived as disrespectful.

2. Do not mimic Black girls' hairstyles, especially if you are not Black. Appropriation and exoticism can lead to the displacement and objectification of Black girls.

3. Do not inquire about Black girls' hair maintenance. Haircare is a distinct cultural practice for many Black girls and should not be debated nor disparaged.

4. Do not adultify Black girls based on the way they style their hair. Protect the innocence of Black girlhood and treat Black girls like the children they are.

5. Do not use deficit language to describe Black girls' hair (e.g., *ghetto*, *ratchet*, *hood*, *wild*, *unprofessional*). Derogatory language can negatively impact Black girls' esteem.

CHAPTER 27

I Am Not My Hair

Donovan Griffin-Blake

I facilitate a girls' circle (like a girls' group) at an alternative school. The group consists of Black and Latinx girls. In one session, the girls came in very upset. They explained they feel that their teacher is racist. I ask them to share their evidence, grab a notebook, and jot down their statements. Donna shares, "So I am wearing my niqab today because it is Ramadan. When I walked into class, some boys yelled, "boom" and the teacher laughed with them. She is so mean." Melanie chimes in, "Yeah, and one day I was wearing this cute outfit with my Gucci purse and she had the nerve to ask me if it was real!" Tanya states, "At least she didn't call home to tell your parents that she saw you in class with a lot of money and was concerned if you were involved in illegal activity!" I explain to the students that I understand what they are saying about the teacher. I explain to the girls that what they are describing are *microaggressions*.

Microaggressions are identified as the verbal and nonverbal actions and environmental slights, snubs, or insults—whether intentional or unintentional—that create hostile, derogatory, or negative messages that target persons based solely upon their marginalized group membership (Sue et al., 2007). Unfortunately, Black girls are subjected to microaggressions in school, often by the administrators and teachers who are supposed to be educating them (Nittle, 2020). These students will continue to encounter microaggressions as they move through life and in the workplace. I shared with the girls that I too have been subjected to this teacher's verbal bias. Most days, I wear my natural hair, which is big and curly. Whenever I straighten my hair, the same teacher makes a point to compliment my hair. My students began to express that they feel like all white teachers make rude statements or inappropriate jokes about their hair. Clearly the behavior of the white teachers towards the hairstyles of Black females has sent a clear message that Black beauty is only acceptable when it resembles the aesthetic of white society. For the next month, we talked about Black women's hair.

Our next sessions encompassed the history of Black hair. I showed them photos of queens and kings from countries in the African continent from the 1400s. We discussed how, in the African continent, a person's hairstyle was directly related to their geographic identity (Byrd & Tharps, 2014). I had them pay attention to the elaborate hairstyles in pictures. I explained to them how proud Africans were of their ornate hairstyles. We discussed how white settlers purposefully shaved the heads of new slaves to take away their African identity as they came to the "New" World (Byrd & Tharps, 2014).

In the 1800s, there were light-skinned and dark-skinned slaves. The white slave owners noticed they got more money for the lighter slaves with the straight hair than they did for the dark slaves with the coarse hair. Even after slavery, white America made straight hair the only acceptable standard of beauty for Black women. We went on to examine what the slaves did when they did not have the equipment to maintain their traditional hairstyles and how this dilemma led to the birth of Black female entrepreneurs and the first female self-made entrepreneur, Madame C. J. Walker, in the 1900s. Madame Walker created a line of hair care products for Black women to maintain their straightened hair. We studied Madame Walker's business model with her army of sales representatives and the training she gave aspiring beauticians through her beauty school (Bundles, 2001). I shared the beauty of the 1960s through visual images in magazines, television, and movies that reintroduced the beauty of the African hair aesthetic into our society. Many of these facts were new information for my students, as this is not often taught in schools.

The controversy of Black American hair aesthetics has been ongoing in Black media. In 1988, filmmaker Spike Lee dramatized the issue in his movie *School Daze*. In the movie, colorism was a major theme, and the concepts of "good hair" and "bad hair" took center stage (Lee, 1988). In the early 1990s, Afrocentric styles were at the forefront of Black hair culture, including various types of braids. Director John Singleton captured the braided hairstyles of the female characters as they tried to find love in a loveless urban setting in his films, *Boyz N The Hood* (Nicolaides & Singleton, 1991) and *Poetic Justice* (Singleton, 1993). Chris Rock produced *Good Hair*, a documentary that explored the various hairstyles of Black women. Recently, Kenya Barris wrote and produced an episode of his hit show *Black-ish* that unpacked the youngest daughter's (Diane's) struggle with deciding if she should keep her hair natural or get a perm (Barris, 2020). The plight of the hair conundrum, for Black women, is still present and relevant in Black culture.

As a Black educator in a suburban school district, I have always been conscious about my hairstyle. In the past, I have worn hairstyles that were deemed acceptable and nonthreatening to white Americans. It is difficult as a teacher to encourage my students to love themselves when I don't show them that I embrace my natural beauty. For the past three years, I have been wearing my naturally curly hair in the classroom. I have taught all of my students that my hairstyle is my choice, and we have discussed what that means to me and them. I have noticed that more of my Black girls and colleagues have started wearing their natural hair more often. I know that my decision to wear my natural hair to work is not viewed as respectable by administrators across the school district, but it was a risk I was willing to take on. This controversy is being debated through the nation via the CROWN Act. The CROWN (Creating a Respectful and Open Workplace for Natural hair) Act (2019) is based on the CROWN research study (Joy Collective, 2019), which surveyed working Black and white women to measure workplace discrimination against individuals with Black natural hair. In November 2019, the CROWN Act was passed in our county, and I now have the legal right to truly be my natural self without fear of reprimand. The CROWN Act has been implemented by only 8 states in this nation. This is still an injustice, and we still have a long way to go!

If hairstyles impact Black women on such a large scale, imagine what Black girls are subjected to. In the American education system, Black girls are penalized for their hair choices under the guise of dress code violations. Black girls should not be denied access to their education nor disciplined because a white school employee does not like their hairstyle.

At Mystic Valley Regional Charter School, two sisters were disciplined for wearing box braids. The girls had to serve detentions, were ejected from their sports teams, and were excluded from participating in the prom (Mettler, 2017). A 12-year-old Black girl at Orlando's Faith Christian Academy in Florida was told her Afro was a distraction to other students in the classroom (Kim, 2013). Imagine your child's daycare teacher sending a note home to say that the child's hair smells bad due to the hair products being used and requesting that you refrain from using those products. That happened in Chicago to Tionna Norris, who received such a note about her three-year-old daughter, Amia (Capatides, 2016). In Terrytown, Louisiana, a Black middle school girl was sent home because she had extensions in her hair. The officials at Christ the King Catholic School stated that the student violated the dress code by not wearing natural hair (Adams, 2018). There are many more discriminatory acts such as the ones listed above that are not reported.

All the background information that I have provided is an attempt to educate white teachers on how hair-based microaggressions have a massive impact on Black girls. Black girls are consistently labeled in school as loud, angry, rude, and hostile, and now their hair is being viewed as a threat to learning in the educational environment. A paper written by Rebecca Epstein, Director of the Georgetown University Law School Center for Poverty and Inequality, and her colleagues reported that Black girls as young as five are viewed as being more sexually mature, more knowledgeable about adult issues, and less innocent than their same-age/different-race peers (2017). Epstein coined the term *adultification* to describe the effect on these children, who are perceived as and/or behaving as adults (Epstein et al., 2017). Teachers, administrators, and other authority figures in American education do not have the right to take away the innocence of Black girls. Schools are guilty of adultifying Black girls through their zero-tolerance dress code policies, which allow these students to be harshly admonished for their hairstyles by white administrators. Currently, Black girls are more harshly disciplined in schools, which is negatively impacting their academic success and is making them the fastest-growing population in the school-to-prison pipeline (Hill, 2017).

To improve the learning environment for Black girls, white teachers need to be aware of their biases towards these students. I challenge teachers, content teams, professional learning communities, department chairs, and administrators to examine their biases. Here is an activity that I do quarterly with my team to discuss our beliefs and attitudes that may impact our teaching.

Activity

This activity can be done individually or in a small group.

- Go to the Project Implicit webpage to take the Implicit Association Test (IAT). (https://implicit.harvard.edu/implicit/takeatest.html)

- Click on the tab, "Take a Test."

- Click on the IAT test that you wish to use to examine for biases within yourself.

- Once you get the test score, you can write a letter to yourself or share with trusted colleagues about how you can be more culturally responsive in your instruction to students who may be impacted by your bias. Then start to mindfully implement culturally responsive strategies into your lessons.

- Reflect frequently on the equity of your instruction to ensure learning for all students.

When I train other teachers on racial microaggressions, I use a clip of Ms. Morello, the teacher in the television show *Everybody Hates Chris* (Rock, 2006). Ms. Morello constantly treated Chris unfairly due to her stereotypical beliefs about his family because they were Black. After showing teachers various clips of Ms. Morello, teachers either laugh because they know a teacher who acts like Ms. Morello, or get silent because they have been Ms. Morello. When they see Ms. Morello and hear Chris narrate how it makes him feel, it is usually a great wake-up call for teachers who were unaware that they have some bias. Whenever I do training relating to race, I love to use video clips to frame our racial conversations. Here are my favorite go-to resources to get video clips to discuss microaggressions:

- Trevor Noah on *The Daily Show*—He uses satire to illuminate racial issues.

- *Black-ish*—Black dad assesses his cultural identity while raising his family in a white upper-class environment.

- *Adam Ruins Everything*—a research-based comedy sketch show that explains the policies in the United States.

I encourage secondary teachers to find episodes (from my resource list) on YouTube that address specific topics. Please remember to review the media resource guidelines for your school district before sharing with the students/staff. For primary teachers, I highly encourage the teaching of diversity using books and stories that teach acceptance. Here are a few examples:

- *Skin Again*, bell hooks

- *Hair Love*, Matthew A. Cherry and Vashti Harrison

- *I Am Enough*, Grace Byers

- *Antiracist Baby*, Ibram X. Kendi

White teachers must keep an open mind and heart to address their biases, in an attempt to be culturally responsive. In their book, *Courageous Conversations About Race*, Glenn Singleton (2015) provides guidance on how to handle these uncomfortable discussions. They recommend that educators follow the four agreements:

- Stay focused

- Speak honestly

- Practice uneasiness

- Prepare for ongoing discussions

The girls circle decided to share their new knowledge with our school community. They made posters of some of the microaggressions they experience in school, and we posted them in staff spaces (staff lounge, copy room, staff restroom, mailroom). They did a presentation called, "I Am Not My Hair" for the school community during Black History Month. Several teachers started to ask the girls about their hair, but we are still working on the initial teacher that we were discussing. We are going to give up on her as we continue the conversation.

As readers learn from this section, hair is a primary component of Black girl identity. To conclude the section, "Covered Girls" demonstrates how covering one's hair by choice is just as important as styling and deserves space in the Black hair narrative. Drs. Arki and Phelps offer personal stories in an effort to share with educators the various reasons why Black girls "wrap" and to also help educators understand and honor the practice, as opposed to creating rules that further marginalize the practice itself and the Black girls who choose to engage in it.

Vignette: Covered Girls

Shemariah J. Arki, Erin K. Phelps

In 2019, the *Cleveland Plain Dealer* named Cleveland, Ohio, one of the worst cities in America for Black women. As a proud Cleveland native, this is something that I knew and experienced daily—essentially, this is not new news. Shortly after this headline was published, a local arts and culture magazine reached out, inviting me to be a part of a story centering the lived experiences of Black women in Cleveland. I was pleased to share space with a dope group of Black women, from my good sista friend of over 20 years to the daughter of one of my mentor educators from my early youth development days. We met at a local coffee house and kiki'd over the current sociopolitical context while symbiotically holding space and lifting one another up.

At the end of our time, the author announced this would be a cover story and asked us to coordinate a time for the photo shoot. Just home from my first trip to Ghana, West Africa, I was excited and proud to rock one of my new Ankara prints to wrap my hair for the cover shoot. A few weeks after the issue ran, I was in a meeting with a Black woman colleague, and she shared a story with me:

> I was out in the streets and saw your magazine cover, and guess what happened? There was another [Black] woman and her daughter who were getting a copy. The little girl, who had on the cutest 'lil headwrap herself, said to her mom: "Look mom, it's me on the magazine."

I tried to keep it together, but I couldn't. My colleague embraced me as I wiped my tears and attempted to remain professional, grateful for this mom and daughter, grateful, in this moment, for being seen.

In the wake of "wokeness," womxn of color have interrogated controlling images of how hair is inherently political for womxn of color. From conversations surrounding colorism and texture discrimination, scholars and nonscholars alike have problematized dominant hair narratives. Oftentimes, however, left out of these conversations are those who cover or wrap their hair for personal, cultural, and/or religious reasons. Because many cultures utilize various types of head coverings in everyday life and/or for special occasions, a direct look at the most marginalized within this group is necessary via a black feminist politic. Many womxn and femmes also wear their headwraps to imply group affiliation or expression of personal ethos.

Reasons I wrap are plenty: to protect my energy (spiritual), to remind myself and those who I am in relationship with who and whose I am, and for support when I am working as I am on the line for my people. In an attempt to break away from

(Continued)

(Continued)

the dichotomous narrative of relaxed or natural, covered or uncovered, oppressed or liberated, I share this story with the intent to outline the sociopolitical contexts behind different head wrapping techniques, provide context for how womxn and femmes wrap their hair in modernity, and nuance discussion on Black girl bodies as sites of political action. In the words of Mona Haydar, rapper-poet-activist-chaplain of the protest anthem "Hijabi" (2017): "Covered up or not, don't ever take us for granted."

I Am Enough, by Grace Byers, illustrated by Keturah A. Bobo

Grade Level PreK–5

Contemporary Realistic Fiction

Book Review by Omobolade Delano-Oriaran

I Am Enough (Byers, 2018) is a book of hair beauty, hair expression, courage, self-love, perseverance, boldness, determination, and more for Black girls. The Black and Brown girl characters are depicted in realistic roles and demonstrate they can dream, rise, win, and be persistent. The storyline compliments the realities of Black girls by using rich, colorful illustrations that mirror authenticity as the characters play with each other, climb the ladder, master karate, run track, play double Dutch, play patty-cake, practice handstands, and read books. Illustrator Keturah A. Bobo masterfully shows Black and Brown girls in authentic and culturally engaging ways, with variances and differences in Black racial skin tones and hues. The realistic characters depicted are Black-centric, culturally authentic, and engaging.

The power in the rich expressions of hairstyles—from braids to top knots to curly 'fros and Afro puffs—"celebrate[s] and affirm[s] the normalcy of Black hair" (Brooks & McNair, 2015, p. 300). The curvaceous hips mirror the reality of many African American girls. Keturah A. Bobo authentically illustrates a Black girl with caramel, ebony, melanin skin tone and a pineapple ponytail hairstyle, sparring in her green belt karate uniform like "the Champ . . . here to fight." Another bonus to this book is that the author and illustrator integrate a multicultural focus by depicting girls from a variety of racial backgrounds with physical disabilities. The storyline unquestionably sends uplifting messages to Black girls of all skin tones and shapes.

PART IV

"WE WANT TO TURN VICTIMS INTO SURVIVORS—AND SURVIVORS INTO THRIVERS."

—Tarana Burke

When one looks in the mirror and sees a reflection that is judged before a word is spoken, or forgotten and disregarded by a glance, it is difficult to face each day knowing what is to come. The author of the following vignette, Samuella Bowden, helps readers begin to feel this experience viscerally in their bodies, while simultaneously demonstrating the strength and perseverance required to move through it. "I just want to be seen for who I am," she says. Her vignette cries out for change in our classrooms.

Vignette: Mirror, Mirror

Samuella Bowden

I wake up in the morning, and I look at my reflection in the mirror. A young Black woman stares back at me. I look at my dark skin that is seen as criminal and dangerous. I look at my dark skin that is seen as ugly and dirty. I look at myself and know that my skin has brought upon me some of the worst judgements known to mankind, so I know I must do everything in my power to push those judgements down.

(Continued)

(Continued)

I know that I have to hold myself to a certain standard, because the slightest mistake could end me. I know that I cannot afford to get caught up in what some would call "kids being kids," because I will be seen as an adult. I must remember that I cannot be too passionate about a situation, because I become "angry" and "aggressive" by default. I move through the world consciously, because I know I am being watched carefully, and second chances will not be given to me. I look at myself in the mirror and promise the girl staring back at me that I will not mess up. James Baldwin once said, "To be a Negro in this country and be relatively conscious is to be in a rage almost all the time." During high school, I felt this rage constantly.

Rage is what I feel when I change my hair because I want to, and my colleagues decide to pull, tug, and pet me as they gawk at my hair like I am some rare animal. Rage is how I feel when a group leader changes their vernacular when talking to me, because before I even open my mouth, a narrative has already been written for me. Rage is the feeling that consumes me when a teacher who has known me for four years stares me in my soul and proceeds to call me some other Black person's name. What upsets me even more is that they don't realize that they have just looked me in my eyes and not seen me for who I truly am.

Most people think it's just a harmless comment or an ignorant action, but truly those harmless comments add up. It isn't about having my feelings hurt, it's about my feelings being disregarded, insulted, and invalidated, and that contributes to the rage already brewing in my heart. The rage that is almost impossible to not feel. The same rage I have to cast away because it is unhealthy to feel. This does not mean that I am angry with anyone. This means that I want to be seen for who I am. This means that I want people to look me in my face and acknowledge my blackness. This means I want my colleagues to try to understand my culture instead of closing their minds off to it because they are "uncomfortable." This means that I want you to see who I see, Sam.

The actions and reactions towards Black girls in the classroom have far-reaching consequences, as readers will learn in the following chapter. Ariel Shivers-McGrew, counselor and advocate, shares personal experiences of being a Black woman in the workplace who struggles to be seen for her intelligence and ability to accomplish her work. Instead of recognition, she is relegated to meaningless tasks to remove her from the table, and told explicitly that her job was, in essence, created for her so there could be diversity in the workplace. As you read this chapter, imagine the emotional toll of being there every day and the strength it took to move past those moments. What skills and support might students need to grow through these moments as they progress through their educational and professional careers? What preparation can a white educator provide to help students refuse such treatment throughout their lives?

CHAPTER 28

Voice Activation and Volume Control in the Workplace

Ariel Shivers-McGrew

While the United States has made significant progress towards giving women space in the workplace, there are obvious gaps between women's employment rates, wages, and economic security, and the advantages men are afforded. Now, add the additional layers of race, sex, religion, age, and education, and you have common themes across the narrative of the intersection. If you are young, Black, and gifted, you will have a work experience that activates your voice, I guarantee. The difficulty will come with learning to control the volume. I recently had to acknowledge the painful reality of what it meant to be in a space where my distinctiveness was high, but belongingness was low. I was expected to hold space for others when their actions were disrespectful, minimizing, and disregarding towards me.

What made this situation unique was my multiple attempts to offer my perspective free of emotion. I stated my observations out loud with a smile on my face. I highlighted the reality of unconscious bias at play—or at least that's what I wanted to attribute to the fact I spent 29 calendar days in the office without interaction with my colleagues. I wanted to believe it was not intentional. I tried to think that if I referenced the job description, I could understand why I was the first minoritized employee at this organization (as a checked-off representation box) who was experiencing social exclusion, because the organization's choice to supposedly be inclusive with my hire was a foreclosed opportunity.

When there were opportunities to interact with other staff, the scenario would go a little something like this.

"Please join us." I'd sit long enough to hear all the introductions made. Not too long after all the presentations were made, I would be asked to make copies, print documents, put swag bags together—in other words, get up from the table because I did not have a seat. I'd sit in as an outlier listening to learn while seething with complete disdain for the dynamics at play. I decided to become tactfully disruptive. I began to control the tone of my awareness. One thing I knew based on observation and interaction about my work peers was they were not the least bit interested in me as a person and what I brought to the table. I do not think anyone ever cared to consider I was, in fact, a qualified mental health professional, trained in equity and workforce trends, and certified in nonprofit management and leadership.

That experience activated my interest in workplace incivility and my voice on DEI (diversity, equity, and inclusion) shortcomings in a professional setting. I needed to know how and when I would decide to advocate for myself if I could not clearly express it. The desire of individuals to be in charge; their need to humiliate others; and their jealousy, envy, and hatred date back as far as human society, while the various pressures these needs and desires put on people's moral, mental, physical, and other types of integrity represent an ancient category (Arnautović, 2013). Targets of workplace harassment may experience stress, depression, low self-esteem, loss of sleep, and even posttraumatic stress disorder (Lewis et al., 2002). Ferris (2004) asserts that few employees seek internal assistance regarding workplace bullying. This may be because they have an intuitive understanding of the consequences attached to seeking support in the workplace. According to Sperry and Duffy (2009), the typical mobbing victim is traumatized and feeling powerless, humiliated, and filled with self-doubt. Naming the experience and describing its effects on the victim's life is a practical action that can begin, but not complete, the restoration of personal agency.

To date, there has been little to no published research directly assessing the relationship between emotional intelligence and workplace incivility (Kirk et al., 2011). Van den Brande et al. (2017) aimed to bridge the research lines of work-related and individual-related antecedents of workplace bullying by investigating the interaction between work stressors and employees' coping strategies in association with exposure to workplace bullying (p. 2). Namie (2003) has conducted research that shows workplace bullying crosses boundaries of gender, race, and organizational rank, in other words, "status-blind" interpersonal hostility is deliberate and sufficiently severe to harm the targeted person's health or economic status. In many instances, workplace bullying is often painful to identify by one or two individual explicit acts, thus creating a challenge for the target, bystander, and manager (Keashly, 2010).

Workplace bullying is a case of workplace aggression. Like bullying, workplace aggression is not a random and unpredictable event—it focuses on specific targets (Neves, 2014). When employees perceive themselves as targets of incivility, they must quickly determine how to react (Porath & Pearson, 2012). But that's it—even as I recount my own lived experience, and I was subjected to what felt like a full-on workplace angry mob. I recall one of my coworkers walking up to me with a sly smile on her face and telling me, "Your job doesn't even really exist anymore." This is where you learn to control your volume as a Black woman in an all-white work environment. As I understood, during the moment in which she made the statement, she felt she could confidently say what she wanted without consequence, passively intending for me to get the message. I heard her, but I was going to make her work to put her insecurities to rest. Consequently, a few months later I was told, "We'll pay you to look for a new job. Don't worry about dropping the ball. If it falls apart it just falls apart—we'll figure it out when we get there."

Here is where I turn up the volume. It was time for my annual review, and I had made my mind up. I applied to be the community outreach and support manager, and instead, I was being pushed into a catch-all administration role. I was playing modern-day blackface and was not going to stand for it. My anger had nothing to do with whether or not I got the position, could perform it, or even wanted it. It was evident my peers were choosing to preserve comfort dynamics over doing the right thing. It did not matter how many instances of unfair and organizationally misaligned values on display I gently nudged at—I had become the problem woman of color, and to others, the Angry Black woman.

I advocated for myself and my ideas, and I resisted the reality that some folks would rather have me in the room than in a seat at the table (diversity vs. inclusion), because that was much more comfortable for them. For every brilliant Black girl who brings value to the table, believe me when I say it is not okay to watch your value swept onto the floor.

Their years in middle school are a time when youth are learning about and experimenting with sex in a diversity of ways. But what about when you don't want to engage, aren't ready, or just aren't interested? How do you say no? And as a Black girl who is adultified (a term used to describe the way Black youth are routinely perceived to be four to five years older than their actual age), how does a 12-year-old Black girl convince herself that all of her feelings are valid, that none of the things happening to her are OK, and that it is critically important to use her voice to say NO? Dr. Alice Ragland invites readers to think about the assumptions they make of Black girls in the classroom, as these assumptions relate to these girls' bodies and the historical and sociopolitical contexts in which Black girl bodies are viewed. Let us all remember, the founder of the #MeToo movement, Tarana Burke, is a self-identified Professional Black Girl.

Vignette: Black Girls Say #MeToo

Alice Ragland

I went to school in the days before #MeToo.[1] Before discussions of consent and toxic masculinity appeared in commercials, on TV shows, and on the nightly news. Before women marched on Washington with knit cat-ear hats and THIS PUSSY GRABS BACK signs. Before high-profile persecutions of serial abusers garnered media attention. It wasn't until the conversation on sexual misconduct made it into the mainstream that I realized that much of what I experienced from elementary school through young adulthood was actually considered sexual harassment or assault.

I remember boys in elementary school pointing to girls in the hallway and loudly categorizing our budding breasts as "eggs" or "marbles," as well as loudly declaring what kind of bra they suspected us to be wearing. I remember girls being bullied and shamed in middle and high school for being sexually active or for being suspected of sexual activity, while the boys were celebrated for "hitting" as many girls as they could. I remember how Black girls in my high school were called thots, set-outs, swooties, and every variation of bitches and hoes. I remember the resounding silence of teachers, counselors, and principles as all of this was happening right in front of their faces. Some of them even joined into the chorus of "she's fast" or "these girls are nasty."

Sex-ed class didn't tell us that someone asking for sex over and over until we give in does not count as consent. Neither does making us feel so guilty that we do it out of pity. Neither does the threat of "if you don't do it, I'll find someone else who will." Black girls at my school were coerced and pressured into sex because people simply felt *entitled* to our bodies. Often, we fell into the belief that we owed somebody sex. On top of that, for some of us, our sense of self-worth was tied up in male attention. Many of us came out of our abstinence-only health class thinking that sex whenever and however, whether we actually wanted it or not, was the way to get someone to like us or to stay interested.

Within this landscape of normalized physical and psychological violence, Black girls at my school were humiliated and punished for "having an attitude," for fixing our hair, and for defending ourselves against those who harassed us. We were shamed and scrutinized by students and adults for being too dark, too light, too loud, too quiet, too big, too thin, too boyish, too tall, too short, too hood, too proper. Black trans girls at my school were bullied and subsequently expelled for "being a distraction."

---

[1] #MeToo is a movement and hashtag spearheaded by Tarana Burke, a Black woman. Often Black women do not get credit for their contributions, so it is important to mention her name.

#MeToo is for the Black girls and women who have experienced any and all of this. It's for those under-the-radar moments of discomfort and shaming that don't get a lot of media attention. It's for those unwanted and unwarranted interactions steeped in the deep history of objectification and open vulnerability of Black bodies. Too many of us have had to say #MeToo.

A Note for Educators: In order to interrupt the silence surrounding violence against Black girls and engage others with this issue, it is critical to check your own prejudices about Black girls. We are all exposed to negative perceptions of Black girls and women, so it is imperative to recognize and unpack your biases. Also, sexual violence against Black girls is a systemic issue based in a history of oppressive structures. These unjust structures are so inundated in our society that they often seem invisible. It's vitally important to educate yourself and others as much as possible about the systems of oppression that perpetuate violence against Black girls and women. I implore all educators to play a role in breaking the silence and interrupting the cycle of shaming and sexual violence against Black girls. Listen and speak up when they say #MeToo.

PART V

"FREEDOM IS A CONSTANT STRUGGLE."

—Angela Davis

Black Girls, White Places, Curating Our Space. Black girls continue to encounter multiple and intersecting layers of discriminatory and oppressive practices compounded by being in white spaces. There's something extra that Black girls must face in white spaces. Something beyond what white girls face. Something beyond what they face in Black spaces. And something beyond what Black boys face in those same white spaces. While Black boys face stereotypes and discrimination, they have access to certain social capital when they are athletic, when they are charismatic, when they are handsome. Black girls face contentious relationships with their white girl peers, tension from their white teachers who expect "girls" to act a particular way, and beauty norms that are based on whiteness. In short, Black girls are constantly struggling for freedom. The following chapter by Dr. Katy Swalwell and her students Vashalice and Nya demonstrates the extra oppression high-achieving Black girls face in suburban classrooms. The subsequent chapter by Ivy Anastasia Alphonse-Crean further illustrates this dynamic in predominantly white independent school spaces. The section closes with a sankofa (ancient Ghanaian proverb that loosely translates to "return and fetch it") moment: a vignette by Cordenia Paige describing her return to such a space, working to make things different for the Black girls who, like her, are often the only one.

CHAPTER 29

When She's The Only One

High-Achieving Black Girls in Suburban Schools

Katy Swalwell, Vashalice Kaaba, Nya Bottley

Being in AP literature felt like the pinnacle for me. I felt like I was finally in a space where I could be "smart" without the fear of having to switch between my two identities (Down-Home Black Girl with my friends and Smart Black Girl at school). Being smart was everything to me, the key to unlock everything my mother and grandmother prayed for me. My AP literature class was the door. I soon realized I was the only Black girl in class. When you are the only one, in an honors class particularly, you are expected to be a proud representation of your entire race. I knew the message: How dare you, a Black girl, simply learn for learning's sake? You must "represent" your entire race, because you are one of the chosen few who are tasked with being "smart." You should be grateful for tokenization—like when a Toni Morrison piece will be read because she is one of the few Black authors whose works are accepted into the pantheon of books considered to have "literary merit." Morrison, even in all of her literary glory, was "othered" and the only one, just like me.

Luckily, my white female teacher instinctively knew this, and through her teaching pedagogy, reminded me each and every day that I was only obligated to be smart for me. I did not have to shoulder the burden of an entire race of people on my back. I did not have to perform "Blackness" for my white classmates, who sought it and expected a stereo-typical version of it. She gave me the freedom to be me. She did not tokenize me or Black women. There was safety in her class. Her social and racial privilege was used as a weapon and shield to defend me from my other classmates and the system that tried to take me out. For a Black girl, this is especially important when she is the only one.

—Vashalice Kaaba.

Given the persistent racial segregation in public schools throughout the United States (Billingham, 2019), there are many classrooms across the country in which a young Black woman like Vashalice may look around and see no one who shares her racialized identity. This is especially true for advanced placement and other "gifted" courses, even in schools that are more racially heterogeneous overall (Ford, 2010; Whiting & Ford, 2009). What are Black girls' experiences likely to be in such isolating contexts, and what should educators do in order to support their success?

CHALLENGES BLACK GIRLS IN SUBURBIA FACE

In suburban and rural schools that have been historically white thanks to de jure and de facto racial school segregation and discriminatory real estate practices intended to create and protect white communities, racial demographics are only recently beginning to shift (Lewis-McCoy, 2018). Educators in these schools (often white themselves) have opted to respond in a variety of ways. Some have engaged in outright hostility, working with white families to maintain segregation. Listen to, for example, the brilliant journalism by Nikole Hannah-Jones in the podcast series *This American Life* two-part episode "The Problem We All Live With" (Glass & Hannah-Jones, 2015a, 2015b). In it, she documents the flagrant efforts of white people in the overwhelmingly white district of Francis Howell to keep out Black students when the state closed the overwhelmingly Black district of Normandy in 2013. Other educators claim to support Black students (and other students of color), but do so through color-blindness or evasiveness and a support of "race neutral" policies (Welton et al., 2015)—despite evidence that these approaches actually *perpetuate* rather than disrupt disparity (Diem et al., 2016).

For instance, a national study by Siegel-Hawley and Frankenberg (2012) found that teachers in "overwhelmingly" white schools were less likely to acknowledge racial disparities and tracking patterns and thus struggled with "guarding against discriminatory practices" (p. 29). Multiple studies have documented the consequences of this stance: Black girls in majority white schools experiencing teachers (especially white teachers) who disrespect them, ignore them, exclude them from the curricula, underrecommend them for accelerated classes, permit microaggressions against them, hold lower expectations of them, reprimand them at higher rates than their white peers for the same infractions, and fail to build meaningful relationships with them or their families (e.g., Campbell, 2012; Chapman, 2014).

Troublingly, one study found these effects to be especially damaging for Black girls with "higher race centrality" (p. 1344), or an especially strong sense of racial identity and pride (Leath et al., 2019). Some teachers may think they are being more thoughtful about noticing racial differences, engaging in what Carter Andrews (2012) calls "racial spotlighting" that puts the lone Black girl on the spot as a representative of her race during conversations in which the teacher deems her identity relevant. Also problematic is how others appropriate, imitate, and essentialize cultural practices they attribute to Black girls in ways that further exclude and marginalize these students (Hyland, 2005).

Black girls' interactions with their white peers in these contexts are often just as stigmatizing.[1] For example, Ispa-Landa (2013) found Black girls bussed to a majority white suburban school saw their white peers frame their Blackness and urbanness as "social liabilities" (p. 227), characterizing them as loud, aggressive, and "ghetto." Similarly, Eggleston and Miranda (2009) found that while Black girls raised within a majority white district similarly stigmatized Black girls who had moved there from the city, *all* felt pressure to assimilate into white cultural practices and norms. Frustratingly, Russell (2015) found that Black girls in predominantly white suburban accelerated classes were particularly vulnerable to what Fordham (2016) calls "friendly fire," symbolic violence enacted upon them by white girls and women.

Frustratingly, Black girls can be disciplined and punished rather than supported for the ways that they navigate and respond to this type of community and interpersonal violence in schools (Morris, 2016). For example, Wun (2016) studied the experiences of Black girls in a suburban school and found them to be subject to punishment for nonviolent infractions like "disobedience" and "defiance." As she notes, "Behaviors that were being characterized as forms of disobedience were [Black girls'] way of demonstrating that they had or were suffering some type of violence outside of school.... Although the girls were often under constant surveillance, their stories of injury, self-defense, and survival were ignored. Instead, the girls were punished" (Wun, 2016, p. 191). There are also constant microaggressions, including the mispronunciation of names, the policing of dress code violations based on the curviness of a student's body, and touching of hair without permission.

How Black Girls Respond

Black girls must thus perform a complicated juggling act of fending off and navigating unique combinations and cycles of racialized and gender violence in schools, expending more energy into coping than engaging in school. They (understandably) tend to isolate themselves socially and academically (Ispa-Landa, 2013) and/or resort to employing code-switching strategies in order to assimilate into a white school culture to avoid these negative repercussions. Code-switching (Myers-Scotton, 1993) can be illustrated in dress, attitude, or even knowing which cultural capital is more valuable given a particular setting. Social code-switching with peers is used to maintain cultural relationships and keep a connection to self and community. Systematic code-switching within the larger system is to leverage the use of dominant culture norms to ensure mainstream success in predominantly white schools. An example of this would be Vashalice (mentioned in the opening story) leveraging her begrudgingly gained working knowledge of white "classic literature" to prove herself "well read" and capable of rigorous academic aptitude.

Both coauthors, Nya and Vashalice, have witnessed or experienced these and other defense mechanisms, supported here by excerpts from focus groups of Black girls at a suburban high school in the Midwest. First, some students silence themselves out of racial fatigue combined with a lack of trust in adults at the school to hear their concerns or take meaningful action. As one student said, "We go out of our way to talk to a teacher or counselor and say, 'Hey. I'm not comfortable. Could you do something about it?' It will go in one ear and come out the other. They don't care. . . . The next day, the same problem. It builds up." Another reflected, "When you're around your friends, it's easy. When you're around other people, you just know when to turn on that switch—to act more proper. [And sometimes] you just don't want to hear anything from anyone today. You just don't want to, so you just turn it on. There comes a point where you just get tired and you just give up."

There is also silencing in class after enough uncomfortable moments like the one this student describes: "During the slavery unit in U.S. history, [my teacher] asked if we'd rather be in the Chesapeake or New England. I asked, 'Would I be a slave?' because technically if we're going to be time-period correct, I would be a slave. Everybody laughed and didn't take into account that it would have been a possibility. That was a really uncomfortable moment and that whole unit was uncomfortable with slavery and civil rights." In addition, Nya and Vashalice note that Black girls respond to social pressure (often along class lines) by "choosing sides," with assimilation (through speech, dress, etc.) the option most celebrated by the school—even when it is damaging to their physical, mental, and emotional health (like using hair relaxers). They also note how Black girls avoid disciplinary action by engaging in respectability politics with the belief that conforming will somehow protect them from racism within the school—even though it rarely does.

What Can Teachers Do?

What can teachers do to disrupt the structures and systems that produce these troubling circumstances? The following list offers some specific suggestions for how teachers can do right by Black girls in their classrooms:

- Ensure that teachers understand how white supremacy and racism has operated throughout the history of education and schooling, so they can better identify and disrupt problematic policies and practices.

- Incorporate attention to anti-Black racism *and* Black joy into the curriculum (King, 2019), which includes providing a complex picture of Black women throughout *all* units that honors their diversity and contributions.

- Hire Black women to be educators, and empower them to use their unique perspectives to engage in transformational, antioppressive practices (Vickery, 2016), while recognizing that staff who identify as people of color may not always serve as allies. Even for those who have not internalized oppression, there are unwritten rules to be navigated for when they are in positions of power that constrain the degree to which they can be visible allies to Black students. Work to remove these barriers.

- Relatedly, white teachers must build meaningful relationships with Black girls in order to support and advocate for them, so that it does not fall exclusively on people of color in the building to love and cherish these students.

- Create and protect affinity spaces for support and validation, not for tutoring, remediation or other efforts to force assimilation. Do not advise girls to avoid being "stereotypically Black" or to perform whiteness in any way, which feeds narratives of respectability politics and can pit Black girls against each other. In other words, reduce the need for code-switching to allow Black girls to live their Blackness, their girlness, and other identities and interests in all of their complexity (e.g., Hill, 2009).

- Do not dismiss students' concerns or gaslight them. When they express frustration with microaggressions, lowered expectations, and other problematic behaviors, take them seriously, investigate, and take action in solidarity with them.

- Last, it is imperative that suburban schools prioritize the health and well-being of their most marginalized students over preservation of their "good" reputations. One focus group student shared a story of how the school leaders warned students not to make the school look bad in relation to an explicitly racist incident. "Really?" she exclaimed as she explained what happened, "You're just worried about how the school looks? Not about how to fix the problem inside of it?"

Note

1. These are strategies that co-authors, Vashalice and Nya believe have helped them (or would have helped them) feel a stronger sense of belonging, comfort, support, and efficacy at school.

CHAPTER 30

Liminal and Limitless

Black Girls in Independent Schools

Ivy Anastasia Alphonse-Crean

Tamarind Soda

In preschool, I loved lunch. My friends and I, muddied from time outside, would sit at large wooden tables and compare the lunches our parents and nannies had fixed us. My mother was known for sending me to school with lunches I loathed. She'd put large chunks of roast chicken in my sandwiches when I wanted aerodynamic lunchmeat. She gave me sharp cheddar cheese, not American, and forbade any of the "cool" lunch treats my friends enjoyed. For my birthday, Momma packed me something exciting: Goya tamarind soda and birthday cake. I was elated and eagerly showed off the sprinkles to my friends.

My teachers, accustomed to cajoling me into finishing my healthy meals, eyed me warily. "That's your lunch?" One asked in an unfamiliar voice.

At pick-up, the teacher pulled my mother to one side. He muttered "lunch" and "substantial." He was telling my mother that what she'd packed was wrong. For the first time, I was wrong at school, weighed down by shame. My teacher stood with his arms crossed, towering over my polished Black mother, unnerving me. Birthday cake and tamarind soda remain anchored within me. My mother still recalls feeling "lesser."

My education has been elitist, siloed and sequestered. I am the product of independent schools. I have only taught in independent schools. I have benefited from well-stocked libraries, one-on-one tutorials, and state-of-the-art buildings. Though I am thankful for these resources, I, a Black girl, acknowledge the shadow side of my education.

I view the environments that I experienced through Pierre Bourdieu's notion of *habitus* (Bourdieu & Passeron, 1990). Habitus describes the modalities that make up one's social and cultural awareness, which lead to a transfer of power between those who play the game and those who do not. Our position in society is internalized and unconsciously enacted, just as society enacts its influence on us. Black girls in the habitus of independent schools occupy an interrogated space. This chapter will examine this space. I also suggest that predominantly white public schools share similar patterns in their treatment of Black girls.

THE PIPELINE TO PRISON

My analysis of Black girls in schools stems from within in the independent school community. Public and charter schools are not exempt from pigeon-holing Black girls. Along with mental exhaustion, these schools bring harm to the Black female body. The school-to-prison pipeline, given life by zero-tolerance policies and police in public schools, is a tangible force tracking Black girls toward incarceration under the guise of education. At schools that employ these measures, "being suspended or expelled from school increase[s] the likelihood of arrest in that same month" (Monahan et al., 2014, p. 110).

In my experience, independent schools psychologically restrain and imprison their Black girls. In the 1980s, independent schools and the National Association of Independent Schools (NAIS) led the charge to diversify (Brosnan, 2001, p. 472). Entry was given into the ivory tower.

The ivory tower, "a place of disengagement," is something physical—difficult to enter, but easily identified (Shapin, 2012, p. 6). A school's habitus is so ingrained with norms subtly permeating the air that one must inhale them and live them to see them. You decode cues that your presence is being called into question but lack the words to point to the source of your plight.

The effect of independent schools on the Black-girl psyche can mimic gaslighting. Towers are easy to point out, but it is much harder to get a grip on an avalanche of cultural cues and subtle snubs. The ivory tower is nothing more than smog.

THE ASSAULT ON BLACK GIRLHOOD

As both a student and faculty member at three different independent schools, I see patterns that occur when independent schools "commit to diversity." The patterns echo William Cross's (1991) theory of nigrescence or racial identity development, as well as John W. Berry's (1997) notion of acculturation, with a more specific micro lens. My framework for the assault on Black girlhood is founded on my own experiences and those of my Black girl colleagues, friends, and students. It applies to both students *and* adults. While this is not a research-based theory, I am hopeful that independent school educators might recognize these reactions in their own schools and take steps to change them.

1. "TOLERANCE"

Many independent schools seem motivated to scout out and admit Black girls, bearing in mind that Black students make up only 6.6 percent of the student population of NAIS member schools currently (NAIS, 2012, 2019). While Black girls are *physically admitted* into the independent school environment, upon admission, they are barely tolerated, not accepted, as learning environments rarely shift to accommodate or center the learner. In her book *Pushout: The Criminalization of Black Girls in School* (2016), Monique W. Morris describes how "expressions of Black femininity. . . are pathologized by school rules" and that "in our haste to teach children social rules, we sometimes fail to examine whether these rules are rooted in oppression" (Morris, 2016, p.178). By examining the biases associated with school policies, faculty and administrators can provide Black girls with an environment that supports rather than polices their behavior.

2. FALSE ENTHUSIASM

Black girls are told that the school is happy to have them. They are given apparel, buddies, and tokens of future affluence such as laptops. John W. Berry (1997) describes how, when people are forced to assimilate, the melting pot becomes a pressure cooker (p. 10). Receiving attention seems harmless, but when that gesture separates the Black girl from her culture, while denying her full entry into a school's culture, a reckoning occurs. It's not that the swag bag is wrong, but many of us don't feel a part of the community, in spite of the sweatshirts and customized cell phone cases. Are swag bags relevant to the cultural lives of the students? Is a student's acceptance of a swag bag a form of assimilation?

3. RECKONING

When does a Black girl feel out of place in the independent school environment? Maybe she wears the wrong thing, or gets her hair touched, or realizes that the habitus at play is something she knows nothing about. This is a disruptive moment of forced exclusion, which will both overshadow and underscore any academic work she may be doing (Berry, 2003, p. 18). When the Black girl's position in the school is called into question by others, subtly undermining her identity, she is reminded that she does not belong and that the environment was not made for her in the first place. Additionally, forced assimilation combined with forced exclusion (segregation) leads to feelings of marginalization, where a student is neither comfortable with their school culture, nor comfortable as they were prior to encountering it (Berry, 1997, p. 10). The Black girl feels pulled to adopt the dominant culture of her school environment while being reminded of the inferiority of her home culture. At the same time, through policy and baseline makeup of her school, she is excluded. She burns the candle at both ends.

4. SURVEILLANCE

Surveillance is the shadow side of enthusiasm. Before matriculation, there was hyperactivity around the potential of a Black girl; now the hyperactivity centers around her daily habits and perceived missteps. She will be brought up disproportionately during meetings. She will be overpraised and simultaneously held to lower standards than her peers. There will be a lens on her under the guise of "support" that serves to highlight flaws. Author of *Pushout* Monique W. Morris states: "It's not about what they did, but rather, the culture of discipline and punishment that leaves little room for error when one is Black and female" (as quoted in Anderson, 2016, para. 8).

5. DISMISSAL

Dismissal is physical and social. Perhaps the Black girl has become a struggling student, and her teachers know it. Her narrative is filled with subjective comments and subjective data ("She's delightful, but scored a 62 percent on her test due to lack of preparation.") Once a Black girl has been dismissed, her story edited, her narrative is nigh unchangeable as faculty pass along "observations" from year to year.

Gendered expectations and racial biases puts Black girls into a chokehold. According to Gaztambide-Fernández, 2010, "the "culture" of an essentially racist institution . . . positions students of color in a discursive space they can hardly occupy" (p. 167). We know when "the amygdala gets the information that it's not socially, emotionally, or intellectually safe," it "sends out a distress signal to the body" that produces "stress hormones that make learning nearly impossible" (Hammond, 2015, p. 45). Teachers (over)react based on the expectations and biases they place upon the Black girl without awareness of the constant pressures their students face in the classroom, and the very real physical consequences of those pressures. Black girls may disengage from the learning process, or just not work to their personal best once they have been dismissed (social), which may lead to their removal from the community (physical). In a punitive setting, which encompasses many of our public schools, the reaction to disengagement is often swift and harsh, further shuffling Black girls forward in the school-to-prison pipeline. At independent schools, they are slowly pushed into the role of someone that does not "fit."

COMBATTING THE SMOG

Dr. Beverly Daniel Tatum (1997) describes "cultural racism" as "smog in the air. Sometimes it is so thick it is visible, other times less apparent, but always, day in and day out, we are breathing it in" (Tatum, 1997, p. 95). Educators may default into the above reactions without realizing that they are, in fact, breathing in the smog. For true inclusion to occur, institutions must evolve for their students.

Educators should occupy the role of "lifelong learner" themselves to make real change in our schools. We must remain culturally humble and aware that there is always work to be done in combating our own biases. As Zaretta Hammond describes in her book *Culturally Responsive Teaching & The Brain,* educators must acknowledge the surface culture of their institution and the unspoken schema or "deep culture" that makes up the brain's software (Hammond, 2015, p. 23). Accommodating students of color within *any* institution that houses predominantly white educators requires deprogramming of the unconscious.

After reflecting on internalized cultural values, teachers and administrators are charged with examining school policy, particularly those rules based on common sense or tradition. Consider that a Black girl's presentation in *your eyes* is still filtered through a potentially biased lens. Ask yourself if your judgement is accurate. Respectful classroom conduct is equated with behaviors like punctuality. Time-as-commodity is, arguably, a white cultural value (Katz, 2009, p. 44). Punishing tardiness is how grading practices "actually promote and authorize our biases to operate" (Feldman, 2019, p. 111). By incorporating a student's behavior into their grade, we "risk allowing and even helping the education system to continue to hurt students not in the dominant cultures" (Feldman, 2019, p. 120).

By acknowledging cultural gaps within themselves, teachers can empower Black girls to grapple with academically advanced content from a secure vantage point. First, reflect your students in your teaching and decor. Rudine Sims-Bishop states, "When children cannot find themselves reflected in the books they read, or when the images they see are distorted, negative, or laughable, they learn a powerful lesson about how they are devalued in the society of which they are a part" (Sims-Bishop, 1990). Black girls belong to a legacy that has made significant contributions to society; those roots should be reflected in your classroom.

The daily habits of Black girls are normalized when the environment around them is affirming. I am in no way advocating for a monolith, but for more efforts to be made in celebrating the pluralism within Black girl-ness without pathologizing Black girl behavior. Perry Gilmore writes, "Black communicative displays . . . have typically been a class marker for failure in our society" (Gilmore, 1985, p. 120). As an empathetic teacher, counteract that notion. While I, a Caribbean-American woman, struggle with the idea of "Black communicative displays," I acknowledge that there are ways to read and write and demonstrate respectful classroom conduct that don't reflect the Eurocentric academy. White cultural values entrenched in gestures like direct eye contact and a reverence for standard English dominates our discourse around whether students are participating effectively, or displaying an attitude (Katz, 2009, p. 44).

Once you affirm students, then you can begin to empathize with them. This will take preparation and professional development on your part. You will have to unbundle many of your own unconscious assumptions to effectively engage talented Black girls. They will detect, in a heartbeat, statements or actions that do not align with your deeply held beliefs.

Hold yourself accountable. Read books like *Grading for Equity* by Joe Feldman (2019). Evaluate your grading practices, particularly if behavior is factored into grades. Find your school's data on retention of Black girls—it speaks volumes when data is available versus when it is hidden. Acknowledge that you have been doing it "wrong," and do not get paralyzed by this realization; you are not being attacked. The process can be painful for white educators trying to do better, but consider how painful it is for Black girls who feel excluded while being expected to articulate their feelings in perfect, measured prose.

Educators and administrators must provide institutional support systems for Black girls to excel. These might include the following:

1. Formation and funding of affinity groups that students advocate for.

2. Sponsoring peer-to-peer mentorship programs, *including* cross-divisional programming for elementary, middle, and upper school students.

3. Preparing parents to deal effectively with the need to attend events and to make themselves a visible presence in the school community. Parents are not without scrutiny, and, whether relevant or not, parental perception is sometimes brought up when informally discussing students.

4. Providing social outlets for Black girls that do not center academics.

EXPECT EXCELLENCE

When I expect excellence, students perform better than when I suspect failure. It is incumbent on all educators to focus on healing themselves while engaging Black girls in the classroom. The crux of the matter is that Black girls' performance serves as a barometer for our attitudes. Any underperformance is an indictment not only of institutional structures but also of our individual failings that manifest as destructive behaviors.

CONCLUSION

I will never forget Sam Washington, who picked us up from the airport when it was time for revisit day at The Lawrenceville School. He treated my mother and me like family, and, unlike staff at the other schools, did not have a specific tour for "scholarship" students that included step dancing. (I love opera) I believed in Sam because he held no expectations about me, but expected everything *of* me. Shelley J. Correll and Cecilia L. Ridgeway outline this dynamic in their 2003 discussion of expectation states theory. They describe how "performance expectations shape behavior in a self-fulfilling fashion" (Correll & Ridgeway, 2003, p. 31). That is, when someone is expected to perform well in a group setting, they will have more opportunities to do so, and are more likely to be "positively evaluated" (p. 31). One performs to the level one is *expected* to. Additionally, "attributes on which people differ," like gender and race, are "one of the most important ways that actors develop differentiated performance expectations" (p. 32). I, Black girl, needed someone to encourage my success without projecting a narrative onto me.

Extension Activities

1. Read the last set of end-of-term comments you wrote. How did you characterize your Black girls' behavior? Did you use subjective language to offset negative feedback?

2. How does your curriculum promote equity and affirm Black girls? Are these practices ingrained into the majority of your classes, or are they inconsistent?

3. Observe your classroom or office space, and list the images and materials you have on your wall. What visually dominates your space? What message are Black girls receiving about your own attitudes from your space?

4. What are the unofficial rules of your school? Take a day to look around and jot down at least three norms you see, from language to dress/fashion sense to food choices at lunch. Do these norms uplift your Black girls?

5. When was the last time you attended a conference or workshop centered around antiracist teaching or inclusive curriculum? What, if anything, did you implement as a result of it?

Ubuntu ngamu ubutu, or simply, Ubuntu, is a Zulu proverb that loosely translates to this: I am a person through other people; my humanity is tied to yours. While Black girls know this intrinsically, the educational environments they matriculate in don't. Black girls feel this interconnection, know themselves, and know freedom, but cannot enact it as "the only." Fifth-grade teacher Cordenia Paige speaks to the agency of Black girls who return to the classroom as educators and administrators to defy the stereotype of being "the only," and to link themselves—and the Black girls they teach—into the cyclical interdependence of Ubuntu.

Vignette: A Black Woman Who Attended a Predominantly White School Returns to Teach Black Girls in Predominantly White Schools

Cordenia Paige

If I could give my younger self advice it would be this:

> Young Black girl, love yourself in this predominantly white school because you are your ancestors' dream; you may be different and feel awkward, but you are beautiful and worthy of the information and education made available in this institution.

Since I couldn't give the advice to my younger self, I did the next best thing when I graduated with my education degree: I returned to teach in predominantly white schools. I wanted Beautiful Black Girls in white spaces to see a familiar face; a lovingly stern—I'm going to hold you accountable because I know you can—face. What I didn't know was that in the process I would learn so much from my Beautiful Black Girl students about how to love myself fully; I am learning to appreciate the younger me who had survived those spaces, as well as the present me who continues to maneuver these spaces. I also didn't know that I would learn to teach others how to join our campaign to lovingly guide Beautiful Black Girls.

When I was seven years old, my cab-driving Dad took me out of the neighborhood public, all-Black school and drove me *all* the way across town to a predominantly white, private school, where I learned to "talk white" and downplay my Blackness until I returned back home each day. I was so very different from everyone else in this new space. I still recall quietly watching everything in those earliest days feeling a kind of shock and awe. I was different from these kids who sat on desks while the teacher gave instructions and asked us questions. I was even different from the other two Black Girls in my second-grade class, because I was light skinned and from the southeast side of DC. I learned just how different we all were when I went to sleepovers in their huge houses, and I calculated that my tiny house could fit inside of their homes.

Despite the differences I had with the other Black Girls, when we got to fourth or fifth grade, one of the Black office administrators saw enough of a similarity to gather all of the Black Girls in the grade into her office. There was no official announcement, no organized meetings about it that we children were aware of, but about once each week, about five or six Black Girls gathered in this woman's office for lunch and fellowshipping in a small space where we were able to simply talk. I don't recall an agenda or objectives. The woman didn't teach any academic subjects, but she listened to us, doled out hugs, reminded us to stand up straight when she saw us in the halls and provided an oasis in the sea of whiteness. I had no idea how impactful those unorganized lunches would be in my life. I hope that I've made that woman's memory proud as I've returned to white spaces to provide similar comfort and encouragement to the Beautiful Black Girls I encounter. Some of the most powerful experiences I've had as a Black Girl, now Woman, in white spaces have been the simplest, kindest gestures that may seem insignificant and "unorganized."

I start my day greeting my students in honor of that Beautiful Black Woman who doled out hugs and reminders to stand tall. I pour extra care and hugs onto my Beautiful Black Girls. I speak to them lovingly, sometimes sternly, but I am careful not to shame nor embarrass them. If I think I have crossed that fine line of embarrassment, I make sure to reach out to speak to them outside of the classroom away from their peers. There is no way to score or grade the effects of the extra love and care I dole out to my Beautiful Black Girls. However, I have been blessed with insight about the positive influence I have had when former students return to visit and to give me hugs or reach out through social media. I am also thankful to those colleagues who have shared with me when they noticed positive changes in the Beautiful Black Girls in my classroom that they did not observe in earlier grades. These confirmations make me proud and sad at the same time. I am proud to have a positive impact on my Beautiful Black Girl students and sad that present students continue to experience similar social-emotional struggles that I had as a student in predominantly white spaces.

I often wish I could teach all Beautiful Black Girls in order to encourage them to stand tall in who they are. Since I can't be everywhere, I urge those who are teaching Beautiful Black Girls to start with the following few active suggestions:

- Journal about the experience of teaching Black Girls. No one needs to read your journal, but it may be helpful to have one place where you can be honest without judgement.

- After four to six months of journaling about teaching Black Girls, you may discover that you've learned a great deal about yourself as a teacher of Black Girls. You may realize that you're an advocate or clarify what you don't know, and you may learn where you need to tweak your approach to Black Girls.

- If you have questions about your Black Girl students' feelings or anything else that may seem awkward, ask yourself first: How would I ask this of a white student?

- If you still need to ask the question, then approach the child (or their parent if the child is too young) with honesty and candor, preferably in private until you know that you're not going to embarrass the child, their family, or yourself.

- I urge teachers to *actively* seek training for teaching Black Girls. Please do *not* expect your Black colleagues to educate you on being Black or on supporting Black Girls.

- Do your own homework. We live in a time where there are several great places to get this training and support. Google is a great place to start.

A Good Kind of Trouble, **by Lisa Moore Ramée**

Grade Level 5–8

Contemporary Realistic Fiction

Book Review by Marguerite W. Penick

Middle school is all about finding your identity, but when you are Black and your best friends are not supporting you in your Black identity, things can be more difficult, especially when the shootings of Black men by police surround you, and your friends who are not Black, do not understand your anger. *A Good Kind of Trouble* takes on multiple issues from peer pressure to standing up for the Black Lives Matter movement, and it brings to the forefront—where it should be—what it means to believe in oneself and to not let anyone—teachers, administrators, bullies, or best friends—deny the realities of race or your Black identity.

PART VI
"DREAMKEEPERS"
—Gloria Ladson-Billings

The dominant narrative around family structures is steeped in whiteness, situating most Black family structures as irregular or abnormal. The contributions of Miss Ruby and Dr. Mobley offer examples of Black excellence and affirm the right of Black girls to belong in educational spaces. Even within their demanding institutional roles, they treated the Black children and students (and even teachers and professors) they served as family. They created a family-type environment that could see and *hold their students. This display of othermothering is integral for Black girls in all education environments. May the stories of these two Black women educators help white teachers begin to envision how schools and classrooms could be different. This requires the fundamental understanding of how being Black in America is not just a racial identity, but a way of being, knowing, and belonging that is shaped by intergenerational mentoring to buffer the agitation of whiteness.*

CHAPTER 31

Mrs. Ruby Middleton Forsythe and the Power of Sankofa

Marguerite W. Penick

> *My teacher's name is Mrs. Ruby and I like my teacher. She is a nice teacher to everyone. Mrs. Ruby is the second and first grade teacher. Mrs. Ruby has 60 children in her class-room. I like my school, too. And I like Mrs. Ruby. Mrs. Ruby is a nice lady, She is the best teacher a Black child could have.*[1]

> —Third-grade student at Holy Cross Faith Memorial School,
> May 1991 written assignment

I identify as a white cisgender female educator who had the honor of being mentored by one of many extraordinary Black teachers. After teaching in a majority African American, urban, midwestern high school, I became abundantly conscious that the system was unfair for my students. The unfairness wasn't only about the funding inequities, although my $500 debate team budget compared to the $10,000 budgets of the schools we competed against certainly added to the inequities. But more important, it was about the low expectations most teachers in my school held for our students. It was about the deficit language that permeated the environment, especially in the teacher's lounge. Once I was in graduate school, courses in history and sociology opened new ideas for me, and I began to wonder why some teachers could successfully educate Black students while so many others failed so miserably.

---

[1] Unless otherwise cited, all quotes from Miss Ruby were from personal interviews with the author or work produced by students while I was teaching at the school.

Whether by fate or luck, in 1989 I was introduced to Mrs. Ruby Middleton Forsythe (Miss Ruby), who changed both my life and the lives of thousands of students, both hers and mine. Between March 1990 and May 1991, I spent eight weeks teaching with Miss Ruby in her all-Black classroom at Holy Cross Faith Memorial School in Pawleys Island, South Carolina. Miss Ruby's classroom is unique in many aspects. It is a private school and a one-room schoolhouse with about 60 students ranging from 4 years old (The Little Ones) to fourth grade, and Miss Ruby is the only teacher.[2] Students who have graduated from Holy Cross Faith Memorial have become doctors, lawyers, teachers, nurses, and business owners. What Miss Ruby saw in each individual student on a daily basis was Black Genius and Black Excellence. What she expected from her students every day was Black Genius and Black Excellence. What she educated her students for every day was Black Genius and Black Excellence.

> *Now, if we can get them to build within themselves, at an early age an esteem of themselves, a bit of independence, dependability, and a desire not to be dependent on someone else, not to be the tail end, as I tell them all the time. They have it, they can do it, if they only try.*

This chapter is a dedication to an extraordinary woman, an incredible teacher, and to those she taught, and that her legacy continues to teach, about the power of education. It is also an exploration of what white teachers can learn from Miss Ruby's education, philosophy, and experience that will support the future of Black children, and especially Black girls. There is no question that statistics show education in the United States is failing our Black girls (Crenshaw et al., 2015) so this chapter explores four lessons learned from Mrs. Ruby Middleton Forsythe who educated them so well: believing in self and cultivating goodness, the integrity of high academic expectations, black history matters, and learn from the past while looking to the future.

SANKOFA AND LOOKING BACK

> *We had two pot belly stoves that heated the room on cold days. The children would cut the wood, pile them, and they would bring them in each day and we would have a good fire. We would sit here in this building till sometimes ten o'clock at night, Teaching. And we'd send word home to those parents that they had to stay because they didn't have their work. And the parents would come here, sit down, and wait. That's right. They would sit here until they got that work done and they'd sit right down here with the children. And most of the children, the older children, the majority of them, have made it good.* (personal interview of Miss Ruby with Carol Hanley)

---

[2]The school originally had three teachers; one was Miss Ruby's husband, the Reverend William Forsythe, and the third was Mrs. Motry Martin. Mrs. Martin left at integration to join the public schools, and the reverend died in 1974. A few people helped for a year or two, but after that, Miss Ruby became the only teacher in the school, with the exception of her final few years, when Mrs. Carol Wallace was an assistant.

According to the Carter G. Woodson Center for Interracial Education, Sankofa "is an African word from the Akan tribe in Ghana." The literal translation of the word and the symbol is, "It is not taboo to fetch what is at risk of being left behind." If one takes the word apart, the meanings of the individual word parts are *san* (return), *ko* (go), *fa* (look, seek and take) ("The Power of Sankofa," n.d.). The symbol for Sankofa is a bird whose feet face forward while the head faces backward. The implication of Sankofa, therefore, is that one must look to history to see what lies ahead. Similarly, I look at what can be learned by looking back at what Miss Ruby knew, and what she taught that can be brought forward to support and lift up our Black girls.

THE EDUCATION OF MRS. RUBY MIDDLETON FORSYTHE

> The school teacher today has to be mother, father, counselor, everything. The majority of the children have nobody to sit down with them to teach them the little things that are right from the little things that are wrong. Sometimes I have to stop the class, close the book, and sit down and say, "Let's talk." (Lanker & Summers, 1989, p. 86)

Miss Ruby's education began at a private Quaker school run by Mr. and Mrs. Montgomery in Charleston, South Carolina. After graduation, Miss Ruby attended Avery Normal Institute in Charleston, a private school for African Americans. Avery Institute, established October 1, 1864, was one of the "oldest and most influential private high schools in South Carolina" (Gordon, 1929, pp. 92–93). Teacher training at Avery followed the established liberal arts education of northern schools. Miss Ruby took courses in economics, languages, methods of teaching, literature, mathematics, school management, natural philosophy, and physiology. She was very proud of the fact that she played basketball, because she stood just a little over five feet. Following Avery, Miss Ruby attended South Carolina State College, where she received her teaching license.

In segregated schools, the roles of Black teachers and white teachers were quite different (Bullock, 1967). According to Bond (1934), as early as 1861, Black educators recognized the necessity of adjusting the curriculum to the specific needs of the Black child and the incorporation of culture, history, and a relevant curriculum, one that would be taught by loving and caring teachers. This was an important goal of Black segregated schools. W. E. B. Du Bois, PhD, sociologist, historian, and author of *The Souls of Black Folk*, believed a strong academic curriculum, combined with an awareness of African American cultural contributions, was the goal of the Black school (1935). The educational reformers of this time called for teaching Black pride and the ability of Black students to succeed in every field (Woodson, 1919). Carter Woodson, PhD, historian, founder of *The Journal of Negro Education*, and author of *The Mis-Education of the Negro* (1933), claimed African Americans subsequently lost this original goal, and their gains in education, by embracing an educational system aimed at producing Black men who thought and acted like white men.

At Avery Institute, the philosophy of "social uplift" was instilled by the principal, Benjamin Cox, who attempted to "mold his students into cultured, learned and responsive citizens who would involve themselves in the community and serve as examples of their membership" (Drago, 1990, p. 139):

> Every one of you should have an aim, say to yourself, what do I want to do? Who am I? I am somebody. There is nobody here exactly like you, I told these boys and girls that the other day. But if you don't have an aim, or you're not looking out there for something, you ain't going to find it, but don't blame a soul but yourselves, allright, yo listen girls and boys, cause there's a hard world waiting out there, for you, and if you are going through school you got to try and get what these teachers are telling you, you got to feel and think that you are somebody to do something, and you got to try. The more you try, the higher you climb. But when you say "I can't," you put a big block right there and you are giving your brains and your mind to somebody else.

Prior to the Supreme Court decision in Brown v. Board of Education (1954), there were "close to 70,000 Black teachers working in Black schools" (Milner & Howard, 2004, p. 286). Milner and Howard (2004) go on to state that "approximately 38,000 African American teachers and administrators in 17 states lost their positions between 1954 and 1965" (p. 286). Citing the work of King (1993), Hudson & Holmes (1994) states, "African American teachers often serve as role models, surrogate parents, disciplinarians, counselors, and advocates for African American students. By their very presence, they convey to Black schoolchildren the expectation that they can and will succeed" (p. 389). Following in this tradition, what I quickly learned from Miss Ruby, who started her teaching career in 1928, is that elders in the Black community always knew, and still know, how to educate Black children (Du Bois, 1935; Woodson, 1933). Through the words of Miss Ruby and her educational foundation built on the strength and knowledge of countless Black educators, there is much white teachers can learn. Below are just four of the many lessons I learned from Miss Ruby that, when applied with integrity and conviction, will help Black girls know the strength and resilience from which they came. It is critical that we, as white teachers, listen and learn from the experts so we can disrupt the current racist educational system, because, as Miss Ruby would say, "You do it, because if you don't, who will?"

LESSON 1: BELIEVING IN SELF AND CULTIVATING GOODNESS

Now, if we can get them to build within themselves, at an early age, an esteem of themselves, a bit of independence, dependability, and a desire not to be dependent on someone else, not to be the tail end, as I tell them all the time. They have it, they can do it, if they only try.

Miss Ruby had high expectations for how her students should behave. She wanted them to treat each other, as well as other people, with respect. She believed the foundation of a strong student is a strong person. When students entered her classroom in the morning, the first thing they had to do was say, "Good Morning Miss Ruby." If, by some chance, they forgot, they were reminded with a sharp, "What do you say when you walk in that door?" Her students were required at all times to say "please" and "thank you" and "yes, ma'am" and "no, ma'am." Preparing to work with the fourth graders, Miss Ruby informed me they were always to raise their hand and ask permission with a "please." Above all, they were not to talk about each other in a derogatory manner. "I don't allow none of that name calling in my classroom," Miss Ruby said.

> *The most important thing for any child before they can accomplish anything, they are going to have to discipline themselves. And from the disciplining themselves, they are going to have to begin feeling, have a feeling about themselves that they can. That's the next thing. Nothing will be accomplished if that child doesn't have that feeling—"I can." When they learn that—that's the most important thing in a child's life.*

Miss Ruby utilized an activity, historically known as *copy work,* not only for writing assignments but also to provide topics to discuss with the students about growing up. Different grades did different activities, which she posted on blackboards around the room. During one of my visits, the second and third grades were copying, "We Do Better Work When We Keep Our Mouths Shut," and on another visit they were copying, "We Come To School To Work and Learn." One time the fourth grade copy board said, "No One Can Hurt You Like You Can Hurt Yourself. We Are Our Biggest Enemy."

> *But you are goin' to have to make him see that the most important thing is to depend on himself. Feeling that he can if he tries. But if he never gets to the place where he feels he can do it, he's not going to accomplish anything. I always tell my children, "Never say 'I can't,' always say 'I'll try.'"*

LESSON 2: THE INTEGRITY OF HIGH ACADEMIC EXPECTATIONS

> *You must start with the little ones. When they reach five years old, you should already have laid the blocks for them to climb on. If you wait until after five, you are going to have a harder time.*

When asked to give advice to upcoming teachers, the first thing Miss Ruby said was the teacher has to remain the teacher and not become "buddy, buddy." "Yes, sir, that's the problem with these new teachers; they all want to be friends with the children, be their buddies." Miss Ruby didn't view this as the job of a teacher. The job of a teacher is to educate the child. "The teacher is mother, nurse, counselor, and friend, but above all, you are the teacher and you must maintain your position." "These new teachers wear jeans and shorts and try to look like the children, no sir, it's not right."

> *When they went to Georgetown [to complete high school] after they finished here there was nothing for them to get. You see we had foreign languages, French and Latin, They had Math, they had Algebra, and the Sciences, more science, more geography, than they were given in public schools. And my husband taught those. . . . He could speak about five different languages.. . . And those people in Georgetown would always say, we hate for those children from Faith Memorial to come to Georgetown. They were so far ahead of those children who were in their high school.* (Personal interview with Carol Hanley)

The academic curriculum of Holy Cross Faith Memorial at the elementary level reflected a standard curriculum. The dominant subjects started with mathematics, which was taught every day. Miss Ruby stressed, "Math, we do math every day, all right, now every day. They got to know their multiplication, yes sir, every day." Reading was taught four days a week and was separate from English. The first graders, however, had reading every day. English consisted of working on grammar and was taught at least twice a week. The other dominant subject was spelling, which was taught on Monday, Tuesday, and Friday. Other academic subjects, which appeared only once a week in the curriculum, were science, social studies, health, Bible studies, and Black history.

> *The littlest one come here, they gonna do something, if they have to scratch on a piece of paper. Like me, I can't understand what some of them gonna do, but they gonna scratch, and they gonna give me that paper before they go in the yard. Understand, as little as they are, you wouldn't be understanding what they write, it could be one or two, but down in this little group, they're gonna scratch it.*

LESSON 3: BLACK HISTORY MATTERS

Miss Ruby viewed the inclusion of Black history and Black pride as essential to African American education. She taught Black history every Friday and had multiple celebrations throughout the year of Black literature, music, and history. She often remarked to me how she did not feel the public schools were adequately educating Black children on their history, their culture, and their social responsibility.

The cultural difference in Black and white schools has been heavily documented, but African American history is rarely taught in schools (Ladson-Billings 1999; Shade, 1989).

Instead the goal has been to fit the African American child into the "educational process designed for Anglo-Saxon middle-class children" (Shade, 1989, p. 1). The African American child may grow up in a distinct culture different from mainstream white culture. The degree to which this is true varies by family dynamics, play style, ideals of self-concept, verbal requirements, and other factors (Hale-Benson, 1986). Schools need to recognize the children's abilities and cultures and use their strengths to find ways to teach them (Baratz & Baratz, 1989). Accomplishing this goal, though, begins with an understanding of the culture (Cole, 1971).

Miss Ruby claimed integration harmed her people. She said that, because of integration, Black people had lost their leaders. One day I asked her why she thought this. She calmly laid her hand on my arm and said,

> Your people, the whites, have harmed the Blacks through integration, because we have lost all of our leaders, now they are the followers. We need to get our leaders back.

For this reason, plus the fact that she was taught African American history at Avery, Miss Ruby continued to teach African American history to her students. Miss Ruby was a believer in racial identity and pride. W. E. B. Du Bois, in an article "Does the Negro Need Separate Schools?" (1935), discussed the idea of segregation versus integration. Du Bois claimed that if schools would treat African Americans as the intelligent people they were, there would be no need for segregation. However, Du Bois went on to claim that if public schools were going to make the Black man feel inferior simply because he was Black, then schools should be separate for Black and white children. Miss Ruby agreed. She felt that by having an all-Black school she was building a foundation for her students to believe in themselves as African Americans before the public school system destroyed their self-esteem as Black people.

LESSON 4: LEARN FROM THE PAST; LOOK TO THE FUTURE

> But the boy who looks back and reaches, the woman who looks back and reaches, and sees a child and their need, has a heart big enough to help that child or see that that child, sees that he can be somebody, that's who I admire. (Interview with Carol Hanley)

Mrs. Ruby Middleton Forsythe is often referred to by the local community educators as being "a loner," "independent," and "unusual." When I first read the opening quote about Miss Ruby being the best teacher a Black child could have, I wondered about the claim. I have to surmise that the claim relates to the fact that Miss Ruby accomplished many of those very things in her classroom that research (Delpit, 1988; Kunjufu, 2014; Ladson-Billings, 2012) indicates educators should attempt to attain with students, not necessarily just Black students, but all students.

> *When I see my product leave and accomplish something worthwhile, then it gives me the urge to try and do a little bit more for a few more. I see the need of these children today. That's the only reason I am holding on, but I don't know how much longer I'm gonna hold on (Miss Ruby as quoted in Lanker & Summers, 1989).*

Miss Ruby passed away on Friday, May 29, 1992, at the home of her son, Burns Maynard Forsythe. May 29th was graduation day for Holy Cross Faith Memorial School. It would have been Miss Ruby's 54th graduation day. She said the children today were "not getting something they needed," and as long as she could "give it to them," she would. She will be remembered by thousands simply as "Miss Ruby."

> Miss Ruby sat in her chair and looked at the children. There were two Little Ones asleep on the floor at her feet. I don't believe I have ever seen such a look of contentment on anyone's face. Not just content with the day, but with the school, with her life, with herself. Miss Ruby had no doubt about who she was or what she did. She respected herself. (Penick, 1991)

The power of Sankofa. The power to look back, listen, and learn from the elders. The power to change the system for all of those beautiful, brilliant, Black girls, just like Miss Ruby.

> *Never say I can't, Always say I'll try.*

Mrs. Ruby Middleton Forsythe, educator, 1905–1992

Activity 1: Eliminate Deficit Thinking

I Am Enough, by G. Byers, illustrated by K. A. Bobo

Deficit language is hardwired into teaching language. To disrupt it takes time and practice. Through modeling, educators can disrupt not only their own deficit thoughts but also those of their students. Read *I am Enough* out loud to the class. Discuss all the positives in the book. Brainstorm something thoughtful and productive students can do for the community: Create a free little library, plant flowers at a nursing home, buy food for a humane society, give money to a hospital to support children in need. Start a penny jar where students place a penny in the jar every time they say something nice about/to each other. (Be certain to provide pennies for those who don't have any.) At the end of the year, take the money and complete their goal.

Activity 2: Teach Black History

The Undefeated, by K. Alexander, illustrated by K. Nelson

Read *The Undefeated* as a class. Then listen to a recording of the author reading it. Have a discussion about all of the people presented in the book. Assign students to research the people in the book, both the famous ones and the ones who represent times of racism and adversity in the history of the United States. Be certain to give options for the research projects. Students can write songs or poems, draw pictures, create videos, interview elders, or if they wish, write a traditional paper. No limits, let the students share the information in whatever means they wish; it is about learning the material, not fitting into a format.

Activity 3: Teach the Power of Goodness

Each Kindness, by J. Woodson, illustrated by E. B. Lewis

Have students create a list of things they do to be kind. Then have them make a list of things they have done, or seen done, that could be considered unkind. Read *Each Kindness* out loud. Post a large picture of each page of the book around the room. Have students do a gallery walk and put sticky notes on each page describing the unkind action on the page. Then, as a class, brainstorm ways to change the unkind actions to kind actions. At the end have students brainstorm ways they can interrupt unkind actions in their school. Create a bulletin board for the whole year where students post their actions. When unkind actions occur throughout the year, return to the book and discuss methods of interruption of unkindness.

Vignette: A Black Woman's Reflections on the Road I Made While Walking: Remarks From My Retirement Ceremony

Marilyn Sanders Mobley

(as amended from speech)

I thank God for this opportunity to share such an important moment in my life with so many people who have been part of my life narrative. I pause to acknowledge the land we are on and the indigenous peoples who were on this land before us, and I also pause to acknowledge my own ancestors whether enslaved or free who paved the way before me and on whose shoulders I stand. I thank God for two loving parents who gave me a foundation of faith and who taught me to value education and to use it as a passport to the life I wanted to live!

As I came up with the vision of inclusive thinking, mindful learning, and transformative dialogue for our office, I was thinking about what I call the three existential questions—who am I? What is my work? and How will I contribute? (Those are questions of identity, calling, and service.) I tried to keep those questions in mind whenever I was leading a program, teaching a class, or meeting with colleagues.

I came here thinking about Dr. Beverly Tatum's idea that inclusive excellence requires that we remember our ABCs:

- **A**ffirming identity
- **B**uilding community
- **C**ultivating leadership

Our students, faculty, and staff need us to live out these core values if our communities are going to survive and thrive. The work of antiracism—of fighting against bigotry, injustice, homophobia, xenophobia, and other forms of hatred on the basis of race, ethnicity, gender, sexual identity and expression, religion, age, class, or nation of origin—must continue and be taken to another level.

As I think about my work here over the past 10 years, I'm reminded of Toni Morrison's essay "Home" in the book, *The House That Race Built* (Lubiano, 1997). She speaks of home as a space that is both snug and wide open. As a both/and thinker, I have wanted CWRU (Case Western Reserve University) to be that kind of space—snug, comfortable for everyone (faculty, students, staff, alumni, community friends) to feel a sense of belonging, *and* wide open enough for everyone to be able to "think beyond the possible" (in the words of our university tagline) and do what they came here to do. I know that work will continue because of the people at this university who have demonstrated their commitment to the work. My faith, my family, and my circle of friends ... have made the last 10 years some of the most important years of my life. I thank you all for being part of my journey and I count it a blessing to have had you here with me today. Thank you.

Voice of Freedom: Fannie Lou Hamer—Spirit of the Civil Rights Movement, by Carole Boston Weatherford, illustrated by Ekua Holmes

Grade Level 5–7

Nonfiction—Biography

Book Review by Marguerite W. Penick

Fannie Lou Hamer is a name that should be known and respected by all Americans. Her compelling story rings of Black America's fight for freedom and equality. Told

(Continued)

(Continued)

in first person by Carol Weatherford and dynamically illustrated by Ekua Holmes, *Voices of Freedom* is the story of a remarkable freedom fighter, too often left out of lessons about the civil rights movement, who jumps out of the pages and into your gut. Hamer started picking cotton at six years old, inculcated too young into the harsh realities of white supremacy. From that first moment in the book, Wetherford never lets down on Hamer's identification and recognition of what Black Americans deserve as human beings, from voting rights to education to the right to assemble and the right to lead. Holmes uses vibrant colors contrasted with the diverse hues and tones of Black America. Readers will be amazed and inspired by this woman who stood up to President Johnson, was beaten and still ran for Congress, was sterilized for being Black and poor and still became a mother. Readers will question that this remarkable woman is not well known or taught about in white schools, and they will hopefully not only teach about Fannie Lou Hamer, but do what she believed in most fervently: become actively engaged in the fight for freedom.

CONNECTING

PART I

"SUCH AS I AM, A PRECIOUS GIFT"

—Zora Neale Hurston

The Connecting section focuses on how to authentically engage with Black Girls in schools. Furthermore, this sections explores ideas for educators to reimagine their everyday practices so Black Girls can excel and thrive. This section begins with a precious gem of a chapter by Drs. Raedell Cannie and Geneva Gay, who fill the readers' senses with vivid stories of the myriad ways Black girls "got it goin' on." They help readers understand the history, culture, and resilience that lead to the manifestation of what is Black girlhood and womanhood today. Their framing is itself a gift to the reader, who will not see Black girls and women in the same light after reading this chapter. But Dr. Cannie and Dr. Gay do not leave it there. They instruct readers to take what they have learned and ensure that every Black girl in their classroom has access to these examples of Black beauty and brilliance, sharing strategies for incorporation into the classroom. They contextualize Black beauty and brilliance in the way the title of this book intends for it to be understood, writing, "Black beauty ... is more a style or way of being, a strength of character and will, than a physical trait, and brilliance is more about ingenuity than intellectuality." They raise the bar for what it means to teach Black girls in a way that helps them to access their beauty and brilliance. This seminal chapter is followed by a vignette by transformational school leader Samantha Pugh, who asks educators to "breathe breath" into Black girls to animate their magic, recognizing the plethora of forces working to suppress the possibilities Black girls hold.

CHAPTER 32

Black Girls Got it Goin' On, Yet Their Best Can Be Better

Raedell Cannie, Geneva Gay

A strong indicator of Black girls' beauty and brilliance is their thriving instead of mere surviving in the midst of recurrent psychoemotional hostilities, economic and educational oppression, and assaults on their human dignity. Despite these circumstances across time, they have cultivated (and continue to do so) a style of being that radiates vitality, strength, and finesse—a persona that often defies mainstream U.S. society's predictability and probability. Given the racist and sexist atrocities that they have endured, one might assume that Black girls (i.e., females, women) would be weak, helpless, perpetually powerless, dependent, and defeated. Quite the contrary is true. Black girls have an inner strength of their own making that radiates grace and dignity. This is especially true of those who are psychoemotionally healthy with regard to their cultural and racial identities, even though at first glance they may not appear to be so. Their strength does not mean being superhuman or having stoic endurance. Instead, it is about creativity, resilience, imagination, and ingenuity in daily living. As Maxine Greene (1984) might say, this beauty is embracing and expanding the aesthetics of one's own being, which is continually complex and incomplete, because "there are always horizons to be breached, there is always a beyond" (p. 124). That is, there are always other possibilities for imagining and seeking what is, what can be, and what is not yet. Applied to Black girls, this means they are repeatedly transcending prevailing oppressive and restrictive conditions and conceptions; creating their own ways of being aesthetic, graceful, and productive; cultivating and evoking their multiplicities; and always evolving, both individually and collectively.

For us these skills and ways of being are the essence of Black girls' beauty and brilliance. Because they are encoded and enacted culturally, they often defy recognition and appreciation by outsiders, or if acknowledged they are frequently considered undesirable. Still, within their own African American cultural standards and contexts, psychologically and culturally healthy Black girls got it goin' on. This idea is consistent with Beverly Bond's (2017) notion that "Black girls rock!" (https://www.bet.com/shows/black-girls-rock.html) Not all Black girls are so fortunate; some need serious attention and intervention by educators and health care professionals. But, because these needs are beyond the boundaries of our expertise—and because we don't hear enough about culturally healthy Black girls—we chose to focus our energies here on the latter.

In this chapter we present some case examples of Black girls' beauty and brilliance as embodied in ideas and actions, and suggest some ways they can be further affirmed and enhanced in teaching and learning. In so doing we are intentional about mixing the past and the present, the self and the other, the exceptional and the ordinary in performative behaviors to illustrate conceptual ideas. We do so because Black girls' beauty and brilliance result from these multidimensional influences and are manifested in ways beyond mainstream U.S. societal conventions. Throughout the chapter we occasionally "speak" stylistically in ways similar to those whom we write about to further confirm the validity of their own self-presentations. The suggested resources and strategies included are not limited by age, subject, or school level, since they are applicable across these contexts with appropriate developmental adaptations, However, we strongly encourage our readers to be diligent about maintaining cultural and conceptual authenticity as explained here in making necessary adjustments for various intended users and contexts.

An Idea Personified

Sometimes it's best to begin teaching ideas and issues about racial and cultural differences that are beyond our immediate and personal experiences with actual examples. Toni Morrison serves this function for us. She exhibited Black girl beauty and brilliance powerfully and persistently, and exemplifies our counterintuitive conceptions of these attributes. To capture some of the essence of these accomplishments, to understand why she is worthy of emulation, and to be consistent with our notion that Black beauty is communally constructed and culturally contextual, we include some testimonials from several other individuals. They serve the dual function of helping to construct a Morrison portraiture and themselves providing opportunities and guidance for our readers and Black girls everywhere to access their legacies of beauty and brilliance, own them, embellish them, and then pass them on.

In both her personhood and authorship, Toni Morrison was unapologetic about her Blackness. She engaged and propelled the beauty and complexity of being

Black in the midst of dire circumstances and in the face of opposition. She wrote BLACK in topic, content, and tone, not so much in rejection of ethnic others, but in centering her own ethnic people, cultural experiences, and ancestral heritages. She was diligent about developing repertoires of complexity and multidimensionality in crafting her stories and characters to counter the literary and experiential tendencies of many others to present African American people as monolithic. Her Black characters and stories were never only victims or warriors, idiots or geniuses, hopeless or miraculous, criminals or saints, but were presented as striving toward the fullness of being in anything and everything (Abdurraqib, 2019; Evans, 2019; Fokenflik, 2019).

Another aspect of Morrison's Black beauty and brilliance was her celebrating and promoting Blackness about and for her cultural, gender, and racial kinfolks. She understood and embodied the Ubuntu idea that "I am as we are." That is, recognizing that Black people are inextricably linked together; that one helping others is a necessary factor of Blackness; that "when the many achieve so does the one," and conversely so. In praising this aspect of her beauty and brilliance, her perpetual becoming better at being herself, Hanif Abdurraqib (2019) said Toni Morrison was genuine in her Blackness. This was not always an easy or desirable thing to accomplish in the United States, where so much trepidation and temptation exist to cover up, mask, or create edited and restricted versions of Blackness for public consumption. In resisting these demands and temptations, Toni Morrison was indeed beautifully and brilliantly BLACK, a benchmark for others' aspirations.

Cross-generational Black girls can also find inspiration in Morrison's willingness to share the stage and the spotlight with other Black people, especially those who were not her accomplishment peers. One of her admirers described this proclivity as holding the doors of opportunity and possibility open as wide as she could and for as long as she could, so that others could enter. Hence, on "leading" she was committed to being a partner and a helpmate.

In her tribute to Toni Morrison, Michelle Obama noted that she showed us the beauty in being our full selves, the necessity of embracing our complications and contradictions. "And she didn't just give us permission to share our own stories; she underlined our responsibility to do so . . . , she was . . . deliberate in proving that our stories are rich and deep and largely unexplored" (Obama, 2019, para. 3 & 4).

Expressing similar sentiments, Leah Wright Rigueur said Morrison told us to "wrestle with both the beautiful and the horrifying parts of blackness, and to do it with clarity, love and empathy. She constantly reminded us that writing us "whole," in all our intricacies and silences, was a necessary part of freedom" (Rigueur, 2019, para. 6).

Danielle Cadet (2019) added that "Morrison's legacy doesn't only live on through her words. It lives on through . . . the license she gave Black women to tell our stories, not for others but for ourselves" (para. 6). In her self-explanation of how she dealt with a society that tried to restrict her options and limit her potentiality, Toni Morrison (n.d.) said, "I stood at the border [margins], stood at the edge and claimed it as central. I claimed it as central, and let the rest of the world move over to where I was" (https://www.goodreads.com/quotes/9866511).

BLACK "GIRLS" ARE INVENTIVE

Across time and circumstances the inclinations of Black females to create may have been prompted not so much by deliberate design or personal initiative as by the demands of living in psychologically hostile and economically underresourced circumstances. Thus, for them, adversity and necessity have been catalysts for ingenuity, imagination, and creativity. Toni Morrison made a similar observation in noting that "out of the profound desolation of her reality [the Black woman] may very well have invented herself."

We believe that human dignity cannot be repeatedly assaulted without generating some kinds of counter actions if the victims are to live psychologically healthy and productive lives. For Black females these natural tendencies toward survival and self-protection have generated a rich variety of "reconstructions of self"—of recovery and renewal! They are evidence that Black females do not simply endure the challenges of living in stressful environments; they create in that they develop skill sets that allow them to live better both within, and beyond, the constraints imposed on them. The strength, imagination, and ingenuity that underlie these continuing "reinventions of self" are the essence of Black girls' beauty and brilliance.

Maya Angelou (1994) captures some of these legacies and abilities of "going beyond" past and present circumstances, and constructing positive narratives of Black femaleness, in her poem "Still I Rise." Her message is that "you can't keep Black females down"; they keep rebounding, recovering, and renewing. Like the phoenix they rise again and again! This means that Black females are not just resilient in that they recover or bounce back to the same state of being where they were before encountering hostility and hegemony. Rather, they go beyond in recreating themselves. In so doing they construct new, evolving variations of their beauty and brilliance. Some of these constructions are so performance-based that it is difficult to capture their essence in words. To be fully understood and appreciated, they have to be observed *being enacted within context*, and viewed through the filters of African American cultural competence. This is understandable because African American culture is grounded in and manifested through oral traditions, or "Nommo, the generative power of the spoken word" (Hamlet, 2011, p. 27). Therefore, it is not surprising that much of Black girls' beauty and brilliance are transmitted through literal and symbolic "performed talk" (Atwater, 2010; Hamlet, 2011; Jackson & Richardson, 2003). Internet media documentations of the "Black Girls Rock" projects since their beginning in 2006 (such as www.huffpost.com;

www.bet.com; www.youtube.com) are valuable resources for these efforts. They allow the viewer to "see" Black beauty and brilliance both in accomplishments achieved and "real time being," or "in the moment of occurrence."

Over time, Black females' brilliance has generated an impressive repertoire of "gifts" of imagination and ingenuity for fighting back and making everyday living more graceful and endearing. These gifts are both tangible and intangible. Black females continually create alternative forms of their own aestheticism and productivity to counter other people's negative perceptions and assessments of their value. These creations are particularly evident in "performative talking" through body adornment (undoubtedly a response to an aspect of Black female being that is especially targeted in racist-based psychological attacks), and transcending constraining economic conditions.

One noteworthy area of body presentation in which Black females have turned other people's conceptions of ugly into their beautiful is hairstyling. According to Thomas Gale (2006), historically hair type rivaled skin color as one of the most distinguished and targeted features of Black women, and "nappy hair" was considered the antithesis of beauty that placed primacy on white skin and straight hair. Over time Black women changed "nappy hair" into "the natural," and in so doing conveyed the idea that its texture was normal for them, and there was no need to be ashamed of it, to disguise it, to distort it, or to always make it an imitation of White standards. They made routine hair care into an artistic endeavor characterized by a multitude of imaginative styling processes and designs, combining creativity with naturalness. A case in point is the creativity and complexity Black females have vested in braiding. The utilitarian plaits of old are replaced with intricate and artistic braiding designs, twists, cornrows, and dreadlocks that capture the attention and applause of wide reaching and diverse audiences, and even sometimes imitations. But the results are often less than adequate. Black women also are known for experimenting with and frequently changing their hair styles as if to convey the idea that "I am versatile and cannot be easily or singularly defined because of my complexity." Their body beautification and presentation inventions suggest that Black females are continually evolving, experimenting and adding to the canvas of their own being. They are creating themselves according to their own existential texts and cultural standards. These transcendences, or "going beyond . . . ," are symptomatic of their beauty and brilliance. Studies of the history, science, art, aesthetics, politics, and economics of African American female hairstyling will be valuable for contemporary girls in better understanding, appreciating, and extending these legacies.

Another inventive form of Black girls' brilliance is cuisine, or "soul food." This includes preparation styles as well as the food itself. An example of this is stretching food items by adding filler ingredients—such as potatoes, vegetables, dumplings, and pasta—to meats to make stews, and cooking rice in beef or chicken stock, and mixing beans and/or vegetables with it to increase its nutritional value. Hannah Giorgis (2018) captures the essence of these inventions in her observation that

> Black people in America and beyond have always made feasts from scraps, transformed the discarded [food items] into the divine. Ham hocks, neck bones, gizzards, [chittlings], and other animal parts unwanted by White families found their way into Black kitchens by necessity; unsung Black cooks turned these disparate bits into craveable dishes. (para. 10)

Invariably, the curators of these edible inventions were Black females. What historically began as necessary resourcefulness to sustain life has become a staple in African American cultural cuisine, and, in some instances, even novelty or adventure foods for others!

A third illustration of Black girls' economic ingenuity has to do with making their homes more liveable spaces and places of physical comfort, with quilting! There is an impressive body of published scholarship on the history of African American quilt making, but it focuses more on "publicly known" quilters and artists (like Harriet Powers, Faith Ringgold, the Gee's Bend quiltmakers, Carolyn Mazloomi, and Daughters of Dorcas and Sons), and highly stylized renditions, such as those reported by Floris Bennett Cash (1995), Roland Freeman (1986) Maude Wahlman (1993), and Cuesta Benberry (1990). These legacies should be part of Black girls' heritages and repertoires of beauty and brilliance, because

> quilts can teach us about the culture in which they are made and about the people who made them—from the materials used and patterns selected, these particular quilts are windows into the migration, cultural heritage, and experiences of African American families in this country [USA] (Carey 2019, para. 2).

We give praise to the motivations and effects of "privately unknown" quilters such as our grandmothers and their peers. They are reminiscent of those in the stories told by Patricia Leigh Brown (1996) in "Life's Threads Stitched Into Quilts" about different girlhood memories of experiencing quilting. Back in the day, many patchwork (or "scrap") quilts were made by poor Black women for their own families' use out of necessity, not aesthetics. With little or no money to buy blankets for bedtime warmth, they had to evoke invention instead. They responded to this need by using salvageable scraps from worn-out clothing and turning them into quilts. Creating these quilts was a communal process with females from different families working together on these constructions, first for one household and then others. The process was as much a social gathering as a construction enterprise, and it was an initiation rite for young girls. The quilts also were family narratives (or story boards), because memories of different family members could be evoked and their stories told through patches taken from unuseable clothes. Over time this necessary activity generated its own aesthetics. Quilters began to create replicable patterns and designs instead of merely stitching the patches together rather haphazardly. Although quilting is now more of a commercial, artistic, and recreational enterprise than an economic necessity, it continues to be a valuable artifact and process for analyzing the legacies of Black girls' brilliance in personal being and transcending imposed circumstances.

Black girls have been inventive in areas of interpersonal care, too. One technique is sharing caretaking responsibilities for those in need. This practice can be centered in nurturing particular children or caring for the community as a whole. Traditionally, older Black girls routinely helped take care of younger siblings. Hence, they learn early about communal parenting and othermothering. This practice can be observed still in young African American female friendships in classrooms, on school playgrounds, and in homes and communities where one member of a group of young children routinely takes charge and directs the flow of interactions and relationships within the group. These roles and responsibilities that often begin in youth continue indefinitely throughout adulthood. "Othermothers" frequently are not biological relatives. Their identity and significance are conveyed through comments such as, "She's not really kin to me; she's just a close family friend, but she is more like a second mother to me." Female Black teachers who engage in othermothering (Greene, 2020) may be noted by Black girls: "Sometimes they act like your momma"; "They care; they listen; they look out for you; they don't play you."

Many other forms of communal caretaking also exist among African American females. These informal assistance efforts have long historical legacies. Graphic ones include abolitionist Harriet Tubman leading enslaved individuals and groups to freedom; house slaves covertly taking food from the masters' kitchens to give to the field slaves; Sojourner Truth and others demanding that their identity as women be recognized and respected; "rent parties" in urban Black communities of the early- to mid-20th centuries to help needy members pay their housing costs; and across time, Black girls of various ages and stations in life speaking up for themselves and other members of their sisterhood. More recent versions of the rent parties are selling dinners out of community centers and churchyards to help raise money to offset the costs of individual needs and neighborhood projects instead of just making financial donations. Organizing and managing these events require cooperative efforts and complementary resources, and they combine recreation, work, and relaxation with building community cohesion. They allow people with different capabilities to make worthy contributions to the realization of common causes and meeting shared needs. Furthermore, they are consistent with African American cultural values about helping the less fortunate in ways that their human dignity is respected and they do not feel like they are just merely being given handouts. Actions such as these are other conveyors of Black cultural beauty as transmitted through and by Black girls. It will be insightful for contemporary Black girls (and their student peers) to investigate current acts of othermothering and communal caretaking among themselves, their families, and community members in both structured and unstructured aspects of everyday living.

FROM CONCEPTUAL IDEAS TO INSTRUCTIONAL ACTIONS

School age Black girls, prekindergarten through college, need to be explicitly and intentionally taught their legacies and heritages of beauty and brilliance. While most of them probably know this heritage intuitively, this is not enough for their maximum well-being in a society and world that continue to foist psychological abuse upon them. Instead, intuition needs to be complemented with intentionality, and implicit knowing needs to be enhanced by explicit identification of attributes and skills that constitute Black beauty and brilliance (such as those described earlier). This can be accomplished in many ways. We offer three possibilities here.

COLLABORATIVE CULTURAL HERITAGE AND DEVELOPMENT STUDIES

Black girls' *cultural heritage and development studies* should be used, in which components of their predecessors' and their own beauty and brilliance are thoroughly examined. A wide variety of observations, self-studies, oral histories, portraitures, testimonies, and literary analyses are useful techniques for these pursuits. Some instructive examples of these are presented by Bond (2017) and Cannie (2018). It is also beneficial for these studies to be collaborative endeavors, thereby continuing the historical tradition of Black females combining resources and efforts to "make a way out of no way," or do the seemingly impossible. Also, educators must hold themselves accountable for intentionally regularizing these learning activities by placing them in the center of *routine* curricular, teaching, and learning activities.

Another useful "selfhood" learning technique for Black girls, proposed by Carter Andrews et al. (2019), is creating *critical conversational spaces* (CCSs). These "spaces" are:

> discussion opportunities that support storytelling and oral history in the African diasporic cultural tradition . . . where experiential knowledge and narrating are encouraged. . . . Black girls' voices [are] amplified in empowering ways . . . [and] their experiences, . . . voices, thoughts, and feelings are . . . valued. (pp. 2536–2537).

Thus, these CCSs can help Black girls of all ages navigate both toxic and constructive living conditions.

ACTIVITY I

POWER OF POETRY

Our content and methods preferences for teaching these Black girl heritage studies and creating critical conversational spaces are reading, writing, and analyzing poetry. By "poetry" we do not necessarily mean this genre as it is formally characterized in a literary sense (although these forms are valuable, too), but as the aesthetic and style of African American thought and speech in routine matters and everyday living. If or when Black girls evoke their cultural communicative proclivities in these conveyances, the results are likely to be poetic! This is so because, as Vertamae Smart-Grosvenor (1982) explained, Black people have

> a way with words. . . . We be word wizards. . . . We're masters of the comeback. . . . Ours is an exciting, practical, elegant, dramatic, ironic, mysterious, surrealistic, sanctified, outrageous, and creative form of verbal expression. It's a treasure trove of vitality, profundity, rhythm–and, yes, style. (p. 138)

In addition to being a communicative form that is highly compatible with African American cultural styles, poetry has some intrinsic attributes that are very conducive to conveying Black girls' unique forms of beauty and brilliance. Poetry captures and conveys feelings along with facts, presents situations vividly and poignantly, and uses language that is at once instructive and aesthetic. Its literal nuances fit well with characterizing Black beauty as something that is more a style or way of being, a strength of character and will, than a physical trait, and brilliance as more about ingenuity than intellectuality. As Vern Kousky (n.d.) suggested, poetry "helps us find our inner voice, . . . lets us positively share our feelings, . . . and provides windows into the thoughts and feelings of others" (paras. 6, 7, and 9). Chris Borris (n.d.) added that "poetry personalizes information" (para. 9). It allows us to speak ourselves from the inside out in imagery rather than descriptive fact. And, Adrienne Rich reminded us that "Poetry can break open locked chambers of possibility, restore numbed zones to feeling, recharge desire," and "poetry is the liquid voice that can wear through stone" (as quoted in Popova, 2016).

Based on quantitative data from psychophysiology, neuroimaging and behavioral responses analysis, Wassiliwizky et al. (2017) demonstrated scientifically that poetry is a powerful stimulus for eliciting peak emotional and corollary physiological responses in the body and brain. Certainly, scrutinizing conditions that obstruct Black girls' beauty and brilliance, and reconstructing them, requires more than factual information conveyed in descriptive language. Instead, the language of conveyance should approximate the issues and audiences of concern. If finesse, style, and imagination are endemic to Black girls' intuitive senses of beauty and brilliance, then similar attributes should be present in the explicit and intentional techniques used to further develop these abilities. Poetry (in content and form) offers these compatibilities, and thus is a viable tool for teaching Black female identity and efficacy past, present, and future.

ACTIVITY 2

A MANIFESTO FOR ENHANCING BLACK GIRLS' BEAUTY AND BRILLIANCE

We also recommend developing and teaching a *culturally appropriate manifesto* for teaching to and about Black girls' beauty and brilliance. It should include the three key components of *beginnings, being,* and *becoming,* since they are dynamic, contextual, and continually evolving. We borrow some ideas from Margaret Burroughs (1968/1992), Stephanie Lahart (n.d.), and Danielle Milton (2014), respectively, to describe the key features of each component of the proposed manifesto. The "beginnings" part of the manifesto deals with the beautiful and brilliant heritages of Black girls. In "Homage to Black Madonnas," Burroughs (1968/1992) reminds contemporary Black girls of the many different personas and identities their predecessors have inhabited over the years, and why these are equivalents of beauty and brilliance. Throughout the poem she praises Black women for their magnificence, humanity, struggle, endurance, gentleness, perseverance, resourcefulness, militancy, discretion, genius, courage, vigilance, dignity, vibrancy, and optimism. In part, she says,

> Black women of genius, brilliant women
>
> Walking through the hateful valleys
>
> In dignity, strength and such serene composure
>
> That even your enemies tremble insecure. . . .

Stephanie Lahart (n.d.) offers Black girls some worthy advice about how—and why—they should *be* in the here and now of their self-perceptions, expressions, and behaviors. The underlying message is that Black girls should judge their own racial and personal worth by their African American cultural standards and experiences rather than by outside impositions. In other words, they should never be apologetic about or compromising of their Blackness. Specifically, Lahart advises Black girls to

- Not be afraid to speak with boldness, conviction, and purpose; your thoughts, feelings, opinions, and ideas are just as important as anyone else's

- Be courageous, confident, and truthful to yourself

- Live life fearlessly but responsibly and respectfully

- Stand out from the crowd and dare to be different

- Embrace your raciality, and remember that your skin tones represent beauty

- Always believe in yourself whether others do or don't

- Be confidentially and genuinely yourself

- Always be your best self

- Love, respect, and be good to yourself

- Be persistent in all that you do, never give up, and always push for that which is important to you

- Be mindful that not everyone will be supportive of you and your best interests

- Be happy for yourself and always focus on the best of yourself

- Be realistic about who you are now and your potential to become

- Let your beauty and strength shine from within

In her letter to her future daughter, Danielle Milton (2014) cautions Black girls about challenges they are likely to encounter to their cultural identity, integrity, and authenticity in the course of everyday living as they matriculate through different levels of education. She also offers some explanations for why it is important to resist these challenges, and how to do so. Her warnings emphasize the need to reaffirm historical legacies of Black femaleness in crafting future variations of Black girls' beauty and brilliance. In so doing she gives operative meaning to the *becoming* dimension of our imagined manifesto. The poignant messages are underscored by the recurrent reframe, "Don't lose yourself, little Black girl" throughout the letter, along with places and interactions that are potential sites for Black girl students to lose their cultural selves and, conversely, where their beauty and brilliance can be revived and renewed. These include

- Both formal and informal interactions in the halls, classrooms, and playgrounds of elementary schools

- In the midst of predominately White educational environments across different levels of schooling

- While questioning your beauty and worth during the adolescent years and while experiencing high school

- Processing college admissions requirements such as taking standardized tests

- Living on college campuses, joining organizations, socializing, and building friendships

- Engaging in various technological means and social media

Milton (2014) also offers some protections for Black girls against the possibility of losing themselves. These protections include being bold, fearless, and phenomenal; recognizing their beauty; and always remembering their heritages, uniqueness, radiance, strength, and brilliance.

The sample texts in the list that follows speak to and about females across the age spectrum, and offer diverse centers of emphasis for teaching and learning Black girls' beauty and brilliance. They also can be complemented by works in other literary genres, such as books for young Black girls about their racial and cultural identities, inspirational quotes, and contemporary praise songs. Some other valuable poetry references by and about Black women and girls are

- "The Agony and Ecstasy of Being Black and Female: A True Voice of African American Women Poets" (Raman, 2011)
- "My Black is Beautiful" (n.d.)
- "I am a Black Girl" (theonlychase, 2017)
- "Dear Black Girl: Letters From the Souls of Black Women" (Harris, 2015)
- "Must Read Poetry Books by Black/African American Women" (Canyon, 2019)

ADDITIONAL IDEAS

Teachers, parents, and friends should help African American girls (and others, too!) to personalize the ideas and images embedded in our manifesto by analyzing the extent to which they apply to themselves. These girls also can create their own dialogic poetry by "telling their own stories"; analyzing the "beauty and brilliance" perceptions and presentations of other female visual, vocal, literary, and performing artists and scholars; and conducting interviews with female family members, neighbors, community residents, and agemates about their own beauty and brilliance, and then converting the results into praise narratives. Questions for the interviews can be based on some of the observations made by authors such as those we referenced. For example, (1) what does it mean *behaviorally* for Black girls to be bold, brilliant, beautiful, radiant, strong, ingenious, imaginative, and have style and finesse; and (2) to what extent are the responses similar across age, socioeconomic status, residential location, educational level, and other demographics? While we imagine this "research" being conducted primarily by Black girls about, with, and for Black girls, because they should be primary in creating their own self-definitions, it might be instructive to include perspectives of diverse Black males on Black girls' beauty and brilliance as well. If students are a bit intimidated about writing poetry, then they can use other expressive genres such as songs, spoken word, letters, art, sociodramas, and interactive dialogues. The point of these "self-constructions" is to create counternarratives to attacks on Black girls' claims to beauty and brilliance.

Another valuable teaching and learning technique is to have Black girls make "self-application contracts" to enact and exemplify different aspects of their own and each other's beauty and brilliance. In these contracts, the Black girls would declare behavioral commitments and specify consequences for violating the terms of them. In other words, they make contractual agreements to being their genuine selves, according to African American cultural criteria, and to holding each other accountable for doing likewise. Thus, they become mindful that constructions and manifestations of Black girls' beauty and brilliance always involve combinations of individuality, collectivity, complexity, and, to an extent, productive uncertainty (Brown, 2013; Bond, 2017).

Furthermore, teachers can use these various texts and techniques to learn about Black girls' beauty and brilliance first for themselves, and then incorporate the resulting insights into school curricula and instruction to make them more culturally reflective of and empowering for Black girls. These changes will challenge pejorative notions (or stereotype threats—Spencer et al., 2016) about Black girls and many conventional educational practices that they are supposed to accommodate, and rightfully so. After all, Black girls have to navigate school and societal "normalcy" every day of their lives, so some reciprocity is due. Moreover, teachers can find some consolation in knowing that the more they challenge the status quo and engage in culturally responsive teaching for Black girls (and other diverse students, too), the more normal, natural, and easy it becomes. Eventually (and hopefully!) a "new normal" will emerge in which Black girls' *own* culturally defined beauty and brilliance are paramount.

Vignette: Black Girls Are Precious Gifts: Educators, Don't Be Kryptonite

Samantha Pugh

As a leader and a teacher I want my students, especially the Black girls, to have breath breathed in them to awaken their magic. Many have asked me what are the conditions that make Black Girls. I remind them that Black Girl Magic can't be bottled up and sold, but there are culturally relevant best practices that teachers, especially white teachers, can do to not be kryptonite to Black Girls. Here are a few:

1. Believe for Black Girls even when they can't—speak aspirations and inspiration every day. Tell them who they are and who they can and will be, even when Black Girls are showing up under their invisible cape of pain and trauma. They need this in a world where they are surrounded by images that are anti–their magic.

2. Remember Black Girls are children—handle them with childlike (not childish) love and admiration. Far too often, Black Girls are treated and seen as adults, especially by those of us who had to grow up quickly because of what was happening in our own homes and communities. Humanize them and teach them.

3. See Black Girls and their humanity for all the greatness that it is—color-blind teaching negates the rich and excellent herstory that is ours. Learn about it, teach it, and celebrate it every day. Show them images of people that look like them; read stories of characters who have experiences similar to theirs.

4. Check yourself and your privilege, and be OK when corrected/challenged—children, Black Girls come to us with greatness; it's in their history and DNA. So, your job is to cultivate that and bring it out. You aren't there to save Black Girls or give them what they already have.

5. Teach Black Girls and love doing it—there's nothing better than seeing teachers who are excited to teach and excited to see kids learn, even if they struggle. When you value teaching them, they will value who and what you are teaching. Let kids see that you love learning, and you *love* learning about them.

6. Advocate for Black Girls and take risks for them. Loving Black Girls can't start and end behind the walls of a school. You have love, support, and advocacy in your homes, with your friends, where you go, and in everything that you do outside of the school. Use your superpower of privilege to make cultural, community, and systemic change. Have courageous conversations about race and classes. Don't be afraid to lose a few friends and family members. Speak up and out about racism, even when it's not popular.

7. Take what you do seriously, and handle it with care—in your classes you have Kamala Harris, Michelle Obama, Martin Luther King, Jr., Sojourner Truth, and Ida B. Wells, but you also can have Sandra Bland, Emmett Till, Breonna Taylor, et cetera. The decisions that you make about your teaching and what you say either lifts up or tears down. You have the power to breathe life or death into our children. That should be taken seriously. Be willing to be challenged and called out if you aren't. Leverage those challenges to learn more about the community and the Black Girls that you serve. Use them to learn about yourself and make necessary shifts to add onto kids' lives. You can't love our rhythm and hate our blues.

8. Focus on teaching Black Girls, not teaching the curriculum. Know and understand what the Black Girls you are in contact with need, and act on this knowledge. Study and ask them what they want to learn and how they learn best. No matter how much material you cover, if Black Girls don't learn, then you have failed them.

(Continued)

(Continued)

9. Understand the movement of Black Girl Magic, but know that it takes more than magic to educate and inspire Black children. You have to work hard at it; you have to be intentional and relentless. This is marathon work, not a sprint, and it's certainly not automatic. It takes time, effort, passion, drive, courage, humility, and expertise to "make the magic happen."

In the book. *The Alchemist*, Paulo Coelho says, "The simple things are also the most extraordinary things, and only the wise can see them." Take time to see the magic; it's really easy to see if you take the time to look. When you realize how simple it is but understand our complexities, you have the power to shape and change the world. If you had the power or magic to do that, wouldn't you?

My name is Samantha Pugh, I am an educator and leader. My superpower is Black Girl Magic. What's yours?

The subsequent vignette, by educator Shannon Gibney, employs her eighth-grade voice in a letter to her social studies teacher, explaining what neither he nor her other teachers could see of her experience in school. The view from inside her eighth-grade body is so clear, and her suggestions for change so tangible, it is impossible to walk away from this vignette without the motivation and intention to begin making change. Educator Judy Osborne's vignette follows, with a description of what empowerment felt like to her as a third grader, with an evocative and generative description of a teacher who modeled so many of the strategies laid out in this book.

Vignette: Dear Mr. Guillen

Shannon Gibney

Dear Mr. Guillen,

Eighth grade sucks.

Universally, this is true, but for a nerdy mixed Black transracially adopted girl like myself, the suckage is tenfold. The fact that I don't even know what half of these words mean yet, or how and if they connect to my identity in any way, should tell you all you need to know about why I will always look back on this year and the year before it as the worst years of my life.

The way the Black girls snicker when I walk by with my too-frizzy hair, too-skinny body, and too-light skin. (This last part I will only realize years later, when I learn about color-struck Black communities.) The way the Black boys look at each other knowingly when I speak in class, and once it is over, yell, "Oreo!" as we leave class and enter that interstitial space called the hallway. Teachers walk through the hallway, but somehow they are not *teachers* there. They don't hear the verbal sparring between popular kids and the outcasts, and they are somehow blind to even the minor physical altercations that are impossible to miss. But the power of invisibility that is mysteriously bestowed upon the socially powerful is elusive to kids like me. No, my skin and hair and *white speech* mark me like a siren in the hallway. There is no escaping the name calling and bullying, except when I hide in the bathroom stall.

The one thing I have going for me in the brutal social hierarchy of middle school is my athleticism. I can run harder, longer, and faster than many of the boys in my grade, and in gym class I am still always the first girl picked on volleyball, kickball, soccer, and even baseball teams. This continues the long-standing trend from elementary school. I will not "lend" my homework to other kids to copy, and I don't show off, but I don't hide my academic abilities either. I care about how I look, but I don't understand fashion or how to dress in a *cool* way, and my parents will not buy me expensive brands like Esprit, Benetton, or Guess! Nor will they let me wear makeup, although that seems like too much trouble anyway.

I'm not saying that any of this is your fault, Mr. Guillen. I want to be clear about that. You did not create the fascist cesspool that is Clague Middle School in Ann Arbor, Michigan, in 1988. And you are not responsible for the endemic *meanness* that seems to be bred into the very marrow of the American preteen. When I look back on some of the things I said to some of my peers who were as precariously located on the social ladder as I was, I can say without a doubt that I was not only a victim of this system, but also a perpetrator in my more insecure moments. Plus, you were not only my homeroom and social studies teacher, you were also the only Latino male teacher I remember having in school. Ever. So, I can only imagine how hard that must have been, especially in the 1980s. I mean, the term *microaggressions* didn't even exist yet! But I'm sure that even though they didn't exist yet, the micro-aggressions were flying faster than the spitballs across the room, from students as well as your peers. I think that's why, all these years later, you were the only middle school teacher I felt any kind of connection to. I could not have said it at the time, but we were both brown, and both structurally, socially, and even culturally alone within the ecology of that school. This mattered to me, although again, I never could have articulated it at the time. And it matters now, too.

I know you had to teach us about the politics and cultures of the Middle East, the one child rule in China, and the bifurcated German state that resulted from the

(Continued)

(Continued)

Cold War. I was 12 and 13, and had basically seen and imagined only the American Midwest at that point. But I wish we could have also spent some time discussing American racial politics, the Great Migration, even the complexity of American families in your social studies class. Because what had been an itch, a minor irritation during my elementary school years, was now a full-blown disease: This white family who loved me, who I loved in return, but who understood nothing of what it meant to be Black in America, and who therefore could not pass on this essential knowledge to me, because they didn't know it themselves. It was beginning to feel like an uncomfortable, semipublic secret, this white family of mine who had a mixed Black transracially adopted daughter.

I knew no one like me, and had begun to fall into the understanding of myself as something of a freak. This is what happens when you don't know that your socially determined identity is structurally isolating through no fault of your own. Perhaps we could have written some first-person ethnographies of our classmates, to create more empathy between us. And then followed it up by discussing the individual in terms of their understanding of their socioeconomic, religious, racial, linguistic, gender, and yes, racial identities. Maybe we could have even expanded the project outward, so that we could have also interviewed some older folks in our community about their experiences with identity, folks who had lived through social movements like the civil rights movements or gay rights. I think that would have given me some perspective. Made me see that I was not a freakish aberration that had just basically fallen from the sky, but rather, just one point in an interlocking set of ongoing historical processes.

I know that back then, we didn't have books like Mariama Lockington's middle grade novel *Black Like Me*, or my own young adult novel *See No Color*, which I basically wrote for my 12-year-old self. But what if we had? What if I had had the chance to see myself, a Black transracial adoptee tween, as the protagonist of my own story? How would that have changed my confidence and my profound sense of social dislocation from my middle school peer group, as well as my growing antipathy to Black kids, Black adults, and Blackness itself? I think I would have at least had a starting place for processing my experience, which is so unlike 99 percent of my peers—Black and otherwise. I think I would have been able to begin to see Black culture as an unfolding process and set of expressions *that I could choose to participate in*, rather than feel confused and oppressed by. I think I would have begun to see that the many ways of being Black could include mine, too, however tainted it was by whiteness, and middle-classness, and a multiracial family. As it was, I had hints of these truths from writers like James Baldwin and academic competitions like the NAACP's ACT-SO (Afro-Academic, Cultural, Technological and Scientific Olympics) in high school, but they were few and far between, and I still always had to make the effort to extrapolate *that* kind of Blackness to my own. And it really wasn't until college that I began to accept that my particular *mixed Black girl raised by white people in a majority white college town Blackness* was legitimate. It took until my late 20s to locate my identity as an adoptee within the context of my Blackness.

I could go on, Mr. Guillen, but I won't.

I know you have things to do, books to read, grandchildren (maybe even great-grand-children?) to tend to. I know that, like all of us, you did the best you could with the resources and information you had at the time. And support. And lack of support. So, this letter is neither complaint nor revisionist history. It is merely meant as an invitation to conversation. A shared imagining of how you and I and others might do it differently now—engage all our students, including those who may be Black transracial adoptees—in the fullness of who they are in the classroom. I teach writing at an urban two-year college in downtown Minneapolis now, and though my students are adults, I do have some who are adoptees. So, in some way we all eventually become subjects and objects in what Paulo Freire and bell hooks would call "liberatory pedagogy." We have to help our students learn to tell their stories in a way that makes them more free, so that they can see themselves and their own power. That's what I wish I would have had access to when I was 12 and 13. Would eighth grade still have sucked? Absolutely. But would I have had to go it so alone? Would I have realized that it wouldn't always be that way? And would I have had a better understanding that I was not actually a freak, but actually a "normal" mixed Black transracially adopted young woman trying to find her way in the world, and that that was always going to be a messy and difficult process? Probably.

Sincerely,
Shannon

Shannon Gibney lives and writes in Minneapolis. She is the author of Dream Country *and* See No Color, *which both won Minnesota Book Awards. She teaches writing at Minneapolis College.*

Vignette: So You Wanted to See the Wizard

Judy Osborne

> *So you wanted to see the wizard. Let me tell you that you've come to the right place.*

—The Wiz

(Continued)

(Continued)

The year is 1975. I am a lanky, wide-eyed third grader in the rebellious city of Newark, New Jersey, a place of young, riotous protest and a spirit demanding survival of the fittest. I am one of 30 Black youngsters in Ms. W's dynamic classroom. Ms. W. is a beautifully chocolate, Afro-haloed, no-nonsense powerhouse of a teacher. She, who fills our classroom with bright smiles, resistance poetry, finger snaps, and pointed questions: "Are you *sure* about that, or do you want to think about it some more?"

The big day has finally arrived. We are noisy eight-year-olds, jittery with excitement, boarding a yellow bus on a cold winter morning. There is a Tony-award-winning Broadway musical just across the George Washington Bridge in New York City that we will be lucky enough to witness. None other than *The Wiz*. By then we had all seen some version of the original *Wizard of Oz* on television with Dorothy and her trusted crew sorting themselves out. But as we were warned in the days leading up to the journey, *this time* would be different.

We are not disappointed. Nearly everyone on the stage is a varying shade of me: ebony blacks, cocoa browns, and bronzy tans. It is absolutely electrifying. The lyrics dance with sky-high riffs and low, soul-stirring runs. There's sashaying of hips, stomping of feet, golden lights flashing, emerald sequins flying *everywhere*. I cannot sit still. For the first time that I can remember, I am completely in love with myself.

Back at home in the privacy of my room, I am immediately in front of the mirror, hair freshly cornrowed for the day's excursion. A comb becomes a microphone. I see myself so clearly. No more Hollywood imaginings of *The Brady Bunch* or *The Partridge Family*. I am smart and beautiful and brilliant and free. Spinning around and around and around . . .

The year spent in Ms. W's class and that unforgettable Broadway visit in 1975 were both powerful and empowering educational experiences for this Black girl. By that time I had already had three young white women as teachers in kindergarten through second grades. Statistics now point to the benefits all students gain when learning from and interacting with teachers of color, but at that time even my eight-year-old self recognized (though perhaps could not articulate) that it just *felt so good*. But why? I remember that she brought her entire self to that classroom, including mannerisms and colloquialisms that were familiar. But she worked equally hard to connect us academically in ways that challenged the mostly white literature and images that seemed to swallow us at every turn. Even a slight expression of interest in poetry earned you a stack of Gwendolyn Brooks poems to take home and memorize. Some connections were organic, but even more were noticed and nurtured. She was a relationship builder. That's super important for teachers to remember. Prior to and beyond the bells and whistles of technology, truly innovative teaching to help Black girls thrive requires vulnerability and authenticity: Are you creating safe enough spaces for relationships to grow?

Racial group differences are not biological, just as race itself is not biological; both are social fictions. Race is a social construct that was created to justify the dehumanization of Black people through systems and institutions and to promote the financial gain and a national belonging of those declared white in the United States. Black children and white children are not biologically wired to learn differently. But learning is not just a reflection of biological wiring; learning, for Black girls, is a practice of freedom. In the next chapter, "Learning to Listen to Her: Psychological Verve With Black Girls," Drs. Darla Scott and Ashley Griffin describe research originally conceived by Dr. A. Wade Boykin, which describes and delineates culturally based learning differences between large groups of Black and white learners. Verve does not explain all learning styles of all children, but he does help clarify why many white educators believe, for example, that a quiet environment is critical to concentration, while many Black educators have a more expansive notion of the different types of learning environments that facilitate concentration. Very few educators have been exposed to the research on verve, which is a concept that will transform how you think about learning spaces that center Black girls. For more background on this concept, see Dr. Darla Scott's chapter in The Guide for White Women who Teach Black Boys (Corwin, 2018).

CHAPTER 33

Learning to Listen to Her

Psychological Verve With Black Girls

Darla Scott, Ashley Griffin

You heard what I said, but were you listening?

Madison has come to her kindergarten class with lots to contribute. She is telling the boys where to sit and repeating the directions for the students who arrived late. While we are supposed to be working quietly and independently, Madison is talking and explaining the assignment to the students near her. How should her teacher address Madison's occasionally "disruptive" behavior?

In his seminal *Culture Matters* piece, Boykin (2001) identifies vervistic instructional techniques, including utilizing rhythmic communication patterns, invoking call and response, varying the pace of instruction, integrating gestures and opportunities for emotional involvement, and making space for lively and spontaneous student input and participation.

Psychological verve is a preference for and receptiveness to relatively high levels of physical stimulation with three dimensions of physical stimulation, namely, variability, intensity, and density (Boykin, 1979, 1982).

In *The Guide for White Women Who Teach Black Boys*, we delved into the empirical support for verve and how it connects to motivation, engagement, and performance for African American students (Scott, 2018). Schools are cultural spaces that privilege particular repertoires of behavior and sanction others (Milne, 2013; Wood & Lemley, 2015). While many public education settings promote white, middle-class norms (Ellison et al., 2000), the cultural norms in Black households are different, cultivating a preference for more high-energy activities and related behavioral displays among girls like Madison (Tyler et al., 2008).

For Black girls, psychological verve looks different from the behavioral displays of boys. Some researchers have concluded that verve is more important for African American boys than African American girls (Corneille et al., 2005). This chapter argues that Black girls are highly responsive to vervistic learning practices, for example, creative, spontaneous, and varied stimuli and activities. In fact, Carter et al. (2008) found that African American girls had statistically significantly higher levels of verve than African American males, with a strong effect size (d = 0.71) (p. 37). One key difference is that verve can be expressed more orally in Black girls and more behaviorally in Black boys. Quite often, Black girls may be viewed as passively defiant in how they engage in the class environment. Specifically, teachers may observe Black girls engaging in excessive talking, lively interactive bonding, or animated noisy work groups (Carter & Larke, 2003).

A Call for Verve

While African American males get more attention in the discipline disparity literature, Black female students are more likely to be suspended from school than White or Hispanic girls across secondary and primary school (George, 2015; Raffaele Mendez et al., 2002). Furthermore, specific common infractions (such as defiance, disrespect, disruptive behavior, profanity, and fighting) led to suspension more often for Black girls relative to their racial-ethnic representation in one school district (Morris, 2012; Raffaele Mendez & Knoff, 2003). There is data to suggest that teacher referral bias, inexperience, and inadequate classroom management techniques are at the root of the disproportionate discipline sanctions and referrals for Black children in general and Black girls specifically (Morris, 2016; Skiba et al., 2002). Several researchers have suggested that vervistic learners can be misinterpreted by their teachers as being off task, passive aggressive, and inattentive in class (Boykin, 2001; Carter et al., 2008).

By examining discipline data for Black girls, we can see critical areas of confusion in looking at the behavioral displays of these young ladies. Unfortunately, stereotypes about Black girls such as the so-called Jezebel (hypersexualized woman) or Sapphire (angry Black woman) can lead to these girls' behavior being interpreted by their teachers as argumentative, defiant, and disrespectful (West, 1995). In reality, Black girls and women are raised to be strong caretakers within their family and social circles (Ward, 1996), as can be seen in the idea of othermothering (Collins, 1990). Othermothering becomes evident when Black girls accept responsibility for each other, other children, and the larger Black community (Collins, 1990). As was highlighted in the vignette above, Madison is known for telling the other children which games they are playing and when to play those games out on the playground. These social bonds could be highly effective for a collaborative learning exercise or creating positive peer pressure around academic success. Furthermore, incorporating chants, role-playing, drama, or poetry into formal instruction would also build upon this asset in Black female learners.

DO YOU GET ME?

Celissa chatted with her peers while she waited for her third-period class to begin. Although she was texting and listening to music, she was still able to keep her conversation going with her girls. How does her third-period teacher utilize her preference for density in the learning strategies that she offers to Celissa?

Psychological verve includes the dimensions of variability, density, and intensity, which takes a unique form for Black girls (Carter et al., 2008). Variability with these girls looks like alternating between conversational topics with ease and enjoying multitasking while learning. Integrating variability into instructional practice could include practices such as providing multiple practice formats for students to choose from to practice the focal skill. It is critical to look for opportunities to introduce voice and choice into the learning environment. Voice is allowing Black girls to have input into what they learn and how they learn in meaningful ways, and choice involves allowing a measure of autonomy and promotes metacognitive thinking. For Black girls, intensity can be observed in loud conversations, hearty laughter, and exuberance during in-class performances, which can be used by Black girls to "carve out free spaces in oppressive locations" such as classrooms (Richardson, 2013, p. 755). Therefore, educators are challenged to bring in and validate these behaviors in ways that allow our Black girls, like Celissa, to demonstrate a high level of engagement and persistent academic performance. Integrating intensity into your instruction for your Black girls could include incorporating gesturing for reacting to the lesson or symbols and movements when providing answers and responses. Martin and Murtagh (2015) offered the active classroom lessons as a great way to bring in intensity and boost engagement among students, which would be especially impactful for Black girls.

Density is manipulated by introducing a multitude of simultaneous activities, such as station work with voice and choice. Imagine that we are working on learning about adding fractions; a learning station framework would involve a manipulatives center (with fraction pieces and problems to solve), a fraction word problems center, and a paper practice station. Then, the students can decide which station to start at and are allowed to move to a station of their choice, understanding that there are to be no more than five students at each station, and each student must finish all three stations. We can also look at density in instruction through graphics-rich environments and mind-mapping tools such as teaching with pictures, webbing organizers, and 3-D diagrams.

CAN YOU SEE ME?

> *Sheila's hand is always raised. She wants to answer all of the teacher's questions very loudly! Sheila needs clarification about the fractions problems, and she wants the teacher to look at her solutions to confirm that she got the answers right. At times, Sheila is out of her seat, coming to the teacher's desk with questions. What can Sheila's teacher do to help her know that she is seen?*

Black girl magic is an empowering construct for highlighting what some call the superpowers of Black women and girls, but the traumas and tragedies that these girls bring to the classroom need space and voice so that healing can take place. Although a preponderance of Black girls are very talented and strong, the pressure to be strong and beautiful at all times can be a heavy burden for young women as they are developing their identities throughout their schooling experiences. Understanding Black girls like Sheila requires talking to them and hearing their concerns seriously, which gives space for girls to speak their opinions without being misunderstood as angry Black women (Morris et al., 2018).

Although some teachers see understanding conflicts between students as a waste of time, listening to the root of the interpersonal challenges that your Black girls are facing will help you to connect with them and help them to feel understood. While vervistic learning may feel like a disruption to your quiet and orderly classroom environment, psychological verve is an untapped asset in finding useful spontaneity and creativity to build engagement into the lesson structure. For example, creating spaces for displaying information in a unique and creative way is helpful for your Black girl students. As natural caretakers, Black girls may seem precocious and mature due to familial responsibilities. There is literature to highlight the fact that Black girls want to be connected to their teachers and taught by them in relational ways (Ladson-Billings, 2009). Many Black girls are emotional and expressive and need creative outlets for their feelings (Richardson, 2013). The critical question of this chapter is "How could you utilize verve in your classroom?"

Did you hear her? Madison is communicating a commitment to her community of learners. Celissa is asking us to give her more hands-on and engaging activities. Sheila is telling us to challenge her with high expectations and demanding warmth. Perhaps, you heard her. But are you listening?

Small Group Exercise 1: How I learn to listen.

In a group of six to eight teachers, after reading the chapter, ask participants to identify what issues and topics engage their Black female students in the learning process. What are their Black girls interested in learning about? Bring those issues and topics to the meeting to share, and then answer the following three questions on your own paper in the same space (questions adapted from Ford et al., 2000).

1. How much time and effort am I willing to devote to teaching in ways that connect and resonate with my Black girl students?

2. How much effort am I willing to commit to getting to know my Black girl students better? What are my roadblocks or beliefs that hinder those efforts?

3. How can I use my Black girls' assets and backgrounds as scaffolding for teaching in my class? What change am I prepared to make today and this week in class?

Small Group Exercise 2: How you learn to see me.

In a group of 8-10 girls, ask the girls to brainstorm a list of adjectives they would use to describe themselves. After they have created that list, ask the girls to generate a list of adjectives they believe that their teachers would use to describe them. Discuss the overlap or divergence.

Postexercise Reflection. Think about the lists generated in the small-group exercise. Do you understand why those points were raised? How can you realign your perceptions of your Black female students? What work needs to be done?

The following vignette by college student Kay Hinderlie offers another window onto what our students—even the most outspoken and self-confident among them—are often thinking in moments of vulnerability and uncertainty. Kay's piece demonstrates the complexity of intersectionality in the lives of students, who may have access to safe spaces for their Blackness, or safe spaces for their queerness, but nowhere for their Black queerness. Kay opens her piece describing how the inaction from her past teachers continues to place the onus on students to self-advocate for their Black spaces to be queer friendly and their queer spaces to be antiracist. Kay's experience invites us to think in more complex ways about the magnificent young people we teach, and suggests that when we listen without defensiveness or pretense, the path forward is clear. To close this section, we hear from Miss Jay, as identified by her students, on how transmisogynoir shows up in school. Through the recitation of her own story, with help from Audre Lorde, she demonstrates how all Black girls, including trans Black girls, are deliberate and afraid of nothing!

Vignette: Creating Safe Spaces for Black Queer Girls

Kay Hinderlie

I watch my feet as I walk to her desk, take a seat. Am I overreacting? Is it my place to discuss this? Will my words reach her? In and out, I take a deep breath. I look up and see her kind eyes looking into me. I hope I reach her. Even if she can't empathize, she might listen. She has the opportunity to advocate for me, to affirm me and my experience. And yet, she may also turn away from my request to let my voice be heard, like many others before her. Even with all the times I've been shot down by educators in the past, I can't help but believe *it could be different this time.* If I speak up, I could be rejected, but if I don't, I'll never know what could've been. I take in the smell of freshly printed paper, and I open my mouth. Words come out.

I tell her about our GSA, the club she supervises. I tell her about the voices that are heard and the voices that are silenced. The coincidence that people like me don't get to speak of our experiences if they differ from those of the white cisgender male copresidents. The frustration I feel as a junior seeing queer underclassmen of color be denied a space for community and growth. I tell her how a room full of Black and Brown faces struggling to make sense of themselves have to sit through conversations that don't engage their multiple intersecting marginalized identities. My voice catches when I tell her of a space that hasn't adjusted based on its needs. My eyes well up and all I can manage to say is, *What do I do?* I can't help but wonder if she, a white straight cisgender woman, has a solution.

My shot in the dark is welcomed by a warm embrace of affirmations and validation. My words, they stretched out like vines to her, and she gladly tends to them instead of pulling them out at the root. Blood rushes out of my ears to fill my heart as relief takes over. *She* heard *me. She heard* me. She turns to pick up a pen and paper, and only then do I finally believe that she—no, that we—plan to take action.

It was not until my junior year in high school that I was fully heard and accepted as a queer Black student. As a result of her openness, I as well as the other members in the club evolved to create a more inclusive and radical space that even now continues to morph and evolve. As many years have passed, I finally recognize that she was one of the educators I can count on one hand who volunteered to stand in my corner. I realize now that out of countless educators, she is the one that made a "safe space" mean more than a sticker on a classroom door. Because of her, I know to demand the same respect and understanding from others. As a being navigating multiple intersecting marginalized identities, I deserve to receive the support and love I ask for.

Vignette: Being a Trans Black Girl: "Fighting Transmisogynoir"

Dee Johnson

Of the many conversations I've had over the years with my Black girl students about resilience and finding their purpose, one stands out in particular, a conversation with a Black girl student during my first month as director of equity and inclusion at a California independent school. We had only met casually before in the corridor, until one day she came to my office in tears. She said, "Miss Jay, if it's not my skin, it's my hair. What am I going to do? I have three more years of this place and. . . ." The tears choked her before the rest of the words could escape her mouth. It broke my heart to see her this way, and so I held her. As she sobbed in my arms she asked, "How are you so brave all the time? Was school like this for you, too?" I told her that I, too, get overwhelmed and frustrated, but that "when I dare to be powerful—to use my strength in the service of my vision, then it becomes less and less important whether I am afraid." She looked up at me and we both said, "Audre Lorde." We chuckled ever so slightly and chatted for about 20 minutes. Before we knew it, the bell rang, and as she grabbed her book bag and squeezed me one last time, she invited me to the Black Student Union meeting that afternoon at lunch. She said that the group could use some love and inspiration and that me sharing more about what I do might help boost morale. I agreed and then released her into a sea of white and ethnically ambiguous children, all of whom seemed to track the bounce of her 'fro as she waved goodbye to me down the corridor.

When I got to the affinity group meeting that afternoon, the room was overflowing with just about every student of color in the school. We didn't have a long lunch period, so I wasted no time. I started by sharing that how and why I do my job is just as important as who I am while doing it. I told them that I knew I wanted to be an educator by profession when I realized that not only was I vastly different from most of my peers at the very white schools I attended, but also when I realized that all the adults in my life—my family members and teachers—were ill-equipped to help a person like me imagine a future. A person like me: a poor, Black, fat, now asylum seeking, trans woman from Jamaica. No one in my life knew how to help me feel safe and powerful in my own body.

I came out to my students as a Black transgender woman that day. I shared with them that I was the only person in my family to attend private school, and that I was also the only one who made it to college. Before I shared my story in detail, I reminded them, "Pain is important: how we evade it, how we succumb to it, how we deal with it, how we transcend it." I wondered if the student from earlier also knew that was me borrowing from Audre Lorde. My eyes searched for her in the room. She had a smile on her face, and so I continued, but not before a boy at the back of the room exclaimed, "Yooooooo!" when I revealed that I was transgender. I watched the students, particularly the Black boys, disassemble me and put me back together with their eyes—but I kept going. I explained to them that I do this work for the next generation of Black trans women who are now, as girls, being expertly primed for erasure and to be passive, complicit even, in the transphobic violence they will experience deep into their adulthood. I told them that I also did this work for the Black trans students who didn't make it to adulthood, for the ones who did but were already lost, *and* for the times I felt powerless and unseen as a child.

I shared that as a Black independent school alumna who is now an independent school diversity practitioner, my job isn't just about informing school leadership about the ways in which their people, programs, and practices sustain white supremacy, cissexism, and capitalist patriarchy. It's also about the deeply vindicating and healing work of helping adults in our community reflect on the fact that most Black students, especially Black girls and femmes, learn to feel invisible and unworthy at Predominantly White Institutions. I watched the students all nod in agreement as I punctuated my statement with the fact that this was not only backed by research, but also by the personal testimony I was about to share.

Before I moved any further, however, I felt the need to underscore the fact that what I was going to share wasn't *just* about being Black at a private school, that there are other forces at play in the world to which we are socialized at school. Instead, it was going to be about the fact that we don't live single-issue lives, and that while we work to end anti-Black racism and white supremacy at our school, we must also develop a more intersectional understanding of the multiple marginalizations faced by our community. I referenced the comment after I came out as transgender as being symbolic of this truth. I also explained that I wasn't looking for an apology but rather an active commitment to "moving against not only those forces that dehumanize us from the outside, but also against the oppressive values that we have been forced to take into ourselves." I then described the three major interventions that would have had the greatest impact on improving my belonging, safety, and mental health when I was a child in independent school: trans representation in the curriculum, trans-inclusive policies and practices, and more expansive parent gender and sex education.

I shared that as a child, I always had a strong internal sense that I was not in alignment with the gender I was assigned at birth. My body felt foreign and offensive to me. By the time puberty hit, I had started experiencing extreme body dysmorphia and thoughts of self-loathing. I found myself averse to looking at myself in the mirror, to wearing a boy's uniform, and to keeping my hair short and "well-groomed," which I interpreted as code for "no Blacks, no femmes at our school." I resented the hairs that sprouted from my face and chest, not to mention the deepening of my voice. I grew distant from my own body and, on the rare occasion that I'd catch a glimpse of my reflection in the mirror, I noticed that I did not recognize the person staring back. I remember going straight to my mother the first time it happened. Not only did she dismiss my concerns as me being dramatic, but I also believed that she neither had the capacity nor the desire to support me through

(Continued)

(Continued)

what I now know to be transgender dysphoria. To be fair though, our culture didn't permit her to believe that any child of hers could be transgender.

The next day, I decided to take my issue to our school's counselor, and to my horror, she also dismissed my concerns, replying with something to the effect of "puberty is a difficult time for everyone." "It will get better," she lied. It never did, and neither did the bullying I experienced for being effeminate. Despite the dismissal I felt that day, I still looked forward to the counselor's gender and sex education class, hoping that I would hear about, read about, or talk about what was going on with my person. At the very least, I hoped to see if anyone else was experiencing something similar. That also did not happen. There was no BIPOC[1] representation in her slides or in the video she shared with us. She barely spoke about gay, lesbian, and bisexual persons, and there was no mention of transgender or gender-independent folx, our love, intimacy, or bodies. There was nothing that signaled that people like me existed, desired love, and even worse, that we deserved to be loved. I distinctly remember thinking that there must have been something so abnormal and so shameful about me, that no one—not even my own mother—cared to see me and my struggle.

As I began to do my own research, to ask more questions and became more vocal about my differences, I realized that my friends began to disappear. Even my Black friends, most of whom came from very religious families, started to drift away. Soon, the very same persons who confided in me about the racist things they experienced on a daily basis at school began to bully me. I was systematically uninvited from parties and ostracized on field trips; no one wanted to sit next to me on the bus, and no one wanted to be roomed with me on overnight trips. I stopped attending field trips altogether because of it.

Over time, I realized that this scornful erasure would perhaps last well into my adult life and that I would have to make peace with it. Even more horrifying, however, was the realization that the education my peers and I were receiving was both woefully inadequate and reductive, and that because of it, people like me would be exposed to unspeakable violence, perhaps at the hands of my classmates, many of whom I'd known since birth.

By the time I graduated high school, I could see that we had missed opportunities in biology class to define and discuss biological sex; the effect of hormones on the human body outside of puberty, cishet[2] pregnancies, and menstruation; the fact that intersex people existed; and the fact that some persons elect to have their sex surgically reassigned. From my history lessons, I could have also easily been led to

---

[1]black, indigenous, people of color

[2]cisgender and heterosexual

think that the only movers and shakers in history were European men and women and Black cishet men like Martin Luther King Jr. and Malcolm X, and that the limits of progressive education were met by the addition of Rosa Parks to the curriculum. I had to wait until I was 18 to learn about the history of Black trans women fighting for LGBTQ rights at Stonewall. I was also the same age when I read my first novel with a trans protagonist. I now think to myself how empowering it would have been to grow up reading books with trans characters, to learn about Marsha P. Johnson and Sylvia Rivera alongside MLK Jr. and Rosa Parks, as well as the possibility of lifesaving medical interventions that could help bring my gender and body in alignment. I also realized that it is because of all these missed opportunities that the murderers of trans women were unlikely to ever be held accountable for their crimes. Society would see them as victims, unable to move past the falsehoods of "she tricked me" and "but I'm not gay." Unable to move towards addressing the fact that we are socialized to not see trans people as human, as real, and that most people are socialized to love genitalia more than the persons to whom they are attached.

I told the students in the room that day that because of these experiences, I knew personally why Black trans youth and adults battle extreme mental health crises, and why routine maiming by transphobia is the chief contributing factor to the disproportionately high rates of death by suicide among trans persons. I also let them know that not feeling power and ownership over our bodies is also one of the major contributing factors to the sexual violence we experience. "Say more about that, Ms. Jay," said a voice, again from the back of the room. I responded by saying that no trans person should experience their body for the first time at the hands of another who has had the time to explore their own power and sexual agency, and that this is what cisheteronormative sex education facilitates. I explained that it creates a power imbalance during the initial romantic encounters that trans persons have, and because of this, these encounters cannot truly be consensual. I told them that many trans youth and adults participate in survival sex work because of homelessness and family rejection. The room fell silent. These considerations are what I take into account when I train counselors and provide them with a checklist to help support trans students through sex education and general counseling. I then continued by saying that this attention to sex education curricula is also for cis persons of all orientations. In not knowing how to engage with trans folx and our bodies in ways that leave us feeling whole, the world for cisgender folx shrinks.

It brought me great joy that day to know that I was able to illuminate for my cishet students the fact that the current curriculum at most schools was providing them few opportunities to understand and to interrogate not only [their] Blackness and the very white world around them, but also social constructs like gender, sex, and class, issues that further complicate our collective struggle for freedom as Black people. In that moment I invited the students to work through their intersectional

(Continued)

(Continued)

identities, to demand better content and pedagogy from their teachers, and to be mindful of the prejudices they'd taken on in order to feel power over others because of their own sense of impotence; things like homophobia, xenophobia, transphobia, and misogynoir. I also shared a personal meditative practice with the students to help them visualize a future that is beautiful and free enough for all of us to exist and thrive. The questions I shared were these: "What are you going to do now and/or when you are free enough? How will it feel to have arrived at that place? How will you be transformed not just by the state of your growing freedom, but also by the promise of sharing its joys with others? Who will stand next to you in this future? Who will you carry? How will you make yourself a blessing to everyone you meet today in service of this future?"

At that very moment, I looked up at the clock and realized that lunch would end in five minutes. In a state of panicked disappointment, I quickly rattled off the policies and practices that I believed would best serve trans students: trans students being allowed to use the bathrooms and locker rooms that best align with their gender; schools establishing transinclusive protocols for overnight field trips; the creation of explicit antibullying policies that protect trans students; and the crafting of advisory programs that teach *all* students about pronouns, misgendering, and deadnaming; as well as how to support students and adults transitioning. I also alerted them to the fact that there was a bin of clothing in my office just in case someone needed a change of gender-affirming clothes during the day. Thank the heavens we don't have a uniform. Before the students ran out the door that day, though, I also told them that their parents also needed to learn more about their intersectional experiences, especially the parts of themselves that fall far outside the scope of their family's cultural worldviews. I reminded them that there is no manual for parenting, nor is there a manual for raising gender-diverse Black children in a world that is vehemently anti-Black and anti-LGBT. I told them that students and their parents need opportunities to learn how to love in more radically healing and liberatory ways, and that it was up to them to call their parents into the conversation.

And just like that, the bell rang, unleashing us all into the corridors and into the final two years of high school for the beautiful Black girl that came to my office that morning. Today, as I'm writing, she's now a graduate of our school, and so too is that Black male student who took issue with me being transgender. Before they both graduated, however, their families sent me a beautiful love note thanking me for making their worlds bigger, more beautiful, and more expansive. And that, friends, is how and why I do this work. It's what keeps me brave. It's what keeps me hopeful. It's what keeps me telling my story.

For those who lived, for those who didn't, and for those who will. #BlackTransLivesMatter

PART II

#1000BLACKGIRL BOOKS

—Marley Dias

There is little doubt that the books read in most schools and classrooms in the United States are not representative of the diversity of the school-age population. Statistics from the Children's Cooperative Books Center in Madison, Wisconsin, show 41.8 percent of books published in 2019 were about white protagonists, and 29.2 percent featured animals as the main characters. Of the 12.2 percent published with Black lead characters, less than half were written by Black authors. This being said, there is also a plethora of exceptional books by remarkable Black authors and illustrators, as can be recognized by the movement of Marley Dias. At 12 years old, Marley set out to find 1,000 Black girl books, because she was "tired of reading about white boys and their dogs" (McGrath, 2017, para. 1). Dias traveled the country, spoke at conferences, met politicians, and exceeded her goal of 1,000 Black girl books. What will Marley do next? Will she have to continue her campaign in order to find books to read at 13, 14, 15? No child should have to launch a national campaign in order to see themselves in literature, yet, Dias's agency demonstrates the ingenuity and capacity of Black girls to state, seek, and pursue what they need to survive.

This section highlights factors to consider in selecting books that are authentically engaging, relevant, and culturally responsive. Authors share the hows (methods for selecting books) and whats (samples of books) that counter the stereotypical images of Black girls. Dr. Delano-Oriaran details the lack of representation and very specific information for teachers on how to select BACE (Blackcentric, authentic, and culturally engaging) books that educators can use to assess both their classrooms and school libraries. Books that affirm Blackness are critical, serving as mirrors for Black girl students and windows for all girl students. The selection of specific, high-quality books encouraged by this chapter will help teachers curate a classroom library that supports all students to have an intersectional perspective of the world, their peers, and themselves.

Selecting and Using BACE (Blackcentric, Authentic, and Culturally Engaging) Books

She Looks Like Me

Omobolade Delano-Oriaran

> *"She looks like me, Mummy." That is precisely what daughter Feyikemi keeps saying to me when we read books that depict authentic Black, African, and African American images and characters that look like her. Feyikemi lights up when these images mirror her lived realities and identities, and she connects with these characters because, just like my daughter, they are Black, brilliant, beautiful, assertive, courageous, and determined.*

This chapter presents a set of criteria that can be used in selecting books that authentically mirror the intersectional identities that Black Girls bring to the classroom: Black, authentic, and culturally engaging (BACE). This metric is influenced by a number of factors, including the works of Rudine Sims Bishop (1990a, 1990b, 2011). I created BACE as a tool to guide educators so Black Girls and Black Boys can be exposed to books that mirror, or reflect, the universality of their racial and cultural identities and experiences. These criteria are also designed to position educators to select books that provide windows for students who are "other" than Black or African American to "come to know people whose cultures [races] are different from their own" (Bishop, 1990b, p. 7). This window is key to evoking empathy, critical thinking, and understanding in readers (Aronson et al., 2018; Johnson et al., 2018), and sometimes to challenging students' thinking.

HERSTORIES: BLACK GIRLS TELLING THEIR STORIES IN REPRESENTATIONS OF AUTHENTIC SELVES

In 2018, there were limited publications that accurately reflected many aspects of diverse cultures and identities. Horning et al. (2019) noticed

> how many picture books feature brown-skinned protagonists with no specific cultural or ethnic identifiers as part of the depiction, and wonder whether these books truly serve as what critic and scholar Rudine Sims Bishop calls "mirrors, windows, and sliding glass doors." We're skeptical, even as we appreciate many of them for their stories, and for the decision to not default to white protagonists (paras. 9–10).

In 2019, two sisters from Delaware—Zaria, 13, and Hailey Willard, 8,—started Zaria X Hailey, a live bedtime story session on social media, and intentionally "picked books with characters who look like [them], because not a lot of kids see books with characters who look like [them]" (Morrison & Cirillo, 2019, para. 4). In November 2015, Marley Dias established the #1000BlackGirlBook campaign (GrassROOTS Community Foundation, 2019) that featured Black Girls as the main characters because she "was sick of the books she was being given in school . . . and as she'll tell you, they were all about white boys and their dogs" (McGrath, 2017, para. 1). A further online search of books dedicated to Black Girls, that is by no means exhaustive, includes lists like "Broadening the Story: 60 Picture Books Starring Black Mighty Girls" (Katherine, 2020); "Black Girl Magic: 33 Picture Books Featuring Black Female Protagonists" (Gordon, 2017); "25 Empowering Books for Little Black Girls" ("25 Empowering Books," 2013); "20 Books that Inspire Black Girls to Strive Toward Greatness" (Griffin-EL, 2018); "13 Books Every Young Black Girl Should Read" (Dior, 2018); and "Brown Girl Bookshelf: 10 Books to Read to Our Daughters" (Foxx, 2013). Yet what some of these lists may not reveal is how these books were selected or what to look for in determining how these books are authentic and mirror balanced representations of African American/Black Girls.

BACE Books that Mirror Black Girls: What Are They?

BACE books are those that authentically center and depict Blacks in active and affirming roles. They are about Blacks and African Americans, usually written by Blacks (with some exceptions), and are based on the author and illustrator's experiences and knowledge base. They depict Blacks as protagonists and illustrate the universality and uniqueness of Blacks as informed by their racial, ethnic, tribal, and national identities, as well as by the intersections of identities such as gender, religion, language, sexual orientation, ability, and a host of social and cultural groups. BACE books reflect what Bishop (2011) called *culturally conscious* books, and they show "distinctively African American ways of living, believing, and surviving" (p. 227). They educate, entertain, and instill Black racial consciousness, her/history, contributions, and pride (Harris, 1990). Informed by W. E. B. Du Bois's 1919 *The Brownies' Book*, the first magazine for African American children (McNair, 2008), BACE books should result in

1. Instilling in all children that Black is beautiful.

2. Familiarizing all students regardless of race or cultural identities with the herstories and histories, accomplishments, struggles, and resistance of Blacks in the context of the United States of America.

3. Providing children of various races other than Black and all genders the opportunity to develop an in-depth appreciation, awareness, and respect for Black Girls and women (Griffin-EL, 2018).

4. Understanding that Black folx have been and continue to be successful in a variety of ways and that they are famous in the global world due to contributions they have made to society.

5. Infusing authentic depictions of Black folx into schoolwide curriculum consistently and continuously—*not* simply regulating such depictions to Black History Month in February and/or isolating them to a section in a curriculum for Blacks or women.

Why Is There a Need for BACE Books?

Black Girls are being stripped of their innocence and brilliance as they go through traumatic experiences in U.S. schools. They are "depicted as hypersexual, emotionally unstable, and uneducated in comparison to the positive images of White girls and women seen in magazines, movies, and television shows" (Jacobs, 2016, p. 226). Black Girls continue to be marginalized, and experience what some have called the invisibility syndrome paradigm (ISP), a process in which they struggle internally with not being validated, recognized, acknowledged, and/or valued

(Haynes et al., 2016). It is important that the narrative is disrupted and Black Girls have affirming educational experiences such as those provided by books and instructional practices that mirror their lived experiences in their school environment. When used in a balanced way, BACE books should counter societal stereotypes about Black Girls.

FACTORS TO CONSIDER IN SELECTING BACE BOOKS FOR GIRLS: "SHE LOOKS LIKE ME"

Using BACE books positions educators to adopt a critical lens to select books that are authentic for Black Girls. Table 34.1 outlines a set of criteria for selecting BACE books. This guide is not an exhaustive list of questions, but is intended to critically engage educators and readers to know how to select BACE books that are culturally relevant to Black Girls. These criteria have been created so the reader's findings result in the affirmative in the Yes column, "Yes, I can use the book, as it is a BACE book!" If there are multiple No's for the book you want to use, consider self-reflection and exploring how you can improve your choices as an educator. What do the No's demonstrate about how you make choices about books that authentically depict Black Girls?

TABLE 34.1   Criteria for Selecting BACE Books

		YES	NO	N/A
I.	**About the Book**			
	a. *Is the copyright date recent, within 5-10 years?*			
	b. *Did the book receive a race-based/social justice award (such as the Coretta Scott King Book Award)?*			
	c. *Does the setting counter stereotypes about Blacks?*			
II.	*Protagonist*			
	a. *Is the protagonist a Black female? (Identify the race of the protagonist based on online reviews.)*			
	b. *On the book jacket, is the protagonist presented at a "close, intimate distance with head and shoulders visible to readers"? (Cueto & Brooks, 2019)*			
III.	*Author/Illustrator*			
	a. *Does the author identify as Black/African American (based on online book reviews or biography)?*			
	b. *Does the illustrator identify as Black (based on online book reviews or biography)?*			
	c. *Does the illustrator demonstrate knowledge about experiences Black Females have? (Check out biographical material about the illustrator to determine their experiences as or of African Americans.)*			

(Continued)

TABLE 34.1 (Continued)

		YES	NO	N/A
IV.	*Countering Stereotypes of Black Females*			
	a. *Does the storyline avoid depicting Black Females as stereotypes like Mammy, Jezebel, or Sapphire? (big-bosomed, promiscuous, hostile, and hypersexualized images; Frank, 2016)*			
	b. *Does the author avoid depicting Black female characters as helpless? (Myers & Bersani, 2008)*			
	c. *If the storyline illustrates various professions, does it depict Black female characters in balanced roles that reflect the diversity of society, such as scientists, congresspersons, teachers, lawyers, doctors, artists, laborers, barbers, et cetera? (Smith-D'Arezzo & Musgrove, 2011)*			
	d. *If the storyline illustrates various professions, does it depict Black female characters in roles/professions traditionally socialized as male (moms working outside of the household, principals, engineers, doctors, pilots, women playing sports, construction workers, astronauts, et cetera? Smith-D'Arezzo & Musgrove, 2011)*			
V.	*Illustration of Physical Qualities*			
	a. *Does the book depict multiple Black female characters with a variety of facial shapes? (If you have Black Females in your class, do they see representations of these characters in themselves?)*			
	b. *Does the book depict Black female characters with various shades of Blackness/skin tones? (e.g., check out Halle Berry, Misty Copeland, Khoudia Diop, Diandra Forrest, Marsai Martin, Lupita Nyong'o, Kheris Rogers, Issa Rae, Jill Scott, Jerricha Hoskins, Alexis Wanguhu, and many more. . . .*			
	c. *Does the storyline depict Black female characters that have darker shades and skin tones in positive roles?*			
	d. *Does the book depict multiple Black female characters with a variety of body shapes? (e.g., check out Marsai Martin, Gabourey Sidibe, Lupita Nyong'o, Lizzo, Jordyn Curet, Nikita Pearl Waligwa, Uzo Aduba, Lena Waithe, Simone Biles, Venus Williams, and Mo'Nique)*			
	e. *Does it depict multiple Black female characters with a variety of nose shapes?*			
	f. *Does it depict multiple Black female characters of a variety of heights?*			
	g. *Do the illustrations accurately reflect the time period of the setting?*			
VI.	*Hair Texture*			
	a. *Is the hair of the Black female characters depicted in any of these styles: curls, braids, twists, cornrows, locs, Afros, and/or puffs? (Brooks & McNair, 2015) Check out hairstyles in the book* Hair Love *(Cherry, 2019). (Check out a google image search of hairstyles of Chimamanda Ngozi Adichie.)*			
	b. *Are the braids, cornrows, locs, or Afros portrayed positively?*			

	YES	NO	N/A
VII. Storyline			
a. Does the storyline depict Black female characters in active roles?			
b. Does the storyline depict Black Females as courageous, or does it invoke courage in Black Females?			
c. Does the storyline affirm the self-image of children who identify as Black/African Americans?			
d. Do some of the Black Females in your classroom/setting (if any) see themselves in the book?			
e. Does the storyline highlight the present-day contributions of African American/Black women?			
f. Does the storyline highlight past contributions of African American/Black women?			
g. In the storyline, are Black Females' achievements or successes based on their initiative and intelligence? (Derman-Sparks, 2016)			
h. In the storyline, does the author avoid depicting Black Females' achievements based on their relationship to White characters or males? (Derman-Sparks, 2016)			
i. Does the storyline transmit appreciation for Black people or experiences?			
VIII. Literary Quality			
a. Does the book have a well-constructed plot?			
b. Does the book foster socioemotional development?			
c. Does it provide readers with opportunities to develop opinions about the storyline or topic? (Crippen, 2012)			
d. Does the storyline accurately reflect the lived experiences of Blacks during the time period in which it is set?			
IX. Linguistic Patterns and Terminology			
a. Do the characters "speak with various linguistic patterns" (Brooks, 2006, p. 375), including but not limited to African American vernacular English, rural dialects, languages from various African countries, and Southern dialects?			
b. Is the terminology used in the book authentic and reflective of the diversity of Black/African American language? (e.g., Mama, Ma, Grandma, Mummy, Mum, Papa, Dad, Daddy) (McNair, 2010)			
c. Does the book use appropriate terminology to depict Black females (e.g., fire woman, policewoman, shero, congresswoman)?			
d. Are the Black female character names used in the book authentic and reflective of the diversity of culture of Blacks and African Americans? (e.g., Ade, Aisha, Ayesha, Michelle, Nene, Tamika, Zenab, Khadija, etc.)			
e. Is it devoid of derogatory words?			

Additional recommendations to consider in selecting BACE books for your collections are the following:

- Books showing Blacks/African Americans persevering and surviving in the current and past periods. Referencing the works of Rudine Sims Bishop, who argues that books "show young African American readers [all readers] that Black people as far back as slavery days have always been resilient in the face of overwhelming odds" (as described by Rogers, 2015, p. 78).

- Books that include present and past Black her-his-our (Black herstory, Black history, Black ourstory) stories. Black her/history did not start with slavery, as Black history "for and by Black folks, has successes independent of Europe" (Knott Dawson, 2020, para. 3).

- Books that depict various settings, economic diversity, and family units that are realistic representations of society.

- Books that illustrate the importance of family among Blacks folx.

Writing as a Black woman, Black Girl, educator, scholar, activist, mother to a Black Girl, and many more, I assert that balanced representations of authentic characters that mirror the intersections of lived experiences and cultural identities of Black Girls are essential. Black Girls are beautiful! Black Girls are brilliant! Black Girls have many more talents waiting to be unleashed. I strongly advocate that all educators, school districts, schoolwide partners, families, and communities use what I consider to be Blackcentric, authentic, and culturally engaging (BACE) books that result in Black Girls saying, "She looks like me!"

NOTE: Sincere appreciation to these members of the Delta Sigma Theta Sorority, Inc.: Roni Becton, Chrystal Cannon, Cindy Clark, and Keisha Jones of the MidsUp Worldwide Facebook page for their January 2020 recommendations of Black women that depict diversity in sistahs.

Continuing with the critical theme of literature and curriculum in the lives of Black girls and their classroom peers, the next chapter, by doctoral candidate Cierra Kaler-Jones and teacher educator Rosalie Reyes, explores the critical importance of literature that celebrates the diversity of hair representation. Readers will take away a wealth of knowledge and practical application to enhance their ability to create truly inclusive classrooms where individuality is honored and respected. Given many of the racial aggressions Black girls face in schools are related to hair, it cannot be emphasized enough that Black hair awareness and respect must be required if we are to center Black girls in our classrooms. This chapter also supports teachers in selecting hair-affirming books that also provide windows and mirrors into the Black hair experience.

CHAPTER 35

Hair Representation Matters

Selecting Children's Books for Black Girls

Cierra Kaler-Jones, Rosalie Reyes

As I prepared to meet a group of three- to five-year-olds for our creative movement dance class, I heard one of the caregivers enter the room, and her daughter peered at me shyly from behind her mom's leg. As the mom greeted me she exclaimed, "Miss Cierra's hair looks like yours!" The girl stepped closer to me to get a better look at my hair. When I bent down to talk to her, she patted my curly bun and then tapped on her own bun with her tiny fingers. I soon realized this wouldn't be the only time where representation played a significant role in creating classroom spaces where my Black girl students felt affirmed.

Seeing positive representation from a young age can help shape what children imagine as possible and influence how they view themselves. Because of this, I started to incorporate children's books into dance class, showcasing and highlighting Black dancers such as Misty Copeland and Debbie Allen, as well as books about various types of hair like *I Love My Hair!* (Tarpley, 1998) and *Hair Love* (Cherry & Harrison, 2019). As I read the pages out loud, the students would jump up from their seats and touch the pages, "That's me! That's me!" they would shout. Children's books, specifically ones where students see themselves represented, enables them to see their identities dance off the page.

Children's Books on Hair as Hopescapes for Black Girls

As educators, we must create spaces where students see themselves and their experiences reflected in classroom materials and pedagogy (Ladson-Billings, 2000). Carefully selecting and analyzing children's texts can provide what Rudine Sims Bishop (1990) calls "windows, mirrors, and sliding glass doors" to readers' multilayered identities. Children's literature can be a window to show what the possibility of new worlds could look like, as well as sliding glass doors to encourage children to use their imaginations to enter those worlds. Toliver (2018) expands this to include *hopescapes* for Black girls, drawing on Hamilton's (1987) original definition, that hopescapes showcase the rich traditions, history, and culture of Black communities and counter stereotypical narratives that dehumanize Black people.

Unfortunately, there are only a small number of children's books that feature Black characters. According to the Cooperative Children's Book Center (2020), only 12.20 percent of children's books published in 2018 featured Black characters. Because there are so few books featuring Black characters, it is even more imperative that we highlight positive representations of Black girls and their hair in literature.

Hair is a racial and ethnic signifier and a cultural practice among Black women and girls (Banks, 2000; Rooks, 1996). Societal understandings of beauty have historically valued straight, thin, long hair (Jones-DeWeever, 2009). These beauty standards are communicated through school policies and media messages, and they have served as another mechanism to sustain racial hierarchies. Brooks and McNair (2014) discussed how the first body issue that affects Black girls' identity development, in addition to skin color, is hair texture. Research has shown that Black women and girls are negatively impacted by the internalization of media images that do not feature their hair textures and styles (Capodilupo, 2015). For Black girls who have thick, coarse, and curly hair, a lack of representation can contribute to how they perceive the world, and in turn, themselves.

Recognizing that hair played a significant role in our (the authors') interactions with our students as early childhood educators, we developed a workshop on hair representation in children's books in partnership with the National Museum of African American History and Culture. In this chapter, we share some of the strategies from the workshop, including guiding questions for assessing books, a reader's theatre lesson, and recommendations for talking to children about hair.

Assessing Books Using a Critical Lens

Using Louise Derman-Sparks's (2013) *Guide for Selecting Anti-Bias Children's Books* as a foundation, we crafted guiding questions to assess children's literature about hair.

CHECK THE ILLUSTRATIONS

Does the book accurately illustrate many and diverse styles, textures, and colors of hair? Are they realistic? What hair textures and styles are missing? Even if the book doesn't directly talk about hair, do the illustrations show examples of natural hair?

EXAMINE THE LANGUAGE

Are terms like *nappy*, *wild*, or *crazy* used to describe hair? If those terms are used, are they used in an affirming way, and do they reclaim the historically negative connotation of the word (e.g., bell hooks's [1999] *Happy to Be Nappy*)? Does the book appropriate a hairstyle that has historical grounding in another culture without discussing the history, such as a mohawk or a fro-hawk? Does the text refer to hair in comparison to animals, or does it use other dehumanizing metaphors? Is the language overall celebratory?

CONSIDER HOW THE BOOK AFFECTS CHILDREN'S SELF AND SOCIAL IDENTITY

When selecting children's books on hair, does your selection include characters of various races and ethnicities? For example, are Afro-Latinx communities represented? Are there representations of communities that cover their hair? Are there discussions about various hair textures? It is important to highlight the diversity of textures (i.e., there are many types of natural hair, and there are different classifications for the various curl shapes and patterns).

READER'S THEATRE LESSON

In more recent years, there has been an increase in the number of children's books that amplify positive representations of Black girls and their hair. Natasha Anastasia Tarpley's (1998) *I Love My Hair!* is a powerful text to use for reader's theatre. In this story, a young Black girl named Keyana discovers the versatility, strength, and resilience of her hair. Throughout the book, she touches on the special bond she has with her mother through doing hair and how a teacher reminded her of how their ancestors used hair as a form of resistance and power.

Reader's theatre lessons have the ability to "transform children's literature into active lessons where students read/recite lines from scripts transferred from an existing text or created scripts from their original stories" (Jeffries & Jeffries, 2014, p. 3). Studies have shown that students who engage in reader's theatre lessons better grasp content and feel more comfortable talking about important, but sometimes difficult, issues (Cueva et al., 2012). This reader's theatre activity, coupled with call-and-response prompts and pre and post reading and reflection questions, can facilitate dialogue in the classroom about the acceptance and celebration of many hair types and textures.

EXAMPLE

- Start by asking prereading questions such as, "Who does your hair? What is your favorite thing about your hair? Why do you love your hair? Was there a time you did something special with your hair?"

- After having a discussion, break students into small groups, and ask them to select three pages of the book *I Love my Hair!* to act out to the larger group. Help students determine which characters they might need to be, depending on the scene they select. For example, one of the pages reads, "But my teacher made me feel better. She said that when she was growing up, folks counted their hair as a blessing. Wearing an Afro was a way for them to stand up for what they believed, to let the world know that they were proud of who they were and where they came from" (Tarpley, 1998, n. p.). In this scene, students can be Keyana and Keyana's teacher to act out a performance where Keyana is dreaming of and envisioning her ancestors being proud of their hair.

- This reader's theatre lesson can be adapted for different age groups. For example, for the youngest readers at the early childhood level, educators or caregivers can read to them and have them act out each page. Older readers at the upper elementary level can read the book and create a new scene to act out or write their own related scene to perform.

- After reading the book, follow up with additional questions and statements such as, "Why do you think Keyana loved her hair? What did you learn about the many ways that Keyana styled her hair? Did you learn something new about hair? Now everyone say ...I LOVE MY HAIR!" For older students, you can also ask them to reflect on why they chose a certain scene.

For additional books that we recommend on hair, please view the hair booklist on Social Justice Books: https://socialjusticebooks.org/booklists/hair/.

RECOMMENDATIONS FOR CONVERSATIONS WITH CHILDREN ABOUT HAIR

- Do stay away from language that emphasizes that differences in hair type and texture don't matter. This takes away from the rich diversity of the many types of hair. When we approach conversations about physical differences from a place of color evasiveness, we willfully tune out information about a person that includes their history, background, and racialized and ancestral experiences. It also reinforces the conscious avoidance of talking about race to further perpetuate the status quo (Annamma et al., 2017).

- Do have conversations with students about consent and hair. Even if some might regard it as complementary to be fascinated by someone's else's hair, it is still someone's body and should not be touched. For Black girls, hair is part of our identity, and it is sacred. Touching hair is a violation of personal space. Encourage Black girls to assert their agency, and reinforce that it is always okay to say "no." Talk to all students about respecting boundaries. Sharee Miller's (2018) children's book, *Don't Touch my Hair!* is a helpful text to open up a conversation about consent and agency in an age-appropriate way. In the book, Aria talks about how it makes her uncomfortable that people give her hair a lot of attention. She then tells everyone to not touch her hair, asserting that it is hers, she loves it, and they can look, but not touch without her permission (Miller, 2018).

- Answer questions with honesty and genuineness. By preschool, children notice differences in physical features such as skin color and hair texture (Derman-Sparks & Edwards, 2010). Young children may believe that talking about race is wrong if you shy away from answering their questions directly (Tatum, 1997). Talking about differences openly and through an antibias lens encourages critical thinking about stereotypes, prejudice, and discrimination; creates space for comfortable and respectful interactions with a wide range of people; and gives children a tool to resist negative messages about their identities (Derman-Sparks & Edwards, 2019).

- Do highlight the beauty and uniqueness of various hair textures. For example, Black girls' hair can take many shapes and forms, such as braids, locs, twistouts, and more. Don't use language that fetishizes hair or describes hair as being "exotic." Help all students see the beauty, history, and normalcy of Black hair. For example, in the early 15th century, West African people would use hair as a way to share messages about their identities, such as marital status, wealth, or role within their community (Byrd & Tharps, 2014). Grooming hair with intricately carved combs was also a community-building process that had been passed down for generations. We see this practice still used today in families like Keyana's in *I Love My Hair!* as a way to build sisterhood, strengthen familial bonds, and tie Black girls to their ancestors (Brooks & McNair, 2014).

- Do share facts about hair that are universal, such as hair comes in different colors and textures, hair has a root and shaft, and hair is something that can be cut, styled, and covered, depending on personal, cultural, and religious preferences and values. As young people become familiar with some of their own features and those of their classmates, help them to have vocabulary and ideas to understand sameness and difference.

- Ask young children questions about what they love about their own hair and affirm the positive qualities of their hair. This helps support children to feel confident, comfortable, and strong in who they are without feeling or expressing superiority towards anyone else (Derman-Sparks & Edwards, 2019).

These strategies can be adapted to fit the unique needs of students and used as a guide to begin or deepen conversations about hair using children's books. Black girls, and the way they show up in the world, must be affirmed and celebrated in classrooms.

The Night Is Yours, by Abdul-Razak Zachariah, illustrated by Keturah A. Bobo

Grade Level PreK–2

Contemporary Realistic Fiction

Book Review by Omobolade Delano-Oriaran

The Night Is Yours is about Amani, a brilliant girl who lives in a neighborhood, surrounded by her friends and family. The setting illustrates an apartment complex that symbolizes the living digs where the author once resided. Zachariah depicts the peaceful setting of Amani's neighborhood. She plays with friends, family, and others in her community. This BACE book weaves culturally authentic and engaging images of Black girls of various hues. The authentic setting counters the many layers of stereotypical imagery of Black and Brown communities, as it's devoid of violent turmoil and "chaos." It is rich in the ambiance of peace, calm, and strength in Black families, as children play hide and seek and double Dutch while their parents and neighboring adults watch from the windows of their apartments. The apartment complex shows the role of porches. In some communities, porches are "like the quietest family member; a gift where community lives and strangers become neighbors" (Burch, 2018). In this context, the children sit on the steps and play, and when they get tired of sitting, they play hide-and-seek during the calm nights of their beloved neighborhood.

The authentic name of the book's protagonist, Amani, which means wishes, faith, and aspirations, possesses Islamic and African origins popular among many African American families. The hairstyles illustrated in the book show the beauty and love of Black hair; curls, braids, twists, Afros, and puffs.

The book counters the stereotypical images of Black girls and manifests their brilliance. Amani's active role as the protagonist reflects the innocence and authenticity of young Black girls, "Little one, so calm and so happy. . . . You are very real tonight," as compared to the hypersexualized images of Sapphire and Jezebel often shown in mainstream literacy and/or media. Zachariah shows Amani as a critical thinker with "you are patient, and you think. I can tell you're running through every possible idea." This demonstrates the inner beauty, strength, and brilliance of young Black girls with, "Go ahead . . . show everyone else . . . teach them how to be a night-owning girl like you. . . . You, Amani, are 'it.'" Zachariah and Bobo show the village, love, and strength in the Black family and community, as children "hear a chorus of adults and big siblings yelling out windows to call them [children] inside," as the book concludes, ending the night with Amani, Mum, and Dad reading away with joy and imagined love.

National certified teacher librarian Sabrina Carnesi continues the theme of authentic representation for Black girls in literature but moves the conversation into young adult literature. Sharing how to select authentic young adult literature that expands the representation of Black girls into multiple literary genres grows the diversity of reading opportunities for readers of all ages. Carnesi clearly lays out the strengths of multiple texts and includes not only titles but also annotations to guide classroom incorporation. In addition to the multiple texts recommended by Carnesi, the chapter is followed by a book review of Children of Blood and Bone written by Tomi Adeyemi, the bestselling fantasy novelist.

CHAPTER 36

Teaching Reading to Beautiful and Brilliant Black Girls

Building a Strong Culture of Engagement

Sabrina Carnesi

This chapter focuses on the critical need to select high-quality, authentically voiced books that reinforce the agency needed for young Black girls to feel beautiful, brilliant, and strong. School and classroom libraries can play a major role in providing equitable access to books that are culturally relevant and that authentically tell and reflect Black Girls' stories and world experiences. Culturally relevant texts, also coined as *mirrored texts,* affirm the reader's existence by speaking the same language as the reader and showing reactions to commonly experienced situations in the same manner as the reader or someone the reader knows (Ladson-Billings, 2009). In many instances these types of books can also serve as guideposts to help the reader pull out of situations they have trouble coping with (Tatum, 2017). When books such as this are not available to readers, it "negatively affects their identity development" (Hughes-Hassell et al., 2017, p. 8), and can also alienate them more than they have already experienced as students of color.

HOW TO SELECT HIGH-QUALITY, AUTHENTICALLY VOICED BOOKS

Given there is a large variety of authors who write books that feature African American and other girls of color as protagonists, it is important to ensure the authors are authentic. In other words, own-voiced authored titles, or books by authors sharing the same cultural background as the readers they write for, should be included in the selection. Texts can also be considered own-voiced if they are based on life experiences that have intersected with or centered on the diverse group the authors are writing about, because this has allowed them entrance into the worlds of those they write about. This will ensure accuracy in the presentation and avoid the chance of stereotyping. Such actions as these are critical components of culturally responsive pedagogy, which allows a learner to "maintain cultural integrity, while succeeding academically" (Ladson-Billings, 1995, p. 476).

SUGGESTED BOOKS WITH REPRESENTATION

Until recently, there were few contemporary young adult fiction titles that directly addressed the issues of identity, cultural history, and self-esteem for young Black girls as strong as Sharon Flake's *The Skin I'm In* (Jump at the Sun/Hyperion, 1998) and Mildred D. Taylor's *Roll of Thunder, Hear My Cry* (Puffin, 1976). Still a very popular time-proven title, *The Skin I'm In* is concerned with 13-year-old Maleeka Madison, who overcomes being teased for the clothes she wears and her dark complexion. Another time-proven title is *Roll of Thunder, Hear My Cry*, which combines 12-year-old Cassy Logan's struggles with self-esteem and identity with the Depression-era social injustices of Mississippi. Over recent years, several titles to touch on these same concepts have been published. *Tiffany Sly Lives Here Now* (Davis, Harlequin Teen, 2018) and *Genesis Begins Again* (Williams, Atheneum, 2019) are realistic titles that feature a Black female protagonist in either high school or middle school who struggles with social acceptance and issues surrounding hair texture and styles, as well as skin tone. Along with the previously mentioned titles, other suggested fiction and nonfiction titles of interest to Black girls are listed in Table 36.1 below. The list consists of 11 middle school and 8 high school titles that are currently or soon-to-be in print at the time of this writing. Each title is presented in a variety of settings and age groups which, among other subject matters and themes, address issues of beauty and self-value for Black females. All titles but one feature a protagonist between the

TABLE 36.1 Suggested Titles for African American Girls Based on Identity Struggles

MIDDLE SCHOOL	HIGH SCHOOL
Colorism	
Camo Girl by Kekla Magoon (Aladdin, 2011).	*Dread Nation* by Justina Ireland (Balzer + Bray, 2018).
Genesis Begins Again by Alicia D. Williams (Atheneum, 2019).	*Tiffany Sly Lives Here Now* by Dana L. Davis (Harlequin Teen, 2018).
Tameka's New Dress by Ronnie Sidney II, Traci Van Wagoner, & Kurt Keller (Creative Medicine-Healing Through Words, 2016).	*Shadowshaper* by Daniel José Older (Levine, 2015).
Like Vanessa by Tami Charles (Charlesbridge, 2018).	*Black Enough: Stories of Being Young & Black in America* by Ibi Zoboi (Balzer + Bray, 2019).

(Continued)

TABLE 36.1 (Continued)

MIDDLE SCHOOL	HIGH SCHOOL
Hair	
Like Vanessa by Tami Charles (Charlesbridge, 2018).	*Tiffany Sly Lives Here Now* by Dana L. Davis (Harlequin Teen, 2018).
Genesis Begins Again by Alicia D. Williams (Atheneum, 2019).	*Shadowshaper* by Daniel José Older (Levine, 2015).
Body Image	
Like Vanessa by Tami Charles (Charlesbridge, 2018).	*The Poet X* by Elizabeth Acevedo (HarperTeen, 2018).
Genesis Begins Again by Alicia D. Williams (Atheneum, 2019).	*Who Put This Song On?* by Morgan Parker (Delacorte, 2019).
Cultural History and Self-Awareness	
Roll of Thunder, Hear My Cry by Mildred D. Taylor (Puffin, 1976).	*The Poet X* by Elizabeth Acevedo (HarperTeen, 2018).
Akata Witch by Nnedi Okorafor (Viking, 2011).	*Shadowshaper* by Daniel José Older (Levine, 2015).
The Gaither Sisters series by Rita Williams Garcia (HarperCollins): • *One Crazy Summer* (2011). • *P. S. Be Eleven* (2013). • *Gone Crazy in Alabama* (2015). *Brown Girl Dreaming* by Jacqueline Woodson (Nancy Paulsen, 2014). *As the Crow Flies* by Melanie Gillman (Iron Circus Comics, 2017).	*An Unkindness of Ghosts* by Rivers Solomon (Akashic, 2017). *Black Enough: Stories of Being Young & Black in America* by Ibi Zoboi (Balzer + Bray, 2019). *All the Days Past, All the Days to Come* by Mildred Taylor (Viking Books, 2020). *The Hate You Give* by Angie Thomas (Balzer + Bray, 2017). *You Can't Touch My Hair: And Other Things I Still Have to Explain* by Phoebe Robinson (Plume, 2016). *More Than Enough: Claiming Space for Who You Are (No Matter What They Say)* by Elaine Welteroth (Viking, 2019). *Who Put This Song On?* by Morgan Parker (Delacorte, 2019). *Outburst* by Patrick Jones (Darby Creek, 2014).

ages of 11 and 16 and center issues such as colorism, body image, hair, and cultural history and identity. Rivers Solomon's *An Unkindness of Ghosts* (Akashic, 2017) is a science fiction dystopian adult title with high interest among teen readers.

A READING STRATEGY TO PROVIDE OPPORTUNITY FOR VOICE AND AGENCY

It is not enough for students to simply be given the opportunity to experience mirrored, windowed, and entryway text in an academic setting when trying to produce successful growth with literacy. To experience such growth requires resilience in readers, so they can rise above their daily "environmental disadvantage and stress" (Hughes-Hassell et al., 2017, p. 62) and perform well in school (Ladson-Billings, 2009; Miller & McIntosh, 1999; Tatum, 2017).

GRAFFITI TEXT ENCOURAGES VOICE AND AGENCY

Graffiti text is a reliable strategy that acts as a gateway to strengthen resilience and provide opportunity for student voice and agency before reading begins. Sandra Hughes-Hassell, Pauletta Bracy, and Casey Rawson's *Libraries, Literacy and African American Youth: Research and Practice* (2017) contains several examples of instructional methods for promoting voice and agency with youth who normally show reluctance to participate. One successful method is referred to as "written conversations" (p. 78), which are unspoken "powerful interactions among youth of all ages" (p. 79). The *Teaching Tolerance* website suggests this in the form of graffiti text, which provides an out-of-context preview for newly assigned reading (Text Graffiti, n.d.). The strategy can be implemented either in person or virtually. The use of online discussion bulletin boards such as Padlet, Twitter, Google+, and QuickTopic are types of digital tools that can be used for virtual conversations.

STEPS AND PROCEDURES

Steps in carrying out this strategy require each student to respond to a random quote they have been assigned from the text they are planning to read, following the particular guidelines set by the teacher. When students are finished writing their individual response to their assigned quote at their own desk, they leave their quote and response there, and move to another desk, where they respond to another quote and another student's comments about it. Then they move to another desk, and respond to another quote and its comments. Students are encouraged to select an idea that was generated from their responses in oral dialogue. This exercise can be carried out in whole and small group settings.

DEBUNKING THE HYPOTHETICAL STEREOTYPE

Scholarly awareness of the uniqueness of Black girls has shown a consistency that debunks the stereotype, which historically portrayed them as loud, angry, and aggressive (Crenshaw et al., 2015; Love, 2019; Morris, 2007; Morris, 2016). This is the hypothesis behind the attitude that often causes Black girls' actions and behaviors to be misunderstood, leading to them be "overdisciplined" compared to their white counterparts (Crenshaw et al., 2015, p. 29). As a school librarian, I have had the opportunity to observe this on numerous occasions. In my current school library, several girls have shown this behavior with some of their teachers when they make use of the library. One student, in particular, is notorious for what teachers define as "outbursts." I have encountered this same student in the hallway and in classrooms conducting herself in the same manner but noticed that when she is approached in a quiet, loving manner, even in the midst of a vexed moment, she is quiet in her response. I have also noticed that when she is involved in a well-planned challenging lesson that incorporates small groups, mobility, and a variety of technologies, she is on task and even volunteers to assist other students who are in need of better understanding.

My assessment is that she is bored with the simplicity of the assigned tasks in class and probably feels the animosity from some teachers who either ignore her or send her from their classrooms when she gets bored. In the meantime, I question whether or not her teachers forget that they are dealing with a 12-year-old girl. While she is tall, verbally expressive, and full-figured, we must not forget that she is only a 12-year-old, seventh-grade girl who is yearning to be treated as such within an environment that appreciates the manner in which she thrives academically. When I had a chance to use graffiti text in this same student's English class, she was very animated and engaged. The participation she displayed showed her enthusiasm and desire to learn. It also portrayed, to some degree, how she had been mishandled, misunderstood, and marginalized.

While advocacy for diversity in book publishing for children and young adults has improved, this nation's publishing world for children's literature is still dominated by white publishers and editors (Jimenez & Beckert, 2020) who can't relate to the lived worlds that authors of color write about (Nel, 2017). Such control places them in the position of gatekeepers with power to allow or reject ideas and perspectives. When Morgan Parker wrote her semibiographical story *Who Put This Song On?* (Delacorte, 2019), she wanted to bring to the forefront the problems behind the aggressive behavior and emotional breakdowns some Black girls display in school and other public places. Using her personal journals and her 17-year-old self as protagonist, the author was able to present a Black, middle-class girl who battles with the trauma of someone who tries hard to maintain a sense of sanity in an all-white world that has made her Blackness invisible. Patrick Jones's *Outburst* (Darby Creek, 2014), which is part of *The Alternative series*, shows the consequences faced by 17-year-old Jada Robinson, whose anger got so out of hand it caused her to be placed in foster care after serving time in juvenile detention. Both of the above-mentioned books mirror the experiences many Black American girls have as the highest recipients for discipline referrals among female students in this nation's K–12 schools (Butler-Barnes & Inniss-Thompson, 2020; Crenshaw et al., 2015).

CONCLUSION

At this point, we are witnessing a public school population that shows a rapidly increasing growth of youth of color, who are now the majority population (Geiger, 2018; Rabinowitz et al., 2019), and a continuing lack of teacher diversity in public schools (Hansen & Quintero, 2019). Some 40 years have passed since teacher education programs have considered the homogeneity of the teaching force in a less than flexible American school culture (Garcia & Ortiz, 1988; Hilliard, 1980). Considering this, standard test scores and discipline reports show there is still evidence of failure, particularly in the language arts. In a Red Table Talk episode, host Jada Pinkett Smith quoted the late Malcolm X on the systematic pattern of neglect society shows to young Black women, saying they "can be the most disregarded and disrespected creatures on the Earth" (Smith, 2019, 00:11:32).

In an excerpt from the original 1962 speech quoted by Smith, Malcolm X presented a series of hypothetical questions concerning Black identity that has not changed with the passage of time for the Black female, for example, "Who taught you to hate the texture of your hair?" "Who taught you to hate the color of your skin?" "Who taught you to hate the shape of your nose, and the shape of your lip?" "Who taught you to hate yourself from the top of your head to the soles of your feet?" (Educational Video Group, 2014, 00:00:22 to 00:00:38). If this is evident among women, could it not also be a truth for school-age girls in our society? A major question that arises is how well are school library and teacher educators prepared to develop the expertise for making the complex judgments needed to determine reading text selections that mirror this population's world?

Additional findings are also needed from studies on Black girls who are experiencing text disengagement and school disconnect due to environmental trauma stemming from being mishandled and misunderstood. Edim's *Well-Read Black Girl: Finding Our Stories, Discovering Ourselves* (Ballantine, 2018) shares stories of the disappointments Black female authors experienced from the sparse availability of mirrored texts in their childhood. The impact Black females have experienced in a world that has made them feel invisible and voiceless provides the reader with food for thought in Morgan Jerkin's *This Will Be My Undoing: Living at the Intersection of Black, Female, and Feminist in (White) America* (Harper Perennial, 2018) and Brittney Cooper's *Eloquent Rage: A Black Feminist Discovers Her Superpower* (St. Martin's, 2018). Both books address the systemic issues Black females cannot avoid when they strive to succeed. Such issues have them existing in a constant state of being misinterpreted and misunderstood in their world of work, academics, and personal relationships, thus revealing a cradle-to-the-grave chronic attack against the basic trajectories needed for sustainability.

Annotated Bibliography for Literature Titles

Acevedo, E. (2018). *The Poet X* (book in verse). HarperTeen.

Xiomara is a 15-year-old New York City Dominican teen. She lives in a world where her mother tries to control her, which results in constant shaming about her full figure, something natural that X cannot control

(Continued)

(Continued)

Charles, T. (2018). *Like Vanessa*. Charlesbridge.

Thirteen-year-old Vanessa Martin has an extraordinary singing voice and daydreams of being Miss America just like the current Miss America Vanessa Williams. Her only drawback is that she can't rise above her painful dissatisfaction with her full figure and dark skin.

Cooper, B. (2018). *Eloquent Rage: A Black Feminist Discovers her Superpower*. St. Martin's Press.

A collection of biographical essays that leads the reader through the complications faced by those who identify with Black feminism in a misogynistic society that interprets beauty in accordance with European standards.

Davis, L. D. (2018). *Tiffany Sly Lives Here Now*. Harlequin Teen.

A 16-year-old relocates to her estranged father after the death of her mother. Due to stress, Tiffany suffers hair loss and wears braid extensions. Her father's religious rules don't allow such practice, and he forces her to remove the braids. Not able to withstand living in a home with the daily images of her mixed-raced half sisters and their long flowing hair, Tiffany secretly seeks out help from a neighbor.

Edim, G. (2018). *Well-Read Black Girl: Finding Our Stories, Discovering Ourselves*. Ballantine Books.

A collection of essays written by black female authors on their early encounters with literature and the sparse opportunities to find books that allowed them to see characters, communities, and situations reflective of the experiences they had.

Flake, S. (1998). *The Skin I'm In*. Jump at the Sun/Hyperion.

Seventh grader Maleeka Madison is 13 years old, model tall, and dark skinned. Her problem is she suffers from severe low self-esteem and is not able to see her beauty or her greatness.

Francois-Madden, M. (2019). *The State of Black Girls: A Go-To Guide for Creating Safe Space for Black Girls*. Self-Published.

A resource written by Francois-Madden, a licensed clinical social worker who specializes in mental health and self-care, that directly addresses Black girls on what to do in case they or others they know are experiencing issues such as depression, anxiety, or any known variety of abuse.

Gilman, M. (2017). *As the Crow Flies*. Iron Circus Comics.

Thirteen-year-old Charlotte "Charlie" Lamonte is complicated: She's queer, Black, and questioning the Western views of Christianity from a racial and feminist perspective. With such ideas running through her thoughts, she's not enjoying her week-long summer vacation at an all-white-all-girls

Christian camp too much. If it weren't for making friends with Sydney, her whole week would be lost.

Ireland, J. (2018). *Dread Nation*. Balzer + Bray.

Issues of gender binary and colorism are embraced in the text of this historical fantasy set in a twisted Reconstruction era that presents the reader with a question: What if slavery had been brought to an end, and all people of color had to be educated and socialized to the highest levels?

Jerkin, M. (2018). *This Will Be My Undoing: Living at the Intersection of Black, Female, and Feminist in (White) America*. Harper Perennial.

A collection of essays that show what life has been like for the author growing up and striving to succeed in this nation's white-dominated society—being misunderstood and misinterpreted in the world of work, academic studies, and personal relationships.

Jones, P. (2014). *Outburst*. Darby Creek.

When 17-year-old Jada Robinson refuses to curb her anger management issues, she suffers the consequences of juvenile detention and foster care, with no opportunity for change, until she changes her attitude and controls the loud outbursts she's known for.

Magoon, K. (2011). *Camo Girl*. Aladdin.

Eleven-year-old Ella is so damaged from bullying, due to the skin condition vitiligo, that she can't stand her reflection in the mirror. Her isolation is further compounded by her being the only Black student in her school, until a new boy arrives.

Morris, M. W. (2017). *Pushout: The Criminalization of Black Girls in Schools*. The New Press.

An exploration of how Black female students' behavior in school is increasingly criminalized and becoming a pipeline to feed the incarceration of girls in the juvenile justice system.

Morris, M. W. (2019). *Sing a Rhythm, Dance a Blues*. The New Press.

Provides guidelines on how to serve young Black and brown girls who have or are experiencing trauma from punishment and abuse and need to find a space of safety and understanding.

Okorafor, N. (2011). *Akata Witch*. Viking.

In this fantasy, 12-year-old Sunny is an American-born Nigerian whose parents have moved her back to Nigeria. She stands out because she is albino and has to deal with the taunt "akata," which means "wild animal," because she is from America. Her newly acquired powers put her on a fast course to learn the ancient secrets that involve the mystery of a grandmother she's never met.

Older, D. J. (2015). *Shadowshapers*. Levine.

In Book 1 of this sci-fi series, the reader is introduced to Sierra Santiago,

(Continued)

(Continued)

a Puerto Rican American who is not only proud of her African ancestry, but embraces it by wearing her hair in its natural state, despite antagonism from her aunt.

Parker, M. (2019). *Who Put This Song On?* Delacorte.

A semibiographical narrative of the struggles the author experienced as a Southern California teen who grew up in a majority white suburb and attended a mostly white private Christian school that treated her Blackness and impulsive angry outbursts as something invisible, instead of something in need of attention.

Robinson, P. (2016). *You Can't Touch My Hair: And Other Things I Still Have to Explain*. Plume Publishing.

A compiled set of biographical essays in which author-comedian Phoebe Robinson humorously shares what it's like to be Black and female in America, especially when it comes to wearing hairstyles that showcase the natural curl of Black hair.

Sidney, R., II, Van Wagoner, T., & Keller, K. (2016). *Tameka's New Dress*. Creative Medicine–Healing Through Words.

In this graphic novel, middle school student Tameka has been fostered out to her grandmother due to the substance abuse of her mom. Unbeknownst to anyone, she is being bullied daily by another student because of her skin tone. The daily bullying is causing additional trauma in Tameka's life.

Solomon, R. (2017). *An Unkindness of Ghosts*. Akashic.

In this postapocalyptic 400-year-old world, Aster is a Black intersex autistic woman who lives on a theocratically run spaceship, where she is treated as a slave because of her race. Aster, however, has found a way to tear the oppressive society down due to a note left by her dead mother.

Taylor, M. D. (1975). *Roll of Thunder, Hear My Cry*. Puffin.

Twelve-year-old Casey Logan learns to cope with the racial hardships of Depression-era Mississippi, while struggling through the pains of growing up and becoming more independent of mind and making choices in life.

Thomas, A. (2017). *The Hate You Give*. Balzer + Bray.

Sixteen-year-old Starr Carter lives in Garden Heights, a low-economic neighborhood, while attending Williamson Prep, a private school in a more elite neighborhood. After witnessing the fatal shooting of her childhood friend, Khalil, she grapples with the weight of keeping her position as the eyewitness a secret and her desire to keep her prep school identity separate from her Garden Heights identity.

Welteroth, E. (2019). *More Than Enough: Claiming Space for Who You Are (No Matter What They Say)*. Viking.

Welteroth, who became the first person of African American origins to man the chair of editor-in-chief at the illustrious *Teen Vogue* fashion magazine at the age of 29, shares with readers how to claim your space at the table of opportunity while ignoring the biased behavior that will leave you thinking less of yourself.

Williams-Garcia, R. (2011). *One Crazy Summer*. HarperCollins.

Sisters Dalphine, Vonette, and Fern discover the importance of family bonds as they spend time with a variety of family members from their Brooklyn neighborhood to Oakland, California, and then the rural countryside of Alabama. Hard lessons of reality are presented to readers with both humor and depth in this trilogy.

Yoon, N. (2015). *Everything, Everything*. Delacorte.

Seventeen-year-old Maddy Whittier is severely inhibited from exposure to many things outside the walls of her home due to her immune deficiency syndrome. When a new family moves in next door, Maddy and the son become romantically involved, ignoring what could happen should Maddie leave the confines of her home.

Children of Blood and Bone, by T. Adeyemi

Grade Level 8–12

Fantasy

Book Review by Marguerite W. Penick

Stepping into a fantasy never felt so real as *Children of Blood and Bones* does when looking at the racism and fear that permeates today's society. Adeyemi creates an intricate world and strong female characters who battle for the right to be who they truly are. As a fantasy, *Children of Blood and Bones* creates a magical world where right battles wrong as Zelie fights to bring magic back to the diviners. Filled with riveting imagery, a magically beautiful and chilling backdrop, and characters who evoke a multitude of emotions, readers enter a world they both hate and love, a remnant of present-day society. As Adeyemi acknowledges in the author's note, Don't forget to "cry for the innocents like Jordan Edwards, Tamir Rice, and Aiyana Stanley-Jones" (p. 526). The battles being fought today are every bit as real as those in *Children of Blood and Bone*, making the fantasy scarily real.

PART III

"I AM DELIBERATE AND AFRAID OF NOTHING."

—Audre Lorde

Dr. Monique Liston boldly introduces readers to the idea of Black Girl Priming and gives teachers, especially white teachers, ways to recognize this behavior in the classroom. In an effort to keep Black girls grounded in the ideals of sisterhood, the classroom must exist as a place to learn and *practice the skills necessary to acknowledge and resist the part of the oppressor that lives within each of us. Using her personal life as a backdrop to the realization of her own brilliance, Liston's chapter is critical for teachers to understand the expansive extent to which society has impacted Black girls and the lengths to which teachers must go to create spaces in which they can overcome the negative priming they've received. This chapter invites educators to take a good hard look at the physical environment of their classrooms, the relationships of the students who inhabit them, and the pedagogical leadership that is critical for creating spaces for sisterhood. Additional strategies for doing so can be found in the subsequent chapter penned by independent school administrator Erica Snowden, well-practiced at helping teachers interpret and shift the microaggressions they have with Black girls students. Snowden shares her perceptive lens and her practical, applicable strategies in this relevant piece.*

CHAPTER 37

Black Girl Sisterhood as Resilience and Resistance

Monique I. Liston

There were four girls in my sixth-grade class. We did everything together. Did homework, played basketball, cracked jokes. Everything. Together. Always. Ironically enough, in my predominantly white school, there was only one white girl in the group.

Even more ironic, this story is not about her; it's about Chico. To this very day, I have no idea why we nicknamed her this, but that is what we called her . . . and always will. If I see her tomorrow, I will exclaim "CHICO!"

The white girl of course had straight hair, as did I, and so did one of the other Black girls. However, Chico did not. She had natural hair that she wore in large poofy braids. As an 11-year-old, I did not get why her hair was not relaxed like ours. I mean, pigtails were for little girls, and we were *not* little girls. I remember distinctly saying, "Chico, when you gonna get a perm!?" I was literally exasperated at the thought of her natural pigtails bouncing all around.

Chico went to a different school the next year. It was the 1990s, so we didn't have cell phones or social media to remain connected; I didn't know if I would ever see Chico again. I always thought about her when my bus passed her house on the way to school.

Time passed.

I went to high school with all my middle school friends, except Chico. Swept up in a pool of creamy crack goodness (chemical relaxers to make my curly thick hair limp and straight), I got my hair done weekly. At the same time, my consciousness around Black culture and history grew. During my senior year, I got really bold and told my mom that I was done with the creamy crack and wanted to wear my hair natural. I was not bold enough to do it before graduation. All the Black girls in my medium-sized, predominately white high school had relaxed, straight hair. In my day-to-day learning, I did not see any Black women who were not relatives or parents of friends. I did not see any Black women who did not have chemical relaxers in their hair.

I got my final relaxer to style my hair for senior prom and graduation.

I graduated in June of 2004, left my hometown, and moved to Washington DC as a freshman at Howard University. After I finished fall exams, I sat in my room struggling to take out yet *another* set of braids. With pain, agony, and frustration, I called in my RA and asked her to help me *cut* my braids off. At 1:00 am on December 17, 2004, we cut *all* of my hair off. The affirmation of identity I saw and absorbed while on the campus of Howard University allowed me to find comfort and beauty in my hair as a symbol of my Blackness and girlhood. When I returned home for holiday break, my new style was well received.

My philosophy on Black hair now is completely different than it was at that time. I am not the one to say all girls with naturals are *down* for the cause, and all relaxed sistas are confused about their Blackness. But I will readily admit that I held judgements like that for many years.

To this very day, I still feel bad about my insistence for Chico to relax her hair. I've always wanted her to know that I feel different now. Not that she cared, not that she even remembered; I just want to say that is not how I feel anymore.

A few years ago, I was on Facebook . . . procrastinating, as usual . . . and a friend suggestion was in my mailbox.

You will not believe who it was. . . . . (yeah, you will).

Yup, Chico.

It's been over 10 years. . . . and there's her picture. . . . and her hair. . . . relaxed!

Her hair is beautiful, but when seeing it relaxed, I still feel guilty.

Chico, I'm sorry for ever being in your ear in the sixth grade telling you to get a perm. I shouldn't have done that, but I didn't know any better at the time. I love your hair then, NOW . . . more than ever. Nevertheless, I'm glad to see you on Facebook. Glad to see you doing well! Peace, Monique

What is Black Girl Priming?

A primer is an elementary textbook that serves as an introduction to a subject. Youth typically receive lessons about race and relationships through family interactions, television and movies, and even preschool interactions. Elementary school experiences for young Black girls often serve as more than lessons or instructions; they are primers on "How to be Black and Girl in This World." To be Black and female within the learning environment means that you are constantly negotiating and navigating intersectional oppression in order to learn. Your Blackness is interpreted as a threat. Your femaleness means that you are to be controlled. As a result, Black girls are taught to see those same hateful concepts in themselves and others. Black girls are taught to resent what is culturally Black and feel trapped by social definitions of *girl* and *woman*. I refer to this process of internalized hatred as Black Girl Priming. Psychologists refer to priming as the process of preparing something or someone to respond unconsciously to a stimulus. Priming for Black girls is related to gender and race-shaped stereotypes (Rudman & Phelan, 2010; Steele & Ambady, 2006) and criminality (Dixon & Maddox, 2005). In other words, priming occurs when something or someone responds to the world around them without critical thought or analysis. For Black girls, priming occurs to shape their response to *Black* and *girl* as limited, and in many circumstances, it is punitive.

Black Girl Priming is the hidden curriculum of race and gender that pits Black girls against other Black girls in the classroom. Black girls are primed to emotionally reject and physically demonstrate their opposition to cultural Blackness. Black girls learn implicitly that skin color, height, weight, savviness, a sharp tongue, and so much more are measures of their relationship to Blackness and acceptability. In this chapter, we will explore the roots of Black Girl Priming, outline how sisterhood challenges Black Girl Priming, and offer ways white educators can resist perpetuating this harm through radical self-awareness, consciousness raising among other white educators, and offering tangible spaces for Black girls to build sisterhood in the classroom.

Anti-Blackness is the psychosocial and sociopolitical denial of dignity to Black people. Frank Wilderson (2010) argues that Black humanity is a "paradigmatic impossibility" in our society. Because of that, Black humanity is fractally represented in our education system. In other words, because of racism, there is an infinite repetition of dehumanization that makes Black humanity smaller and smaller as education cycles continue. There is no room to see Black people as deserving of all rights afforded citizens, members, or people within the American social context.

As a result, Black people are left to be constant negotiators of their own existence, perpetually engaging in dialogue to merely assert their humanity. There is no fourth-grade social studies class where students learn that "white is right" and

"Black is whack," but there is a tacit curriculum of socialization that punishes students for being Black and worse, being Black and female without apology. In my story, the hidden curriculum had taught me that the natural hair texture of Black girls needed to be altered to show maturity and acceptability within the world. As a young girl and product of Black Girl Priming, I made fun of another student. As a hidden curriculum, Black Girl Priming operates as a duplicitous tactic of unchecked anti-Blackness within our educational systems. Recent literature on Black girlhood studies explains how Black girls are denied their adolescence (Epstein et al., 2017) and are often in search of people and spaces to affirm their self-identification and self-authentication (Rambo, 2015; Rosenberg, 1987). Consider each commencement ceremony as another layer of anti-Black denial.

Black students have been historically disenfranchised by the American education system. Black students are tacitly taught they are less valuable, most vulnerable, and least deserving of an education. They rarely get to access a system that sees their inherent value, offering them a sense of dignity without contingency or apology. In a simultaneously humiliating effort, girls are socialized to operate within a narrow spectrum of gender normativity. They are expected to behave, respond, and react to their surroundings in ways that remain unchecked for most male-identified students. Kimberlé Crenshaw (1990) gave us intersectionality as language to frame the ways that Black girls and women experience the impact of race and gender at the same time and as consequences of one another. Black girls are primed to not understand themselves at the intersections, as their intersectional identities are constructed as threats instead of opportunities. Instead of praising Chico for her beautiful hair, I used it as a catalyst for jokes. I exploited her hairstyle as a threat and made fun of her for not following the curriculum that Black Girl Priming laid out for us.

Institutions, such as schools, have been slow to engage anti-Blackness head-on as a barrier to success for Black students. The dehumanization of Black girls as students has been marginally addressed through cultural competence, diversity, inclusion, and most recently equity. Black Girl Priming reminds Black girls that they are responsible for managing their Blackness and their girlhood, and if they do not manage it properly, they will face consequences that could be dehumanizing at best or fatal at worst. This puts Black girls at odds with one another. There is only so much space within the small, crafted intersection of Black girlhood that the slightest deviation is an opportunity to distinguish oneself as "following the rules" of an unwritten curriculum. To practice equity, a redistribution of power and responsibility has to occur. The responsibility needs to shift away from Black girls. In the classroom setting, Black girls need to be released from the suppression of their own dignity. The responsibility for managing race and gender intersections should not be a threat that Black girls are navigating, it should be an opportunity to disrupt oppression, mitigate the harm of anti-Blackness, and affirm the dignity of Black girls.

WHAT WOULD HAVE BEEN DIFFERENT IF WE HAD AN EDUCATOR WHO WAS EQUIPPED TO DISRUPT BLACK GIRL PRIMING FOR CHICO?

For Black girls, disrupting Black Girl Priming is a *resilience practice*. It took me getting an education at a historically Black college to undo some of the damage Black Girl Priming had done to me. But what about the other 14 girls from that class that did not get that lesson or exposure? If it were left to the current Eurocentric education systems to undo the psychological and emotional harm of Black Girl Priming, our success rate would be 1 in 15. If the educators in our school building had any knowledge of how building sisterhood among the Black girls in the classroom could change the trajectory of their lives, our educational experiences would have been vastly different. I could have affirmed Chico without apology. I could have learned to love myself without the mitigating concern of how I am "supposed" to look for the sake of a commercialized white-appeasing or a white-appearing aesthetic. Mendelberg (2008) shared in an article addressing racial priming in media, "Racial cues racialize people's responses even though— and especially when—people are unaware that they have been exposed to racial cues, and that their decisions are shaped by racial stereotypes or attitudes" (p. 111).

For white educators, disrupting Black Girl Priming is a *resistance practice*. When white educators disrupt Black Girl Priming by increasing opportunities for sister-hood among Black girls, they are actively resisting the systems of inequities that have caused Black students to see themselves as less than or other than. As a result, white women educators need a new grammar of praxis for our educational spaces. Anti-Blackness disruption must situate Black girls in classrooms as assets to one another and give them opportunities to cultivate relationships with one another that affirm each other despite the Black Girl Priming curriculum.

Classroom Actions

In your work as a classroom leader, you can give Black girls the opportunity to create their own narratives about their individual and collective identities. Through these exercises, you have an opportunity to practice centering youth voices and using their own skill sets to create and define narratives of themselves and their relationships.

These exercises can be paired with lessons in any subject area to highlight students' skills in literacy, oracy, and the arts.

- Self Portrait Gallery—Have Black girls take selfies with their classmates. Print those pictures. Have the students write short narratives about their relationships with the other girls. Artists such as Emma Moss, Tschabalala Self, and Kara Walker might be useful to explore.

- Photovoice Project—Have students take pictures of Black women in groups in their school or broader community. Have the students interview others to talk about the people in the pictures and their relationships with one another. This is a great time to engage students in their use of social media. Perhaps hashtags, snaps, or threads might be useful for their engagement.

- Research Project—Have students research Black women groups or collectives such as Sister Song, The Combahee River Collective, and/or Black Greek letter organizations and present them to the class.

Reading Group Exercise

- Mapping Your Own Identity Development—As an instructor, create a timeline of events in your life that allowed you to understand your own intersectional identity. What led you to understand your race? When did you become first aware of your race and gender? How does your experience align with what was presented in this chapter?

- Write a thank-you note to a Black woman-led organization, group, or collective expressing appreciation for their protection and celebration of Black Girlhood.

CHAPTER 38

Respect Black Girls

Prioritize, Embrace, and Value

Erica Snowden

It's a normal school day, and Kara[1] is in the classroom and being told to transition quickly from one task to the next. Trying her best, the teacher begins to give Kara a lecture about organization and responsibility. Kara does not look at the teacher while she is lecturing; she continues to try to gather her belongings and transition. "Kara, do you see why having a neat desk will help you?" says the teacher. No response from Kara. "Kara please look at me," responds the teacher. "I hear YOU!!!!" yells Kara with her hands in the air and her eyeballs rolled to the sky.

The incident between Kara and the teacher quickly moves from an issue of transitioning—according to the teacher—to one of disrespect. As the administrator in this scenario, I understand how Kara's behavior could be interpreted as disrespectful. I also know that such an interpretation doesn't take into account racial and cultural differences; in many Black households, children are taught to be respectful by *not* looking adults in the eye, questioning them, or "talking back" (Feldman, 1985). This centuries-old behavior is part of what Dr. Joy DeGruy (2005) calls *post traumatic slave syndrome*: "In the slave environment, and continuing through the period known as reconstruction and the long night of Jim Crow, it was inherently unsafe for a Black child to stray, wander, or question white people. Such behavior could result in severe punishment or even death" (p. 10). Such behaviors were used as a means to survive.

---

[1] Not her original name

Kara is trying to show that she is responding to authority, and she wouldn't dare stop her original task of getting her materials, which is what got her in trouble in the first place. The teacher reads her lack of eye contact, yelling, and eye rolling as disrespectful and rude. Who wouldn't be frustrated if they couldn't find their belongings, received a lecture for not finding their belongings, and then found themselves interrupted in the process to look at the lecturer? All of this could possibly go against what Kara has been taught both implicitly and explicitly at home. Kara was asked to take a break in this instance.

Black girls usually learn to code-switch before their white teachers even realize they're doing it. Morton (2014) states, "Code-switching could be characterized as the ability to adapt one's behavior as a response to a change in social context...." (p. 259). As Howard Stevenson (2014) has written, schools are not raceless or cultureless spaces: "Schools are centers of racial socialization and represent the one place where social ethics, economic warfare, national politics, and racial conflict emerge, collide, erupt, or lay hidden daily" (p. 60). Educators have the responsibility and opportunity to help students shape a new narrative by disrupting deeply held racial stereotypes; first, they must know what those stereotypes are.

For many Black women and girls, our deep culture and deep racial socialization has been peppered with a lesser-known but deeply pervasive stereotype, and reclaimed by Cooper (2018), as *eloquent rage*. Rage, sassiness, and backtalk are all aspects of Kara's response that were described by the white teacher. Dr. Joy DeGruy (2005) calls it *ever-present anger*. Kara's reaction, the rolling eyes and a loud voice, unfortunately earned her the stereotypical label of angry Black girl, a "Sapphire."

The most deeply pervasive stereotype to impact Black women is the Sapphire caricature, sometimes referred to as the *sassy black woman* or the *angry black woman* (ABW). "The Sapphire Caricature is a harsh portrayal of African American women, but it is more than that; it is a social control mechanism that is employed to punish Black women who violate the societal norms that encourage them to be passive, servile, non-threatening, and unseen" (Pilgrim, 2008/2012, para. 1). The Sapphire caricature is, essentially, punishment for Black women who do not act white.

How many times have Black girls heard teachers ask the following questions and make similar statements? "Why is she upset?" Or "angry"? Or "loud"? "She always has an attitude." "She rolls her eyes any time I give her a redirection." "She never seems happy." "She's disrespectful." "She just doesn't stop talking." (Fordham, 1993). The funny thing about stereotypes is they only need a kernel of truth to hold value and carry on a legacy that gets it wrong more than it gets it right. Maybe you as a white teacher did have a Black female student who talked all the time and was rude and rolled her eyes. However, when the next Black female student came along, did you look into your mental Rolodex of racial encounters and say, " I know this kind of student, I've seen this before!" Because Black folk do not get the privilege of being individuals and are often seen as a collective, every Black female student who comes after that first one may be seen through the lens of those previous negative experiences. The relevant critical question to explore is, What can educators do? I offer the following three skills as a means of starting the process of implementing relevant culturally responsive practices for positioning Black girls to thrive and hone their Black Girl Magic in your classroom.

PRIORITIZING

Educators have to emphasize that Blackness should be celebrated. Black girls are valuable. Black girls belong. What this means is educators need to make it okay for Black girls to engage and lead with the identities they present in the classroom. If you are a Black teacher, it is not enough to just be there as a mirror. You must engage as a mirror, tell your story, wear your natural hair, incorporate your culture and language. These acts model and teach Black girls that they belong in the school space; they don't have to change to fit in. If you are a white teacher, it means supporting Black colleagues as they provide these mirrors where support may not come naturally and may push you outside your comfort zone.

Support looks like affirmations of Black identities in images throughout the school on the walls, in the texts students read, in the artwork showcased, in the music learned and played, and in the curriculum taught. Teachers who take the time to learn students' names and how to pronounce them correctly, and who decipher one Black girl from the next, can be impactful. Building real and genuine relationships with Black girls matters. You do not have to act like you like their music, but you can honestly inquire and listen. Reading articles, listening to podcasts, and watching documentaries on your own can help to build understanding, empathy, and knowledge. Possible examples include the podcasts Teaching While White (https://www.teachingwhilewhite.org/podcast) and Code Switch (https://www.npr.org/podcasts/510312/codeswitch), and the video *Pushout: The Criminalization of Black Girls in Schools*. Put yourself purposely in Black spaces. Attend a Black festival, concert, or event. Marvel in the hairstyles, adornments, fashion, and culture with the intent to gain a greater appreciation.

EMBRACING

Embracing Black girls for all that they are and encompass is paramount. So often, Black girls are put into a box that presents a strong binary of either/or, often landing on the negative end. Like the Sapphire caricature, Black girls are portrayed as angry, therefore not happy. In schools, it becomes a division between girls who smile and get along and those who do not (Fordham, 1993). Black girls are seen as strong, and therefore not soft. Serena Williams plays tennis with a dominant or overpowering presence, which has been called "manly," to which Williams replies, "Only a woman can be this strong." All of these binaries that are mostly based on stereotypes do not allow educators to embrace Black girls for all of their magic. There is room for both/and.

Black girls are entitled to all ranges of emotions and should be acknowledged as emotionally intelligent. To characterize their anger as "over the top," uncalled for, or disrespectful is a threat against their true and authentic feelings and a form of oppression in and of itself. How can educators affirm Black girls' gifts as superpowers and teach Black girls how to wield their magic? Instead of calling students argumentative, show them how to debate and persuade others to accomplish a goal. Show them that anger can be a change agent, impactful, and action oriented. Teach them to use their magic to disrupt and dismantle systems. Cast them in a school play or hosting position to use their resounding oratorical skills. Create space to showcase #BlackGirlMagic all year long, not just during Black History Month, and to think outside of the normal Black (s)heroes. If you talk about Rosa Parks, first talk about Claudette Colvin (Hoose, 2009), who inspired Rosa by being the first to be arrested for sitting in her seat. Share that Harriet Tubman was more than the Moses of the Underground Railroad, and that she later became a spy during the Civil War (Weatherford, 2006). When Black girls are quiet in math classes, lift up Katherine Johnson and other "hidden figures" to exhibit math genius (Shetterly, 2016, 2018). As we enter the 2020s, and many discuss the Great Gatsby during the Roaring Twenties, promote in addition the Harlem Renaissance, filled with fashion, art, and literature from Zora Neale Hurston. Embrace Black women from their ultimate creativity to their scholarly critiques.

I have started collecting Barbies in my office. Most of them are Black or racially ambiguous, and that is intentional. I use them to engage students in conversations, and most always we talk about skin tone, hair texture, body types, and differences. Mattel is attempting to create dolls with curvy bodies, hair that is not straight, varied complexions, and different abilities. In addition to Mattel, Black women such as Yelitsa Jean-Charles (healthyrootsdolls.com) and Ozi Ikuzi (ikuzidolls.com) are creating companies that represent the diversity of Black girls and highlight the glorious curls in their hair and curves in their bodies. While I do this for my students, it helps me to embrace my identity, as these images were not readily available when I was growing up. Now I get to watch young eyes light up with joy when they see dolls that look like them, read books with characters like them, and learn from teachers who look like them and understand them.

VALUING

Malcolm X said, "The most disrespected person in America is the Black woman. The most unprotected person in America is the black woman. The most neglected person in America is the Black woman" (Yonan, 2020, p. 6). Valuing Black girls in schools is a way to move the needle in a more positive direction. Instead of repeating the sidelining of Black women in the civil rights movement, the feminist movement, and even in the Black Lives Matter movement, seek out and make the effort to lift up their value in these movements and others. Compliment the Black girls in your class, shedding light on what they bring to the classroom community. Do not talk over them or let others interrupt them. Repeat their salient comments and inquire about their ideas. Show Black girls their value in the classroom, and tell them about it.

Reiterate high expectations, and hold Black girls to them. Give them grace when they don't meet the standards, and help them to improve. Acknowledge their efforts, and impress upon them a growth mindset. Encourage them to do their best, and highlight women like them who can serve as mentors. Show them how Black women have endured greatly and have been the backbone of what we call America. Pay attention to and speak out against media outlets that devalue Black women and Black girls. Support the Black women you work with, and consider how you might need to change some of your own behaviors. Are you cutting them off in conversations? Do you speak out when others use their ideas as their own? Do you disrupt when they are being tokenized?

Prioritizing, embracing, and valuing Black girls has to be more than lip service. It has to be a way of life that is done with integrity. Are you doing it even when no one is looking? Kara didn't need a lecture in the story above. She needed time and compassion. What could the teacher have considered to respond in a culturally responsive way? Is Kara often disorganized, in the teacher's opinion? If so, she could ask herself, "What can I do to help her learn organization? Does she need advance notice of what is coming next?" What if the teacher asked, "Is there anything I can do to help?" Would alerting the class to Kara's lack of preparation cause humiliation? Try this the next time you transition, and notice some students aren't ready. "Alright students, I'm going to give myself some wait time to transition my thoughts, and if anyone, like me, needs more time, please let me know how I can help." When you care about Black girls and prioritize, embrace, and value them, everyone wins.

In the following chapter, Dr. Darla Scott explores the topic of understanding the intersecting identities of Black girls, as this directly impacts how they show up in the classroom. Scott points out how white women teachers interact with and respond to Black girls through a one-dimensional perception of Black girls we all have been socialized to believe. This approach stifles the full capacity of the white educator to fully see and connect with Black girls as full and distinct beings. Exploring the experiences of two students, Rae and Jewel, Scott provides a lens into each girl's experience, showcasing the diversity of Black girl needs in the classroom. Scott states, "Developing an understanding of the complexity of Black girls takes time and attention." She implores white teachers to do their own identity work, as this will help them learn about themselves and their biases. Scott states, "This is the critical first step to educating Black girls."

Penned by activist and educator Sharif El-Mekki, the next chapter shares practical strategies for doing just that. El-Mekki offers suggestions for supporting the intersectional identities of girls who identify as Black and Muslim. Supported by an additional vignette by high school student Ha Lien Gaskin, the section continues to demonstrate the complexities of Black girls, specifically those who identify as "Blasian" (Black and Asian). Readers continue to learn how whiteness and colorism impact a Black girl's self-worth, in spite of her conscious attempts and deep longing to affirm and love herself.

CHAPTER 39

Understanding the Intersecting Identities of Black Girls

Darla Scott

Ms. Maggie, a white woman educator, is working with two Black girls, Jewel and Rae, who are struggling learners in her fourth-grade class. She understands that they come from working-class homes with limited resources, so she redirects these girls' off-task behavior less frequently and allows them more time to complete less-difficult classwork. However Ms. Shonda, a Black paraeducator, often redirects and corrects these girls in Ms. Maggie's class and tells Ms. Maggie that she is "not doing them any favors" by adjusting their assignments. What is the root of the conflict between Ms. Maggie and Ms. Shonda, the teachers?

Intersectionality is a framework for acknowledging how power structures promote interconnected, overlapping, and compounded experiences of oppression for minoritized populations with multiple marginalized identities (Crenshaw, 1991). This construct provides a way of thinking about identity as it relates to power, which underscores concerns traditionally left invisible by existing social structures (Cho et al., 2013). Intersectionality highlights the complexity of understanding who we are individually, and it can serve as a tool for identifying strategies for achieving equity (Collins & Bilge, 2016). This chapter examines how one-dimensional perspectives on Black girls oversimplify their nuanced selves and frustrate our efforts to connect with and understand the Black girls taught by white women in our classrooms.

Jewel and Rae

Jewel has been visiting her local place of worship more frequently now that her parents are divorcing. In many ways, she is wondering how Rae and her other friends at school will treat her if she adopts a hijab. While her parents seem supportive, she is concerned about how she will be viewed and treated at school.

Rae's eyes have been bothering her for months, but she knows that she is smart and doesn't want to talk about her vision problems. Normally, she would tell Jewel about it, but Rae is embarrassed that her eyes are not working properly. While Rae likes Ms. Shonda, she does not want to be one of the "kids" that Ms. Shonda comes into class to help.

As educators seeking to provide culturally responsive instruction, our goal is to understand Black girls within the contexts of their intersecting identities and do the work that will help us to connect with them. Black girls are Christian and Muslim and Jewish and Buddhist and atheist and agnostic—and more. Black girls are making choices about other aspects of identity beyond their Blackness, and—like all teens—they are asking big questions about who and how to be. Keeping it simple by focusing only on one aspect of identity is a heuristic, which allows Black girls to fit neatly into our schema for who they are and what they should care about. Developing an understanding of the complexity of Black girls takes time and attention; it is not easy work.

Ms. Shonda

Ms. Shonda remembers when she was in school and her white teachers never really expected much from her. It bothers her to see Ms. Maggie giving Jewel and Rae "easy" work when they are capable of much more! Even though she sees Ms. Maggie's pedagogical practices as a violation, Ms. Shonda understands her role as a paraprofessional in Ms. Maggie's class makes it hard for her to do anything to really address this situation, even though she feels a responsibility to do so. In what ways are past traumas and current power structures impacting Ms. Shonda's pedagogy? How does this manifest in her relationships with Jewel and Rae?

In her theory of engaged pedagogy, hooks (1994) outlines a useful framework for authenticity in academic instruction and bridging the gaps of oversimplification of our Black girls in the classroom. Indeed, it has been suggested that the teacher's chief goal should be to inspire Black girls (and all students) to "transgress" or intentionally violate the class, sexual, and racial boundaries that have been established to perpetuate inequity in education and opportunity (hooks, 1994). These types of practices return to the transformative, revolutionary, and abolitionist aims in presegregation Black education, while centering the lived experience of today's youth in the wake of #BlackLivesMatter. In order to connect, today's educators must complete a personal preparation process before engaging in the authentic teacher-led disclosure that builds trust and creates critical engagement and power shifts in the classroom (Arki, 2016).

First, white female teachers must read and critically examine articles and book chapters that center themselves in a reflexive process by highlighting issues of power and privilege (titles such as *Waking Up White* by Irving, *White Woman's Work* by Hancock & Warren, and *White Fragility* by DiAngelo & Dyson). It is imperative that white teachers do their own identity work! Knowing yourself and your own biases is a critical first step to successfully teaching Black girls. There are several chapters in this volume that highlight the developmental and cultural considerations for marginalized Black girls. White teachers should reflect on their own developmental process, identity, roles, and responsibilities, and on how these connect with what they learn about Black girls. Teachers modeling vulnerability in the classroom can foster a climate of trust and create safe spaces for this dialogue (Berry, 2010).

Invested educators must engage a community of learners to share current challenges with reaching and understanding Black girls, using a model like the SCRR (self collective root responsibility) dialogue organization framework (Sankofa Community Empowerment, 2001; Williams et al., 2012). As laid out in Williams et al. (2012), the SCRR framework requires you to begin by considering your experiences (positive and negative) with Black girls (self) and then consider the implication and impact of those experiences for others (collective). Finally, you look for the causes of the challenges (root) and consider how you can be active in addressing the challenge (responsibility).

Using the SCRR framework, Ms. Maggie could reflect on her experiences with Jewel and Rae, her Black girl students, and with Ms. Shonda, her paraprofessional. What assumptions are driving her treatment of her students? What questions would you think to ask Ms. Maggie?

- Self: What identity is Ms. Maggie focused on? What identities is she missing? What does Ms. Maggie overlook in this situation? Because of her biases and lack of familiarity with issues facing Black people, how does she misread their needs, many of which Ms. Shonda can see clearly?

- Collective: What messages does she send her Black girls by not redirecting their off-task behavior? How do Ms. Maggie's actions (and inactions) serve as triggers for Ms. Shonda?

- Root: What is the long-term impact of giving the girls less-difficult work? What attributions could Jewel and Rae make about the work they are receiving from Ms. Maggie? How do historical injustices lead to the power differential between

Ms. Maggie and Ms. Shonda? How could Ms. Maggie elevate and listen to Ms. Shonda's voice, even though Ms. Maggie has more institutional power?

• Responsibility: How do the Black girls respond to Ms. Shonda's redirection? How can Ms. Maggie and Ms. Shonda work together to utilize their collective and complementary strengths, in spite of their institutional power differences?

Moving through the framework, Ms. Maggie would consider the impact of her actions on others and ultimately work down to the root of the issue, as well as identify specific steps to address the issue. While this type of situation may be uncomfortable, it is critical that we courageously engage in complex challenges. If Ms. Maggie chooses to not respond or to ignore this issue, then Jewel and Rae, the 10-year-old Black girls, pay the price.

"Confronting one another across differences means that we must change ideas about how we learn; rather than fearing conflict we have to find ways to use it as a catalyst for new thinking, for growth" (hooks, 1994, p. 113).

> Ms. Maggie has been working with working-class children for 10 years, and she is confident in her ability to teach her students. Although she was raised in a predominantly white community, Ms. Maggie says that she does not see color, loves all cultures, and only sees the individual children. Ms. Shonda's comment that she is not challenging Jewel and Rae really bothered her, and Ms. Maggie feels offended that Ms. Shonda would suggest that she is not working for the betterment of both Black girls. What would you tell Ms. Maggie to consider in this situation?

Ladson-Billings (2009) would see Ms. Maggie's color-blindness as a form of "dysconscious racism," which equates equality with sameness and accepts white cultural standards as norms (p. 36). There is research to suggest that inner strength and relationship identities are central to understanding the intersectionality of Black women and girls (Shorter-Gooden & Washington, 1996).

As we see in the vignettes, Rae wants to show strength, and Jewel wants to be a good friend. For Black girls, identity intersections are born out of a commitment to excel in their multifaceted roles in ways that affirm their strength, passion, and commitment to their communities, whether adaptive or maladaptive. Black girls are sisters, daughters, friends, othermothers, lovers, wives, and mothers taking great pride in their ability to shine in these spaces (Collins, 1990).

Given all of this, how can invested educators learn more about the complex intersectional identities of their Black female students? They can start by recognizing the educational trauma that Black girls bring into their classrooms before they even meet. Cultural mistrust can serve as a barrier for Black girls to open up in class due to past traumas and negative interpersonal experiences in class.

For example, low-income Black female college students reported significantly less interpersonal trust than white male students (Terrell & Barrett, 1979). Stigma is another factor that needs to be considered when inviting Black girls to take part in small group discussions. One way to address this issue is to maintain open participation in identity discussions. Project Sister Circle offers a model for empowering Black girls to become change agents and advocates by beginning with centering exercises (e.g., yoga-type stretches and affirmations) and continuing with group discussion (e.g., healthy relationship with others), project work (e.g., identifying ways to address their systemic challenges), and journaling as a stress coping tool (Williams et al., 2012).

Developmentally, Black girls come with diverse concerns based upon their age, maturity, and lived experiences such as adultification (Blake et al., 2011). A recent study of adultification demonstrated that Black girls tend to be seen as less innocent and less in need of protection than their non-Black peers, and that this perception can contribute to their overrepresentation in exclusionary discipline processes (Epstein et al., 2017). Thus, it is critical to provide journaling and open forums for Black girls to communicate about their identities and be guided through an understanding of the power systems that impact them in those spaces. For example, during middle school, it is critical that Black girls learn self-advocacy and are validated in their attempts to establish and maintain healthy relationship boundaries. During this transition, there is a risk for inner-city Black girls, like Jewel and Rae, to refrain from externalizing behaviors and, instead, to simply conform to gender-role expectations and social pressures (Thomas et al., 2003). While externalizing behaviors (e.g., arguing or talking loudly) are typically viewed as negative, Black females need to be validated in their efforts to address and disrupt the oppressive systems in their daily lives. In sum, Black girls navigate identities and worlds that touch them but feel and look very different for them. Invested educators must be willing to engage in disrupting power structures and perceptions that reinforce intersecting systems of bias and oppression.

A note about identity work exercises: There are many thought-provoking exercises, and it is not my intention to oversimplify this arduous process by providing a nominal interaction exercise so that anyone can check the box of identity work. But the following exercise holds merit as an introductory exercise.

Identity Work Exercise: Unpacking the Invisible Knapsack

Exercise by Peggy McIntosh (https://www.racialequitytools.org/resourcefiles/mcintosh.pdf)

In a group of three to five teachers, complete the reading, examine the list of daily white privilege, and then identify the systems that work to support that privilege. Consider how these privileges have shaped your identity and expectations.

Exercise modified from Goldbach (2019)

Working with a small group of Black girls, the teacher begins by writing their name and its meaning on one side of a 3X5 index card. They write the top three social identities that they feel closest to on the back of the index card. The teacher also shares why they picked those identities. Then they pass out index cards to their Black girl students and ask them to do the same: Write down their name and its meaning (if they know it), their three most important social identities, and why they chose those identities.

After doing this as a small group exercise, it can be done with the whole class as trust develops. Ask the students to identify the three most common social identities, and then as a class offer suggestions to complete a Venn diagram with challenges classmates face in those roles, and fill in the overlapping spaces with challenges that are shared between roles. Guide the class in a discussion of how they (as a class) make it easier or harder to have a particular social identity. What can they do to better support each other?

Postexercise Reflection

Within a group of three to five teachers, share and think about the common challenges: How can you overcome these issues in class to maximize authentic engagement? Generate a list of strategies, and share it with your own community of learners. How can you create safety nets of supports for the common challenge areas?

Vignette: Just Educational Ecosystems for Black Girls: Educators, Here Are Eight Ways You Can Support Black Muslim Girls During the School Year

Sharif El Mekki

A few years ago, one of our students, a Black Muslim girl who also happened to be a scholar-athlete, was banned from a playoff basketball game because she refused to remove her hijab. Our community rallied around her. I wrote about it for Phillys7thWard.org and the *Philadelphia Citizen*.

> *Freedom fighting heroes come in all ages. At Mastery-Shoemaker, we have been blessed to have <u>several students</u> who lead and serve in their communities on a consistent basis—in small and huge ways.*
>
> *Recently, one of our students made the brave and insightful decision to stand up by sitting down.*

(Continued)

(Continued)

Nasihah Thompson-King is a varsity basketball player. She is a Muslim and wears a hijab. During the playoffs this past winter, Nasihah was told by the referee, Sandra Yost, to remove her scarf or she <u>would not be able to play</u>.

Nasihah had an important decision to make within a few short minutes. Our team was marching towards the championship. If she refused to remove her hijab, she wouldn't be able to play. She didn't want to let her teammates down. But, Nasihah also knew what religious freedom meant and chose to take a stance against religious intolerance and cultural bias.

<u>*She sat out of the game.*</u>

The referee made a colossal mistake and demonstrated a callous form of hubris and ego. She was not accustomed to Black Muslim girls, and she used her own ignorance to do what other referees (Nasihah had been playing competitive basketball for years and had never been accosted in such a way) had simply refused to do—use her power to discriminate.

I am an activist who chose to become an educator. With that, I am deeply interested in addressing the inequities that students face in and outside of schools. Too many students have negative school experiences that undermine their self-worth and identity—two areas that are the very foundations for optimal learning. We need more people to advocate for students, all students, and especially students who are marginalized most consistently. Black Muslim students are a part of this marginalized group of students. As educators claiming that Black Lives Matter, we must insist that *all* Black Minds Matter as well.

Our students must have better environments to study in, better buildings and classrooms, and a far better, and more just, educational ecosystem for them to reach their highest potential. In order for us to ensure we are positioning our schools and classrooms as these optimal learning environments, we must insist that we ask those marginalized students, what is your experience like as a Black Muslim girl/ young lady in our school? In my classroom? What should I start, stop, and continue doing to ensure you feel seen, heard, and whole?

Arundhati Roy said, "There's really no such thing as the 'voiceless.' There are only the deliberately silenced, or the preferably unheard" (Roy, 2004, para 4). To that end, when we think of our Black Muslim girls, we should know that they may be experiencing challenging situations that need to be discussed and heard. We don't need to give them a voice—we need to stop ignoring them and ensure they have access to the platforms most often relegated to white teachers and systems.

We know that many schools struggle with how to support Black children in general and Black Muslim girl students specifically. During the school year, Black

Muslim girls and young ladies may need additional resources, and the adults who have signed up to work with them need a better understanding of how to support their Black Muslim girl students, now and in the future.

Here are eight things that we can do to see, hear, and understand our Black Muslim girls.

(1) Understand the history of Muslims and Islam in the Americas: While many Americans think that Islam is a new and recent religion on these shores, there's evidence that seafaring Muslims came and peacefully interacted with Native Americans long before Columbus. There's also evidence that up to 30 percent of the enslaved west Africans were Muslims, and many, in the resiliency consistent with African people, practiced Islam in whatever ways they could on these shores. They led rebellions, and there is evidence that some of Denmark Vesey's conspirators identified as Muslims.

(2) Many Black Muslim girls wear a scarf, or hijab. Many may wear it sometimes, others all the time, and many may wear it when they feel like it. It is not your job to ascertain if this coincides with their level of faith in Islam. If anything, consider how you have deliberately ensured they know it is safe to wear their hijab and any other modest clothing. Too many Muslims and non-Muslims believe it is their place to police what Muslim students are wearing. That is not your place. Rather your place is to ensure your space is one of safety and acceptance.

(3) There may some Black Muslim girls who tend to be quiet and reserved, or who choose not to be assertive all the time—which is their prerogative. However, when I have seen girls from other faiths demonstrate a level of humility and shyness, they are spoken about in glowing terms. When I see Black Muslim girls exercise their own freedom to choose when to be assertive or not, they are often characterized as oppressed by their religion. The oppression in these circumstances are the judgmental gazes and assumptions. Also, not every Black Muslim girl is comfortable in a mixed-gender group. They may decline to speak about health or sex education in a mixed gender group.

(4) Many Black Muslim girls may need safe spaces and quiet places to pray and observe their fasting during the Islamic holy month of Ramadhan. The month of Ramadhan will be during the school year for several years to come. The Islamic calendar is based on a lunar calendar, so the start of the month of Ramadhan changes each year. Rusul Alrubail (2020) wrote a great piece that shares how schools can support Muslim students during the month of Ramadhan. She describes how school staff can show understanding and empathy. It is also important to create a judgement-free zone. Again, every

(Continued)

(Continued)

Muslim student may not fast, for a variety of reasons, and it's none of your business, *unless you* are the reason Black Muslim girls feel reluctant to fast, pray, or observe any other Islamic ritual they may want to. Consider that Christian and Jewish privileges may deeply influence how educators think about religion, holidays, and rituals. It takes a level of cultural humility to understand how this privilege may negatively impact interactions with Black Muslim girls. Sister Salima Suswell and many others, including many Black Muslim girls, challenged our city's schools and districts to ensure their two main religious holidays were recognized and celebrated on the official school calendar. Black Muslim girls and their families no longer had to take off from school when one of the two Eids came around on the calendar. They, and all the other students, were off. Jummahs, Friday prayers, are midday prayers that many Black Muslims attend. Yes, it is in the middle of a school day, but we don't have off like Christians do each Sunday. So, accommodating the needs of all students is a part of an inclusive learning environment.

(5) Like all children, Black Muslim girls need to have a sense of belonging in their schools. Regardless of how they look, dress, and practice their faith, these students, like all students, should feel respected, engaged, and whole every single day. While it is not their job to teach you, many will be open to giving feedback about their experience as Black Muslim girls and young ladies. The conditions for Black Muslim girls to be forthcoming and honest about their experiences are within the adults' locus of control.

(6) Black Muslim girls should be able to find spaces that reflect them. There are literally hundreds of books, young adult books written by Black Muslims, which center Black Muslim characters. Are any in your school and classroom? On another level of consciousness, are any in your home? When we ponder the idea of the mirrors and windows experiences of Black Muslim girls in our schools and classrooms, we are not only thinking of whether we have any Black Muslim women staff, but we are also thinking of how Islam is taught, and how often positive images of Black Muslim girls and women are hanging on our walls and exist in our literature, history, science lessons, et cetera. We are considering what messages of belonging and respect are shown to Black Muslim girls in our schools. We know with full certainty that a white Christian girl's positive identity will be reinforced and celebrated many times over throughout a 180-day school year. How often can we say the same thing about Black Muslim girls and young women?

(7) Belonging can be increased by recognizing Black Muslim girls' unique and collective experiences. Husnaa Hashim, another one of our former students, was Philadelphia's Youth Poet Laureate. She is an author and artist whose

work is prominent in some schools and not in many others. Black Muslim girls may need school staff (or an outside partner) to support the creation of a Muslim and interfaith student group or some other type of space for Black Muslim girls to congregate, share, and contribute. Some students may want to formalize their work through a Muslim student association (MSA). This is all perfectly legal. Some people think that religion can't be discussed or religious groups are prohibited in public schools—nothing could be further from the truth. Student groups should and must be supported in schools.

(8) Over the years, I have spoken to many students who identify as Black Muslims who felt marginalized during lunch, cookouts, and any other school ritual or routine that had food as a part of it. This is because Muslims don't eat pork products (gelatin, pepperoni, ham, etc.), but they are not thought of when orders are being placed. Many Muslims only eat halal meats, which means they only eat meat from an animal killed in the Islamically prescribed way. Being aware of this, knowing where halal stores may be in your community, and even just having the foresight and cultural proficiency to ask the students' families would go a long way to inclusivity and creating a sense of belonging in the educational ecosystem.

To implement these suggestions, one must be committed to ensuring an inclusive and culturally responsive and sustaining educational program. The school leaders and staff must have a level of cultural humility and open-mindedness to ensure success.

Let us all commit to making our schools safe places and supportive of the communities that they serve. Islam is the fastest-growing religion in America and in the world—and it is here to stay. Our job is to ensure that our Muslim students feel as welcomed as every other group of students. The commitment to educational justice and a mindset that embraces and supports all students are the first steps in ensuring that Black Muslim girls experience a just educational environment to learn and thrive in.

Recommended Resources

https://afomaumesi.com/muslim-ya-books/

https://www.teenvogue.com/story/salaam-reads-aims-muslim-ya-books

https://www.pbs.org/newshour/author/rusul-alrubail

https://phillys7thward.org/topics/muslims/

Vignette: The Skin I'm In

Ha Lien Gaskin—High School Student

I am Vietnamese and African American. Sometimes in our family we call it Blasian, a mashed-up mix of Black and Asian. At first glance, I look clearly "exotic, so unique!" as strangers often comment cheerfully in the street. I have curly-ish hair, caramel-darkish-I-don't-know skin color, and you can't tell anymore, but I dyed the tips of my black hair blue. My eyes squish into slants when I smile, and my lips are full and pouty, even when I don't mean them to be. I love my skin, my hair, my eyes, my nose.

One cool autumn day, though, I found myself walking alongside my friends on busy Franklin Street. In a particularly shiny window that we pass, I noted with a little surprise that my skin is a few shades darker than the pinky pale colors of my friends. I grimaced sourly. I wished for a second that I was someone else—tall and willowy, long straight hair, small nose, and lighter. Just a shade or two lighter. I blinked. I was still small, slightly stubby. My face was still burnt-chicken-nugget-brown, haloed by my black frizz of hair. I sighed and kept walking.

Later, I was still thinking about what I had thought privately. I was disappointed in myself. I thought that I was immune to the pitfalls of racism, that I had somehow transcended the everyday microaggressions that supposedly plague our society. I was perfectly willing to point out racism from afar, but finding it in myself was something different all together. Racism had permeated me, burrowing under my skin and bubbling up through the pores of my brain. I was shocked that I had thought those things, let myself be influenced by subtle colorism that is hidden in every part of our society.

I wonder if my subconscious will always think that my rich mixture of Blasian features is ugly. I wonder if I'll ever feel like I belong in my classes. I wonder if my black friends know they are worth teaching, that they are intelligent and capable of amazing things, not because they are black, but because they are them. I wonder if I'll ever escape my skin and the responsibilities that come with it.

In the following chapter, "#StudentAsSignMaker," Dr. Shemariah J. Arki helps readers dive deeply into Black racial identity development, offering three questions that all Black girls ask as they begin to make sense of their identities: (1) How do I understand and see myself? (2) How do I understand and see the world? and (3) How does the world see me? By positioning students as sign makers, we can interpret their lived experience as empirical evidence to structure learning environments to ensure all students are connected, respected, and valued.

CHAPTER 40

#StudentAsSignMaker

Curating Classrooms
for Identity Development

Shemariah J. Arki

Ushering in a new generation of young folks as front-line activists and organizers, #BlackLivesMatter (#BLM) has become a radical movement for social
change led by young folks, thus its significance to classrooms, curriculum, teaching,
learning, and leadership. By centering the voices of the most marginalized and
intentionally uniting those voices on the front lines, the activism and organizing
of #BLM extends beyond the killing of Black folks at the hands of state violence—
to include advocacy of all othered identities through the practice of intersectionality. In the sociopolitical context of #BLM, teachers must approach teaching and
learning through a critical lens.

The chapters and vignettes included in this book contribute the lived experiences
of Black girls in the classroom as empirical evidence of classrooms as spaces of
radical transformation. Black girls cannot come to school with the assumption
they are included in the societal view that education is *free and compulsory to all.*
They intrinsically understand this is not true for them, and they must engage in a
separate process of decoding and recoding (Freire, 1970/2000). Black girls are
forced to wrestle with the dichotomy of both schooling and education, and teaching and learning, as they move between the roles of student and teacher, often
unwittingly defying tropes and stereotypes meant to demean them. Black girls in
today's sociopolitical context must learn how to operate as hypervisible and invisible, as they are inundated with images that say "all are welcome" and systemically
silenced by "I don't see color" sentiments. This chapter will share parts of a research
study where critical discourse analysis (CDA) was used to answer the central

question: How are the lived experiences of today's public school students reflected through their submission for Stop the Hate–Youth Speak Out essay contest?

#StudentsAsSignMakers

The selected methodology for this research project was qualitative, critical discourse analysis. This methodology is aligned with research questions by allowing the lived experiences of participants, Black girls, to be used as empirical data (Rogers, 2011a; Schwandt, 2000). In this project, the lived experiences of Black girl students serve as the counternarrative, as they are analyzed through the socio-political context, #BLM, which intentionally requires a critical analysis of power (Banks, 1974; Daniel, 2009; Kumashiro, 2000; Ladson-Billings, 1999).

Rogers (2011a) defines *critical discourse analysis* (CDA) as a "problem-oriented and transdisciplinary set of theories and methods that have been widely used in educational research" (p. 1). Based on this definition and its inherent commensurability, CDA allows for an analysis of power not just in the data, but within the process itself (Rogers, 2011a, 2011b). Through reflexive tendencies of CDA, researchers are able to identify as mediums, or multimodal social practice participants who ultimately serve at the liberty of the communicator (Rogers, 2011a). Gunther Kress, seminal CDA author and critical linguist, permits researchers to view "a speaker as a socially located individual who uses semiotic systems to achieve particular functions or goals" (Rogers, 2011a, p. 13).

CDA is also informed by the work of James Gee and Norman Fairclough, interdisciplinary linguists who understood that schools are often microcosms of the communities in which they are located, positioning "schools, classrooms, and educational practices [as] sites for studying not only the micro-dimensions of classroom talk but also the ways in which social structures are reproduced at macro-levels" (Rogers, 2011a, p. 3). The use of CDA as methodology in this study seeks to allow the researcher to serve as analyst to "describe, interpret, and explain" (Rogers, 2011a, p. 3) the sociopolitical context, which was earlier identified in this research as #BlackLivesMatter. Upon this foundation of researcher as analyst, an amalgamation of intersecting identities requires a "deep exploration into power" (p. 1). This chapter situates critical race theory (CRT), specifically its tenets of counternarrative and whiteness as property, as the framework for the voice of the student. Researchers/analysts must then affirm "oppression and liberation are twin pillars of concern" (p. 4) and that their insidious operation affects us all based on our identities, independent of our role or responsibility (Rogers, 2011a). Therefore, the amalgamation of the theories and frameworks presented allows the researcher/analyst to position students as *sign-makers,* which means individuals who centered their own lived experience through a double hermeneutic identity development process to make sense of the world and determine how and when to engage in it.

According to Schwandt (2000), there is no separation between understanding and interpretation, and therefore the process of sign-making requires Black girls to wrestle with their own biases in pursuit of equity for all. In a process similar to what Lorde (1984/2007) describes as the "outsider within" phenomenon, Black girls in the classroom must understand their actions as interpretations of the cultures, systems, and traditions of the dominant culture (Schwandt, 2000), and their role in continuing to curate a new vision for what these things say about and do for the Black girls who will come after them. The American education system often requires Black girls to "step outside" (Schwandt, 2000) of their skin in order to make sense of the world. By positioning Black girls as sign-makers, the researcher/analyst privileges the voice of the student and allows that voice to make meaning of their world, on their own terms. "Understanding is participatory, conversational and dialogic" (Schwandt, 2000, p. 195), making language the key transmitter to dialogue (Gallagher, 1992). In other words, a double hermeneutic process allows those who hold intersecting oppressed identities to understand and interpret information in a desire for liberation from the dominant narrative:

> The practice of social inquiry cannot be adequately defined as an atheoretical making that requires only methodological prowess. Social inquiry is a distinctive praxis, a kind of activity (like teaching) that in the doing transforms the very theory and aims that guide it. In other words, as one engages in the "practical" activities of generating and interpreting data to answer questions about the meaning of what others are doing and saying and then transforming that information into public knowledge, one inevitably takes up "theoretical" concerns about what constitutes knowledge and how it is to be justified. . . . In sum, acting and thinking, practice and theory, are linked in a continuous process of critical reflection and transformation. (Schwandt, 2000, p. 191)

Understanding this double hermeneutic process that Black girls are engaging in is critical for teachers, who are likely, unwittingly, part of "the world," which does not see Black girls as they see themselves. Researchers agree that many teachers are not prepared to educate today's urban youth, specifically in the wake of #BlackLivesMatter (Arki, 2016; Love, 2019). Teacher preparation programs fail to connect, respect, and value the empirical evidence Black girls' lived experience provides, particularly in the context of teaching and learning (Arki, 2016; Evans-Winters & Bethune, 2014; Love, 2019). This next section will highlight two of the five central tenets of CRT (counternarratives and whiteness as property) to understand the three questions central to Black girl identity development: (1) How do I understand and see myself? (2) How do I understand and see the world? and (3) How does the world see me?

How Do I Understand and See Myself?

By positioning Black girls as sign-makers, one of the first realities educators must face is that the dominant narrative shifts to amplify the voices of the most marginalized. In tandem, a reality for Black girls in the classroom is for them to—in the words of Chief Kofi Attu, Akpafu Todzi, Oti Region, Ghana, West Africa—"See yourself. Then see yourself again." As defined in CRT literature, counternarratives are the stories, voices, and lived experience of people with marginalized identities (Delgado et al., 2012; Ladson-Billings, 2013). Counternarratives are also referred to as the simple stories or oral traditions passed down throughout history to preserve one's deep connection to family history and culture (Delgado et al., 2012; Ladson-Billings, 2013). By sharing counternarratives, Black girls have an opportunity to expand conversation and dialogue through praxis. Black girls use counternarratives, or storytelling, "as a way to illustrate and underscore broad legal principles regarding race and racial/social justice," or as CRT theorist bell hooks states, "a practice of freedom" (as quoted in Ladson-Billings, 2013, p. 42).

In the classroom, I have my students engage with counternarratives through the work of Paul Laurence Dunbar using his famous work, "We Wear the Mask." In this lecture, we read the poem aloud, and students are instructed to underline the line in the poem that has the most impact on them. Next, I arrange the students in small groups and have them rewrite the poem, but only using the lines they have underlined. We then read the reconstructed poems aloud to open the discussion on mask wearing. After a few students share some low-risk stories on mask wearing, I draw their attention to a hip-hop song by Atlanta-based rapper Future, entitled "Mask Off." With a close read of some of the lyrics, the students begin to conflate the ideas of Dunbar's mask, Future's mask, and now their own. By using hip-hop, students are able to make relevant the concept of mask making and wearing as a tool to interrogate their own identities.

By understanding how the world sees them, Black girls have a distinct advantage over other students of color, as they are symbiotically able to negotiate and perform their identity, which is a privilege for some and a constant negotiation for others. In short, they know when to put the mask on and when to take it off. They have mastered this negotiation as a point of privilege—being able to successfully matriculate in mostly white educational spaces. It is important to note that while all Black girls do not attend schools where the students are majority white, the educational system has the same impact for *all* students, independent of where they matriculate. By centering counternarratives, this experience affirms their experiential expertise in an academic setting.

How Do I Understand and See The World?

Upon positioning students as sign-makers, we can posit their signs as tools of inquiry to serve as the social and cultural frameworks for understanding how people use language to accomplish social goals (Rogers, 2011a). Educators can thus connect their assertion of establishing humanity in their students as the first step in curating intersectional classrooms that center Black girls. Amani, a student from the study, describes her journey of going inside herself to find some answers after a classmate compared the achievements of African Americans to t-ball, "I remember not speaking very much that day. I remember my friends being frustrated with my silence (Hill, 2015, p. 6)." It is important to note that this internal action constitutes action, even though at this moment it does not include anyone other than the self. Based on Amani's new positionality as sign-maker and the repositioning of the dominant narrative towards a counternarrative, internal action must preface external action.

One key method for drawing the parallels between CRT and education rests in the perceptions of property ownership, which is the foundation for whiteness. Outlined by Ladson-Billings (1999) in her discussion on curriculum, she argues against the concept of a color-blind curriculum that supports the status quo and reinforces whiteness as good, normal, and acceptable. Additional research discusses considerations of normalcy, which are based in whiteness, around acculturation and assimilation of watered-down approaches to discussing issues of race, class, and gender in an educational environment (Daniel, 2009). Therefore, whiteness in the curriculum and whiteness itself are a form of property, or ownership, which increase the social and educational capital of white students. Because Black girls by definition cannot own this property—or cannot do so except by enduring exceptional harm—they are a priori limited in the academic success and access that we experience.

By utilizing the principles of CRT in educational research, students, teachers, and administrators alike can draw deeper connections from the current state of public education to American history. Black girls reach out to teachers, counselors, and other students in pursuit of creating educational environments where all students are connected, respected, and valued. Amani states, "I joined the Student Group on Race Relations. . . . I created activities to highlight . . . micro-aggressions. . . . I became a mentor to other young [minoritized] girls. . . . I created the CATALYST Student Group to emphasize the need for education in all areas." (Hill, 2015, p. 6).

As Black girls continue to negotiate their identity, they are embodying Ujima, the Kiswahili phrase that translates as "collective work and responsibility," the third of the seven principles of the Nguzo Saba (Karenga, 2008). Developed by Dr. Maulana Ron Karenga, the Nguzo Saba stands at the heart of the origin and meaning of Kwanzaa (a celebration created to introduce and reinforce seven basic values of African culture); it is these values that serve as the foundation and fortification of the Black community (Karenga, 2008). Through the practice of Ujima, Black girls in the classroom, including Amani, recognize and inhabit the role of the sign-maker to move beyond the recognition of the need for unification and position themselves as examples of the transformation. Ujima requires all oppressed populations to work together across lines of difference in pursuit of a common goal—according to the counternarrative—of liberation from all oppression. When positioning students as sign-makers, all of these actions continue the cycle of sign-making while challenging traditional classroom power dynamics. Black girl students understand the power of the collective and their ability and responsibility to curate culturally relevant strategies that amplify the message of the most marginalized, even when it's themselves, in their school community.

How Does The World See Me?

Arguably, the most important concept of Black girls' identity development has to do with understanding what the dominant narrative has to say about Black girls—even though it is the point of their identity that is outside of their control. Knowing and understanding how the world sees Black girls can be heavy for them, yet also freeing. Perhaps this, in whole or in part, is the pedagogical approach that was employed by the students in the Stop the Hate essay contest.

Melissa Harris-Perry (2013) opens *Sister Citizen* with the analogy of the crooked room, speaking to the historical and sociopolitical context for Black girls in the United States. Her work goes on to center itself in a politic of misrecognition of Black women and girls by the dominant narrative. Qualitative and quantitative data from prominent researchers (Morris, 2016; Crenshaw, 1995), including many featured in this book, tell the stories of countless Black girls and their engagement with unequitable school policies and procedures, from discipline to dress code to classroom management Harris-Perry (2013) states:

> When they confront race and gender stereotypes, [B]lack women are standing in a crooked room. Bombarded with warped images of their humanity, some [B]lack women tilt and bend themselves to fit the distortion . . . Jezebel . . . Mammy . . . Sapphire. . . . To understand why [B]lack women's public actions and political strategies sometimes seem tilted in ways that accommodate the degrading stereotypes about them, it is important to appreciate the structural constraints that influence their behavior. It can be hard to stand up straight in a crooked room. (p. 29)

Whether it is a crooked room, stopping the hate, or being an upstander, Black girls in the classroom have a clear community and counternarrative that centers them as the agent of their own liberation. The empirical evidence (i.e., lived experiences of Amani and all Black girls in the classroom) is more true a measure of a teacher's pedagogy than any standardized tests; their lives and voices show that when it comes to Black students facing discrimination in the face of #BlackLivesMatter, the identity development of the student becomes the primary resource available to the student dealing with and responding to the incident. The white silence perpetuated in today's classrooms by unprepared teachers has the potential to completely subjugate a Black girl's classroom experience. In an earlier study of Amani, I cite Kevin Kumashiro, antiracist educator, as he acknowledges "the complex nature of systems of whiteness as they affect curriculum, pedagogy and educational policy, thus making room for a myriad of liberatory praxes originating from specific social identifiers: feminist, queer, multiracial and so on" (as quoted in Arki, 2016, p. 243). Therefore, the role of the student must shift in order to combat oppression in the classroom.

We Have a Duty to Fight for Our Freedom

According to educational theorist Dr. Bettina Love (2019) in *We Want To Do More Than Survive: Abolitionist Teaching and the Pursuit of Educational Freedom*, all of us must work to save education. By positioning the classroom as a place of radical transformation, Love begs of all of us—teachers, administrators, students, parents, et cetera—to approach educational systems change as an act of abolition. In doing so, we must position the current system of American education as a survival complex, which constrains us to a struggle-based praxis grounded in the long and oppressive history of BIPOC in America (Love, 2019). Upon the interrogation of our hidden assumptions, teacher-activists are able to map the margins of the permanence of racism, thereby clarifying and/or repositioning the relationship between our identities, roles, and responsibilities. Such duality is necessary for those of us matriculating in systems and institutions that were not designed for our matriculation, let alone our success. An abolitionist teaching framework allows teacher-activists to adopt a pedagogy in the interruption of both unconscious *and* implicit bias.

By starting the work within our own identity development process, or what Love (2019) refers to as "freedom dreaming," teacher-activists stand in the tradition of abolitionists, Black feminists, and all those serving as front line soldiers in the fight for educational freedom:

> The ultimate goal of abolitionist teaching is freedom. Freedom to create your reality, where uplifting humanity is at the center of all decisions. And, yes, concessions will be made along the way, battles will be lost, and sometimes teachers, parents, and community members will feel like they are not doing enough, but the fight is fought with the indomitable spirit of an abolitionist who engages in taking small and sometimes big risks in the fight for equal rights, liberties, and citizenship for dark children, their families, and their communities—this is fighting for freedom. (Love, 2019, p. 89)

When Black girls have the opportunity to freedom dream, our identities become our most important tool in pursuit of liberation.

> *In the next vignette by Usherla DeBerry, a Black girl who identifies as Deaf, readers will learn strategies for both hearing teachers and white teachers to consider as they work to build classrooms in which Deaf Black girls will thrive.*

Vignette: Beautiful, Brilliant, Black, and Deaf

Usherla DeBerry

I grew up oral. American Sign Language was not being used in the classroom nor at home. I read lips most of my childhood. I did watch for patterns of behaviors in the classroom and was reluctant to ask questions. Because of my hearing loss, I was isolated and had trouble making friends and keeping friendship. It was my only friend, Elizabeth, who realized I was Deaf before everyone else, including my family and the teacher. Teachers need to notice signs of potential hearing loss (e.g., a student speaks differently, turns off volume, asks the teacher to repeat, complains of noise, responds inappropriately to questions, watches how others are acting/imitates behaviors, etc.). Elizabeth and I had a great bond that baffled everyone. Between my hearing loss, Elizabeth's sense of responsibility, and our intuitive sense of one another's needs, we simply connected.

During kindergarten, Elizabeth was removed from our class by the special request of her parents. When I asked my white teacher about why Elizabeth had left, she instantly called my mother. My mother came to the school, and my white teacher asked me to step outside of the class in the hallway to speak with my mother. Immediately, I assumed I was in trouble. My mother explained that she was present because I kept asking about "Elizabeth." I looked at her with a baffled face to figure why she would be the one to explain this to me.

Then mom asked me a seemingly unrelated question that I could not understand. "What color are you?" I responded, "I am brown." She stated, "No you are Black." I responded, "No, I am not." She then asked, "What color do you want to be?" I responded, "Golden brown." She said, "There you go. Now what color is Elizabeth?" I said, "White." And mom showed a sense of relief and said, "And that is why you cannot play with her, and that is why she is no longer in your class. She has been moved to a different class, a class across from the hallway, you see?"

It was hard for my mother to play a dual role, being a parent and educator. Teachers need to be able to address and confront racism for the sake of the students as well as parents. Racism should not be the sole responsibility of Black parents. In this situation, the students could have written letters, drawn pictures to the school to change the trajectory of the school, and helped to promote conversations inside and outside of the classroom. How do we teach our Black girls at such a young age the abstract thoughts that appear to be acceptable to our society? It is okay to have the conversation. Just be sure you are not sugarcoating it, so when it comes up again, you are merely reviewing it as a refresher. What is the actual responsibility of a white teacher in my situation? This is a social responsibility for everyone, not a responsibility only for the Black parents. It should also be the responsibility of all the non-Black parents in that classroom community.

I share these stories to give you a small glimpse into my life as a Black Deaf woman, with the hope that you will acknowledge their existence and experiences in your classrooms and communities. Lundqvist et al. (2012) stated that stories fascinate people and often render facts easier to remember. I agree. Teaching our brilliant and beautiful Black girls is an exceptional task. There are some things that our Black teachers and families will share with us that the white teachers may not latch onto or see as being crucial. In this piece, I will share strategies for supporting students who are brilliant, beautiful, Black, and Deaf.

1. Even Deaf Black girls are seen first as Black. Being seen for her deafness will come later, as soon as the person meets her and understands her need for communication access.

2. Black Deaf female students are often underrepresented in classrooms, books, and curriculum. Very rarely do they learn about Black culture at school. Race or racism is an uncomfortable topic for many, and many families do not talk about it in their homes as well. Schools rarely address the disproportionate numbers of Black and Brown people on probation or rearrested in the United States in their history or government classes.

3. White teachers do have bias, and this can be hard for Black Deaf female students. Sometimes they can't even see it. If they live in racial isolation, or internalize the racism they experience, they may assume that the bias they experience is simply the status quo. Countering bias requires incorporating Black Deaf female culture into the schools as well as at the residence halls and dorms for those that lived a certain number of miles from the campus. Teachers need to be able to help students unlearn the common sentiment, "I do not see color; I see people."

4. Black Deaf girls are often misunderstood by teachers and administrators. They may seek recognition at school because their hearing parents are still trying to figure out their parental roles as parents of a Deaf child, along with

(Continued)

(Continued)

her educational goals. Often parents are not included in the student's IEP (individualized educational program), and teachers do not transparently share with the student and parents what they are doing in the classroom to help the student master the goals set for her.

5. With IEPs, it is imperative to include the students in the plans to help the students understand their progress and goals. Black Girls can be part of the decision making by sharing their future goals. This would help them have a clear map for where they are going with their education, and to speak confidently.

6. Teachers of Black Deaf girls should consider embracing American Sign Language (ASL) in the classroom and at home. Research shows that 98 percent of our Black Deaf students have hearing parents at home, and the first language is English. ASL may be viewed as a foreign language. Even when students are mainstreamed, they should have the opportunity to take ASL. Hearing and Deaf students alike should have the opportunity to learn and embrace ASL as they would any other second language.

7. Some Black Deaf girls do not participate actively in class, particularly when they are integrated with hearing children. In these cases, they need to be encouraged to speak up and be called on often. Otherwise, you risk promoting quiet Black girl syndrome. What often happens is that a student is called a "good girl" because she is quiet in class and does not have to be dealt with. We expect Black girls to behave all the time. Call on them just like you call on everyone else, and take on the hard conversations; do not expect them to be "good."

8. Some students read lips, and this requires a great deal of patience and time for the teacher to set out reminders throughout the day to ensure these students are not missing anything and are staying on task. Those students should not be assumed to be helpless or less competent. They often have excellent cognitive skills, but their hearing loss gets misinterpreted as a deficit. It is imperative to ensure that the learning environment is inclusive for Deaf students or students with a hearing loss.

9. Understanding diversity is important as we deal with the movements of Black Lives Matter and the new Jim Crow. This would help the teacher see many Black students' perspectives on social relations and their communities. White teachers and white students may be cautious in their attempts to proceed, in order to avoid white fragility. They may be intimidated when a Black Deaf female student has started using her voice, sharing her true feelings with the class. In this case it is important to listen and learn.

10. Finally, it is imperative to gain access to communicating with the Black Deaf female student. Once the teacher has access, the teacher will be able to implement various learning approaches based on the student's unique needs, and the Black Deaf female student will be able to respond accordingly.

The subsequent chapter, by PhD candidate T. Donté McGuire and Dr. Keon McGuire, demonstrates the powerful impact when Black men do their own work to unlearn misogynoir, or sexism perpetrated by Black men onto Black women. These authors guide us through an intricate depiction of how aspects of their socialization as Black boys impacted their relationships with Black girls and women throughout their lives. Examining their positionality as Black and male has enabled them to show up in ways that center Black girls and women. They end their chapter with strategies that educators can use to do a similar self-assessment in the context of their school or department.

CHAPTER 41

Black Men Educators Teaching Brilliant and Beautiful Black Girls

T. Donté McGuire, Keon M. McGuire[1]

As we prepared to write this chapter, we wondered, "What can we as Black men offer to the topic of teaching brilliant and beautiful Black girls?" We realize anything we write has likely already been written by Black girls and women.[2] So, novelty is not our goal. What we will share are some of our experiences (un)learning what it means to teach, learn from, and ultimately be in healthy relationships with beautiful and brilliant Black girls and women. We say Black girls and women because we believe that the ways Black men educators engage Black girls in their classroom is directly connected to the ways they engage their Black women colleagues and supervisors. We hope sharing our stories provides some examples of how Black men[3] can help to make schools places where Black girls and women can

---

[1] We want to give a special shout out to our partners Terri Y. McGuire and Meskerem Glegziabher, who reviewed our chapter and who are, if nothing else, brilliant and beautiful Black women!

[2] Black girls and women are incredibly diverse in terms of gender identity and expression, faith, class, and ability, and much more. When we write "Black girls and women," we are speaking broadly about our efforts to create educational spaces that welcome, affirm, and value *all* Black girls and women.

[3] When we say "as Black men," we are speaking to our specific lived experiences of working in predominately White institutions, which are shaped by our various identities, including identifying as cisgender, heterosexual men.

be free. While today we are better able to identify and challenge systems that oppress Black girls and women, at a very young age we were unknowingly being socialized to invest in and perpetuate those very systems.

"Boyz n the Hood, Girls in the House"

When we were children, we spent a lot of time with two of our cousins, who were more like siblings. Both were older than we—one was, like us, a young boy, and the other a young girl. We all enjoyed playing sports, especially basketball any chance we could get. This was also around the time the classic movie *Boyz n the Hood* (Nicolaides & Singleton, 1991) came out. One day while the three of us boys were playing basketball in the driveway next to the house, our girl cousin came outside wanting to join the game. But we said "No." Instead, we began to mockingly say to her, "boyz n the hood, girls in the house," over and over. She went to get our mother and grandmother to tell how we were mistreating her, and while neither of us can remember what happened next or how everything ended, that day still stands out in our memory.

We did not know words such as *sexism* and *patriarchy* at the ages of seven and eight, but looking back, it is clear that we were learning some of the rules of a sexist and patriarchal society. We *understood* that girls and boys had their own, separate spaces, and that a girl's place was inside the house, specifically the kitchen, and not playing sports. We also *understood* that we, as boys, had both the right and responsibility to tell girls their place and keep them from places we felt they did not belong.

There are more stories that we could share that would reveal the deeply harmful ways we were taught to be in relationships with the Black girls and women in our lives. To be clear, the systems that encourage and reward us, as Black men, to invest in and perpetuate systems that oppress Black girls and women still exist today. Therefore, as Black men educators who are committed to creating educational spaces that welcome, affirm, and value Black girls and women, the work we do to better recognize and resist these systems of oppression as they manifest in ourselves, our relationships, and our institutions of education is not only important personal development, but imperative professional development. Sometimes we have been able to predict how our own development will progress, such as when we read Brittney Cooper's (2017) *Beyond Respectability: The Intellectual Thought of Race Women*. Other times, as this next story suggests, our learning came as a surprise.

Moving Closer to Black Girls and Women

A few years ago, Donté[4] participated in a multiday professional development experience that aimed to help social justice educators deepen their understanding of race and racism. During one activity, the session leader asked for a group of participants

---

[4]In this section, "I" refers to Donté McGuire.

to serve as volunteers, and I volunteered. The group was taken outside of the room to receive our instructions. Our job as volunteers was to return to the room, form the tightest circle possible by locking arms, and not allow any of the other people inside our circle. Having participated in and facilitated this experience several times before, I was confident I knew how the experience would play out. We would do our best to keep others out, while those on the outside would become increasingly creative in their attempts to enter our circle. Eventually one person would find their way inside before several others followed, and ultimately the activity would end.

Then, in the middle of the activity, as I tried my best to keep our circle intact, I looked over my shoulder and saw the person I was keeping out at the time was a Black woman. In that moment, the activity slowly began to transform from a familiar game into a metaphor of the systems of oppression that seek to separate Black people from one another in predominantly White educational spaces. I began to reflect on the messages that I received in those spaces, both explicitly and implicitly, that the "rules of the game" were to keep Black women out and to be "successful" by distancing myself from Black women. I reflected on how climbing an organizational ladder meant being in rooms that had fewer Black women. And how those rooms were often places where the voices, concerns, and perspectives of Black women, particularly if they went against the norm, were rarely taken seriously. I realized that the tension and resistance I previously felt towards efforts to center the concerns and increase the presence of Black girls and women and/or Black Feminist perspectives in these rooms were neither imaginary nor random.

From that moment, I have tried to be an educator that moves closer to and with Black girls and women. I try to consistently assess the well-being of Black girls and women in any space that I am in; increase the presence of Black women and girls in any space that I am in; listen to and amplify the voices and perspectives of Black girls and women; and perhaps most important, support, advance, and increase Black feminist leadership. Even with the best intentions, I realize that trying to maintain these commitments is not something I can or should do alone. Instead, I have found it necessary to be in community with other folks who share similar commitments, including other Black men.

Translating Awareness to Practice

While it is important to increase our awareness of the systems that oppress Black girls and women, it would be insufficient to simply identify these systems without attempting to intentionally resist them in ourselves, our relationships, and our institutions of education. First, any sincere efforts of Black men educators "teaching beautiful, brilliant Black girls" must examine, interrogate, and heal from our own patriarchal socialization and complicity. Men (like us initially) who do not believe Black men possess any "real" form of privilege may consider engaging with Jewel Woods's (2009) Black male privileges checklist. It offers a point of entry for the everyday ways Black cisgender heterosexual men benefit from their gender and sexual identities.

Second, educators may attempt to track their reflections and intentions, and follow through on supporting Black girls and women in education. Highlighting some of the issues discussed earlier, we offer the table below as an example:

TABLE 41.1 Reflecting on Commitments to Beautiful Brilliant Black Girls

What Are the Realities of Black Girls and Women in My Educational Setting(s)?	What Messages Does This Send About Black Girls and Women?	How *Can* I Interrupt or Challenge This Narrative in My Classroom and/or School? *Be Specific.*	Reflecting on What I Said I Could Do, How *Have* I Actually Interrupted or Challenged This Narrative in My Classroom and/or School? *Be as Specific and Honest as Possible in Your Own Reflections.*
The curriculum either never or only rarely includes content that centers Black girls and women as brilliant and beautiful.	Black girls and women are not people we look towards to find brilliance and beauty.	Develop grade-appropriate lessons that centers on the questions, What makes Black girls/women brilliant? What makes Black girls/women beautiful?" *Do this outside of Black history month.*	
Black girls' voices, concerns, and perspectives are questioned, undermined, or challenged when they speak their truths.	Black girls' words and actions should consistently be questioned, challenged, and critiqued, and do not require our sincere curiosity, concern, or care.	Track how many times you question, challenge, or critique Black girls in your classroom, compared to the number of times you affirm the value of their perspectives. Ask curious, open-ended questions that allow Black girls and women to share more of their truths in your classroom. Receive feedback from Black girls and women without being defensive. Name out loud when you notice other students, colleagues, or administrators being overly critical of Black girls.	

(Continued)

What Are the Realities of Black Girls and Women in My Educational Setting(s)?	What Messages Does This Send About Black Girls and Women?	How *Can* I Interrupt or Challenge This Narrative in My Classroom and/or School? *Be Specific.*	Reflecting on What I Said I Could Do, How *Have* I Actually Interrupted or Challenged This Narrative in My Classroom and/or School? *Be as Specific and Honest as Possible in Your Own Reflections.*
Black women are not well represented in leadership positions.	Black women are not fit to lead.	Offer Black girls leadership roles in the classroom early and often, and hold other students accountable for supporting them in those roles. Teach your students about the Black women educators who have helped you become a better educator. Advocate for more Black women leaders within your school.	

We invite educators to create a similar table for themselves and share it with trusted colleagues for affirmation and accountability.

Third, educators can start their classes by specifically centering Black girls and women. Where we start matters, and by centering Black girls and women in the beginning, educators signal to the class as a whole, and to Black girls and women in particular, that their experiences and perspectives matter. For example, any math course could be structured to begin each class by highlighting a significant mathematician(s), and one class could highlight Katherine Johnson, Dorothy Vaughan, and Mary Jackson, three Black, women mathematicians popularized in Margot Lee Shetterly's (2016) book *Hidden Figures* for their critical role as NASA "human computers."

Last, and arguably most important, Black men educators must assume responsibility in interrupting, challenging, and reframing sexist ideas when communicated by students and colleagues, through education, dialogue, and accountability. Relatedly, we as Black men educators have a responsibility to disrupt, challenge, and interrupt sexist and patriarchal thinking and behaviors among men colleagues, especially those messages and behaviors that occur in private, all-men spaces.

IF BLACK GIRLS AND WOMEN WERE FREE, WE WOULD ALL BE FREE

We realize that many educational institutions and educators can be considered successful without evidence that they adequately educate Black girls and women. Therefore, many of us must set a new bar, for ourselves and our colleagues, that honors the beauty and brilliance of Black girls and women. Not only because it is right, but also because educating *all* Black girls and women means educating everyone.

We agree with the Combahee River Collective, a group of Black, lesbian, feminist scholars and organizers, who said, "If Black women were free, it would mean that everyone else would have to be free since our freedom would necessitate the destruction of all the systems of oppression" (Smith, 1983, p. 270). We believe the collective's vision for freedom is as true today as it was when it was written (Taylor, 2017).

As educators seeking to challenge multiple systems of oppression, embracing this perspective calls us to begin our educational approaches with Black girls and women in mind. This reverses the norm of completely excluding or marginally considering Black girls and women. This approach does not exclude other groups. In fact, it is more inclusive than the statement might suggest, as Black girls and women exist across a spectrum of experiences and identities, including but not limited to socioeconomic status, gender identity and expression, ability, religion, and nationality. Therefore, an educational investment in Black girls and women is an investment in all students.

This section ends with two evocative, inspirational pieces. First, a vignette by Dr. Sabrina Robins describes the highs of parenting a child who is gifted with academic prowess. She describes the profound lows of negotiating with a school system that refuses to acknowledge that her daughter is triple gifted—Black, gifted and with autism. Robins's words lead teachers to pay attention to displayed traits and behaviors of autistic Black girls that often go misinterpreted. (For a more comprehensive introduction to Sabrina's daughter, see Simone Robins's vignette in this very book!) This piece is followed—so appropriately—by Dr. Tangela Serls's discussion of her research on Black Girl Magic and how to develop (or get out of the way of) a Black girl's voice.

Vignette: I Wish You Believed in Magic

Sabrina Robins

My daughter was diagnosed with autism at 10 years *young*. I hadn't known the word, its meaning, or the weight it was going to place onto my husband and my heart. Together, we became a train on the verge of derailing—or so we thought. Our talented, gifted, autistic, *Black* child grew, evolved, and transitioned into a triple threat.

Ever since my daughter was two years young, she was as bright as the sun on the first day of the summer solstice, and eager. She studied Black her/history, numbers, the alphabet, our solar system, the color charts in many cases in English and Spanish; you name it, we did it! Each time, she'd have this gleam in her eye that kept you there, held you there, invested in her. It was rather easy to envy her excitement and joy.

Sundays were bright days, days we called "Science Sunday." She'd throw on her lab coat, a white Oxford shirt with "Dr." written on a piece of masking tape, and we'd perform these "science-in-a-bag" experiments. It wasn't until we bought her an iPad and taught her how to research that we discovered she had developed a love for theater arts.

> It was magic, watching her perform.
>
> She was, indeed, gifted.

We enrolled her in a private school that had an international-focused curriculum. She took placement tests and tested out of kindergarten, and read at a high school level, at only five years *young*. The school recognized how gifted she was and created an individualized learning plan. They even requested she be placed into second or third grade, but we settled for first. We did not wish for her to experience a social and age gap.

> They knew she was gifted. They recognized her potential. They acknowledged her magic.

My daughter's teachers allowed her to work at her own pace. The nature of her curriculum allowed her to acquire Spanish, French, Chinese, and Japanese, speaking with such comfort one would believe such languages were her native tongue. I thank the diversity of the school, giving her a variety of cultures to appreciate. Watching her flourish, watching her contagious magic bring joy to others, bestowed self-confidence in her. Unfortunately, all great things come to an end, sometimes. Due to financial reasons, this wonderful school had to close its doors.

Everything changed.

By fourth grade, we enrolled her in a traditional school and learned that she couldn't sit for long periods of time. She'd move about or rock back and forth in her chair. Her teacher found this behavior a distraction. Sometimes, my daughter didn't complete her standardized tests or in-class assignments. She became such a daydreamer.

By fifth grade, we became committed to get her back into an international school. That's around the time we found out that our zany, smart, beautiful, magical daughter was autistic. I became obsessed with learning everything I could about autism, looking at charts of people on the spectrum and even reading about the school experiences of people with disabilities.

Not my magical girl. It just—couldn't be.

A plethora of negative, anxiety-induced emotions began to overwhelm me. I just remember thinking, "Oh, my goodness. School is going to be difficult for her." She had low social skills relative to others in her age group, and we learned that 98–99 percent of students with disabilities are prone to get bullied by both adults and peers alike. I needed to protect her, but how?

I learned her current school didn't provide the special services my dear daughter needed to unlock her full potential of learning. I enrolled her in a public school that became a challenge as I familiarized myself with each of her teachers. I pleaded with them about the help she needed, only to come to the realization that Black students, to begin with, weren't the ones to be treated special nor handled with care. I did all I could to prove otherwise, attended field trips, baked cookies. I did it all. My daughter deserved a chance to have a positive school experience despite the microaggressions towards Black students. It appeared to me that my daughter had lost the designation of being considered talented and gifted and found that other Black parents have experienced similar circumstances. This is my truth!

CHAPTER 42

Black Girl Magic

Beauty, Brilliance, and Coming to Voice in the Classroom

Tangela Serls

> *Pretty women wonder where my secrets lie/ I'm not cute or built to suit a fashion model size/ But when I start to tell them they think I'm telling lies.*
>
> —Maya Angelou

INTRODUCTION

Sashaying across the stage at Walter P. Jones Elementary reciting lines from Maya Angelou's "Phenomenal Woman" is one of my earliest memories of feeling both beautiful and brilliant—two words that are rarely associated with Black girls in mainstream popular culture. When I was a young child, the irony in the opening lines taught me that even though conventional standards of beauty do not include me, I am still worthy of being admired and adorned. Of course my adolescent self might have articulated my understanding differently, but the sentiment was in the performance as I embodied the belief that Black girls are beautiful.

Not only is reciting Angelou's poem one of my earliest memories of feeling beautiful and brilliant, it is also one of my earliest memories of coming to voice. I have other memories of developing my voice. (For example, in elementary and middle school I participated in a number of Black History "Month" oratorical contests, and I delivered remarks at both my high school commencement and undergraduate commencement ceremonies as salutatorian and valedictorian, respectively.) However, the truth is even though I consider myself to be a decent orator, I sometimes struggle to develop and use my voice. In those moments, I rely on the collective knowledge and wisdom of Black women and girls who have come before me, and I find the courage to speak.

It is important for Black girls to develop their voices, because in doing so they contribute to the intellectual legacy and the ongoing production of Black girl epistemology (knowledge). As Audre Lorde writes in "A Litany for Survival" (1978), "We were never meant to survive (line 24). . . so it is better to speak" (line 42). Heady and solemn, Lorde's litany is a communal prayer that notes the importance of self-expression in a world where Black girls are routinely silenced. Furthermore, Lorde alludes to various systems of oppression that intersect and ultimately seek to silence us. As Black girls living in a world of racist, sexist, and homophobic systems (among others), we were not meant to live and triumph, but we do. Despite the insecurity, instability, and anxiety that sometimes shroud us, it is important for Black girls to speak and recognize the power in our individual and collective voice.

BLACK GIRL MAGIC AND DEVELOPING VOICE

Black girl magic represents excellence in mind, character, and action and is an expression that resonates with a lot of Black girls. Clover Hope maintains, Black girl magic "ritualize[s] black female brilliance in three words" (2017, para. 45). Black girl magic and the corresponding virtual platform #BlackGirlMagic[1] allude to the collective knowledge shared by Black women and girls. The magic is an intergenerational appreciation, acceptance, and recognition of our beauty and brilliance. The concept recognizes the knowledge Black girls cultivate—particularly in the face of fading hope—and it celebrates our perseverance as we use our knowledge to become the best version of ourselves.

In 2013, CaShawn Thompson used her virtual platform on Twitter and declared, "Black Girls Are Magic." She has since been credited as the woman who popularized the #BlackGirlMagic movement on social media. In an interview with the *Los Angeles Times,* Thompson revealed, "I say 'magic' because it's something that people don't always understand. . . . Sometimes our accomplishments might seem to come out of thin air, because a lot of times, the only people supporting us are other black women" (as quoted in Thomas, 2015, para. 6). Thompson points to her own circle of friends as early supporters of her #BlackGirlMagic platform.

In an online article for *Elle,* Ashley Ford explains the "magic" in black girl magic "is about *knowing* (emphasis added) something that others don't know or refuse to see" (2016, para. 5). Ford's definition points to the intellectual legacies Black girls have inherited, which, though they have been carefully cultivated, appear to be magic to others. According to Ford, #BlackGirlMagic, "has never been about being in possession of superhuman mental or emotional strength . . . it's about claiming

---

[1] The hashtag #BlackGirlMagic is used intentionally here and other places in this work to distinguish the virtual platform for Black girl magic versus the notion of the concept itself.

or reclaiming what others have refused to see" (2016, para. 6). Ultimately, Black girl magic and the virtual platforms are examples of the expanding range of Black women's and girls' loving relationships as we tap into new possibilities for empowerment and coming to voice.

Black schoolgirls are stifled as they attempt to hone their voices, and the issue of voice is prevalent in studies on gender inequity in education. Similarly, in the field of girls' studies, the issue of voice has been linked to legitimate concerns about girls' self-esteem (Johnson, 2015). Black girl magic—including the knowledge Black women have passed down for generations, the studiousness contemporary Black girls display in our chosen fields, and the inspiration that motivates us along various courses of action—could be used in the classroom to empower Black girls. As educators, we have an opportunity to celebrate and support Black girls as they develop their voice in the classroom.

TIDBITS FOR TEACHERS

The next section contains information educators can use as they seek to empower Black girls and help them develop their individual and collective voice.

- **Learn more about Black women and girls from both a historical and contemporary context, and share that knowledge with students**. When considering the historical, start with the history you know, and then look for the *herstory*. For example, many people do not know that Rosa Parks worked as an investigator for the NAACP prior to refusing to give up her seat in an act that prompted the Montgomery bus boycott. Similarly, Tarana Burke—Black girl advocate and founder of the Me Too movement—has been raising awareness about the prevalence of sexual assault in communities of color for well over a decade. However, it was not until #MeToo went viral—from Alyssa Milano's tweet—that people learned about her and her work. For all students, but for Black girls specifically, *herstory* is important, because it can serve to empower them as they develop their voice.

Tidbit: Many of the stories in Blair Imani's book *Modern Herstory: Stories of Women and Nonbinary People Writing History* (2018) can be read in five minutes or less. There are a number of ways educators could use the stories in the classroom (e.g., to introduce other relevant course content or to have a discussion about policies and current events).

- **Recognize and understand there is diversity among Black girls' experiences— educational and otherwise.** Instead of race, ethnicity and nationality factor more heavily in a person's identity in some cultures. Thus, many Black girls of the African diaspora—particularly those who may not have been born in the United States—go through a process of accepting the label "Black." Black girl cultures are paradoxes; they can be both universal and particular to a specific state, region, or part of the world. For example, Jamaica Kincaid's "Girl" (1978) is universal in that it recounts the story of a young Black girl passively absorbing information and in the end coming to voice under the guidance of an older female character. However, a number of examples in the narrative are culturally specific and would likely resonate more with Black girls who are familiar with West Indian culture.

Tidbit: Ruth Nicole Brown is an academic who studies gender and race dynamics as they relate to Black girlhood. Check out her books *Black Girlhood Celebration: Toward a Hip Hop Feminist Pedagogy* (2009) and *Hear Our Truths: The Creative Potential of Black Girlhood* (2013). You should also check out the work she does with SOLHOT (Saving Our Lives, Hear Our Truths), a "practice-based, publicly engaged, collectively organized space for Black girls to envision Black girlhood anew" ("The Visionary," n.d., para. 1). Not only will Brown's work introduce you to tools to empower Black girls in the classroom, it will also help you transform the learning experience for other students as well.

- **Acknowledge the diligence Black girls display when triumphing within their fields, and inspire the students in your class to blaze their own trails.** Although verbal expression is absolutely a part of developing one's voice, there are a number of other nonverbal expressions that Black girls may find equally empowering. This chapter places an emphasis on verbal expressions; however, it is important to acknowledge other expressive forms (e.g., writing, painting, dancing, photography, etc.).

Tidbit: Black Girls Rock is a nationally recognized youth empowerment and mentoring organization that has hosted an annual awards show and Black girls leadership conference for over a decade. The names of nominees and winners in various categories can serve as useful examples when inspiring Black girls in your classroom to blaze their own trails. The list of names could also be used to complete the web investigation assignment described at the end of the chapter.

CONCLUSION

Growing up I had teachers who recognized the importance of creating a space for little Black girls to develop their voices. For example, I remember having a few assignments throughout my K–12 educational experience where I was responsible for learning a passage and reciting it from memory. Moreover, we often read aloud as a class. And even when we stumbled in our delivery, we felt affirmed, because our teacher had taken the time to cultivate a sense of community within the class. Though I had a relatively positive educational experience, I understand that there are systemic injustices that exist and influence the ways Black girls experience educational systems in the 21st century (see Morris, *Pushout: The Criminalization of Black Girls*, 2015). However, as Donna Marie Johnson notes, "It is important to remember that despite obstacles, African American girls are more than their challenges. They have strengths, and there are a significant number of . . . Black girls who continue to excel academically, and who are successful in school" (2015, p. 43). Empowerment and the development of voice are likely to ensue when students feel valued by their teachers. Thus, it is important that educators approach teaching Black girls from a place inspired by Black girl magic, a place where they truly believe Black girls are beautiful and brilliant.

Web Investigation Assignment

Directions: Students should complete the following web investigation and prepare a one- to two-page response. *(Instructors can assign the page count/word count that fits their needs.)*

- **Do an internet search on two or three of the following women:** *(It is a good idea for instructors to do a preliminary search on the people they assign to make sure students will find relevant information. The following is a sample list; however, instructors should list Black women and girls who best fit the needs of their lesson.)*

  - Tananarive Due
  - Jacqueline Woodson
  - Eve L. Ewing
  - Ibi Zoboi
  - Warsan Shire
  - Lorna Simpson

- **After you've completed your internet search, write a one- to two-page response to your findings. Be sure to include information on the reference(s) used.**

Here are a few questions you may consider as you write your response:

What did you learn about the women? Did you learn anything that reminded you of material we have previously covered? Was there a quote from the person that inspired you? If so, discuss it. *(Instructors should modify questions to fit the needs of their lesson.)*

- **Bring a printed copy of your assignment to class. You will be paired with two to three classmates, and you all will discuss your findings.** *(Students should not read directly from their paper, but rather use their document as a guide as they have a small group discussion. Follow up with a large group discussion, and encourage individual students to share with the larger class. In the large group discussion, instructors can synthesize students' findings and explain the differences in the types of sources the students used to gather their information. This assignment helps students develop their voice and ideas as they share their knowledge with their peers.)*

PART IV

"PERSEVERANCE IS MY MOTTO."

—Madam C. J. Walker

Knowing who we are and what we bring as Black girls is something that can at times feel like a rite of passage as we navigate the white supremacist society that we live in. As Black girls are constantly negotiating their identities, both inside and outside of school, it is important that the adults in their lives provide spaces of dynamic teaching and learning outside of the classroom. The following chapter opens with words from two professional Black Girls, Toni and Jada—students from Joan of Arc High School—who share their lived experience in the classroom of one white teacher. Authors Dr. Monique Lane and nonprofit executive Kendra Carr then show us how the pedagogical practices of Powerful Beyond Measure, an out-of-school-time program that centers on identity development, leadership, and resistance, supports the overall growth, academic achievement, and personal development of Black girls.

Vignette: #Professional Black Girls: An Interview With Dr. Yaba Blay

by Shemariah J. Arki

In the classroom, Black girls suffer from being invisible and hypervisible at the same time. According to multiple Black feminist scholars, Black girl bodies serve as a site of knowing and becoming, not just for themselves, but also for the spaces and places at which they matriculate, including classrooms. Therefore, curriculum and pedagogy matter. Schools and other education-based institutions can no longer feed culturally irrelevant information to our Black girls without anticipating pushback. There is something that happens to us, to our girls, when we don't intentionally teach students about privilege and oppression and how they operate in American society. Black girls who don't learn about the intricacies of white supremacy, white privilege, and whiteness often fail to see themselves as the mere perpetuation of a trope—angry, emasculating, or hypersexed.

(Continued)

(Continued)

In the following interview, I speak with Dr. Yaba Blay, creator and curator of #ProfessionalBlackGirl, a multiplatform digital community that celebrates the everyday, round-the-way culture of Black women and girls. As a proud member of this community, I felt it necessary to include this asset-based identity narrative for teachers to understand. Many times in my own educational career, particularly as a graduate student and early career professional, I have been boxed into the infamous Black girl tropes mentioned above. When interpreted through a lens of whiteness and white supremacy, particularly without any attention to the interpreter's self-awareness, my good deeds and attempts at securing equity for myself and those whom I'd chosen to identify would be seen as selfish, elitist, and exclusionary. Ultimately, #ProfessionalBlackGirl gave me the language, tools, and resources to survive and help others who identified as such to do the same.

Shemariah:	Why "Professional Black Girl"?
Yaba:	This #ProfessionalBlackGirl thing started with me being on Instagram way too much and continually saying I love Black girls. And when I say that, I mean that I experience joy every single day simply from looking at Black women and girls on social media— I promise you that. It's so nice seeing videos . . . little girls dancing and getting it! I want to encourage their spirit of freedom. We talk about freedom so much as Black people, and yet many of us have no idea what it really means to be free. We're only thinking about a situation of freedom. Freedom starts here with your ability to control what you do with your body. That's a type of freedom.
Shemariah:	Yassss! We must reimagine freedom. bell hooks reminds us that education is a practice of freedom. Hair styles, making up dances, wearing uniforms (or the intentional interruption of them)—for Black girls in school, these acts are certainly operating as attempts at freedom. These are things schools and other education-based institutions are policing through unequal and oppressive structures, rules, policies, procedures, and practices. When Black girls are seen as acting out or being defiant, they're simply practicing freedom.
Yaba:	Hashtag Professional Black Girl! She's a professional. And that professionalism has nothing to do with training. . . . Who trained us how to put baby hairs down? And if there is training, it is something that we train each other in, because it's our culture. That's what makes us who we are—not these degrees, and not this classroom.
Shemariah:	Yes, the concept of Black Girl Priming is discussed by Dr. Monique Liston in this text. We must understand the dominant narrative and how we have been socialized into behaving this way with one another. So, #ProfessionalBlackGirl can actually serve as a primer

for those of us who are navigating educational systems. Reimaging, redefining, and curating spaces for ourselves in places that were not designed for us to exist, let alone live, survive, or thrive.

Yaba: When I thought about Professional Black Girl and even using the language of *professional* as subversive, it came out of that space of being a Black girl with a PhD and recognizing what privilege comes with folks calling me *Dr. Blay*. I was trained in black studies and women's and gender studies, and we were talking about *us* . . . but in a way that was only accessible to those of *us* with that ivory tower privilege. I had questions, like, how do you come to be the voice of Black people? How do you come to be the voice of women? How do you come to be the voice of Black children? What were your receipts? I had to ask myself *why are we doing this work and who is the work actually for?* Since then, I've been committed to figuring out ways to translate this work outside of the classroom. I understood the privilege of being *Dr. Yaba Blay* and how that somehow validates what others are willing to hear about Black women and girls' experiences. And so with that privilege, I'm not coming to you buttoned up. I'm not coming to you saying words that you have to look up to even understand what I'm saying. I'm talking to you as Yaba, not Dr. Blay.

#ProfessionalBlackGirl comes out of a space of knowing what people think *professional* is, and then seeking it as a goal. I was teaching at an HBCU, I was watching my Black women colleagues train our Black girls away from themselves . . . that you have to wear your hair a certain way, you have to dress a certain way, you have to speak a certain way, in order to be accepted in the real world.

Shemariah: That training or priming can also be likened to the conversation in our community on respectability politics and how it will only get you so far. It's important for us to teach Black girls that independent of how we see ourselves or the world, we must understand how the world sees us. It has nothing to do with who we really are; this vision of us represented in the dominant narrative is of who they think we are, and how they must respond to us to maintain their power.

Yaba: And so what I'm telling you is about playing a game. But the game is not about taking on an identity and becoming someone else. It's about playing a game you cannot win. And in this game, I've decided to be the best me I can be: a #ProfessionalBlackGirl. When I see grown women dressed a particular way, doing certain things, speaking to each other in our own tongue, our mother tongue—that's the energy I place behind the use of *professional* in

(Continued)

this context; it is intentionally subversive. It's a middle finger to all of these standards that whiteness, white privilege, and white supremacy put on us that absolutely takes us away from ourselves. We are reclaiming. Nope, I'm not gonna say reclaiming because we never let it go. We're holding on to ourselves.

Shemariah: When thinking about Black girls in the classroom, what's top of mind for you?

Yaba: I think about so many questions that they're probably having in terms of who they're supposed to be in that classroom. I know that a general broad conversation about high school students is just a general broad conversation about female high school students. I don't know if there's enough conversation about Black female high school students because there's so many ways we show up in the classroom.

So many areas that could be impacting their lives. And I don't know that we give culture enough credit in that dynamic, you know? Questions like: What are they culturally expected to do? Who were they culturally expected to be as Black girls? What is it that they're experiencing, and where are their role models, demonstrating what or who they can aspire to be? Questions they may ask themselves: If I'm the smart Black girl, am I gonna have any friends? If I'm the ratchet Black girl, am I even going to get out of this school? Can I afford to be myself if I'm trying to fit in with these other Black girls? Maybe I'm not; maybe I am distancing myself from those Black girls because I don't want all of that on me.

Then there are hormones! So on top of learning what they're responsible for, they've got to have on the right clothes that fit a certain way to be cute and to be seen. To not only have homegirls and girlfriends, but to also catch the attraction of some of the boys, because that's what happens too. And in the right moment, this might supersede all of the learning that is supposed to happen at school.

As an educator myself, I can think of the Black girl who is the teacher, who also has questions about who she is supposed to be at that moment. She may think, "Oh, I don't want to take on a Mammy character and be your caretaker because I'm responsible for teaching you," or she may be anxious about what these students might think when they see a Black woman's body and how they might think they can behave in her presence. In order to be successful, she knows she must come outside of herself and be somebody else. Just like the high school girls, similar questions arise for the Black girl teacher. What are my colleagues thinking? Am I gonna be able to keep this job?

Shemariah: What do you think teachers should know about the #ProfessionalBlackGirl who shows up in their classrooms?

Yaba: I just think, again, it comes back to truth. I think we must honor the brilliance of our children. We don't honor their humanity. We don't even allow their personalities to be genuine to them. . . . And there's so many parents who want to create a box for their children to stay in. As a daughter, mother, educator, and Black girl, I get it! We live in a society, we gotta act right, but we also must be intentional about holding on to who we are.

Shemariah: I believe that parents are our first teachers and they certainly hold part of this responsibility. In addition to and in conjunction with the role of parents and families, as educators and administrators, folks who proudly identify as *professionals*, you must do your own work as an adult in a position of power, an employee, a white person and an overall decent human being. We know the majority of today's teachers identify as white women, therefore we must be intersectional and employ antioppressive frameworks in our approach to curating classrooms as spaces of radical transformation, particularly for Black girls and femmes.

***

As #ProfessionalBlackGirls, we give each other the ability to think, to infer, to concur or not with ourselves first, and then one another. This opens the door to dynamic ways of knowing and becoming. By intentionally identifying as a #ProfessionalBlackGirl, Black girls are able to position the classroom as a place of radical transformation. Radical, meaning getting to the root of issues like anti-blackness and patriarchy and transformation in the sense of not being able to be recognized, or being new. The classroom should be a place where Professional Black Girls can be seen and loved, out loud.

Teachers, I encourage you to visit the website (https://professionalblackgirl.com/web-series/) to view both seasons of the web series to hear from professional Black Girls themselves to learn more about how we show up in your classrooms and learning spaces as students, peers, and colleagues. As you view each episode, ask yourself the following questions:

- If she showed up in my classroom, would she feel welcomed?
- When she shows up in my classroom, what's my role in supporting the identity development of this #ProfessionalBlackGirl?

CHAPTER 43

Listen to Her!

Black Girls Constructing Activist Identities in a School-Based Leadership Program

Monique Lane, Kendra Carr

> Whenever I would share, the teacher would overlook what I said or make it seem like I was being unclear. I relate my comments to what's happening in society, and I keep it real. My teacher looks like she doesn't know what to say. Someone else would say the same thing I just said, but they would say it "smarter" and get credit for it. I have learned how to maneuver being Black at this school.
>
> —Toni, Joan of Arc High School student

> My teacher said the N-word because she said it was OK that it was in literature. I wish we could have a slave come to campus and talk to us, because they don't hear it from us. . . . People want respect for their culture but don't give respect to Black girls. We aren't even that ghetto, and we have this label of ghetto. Being Black on *us* is ratchet, and being Black on *them* is hip. It's like being attacked 24-7.
>
> —Jada, Joan of Arc High School student

INTRODUCTION

Toni and Jada offer a sobering depiction of the curricular practices and schooling experiences that adversely affect Black girl learners throughout the nation. Since

African American female youth are more likely to live in economically depressed communities and attend poorly funded schools (Crenshaw et al., 2015)—and experience racist, sexist, and socioeconomic oppression in our larger society (Evans, 1988; Grant, 1984)—they endure heightened exposure to educational resource [mal]distribution, deficit teacher ideologies, and culturally irresponsible academic instruction (Lane, 2017; Morris, 2016).

Empirical studies have drawn attention to how white women-identified practitioners—the leading population of preK–12 educators in the United States (U.S. Department of Education, National Center for Education Statistics, 2019)—inflict daily indignities upon culturally marginalized students (Harris et al., 2020; Juárez Harris et al., 2016; Levine-Rasky, 2000). The stereotype of the strong Black woman romanticizes the resilience of African American female youth and results in excessive and undeserved reprimand (Morris, 2016). Well-meaning teachers may actually be unable to recognize Black girls' educational needs and cultural subjectivities—this is typically communicated as benign neglect to African American girl learners (Lane, in press). Alarmingly, African American girls and women (a) are commonly excluded from advanced placement (AP) and college preparatory courses, (b) are less likely to graduate from high school on time, (c) are overrepresented in community colleges, and (d) matriculate at four-year institutions at lower rates than other racialized women (Archer-Banks & Behar-Horenstein, 2012; Evans-Winters, 2011; The NAACP Legal Defense and Educational Fund & The National Women's Law Center, 2014).

As Black women scholars who center Black girl learners in our research, we draw on Black feminist pedagogy (Collins, 2000; Lane, 2017) and critical race feminism (Evans-Winters & Esposito, 2010) to highlight a service-learning program opportunity for Black and Latina students. In this program, Powerful Beyond Measure, the girls journeyed to Kenya for a three-week transformational trek, in which the young women scholars lived and learned alongside their African peers at an all-girls boarding school. Upon return, the students designed and created service-learning projects in their communities. This chapter will offer pedagogical imperatives that are critical for white readers who desire to develop a program such as this one. *If* put into practice by white women teachers, these imperatives *may* be received by Black girls as invitations to engage in the curriculum with a sense of safety and willingness to do the hard work of self-discovery and intellectual growth.

Pedagogical Imperatives for White Women Teaching Black Girls

From a previous study by one of the authors (Carr, 2020), we share two ideological imperatives upon which white women should orient themselves as educators of Black girls. First, as white dominance continues to pervade our global society, white teachers must create buffers—safe and nurturing classroom spaces where these young women can explore and negotiate their identities. Second, Black girls have a boundless capacity to exercise their voice and influence community change.

DIRECTIVE 1: IDENTITY WORK IS NOT OPTIONAL

The emotional and psychological safety of Black girls depends in part on our willingness and ability to see them as treasures. Veritably, these learners need safe and validating classroom environments that encourage them to explore their particularities—and relief from stereotypical associations and homogeneous grouping—and discover race, gender, socioeconomic status, physicality, sexual orientation, disability, and religion as aspects of their entangled identities.

These young scholars were both curious and struggling, unclear and certain about who they were. Students self-identified as Black, African American, or biracial. Esther shared, "I'm African American. West African, born in America." While some girls were uncomfortable being Black at school, others praised the efforts at Joan of Arc High School to make all girls comfortable. Critical race feminist scholar Theodora Berry (2010) emphasized, "Commonality of race does not produce commonality of self-identity" (p. 24). Thus, we listened carefully to *each* of the girls shed light on her needs, and how she juggled feelings of pride and isolation as she moved through the world in a racialized, gendered body.

In journal entries, the scholars conveyed *pride* in myriad aspects of their identity, including their race and culture. Antoinette identified what she was most proud of: "skin color, I love being Black. The part of my identity that is most important to me is protecting my culture." Sierra shared, "I am most proud of my race. I am proud to be African American. It is important to me because I am judged about it whether I want to be or not." Additionally, Jada singled out her growth in her "relationship with God" (Jada, journal entry); Toni named "good morals" (Toni, journal entry); and Davia highlighted "being a leader, outspokenness, [and the] ability to smile through hard times" (Davia, journal entry).

The scholars' narratives also depicted the ways in which students felt *isolated* and invisible within their school community, which led to student disengagement. For instance, Sierra stated that she regularly experienced discomfort when classmates joked about her "economic standing" and severely limited material resources. Clonan-Roy et al. (2016) explain that:

> for girls of color, self-worth and self-esteem are often connected to their sense of belongingness and acceptance in their communities and schools, their sense of feeling respected and their experiences validated, and their sense of others' seeing them as having intelligence (p. 107).

Educators have the power to initiate opportunities for students to be seen in their classrooms.

DIRECTIVE 2: NURTURE BLACK GIRLS' POWER THROUGH LEADERSHIP AND RESISTANCE

For generations, elders within African American communities have passed down ancestral wisdom situating education as a means of personal and community uplift. Yosso (2005) defines this particular form of community cultural wealth as *resistance capital*, which encompasses both the knowledge of racism, sexism, and systems of marginalization, and the skills and "motivation to transform such oppressive structures" (p. 81). Resistance capital is often unrecognized and overlooked in schools, yet it undergirds the very purpose of education for African American communities. Based on a tenet identified by Mitchell (2010), Carr's (2020) inquiry requires students to design and implement a service-learning project to cultivate their leadership capacities and create solutions to social justice issues in their communities.

By the end of our service-learning program, each young woman personally identified as a leader, sensed that she was becoming a leader, or was actively developing stronger leadership skills. Davia shared:

> I have grown from being a shy girl who was afraid to speak and I thought that I would never find my voice. Now, I have found mine and am able to help those who have not found their voice yet.

Students' expression of "becoming" relates directly to Lane's (in press) conceptualization of #BlackGirlJoy. According to Lane, #BlackGirlJoy is "tied to Black women and girls' *conscious unfolding*—namely, the journey to self-define and evolve—in the face of abundant systemic injustices" (p. 8). The author urges educators to support, adopt, and sustain spaces in which Black girls can safely *be in process*.

Strategies for Transformative Classroom Practices

1. Incorporate *multiple modes* through which Black girls can engage in identity work, such as different journaling prompts, activities, and discussion circles. For example, the Social Identity Wheel activity, made accessible through the University of Michigan's Inclusive Teaching Initiative, allows students to share aspects of their identity that point to empowerment *and* alienation ("Social Identity Wheel," n.d.).

2. Developing sustained counterspaces within the curricular structure invites Black girl learners to *systematically* analyze their lives *frequently* and over an *extended* time. For example, divide the class into pairs, and

(Continued)

(Continued)

provide a prompt (e.g., *When I walk through the halls, I think people see,* or *I feel strongest when . . . because . . .*). By giving students equal time to speak and respond to the prompt, you can foster empathy and connection; instruct partners to deeply listen and make note of the speaker's unique story and strengths.

3. Encourage Black female learners to develop a *community of support and care* amongst themselves, outside of the surveillance of white and male peers. Offer your classroom as a space for a lunchtime or afterschool club that centers the experiences and needs of African American girls. Identify students who would like to lead this group, and be a resource and advocate for them within the school community.

CONCLUDING THOUGHTS

One outcome of the authors' engagement with the Powerful Beyond Measure participant narratives is a razor-sharp discernment of young Black women's curricular consumption and socialization in U.S. schools. Carr's (2020) endeavor to (a) center Black girl learners' identity work and (b) cultivate students' leadership capacities through service-learning increased the girls' intellectual curiosity as well as their cultural and critical competencies. Thus, the research findings are illustrative of Ladson-Billings' (1995) "pedagogy of opposition" (p. 160). Through their participation in Powerful Beyond Measure, African American girls defied the ideological and institutional forces that condition these youth to be passive recipients of schooling. To cultivate a transformative praxis (Freire, 1970/2002), white female practitioners—and any educator who takes up this work—must engage in recurring critical self-examinations while implementing innovative curricular strategies.

Extant scholarship has established that (a) deeply listening to Black girls' perspectives, (b) valuing their experiences, and (c) taking *action* that is guided by students' insights are fundamental to pedagogical love (McArthur & Lane, 2018). Social media and rhetoric that positions African American female learners as irrationally hostile, sexually immoral, and ratchet compromise these students' humanity and threaten their budding identities (Love, 2017; Morris, 2007; Sealey-Ruiz, 2007). For this reason, we conclude with a rallying call for practitioners to *listen* to Black girls!

I (Ali Michael) met the authors of the following vignettes at the Color of Education Summit at Duke University in 2019. The students were presenting a workshop and tabling to participants, which was composed mostly of educators and educational policy makers. I was so impressed with the way they talked about the urgency and importance of their work with the Equal Justice Initiative, memorializing the genocidal violence that took place in their communities throughout history, so that nobody would forget. I was struck that through the Equal Justice Initiative, it could be possible for students in any county to get involved in advocacy and mobilizing power in this way. Most teachers are likely to be intimidated by this type of historical investigation, perhaps believing that the content would be too much for young people to handle. But KaLa, Sammi, and Ny—the authors of the following vignette—were actively teaching content to rapt teachers and administrators who were attending the conference. And for these students, knowledge was power. It enabled them to acknowledge what came before them so that they could confront the present with honesty, clarity, and agency.

Vignette: Black Girls as Leaders

Samarria Tucker, Nyee'ya Williams, KaLa Keaton

We are two out of six high school students,[1] known as the Freedom Struggle Committee, who are committed to developing a permanent public acknowledgment of the victims of lynching in our state. Beginning during the fall of 2016, former committee members[2] worked with community leaders and local government officials to make our vision a reality. Our project is to build a physical memorial in remembrance of victims of lynching in North Carolina. It will consist of two sheets of granite placed together to appear like an open book. A bronze tree will come out of the middle of the two open sides. We will include a brief history of lynching in North Carolina. On the memorial we will include a list of the names of all known lynching victims in North Carolina, and this phrase: "and to those unknown but not forgotten." We hope that this memorial will bring forth the truth of our dark history as well

(Continued)

---

[1]The other students include Kelly Blackman, Allison Jemerson, Saadhvi Mamidi, and Richie Bryant.

[2]Former committee members include Kana Parker, Lucy Murray, Alissa Meyerhoffer, Christina Jones, and Steven Powell.

(Continued)

as stand as a testament to our tenacity and hope for reconciliation. As Black women in America, it makes us feel more important, because a lot of the time, in history we are ignored. It feels like someone cares about the things that happened in the past and wants to recognize the truth. It is time to face the past, and this makes us feel like we're doing just that.

—Samarria Tucker, Nyee'ya Williams

I've lived in Wake County my entire life. The extent of my knowledge about Black history in school began with Harriet Tubman, skipped a century or so, and ended with Dr. Martin Luther King Jr. Before the ninth grade, when I first became involved with the lynching memorial projects, I felt detached from real-world issues that would affect me as a Black girl. I thought, it happened 200 years ago, or, it didn't happen here. It was the local history, the history just a 30-minute drive away, that opened my eyes. I feel that everyone should wake up, too. At Middle Creek High School, we demonstrated this principle into our African American literature class. The course was aimed at learning not only the different literature forms seen in black culture but the hidden history that created them as well. When we were not doing "traditional" work; we worked on recognizing Wake County's only recorded lynching victim, George Taylor, with the Equality Justice Initiative. Now, we have expanded the course and added a second class. Our block was made primarily of Black women, and we all loved this work. We felt empowered, strong, and like we were making a difference. Often, we feel overlooked and underrepresented in our community, especially when attending predominantly white schools. This experience, along with opportunities that resulted from our project, gave us Black girls the support, attention, and recognition we deserved after years in the education system.

—KaLa Keaton

The next chapter and vignette illustrate the need for effectual visual and environmental cues to let Black girls know they are seen, they are heard, and they matter, as well as what happens when they don't get those cues. In "When You Imagine a Scientist, Technologist, Engineer, Artist, or Mathematician, Imagine a Black Girl," Dr. Ansley Booker advises educators to cultivate a strong science identity in girls as early as possible through books, toys, and visualization. Dr. Booker uses STEM and STEAM because both in addition to STREAM are critical for, and to Black Girls. The book review that follows illustrates the endless possibilities when we do. The subsequent vignette by student Sinclair Robins demonstrates what can happen when we do not.

When You Imagine a Scientist, Technologist, Engineer, Artist, or Mathematician, Imagine a Black Girl

Ansley Booker

Never be limited by other people's limited imaginations!

—Mae Jemison, astronaut

This chapter seeks to examine what role gender, race, and digital media have on a Black girl's perception of science, technology, engineering, arts, and math (STEAM) disciplines. This chapter is a collection of literature detailing the current mediums used to display young African American girls in STEAM. Researchers state that Black girls must determine a science identity in STEAM disciplines as early as middle school to ensure a definitive career path (Brickhouse et al., 2000; Burke & Stets, 2009). Yet by fourth grade, how many positive STEAM images have been provided for these African American girls? Currently, very few forms of digital media have navigated the complexity of Black girls in STEAM. This chapter is a review of media platforms such as television and movies, highlighting some characters that are breaking gender, economic, cultural, and social barriers in STEAM education. These sheroes include a child doctor, Doc

McStuffins, an engineer/inventor from Wakanda named Shuri, a young scientist named Meg Murry, Barbie dolls, and "Hidden Figures" such as Katherine Johnson, Mary Jackson, and Dorothy Vaughn. Last, the effects of digital media on the perceptions of African American girls entering into STEAM is explored utilizing various identity development constructs.

BACKGROUND

Historically, the United States has been viewed as a world leader in technology, engineering, and innovation. However, to maintain this status, the government must repair the STEM pipeline in K–12 education. Currently, the U.S. Department of Education has several STEM-based initiatives to improve the number of students interested in STEM, including the "Educate to Innovate" campaign. Former president Barack Obama developed this campaign in 2009, collaborating with over 13 agencies to form the Committee on STEM Education (CoSTEM). The objective was to help strategize ways to increase and sustain public and youth STEM engagement, increase federal funds for K–12 education, improve undergraduate STEM experiences, increase outreach for underrepresented populations, and improve graduate education for the STEM workforce (U.S. Department of Education, n.d.).

Nevertheless, despite these newer efforts, the numbers of African American women continue to decline in computer sciences, mathematics, and statistics, and engineering. Yet, the question remains, "Why are so few African American women earning degrees or pursuing careers in STEAM?" Most of the answers are attributed to academic unpreparedness, lack of science and engineering exposure, and systemic/social/cultural barriers, including stereotypes and implicit biases (Settles, 2014). Last, research shows that many minorities do not have equal access to STEAM courses and, as a result, many fail to maintain an interest in STEM or are inadequately prepared to pursue STEM academics on the collegiate level.

SCIENCE IDENTITY

One important solution to this problem is the establishment of a solid "science identity." Research has shown that young girls must make a connection to STEAM as early as elementary school to pique their interests in scientific disciplines. A science identity is related to students' interest in science, their enrollment in science courses, their desire to pursue a science career, and even their choice to enter and graduate from a science program (Lee, 1998; Merolla & Serpe, 2013; Merolla et al., 2012). When young girls fail to establish a STEAM identity by the age of 12, they tend to lose interest in STEAM disciplines (Steinke, 2017). As a solution, Hom (2014) pointed to a blended learning method, which highlights the utilization of STEAM in everyday life applications to improve these connections as early as elementary school. This method focuses on using the scientific method to solve problems with practical applications.

STEAM education through blended learning must be established by elementary school. During these developmental years, students need to be exposed to introductory STEAM courses, fields, and occupations. The goal is to get the students acclimated to the different disciplines and opportunities. As the students progress, the intensity and significance of STEAM-related careers, jobs, and academic pursuits should be stressed throughout middle and high school (Hom, 2014). These initiatives are utilized to prevent drop out and disinterest by students as they mature.

BOOKS

Very few books are aimed at young girls interested in STEAM. Books aimed at this specific audience include the following:

- *Little Leaders: Bold Women in Black History* by Vashti Harrison
- *Ada Twist, Scientist* by Andrea Beaty
- *Rosie Revere, Engineer* by Andrea Beaty
- *Goodnight Lab* by Chris Ferrie Books
- *Wonder Women: 25 Innovators, Inventors, and Trailblazers Who Changed History* by Sam Maggs
- *Changing the Face of Engineering: The African American Experience* edited by John Brooks Slaughter, Yu Tao, and Willie Pearson Jr.
- *Hidden Figures: The True Story of Four Black Women and the Space Race* by Margot Lee Shetterly

One of the books highlighted is *Wonder Women: 25 Innovators, Inventors, and Trailblazers Who Changed History*. The book details the story of these prominent women in their respective fields, including those that were doctors, mathematicians, spies and forgers, writers, soldiers, and inventors from around the world (Maggs, 2016). Maggs highlights the struggles of Black women, particularly stating several inventions were not credited to them because of their race. The book entitled *Hidden Figures: The True Story of Four Black Women and the Space Race* tells the stories of four Black women through the 1940s–1960s as they work for NASA as "human computers" (www.hiddenfigures.com). The book was turned into a movie in 2016; it focused primarily on the stories of Katherine Johnson, Mary Jackson, and Dorothy Vaughan. Their stories revolved around navigating bias, gender norms, segregation, racism, sexism, gender pay gaps, and inequality. All of these books can be used during story time or serve as research subjects for book reports in the early grades.

Toys

Children of color have had difficulty finding toys—specifically dolls—within their racial identity. Several manufacturers now offer dolls in many nationalities and ethnic groups. However, one manufacturer, Mattel, has made some improvements in making toys that reflect not only varying races but also varying gender roles. Mattel is the company that manufactures Barbie, a doll that has been an icon since the 1950s. She is now breaking barriers and making another iconic statement as a modern-day career professional.

On March 6, 2018 (International Women's Day), Mattel announced that Katherine Johnson and 16 other inspiring women would receive Barbie dolls modeled after them. Mattel says Johnson's Barbie "celebrates the achievements of a pioneer who broke through barriers of race and gender" (Boyle, 2018). Barbie is also reinforcing the STEAM career identity by highlighting dolls as vets, bee-keepers, astronauts and space scientists, scientists, zoologists, builders (engineers), paleontologists, and dentists. Also, Mattel has a partnership with Tynker, which is the number one kids' coding platform ("Barbie + Tynker," n.d.). This collaboration allows young girls to learn basic programming. The coding platform is similar to computer applications or computer science but explores career occupations. In addition, the coding platform can be used in the classroom to teach basic coding and diversity in careers.

Lego has also made strides towards improving toys centered on STEAM occupations, including the collection of Lego minifigures to include "Women of NASA." The figures include Katherine Johnson, Sally Ride, Nancy Grace Roman, and Mae Jemison. The women of color include Dr. Mae Jemison, the first African American woman in space, in 1992 aboard the space shuttle Endeavour; and Katherine Johnson, a NASA mathematician and physicist who calculated the trajectories for the Mercury and Apollo programs (Boyle, 2017).

Visualization

Young girls must be able to establish a connection to STEAM careers through a role model, mentor, or representative. These role models can be used to combat the negative stereotypes or break gender norms that young women have previously been exposed to by society. Another major component of developing a science identity is to visualize yourself in the occupation. Visualization is very important, especially when looking for role models, and has been identified as a successful recruitment and retention tool for girls and women in STEAM disciplines. (Rosenthal et al., 2011). The exposure to role models, if not obtained directly, can be achieved visually through television, movies, books, or other media platforms. STEAM role models can also be established by having female scientists, engineers, artists, et cetera visit the classroom to tell their STEAM story.

Television

There are very few animated television programs that reflect the diversity in America. One of the first to explore the phenomenon was Disney's Dottie "Doc" McStuffins in 2012. This television show was centered on a six-year-old Black girl who wanted to be a doctor like her mother (Ashby, 2012). Doc McStuffins has many patients, including Stuffy the Dragon, Lambie, Hallie the Nurse, and Chilly the Snowman. The show inspires children to work through their problems while utilizing critical thinking and resources at hand. A large emphasis is placed on personal healthy body habits. Many reviewers including parents were excited about the diversity and inclusivity the show has brought, including highlighting a young Black girl who wants to be a doctor like her mother. Gary Marsh, president and chief creative officer of Disney Channels Worldwide said, "What we put on TV can change how kids see the world, and that is a responsibility that I take very seriously" (Barnes, 2012).

Cinema

As is the case with television, there are very few African American female STEAM characters in cinema. The 2018 blockbuster *Black Panther* introduced the world to the fictional Shuri, a smart and gifted young woman who has faced adversity for her intellect but has utilized it to advance her nation with the use of several STEAM disciplines. In the movie, Guyanese actress Letitia Wright portrayed Shuri. Wright is only 24 years of age, which has allowed even younger girls to visually identify with her. Shuri has a genius-level intellect and is one of the smartest humans in the world. Shuri is also a gifted engineer, having designed "Wakanda's technology arsenal, including weaponry, defenses, communication, and transportation" ("Shuri," n.d.).

The film *A Wrinkle in Time* introduced Meg Murry, a young Black girl who was able to wrinkle time by utilizing mathematical calculations and physics to rescue her father (Berman, 2017). Murry's father is a scientist who disappeared while studying astrophysics and was teleported to another world after solving a question about the existence of humanity. The movie—adapted by Disney in 2018—was based upon a book written by Madeleine L'Engle in 1962. Ava DuVernay, a notable African American female director, directed the movie. DuVernay understood the importance of diversity in Hollywood; therefore, she intentionally decided to cast a Black lead with a Black mother in this adventure movie that features science. Each of these movies, books, and shows is important to increase the visibility of African American girls in STEAM careers and lifestyles. These media can be used to combat stereotypes and influence science identities for young girls inside the classroom.

Conclusion

America has a long road ahead in terms of advancing minoritized populations in all forms of media from television to movies. However, many networks, manufacturers, and authors are making great strides towards highlighting the significance and contributions of African Americans to American history, particularly concerning STEAM innovations. The acknowledgment and visual displaying of these animated characters or real-life pioneers have enabled many young Black girls to visualize and dream of occupations never once imagined. Also, the educational sector must continue to help underrepresented minorities— and particularly Black women—establish a science identity early by providing quality STEAM-based courses rich in science and math. With diligence and a commitment to overcoming barriers, this will ensure there are future generations of Black girls with a fully developed science identity who are engineers, mathematicians, and computer scientists.

Activities for Teachers

1. Develop project-based learning (PBL) lessons by researching educational standards in your state for each grade level. PBL activities can be modified into STEAM Day celebrations or STEAM research symposiums/science fairs. Projects could include robotics team development (Lego League) and computer programming.

2. Design STEAM-based activities, including those centered upon "Bodies: The Exhibition," aquariums and marine biology, and the 4-H STEAM lab. Each of the activities has lesson plans adapted from their websites ("Bodies," 2019; National 4-H Council, n.d.).

3. Multimedia case studies and worksheets are available online for each book and movie title mentioned in this chapter. Use one of these with your class to have an in-depth discussion about the characters and how their work influenced society. Titles include *Hidden Figures, Gifted Hands, Something the Lord Made, The Immortal Life of Henrietta Lacks, Black Panther, Red Tails, Raising Dion, See You Yesterday,* and *A Wrinkle in Time.*]

Multimedia Case Studies Resource Guide

Hidden Figures: https:// techbridgegirls.org/assets/files/ what/publications/Discussion GuideforHiddenFigures.pdf

Gifted Hands: https://quizlet .com/252942463/gifted-hands- quiz-questions-flash-cards/

Something the Lord Made: http://teachwithmovies.org/ partners-of-the-heart/

https://quizlet.com/ 137469757/something-the- lord-made-flash-cards/

The Immortal Life of Henrietta Lacks: http://rebeccaskloot .com/the-immortal-life/ reading-group/

Black Panther: https:// static1.squarespace.com/

static/58b3bac83e00bef9f44
9565c/t/5acedfbe758d
4676cbd647b9/1523507
139967/STEM+and+Black+
Panther+Teacher+Guide.pdf

Red Tails: https://images
.history.com/images/media/
pdf/Double_Victory_FIN.pdf

Raising Dion: None (create
your own)

See You Yesterday: None
(create your own)

A Wrinkle in Time: https://
www.teacherspayteachers
.com/Browse/Search:a%20
wrinkle%20in%20time%20pre

https://www.weareteachers
.com/a-wrinkle-in-time-
activities/]

4. Have a vision board STEAM career
party: Students will leave this
activity having completed a STEAM
vision board detailing their specific
journey to their particular career,
and having identified notable
women from their chosen fields.
They should include S.M.A.R.T.
goals, role models, salary, degree
programs, college admissions,

inspiring quotes, and encouraging
messages. Vision Boards are "a
collage of pictures, text, and other
items that represent and affirm
one's dreams and ambitions,
created to help visualize and focus
on one or more specific aspirations"
(Rock Holdings, n.d.).

5. Questions for further discussion for
your class and/or for yourself

- Why do so few Black girls aspire
to have careers in STEAM?

- What barriers or catalysts are
present when African American
girls are matriculating in schools
that involve the STEAM
academic pipeline?

- How do we define Black girls'
STEAM identity?

- What role do digital media—
including but not limited to
social media, film, television,
and books—play in the
development of Black girls'
STEAM identity?

- What role can I play in ensuring
more Black girls become
interested in STEAM careers
and degrees?

GLOSSARY

STEAM—science, technology, engineering, art, and math (Hom, 2014)

Science Identity—Is related to students' interests in science, their matriculation in
science courses and programs, their desire to pursue a science career, and even the
choice to enter and graduate from a science program. (Lee, 1998; Merolla & Serpe,
2013; Merolla et al., 2012)

Underrepresented Minority—This category comprises three racial or ethnic
minoritized groups (Blacks, Hispanics/Latinx, and American Indians or Alaska

Natives) whose representation in science and engineering education and employment is smaller than their representation in the U.S. population (National Science Foundation, 2017).

SLAY, by Brittney Morris

Grade Level 7–12

Contemporary Realistic Fiction

Book Review by Marguerite W. Penick

To read a story about Black Girl Magic is to read *SLAY.* Kiera is one of four Black students in her predominately white school. She tutors math, she codes, and she is the creator of SLAY, a video game she started to create a safe space where she could be herself, she could be Black, and she did not have to explain, defend, or pretend at every corner. Those who enter SLAY become surrounded by Black history and culture, and as Kiera describes the world when in the arena, "an orchestra of Black magnificence." Racism swirls throughout the book, from outsiders who call it racist to white "experts" who assume because the game is only for Black people that the youth who are "most likely to identify with it are underprivileged kids from low-income families in impoverished areas." An unexpected tragedy throws fuel on the fire as Kiera and the kings and queens of SLAY duel for a world of beauty, acceptance, strength, and pride for the history and resilience of the Black community.

Vignette: Did I Even Matter?

Simone Sinclair Robins

I was in fourth grade. At the time, the class was going over a unit on slavery all around the world. We went through Roman slavery, slavery of Canaanites, and even current-day slavery in our country. One thing that I found odd was that chattel slavery was never mentioned. In a moment of curiosity, I scoured through my textbook to find a portion about it . . . labeled as "forced emigration." At the age of eight, I had never felt such profound feelings of confusion and even anger. I raised my hand as quietly as I could and asked, "Why isn't Black slavery in the book?" The teacher stared at me, and we exchanged an awkward moment of silence. Flustered, she tried to continue the lesson. That only made me more frustrated. I shouted, "Tell me about Black slavery! Where is it!?"

The classroom fell silent as everyone turned to me, eyes wide and mouths agape. The teacher gently set her textbook on the podium. I still remember the look on her face, and it gives me chills. In the coldest tone I had ever heard, she told me to wait outside of the classroom. I obeyed and collected my things. After waiting outside for what felt like an hour, I saw her step out of the classroom. She still had her face from earlier. This was our exchange:

"Simone, do you know why I took you out of the class?"

"Yes, ma'am. It was because I interrupted."

She proceeded to hand me the textbook, but it had a bookmark. The teacher had given me the page number and I turned to it, only to see the page I had turned to earlier. I was so confused. I looked up to the teacher and asked, "But, ma'am . . . black slavery wasn't forced emigration?"

She replied, "It is what the book says; therefore it's what I will teach."

The woman then leaned down to me, eye level.

"What you did in the classroom was very disruptive and disrespectful. Not only were you rude to interrupt the lesson, but you also distracted your classmates from learning. Don't make me take you out of the classroom again, or I *will* send you to the principal's office, and he will tell your mother about your bad behavior. Do you understand me?"

Now, years later, I know that I did nothing wrong. But as an eight-year-old girl, the intimidation of being sent to the principal's office was enough for me to almost cry. I nodded, trying to keep my tears in. The teacher's bright, warm smile returned to her face as she patted her hand on my shoulder.

"Okay! I'm glad you understand."

For the rest of that day, I sat at my desk, powerless as all get out. I felt like the tower of confidence and strength in me was reduced to a pile of rubble. My legs weren't legs, they were moving pillars of lead. My eyes were no longer eyes, they were dams holding back violent torrents of tears. I didn't look at the teacher the same way anymore, nor did I respect her as a confidant. She was merely an authority figure to me. The moment school ended, I didn't stay a moment longer. When I saw my mom driving down the pickup line, I hopped into the car and started bawling. She asked me what was wrong, and I blubbered everything on the ride home. If you had seen her yourself, there could've been steam spewing from her bejeweled ears. I don't remember what happened in school after that, other than how numb I felt, how little I ate or drank, or how long I stared at the ground during recess.

The previous vignette highlights what happens to a Black girl when she feels invisible and how quickly she will disengage thereafter. Robins shows us how one seemingly mild incident casts a shadow on the future of a Black girl's educational career. The following chapter by Dr. Ashleigh Greene Wade showcases how a teacher can curate classrooms using new media literacies for Black girls. If language is the key transmitter to dialogue, teachers must acknowledge new literacies, specifically in the wake of #BlackLivesMatter. Today's students communicate with one another on a much deeper level than youth of yesterday, routinely using multiple modalities including hashtags, emojis, and text talk. However, adding social media to curated classrooms as new media presents its own set of challenges with ethical and privacy considerations, as Wade shows. The subsequent chapter by Dr. Valerie Adams-Bass discusses what happens when these ethical and privacy considerations are strictly institutional and fail at being culturally relevant. In the following section, the authors show how teachers can work through individual and systemic concerns affecting Black girls, with regard to introducing new literacies into the classroom.

CHAPTER 45

Developing an Ethic of Engaging Black Girls in Digital Spaces

Ashleigh Greene Wade

As the field of Black girlhood studies continues to grow, there will be an expansion of research and pedagogical approaches to working with Black girls. While these developments will be essential to responding to the diversity of Black girlhood(s), we must always remember that working with Black girls, or any marginalized group, requires an intentionally ethical approach. Developing an ethics of engaging Black girls, whether through scholarship, pedagogy, or both, requires a level of self-reflexivity that allows researchers and educational practitioners to fully acknowledge the complexities of Black girlhood. One unique thing about working with Black girls in this moment of digital proliferation is having the option to combine visual and discursive analysis with ethnography. While Black girls' digital media content presents new ways to approach the study of Black girlhood, engaging Black girls in digital contexts also presents a number of ethical challenges. While it is important to acknowledge power discrepancies in all areas of teaching and research, the need becomes even more pronounced when teaching and collaborating with Black girls who often experience their environments as hostile in ways that their male and non-Black counterparts do not (Crenshaw et al., 2014). The following essay offers some observations from working with Black girls in digital spaces. I explain the ethical considerations of doing work with Black girls, especially in digital contexts, and argue that developing an ethical approach to engaging Black girls is not only a necessary component of researching and teaching Black girls but also a form of protecting Black girls.

The story of how I started studying Black girls' digital practices starts with a tale of two schools: one public, one private; one coed, one single-sex; both environments where Black girls felt invisible. After finishing my undergraduate studies, I began working as a high school English teacher at a public school in a small town. I had no formal training in teacher education, and my passion to make a difference in students' lives was met with overcrowded classrooms, an abysmal lack of resources, and administrative corruption. The student population was majority Black and majority low income. Additionally, a significant number of students in each class had individualized education programs (IEPs), and most of the students that I taught were far below grade level in reading and writing. While many of the students in this school faced unfair stereotyping regardless of gender, the extent to which principals and teachers saw certain Black girls as a lost cause stood out to me. To combat the blatant dismissal of Black girls, I made sure that the Black girls I taught knew that I saw them as human but that I also saw them as children worthy of grace and compassion.

In some ways, my second high school teaching position seemed like the direct opposite of the first one. This time, I was at a predominantly white, independent, all-girls' school. On the surface, this school had more resources, but these resources did not do much to mitigate Black girls' invisibility. During my first semester at this school, my basement classroom quickly became a "hush harbor" of sorts, where Black girls—many of whom were not even enrolled in my classes—would come in, shut the door, and begin telling me about everything from quibbles they'd had with peers to subtle (or not-so-subtle in some cases) racism exhibited by their teachers or other school personnel. These conversations happened during the same time I sat on two diversity committees at the school. On both committees, members talked about how committed they were to inclusion, but there was a huge disconnection between how we said we were serving all girls and the experiences I heard about from Black girls.

This discrepancy led me to realize one thing that the two schools had in common: They were ignoring the plights of Black girls. In the public school, the Black girls were labeled trouble makers, dismissed as attitudinal, and written off by adults if they transgressed social norms. In the private school, Black girls were seen and not heard. This realization both solidified my commitment to making Black girls' lives better and led me to study Black girls' digital practices, because I wanted to learn more about how (or if) digital spaces might be providing Black girls with places where they could be themselves unapologetically.

One of the first ethical decisions researchers and practitioners have to make in their digital work with Black girls has to do with issues of privacy. On the one hand, nothing on the Internet is truly private; even the "deep web" or "dark web" can be accessed with the right skillset. At the same time, the social media platforms that are popular among Black girls allow for adjustments in privacy settings. These applications give users the option to set their accounts to private or public. For accounts that are private, people have to request to follow the account. This feature allows the account holder to approve or deny such requests, thus offering a little more control over who can see what they post. For accounts that are public, anyone with the screenname can look up the person and look at the content on their account. Each of these platforms also offers an extra layer of privacy in the form of messaging, so even if you can see a person's account, you can't see the messages that they exchange with others. Snapchat, for example, allows users to maintain a story that all of their followers can see but also allows users to send stories, or snaps, to specific individuals.

In my research, I mostly use social media accounts that are available publicly, but what does "public" mean to a teenager or tween? When using public social accounts to learn about and engage Black girls, there are still obligations to protect their identities. For me, the first step in doing this involves having a conversation with Black girls about their social media. I ask them questions about their motivations for posting what they do, and what they want others to learn about them through interacting with their social media. I also ask for permission to use content from their accounts in publications or presentations. However, even in instances where I receive permission, I am careful about which images I choose. While their accounts are public, social media applications allow users to change their privacy settings at any time. Therefore, I would not want to have images of Black girls circulating in the form of publications or presentations after they have changed the privacy settings on their accounts. This is an example of an ethical decision that goes beyond the requirements of the institutional review board (IRB).

Another ethical challenge that presents itself in research involving Black girls is the power differential. While this problem tends to be relevant to most research involving human participants, the power discrepancy becomes intensified when working with Black girls. For one, there is a power discrepancy between children and adults. In most situations, adults have more authority than children based on age alone. Another power differential exists between teacher and student. Teachers have the power to influence a student's educational trajectory. I experienced both of these challenges simultaneously through participant observation. For part of my research, I spent some time volunteer teaching at a high school. During this time, students were my research participants, but I also had to assign them a grade and adhere to classroom management standards. Diffusing power discrepancies helped me to do both of these things without compromising my ethical standards or the educational quality of my course.

As Moya Bailey (2015) points out, the IRB does recognize children as a vulnerable population that might be especially susceptible to unethical research practices; however, when working with marginalized groups, we must expand our ethical considerations beyond those of the IRB. Bailey goes on to describe establishing a collaborative relationship with research participants rather than a paternalistic one. Allowing the students to take ownership of the course motivated them to do the work that was required from the school's perspective. This type of collaborative approach is necessary in doing work with Black girls, because it acknowledges that Black girls are the experts of their own lives (Brown, 2012), and it places Black girls' voices/ideas at the center of the research. Before I started working on my research, several senior scholars suggested that I would have a hard time completing it, because I would have a hard time getting Black girls to open up to me. By explaining to Black girls that they were not my research "subjects" but instead my collaborators, I was able to not only conduct ethical research, but also develop Black girls' interest in the work. In several conversations with Black girls, some of them would thank me for listening to them (because most adults in their lives don't) and for wanting to share their stories.

One of the positive things about my experiences researching Black girls' digital practices is that the girls who decided to collaborate with me were very open and generous with their time and information. But part of being collaborators means maintaining the trust of the people/communities with whom you are in collaboration. Everything about Black girls' lives is not meant to be knowable, and those of us doing research on Black girls have to contend with and respect what Audra Simpson (2014) describes as *ethnographic refusal,* a term that she uses to describe an "anthropological limit" that "tell[s] us when to stop" (p. 113). Simpson theorizes this concept through a discussion of how her research participants avoided certain topics of conversation.

While Simpson's articulation of ethnographic refusal mainly focuses on research participants, I think we also have to engage in a level of ethnographic refusal as researchers and practitioners by not only accepting what is unknowable about Black girls but also by not disclosing everything that we *do know* about them. Many of the Black girls I have encountered in my research have cultivated their own digital spaces where they can play, laugh, talk, and just plain be themselves without the scrutiny of adults—and not just random adults, but adults who have direct influence on their material realities (parents, adult guardians, teachers, school personnel). Because Black girls' relationship to space is often fraught with hostility, it is important to use extreme care when Black girls permit us to enter these spaces with them. Working with Black girls, especially in digital spaces, means maintaining balance between the scholarly impulse to find out what you don't know and the ethical obligation to protect the privacy and sacredness of the spaces that Black girls create for themselves.

Ultimately, the most ethically sound approach to scholarship and pedagogy that engages Black girls has to begin with the premise that Black girls' subjectivities extend far beyond their roles as students. While it is important to understand and apply Black girls' digital literacies to classroom contexts, it is equally important to remember that part of creating culturally relevant curriculum involves protecting spaces that Black girls have created for themselves. To paraphrase singer Solange Knowles: Some stuff is just for Black girls. While our natural inclination as teachers and learners is to seek knowledge, we have to understand the limits of what is knowable about Black girls. Not only do we have to understand these limits, we have an ethical responsibility to accept them.

CHAPTER 46

A Matter of Media

Cultural Appropriation and Expectations of Black Girls

Valerie N. Adams-Bass

During one of the years that I served as a CDF (Children's Defense Fund) Freedom School site codirector, my non-Black colleague suggested that we have the children sing R. Kelly's *I Believe I Can Fly* as a feature of our Freedom School finale. I adamantly disagreed with my colleague, whose voice was beautiful—no competition from me—I love music, but I am not a song-stress. CDF Freedom Schools are modeled on the Freedom Summer Freedom Schools offered by SNCC (Student Nonviolent Coordinating Committee) during the civil rights movement. Music was indeed a significant part of the civil rights movement.

As we prepared for our finale, she pressed for the scholars to sing the song. "The kids love it, it is motivating, let's sing it." My refusal to have the children sing Kelly's song was directly related to his reputation within the Black community of being a pedophile. A trial was occurring near this time. In an attempt to help her understand why my no was a NO, I provided her with this background information. She readily dismissed the additional context and pressed for this song to be the feature of our finale. We did not agree about R. Kelly, but we did not sing this song.

Fast forward, years later, R. Kelly's behavior, practices, and sexual relationships with underage girls is now national news. I share this story because context matters. What message would we have communicated to Black girls about their value if we chose to sing an R. Kelly song? And why was my colleague unable to hear my resistance?

This piece is directed at helping educators develop their cultural literacy, which requires more than *knowing* what kids like, listen to, or watch. Cultural literacy and critical [racial] media literacy require being able to engage with children and youth and even to challenge them to be critical consumers. In challenging your students, you are not correcting or penalizing them, but you are encouraging them to take in messages that are affirming—and to be aware of all the anti-Black messages they might be fed, even by artists who are Black.

Sometimes, in an attempt to relate to Black girls, teachers will draw a comparison between the behavior of Black adult female artists and that of the preteen and teenage girls in their classrooms (Hall & Smith, 2012; Neal-Jackson, 2018). Others will elect to play music from an artist who is controversial within the Black community. This chapter is going to help teachers better understand some of the complex dynamics of Black people and the media, including blaxploitation and beauty standards. Not all media that is commonly consumed by Black youth is necessarily good for them. I will close with what educators can do to better help themselves—and their students—navigate these dynamics in a way that helps Black girls thrive.

MEDIA SOCIALIZATION

Media is widely accepted as a socializing agent. *Media socialization* is defined as the exposure to mass communication (television, radio, internet, newspapers) messages, which teach people socially accepted behaviors that have (a) a direct influence on cognitive ability and behavioral functioning, and (b) a mediating or facilitative indirect influence on learning (Adams & Stevenson, 2012). Media socialization is the foundation for how youth come to develop static or stereotypic representations of themselves and others. Think of it as a dynamic process where you are both consuming and processing what you are viewing, reading, or hearing.

Over the past decade images of Black women and girls have increased in mainstream media, as Black actors and musicians have been elevated to pop artists as a result of their ability to bring in high earnings. Cross-over status—Black artists who are marketed to mainstream audiences—is correlated with the highest earners. Contemporary media images include ratchet representations of Black women and white women who commodify aesthetics that are a norm in the Black community (Bentley-Edwards & Adams-Bass, in press). As Black girls learn to move through a society that often views them as problematic, media presents another layer of messaging that Black girls must learn to navigate and interpret (Adams-Bass & Bentley-Edwards, 2020; Hall & Smith, 2012).

For example, the main character of the ABC prime-time drama *Scandal,* Olivia Pope, was played by African American actress Kerri Washington. As the main character, she is surrounded by a multicultural cast of supporting actors and actresses. Olivia Pope was touted as a "bold new take" and an example of a Black professional woman on a prime-time series. In spite of this, Washington's performance often included a storyline about Pope's personal life that presented her at the intersection of the Sapphire and the Jezebel (Bogle, 2016; Jackson 2006) or the Thug Mrs. (Jackson, 2006). What are the actual power dynamics represented by *Scandal*? What messages are communicated to viewers, especially to Black girls? Mims's 2019 work describes the way Black girls reference and relate to Black female artists as models for motivation, coping, and navigating challenging situations. Countering these images is a challenge when Black children [girls] encounter people that are exposed to this type of media content without cultural context, who endorse these images as representative of Black people (Adams-Bass & Henrici, 2019).

BLACK GIRLS AS CHILDREN

Spencer's theory of human development, the phenomenological theory of ecological systems (PVEST), is a theory that provides an opportunity to map the protective factors and vulnerability Black children [girls] experience. In short, Black children are frequently tasked with developing healthy, positive emergent identities as part of adolescence by navigating around conflicting messages received from media, family, friends, and teachers, along with interpreting racialized experiences and developing necessary coping strategies (Spencer, 1995; Spencer et al., 1996; Swanson et al., 2009). Black girls' developmental experiences are compounded by racial and gender bias, wherein negative racial biases against Black people and females intersect and shape their educational experiences. As teachers, you have the potential to serve as a protective factor that provides opportunities for reshaping their school experience and stories.

REALITY TELEVISION, IS IT REAL?

Much of the human experience relies on storytelling. Critical media literacy (CML) involves identifying the storyteller—behind the media and the associated messages (Kellner & Share; 2007b; Orlowski, 2006). Commercialized and privately owned content often infiltrates the public domain through various types of media. Television and advertising has become a primary source of information and socialization. Reality television shows targeting Black audiences catapulted to the Number 1 genre for youth ages 16–25 with the introduction of *Flava of Love*. Although bachelorette/bachelor-type reality shows are no longer the primary headliner of Black reality shows, distorted depictions of Black women remain a staple of this genre. For example, the *Real Housewives of Atlanta* features a majority cast of Black women who regularly dismiss and denigrate one another. Cardi B is an alumnus of *Love & Hip-Hop*. Educators of Black girls should know these shows are contemporary blaxploitation-exaggerated images of Black men and women that glorify drug dealing, sexual promiscuity, and violence (Sims, 2020).

Comparing Black girls to these images diminishes their childhood by interpreting their behaviors through an adult lens (Adams-Bass & Bentley Edwards, 2020).

It is a good idea to be tuned into the media Black girls are consuming. Black female performance artists such as Beyoncé, Nikki Minaj, and Lizzo are being mainstreamed. Unfortunately, for many, these adult women become references for relating to Black girls. Listening to a Black artist who has music on the Top 40 or watching their videos does not guarantee an understanding of how Black girls relate to these artists, or that you have the ability to relate to the girls via your familiarity with these artists. Without a set of CML skills, you may reinforce stereotypes these girls need assistance countering. Black girls likely appreciate that you're able to recognize the contemporary artists they enjoy and that you too may enjoy these artists, and an awareness of what they are "into" provides a common ground from which to build a conversation. My experience is not to cut off access or conversation about what shows they are viewing or music they are listening to because of the content, but to be selective about media you allow in your classroom. Have a discussion about the artist. When having a conversation about Lizzo, include discussion about body image ideals. You could also speak with students about which Black women are considered acceptable as role models and how they are presented in the media. The ability to relate to your students in this way is an opportunity to develop a discourse with them that may lead to a better relationship and improved lesson plans that are informed by your students who are willing to learn.

BEAUTY AND THE TWEET

With social media platforms like Instagram, Snapchat, TikTok and Twitter, teenagers receive messages that range from body positive and social support to those that produce anxiety to achieve and maintain status with sexualized images. For example, the popularity of white women like the Kardashian sisters and other non-Black women adopting body types traditionally reserved for Black women is a phenomenon Black girls are witnessing. Black girls are responding to messages that simultaneously devalue and adultify their aesthetics while celebrating non-Black women who have bought these features (Adams-Bass & Bentley-Edwards, 2020; Bentley-Edwards & Adams-Bass, in press).

Modern images of beauty evolved from the historical ideals of womanhood; women are envisioned as white, meek, quiet, and slim (Hill, 2001). African American daughters receive messages about body image and self-esteem that are framed by the reality that beauty standards and roles traditionally relegated to white women do not apply to them (Adams-Bass et al., 2014; Buckley & Carter, 2005; Hill, 2001, 2002; Sanders & Bradley, 2005). Black women are more likely to resist mainstream messages of beauty and instead rely on their cultural group's standards of beauty, or more recently, the hip-hop aesthetic, and are passing these perspectives on to their children (Hesse-Biber et al., 2004; Hill, 2001, 2002; Stephens & Phillips, 2005; Yasui et al., 2004). There are body and gender politics Black girls must manage as they experience puberty. The commodification of Black beauty standards adds an additional layer of messaging to be decoded and understood (Bentley-Edwards & Adams-Bass, in press).

CRITICAL MEDIA LITERACY

One way to help students navigate these contradictory messages is to develop CML skills for yourself and with your students. Media literacy is defined as a series of communication competencies, including the ability to access, analyze, evaluate, and communicate (National Association for Media Literacy Education, 2007). CML includes the politics of representation of gender, race, class, and sexuality, as well as a critical understanding of ideology, power, and domination that are absent from definitions of media literacy.

Media and the public education system are the two main sources of information in our society (Orlowski, 2006). Many media outlets are now owned by large conglomerates whose main concern is financial gain. Most companies do not take risks or support the production of stories that offer positive and/or nuanced perspectives of Black artists (Balaji, 2009). Using CML within classrooms, educators have the opportunity to provide a space that allows for counternarratives against the traditionally white hegemonic mainstream media (Orlowski, 2006).

CML helps teachers and students understand how power and media are linked through the lenses of message deconstruction and alternative media production (Kellner & Share, 2007a). This approach also integrates ideas from multicultural, intersectional, feminist, and postmodern theories (Kellner & Share, 2007b). Alvermann & Hagood (2000) also posit that the concepts of audience and popular culture are core when it comes to definitions of CML.

As an educator, attempting to connect with young people, especially girls, through media means becoming culturally and media literate. Do your homework. Really listen to your Black colleagues who offer insight and—as I tried to offer to my colleague—an insider perspective. Listen to the girls; really listen to their spoken and unspoken communication. A number of Black children are able to appreciate and critique an artist. For example, some students like Lil Wayne's music but critique statements he has made about darker-skinned Black women (King, 2011). An awareness of this kind of discourse will help to guide your decision about the music you permit in your classroom and the discussions you have with students about an artist. R. Kelly writes music enjoyed by many, but what message would you be communicating to Black girls about their worth if you play his music in your classroom? If you choose to play his music, what discussion will you have about his behavior with Black girls? It may be one more thing you'll need to do, but your willingness to make the effort to educate yourself on how to interpret media, and the persona of artists young people are tuned into, provides an opportunity for you to become a source of support and will help you to honor the Black girls you teach.

Cultural literacy requires you to take time to learn more about Black girls' (and women's) experiences and the profiles of the performance artists you select as your connector. Do more than find out what or who is "in." Situating audiences and media within a social-historical framework helps to understand media content and the impact of messages within specific populations and cultures. Students appreciate your ability to do the latest dance or recite the lyrics to their favorite song or know the names of their favorite on-screen characters. Using media as a tool to connect with youth is a practical option, but there is a need for you to be culturally and media literate.

CML allows you to ask questions and make conscious decisions about what artists you feature or which of their songs, quotes, or images you integrate or introduce in your classroom. As you learn about the artists and context, I suggest that you expand your classroom by integrating what you learn into your own lesson plans.

Social media can be a resource for you to learn about what is trending for Black girls and a CML tool that you can bring into your classroom. As an educator, by equipping yourself with cultural and CML skills, you will be able to create lessons and engage in conversations with Black girls that increase their protective factors and provide opportunities for them to develop and practice adaptive coping skills, as well as develop counternarratives that protect their individual and group identities and contribute to a healthy self-concept, esteem, and academic engagement.

INCREASING YOUR LITERACY

The ability or willingness to critically engage or question media images is low for non-Black consumers who have no or limited encounters with Black people. Choose a contemporary Black female artist-actress or musician. Follow them on social media and create an alert for this artist. What are you learning? What can you integrate into your classroom and lessons from what you've learned?

Reflection

Who was your favorite artist or favorite TV show and why? What feelings emerged as part of this reflection? How will this help you connect with your students?

Complete this sentence: Black girls are _____. What did you say or write? Why? What influenced your statement? How does this influence your interaction with Black girls in your classroom?

Black girls move daily throughout multiple systems that seek to murder their spirits. Yet they are able to maintain a sense of #BlackGirlMagic, or the ability of a Black girl to transcend her race and gender—which lead to her oppression in a white supremacist society—and use those same identifiers to magically dismantle that same system through the cultivation of deep relationships, the pursuit of excellence, and just enough attitude. As Drs. Anderson and Coleman-King instruct teachers how to "Catch This Magic" in the next chapter, consider the multiple, distinct, and divergent Black girl identities presented in this text; consider how your institution has gotten in the way of gifted Black girls. Next, decide what you will do to help reverse this phenomenon. In the words of actor Jesse Williams, "Just because it's magic doesn't mean it's not real."

CHAPTER 47

"Catch This Magic"

How Schools Get in the Way of Gifted Black Girls

Brittany N. Anderson, Chonika Coleman-King

The problem with identifying gifted Black girls is that teachers don't believe we exist. I have many memories of my experiences in K–12 public schools, but one of my most striking memories is of an experience I had in the fourth grade. My teacher asked the class to write a report. I don't remember having a close relationship with this teacher, or many others for that matter, but I do remember how hard I had worked on my report with the support of my mother. Our family had several sets of encyclopedias in our home at the time—at that time, it was the closest you could come to having your own research library at your fingertips. I sat down with our encyclopedias and my mom to write my report. My mom was careful to ensure that I relayed information in my own words. However, when I read my report aloud in class, my teacher chastised me for cheating. She said I had plagiarized the assignment and that it was not my own work. I cried. I told her that my mom had helped me, but that it was my work. The memory stopped there. When gifted Black girls excel, their intellectual curiosity and academic astuteness are often met with suspicion and hostility rather than support.

FRAMING THE INTERSECTIONS OF BLACK GIRLS AND GIFTEDNESS

As gifted-identified Black women, we position this work from our own experiences as gifted-identified students, and also from our experiences as classroom teachers. We encourage you to let Black girls' "voices and actions form the basis of what [they] call 'Black girlhood'" and gifted "in the context of doing and learning"

(Gholson & Martin, 2014, p. 19). As it pertains to gifted Black Girls, it is imperative educators enact an antiracist, intersectional, and asset-based approach.

In education, the experiences of Black girls and women stand at the paradoxical juxtaposition between oppression and achievement. In current research and theoretical models that address racial inequity and/or gender disparities in gifted education, there is a missing narrative around gifted-identified/high-achieving Black girls as well as their disproportionate underrepresentation in gifted programming, services, and advanced placement (AP) courses (Anderson & Martin, 2018; Evans-Winters, 2014; Harper & Anderson, 2020). Centering intersectionality (Crenshaw, 1991), there must be more attention focused on the missing narrative of Black girls in gifted education, especially regarding their identification for gifted programs and services, talent development in classes, cocurricular activities, out-of-school-time programs, and home-school connections.

Significant research shows how minoritized students have been underreferred by teachers for gifted programs and services (Ford, 1998; Ford et al., 2008; Grissom & Redding, 2016; McBee, 2006). Due to issues of underrepresentation and school marginalization, in 2011, only 10.8 percent of Black girls in the United States were identified as gifted and talented, as compared to 57.3 percent of White girls (Civil Rights Data Collection, 2013). External barriers associated with being a gifted Black girl are difficult to overcome, particularly when conflated with internal identity development issues and sociopolitical barriers, such as culturally incompetent educators, imposter syndrome, and stereotype threat (Anderson & Martin, 2018). Additionally, some gifted Black girls may be unable to relate to peers and teachers in gifted classes and, in turn, will be susceptible to discriminatory, racist, sexist messages, both intentional and unintentional (Ford, 2011, 2013).

In these educational environments, Black girls are consistently exposed to stereotypes about Black inferiority and, therefore, may have lower self-concepts and self-esteem (Greene, 2016; Maxwell, 2007). Despite the potential onslaught of negative stereotypes, several studies have found that academically resilient Black girls adopt a strong positive identity (Evans, 2015; Evans-Winters, 2014; Henry, 1998; O'Connor, 1997). Without adequate success strategies to navigate the nuances of being a gifted Black girl in K–12 classrooms, however, many Black girls enter postsecondary education struggling with socioemotional and identity development issues and battling the nonaffirming cultural norms of an institution (Anderson & Martin, 2018).

Practical Tips for Talent Identification and Talent Development of Gifted Black Girls

Gifted education researcher and equity advocate Mary Frasier (1997) developed a framework called F-TAP (Frasier—Talent Assessment Profile) and tools for identifying and developing the talents of minoritized students. We utilize the *Four A's framework—attitude, access, assessment,* and *accommodations* (what we are calling *adaptations*) and the *traits, aptitudes, and behaviors scale* (TABS) observation tool as a means of identifying gifted Black girls. Both the framework and scale (Table 47.1) are used as points of assessment to create an identification profile for students.

TABLE 47.1 Frasier's Traits, Aptitudes, and Behaviors (TABS) Observation Tool (Frasier et al., 1995)

Guide: This is a guide for observing students in your classroom. As they show evidence of potential, make anecdotal notes about the interactions.

MOTIVATION	INTERESTS	COMMUNICATION SKILLS	PROBLEM-SOLVING ABILITY	MEMORY
EVIDENCE OF DESIRE TO LEARN	A FEELING OF INTENTNESS, PASSION, CONCERN OR CURIOSITY ABOUT SOMETHING	HIGHLY EXPRESSIVE AND EFFECTIVE USE OF WORDS, NUMBERS, AND SYMBOLS	EFFECTIVE, OFTEN INVENTIVE, STRATEGIES FOR RECOGNIZING AND SOLVING PROBLEMS	LARGE STOREHOUSE OF INFORMATION ON SCHOOL OR NON-SCHOOL TOPICS
Forces that initiate, direct and sustain individual or group behavior in order to satisfy a need or attain a goal. Students may: • strongly aspire to be somebody, do something extraordinary. • be an enthusiastic learner. • demonstrate persistence in pursuing or completing self-selected tasks (may be culturally influenced; evident in school or non-school activities).	Activities, avocations, objects, etc., that have special worth or significance and are given special attention. Students may: • demonstrate unusual or advanced interests in a topic or activity. • be a self-starter. • be beyond age-group. • pursue activity unceasingly.	Transmission and reception of signal or meanings through a system of symbols (codes, gestures, language, numbers). Students may: • demonstrate unusual ability to communicate (verbally, physically, artistically, symbolically). • use particularly apt examples, illustrations or elaborations.	Process of determining a correct sequence of alternatives leading to a desired goal or to successful completion or performance of a task. Students may: • demonstrate unusual ability to devise or adapt a systemic strategy for solving problems and to change the strategy if it is not working. • create new designs, invent.	Exceptional ability to retain and retrieve information. Students may: • already know information. • need only 1-2 repetitions for mastery. • have a wealth of information about school or non-school topics. • pay attention to details. • easily manipulate information. • be highly curious.
Inquiry Questions, experiments, explores	**Insight** Quickly grasps new concepts and makes connections; senses deeper meanings.	**Reasoning** Logical approaches to figuring out solutions.	**Imagination/Creativity** Produces many ideas; highly original	**Humor** Brings two unrelated ideas or planes of thought together in a recognized relationship

444

(Continued)

MOTIVATION EVIDENCE OF DESIRE TO LEARN	INTERESTS A FEELING OF INTENTNESS, PASSION, CONCERN OR CURIOSITY ABOUT SOMETHING	COMMUNICATION SKILLS HIGHLY EXPRESSIVE AND EFFECTIVE USE OF WORDS, NUMBERS, AND SYMBOLS	PROBLEM-SOLVING ABILITY EFFECTIVE, OFTEN INVENTIVE, STRATEGIES FOR RECOGNIZING AND SOLVING PROBLEMS	MEMORY LARGE STOREHOUSE OF INFORMATION ON SCHOOL OR NON-SCHOOL TOPICS
Method or process of seeking knowledge, understanding of information. Students may: • ask unusual questions for age. • play around with ideas. • demonstrate extensive exploratory behaviors directed toward eliciting information about materials, devices or situations.	Sudden discovery of the correct solution following incorrect attempts based primarily on trial and error. Students may: • demonstrate exceptional ability to draw inferences. • appear to be a good guesser. • be keenly observant. • possess heightened capacity for seeing unusual and diverse relationships. • integrate ideas and disciplines.	Highly conscious, directed, controlled, active, intentional, forward-looking, goal-oriented thought. Students may: • make generalizations. • use metaphors and analogies. • think things through in a logical manner. • think critically. • think things through and come up with a plausible answer.	Process of forming mental images of objects, qualities, situations or relationships, which aren't immediately apparent to the senses. Problem-solving through non-traditional patterns of thinking. Students may: • show exceptional ingenuity using everyday materials. • have wild, seemingly silly ideas. • produce ideas fluently/flexibly.	Ability to synthesize key ideas or problems in complex situations in a humorous way; exceptional sense of timing in words and gestures. Students may: • have a keen sense of humor, may be gentle/hostile. • see unusual relationships. • demonstrate unusual emotional depth. • demonstrate sensory awareness.

Source: Research for this report was supported under the Javits Act Program (Grant No. R206R00001) as administered by the Office of Educational Research and Improvement, U.S. Department of Education. Grantees undertaking such projects are encouraged to express freely their professional judgement.

This report, therefore, does not necessarily represent positions or policies of the Government, and no official endorsement should be inferred. This document has been reproduced with the permission of The National Research Center on the Gifted and Talented.

Talent Identification using the F-TAP

As a metric to identify the talents and strengths of gifted/high-ability Black girls, Frasier's Four A's can be used as a conceptual framework. *Attitude* refers to the mental position, feeling, or emotion towards a minoritized student (Frasier, 1991). A teacher should use critical self-reflection to analyze their personal orientation, disposition, and perspective toward the gifted potential Black girls exhibit. If an educator views the actions and demeanor of gifted Black girls from a deficit perspective, the likelihood of the girls being referred for gifted programming and services is narrow. For Black girls, the potential for talent usually manifests differently than it does in mainstream populations. Furthermore, teachers generally focus on these students' deficits rather than strengths (Grantham & Ford, 2003; Trotman Scott & Moss-Bouldin, 2014; Wright, 2011).

Access specifies the ways in which culturally and linguistically diverse students are considered for gifted programming and services. For gifted/high-achieving Black girls who often culturally differ from their gatekeeping teachers, access to special programming, acceleration, and coursework that taps into and further develops their talent potential may be limited. *Assessment* refers to the entire process of appraising, estimating, or evaluating the degree in which giftedness is present; assessing giftedness should move beyond intelligence tests and focus on multiple criteria (Ford, 2013; Frasier, 1997).

Adaptations addresses the program design and curricular experiences that support the needs of culturally and linguistically diverse students by creating opportunities for students to demonstrate and develop their potential. Adaptations should stimulate engagement and give students the opportunity to explore, take risks, problem solve, and think critically; and they should provide the necessary accommodations for students to be considered for gifted programming (Hines et al., 2016).

Traits, Aptitudes, and Behaviors of Gifted Black Girls

Frasier and Passow (1994) developed the *Traits, Aptitudes, Behaviors Scale* (TABS) as an observation tool to identify the core attributes of giftedness for minoritized students. The TABS form has a total of 10 core attributes underlying the gifted construct across racial and cultural groups, socioeconomic status, and gender identity/expression (Frasier et al., 1995). The TABS is unlike any other observation scale, because it takes into account nonmainstream gifted behaviors that educators may overlook or misconstrue as evidence that a child is not gifted (Besnoy et al., 2016; Frasier & Passow, 1994).

Frasier et al. (1995) proposed these giftedness attributes would provide a better basis for establishing a process for identifying, recognizing, and planning the educational experiences of minoritized students. These attributes were identified as communication skills, imagination/creativity, humor, inquiry, insight, interests, memory, motivation, problem solving, and reasoning. (For a way to use this scale, see the activities section at the end of this chapter.) This framework is important for identifying the talent potential of high-achieving/gifted Black girls:

> *Before my educators and school system recognized my gifts, my mother had long identified and cultivated my strengths and talents. At school, talent identification was solely based on aptitude and intelligence tests, but my core strengths—reasoning, a strong sense of order/organization, problem-solving, inquiry, and love of reading—started at home. During my formative elementary years, I lived in a rural area with pervasive inequitable practices, where there was a home–school cultural mismatch. My mother pushed for a positive self-concept, had very high expectations, and had a strong sense of Black pride. At school, these traits often were not recognized, and in some cases I was penalized for them. Questioning and interrogating actions and information were viewed as annoying or rebellious by teachers, but were considered strengths in my home. My mother cultivated these skills by providing books wherever she could find them (garage sales, thrift stores), limiting TV consumption, encouraging my love of "playing school," and often giving me leadership opportunities. However, at school, it was perceived that I was "showing off" or being too "headstrong," and I was singled out for my intelligence, compared to my white peers.*

TALENT DEVELOPMENT

Had it not been for our mothers, our educational trajectories might have been much different. Even when our teachers did not see our giftedness, our mothers did, and they fought tenaciously for us to have the education we needed. It was our mothers, *not our teachers*, who, with relatively little insider knowledge of schools, used every tool at their disposal to ensure we had the right opportunities.

> *When I was in the first grade, my mother moved me from the local elementary school to a school across town that had a gifted program. My mother believed that I was capable of advanced work and wanted me to have a chance at attending a gifted program. However, my new school was not within walking distance from my home, nor did the school bus pick up kids from my neighborhood who were not enrolled in the gifted program. Somehow, my parents negotiated for me to get a bus pass to ride the city bus to and from school. At seven years old, I walked four blocks to the bus stop, waited for the bus and rode from Beach 69th Street to Beach 35th Street just for a chance at gifted placement.*

In reflecting on the TABS criteria, it became apparent that most of our opportunities to display what we knew and what we could do happened at home. The narrow, Eurocentric curriculum did not allow for us to share the knowledge we gained from our communities, demonstrate our curiosity, or use inventive strategies, which were criticized rather than encouraged.

Instead of teachers viewing parents' assessments of their child's ability with scrutiny, teachers should be working in collaboration with parents to help them realize the goals parents have for their child. This collaboration includes asking parents about observations of their child at home and taking parents' assessments of their child's knowledge and skills seriously. Teachers must be intent on seeking out Black girls' gifts by focusing on their interests, motivations, goals, and successes—assuming a posture of expectation.

Collaboration with and support of families is pivotal, and educators can play a significant role in helping parents access networks. By encouraging parental participation in networks, educators can help parents gain access to information about how to prepare for assessments, how to complete forms, and how to advocate for their children. Once they have built a relationship with the parents and family, teachers can also visit children in their home to observe them in their own domain, where TABS may be most evident for children whose home and school cultures do not align.

ACTIVITIES

- **TABS Observation:** Complete the TABS for the students in your classroom. This can be done during or after a lesson(s), preferably an interactive lesson. Use the attribute categories to make anecdotal notes of students' responses and interactions with the stimuli and content (Frasier et al., 1995). Teachers should also review these categories with students, to allow students to know their perceived areas of strength, as well as to provide feedback about identified categories.

- **Referrals:** Each reporting period, select two to three students from your class, and refer them to a program either in or outside of the school that will help hone their strengths.

- **Teacher Reflection Questions:** Ask yourself the following questions:
  - Does the curriculum allow opportunities for students to develop or strengthen their talents based on the TABS categories?
  - Who can I envision in my classroom as successful entrepreneurs, teachers, doctors, lawyers, authors, editors, professors, et cetera?

- As you work with gifted Black girls, try to reframe the behaviors you are seeing in your classroom using Table 47.2.

TABLE 47.2 Using Traits, Aptitudes, and Behaviors for Gifted Black Girls

IDENTIFIED BEHAVIORS	REFRAME AS	TEACHER'S ACTION
Exuberance, verve, loud voices, calling out	Engagement and curiosity	Create space for different kinds of engagement styles.
Comments that are perceived as "smart" or disrespectful	Creativity, expressiveness, and effective use of words	Acknowledge the creativity, and channel it in a positive way.
Deviance from academic norms, peculiar interests	Intellectual creativity	Ask questions about their choices; encourage additional exploration.
Scores that are good or near excellent	Potential to meet higher academic standards with additional effort or support	Show recognition of their skill level; offer additional support or suggest enrichment activities to boost performance; create lessons that excite students and prompt them to engage.
Use of multiple Englishes or languages	Knowledge of multiple language conventions, robust vocabulary, versatility	Engage ideas and meanings; allow for creative ways to use language in assignments; introduce multiple modalities through audio recordings that capture language and expressiveness.

For those of us who have deep, personal, and loving relationships with Black girls in our lives; whether it be as a parent, family member, or close friend; it's of vital importance that we guide and reflect back to them a sense of understanding, appreciation, and respect as they learn to navigate a world that isn't always receptive to all that they bring. This section contains a series of vignettes written by Yusef Salaam, John Igwebuike, and Eddie Moore Jr. that speak to the profound value that all of them have experienced in being fathers to Black girls. Each vignette speaks to the deep sense of love, gratitude, and immense joy that their Black daughters have brought to their lives, and shares the wisdom that Black parents impart to their Black daughters as they prepare them for the world.

PART V

"BE THANKFUL THAT YOU'VE BEEN GIVEN THAT GIFT, BECAUSE [BLACK] GIRLS ARE AMAZING."

—Kobe Bryant

Vignette: Black Girls Own their Futures!

Yusef Salaam

> *Dr. Yusef Salaam is an educator and a member of The Exonerated Five, previously known as The Central Park Five. Dr. Salaam also identifies as a proud Black father of seven amazing Black daughters.*

Black Girls experience wanting to be liked, wanting to have friends, wanting to be—not necessarily popular—but to fit in. I think that's one of the challenges for the younger ones right now. The older ones, I think their challenge is how to navigate racism in the different spaces that they have experienced it. Much of it is covert racism, so microaggressions where you are trying to figure them out, you know something is wrong, and every time you try to confront it, they are like no, I didn't mean that, that's not what "we" were thinking. Black Girls need to know, without a shadow of doubt, that they are the owners of the future.

Juneteenth for Mazie, **by Floyd Cooper**

Grade Levels 1–4

Realistic, Historical Fiction

Book Review by Omobolade Delano-Oriaran

Juneteenth, or Freedom Day, is a commemoration of delayed freedom for African Americans. Although the ratification of the Emancipation Proclamation in 1863 abolished slavery in the United States, the news of Black freedom didn't reach Blacks until 1865 in Galveston, Texas.

Juneteenth is an official state holiday in America, recognized by all but three states (Robbins, 2020). Author Floyd Cooper masterfully introduces Juneteenth to young children through the lens of protagonist Mazie in his book, *Juneteenth For Mazie*, a compelling story of celebration, freedom, liberty, and the abolishment of slavery for Blacks in America.

Floyd depicts Mazie's Dad recounting the story of Juneteenth to his daughter, Mazie, aka Sugar Bear. "We will celebrate the day your great-great-great-grandpa Mose crossed into liberty! The day will be celebrated by us and many more families on a day we call Juneteenth" (n.p.). The rich, brown, poignant illustration of Dad sitting in the chair, his chin resting on Mazie's forehead, and hand on her beautiful black hair, depicts the powerful presence, nature, and love of African American fatherhood in a daughter's life. The story shatters the essence of the stereotypical depictions and narratives of Black men in America and reunites it with the underlying, ignored truth of Black fatherhood.

As "Dad lifts Mazie into his arms," Juneteenth explores the hardships of courageous Grandpa Mose and other slaves laboring in cotton fields, dreaming of new beginnings, praying for freedom, and "ma[king] plans for . . . a better future" as they courageously fought for freedom and "ran north to freedom, following a bright star in the sky" (n.p.).

The illustrations show the tears of freedom and jubilation of both young and old African Americans upon the revelation of the Emancipation Proclamation on "that warm June day in Galveston, Texas" (n.p.). Cooper thoughtfully shares the truth, that "things were still not perfect," with his magnetic illustration depicting African Americans from the 1950s and 1960s to the present day of Blacks who persevere, march for jobs, and profess the importance of voting and learning. The realistic storyline mirrors the struggles and determination of Blacks in America from slavery to Black excellence, periods where Black folx became sheroes and heroes, complemented with images of President Barack Obama's inauguration as the first African American president of the United States of America. This book is heavily layered with authenticity and is engaging for people from all backgrounds and walks of life, or better put in Cooper's words, *Juneteenth for Mazie* is a book "to remember" (n.p.).

Vignette: Love Letter to My Dazzling, Darling Daughters

John Igwebuike

God blessed me with three dazzling daughters—Neziah Igwebuike (b. 2002), Naomi Igwebuike (b. 2004), and Natalia Igwebuike (b. 2005).

Because each of your names begins with *N*, I loved outfitting each of you in your youth with brand new *Balance* running shoes with the emblazoned *N* logo prominently displayed on the side. That common first letter N in your first names is a lifelong reminder that the three of you should stay close, connected, and united. Remember the meaning of your last name: Igwebuike = Unity Is Strength.

It is said that life is God's gift to us, and what we do with our lives is our gift to God. Likewise, my dear and beloved daughters, you are my glorious gifts from God to me. You are so divinely designed (Neziah: piano playing), cosmically created (Naomi: artistic renderings) and magnificently made (Natalia: photogenic theatrical performances). I am so honored that God chose me to be your dad. Being your father is not something I *have* to do; it's something I *get* to do. Indeed, it is a joy that I am called to do, love to do, and am thrilled to do. You are God's gift to me.

To that end, and because of that gift, I have committed my life—every precious moment we spend together—to nurse, nourish, and nurture each of you to the absolute best of my ability.

I particularly appreciate those instances when we are in the car together and happen to come to a stop light. Frequently, the space at the intersection is occupied by a poorly dressed person with a cardboard sign that says, "Need help." When you see him or her, you are quick to speak out for this vulnerable and voiceless person to ensure that he or she is heard. You say, "Daddy, let's help him" or "Daddy, let's give the lady some money." More than you would ever know, you have defined my mission and life's calling through these simple acts of kindness.

If a tree falls in the forest and no one is around to hear it, does it make a sound? Yes! An absolute yes! It makes a precious sound, a unique sound, a valuable, irreplaceable sound. I will always remember going with Mom for her prenatal care visits. I would be giddy with excitement to hear the ultrasound. I would be spellbound listening to the beatific beats of your little hearts. Yes, everybody makes a sound, but your little beats made my big heart beat faster.

As a listening coach, educator, and trainer, I focus on diversity, equity, inclusion, belonging, and "being heard." To that end, and to make the world an even better place for you my daughters, I have devoted my life's work to make our world and the people in it more understanding by way of the positive power of effective listening. Through the Lead Listening Institute, which I founded, we raise awareness, develop programs, and transform cultures to ensure that everyone is heard, listened to, and understood without regard to color or creed. All children are to be heard the way that you my daughters have spoken to me. You are God's glorious gift to me and the world.

Vignette: Love Letter: Sharif El-Mekki

To My Four Daughters,

It is an incredible honor and privilege to be your father. When I think of you, I can't help but reflect on my relationships with the other women in our family: my Mama (who you affectionately call Bibi), Mama Fatima, Mama Shakurah, Aunt Rosie, Aunt Vernie, my four sisters (Deonte, Nzinga, Badia, and Haajar), our aunts, and grandmothers. I also consistently think of the countless Black women who raised me: teachers, coaches, neighbors, and friends.

I had always prayed to God for daughters, because I was deeply inspired by the father-daughter relationships I would see, especially while growing up in Iran. Yes, there are always challenges in raising a family, but my fervent desire is, and has always been, to see you touch the world in a robust and powerful way. This vision provided me with a direction—a North Star if you will.

I must confess to you that as strong as I may appear to you, when I am by myself and think of you, I feel how weak I am. Yes, my love for you is my weakness. I would give my life for you if needed. Without a hesitation, I would walk by your side like a shadow just to protect you against anything that can harm you. I wish I could open my chest to let you see the special place you occupy in my heart. I hope my words, attention, and deeds reflect what I feel for you.

As much as I love you, unfortunately I won't always be able to be physically present in your lives; therefore, I trust you will internalize the advice I give you and use it throughout your lives.

Know, with full certainty, that you are all beautiful. Stunningly so. Our Creator gave you beautiful skin, beautiful hair texture, and most of all beautiful spirits. The media, society, and people you encounter will try to send you messages that you are not gorgeous. That you are lacking something, that Blackness is something to avoid. But, you should revel in your Blackness, embrace your melanin and your heritage. Think of Maya Angelou's "Phenomenal Woman" poem, where she challenges you to be a phenomenal woman, head unbowed. I have to say, Mama Maya Angelou, yes, it does make me proud. I will always be committed to seeing you touch the world as a self-determined, liberated woman. One who is free from oppression. Free from permanent barriers—self-imposed or otherwise. Our fight is so that women like you are able to improve the world without being oppressed as you are doing it.

Or, consider Nikki Giovanni's classic and cool statement in "Ego Tripping (There May Be A Reason Why)," where she lets the world know that she, *and you, can fly like a bird in the sky. . . .*

Daughters, you are all beautiful, bold, and brilliant. You have always given your best in learning and experiencing new things. You are smarter, more thoughtful, and more empathetic than I was at your age. Too often, I acted out of emotion (anger), and it frequently clouded my judgement. I beg you to listen to your heart, but also use your brain!

I ask that you always take care of each other. Stick together like the fingers of a hand, and when necessary, close your fingers and make a fist—a fist protecting a sacred pearl inside of it. That pearl is your relationship. Always have each other's back, and never take your family for granted. You never know when your last moment on earth will be, so please show love to one another and always stay in touch.

I beseech you to make good choices when choosing your friends. A good friend will always give you good advice, care for you, and be there in the moments of need. A bad friend will make you forget who you truly are. If someone is not challenging their friends to be their best, they have ulterior motives. At times, when people do not regard themselves in the highest light, they will want to be around people who also don't see their own light. Be a genuine friend to the people who deserve you. Choose the type of friends that you deserve as well.

Know your worth. Cherish it. Protect it. Hold yourself accountable to safeguard it, and everyone else will fall in line. Know that Arundhati Roy cautioned us that "There's *really no* such thing as *the 'voiceless.'* There are only the deliberately silenced, or the preferably *unheard*" (Roy, 2004, emphasis added). So, do not mistake yourself as voiceless. Do not limit yourself. The world deserves to hear you.

You know that you come from a long line of activists. Your grandparents met and married while in the West Philadelphia branch of the Black Panther Party for Self Defense. Your great aunt, Maryam El-Mekki Abdullah, would listen to Brother Malcolm, our Black Shining Prince, every chance she got, in person or on albums she would gently place on her record player. Your great-grandparents fought against racism in the North and the South. Not only has your family experienced a lot, we have collectively learned a lot from our experiences. Life will not always be fair to you. Antiracism and anti-Blackness have always been in a race. As racism morphs and shifts its shape like an alien in a Marvel comic, you must be prepared to change, innovate, and apply the lessons learned from your ancestors to advance the blood-stained banner of justice.

As Reverend Thomas Threadgill wrote, "No generation can expect to see the end of struggle. Each generation has a responsibility to advance the struggle." And because our work as activists is sacred and important, activists must take care of themselves and each other. It is your duty. Recite our scriptures. Recite Assata's Pledge. Remember Audre Lorde's words: "**Caring for myself is not self-indulgence, it is self-preservation**, and that is an act of political warfare."

The fight is long, arduous, and worth it. The baton is now in your hands. And, with this baton, remember what Frantz Fanon, poignantly taught us: "Each generation must out of relative obscurity discover its mission, fulfill it, or betray it."

(Continued)

(Continued)

And, last, protect your children, my children, and grandchildren. The children who claim our bloodline, the ones who claim our lineage, and the ones who claim our communities. Remember Steve Biko's words, "The most potent weapon in the hands of the oppressor is the mind of the oppressed." Protect the children. Protect their minds—and yours.

I end this love letter with advice from another one of our heroes, Imam Ali Ibn Abi Talib:

> Hate no one, no matter how much they have wronged you. Live humbly, no matter how wealthy you become. Think positively, no matter how hard life is. Give much, even if you have been given little, Keep in touch with the ones who have forgotten you, and forgive who has wronged you, and do not stop praying for the best for those you love. (https://www.azquotes.com/quote/865773)

Things won't always be easy, my daughters, but Allah said, with *hardship comes ease. Verily, with hardship comes ease.* So, even when things seem insurmountable, know that you can fly, like a bird in the sky.

Vignette: Lioness to Bee: A Love Letter to the Pride!

Stevie Jones

LIONESS—I sit today and cypher future messages from deep cracks within my spirit aimed at your future understanding that life will bring you, at times, more than you think you can take. In those moments, hear the voice of your father reminding you that you are as significant to this planet as the queen bee is to her colony. The queen is pivotal to everything that happens within a healthy beehive (her world). When you study the role of the queen bee, take notice of how she's put together, and take special pride in knowing that the universe painted her most noticeable and durable characteristics "BLACK"!

As the lion of our pride, it's my responsibility to teach you that your life is timeless and that you must be mindful of the steps you will take along the expedition; they are numbered. You were sent to earth as one of my most precious gifts, but you must leave as one of the presents your generation could not have moved forward without unwrapping!

I pray that your vision and imagination give you the courage to make every imprint into the earth of great importance to you, for a day will come when you will realize that each step has counted for so much more than you bargained for. The universe has hidden your gift to this planet deep within you; yes, you came to planet earth with this gift to include every required tool necessary to succeed. Heaven lined the walls of your heart with a majestic life-changing ability, because that's the only place she knew you couldn't miss.

Understand humanity has five basic senses: sight, hearing, smell, taste, and touch; the sensing organs associated with each sense send information to the brain to help us understand and perceive the world around us. Perception then gives way to a deeper understanding, which begins to shape the vision of your sight. Vision will produce a source of energy capable of placing your wildest dreams in the palm of your hand. So dream wildly and be patient enough to process all of the data that your senses pull into your mind. If you are to prosper, you must elevate your status; become the best you can be in your chosen field; then turn back to pull your sisters to the same level of liberty.

At some point in this life, you'll have to be exactly who you are; my only prayer is that you discover exactly who that is before life calls on you to respond. A wise woman has cabinets filled with things she uses; her habits sustain her life and blood!

The mirror reflects, even in your darkest moments, a strong, brilliant, courageous, and beautiful young Black woman; Go win! I encourage you to use your senses to charge and empower your imagination in such a manner that your vision becomes the only true guide and GPS for your life as you go on a pilgrimage through this land.

Love, Daddy

Vignette: Aniya

Eddie Moore Jr.

No one lights up the room like you.

Energy, emotion, smiles, tears—it's all so true.

So real, so inspiring, so, overwhelming, so much if you're not prepared.

Unfortunately for some your beauty, brilliance, and truth will make them scared.

I'm writing this love letter to you so that you're encouraged and informed about the world you'll encounter time and time again.

(Continued)

(Continued)

Please, never let anyone shut you down, put you down, or stop you from being genuine.

There will be days and times you'll need to take a deep breath and count to four.

But never let it stop you from reaching the heights; you're equipped to soar.

Many people will see you and judge, hate, degrade, demean, and put you down.

However, you must get up, rise up, and remember nothing should ever control your loud sound.

You are born to lead and take on any challenge and overcome any obstacle.

Scientist. Doctor. Athlete. Scholar. Volunteer. Speaker. Friend. Dancer. Rapper. Just beautiful, brilliant and reaching heights that are outright diabolical.

You should know that right after you were born I was there.

Mom had some complications and we were left all alone there.

We danced, we talked, we slept and will forever be linked.

You've made me into a better person, a better dad, a better professional, and are always making me laugh, breathe, scream, hug, kiss and think, think and rethink.

Listen to me NyNy and hear me loud and clear.

Leaving you to experience the pain, struggle, sexism, oppression, supremacy, and hate in America is something I really fear.

Be Bold. Be Positive. Be Aniya every fucking day.

If you face an oppressor here is what you say.

My daddy taught me to be black bold and strong.

Nothing you say or do would make me do anything wrong.

But know this, although I forgive you and will give you this pass.

However, If you keep pushing #BlackGirlMagic, I might just kick your ass!

Now sweetie please say this only as a last resort.

You must remain focused and not let this system get you out of sorts.

Aniya Marie Moore, this love letter is my gift to you.

Be Beautiful, Be Brilliant, Be Black, Be you!

PART VI

"WE WILL FIGHT TILL THE LAST OF US FALLS IN THE BATTLEFIELD."

—Nana Yaa Asantewaa, Queen Mother of Ejisu in the Ashanti Empire, Ghana

With this final section, our book begins to close, with an intentional curation of the tender, righteous, and courageous words of Black mothers, who demonstrate the utter carnal rawness of the physical connection to Black babies who—still today in 2020—cannot be guaranteed protection. Samaria Rice, a mother of the movement and mother to Tamir Rice, writes to us directly, devastatingly, of the anguish that drives her activism. A neighbor called the police, reporting that Tamir had a gun, but that it was "probably fake" and he was "probably a juvenile" (Dewan & Oppel, para. 7). Minutes later, Timothy Loehmann, a 26-year-old white officer arrived at the park, murdering Tamir within seconds. Ms. Rice reminds us that if educators want to create a world that will protect Black children, we cannot abide the violence, reactivity, and systematic disregard for Black lives embedded in our criminal justice and policing systems.

Centering the lived experiences of Ms. Rice and all mothers of the movement, Dr. Shemariah J. Arki—a mom of two Black sons, a native Clevelander and #BlackLivesMatter scholar seeks to add the concept of motherwork as pedagogy to the canon, centering classrooms as tools for radical transformation. The concept of motherwork suggests that any educator who desires to teach Black girls must also take on

(Continued)

pedagogy of "othermothers" to their Black girl students. This chapter frames all of the pieces in this final section as an invitation to educators to consider the seriousness and sanctity of the othermother role they accept when they say "yes" to teaching Black girls, demanding they see how othermothering Black girls is means for their survival.

The subsequent vignette, Jenga, *by Doraja Lake, illustrates the logistical complexities of Black mothers in academia, particularly when they are solo parenting. This vignette will raise the empathy levels that readers have for Black solo moms, while indicating possible ways in which schools and the academy might consider structural changes that could make their education—and the education of their children—less of a game of chance.*

Vignette: A Mother's Pain To Power

Samaria Rice

My son, Tamir Rice, was only 12 years old when he was murdered by Timothy Loehmann, a Cleveland police officer, in 2014.

I'll say it again. The world needs to not only hear, but also understand the brevity of the words I am saying, the words that no mother should ever have to speak.

My son was murdered in 2014.

Say his name: **Tamir Rice**.

I'm tired of the hashtags. I'm tired of being angry, and yes, know that I am angry, and not that I am sad. I am *angry*. I haven't slept from the PTSD that plagues me as I sit with the rest of my family and eat, staring at the chair that Tamir used to sit in as he pushed his peas away from the chicken with his fork.

He was 12 years old.

He was *only* 12 years old.

My son Tamir was only 12 years old, but because of his race, in this country, in this white commonwealth they call *community* (that doesn't possess any amount of *unity*), they took the nail to him—and as much as I wish to war with other races for this injustice, I only pray for God to come down and manage those whom he calls his children.

But they will do it again. They will.

This will happen again. It has.

We've been allowing this to happen time and time again, electing the same kind of politicians we believe will help us but only condone a civil war to happen; for if such a war were to happen, it would only give more power to the already powerful in which *my* race has *none*.

Tajai, Tasheona, and Tavon, my oldest son, are all I have left. With all the protests happening, many white supremacists and masked anarchists are trying to infiltrate our movement by setting fires and committing vandalism across the nation. When these things happen, our agenda gets lost. Please don't get lost, my dear people. Please don't get lost! For it is not in our nature to destroy, to loot, to burn; we have always been a peaceful people. We must apply, and keep applying, pressure, my young people, to the governors of the law, the Capitol, and the Supreme Court. Ancestors of all who are white must hear our voices while they are privileged with the right to sleep peacefully despite knowing what's happening in our country.

They do not care, but it is our duty to make them. It is our duty to fight for our freedom.

My son, Tamir Rice. *Say his name.*

Ahmaud Arbery. Say his name.

Breonna Taylor. *Say her name.*

George Floyd. *Say his name.*

Many others that we do not know. Say their names.

We do not need white teachers and educators to tell us who we are, for we already know who we are. The minute we allow other races to preach and dictate who we are as Black people, as Black women, specifically, is the moment we hand them more power, but they have enough, and I've HAD ENOUGH.

How about this: I've had enough of white supremacy, telling me I am not a child of God, yet I am, and am a queen as well. I'm tired of them trying to mimic the Black woman yet not seek to support us as Black women. I'm tired of those who don't truly believe that "Black is beautiful," as they steal the world, our world, up from under our feet that have walked the Underground Railroad. I'm tired of dealing with the foolishness of Black versus Brown skin with Madam C. J. Walker, having our names stripped from that which we invented for the common good. I am tired. I am tired.

I—am—tired.

How dare they take our credit?

How dare they mimic us?

But we shall keep our heads up and stand up for what we believe, for we shall overcome. My Black people of this Earth, the Pangea that derives from our very roots of African culture where ALL PEOPLE come from.

Having four children has kept me involved with teaching and schooling them on the narratives they must know and not the narratives handed down by white people.

How dare they dictate the narratives of our people?

We already know the system is not broken, it is doing what it was designed to do: fail us. Their hatred of us is due to our success. For black queens are the greatest threats to white supremacy. They will tighten nooses around our necks before a Black woman dares touch their crowns, crowns that *we* wore, on *our* heads, before *they* knew what a crown symbolized.

So, I watch their teachers closely to ensure that our children, our Black children, receive the proper quality education, including the history of our people, that they are so afraid to share in these predominantly white schools. Our people suffer, which is sad. Our people deserve to know where they come from instead of what culture ruled over them, the same people they must sit next to in classrooms. They've doomed our Black children from the start. Those white teachers hesitate to call us, but if they were Black, they'd tell us what's real.

I'm one of the ones who care, one of the ones you can call, one of the ones invested in better learning for our children, striving to protect them from the racist things said about even our first and only Black president, Barack Obama.

It is a shame my children must feel the sharp end of racism's sword, but the fact is, at the end of the day, they shouldn't have to.

CHAPTER 48

Motherwork as Pedagogy

Shemariah J. Arki

The statement written by the womxn of The Combahee River Collective (a group of Black, lesbian feminists who separated from the National Black Feminist Organization) would create waves in the contemporary Black feminist movement for many years to come. The experiences created by the intersection of marginalized identities (race, class, gender identity/expression, and sexual orientation) provided multiple ways of knowing for Black womxn (Collins, 1990, 1994). By rearticulating a consciousness that already exists, black feminist thought (BFT) offers resistance and agency as inherent traits (Collins, 1990; Kaplan, 2000). BFT is the embodiment of the well-known speech by Audre Lorde (2003), "The Master's Tools Will Never Dismantle The Master's House." Black womxn live this intersection—practicing interruption. . . . practicing freedom (hooks, 1994). From the elementary classroom to the ivory tower, Black girls and womxn live an alternative epistemology contoured by a dual consciousness, Afrocentric and female (Collins, 1990; Du Bois, 1991; Rabaka, 2009). Located in the margin, a Black feminist identity is rooted in the sociopolitical contradictions of social identities for those who identify as Black womxn (Cha-Jua, 2013; Du Bois, 1991; Morgan, 1999). In an effort to survive, many Black feminists find themselves in a constant state of knowing and becoming. Based on the work of Deborah K. King (1995), this "both/and" phenomenon creates space for dueling identities to amicably coexist and ultimately thrive through the transformative practice of motherwork.

At the center of BFT is the love and labor of Black womxn—their "enslavement to this country, to suffrage, to civil rights, and family rights (Sankofa Waters, 2015 p. 13)". In her work, *We Can Speak For Ourselves: Parent Involvement and Ideologies of Black Mothers in Chicago*, Billye Sankofa Waters (2015) advances that motherwork, in theory and method, "blurs discipline lines towards a collective experience" (p. 13). The theory and methods originated by Collins (1990) as BFT are the following: (1) lived experience as the concrete criterion for meaning, (2) using dialogue to assess knowledge claims, (3) the ethic of caring, and (4) the ethic of responsibility. The blurring between disciplines commences with the emergence of following roles and responsibilities of Black womxn practicing feminism. Collins (1990) posits the following five pillars of motherwork:

- Bloodmother, othermothers, and womxn-centered networks

- Mothers, daughters, and socialization for society

- Community othermothers and political activism

- Motherhood as a symbol of power

- The view from the inside: The personal meaning of mothering

BLOODMOTHER, OTHERMOTHERS, AND WOMXN-CENTERED NETWORKS

The acceptance of the inhabitation of the feminine divine is a significant element in one's Black feminist practice. Washington (2013) describes Yemoja—the African goddess of the ocean and the patron deity of pregnant women—as "the most versatile element . . . the essential source of all life" (p. 215). Revered as the mother of all, her "inherent dynamism, malleability and immortality" (Washington, 2013, p. 218) can be realized through Collins' (1990) theoretical interpretation of womxn-centered networks. These networks are communities of womxn who share the responsibility of child rearing; operate as family, either birth or chosen; and remain just as dynamic as their womxn, of whom a significant number identify with multiple oppressed identities (Collins, 1990, 1994). Based in the tradition of Yemoja, these womxn-centered networks challenge the notions of whiteness as property by releasing the dominant narrative of the U.S. middle-class family life (Collins, 1990, 1994; Ladson-Billings, 1998). Womxn-centered networks are built and sustained by womxn with a strong connection to their matriarchal ancestors and their intrinsic connection to the feminine divine.

MOTHERS, DAUGHTERS, AND SOCIALIZATION FOR SOCIETY

Black mothers and daughters often find themselves in the space between theory and practice. Their display of motherwork is often reflexive of the motherwork they witnessed, either from their own mother or their womxn-centered network. Black girls performing in the classroom learn how to operate in the world more from practice than from instruction. Black girls then have the important task of being better and going farther than their own mothers or othermothers; nevertheless, many mothers shield and protect their children from the ugly parts of their past in an effort to keep them safe. Many mothers and othermothers use their view from the inside to provide access to a life most Black children don't have access to.

Black girls show up in the world with a strong sense of self and determination to achieve. For many, it's through the realization and acceptance of their mother's identity as a woman first that they ascertain and transcend the goals they have set for themselves. Wallace (2015) said it best: "Now that I know my mother better, I know that her sense of powerlessness made it all the more essential to her that she take radical action" (p. 98). Black girls, as young as kindergarten, arrive in your classrooms with this sentiment as their plight.

COMMUNITY OTHERMOTHERS AND POLITICAL ACTIVISM

The contention that the world is one person's responsibility can seem extensive when viewed through today's neoliberal context. This deep-seated responsibility to love and nurture the children of the diaspora is rooted in a deep connection to the feminine divine. Community othermothers often out themselves through their language. Freire (1970/2000) theorizes language as the key to dialogue, while hooks (1994) and Hilliard (2013) posit literacy as a key process of coding and decoding said language and dialogue. Community othermothers often speak as if they are a part of a collective, standing on the shoulders of ancestors, and on the front lines with fellow othermothers and activists, shouldering the fight for freedom (Collins, 1990; Guy-Sheftall, 1995; Sankofa Waters, 2015). Black womxn's community activism is often realized through the example of their othermothers, paired with the contention that their "worldly accomplishments" must be put to use for the betterment of their people (Collins, 1990).

Mothering the Mind. The concept of *mothering the mind* is necessary in today's sociopolitical context (Arki, 2016, 2018; Emdin, 2016; Love, 2016, 2019). The desire of mothers and othermothers to help prepare the next generations of leaders has become one of the most important ways in which motherwork takes shape in the wake of #BlackLivesMatter. In theory, mothering the mind connects Black womxn through a shared sisterhood of racial uplift and responsibility to contribute through the role of mother (Collins, 1990). More important, mothering the mind is practiced through one's daily actions (Collins, 1990). Essentially, Black womxn who wake up every day with a desire to be the best mother they can be to all the children of the diaspora are interrupting the dominant narrative and reconstructing the role of mothers and the responsibility of motherwork. Can you imagine how the process of teaching and learning would shift if mothering the mind were a founding pillar of the American education system?

MOTHERHOOD AS A SYMBOL OF POWER

Community othermothers have long been studied through the shared identities of middle-class Black womxn's political activism (Collins, 1990). The labor imparted by many othermothers to move their community forward, however, is often shouldered by many womxn whose names and faces are forever unknown (Collins, 1990). These "strong Black womxn" are the ethos of the continual development of the Black family, the Black community, and the Black radical tradition. This intrinsic sense of power is often traced back to stories of Yemoja and then resurfaces through oral narratives and affirmations such as Sankofa. Sankofa, the Ghanaian principle that loosely translates to "return and fetch it," is spoken or referred to by many Black womxn as an affirmation of their duty as members of the community. Maternal politics often include acting on such feelings of power, when viewed through the sociopolitical context of the times. Motherhood as power most often occurs when a Black woman has and chooses to put forward her privileged identity, as Black girls in the classroom often do in order to just be seen. This position can also be taken up by those who care about Black girls and womxn, nodding to the role of motherwork as pedagogy.

THE VIEW FROM THE INSIDE: THE PERSONAL MEANING OF MOTHERING

To serve in the capacity of mother is one of the highest honors. Reproductive justice has long been an issue that surrounds the activism of motherwork for Black womxn. Throughout the antebellum and Jim Crow eras of the American South, becoming a woman was often tied to biological motherhood, without question around how she was impregnated (Collins, 1990). Despite those conditions, Black mothers willingly sacrifice for their children. They understand the grim nature of their children growing up in Black America. Black mothers and othermothers have strived to meet the physical, emotional, and psychological needs of their children while sacrificing their own.

FOR TEACHERS

Those who perpetuate motherwork as pedagogy are often recipients of the same, whether in their schools or communities. Many can often articulate the story of that one educator who showed them radical love and cared for their wellbeing, just like a mother. These are the stories that become specific points of demarcation, stories that shape a teacher's pedagogy. For example, a hip-hop feminist display of motherwork is very different from that of a second- or third-wave feminist grandmother. One key factor in this difference is the presence of institutional power and the access that is granted based on one's identity (Collins, 1994). This is where the pedagogy opens itself to those who may not identify as Black or feminist, but certainly share the strong desire to leave the world better than how they found it, thus creating new and innovative tools and techniques around teaching and learning in the wake of #BlackLivesMatter. Teachers may use many frameworks to situate their motherwork—whether social justice, African-centered, or hip-hop—to make the point. As an administrator, classroom teacher, paraprofessional, support staff, or volunteer, teachers, through the use of mothering and othermothering, independent of their identities, are able to create classrooms where beautiful and brilliant Black girls are connected, respected, and valued.

Vignette: Jenga: The Game Single Mothers Play in the World of Academia

Doraja Lake

Walking around my campus, I feel as though I am playing a daily dangerous game of Jenga while subsisting on french fries and coffee. As I look back over my life and my educational process, I realize that I am not supposed to be here. It was supposed to be over the moment my parents filed for divorce and told me that there would be no money to send me off to college. I was supposed to go on into the workforce and live life amongst the working class. Higher education was supposed to simply be a dream for me. However, through sheer determination and some very generous benefactors, I am staring down the barrel of my very first bachelor's degree. The journey has been difficult; I have battled illnesses, surgeries, mental health struggles, gaps in educational abilities, homelessness, and a slew of the other daily struggles that nontraditional students encounter. None of those challenges has been as difficult as juggling the blocks on my education tower that being a single mother adds to the game.

Between work, classes, classwork, housework, and the nuances of parenthood, such as parent–teacher conferences and doctor appointments, day-to-day living feels like an intricate mashed up game of Jenga while navigating the pitfalls of my predominantly white institution's campus. This fast-paced, nonstop, high-stakes competition between the classroom and real life leaves little downtime for a nontraditional student. As I began this game, I knew that I'd have to straddle three worlds—motherhood, student life, and Black girlhood—with all of my blocks *while* moving forward. Block 1: I chose my path; therefore, I own my path. Block 2: I balance fixing lunch, parent–teacher conferences, checking homework, laundry, and other household duties with my coursework. Block 3: As a sociology scholar, I know that caring for myself is a revolutionary act, so I have to take "me time." Move a block: Making doctor appointments, attending sports practices, and scheduling play dates makes for a precarious game of nonstop chaos.

As a student, I rearrange the blocks of my Jenga tower by straddling a number of social fences to avoid looking like a bad mother.

(Continued)

(Continued)

As a divorced mother, I rearrange the blocks of my Jenga tower, because I am responsible for every financial decision impacting my life and almost every aspect of my children's lives.

I move forward and add two blocks, because people talk about how amazing it is that I have returned to the classroom and how strong a woman I am. However, I quickly lose one turn because I get confused as to where my social identity as a student, mom, and Black Girl begins and ends.

In order to keep up the appearance of an effortless yet calculated game, I play the supermom card. I add five blocks to my tower by starting my day off at 5:30 a.m. I multitask as I listen to lectures, read articles, and finish cooking a nutritionally balanced dinner. By 8:30 a.m. I have shifted roles to put on the good Black mother hat by engaging with teachers and other parents in the school drop-off line. I try to add one more block to my Jenga tower as I drive to campus, by switching back to my good student hat. I walk with my head high, because I have listened to lectures on the way to the classroom, and I have defied the trope of the lazy black person because I have already completed three hours of work before I clocked in to "work."

On campus and in my classroom, I move one block in my game because the imposter syndrome I'm feeling confirms my physical presence as the "only."

Understanding my place in the line of Black girls who have been the only, I move a block to the top, trailblazing for all future Black single mothers that want a crack at an elite education.

With that knowledge, I waltz to my first three classes and stack blocks onto my teetering tower.

My cell phone rings, and the tower comes crashing down. I head to my son's school to pick him up—he has a fever. The game of life is not over, but today's session of Jenga has toppled to my feet. The board game will be reset tomorrow.

The theme of Black motherhood continues here, with a vignette by a Black girl high school student, Miah Prescod, who sees the vulnerability of Black mothers, Black people, and Black children, and considers whether she can even willingly take on the pain involved in parenting Black children in a world not built for them. Her powerful vignette is followed by love letters, beautiful declarations of love and protection, written by Tanisha Brandon-Felder and Andrea Johnson, whose choices to bear and raise children, who they love so deeply, take on new meaning within the context of risk and loss outlined here.

This section—and the book—end with the poetic words of Erica Snowden, who asks and answers the question, "What should we tell our Black girls about themselves and about the world they have been born into?"

Tell them, Snowden writes, "the world is theirs for the taking." Tell them "their time to shine is now." The time is now for Black Girls to shine - Black Girl Magic, Black Girl, Excellence - Black Girl Genius. Beautiful Brilliant Black Girls Rock - Congratulations to the 49th Vice President of the United States of America, Kamala Harris.

Vignette: Black Girl Fears Motherhood

Miah Prescod, High School Student

Here is a list
     of reasons
          as to why
               I fear becoming
                    a Black mother in America:

One.
A Black woman
is three to four times more likely to die from
childbirth than a white woman.
Should I
decide to have children,
I
am three to four times more likely to die.

Two.
"In North America,
the future of slavery
depended upon black women's reproductive capacity
as it did on the slave market."[1]
my body
no longer my own
never was my own
my body
simply a tool,
means of mass production
furthering slavery,
my body,
has simply never been my body.

---

[1]Hartman, S. (2016). The belly of the world: A note on black women's labors. *Souls: A Critical Journal of Black Politics, Culture, and Society, 18*(1), 166–173. https://doi.org/10.1080/10999949.2016.1162596

(Continued)

(Continued)

Three.
Christina Sharpe:
"The negation or disfigurement
of maternity
turns the womb into a factory
reproducing blackness
as abjection
and turning the birth canal
into
another domestic middle passage."[2]
America turned
my birth canal
into a gateway for their prison system,
my unborn child into another dollar sign.

Four.
Birthing a Black child
a life predetermined
is not something I look forward to
my reality
now a series
of endless funerals,
ones I will never attend
mourning the lives of black souls
gone too soon
watching Fox 12 news from my couch
another Black girl reported missing,
another Black boy gunned down by police,
another Black mother lying on her deathbed.
America has drowned out her screams.

Five.
Childbirth,
is a one-way path to a graveyard
and
in this world, Black babies don't ever survive
in this world, Black babies are not meant to survive
in this world, Black motherhood equals high-risk pregnancy
in this world, Black motherhood equals complications

[2]Sharpe, C. (2014). Black studies. *The Black Scholar*, *44*(2), 59–69. https://doi.org/10.1080/00064246.2014.11413688

Six.
Every time my father tells me
how many grandkids he wants
I cringe on the inside
because
the thought of reproduction as a Black woman
in America
honestly scares the hell out of me.

Seven.
I feel guilty
because everyone talks about the joys of motherhood,
happiness and fulfillment
but no one ever talks about the fears of Black motherhood.

So
before you proceed
to ask
a Black woman
when
she's going to have kids
remember
she is three to four times more likely to die
from childbirth than a white woman.

Vignette: Dearest Bayje

Tanisha Brandon-Felder

It is with an open heart and teary eyes that I write this love letter to you. My heart is open because I know all the wonderful things that lie ahead for you. You are an amazing person. I am excited for every person who gets the honor of spending time with you. You are kind, you are generous, you are caring, you are patient, you are compassionate, you are inclusive. Every person who spends time with you, even when you are in a large group, feels the intimacy of your attention. It is for this reason, that I admire you. Low key, you are my hero. You are the extrovert, and my introverted self admires your boldness and confidence in who you are. You love yourself more than anyone else I know. Well, I might love you a bit more.

My eyes are teary because I know the world is not always kind. Though you've already experienced loss and grief in your young life, I know there is more pain to

(Continued)

(Continued)

come. Why, you may ask? Because we live in a world where people still treat you differently based on how you look and their stereotypical and racist ideas of who you should be. We already dealt with this with one of your teachers this year. He was the one teacher who seemed to not like you. How could that be? As I said before, everyone loves you! But this teacher would find reasons to talk harshly to you, ignore you, and force you to leave the class. Your advocacy of his mistreatment towards you and others only made this worse. Even when I talked to him and implored him to get to know you, his behavior never changed. That was all about him, but he made it feel like it was all about you. I will never forgive him for how he made you feel. To make it worse, he was a Black male teacher. Remember, not all skin folk are kinfolk. But here's the thing, there will be more like him, Black or not, that will forget they have the power to crush your spirit, and you will be tried and tried again. Don't forget who you are. You are amazing. My eyes are the most teary when I think of these moments.

So what do I wish for you more than anything else in the world? I wish for your brilliance to shine. For your love to fill every room you enter, and for you to find a love that fills you up. I want you to push yourself up mountains and to enjoy the peaks, and to be strong enough to endure the valleys and embrace the pits. I want you to know that you are enough. That no one completes you, that you do not need anyone to be successful, and that your words, body, soul, and spirit matter. Please remember that I love you. You are my absolute favorite person in the world.

Love, Mommy

Vignette: A Love Letter to My Daughter Alyse

Andrea Johnson

How fitting that in your 30th year I am sitting here reflecting on you, me, and our journey as mother and daughter. You came into this world on your own terms. After three hours of labor, the nurse came in to check me and said, "You are coming along well, I will be back later." As she got to the door of my room I said, "Come back, I am ready to push." She gave me a puzzled look, and I said, "This is my third child." With that she rushed to get the doctor who got her gloves on just in time as you entered the world. Up until then, I was the mother of boys. I actually assumed you would be a boy and was pleasantly surprised when the doctor said the words, "It's a girl." You and me, the feminine forces in a house full of men. Although we were outnumbered between your Dad, two brothers, and the hordes of football players that seemed to always be at our house during your adolescence, we held our own no matter what.

I worried so much about raising a Black girl in a predominately white community. I wanted you to feel beautiful and to feel truly seen. I remember the joy you had when Taylor moved in and became your first Black girlfriend at school. Sixth grade. Although she moved to another state in the tenth grade, I love that you are still close. Sister-friends. I remember how angry you were when I sent you to Detroit for the summer of your eighth-grade year. That summer we now call "Black Girl Bootcamp." You didn't know then that I needed you to be loved up and schooled by your Black aunties, cousins, and grandmas as you were becoming a woman. I couldn't do it all by myself. I needed you to see yourself—and me—in our lineage; a long line of strong, beautiful Black women. You came back ready to take on the world with the confidence and knowledge of your family.

I know high school wasn't always easy for you socially. The white girls you'd known since kindergarten didn't always include you in their groups. You never complained. You always said, "There's no crying in baseball." You immersed yourself in dance and literally kept it moving. In your senior year, when you decided to go to an HBCU, I knew there was a light at the end of that tunnel. Howard University was Black Girl Bootcamp the remix. That is where you solidified who you are as a strong Black woman.

I am so proud of who you are as a wife and mother. I see you mentoring your goddaughter as she discovers her own Black girl magic. I see you, a feminine force, holding your own, confident in your blackness, making a difference in this world. I am honored that you chose me to be your mom, and I love you, always.

Vignette: Diamonds: Beautiful, Brilliant, Black

Erica Snowden

What shall we tell our girls?
What shall we tell our girls when they are told they have an attitude?
What shall we tell our girls when they are called rude?
What shall we tell our girls when they don't smile?
What shall we tell our girls when they're described as wild?
What shall we tell our girls when they are told they're aggressive?
What shall we tell our girls when their bodies are deemed suggestive?
What shall we tell our girls when they are called angry?
What shall we tell our girls when they are called lazy?
We shall tell them they are fearfully and wonderfully made

(Continued)

(Continued)

Descendants of mighty Queens
If they put their minds to it, they can have anything
We shall tell them they are phenomenal women in the making
The world is theirs for the taking
We shall tell them they stand on the backs of women who came before
That they are resilient, brave, loving, firm, and kind
They've been endowed with strengths from generations before them
They stand on the backs of abolitionists, civil rights activists, politicians,
Black feminists, world-renowned athletes, singers, actresses,
Astronauts, mathematicians, educators, scientists,
Mothers, daughters, sisters, "fass aunties," and more
They are the backbones of our people
They are diamonds in the process of pressure and high temperatures
Their time to shine is now.

A Note from the Editors

We started this journey fully aware that Black Girls are Beautiful and Brilliant. We continue the journey knowing each step is a pathway to Black Girls excelling. Join us in the journey to Beautiful Brilliant Black Girl Excellence!

Video Resources

	Video 1: Recognizing, Embracing, and Understanding the Richness in Black Girls
Video 2: Parents and Families	
	Video 3: Bursting Stereotypes While Being the Only
Video 4: What Spirit Murder Looks Like	
	Video 5: White Teachers Reflect
Video 6: No More Self Doubt	

(Continued)

(Continued)

	Video 7: Comfort and Isolation
Video 8: Supporting Gender Non-Conforming Black Youth: The Time Is Now	
	Video 9: Relationships with White Peers
Video 10: Preparing Black Girls to Rock This World	
	Video 11: It's Not Magic, It's Hard Work and Determination
Video 12: It's My Crown, Don't Touch My Hair	
	Video 13: Affinity
Video 14: Mentorship	

	Video 15: Dear Teacher
Video 16: Advice for Teachers	
	Video 17: See Yourself, Black Girl . . . Then See Yourself Again

References

FOREWORD

Combahee River Collective. (2014). A black feminist statement. *Women's Studies Quarterly*, 271–280.

hooks, b. (1999). Loving blackness as political resistance. In *Black looks: Race and representation* (pp. 9–20). South End Press.

UNDERSTANDING

PART I. BLACK PEOPLE I LOVE YOU, I LOVE US, OUR LIVES MATTER."—ALICIA GARZA

CHAPTER 1: Black "Girls" Are Different, Not Deficient

Angelou, M. (1986). *All God's children need traveling shoes*. Random House.

Angelou, M. (1994). *The complete collected poems of Maya Angelou*. Random House.

Bennett, L., Jr. (1980). What is Black beauty? An appraisal of the grandeur of Black womanhood provides new and starling answers. *Ebony*, *36*(10), 159–162.

Cannie, R. (2018). *Daring to differ: A culturally responsive research study of self* [Doctoral dissertation]. University of Washington.

Carter Andrews, D. J., Brown, T., Castro, E., & Id-Deem, E. (2019). The impossibility of being "perfect and White": Black girls' racialized and gendered schooling experiences. *American Educational Research Journal*, *56*(6), 2531–2572.

Gibran, K. (1926). *Sand and foam*. Knopf.

Gibran, K. (2013). *Khalil Gibran's The Broken Wings: "Out of suffering have emerged the strongest souls; the most massive characters are seared with scars."* A Word to the Wise. (Original work published 1912)

Harris, J. (2015, October 4). *Dear Black girl: Letters from the souls of Black women*. https://www.theroot.com/dear-black-girl-letters-from-the-souls-of-black-women-1790861287

Lagace, M. (2020, March 11). *350 badass Maya Angelou quotes that will blow your mind*. https://wisdomquotes.com/maya-angelou-quotes

Leviton, M. (2020, February). We will be seen: Tressie McMillan Cottom on confronting sexism and classism. *The Sun Magazine*, pp. 4–12.

Parker, M. (2017, February 14). *Four love poems for Black women by Black women*. https://www.buzzfeednews.com/article/poetmorganparker/four-love-poems-for-black-women-by-black-women

Alim, H. S., & Paris, D. (2017). What is culturally sustaining pedagogy and why does it matter? In H. S. Alim & D. Paris (Eds.), *Culturally sustaining pedagogies: Teaching and learning for justice in a changing world* (pp. 1–21). Teachers College Press.

Angelou, M. (2013). *And still I rise*. Hachette UK.

Blake, J., & Epstein, R. (2017). *Listening to Black women and girls: Lived experiences of adultification bias*. Georgetown Law, Center on Poverty and Inequality. https://endadultificationbias.org/wp-content/uploads/2019/05/Listening-to-BlackWomen-and-Girls-v7.pdf

Cara, C. (2012). It takes a village to raise a child: Team teaching and learning journeys. *International Journal of Interdisciplinary Social Sciences, 6*(10), 49–66. https://doi.org/10.18848/1833-1882/CGP/v06i10/52177

Carter, D. J. (2007). Why the Black kids sit together at the stairs: The role of identity-affirming counter-spaces in a predominantly white high school. *The Journal of Negro Education*, 542–554.

Clifford, C. (2018, July 13). *This 11-year-old launched a business with her sister to combat racism—and it's taking off*. CNBC. https://www.cnbc.com/2018/07/11/kheris-rogers-makes-anti-bullying-flexin-in-my-complexion-t-shirts.html

Davis, O. I. (1999). In the kitchen: Transforming the academy through safe spaces of resistance. *Western Journal of Communication, 63*(3), 364–381.

Delano-Oriaran, O. O., & Meidl, T. D. (2013). Critical conversations: Developing white teachers for diverse classrooms. *Journal of Praxis in Multicultural Education, 7*(1), 1–27.

Delta Sigma Theta Sorority, Inc. (2020). *Educational development*. https://www.deltasigmatheta.org/educational.php

Edwards, E., McArthur, S. A., & Russell-Owens, L. (2016). Relationships, being-ness, and voice: Exploring multiple dimensions of humanizing work with Black girls. *Equity & Excellence in Education, 49*(4), 428–439. https://doi-org.snc.idm.oclc.org/10.1080/10665684.2016.1227224

Evans-Winters, V., & Esposito, J. (2010). Other people's daughters: Critical race feminism and Black girls' education. *Educational Foundations, 24*(1-2), 11–24. https://files.eric.ed.gov/fulltext/EJ885912.pdf

Ford, D. Y. (2014). Segregation and the underrepresentation of Blacks and Hispanics in gifted education: Social inequality and deficit paradigms. *Roeper Review, 36*(3), 143–154.

Gay, G. (2002). Preparing for culturally responsive teaching. *Journal of Teacher Education, 53*(2), 106–116.

Goddard, R. D., Tschannen-Moran, M., & Hoy, W. K. (2001). A multilevel examination of the distribution and effects of teacher trust in students and parents in urban elementary schools. *The Elementary School Journal, 102*(1), 3–17. https://doi-org/10.1086/499690

Gorski, P. (2016). Rethinking the role of "culture" in educational equity: From cultural competence to equity literacy. *Multicultural Perspectives, 18*(4), 221–226.

Ladson-Billings, G. (2014). Culturally relevant pedagogy 2.0: Aka the remix. *Harvard Educational Review, 84*(1), 74–84.

McArthur, S. A. (2016). Black girls and critical media literacy for social activism. *English Education, 48*(4), 362–379.

McCarthy, K. (2020, January 3). Black-ish star Marsai Martin shares advice on big dreams. *Good Morning America.* https://www.goodmorningamerica.com/culture/story/black-ish-star-executive-producer-marsai-martin-shares-6804663

Michie, G. (2007). Seeing, hearing, and talking race: Lessons for white teachers from four teachers of color. *Multicultural Perspectives*, 9(1), 3–9. https://doi.org/10.1080/15210960701333633

Move to End Violence. (2016, September 7). Ally or co-conspirator?: What it means to act #InSolidarity. *Move to End Violence.* https://movetoendviolence.org/blog/ally-co-conspirator-means-act-insolidarity/

Muhammad, G. (2012). Creating spaces for Black adolescent girls to "Write it out!" *Journal of Adolescent & Adult Literacy*, 56(3), 203–211. www.jstor.org/stable/23367738

Nunn, N. M. (2018). Super-girl: Strength and sadness in Black girlhood. *Gender & Education*, 30(2), 239–258. https://doi-org.snc.idm.oclc.org/10.1080/09540253.2016.1225013

Nyachae, T. M. (2016). Complicated contradictions amid Black feminism and millennial Black women teachers creating curriculum for Black girls. *Gender and Education*, 28(6), 786–806.

Parrella-Aureli, A. (2019, May 14). *Black girls break bread brings students in mostly-white schools together to share a meal—and empower each other.* Block Club Chicago. https://blockclubchicago.org/2019/05/14/black-girls-break-bread-brings-students-in-mostly-white-schools-together-to-share-a-meal-and-empower-each-other/

Santi, C. (2019, May 13). Student becomes valedictorian after being told Black girls can't. *Ebony.* https://www.ebony.com/news/student-becomes-valedictorian-black-girls-cant/

Schultz, K. (2010). After the blackbird whistles: Listening to silence in the classroom. *Teachers College Record*, 112(11), 2833–2849.

Sealey-Ruiz, Y. (2016). Why Black girls' literacies matter: New literacies for a new era. *English Education*, 290–298.

Woodard, R., Vaughan, A., & Machado, E. (2017). Exploring culturally sustaining writing pedagogy in urban classrooms. *Literacy Research: Theory, Method, and Practice*, 66(1), 215–231.

Young gun control activist talks representation. (2020, January 22). *Brut.* www.brut.media/us/international/young-gun-control-activist-talks-representation-73ac4419-4df4-4110-9341-ab6469f65e77

CHAPTER 3: A Systemic Response to Creating a School Where Black Girls Can Thrive

Bonilla-Silva, E. (1997, June). Rethinking racism: Toward a structural interpretation. *American Sociological Review*, 62(3), 465–480. http://www.jstor.org/stable/2657316.

Bonilla-Silva, E. (2017). *Racism without racists: Color-blind racism and the persistence of racial inequity in the United States.* Rowman & Littlefield.

Booker, C. (2020). *Mastering the Hire: 12 Strategies to improve your odds of finding the best hire.* HarperCollins Leadership.

Digh, P., & Lewis, V. L. (n. d.) *Hard conversations: Introduction to racism* [Online seminar]. https://www.pattidigh.com/racism/

Jackson, B., & Hardiman, R. (2013). *Continuum on becoming an anti-racist multicultural organization.* Adapted from original concept by Baily Jackson and Rita Hardiman, and further developed by Andrea Avazian and Ronice Branding; further adapted by

Melia LaCor. https://www.aesa.us/conferences/2013_ac_presentations/Continuum_AntiRacist.pdf

Kendi, I. X. (2019). *How to be an antiracist*. One World.

Sue, D. W. (2010). *Microaggressions and marginality: Manifestation, dynamics, and impact*. John Wiley & Sons.

Book Review: *Hey Black Child*

Friedman, R. E. (2018, June 1). Hey, Black Child [Book review]. *School Library Journal*. https://www.slj.com/?reviewDetail=hey-black-child

Perkins, U. E. (Author), & Collier, B. (Illustrator). (2017). *Hey Black child*. Little, Brown.

PART II "NAH"—HARRIET TUBMAN

Vignette: Where Does the Sapphire Caricature Come From?

Taylor, S. R. (2018). *The body is not an apology: The power of radical self-love*. Berrett-Koehler.

CHAPTER 4: My Eloquent, Angry, Black Rage

Cooper, B. (2018). *Eloquent rage: A black feminist discovers her superpower*. Picador.

Crenshaw, K. (1994). Mapping the margins: Intersectionality, identity politics, and violence against women of color. In M. A. Fineman & R. Mykitiuk (Eds.), *The Public Nature of Private Violence* (pp. 93–118).

Fordham, S. (1993). "Those loud black girls": (Black) women, silence, and gender "passing" in the academy. *Anthropology and Education Quarterly, 24*(1), 3–32.

Howard, M. L. (2016). *Nzinga: African warrior queen*. Jungum Press.

Hurts, F. (2004). *Imitation of life*. Duke University Press. (Original work published 1933)

Idang, G. (2015). *African culture and values*. UNISA Press.

Jones, T. A., & Norwood, K. J. (2017). Aggressive encounters and white fragility: Deconstructing the trope of the angry Black woman. *Iowa Law Review*, 2017–2068.

Laemmle, C., Jr. (Producer), & Stahl, J. (Director). (1934). *Imitation of life* [Motion picture]. Universal Pictures.

Lee, H. (2006). *To kill a mockingbird*. Harper Perennial Modern. (Original work published 1960)

Mitchell, M. (1999). *Gone with the wind*. Warner Books. (Original work published 1936)

Pilgrim, D. (2012). *The Sapphire caricature*. Jim Crow Museum, Ferris State University. https://www.ferris.edu/HTMLS/news/jimcrow/antiblack/sapphire.htm (Original work published 2008)

Prasad, R. (2018). *Serena Williams and the trope of the angry Black woman*. BBC News. https://www.bbc.com/news/world-us-canada-45476500

Seales, A. (2019). *Small doses: Potent truths for everyday use*. Abrams Image.

Selznick, D. (Producer), & Fleming, V. (Director). (1939). *Gone with the wind* [Motion picture]. MGM.

Stowe, H. B. (1999). *Uncle Tom's cabin*. Wordsworth Classics. (Original work published 1851)

Swartz, E. (1993). Multicultural education: Disrupting patterns of supremacy in school curricula, practices and pedagogy. *The Journal of Negro Education, 62*(4), 493–506.

Tatum, B. (1997). *Why are all the Black kids sitting together in the cafeteria? And other conversations about race*. Basic Books.

Twain, M. (2002). *The adventures of Huckleberry Finn.* Penguin Classics. (Original work published 1884)

Tyldesly, J. (2006). *Chronicle of the queens of Egypt.* Thames and Hudson.

CHAPTER 5: The Right Kind of Black Girls

Burch, T. (2015). Skin color and the criminal justice system: Beyond black-white disparities in sentencing. *Journal of Empirical Legal Studies, 12*(3), 395–420.

Collins, P. H. (2009). *Black feminist thought.* Routledge.

Dace, K. L. (2012). The whiteness of truth and the presumption of innocence. In. K. L. Dace (Ed.), *Unlikely allies in the academy: Women of Color and white women in conversation* (pp. 42–53). Routledge.

hooks, b. (2000). *Feminist theory: From margin to center.* Pluto Press.

Maddox, K. B. (2004). Perspectives on racial phenotypicality bias. *Personality and Social Psychology Review, 8*(4), 383–401.

McGee, E. O., Alvarez, A., & Milner, H. R., IV. (2016). Colorism as a salient space for understanding in teacher preparation. *Theory Into Practice, 55*(1), 69–79.

Mendes, W. B., Blascovich, J., Lickel, B., & Hunter, S. (2002). Challenge and threat during social interactions with white and Black men. *Personality and Social Psychology Bulletin, 28*(7), 939–952.

National Center for Education Statistics. (2017). *Fast facts.* https://nces.ed.gov/fastfacts/display.asp?id=28

National Women's Law Center. (2017). *Let her learn: Stopping school pushout.* https://nwlc.org/resources/stopping-school-pushout-for-girls-of-color/

Patton Davis, L. D., & Winkle-Wagner, R. (2012). Race at first sight: The funding of racial scripts between black and white women. In. K. L. Dace (Ed.), *Unlikely allies in the academy: Women of color and white women in conversation* (pp. 181–191). Routledge.

Pilgrim, D. (2012). *The Sapphire caricature.* Jim Crow Museum, Ferris State University. https://www.ferris.edu/HTMLS/news/jimcrow/antiblack/sapphire.htm (Original work published 2008)

CHAPTER 6: Colorism in the Classroom

Associated Press. (2019, January 7). *Colorism reveals many shades of prejudice in Hollywood.* NBC News. https://www.nbcnews.com/news/nbcblk/colorism-reveals-many-shades-prejudice-hollywood-n959756

Banks, T. L. (2000). Colorism: A darker shade of pale. *UCLA Law Review, 47,* 1705–1745.

Baxley, T. (2014). Taking off the rose-colored glasses: Exposing colorism through counter narratives. *The Journal of Culture and Education, 14*(1), 20–35.

Blake, J. J., Keith, V. M., Luo, W., Le, H., & Salter, P. (2017). The role of colorism in explaining African American females' suspension risk. *School Psychology Quarterly, 32*(1), 118–130.

Capodilupo, C. M., & Kim, S. (2014). Gender and race matter: The importance of considering intersections in Black women's body image. *Journal of counseling psychology, 61*(1), 37–49.

Graham, L. (1999). Our kind of people: Inside America's black upper class. New York: Harper Collins.

Hunter, M. (2007). The persistent problem of colorism: Skin tone, status, and inequality. *Sociology Compass, 1*(1), 237–254.

Hunter, M. (2016). Colorism in the classroom: How skin tone stratifies African American and Latina/o students. *Theory Into Practice*, *55*(1), 54–61.

Jackson-Lowman, H. (2014). An analysis of the impact of Eurocentric concepts of beauty on the lives of African American women. In H. Jackson-Lowman (Ed.), *Afrikan American women: Living at the crossroads of race, gender, class, and culture* (pp. 155–172). Cognella Academic.

Jordan, W. (1968). *White over Black: American attitudes toward the Negro, 1550–1812*. University of North Carolina Press.

Keith, V. M., & Monroe, C. R. (2016). Histories of colorism and implications for education. *Theory Into Practice*, *55*(1), 4–10.

Knight, D., & Meyer, I. (2015). What's 'colorism'? *Teaching Tolerance*, *51*, 45–48.

Ladson-Billings, G. (1995). Multicultural teacher education: Research, policy and practice. In J. Banks (Ed.), *Handbook of research on multicultural education*, 747–759. New York: Macmillan.

McGee, E. O., Alvarez, A., & Milner, H. R., IV. (2016). Colorism as a salient space for understanding in teacher preparation. *Theory Into Practice*, *55*(1), 69–79.

Nyong'o, L., & Harrison, V. (2019). *Sulwe*. Simon & Schuster Books for Young Readers.

Omi, M., & Winant, H. (1986). *Racial formation in the United States*. Routledge.

Stevenson, B. (1996). *Life in black and white: Family and community in the slave South*. Oxford University Press.

Sweet, F. W. (2005). *Legal history of the color line: The rise and triumph of the one-drop rule*. Backintyme.

Thompson, M., & Keith, V. (2001). The blacker the berry: Gender, skin tone, self-esteem, and self-efficacy. *Gender & Society*, *15*(3), 336–357.

Wilder, J. (2010). Revisiting "Color names and color notions": A contemporary examination of the language and attitudes of skin color among young black women. *Journal of Black Studies*, *41*(1), 184–206.

Williams, A. D. (2019). *Genesis begins again*. Simon & Schuster.

Williamson, J. (1980). *New people: Miscegenation and mulattoes in the United States*. Free Press.

Book Review: *The Skin I'm In*

Flake, S. G. (2007). *The skin I'm in*. Hyperion Books

PART III. "SPIRIT MURDERING"—BETTINA LOVE

CHAPTER 7: Visible Black Girls…Powerful Beyond Measure

Applebee, A. (1996). *Curriculum as conversation transforming traditions of teaching and learning*. University of Chicago Press.

Cain, S. (2013). *Quiet: The power of introverts in a world that can't stop talking*. Crown Publishing Group.

Cain, S., & Klein, E. (2015, Fall). Engaging the quiet kids. *Independent School*. https://www.nais.org/magazine/independent-school/fall-2015/engaging-the-quiet-kids/

Derman-Sparks, L., & Olsen-Edwards, J. (2010). *Anti-bias education for young children and ourselves*. National Association for the Education of Young Children.

Harris-Perry, M. (2013). *Sister citizen shame stereotypes and Black women in America*. Yale University Press.

Haynes, C., Stewart, S., & Allen, E. (2016). Three paths, one struggle: Black women and girls battling invisibility in U.S. classrooms. *Journal of Negro Education, 85*(3), 380–391.

Holloway, M. (2016, July 20). Why all teachers should advocate for quiet students. *Introvert, Dear.* https://introvertdear.com/news/why-all-teachers-should-advocate-for-quiet-students/

Houston, E. (2020). *Introvert vs. extrovert: A look at the spectrum and psychology.* Positive Psychology. https://positivepsychology.com/introversion-extroversion-spectrum/

Love, B. L. (2016). Anti-Black state violence, classroom edition: The spirit murdering of Black children. *Journal of Curriculum and Pedagogy, 13*(1), 22–25.

Love, B. (2019). *We want to do more than survive: Abolitionist teaching and the pursuit of educational freedom.* Beacon Press.

Milner, R. H. IV. (2006). *The promise of Black teachers' success with Black students.* https://files.eric.ed.gov/fulltext/EJ794734.pdf

Morris, M. W. (2016). *Pushout: The criminalization of Black girls in schools.* The New Press.

Rosen, J. (2016). *Teacher expectations reflect racial biases, Johns Hopkins study suggests.* https://hub.jhu.edu/2016/03/30/racial-bias-teacher-expectations-black-white/

Shulman, R. (2018). Why we need to pay attention to young introverts. *Forbes.* https://www.forbes.com/sites/robynshulman/2018/10/22/why-we-need-to-pay-attention-to-young-introverts/#4aa305ff630e

Simmons, D. (2017). Is social emotional learning really going to work for students of color? *Education Week.* https://www.edweek.org/tm/articles/2017/06/07/we-need-to-redefine-social-emotional-learning-for.html

Students lack interest or motivation. (2020). Carnegie Mellon University, Eberly Center for Teaching Excellence & Educational Motivation. https://www.cmu.edu/teaching/solveproblem/strat-lackmotivation/lackmotivation-04.html

Teaching introverted students: a guide for educators and parents. (2020). Education Degree. https://www.educationdegree.com/articles/supporting-introverted-students

Tomlinson, C. A. (2014). *The differentiated classroom: Responding to the needs of all learners.* ASCD.

Vignette: You Murdered My Rhythm and Blues

Baldwin, J. (1963, December 21). A talk to teachers. *Saturday Review,* 42–44.

CHAPTER 8: Why Does My Darkness Blind You?
Abandoning Racist Teaching Practices

Carter, D. (2007). Why the black kids sit together at the stairs: The role of identity-affirming counter-spaces in a predominantly white high school. *The Journal of Negro Education, 76*(4), 542–554. www.jstor.org/stable/40037227

Crenshaw, K. (1989). Demarginalizing the intersection of race and sex: A Black feminist critique of antidiscrimination doctrine, feminist theory and antiracist politics. *University of Chicago Legal Forum, 1989*(1), 139–167. https://chicagounbound.uchicago.edu/cgi/viewcontent.cgi?article=1052&context=uclf

Douglas, B., Lewis, C. W., Douglas, A., Scott, M. E., & Garrison-Wade, D. (2008). The impact of white teachers on the academic achievement of black students: An exploratory qualitative analysis. *Educational Foundations, 22*(1-2), 47–62. https://files.eric.ed.gov/fulltext/EJ839497.pdf

Garcia, P., Fernández, C. H., & Jackson, A. (2019). Counternarratives of youth participation among black girls. *Youth & Society*, 1–22. https://doi.org/10.1177/0044118X18824738

Gibson, S. (2016). Adolescent African American girls as engaged readers: Challenging stereotypical images of Black womanhood through urban fiction. *The Journal of Negro Education*, 85(3), 212–224. www.jstor.org/stable/10.7709

Huang, J., Krivkovich, A., Starikova, I., Yee, L., & Zanoschi, D. (2019, October 15). *Women in the workplace 2019*. McKinsey & Company. https://www.mckinsey.com/featured-insights/gender-equality/women-in-the-workplace-2019#

Joseph, N. M., Viesca, K. M., & Bianco, M. (2016). Black female adolescents and racism in schools: Experiences in a colorblind society. *The High School Journal*, 100(1), 4–25. https://doi.org/10.1353/hsj.2016.0018

Kang, J., Dasgupta, N., Yogeeswaran, K., & Blasi, G. (2010). Are ideal litigators white? Measuring the myth of colorblindness. *Journal of Empirical Legal Studies*, 7(4), 886–915. https://doi.org/10.1111/j.1740-1461.2010.01199.x

Knittel, M. (2018). *Making the transition from ally to co-conspirator*. Medium. https://medium.com/@knit0371/making-the-transition-from-ally-to-co-conspirator-cc28a5752af7

Lewis, J. A., Mendenhall, R., Harwood, S. A., & Browne Huntt, M. (2013). Coping with gendered racial microaggressions among black women college students. *Journal of African American Studies*, 17(1), 51–73. https://doi.org/10.1007/s12111-012-9219-0

National Center for Education Statistics. (2018). *Fast facts: Historically black colleges and universities*. https://nces.ed.gov/fastfacts/display.asp?id=667

Pérez, R. (2017). Racism without hatred? Racist humor and the myth of "colorblindness." *Sociological Perspectives*, 60(5), 956–974. https://doi.org/10.1177/0731121417719699

Starck, J. G., Riddle, T., Sinclair, S., & Warikoo, N. (2020). Teachers are people too: Examining the racial bias of teachers compared to other American adults. *Educational Researcher*, 49(4), 273–284. https://doi.org/10.3102/0013189X20912758

Sue, D. W., Capodilupo, C. M., Torino, G. C., Bucceri, J. M., Holder, A. M., Nadal, K. L., & Esquilin, M. (2007). Racial microaggressions in everyday life: Implications for clinical practice. *American Psychologist*, 62(4), 271–286. https://doi.org/10.1037/0003-66X.62.4.271

Warren, V. L. (2019). *The experiences of being African American women at a predominantly white religious college* [Doctoral dissertation, Capella University]. ProQuest pubs and Theses Global. https://search.proquest.com/docview/2281307402?accountid=36783

Book Review: *Genesis Begins Again*

Williams, A. D. (2019). *Genesis begins again*. Simon & Schuster.

CHAPTER 9: Finding My Armor of Self-Love

Anderson, B. N., & Coleman-King, C. (in press). "Catch this magic": How schools get in the way of gifted black girls. In O. Delano-Oriaran, M. W. Penick, S, J. Arki, A. Michael, O. Swindell, & E. Moore Jr. (Eds.), *Teaching beautiful brilliant black girls*. Corwin.

Arki, S. J. (2016). Teachers as activists: Using a Black, feminist pedagogy to prevent classroom bullying. In A. Osanloo, C. Reed, & J. Schwartz, J. (Eds.), *Creating and negotiating collaborative spaces for socially-just anti-bullying interventions for K–12 schools* (pp. 241–256). Information Age.

Liston, M. (in press). Black girl priming. In O. Delano-Oriaran, M. W. Penick, S, J. Arki, A. Michael, O. Swindell, & E. Moore Jr. (Eds.), *Teaching beautiful brilliant black girls*. Corwin.

Lythcott-Haims, J. (2018). *Real American: A memoir*. St. Martins Griffin.

Morris, M. W. (2016). *Pushout: The criminalization of black girls in schools*. The New Press.

Steele, C. (2010). *Whistling Vivaldi: How stereotypes affect us and what we can do*. W. W. Norton.

Swalwell, K., Kaaba, V., & Bottley, N. (in press). When she is the only one: High achieving black girls in suburban schools. In O. Delano-Oriaran, M. W. Penick, S, J. Arki, A. Michael, O. Swindell, & E. Moore Jr. (Eds.), *Teaching beautiful brilliant black girls*. Corwin.

Young V. (2011). *The secret thoughts of successful women: Why capable people suffer from the impostor syndrome and how to thrive in spite of it*. Currency.

PART IV. "RECLAIMING MY TIME"—MAXINE WATERS

CHAPTER 10: Girls in the School-to-Prison Pipeline: Implications of History, Policy, and Race

Abelson, R. P., Dasgupta, N., Park, J., & Banaji, M. R. (1998). Perceptions of the collective other. *Personality and Social Psychology Review, 2*(4), 243–250.

American Civil Liberties Union. (2017). *Bullies in blue: The origins and consequences of school policing.* https://www.aclu.org/sites/default/files/field_document/aclu_bullies_in_ blue_4_11_17_final.pdf

Banaji, M. R., Hardin, C., & Rothman, A. J. (1993). Implicit stereotyping in person judgment. *Journal of Personality and Social Psychology, 65*, 272–281.

Bennett, W. J., Dilulio, J. J., Jr., & Walters, J. P. (1996). *Body count: Moral poverty and how to win America's war on drugs*. Simon & Schuster.

Binion, B. (2019, September 23). *Florida police officer fired after arresting a 6-year-old girl for throwing a temper tantrum: Another example of the school-to-prison pipeline, which mislabels kids as criminals*. Reason. https://reason.com/2019/09/23/florida-of- fice-6-year-old-girl-arrested-for-throwing-a-temper-tantrum-school-to-prison- pipeline/

Blake, J., Butler, B. R., Lewis, C., & Darensbourg, A. (2011). Unmasking the inequitable discipline experiences of urban Black girls: Implications for urban educational stakeholders. *The Urban Review, 43*(1), 90–106.

Breslow, J. M. (2015, June 8). Locked up in America: Christel's story. *Frontline*. https:// www.pbs.org/wgbh/frontline/article/locked-up-in-america-christels-story/

Burkard, A. W., & Knox, S. (2004). Effect of therapist color-blindness on empathy and attributions in cross-cultural counseling. *Journal of Counseling Psychology, 51*(4), 387–397.

Dilulio, J. J., Jr. (1995). The coming of the super-predators. *The Weekly Standard 1*(11), 23–28.

Emdin, C. (2016). *For white folks who teach in the hood. And the rest of y'all too: Reality pedagogy and urban education*. Beacon Press.

Epstein, R., Blake, J. J., & Gonzalez, T. (2016). *Girlhood interrupted: The erasure of Black girls' childhood*. Georgetown Law, Center on Poverty and Inequality. https://www.law.george town.edu/poverty-inequality-center/wp- content/uploads/sites/14/2017/08/girlhood- interrupted.pdf

Equal Justice Initiative. (2017, September 14). *Black children five times more likely than white youth to be incarcerated.* https://eji.org/news/black-children-five-times-more-likely-than-whites-to-be-incarcerated/

Evans-Winters, V. E. (2011). *Teaching Black girls: Resiliency in urban classrooms* (2nd ed.). Peter Lang.

Fenning, P., & Rose, J. (2007). Overrepresentation of African American students in exclusionary discipline: The role of school policy. *Urban Education, 42,* 536–559.

Fordham, S. (1996). *Blacked out.* University of Chicago Press.

Fuentes, A. (2011a). Arresting development: Zero tolerance and the criminalization of children. *Rethinking Schools.* Winter 2011/2012, 18–23.

Fuentes, A. (2011b). *Lockdown high: When a schoolhouse becomes a jailhouse.* Verso.

Kaeble, D., & Cowhig, M. (2018, April 26). *Correctional populations in the United States 2016.* NCJ 251211. U.S. Department of Justice, Office of Justice Programs, Bureau of Justice Statistics. https://www.bjs.gov/index.cfm?ty=pbdetail&iid=6226

Kajstura, A. (2019). *Women's mass incarceration: The whole pie.* Prison Policy Initiative. https://www.prisonpolicy.org/reports/pie2019women.html

Gregory, A., & Mosely, P. M. (2004). The discipline gap: Teachers' views on the overrepresentation of African American students in the discipline system. *Equity & Excellence in Education, 37*(1), 18–30.

Inniss-Thompson, M. N. (2017, September). *Summary of discipline data for girls in U.S. public schools: An analysis from the 2013–14 U.S. Department of Education Office for Civil Rights data collection.* National Black Women's Justice Institute. https://www.acsa.org/application/files/5215/0532/2372/NBWJI_Fact_Sheet_090917FINAL.pdf

Losen, D. J. (2012). Sound discipline policy for successful schools. In S. Bahena, N. Cooc, R. Currie-Rubin, P. Kuttner, & M. Ng (Eds.), *Disrupting the school to prison pipeline* (pp. 45–72). Harvard Education Press.

Monroe, C. R., & Obidah, J. E. (2004). The influence of cultural synchronization on a teacher's perceptions of disruption: A case study of an African American middle-school classroom. *Journal of Teacher Education, 55*(3), 256–268.

Morris, E. W. (2007). "Ladies" or "loudies"? Perceptions and experience of black girls in classrooms. *Youth & Society, 38*(4), 490–514.

Morris, M. W., Conteh, M., & Harris-Perry, M. (2018). *Pushout: The criminalization of Black girls in schools.* The New Press.

National Women's Law Center. (2017, April 18). Four ways that educators can let her learn. *National Women's Law Center.* https://nwlc.org/blog/four-ways-educators-can-let-her-learn/

Nicholson-Crotty, S., Birchmeier, Z., & Valentine, D. (2009). Exploring the impact of school discipline on racial disproportion in the juvenile justice system. *Social Science Quarterly, 90*(4), 1003–1018. www.jstor.org/stable/42940652

Office of Juvenile Justice and Delinquency Prevention. (2018). Estimated number of juvenile arrests, 2018. *Statistical briefing book.* www.ojjdp.gov/ojstatbb/crime/qa05101.asp?qaDate=2018

Pane, D. M., & Rocco, T. S. (2014). *Transforming the school-to-prison pipeline: Lessons from the classroom.* Sense Publishers.

Sickmund, M., Sladky, T. J., Kang, W., & Puzzanchera, C. (2017). *Easy access to the census of juveniles in residential placement.* http://www.ojjdp.gov/ojstatbb/ezacjrp

Skiba, R. J. (2002). Special education and school discipline: A precarious balance. *Behavioral Disorders, 27*(2), 81–97.

Skiba, R. J., Peterson, R. L., & Williams, T. (1997). Office referrals and suspensions: Disciplinary interventions in middle school. *Education and Treatment of Children, 20*(3), 295–303.

Smith, E. J., & Harper, S. R. (2015). *Disproportionate impact of K–12 school suspension and expulsion on Black students in southern states.* University of Pennsylvania, Center for the Study of Race and Equity in Education.

Sue, D. W. (2005). *Multicultural social work practice.* John Wiley & Sons.

Winn, M. T., & Behizadeh, N. (2011). The right to be literate: Literacy, education, and the school-to-prison pipeline. *Review of Research in Education, 35*(1), 147–173.

Winter, M. (2013, May 2). Florida teen arrested, expelled over science 'blast.' *USA Today.* https://www.usatoday.com/story/news/nation/2013/05/02/florida-student-arrested-science-experiment-blast/2130381/

CHAPTER 11: How Dare You be Brilliant: The Precarious Situation for Black Girls

Adams, P. (2010). Understanding the different realities, experience, and use of self-esteem between Black and white adolescent girls. *Journal of Black Psychology, 36*(3), 255–276.

Ahmad, F. Z. & Iverson, S. (2013). *The state of women of color in the United States.* Center for American Progress. https://www.americanprogress.org/issues/race/reports/2013/10/24/77546/the-state-of-women-of-color-in-the-united-states-2/

Anderson, M. J. (1988). *The American census: A social history.* Yale University Press.

Aud, S., Fox, M., & KewalRamani, A. (2010). *Status and trends in the education of racial and ethnic groups* (NCES 2010-015). U.S. Department of Education, National Center for Education Statistics.

Berry, M. F. (1982). Twentieth century black women in education. *Journal of Negro Education, 51*(3), 288–300.

Blake, J., Butler, B., Lewis, C., & Darensbourg, A. (2011). Unmasking the inequitable discipline experiences of urban Black girls: Implications for urban educational stakeholders. *The Urban Review, 43*(1), 90–106.

Brown v. Board of Education, 347 U.S. 483 (1954).

Buckley, T. R., & Carter, R. T. (2005). Black adolescent girls: Do gender role and racial identity impact their self-esteem? *Sex Roles, 53*(9/10), 647–661.

Carter, P., Skiba, R., Arredondo, M., & Pollock, M. (2014). *You can't fix what you don't look at: Acknowledging race in addressing racial discipline disparities.* The Equity Project at Indiana University.

Chapman, C., Laird, J., Ifill, N., & KewalRamani, A. (2012). *Trends in high school dropout and completion rates, 1972–2009.* http://nces.ed.gov/pubs2012/2012006.pdf

Chavous, T., & Cogburn, C. (2007). Superinvisible women: Black girls and women in education. *Black Women, Gender +Families, 1*(2), 24–51.

Crenshaw, K. (1989). Demarginalizing the intersection of race and sex: A black feminist critique of antidiscrimination doctrine, feminist theory, and antiracist politics. *University of Chicago Legal Forum, 1989*(1), 139–167.

Crenshaw, K. (1991). Mapping the margins: Intersectionality, identity politics, and violence against women of color. *Stanford Law Review, 43*(6): 1241–1299.

Crenshaw, K., Ocen, P., & Nanda, J. (2015). *Black girls matter: Pushed out, over-policed and under-protected.* https://www.atlanticphilanthropies.org/wp-content/uploads/2015/09/BlackGirlsMatter_Report.pdf

Evans-Winters, V. E. (2011). *Teaching Black girls: Resiliency in urban classrooms* (2nd ed.). Peter Lang.

Evans-Winters, V., & Esposito, J. (2010). Other people's daughters: Critical race feminism and Black girls' education. *Educational Foundations, 24*(1–2), 11–24.

Ford, D. Y. (2013a). Gifted underrepresentation and prejudice: Learning from Allport and Merton. *Gifted Child Today, 36*(1), 62–68.

Ford, D. Y. (2013b). *Recruiting and retaining culturally different gifted students in gifted education.* Prufrock Press.

Gifted and Talented Children's Education Act of 1978, §901, 20 U.S.C. 3311 (1978).

Gilliam, W., Maupin, A., Reyes, C., Accavitti, M., & Shic, F. (2016). *Do early educators' implicit biases regarding sex and race relate to behavior expectations and recommendations of preschool expulsions and suspensions?* Yale School of Medicine, Edward Zigler Center in Child Development & Social Policy. https://medicine.yale.edu/childstudy/zigler/publications/Preschool%20Implicit%20Bias%20Policy%20Brief_final_9_26_276766_5379_v1.pdf

Morales, E. (2014). Intersectional impact: Black students and race, gender and class microaggressions in higher education. *Race, Gender and Class, 21*(3/4), 48–66.

Morris, E. W. (2007). "Ladies" or "loudies"? Perceptions and experience of black girls in classrooms. *Youth & Society, 38*(4), 490–514.

National Center for Educational Statistics. (2010). Indicator 24. Enrollment. *Status and trends in the education of racial and ethnic minorities.* http://nces.ed.gov/pubs2010/2010015/indicator6_24.asp

Renzulli, J. S. (1978). What makes giftedness? Reexamining a definition. *Phi Delta Kappan, 60*(3), 180–184, 261.

Riley, T., Foster, A., & Serpell, Z. (2015). Race-based stereotypes, expectations, and exclusion in American education. In L. D. Drakeford (Ed.), *The race controversy in American education* (pp. 169–189). Praeger.

Squires, J. (2008). Intersecting inequalities: Reflecting on the subjects and objects of equality. *The Political Quarterly, 79*(1), 53–61.

Tyson, K. (2003). Notes from the back of the room: Problems and paradoxes in the schooling of young black students. *Sociology of Education, 76*(4), 326–343.

U.S. Department of Education, Office for Civil Rights. (2016). *2013–2014 civil rights data collection: A first look.* https://sss.usf.edu/resources/presentations/2016/fasp2016/2013-14-first-look-CRDC.pdf

CHAPTER 12: Girl Trafficking Misunderstood: Understanding the Commercially Sexually Exploited African American Girl

Bloom, S. (1995). Creating sanctuary in the school. *Journal for a Just and Caring Education, I*(4), 403–433.

Butler, C. N. (2015). The racial roots of human trafficking. *UCLA Law Review, 62,* 1464–1514.

Emba, C. (2019, January). Black women and girls deserve better. *The Lilly.* https://www.thelily.com/black-women-and-girls-deserve-better/

Epstein, R., Blake, J. J., & Gonzalez, T. (2017). *Girlhood interrupted: The erasure of Black girls' childhood*. Georgetown Law, Center on Poverty and Inequality. https://www.law.georgetown.edu/poverty-inequality-center/wp-content/uploads/sites/14/2017/08/girlhood-interrupted.pdf

Human trafficking defined. (n.d.). Retrieved November 12, 2020, from https://www.justice.gov/humantrafficking

Love, B. (2019). *We want to do more than survive: Abolitionist teaching and the pursuit of educational freedom*. Beacon Press.

Marcus, A., Horning, A., Curtis, R., Sanson, J., & Thompson, E. (2014). Conflict and agency among sex workers and pimps: A closer look at domestic minor sex trafficking. *Annals of the American Academy of Political and Social Science, 653*(1), 225–246. https://doi.org/10.1177/0002716214521993

Morris, M. W. (2016). *Pushout: The criminalization of black girls in schools*. The New Press.

National Association of Black Social Workers. (1972, September). *Position statement on trans-racial adoption*. https://pages.uoregon.edu/adoption/archive/NabswTRA.htm

Office of Juvenile Justice and Delinquency Prevention. (n.d.). *Commercial sexual exploitation of children*. Retrieved November 12, 2020, from https://ojjdp.ojp.gov/programs/commercial-sexual-exploitation-children

Reese, F. (2017, June 15). Sex trafficking's true victims: Why are our black girls/women so vulnerable? *Atlanta Black Star*. https://atlantablackstar.com/2017/06/15/sex-traffickings-true-victims-why-are-our-black-girlswomen-so-vulnerable/

Riddle, T., & Sinclair, S. (2019, April 23). Racial disparities in school-based disciplinary actions are associated with county-level rates of racial bias. *Proceedings of the National Academy of Sciences, 116*(17), 8255–8260. https://doi.org/10.1073/pnas.1808307116

The 7c's: The essential building block of resilience. (n.d.). *Fostering Resilience*. Retrieved November 12, 2020, from http://www.fosteringresilience.com/professionals/7cs_professionals.php

Vignette: Know Your Body, Sis

Banner, J. M., & Cannon, H. C. (2017). *The elements of teaching*. Yale University Press.

brown. a. m. (2019). *Pleasure activism: The politics of feeling good*. AK Press.

Collins, P. H. (2002). *Black feminist thought: Knowledge, consciousness, and the politics of empowerment*. Routledge.

Collins, P. H. (2004). *Black sexual politics: African Americans, gender, and the new racism*. Routledge.

Collins, P. H., & Bilge, S. (2016). *Intersectionality*. John Wiley & Sons.

Combahee River Collective. (1977). A black feminist statement. In Linda Nicolson (Ed.), *The second wave: A reader in feminist theory* (pp. 63–70). Routledge.

Cooper, B. (2018). *Eloquent rage: A Black feminist discovers her superpower*. St. Martin's Press.

Crenshaw, K. (1989). Demarginalizing the intersection of race and sex: A black feminist critique of antidiscrimination doctrine, feminist theory and antiracist politics. *The University of Chicago Legal Forum, 1989*(1), 139–167. https://chicagounbound.uchicago.edu/cgi/viewcontent.cgi?article=1052&context=uclf

Fine, M. (1988). Sexuality, schooling, and adolescent females: The missing discourse of desire. *Harvard Educational Review, 58*(1), 29–54.

Halliday, A. S. (2017). Envisioning black girl futures: Nicki Minaj's anaconda feminism and new understandings of Black girl sexuality in popular culture. *Departures in Critical Qualitative Research, 6*(3), 65–77.

Saar, M. S., Epstein, R., Rosenthal, L., & Vafa, Y. (2015). *The sexual abuse to prison pipeline: The girls' story.* Georgetown Law, Center on Poverty and Inequality. https://www.law.georgetown.edu/poverty-inequality-center/wp-content/uploads/sites/14/2019/02/The-Sexual-Abuse-To-Prison-Pipeline-The-Girls%E2%80%99-Story.pdf

Seales, A. (2019). *Small doses: Potent truths for everyday use.* Abrams Image.

Taylor, S. R. (@sonyareneetaylor). (2020, June 14). *My #PleasureReport aka black joy as survival* [Video.] https://www.instagram.com/p/CBZy4tiAjxm/

CHAPTER 13: Little Black Girls With Curves

Adams-Bass, V., & Bentley-Edwards, K. L. (2020). The problem with Black girl magic for Black girls. In D. Apugo, L. Mawhinney, & A. M. Mbilishaka (Eds.), *Strong black girls: Patchwork stories of remembrance, resistance, and resilience* (2nd ed., pp. 99–117). Teachers College Press.

Barret, K. (2018). When school dress codes discriminate. *NEA News.* http://neatoday.org/2018/07/24/when-school-dress-codes-discriminate/

Bentley, K. L., Adams, V. N., & Stevenson, H. C. (2009). Racial socialization: Roots, processes, and outcomes. In H. A. Neville, B. M. Tynes, & S. O. Utsey (Eds.), *Handbook of African American psychology* (pp. 255–267). Sage.

Bentley-Edwards, K. L., & Adams-Bass, V. N. (2013). The whole picture: Examining Black women through the life span. In H. Jackson Lowman (Ed.), *Afrikan American Women: Living at the Crossroads of Race, Gender, Class, and Culture* (pp. 189–201). Cognella Academic.

Biro, F. M., Greenspan, L. C., Galvez, M. P., Pinney, S. M., Teitelbaum, S., Windham, G. C., Deardorff, J., Herrick, R. L., Succop, P. A., Hiatt, R. A., Kushi, L. H., & Wolff, M. S. (2013). Onset of breast development in a longitudinal cohort. *Pediatrics, 132*(6), 1019–1027. https://doi.org/10.1542/peds.2012-3773

Blake, J. J., Butler, B. R., Lewis, C. W., & Darensbourg, A. (2011). Unmasking the inequitable discipline experiences of urban Black girls: Implications for urban educational stakeholders. *The Urban Review, 43*(1), 90–106. https://doi.org/10.1007/s11256-009-0148-8

Epstein, R., Blake, J. J., & González, T. (2017). *Girlhood interrupted: The erasure of Black girls' childhood.* Georgetown Law, Center on Poverty and Inequality. https://www.law.georgetown.edu/poverty-inequality-center/wp-content/uploads/sites/14/2017/08/girlhood-interrupted.pdf

Herman-Giddens, M. E. (2001). Early puberty: Implications for physical and psychological well-being. *Journal of Women's Health & Gender-Based Medicine, 10*(4), 391–391.

Herman-Giddens, M. E. (2013). The enigmatic pursuit of puberty in girls. *Pediatrics, 132*(6), 1125–1126. https://doi.org/10.1542/peds.2013-3058

Herman-Giddens, M. E., Slora, E. J., Wasserman, R. C., Bourdony, C. J., Bhapkar, M. V., Koch, G. G., & Hasemeier, C. M. (1997). Secondary sexual characteristics and menses in young girls seen in office practice: A study from the pediatric research in office settings network. *Pediatrics, 99*(4), 505–512. https://doi.org/10.1542/peds.99. 4.505

Losen, D. J., & Whitaker, A. (2017). *Lost instruction: The disparate impact of the school discipline gap in California.* UCLA Civil Rights Project.

Morris, E. W. (2007). "Ladies" or "loudies"? Perceptions and experiences of Black girls in classrooms. *Youth & Society, 38*(4), 490–515.

Morris, M. W. (2015). *Pushout: The criminalization of Black girls in schools*: The New Press.

Morris, E. W., & Perry, B. L. (2017). Girls behaving badly? Race, gender, and subjective evaluation in the discipline of African American girls. *Sociology of Education, 90*(2), 127–148. https://doi.org/10.1177/0038040717694876

The NAACP Legal Defense and Educational Fund & The National Women's Law Center (NWLC). (2014). *Unlocking opportunity for African American girls: A call to action for educational equity.* Authors.

Raby, R. (2010). "Tank tops are ok but I don't want to see her thong." *Youth & Society, 41*(3), 333–356. https://doi.org/10.1177/0044118x09333663

PART V. "YOUR SILENCE IS A KNEE ON MY NECK"—NATASHA CLOUD

CHAPTER 14: Whiteness Competency: How Not to Be BBQ Becky

Acuña, R. (2007). *Occupied America: A history of Chicanos* (6th ed.). Pearson.

Alexander, M. (2010). *The new Jim Crow: Mass incarceration in the age of colorblindness.* The New Press.

Allen, T. W. (1997). *The invention of the white race.* Verso.

Anderson, C. (2016). *White rage: The unspoken truth of our racial divide.* Bloomsbury.

Battalora, J. (2013). *Birth of a white nation: The invention of white people and its relevance today.* Strategic Book Publishing and Rights Agency.

DiAngelo, R. (2018). *White fragility: Why it is so hard for white people to talk about racism.* Beacon Press.

Feagin, J. R. (2006). *Systemic racism: A theory of oppression.* Routledge.

Fearnow, B. (2018, May 10). Video: White woman calls police on Black family's BBQ for 'trespassing' in Oakland Park. *Newsweek.* https://www.newsweek.com/lake-merritt-bbq-barbecue-video-oakland-racist-charcoal-east-bay-black-family-919355

Frankenberg, R. (1993). *White women, race matters: The social construction of whiteness.* University of Minnesota Press.

Glenn, E. N. (2002). *Unequal freedom: How race and gender shaped American citizenship and labor.* Harvard University Press.

Harris, A. (1993). Whiteness as property. *Harvard Law Review, 106*(8), 1744–1791.

LaDuke, W. (2005). *Recovering the sacred: The power of naming and claiming.* South End Press.

Lipsitz, G. (2006). *The possessive investment in whiteness: How white people profit from identity politics.* Temple University Press.

Marable, M. (1983). *How capitalism underdeveloped Black America.* South End Press.

Marcius, C., & Annese, J. (2020, May 25). See it: 'I'm going to tell them there's an African-American man threatening my life': White woman calls cops on man in Central Park after he asks her to leash her dog. *New York Daily News.* https://www.nydailynews.com/new-york/nyc-crime/ny-viral-video-central-park-20200526-o7djnjr3fjcsfl2augko6mv7oi-story.html

Omi, M., & Winant, H. (1994). *Racial formation in the United States: From the 1960s to the 1990s* (2nd ed.). Routledge.

Roediger, D. R. (2003). *The wages of whiteness: Race and the making of the American working class* (Rev. ed.). Verso.

Rothstein, R. (2017). *The color of law: A forgotten history of how our government segregated America*. Liveright.

Chapter 15: Can I Do This if I'm White? How White Educators Can Be the Teachers Black Girl Students Deserve

Foronda, C., Baptiste, D. L., Reinholdt, M. M., & Ousman, K. (2016). Cultural humility: A concept analysis. *Journal of Transcultural Nursing, 27*(3), 210–217.

Helms, J. E. (1995). *An update of Helm's white and people of color racial identity models*. In J. G. Ponterotto, J. M. Casas, L. A. Suzuki, & C. M. Alexander (Eds.), *Handbook of multicultural counseling* (p. 181–198). Sage.

Johnson, T. (2020, June 11). When Black people are in pain, white people just join book clubs. *Washington Post*. https://www.washingtonpost.com/outlook/white-antiracist-allyship-book-clubs/2020/06/11/9edcc766-abf5-11ea-94d2-d7bc43b26bf9_story.html

Sealey-Ruiz, Y., & Greene, P. (2015). Popular visual images and the (mis)reading of black male youth: A case for racial literacy in urban preservice teacher education. *Teaching Education, 26*(1), 55–76.

Stevenson, H. (2014). *Promoting racial literacy in schools: Differences that make a difference*. Teachers College Press.

Sue, D. W., & Torino, G. C. (2005). Racial-cultural competence: Awareness, knowledge, and skills. In R. T. Carter (Ed.), *Handbook of Racial-Cultural Psychology and Counseling, Training and Practice* (Vol. 2, pp. 3–18). John Wiley & Sons.

Tatum, B. D. (2017). *Why are all the Black kids sitting together in the cafeteria? And other conversations about race*. Basic Books.

Chapter 16: Not Knowing and Not Controlling: Learning Alongside Black Girl Students

Ahmed, S. (2006). *Queer phenomenology: Orientations, objects, others*. Duke University Press.

Cox, A. M. (2015). *Shapeshifters: Black girls and the choreography of citizenship permutations*. Palgrave Macmillan.

Davis, C., & Phillips-Fein, J. (2018). Tendus and tenancy: Black dancers and the white landscape of dance education. In A. Kraehe, R. Gaztambide-Fernández, & B. Carpenter, II (Eds.), *Palgrave handbook on race and education* (pp. 571–584). Palgrave Macmillan.

DeFrantz, T. (2012). Unchecked popularity: Neoliberal circulations of black social dance. In D. Nielsen & P. A. Ybarra (Eds.), *Neoliberalism and global theatres: Performance* (pp. 128–140). Duke University Press.

Desmond, J. (1993). Embodying difference: Issues in dance and cultural studies. *Cultural Critique, 26*(Winter), 33–63.

Dixon-Gottschild, B. (1996). *Digging the Africanist presence in American performance: Dance and other contexts*. Greenwood Press.

Hook, J. N., Davis, D. E., Owen, J., Worthington Jr., E. L., & Utsey, S. O. (2013). Cultural humility: Measuring openness to culturally diverse clients. *Journal of Counseling Psychology*. https://doi.org/10.1037/a0032595.

hooks, b. (1992). *Black looks: Race and representation*. South End Press.

McCarthy-Brown, N. (2017). *Dance pedagogy for a diverse world: Culturally relevant teaching in theory, research and practice*. McFarland.

Sharpe, C. (2016). *In the wake: On blackness and being*. Duke University Press.

Shuller, K. (2017). *The biopolitics of feeling: Race, sex and science in the nineteenth century*. Duke University Press.

Vignette: Confessions of a White Teacher: Seven Ways I Failed Beautiful and Brilliant Black Girls

Helms, J. E. (2007). *A race is a nice thing to have* (2nd ed). Microtraining Associates.

CHAPTER 17: Not in Our Name: Fierce Allyship for White Women

Hancock, S., & Warren, C. A. (2017). *White women's work: Examining the intersectionality of teaching, identity, and race*. Information Age.

Hoyer, J., & Beesdo-Baum, K. (2014). Prolonged imaginal exposure based on worry scenarios. In P. Neudeck & H. Wittchen (Eds.), *Exposure therapy: Rethinking the model, refining the method* (pp. 245–260). Springer.

Liu, W. M. (2017). White male power and privilege: The relationship between white supremacy and social class. *Journal of Counseling Psychology, 64*(4), 349–358.

Shapiro, F. (2018). *Eye movement desensitization and reprocessing: Basic principles, protocols, and procedures* (3rd ed.). Guilford.

CHAPTER 18: White Teachers, Black Girls, and White Fragility

Banks, J. A., & McGee Banks, C.A. (2010). *Multicultural education: Issues and perspectives* (7th ed.). Wiley.

DiAngelo, R. (2018). *White fragility: Why it's so hard for white people to talk about racism*. Beacon Press.

Jackson, L. M. (2019). *White negroes: When cornrows were in vogue . . . and other thoughts on cultural appropriation*. Beacon Press.

Johnson, E. P. (2003). *Appropriating blackness: Performance and the politics of authenticity*. Duke University Press.

Lindsay, C., Blom, E., & Tilsley, A. (2017). *Diversifying the classroom: Examining the teacher pipeline*. Urban Institute. https://www.urban.org/features/diversifying-classroom-examining-teacher-pipeline

Picower, B. (2015). The unexamined whiteness of teaching: How white teachers maintain and enact dominant racial ideologies. *Race Ethnicity and Education, 12*(2), 197–215.

PART VI. "GIVE LIGHT AND PEOPLE WILL FIND THE WAY."—ELLA BAKER

CHAPTER 19: A Reimagined Pedagogy of Affirmation and Artistic Practices

Collins, P. H. (1990). *Black feminist thought: Knowledge, consciousness, and the politics of empowerment*. Routledge.

Epstein, R., Blake, J., & González, T. (2017). *Girlhood interrupted: The erasure of Black girls' childhood*. Georgetown Law, Center on Poverty and Inequality. http://www.law .georgetown.edu/academics/centers-institutes/poverty-inequality/upload/girlhood-interrupted.pdf

Evans-Winters, V. E., & Girls for Gender Equity. (2017). Flipping the script: The dangerous bodies of girls of color. *Cultural Studies Critical Methodologies, 17*(5), 415–423.

Hines-Datiri, D., & Carter Andrews, D. J. (2017). The effects of zero tolerance policies on Black girls: Using critical race feminism and figured worlds to examine school discipline. *Urban Education*, 1–22.

Paris, D., & Alim, H. S. (2014). What are we seeking to sustain through culturally sustaining pedagogy? A loving critique forward. *Harvard Educational Review, 84*(1), 85–100.

Ladson-Billings, G. (1995). But that's just good teaching! The case for culturally relevant pedagogy. *Theory Into Practice, 34*(3), 159–165.

Love, B. (2019, May 23). How schools are 'spirit murdering' black and brown students. *Education Week*. https://www.edweek.org/ew/articles/2019/05/24/how-teachers-are-spirit-murdering-black-and.html

Morris, E. W. (2007). "Ladies" or "loudies"? Perceptions and experiences of black girls in classrooms. *Youth & Society, 38*(4), 490–515.

Morris, M. (2019). *Sing a rhythm, dance a blues: Education for the liberation of Black and Brown girls*. The New Press.

Muhammad, G. E., & Womack, E. (2015). From pen to pin: The multimodality of Black girls (re) writing their lives. *Ubiquity: The Journal of Literature, Literacy, and the Arts, 2*(2), 6–45.

Nunn, N. M. (2018). Super-girl: Strength and sadness in Black girlhood. *Gender and Education, 30*(2), 239–258.

Omolade, B. (1987). A Black feminist pedagogy. *Women's Studies Quarterly, 15*(3/4), 32–39.

Robinson, D., & Lewis, C. W. (2017). Typologies for effectiveness: Characteristics of effective teachers in urban learning environments. *Journal of Urban Learning, Teaching, and Research, 13*, 124–134.

Walker, A. (1983). *In search of our mothers' gardens: Womanist prose*. Houghton Mifflin Harcourt.

Respecting

PART I. "I'LL BE BOSSY AND DAMN PROUD."—ROSA CLEMENTE

McKinzie, A. E., & Richards, P. L. (2019). An argument for context-driven intersectionality. *Sociology Compass, 13*(4), e12671.

CHAPTER 20: Who are Black Girls: An Intersectional Herstory of Feminism

Arki, S. J. (2016). Teachers as activists: Using a Black, feminist pedagogy to prevent classroom bullying. In A. Osanloo, C. Reed, & J. Schwartz (Eds.), *Creating and negotiating collaborative spaces for socially-just anti-bullying interventions for K–12 schools* (pp. 241–256). Information Age.

Arki, S. J. (2018). Ruminations from a #BlackMommyActivist. In E. Moore Jr., A. Michael, & M. W. Penick-Parks (Eds.), *The guide for white women who teach Black boys* (pp. 270–274). Corwin.

Carlton Parsons, E.R. (2008, March 19). Positionality and a theoretical accommodation of it: Rethinking science education research. *Science Education*, *2*(6), 1127–1144. http://doi/10.1002/sce.20273

Chesimard, J. (1973). To my people. *The Black Scholar*, *5*(2), 16–18. www.jstor.org/stable/41066198

Christian, J. C. (2014). *Understanding the black flame and multigenerational education trauma: Toward a theory of the dehumanization of black students.* Lexington Books.

Collins, P. H. (1990). *Black feminist thought: Knowledge, consciousness, and the politics of empowerment.* Unwin Hyman.

Collins, P. H. (1994). Shifting the center: Race, class and feminist theorizing about motherhood. In E. Nakano Glenn, G. Chang, & L. Rennie Forcey (Eds.), *Mothering: ideology, experience and agency* (pp. 45–65). Routledge.

The Combahee River Collective. (1995). A Black feminist statement. In B. Guy-Sheftall (Ed.), *Words of fire: An anthology of African American feminist thought* (pp. 232–240). The New Press.

Crenshaw K. W. (1995). Mapping the margins: Intersectionality, identity politics and violence against women of color. In K. Crenshaw, N. Gotanda, G. Peller, & K. Thomas (Eds), *Critical race theory: The key writings that formed the movement* (pp. 357–383). The New Press.

Crenshaw, K. (2016, October). *The urgency of intersectionality* [Video]. TED Talk. https://www.ted.com/talks/kimberle_crenshaw_the_urgency_of_intersectionality?language=en

Davis, A. (1995). Reflections on the black woman's role in the community of slaves. In B. Guy-Sheftall (Ed.), *Words of fire: An anthology of African American feminist thought* (pp. 200–218). The New Press.

Fennel, S., & Arnot, M. (2008). Decentring hegemonic gender theory: The implications for educational research. *Compare*, *38*(5), 525–538.

Guy-Sheftall, B. (1995a). Civil rights and women's liberation: Racial/sexual politics in the angry decades. In B. Guy-Sheftall (Ed.), *Words of fire: An anthology of African American feminist thought* (pp. 143–228). The New Press.

Guy-Sheftall, B. (1995b). Maria Miller Stewart (1803–1879). In B. Guy-Sheftall (Ed.), *Words of fire: An anthology of African American feminist thought* (p. 25). The New Press.

Guy-Sheftall, B. (1995c). Preface. In B. Guy-Sheftall (Ed.), *Words of fire: An anthology of African American feminist thought* (pp. xiii–xvii). The New Press.

Guy-Sheftall, B. (1995d). The Combahee River Collective. In B. Guy-Sheftall (Ed.), *Words of fire: An anthology of African American feminist thought* (p. 231). The New Press.

Hansberry, L. (1957). Simone de Beauvoir and the second sex: An American commentary. In B. Guy-Sheftall (Ed.), *Words of fire: An anthology of African American feminist thought* (pp. 128–141). The New Press.

hooks, b. (1994). *Teaching to transgress: Education as the practice of freedom.* Routledge.

Lorde, A. (1984). Age, race, class, and sex: Women redefining difference. In *Sister outsider*, 114–123. Crossing Press.

Love, B. (2019). *We want to do more than survive: Abolitionist teaching and the pursuit of educational freedom.* Boston.

Morris, M. W. (2016). *Pushout: The criminalization of Black girls in schools.* The New Press.

Rabaka, R. (2009). *Africana critical theory: Reconstructing the black radical tradition from W. E. B. Du Bois and C. L. R. James to Frantz Fanon and Amilcar Cabral.* Lexington Books.

Ransby, B. (2014). Foreword. In P. S. Fonner (Ed.), *The Black Panthers speak* (pp. ix–xviii). Haymarket Books.

Ross, R. (2003). *Witnessing and testifying: Black women, religion and civil rights*. Fortress Press.

Stewart, M. M. (1831/1995). Religion and the pure principles of morality, the sure foundation on which we must build. In B. Guy-Sheftall (Ed.), *Words of fire: An anthology of African American feminist thought* (pp. 26–29). The New Press.

Taylor, U. (1995). Amy Jacques Garvey (1896-1973). In B. Guy-Sheftall (Ed.), *Words of fire: An anthology of African American feminist thought* (p. 89). The New Press.

Wallace, M. (1982). A black feminist's search for sisterhood. In A. Hull, P. B. Scott, & B. Smith (Eds.), *All the women are white, all the Blacks are men, but some of us are brave* [Kindle edition]. The Feminist Press at CUNY. https://www.amazon.com

Weisenburger, S. (1998). *Modern Medea*. Hill and Wang.

Book Review: *Crossing Ebenezer Creek*

Bolden, T. (2017). *Crossing Ebenezer Creek*. Bloomsbury.

CHAPTER 21: Navigating Multiple Identities: The Black Immigrant Girl Experience

Allen, K. M., Jackson, I., & Knight, M. G. (2012). Complicating culturally relevant pedagogy: Unpacking African immigrants' cultural identities. *International Journal of Multicultural Education*, *14*(2), 1–28.

Anderson, M. (2015). *A rising share of the U.S. Black population is foreign born*. Pew Research Center: Social and Demographic Trends. https://www.pewsocialtrends.org/2015/04/09/a-rising-share-of-the-u-s-black-population-is-foreign-born/

Anderson, M., & López, G. (2018, January 24). Key facts about black immigrants in the U.S. *FactTank: News in the Numbers*. Pew Research Center. https://www.pewresearch.org/fact-tank/

Arthur, J. (2000). *Invisible sojourners: African immigrant diaspora in the United States*. Praeger.

Awokoya, J. T. (2012). Identity constructions and negotiations among 1.5- and second-generation Nigerians: The impact of family, school, and peer contexts. *Harvard Educational Review*, *82*(2), 255–281.

Blum, L. (2015). Race and class categories and subcategories in educational thought and research. *Theory and Research in Education*, *13*(1), 87–104.

Carter, P. (2005). *Keepin' it real: School success beyond black and white*. Oxford University Press.

Cone, N., Buxton, C., Lee, O., & Mahotiere, M. (2014). Negotiating a sense of identity in a foreign land: Navigating public school structures and practices that often conflict with Haitian culture and values. *Urban Education*, *49*(3), 263–296.

Coutinho, M. T., & Koinis-Mitchell, D. (2014). Black immigrants and school engagement: Perceptions of discrimination, ethnic identity, and American identity. *Journal of Black Psychology*, *40*(6), 520–538.

Crenshaw K. W. (1995). Mapping the margins: Intersectionality, identity politics and violence against women of color. In K. Crenshaw, N. Gotanda, G. Peller, & K. Thomas (Eds.), *Critical race theory: The key writings that formed the movement* (pp. 357–383). The New Press.

Fries-Britt, S., George Mwangi, C. A., & Peralta, A. M. (2014). Learning race in a U.S. context: An emergent framework on the perceptions of race among foreign-born students of color. *Journal of Diversity in Higher Education, 7*(1), 1–13.

Gilbert, S. (2009). A study of Ogbu and Simons' thesis regarding Black children's immigrant and non-immigrant status and school achievement. *The Negro Educational Review, 60*(1-4), 71–91.

Habecker, S. (2016). Seen but not heard: Assessing youth perspectives of African immigrant parenting in the diaspora. *Africology: The Journal of Pan-African Studies 9*(4), 253–270.

Halter, M., & Johnson, V. (2014). *African and American: West Africans in post-civil rights America.* NYU Press.

Johnson, S. (2020). A changing nation: Population projections under alternative migration scenarios. *Current Population Reports*, P25-1146, U.S. Census Bureau.

Knight, M. G., & Watson, V. W. (2014). Toward participatory communal citizenship: Rendering visible the civic teaching, learning, and actions of African immigrant youth and young adults. *American Educational Research Journal, 51*(3), 539–566.

Lee, C. C. (2019). Invite their languages in: Community-based literacy practices with multilingual African immigrant girls in New York City. *International Journal of Multicultural Education, 21*(2), 1–22.

Lee, S. (2005). *Up against whiteness: Race, school, and immigrant youth.* Teachers College Press.

Mugisha, V. M. (2015). Engaged African refugee youth negotiating schooling in America: An inquiry into the influence of culture and social structure. *International Journal of Education, 7*(1), 165–194.

Mwangi, G. C. A. (2014). Complicating blackness: Black immigrants and racial positioning in U.S. higher education. *Journal of Critical Thought and Praxis, 3*(2), 1–27.

Njue, J., & Retish, P. (2010). Transitioning academic and social performance of African immigrant students in an American high school. *Urban Education, 45*(3), 347–370.

Obiakor, F., & Grant, P. (2005). *Foreign-born African Americans: Silenced voices in the discourse on race.* Nova Science.

Peguero, A. A., Shekarkhar, Z., Popp, A. M., & Koo, D. J. (2015). Punishing the children of immigrants: Race, ethnicity, generational status, student misbehavior, and school discipline. *Journal of Immigrant & Refugee Studies, 13*(2), 200–220.

Vespa, J., Medina, L., & Armstrong, D. M. (2018). Demographic turning points for the United States: Population projections for 2020 to 2060. *Current Population Reports*, P25-1144, U.S. Census Bureau.

CHAPTER 22: Yes! Black Girls are Genderqueer and Transgender, too!

Collins, C. & Ehrenhalt, J. (n.d.). *Best practices for serving LGBTQ students: A Teaching Tolerance guide.* https://www.tolerance.org/magazine/publications/best-practices-for-serving-lgbtq-students

Crenshaw, K. (1989). Demarginalizing the intersection of race and sex: A Black feminist critique of antidiscrimination doctrine, feminist theory and antiracist politics. *University of Chicago Legal Forum, 1989*(1), 139–167. https://chicagounbound.uchicago.edu/uclf/vol1989/iss1/8

Kendi, I. X. (2019). *How to be an antiracist.* One World.

Kosciw, J. G., Greytak, E. A., Zongrone, A. D., Clark, C. M., & Truong, N. L. (2018). *The 2017 National School Climate Survey: The experiences of lesbian, gay, bisexual, transgender, and queer youth in our nation's schools*. GLSEN.

Levin, D. (2019, March 28). Generation Z: Who they are, in their own words. *New York Times*. https://www.nytimes.com/2019/03/28/us/gen-z-in-their-words.html

Nealy, E. C. (2017). *Transgender children and youth: Cultivating pride and joy in families in transition*. W. W. Norton.

Payne, E., & Smith, M. J. (2013). LGBTQ kids, school safety, and missing the big picture: How dominant bullying discourse prevents school professionals from thinking about systemic marginalization or . . . Why we need to rethink LGBTQ bullying. *QED: A Journal in GLBTQ Worldmaking, Inaugural Issue*, 1–36.

Pyne, J. (2016). "Parenting is not a job . . . It's a relationship": Recognition and relational knowledge among parents of gender nonconforming children. *Journal of Progressive Human Services, 27*(1), 21–48.

Shriberg, D., & Baker, B. A. (2019). Commentary: Taking a social justice perspective on research supporting LGBTQ students: Same team, different positions. *Journal of Educational and Psychological Consultation, 29*(1), 89–97.

Simmons, D. (2019, October). How to be an antiracist educator. *ASCD Education Update, 61*(10). http://www.ascd.org/publications/newsletters/education-update/oct19/vol61/num10/How-to-Be-an-Antiracist-Educator.aspx

Slesaransky-Poe, G. (in press). When our boys wanted to be girls: A retrospective look at parenting gender nonconforming boys. In D. A. Berkowitz, E. Windsor, & C. S. Han (Eds.), *Male femininities*. NYU Press.

Slesaransky-Poe, G., Ruzzi, L., DiMedio, C., & Stanley, J. L. (2013). "Is this the right school for my child?" *LGBT Youth Journal, 10*(1–2), 29–44.

Smith, M. J., & Payne, E. (2016). Binaries and biology: Conversations with elementary education professionals after professional development on supporting transgender students. *The Educational Forum, 80*(1), 34–47.

Staley, S. & Leonardi, B. (2019). Complicating what we know: Focusing on educators' processes of becoming gender and sexual diversity inclusive. *Theory Into Practice, 58*(1), 29–38. https://doi.org/10.1080/00405841.2018.1536916

Truong, N. L., Zongrone, A. D., & Kosciw, J. G. (2020). *Erasure and resilience: The experiences of LGBTQ students of color, Black LGBTQ youth in U.S. schools*. GLSEN.

CHAPTER 23: Prismatic Black Girls Reflecting African Spiritualities in Learning Environments

Brandt, A., & Chernoff, E. J. (2015, Spring). The importance of ethnomathematics in the math class. *Ohio Journal of School Mathematics, 71*, 31–36.

Eglash, R. (1997). When math worlds collide: Intention and invention in ethnomathematics. *Science, Technology, & Human Values, 22*(1), 79–97.

Long, C. H. (1997). Perspectives for a study of African-American religion in the United States. In T. E. Fulop & A. J. Raboteau (Eds.), *African-American religion: Interpretive essays in history and culture*, (pp. 25–33). Routledge.

Morris, M. W. (2016). *Pushout: The criminalization of Black girls in schools*. The New Press.

Ncube, B. (2017). Mothers, soil, and substance: Stories of endurance from Matobo Hills, Zimbabwe. *Journal of Mennonite Studies, 35*, 223–240.

Ng, R., Staton, P. A., & Scane, J. (Eds.). (1995). *Anti-racism, feminism, and critical approaches to education*. Greenwood.

Olupona, J., & Chiorazzi, A. (2015, October 6). The spirituality of Africa. *The Harvard Gazette*. https://news.harvard.edu/gazette/story/2015/10/the-spirituality-of-africa/

Rymes, B. (2015). *Classroom discourse analysis: A tool for critical reflection*. Routledge.

Shahjahan, R. A. (2010). Toward a spiritual praxis: The role of spirituality among faculty of color teaching for social justice. *The Review of Higher Education, 33*(4), 473–512.

Simpson, J. (Chief editor). (n.d.). *Oxford English dictionary*. Retrieved November 17, 2020, from www.oed.com/view/Entry/186904

Walker, A. (1982). *The color purple*. Simon & Schuster.

Book Review: *Pet*

Emezi, A. (2019). *Pet*. Make Me A World.

PART II. "I AM DESPERATE FOR CHANGE—NOW—NOT IN 8 YEARS OR 12 YEARS, BUT RIGHT NOW."—MICHELLE OBAMA

CHAPTER 24: Black Girl on the Playground

Aboud, F. (1988). *Children and prejudice*. Blackwell.

Aronson, J., Fried, C. B., & Good, C. (2002). Reducing the effects of stereotype threat on African American college students by shaping theories of intelligence. *Journal of Experimental Social Psychology, 38*(2) 113–125. https://doi.org/10:1006/jesp.2001.1491

Buck, C. (2017, May). Let's talk about race [Photo essay]. *O, the Oprah Magazine*.

Cabrera, N. J. (2013). *Minority children and their families: A positive look*. National Black Child Development Institute. https://drive.google.com/file/d/0B2PHh3_OARUTeWp4YlRMWW14cXM/view

Chugh, D., & Kern, M. C. (2016). Ethical learning: Releasing the moral unicorn. In D. Palmer & K. Smith-Crowe (Eds.), *Organizational wrongdoing: Key perspectives and new directions* (pp. 474–503). Cambridge University Press.

Derman-Sparks, L. (2012). *Stages in children's development of racial/cultural identity & attitudes*. https://www.uua.org/files/documents/derman-sparkslouise/1206_233_identity_stages.pdf

Derman-Sparks, L., & A. B. C. Task Force. (1989). *Anti-bias curriculum: Tools for empowering young children*. National Association for the Education of Young Children.

DiAngelo, R. (2015, April 9). *White fragility: Why it's so hard to talk to white people about racism*. Good Men Project. https://goodmenproject.com/featured-content/white-fragility-why-its-so-hard-to-talk-to-white-people-about-racism-twlm/

Diaz-Imbelli, L. (2013). *Soy mi cuento: Latina students bridging multiple worlds in independent schools* [Doctoral dissertation, St. John Fisher College]. Fisher Digital Publications. http://fisherpub.sjfc.edu/education_etd/178

Drake, H. (2018). *Do not move off the sidewalk challenge: Holding your space in a white world*. WriteSomeShit. https://writesomeshit.com/2018/07/12/do-not-move-off-the-sidewalk-challenge-holding-your-space-in-a-white-world/

Gonzales-Backen, M. A., & Umaña-Taylor, A. J. (2010). Examining the role of physical appearance in Latino adolescents' ethnic identity. *Journal of Adolescence, 34*(2011), 151–162. https://doi.org/10.1016/j.adolescence.2010.01.002

Hammond, Z. (2015). *Culturally responsive teaching and the brain: Promoting authentic engagement and rigor among culturally and linguistically diverse students.* Corwin.

Harris-Britt, A., Valrie, C. R., Kurtz-Costes, B., & Rowley, S. J. (2007). Perceived racial discrimination and self-esteem in African American youth: Racial socialization as a protective factor. *Journal of Research on Adolescence, 17*(4), 669–682. https://doi.org/10.1111/j.1532-7795.2007.00540.x

Michael, A. (2015). *Raising race questions: Whiteness and inquiry in education.* Teachers College Press.

McKown, C., & Weinstein, R. S. (2003). The development and consequences of stereotype consciousness in middle childhood. *Child Development, 74*(2), 498–515.

Moll, L. C., & Ruiz, R. (2002). The schooling of Latino children. In M. M. Suarez-Orozco & M. M. Paez (Eds.), *Latinos: Remaking America* (pp. 362–374). University of California Press.

The People's Institute for Survival and Beyond. (2018). *Our principals.* https://www.pisab.org/our-principles/

Staats, C., Capatostos, K., Wright, R. A., & Jackson, V. W. (2016). *State of the science: Implicit bias review.* Kirwan Institute.

Steele, C. M. (2010). *Whistling Vivaldi: How stereotypes affect us and what we can do.* W. W. Norton.

Style, E. (1996, Fall). Curriculum as window and mirror. *Social Science Record, 33*(2), 21–28.

Sue, D. W. (2010). *Microaggressions in everyday life: Race, gender, and sexual orientation.* John Wiley & Sons.

Tatum, B. D. (1997). *Why are all the Black kids sitting together in the cafeteria? And other conversations about race.* Basic Books.

Umaña-Taylor, A. J., & Fine, M. A. (2004). Examining ethnic identity among Mexican-origin adolescents living in the United States. *Hispanic Journal of Behavioral Sciences, 26*(1), 36–59. https://doi.org/10.1177/0739986303262143

Umaña-Taylor, A. J., O'Donnell, M., Knight, G. P., Roosa, M. W., Berkel, C., & Nair, R. (2014). Mexican-origin early adolescents' ethnic socialization, ethnic identity, and psychosocial functioning. *The Counseling Psychologist, 42*(2), 170–200. https://doi.org/10.1177/0011000013477903

Vignette: Who's Going to Sing a Black Girl's Song?

Shange, N. (1975). For colored girls who have considered suicide / When the rainbow is enuf [Choreopoem]. Shameless Hussy Press.

Shire, W. (2011). *Teaching my mother how to give birth.* Flipped Eye.

CHAPTER 25: Black Girls' Voices Matter: Empowering the Voices of Black Girls Against Coopting and Colonization

Bristol, T. J. (2015). Male teachers of color take a lesson from each other. *Phi Delta Kappan, 92*(2), 36–41.

Crenshaw, K. (2015). *Black girls matter: When national initiatives to help youth of color focus only on boys, the needs of our most vulnerable young women become invisible.* Feminist Majority Foundation. https://feminist.org/education/pdfs/26-29_BlackGirlsMatter_lo.pdf.

Crenshaw, K., Ocen P., & Nanda, J. (2014). *Black girls matter: Pushed out, overpoliced and underprotected*. African American Policy Forum & Columbia Law School: Center for Intersectionality and Social Polity Study. https://aapf.org/publications

Duncan-Andrade, J. M. R., & Morrell, E. (2008). *The art of critical pedagogy: Possibilities for moving from theory to practice in urban schools*. Peter Lang.

Emdin, C. (2016). *For white folks who teach in the hood—and the rest of y'all too: Reality pedagogy and urban education*. Beacon Press.

Evans-Winters, V. (2011). *Teaching black girls: Resiliency in urban classrooms* (2nd ed.). Peter Lang.

Evans-Winters, V. E. (2017). Flipping the script: The dangerous bodies of girls of color. *Cultural Studies ↔ Critical Methodologies*, *17*(5), 415–423. https://doi.org/10.1177/1532708616684867

Fahey, K., Breidenstein, A., Ippolito, J., & Hensley, F. (2019). *An uncommon theory of school change: Leadership for reinventing schools*. Teachers College Press.

Fantz, A., Yan, H., & Shoichet, C. E. (2015, June 9). *Texas pool party chaos: 'Out of control' police officer resigns*. CNN. https://www.cnn.com/2015/06/09/us/mckinney-texas-pool-party-video/index.html

Freire, P. (1970). *Pedagogy of the oppressed* (M. B. Ramos, Trans.). Continuum.

Gronn, P. C. (2002). Distributed leadership. In K. Leithwood & P. Hallinger (Eds.), *Second International Handbook of Educational Leadership and Administration* (pp. 653–696). Kluwer Academic.

Kendi, I. X. (2019). *How to be an antiracist*. One World.

King, J. E. (1991). Dysconscious racism: Ideology, identity, and the miseducation of teachers. *Journal of Negro Education*, *60*(2), 133–146. https://doi.org/10.2307/2295605

Kinloch, V. (2018). A pedagogy of love: Black girls and Black liberation. *Education Week*. http://blogs.edweek.org/teachers/classroom_qa_with_larry_ferlazzo/2019/02/response_holla_if_you_see_us_black_girls_in_spaces_we_call_schools.html

Knott-Dawson, S. (2018, February 8). To my military black daughters, nobody can take away your history. *Education Post*. https://educationpost.org/to-my-brilliant-black-daughters-nobody-can-take-away-your-history/

Ladson-Billings, G., & Tate, W. (1995). Towards a critical race theory of education. *Teachers College Record*, *97*, 47–68.

Leithwood, K., & Jantzi, D. (1994, April 19–23). *The effects of transformational leadership on organizational conditions and student engagement with school [Paper presentation]*. American Educational Research Association Annual Meeting, Montreal, QC, Canada.

Love, B. L. (2019). *We want to do more than survive: Abolitionist teaching and the pursuit of educational freedom*. Beacon Press.

Morris, M. W. (2016). *Pushout: The criminalization of black girls in schools*. The New Press.

Muhammad, G. (2018, October 30). *Literacy colloquy: We are more than enough: Toward a Black girls literacies framework to save education for all* [Lecture]. Michigan State University, East Lansing, MI. https://edwp.educ.msu.edu/event/we-are-more-than-enough-toward-a-black-girls-literacies-framework-to-save-education-for-all/

Muhammad, K. G. (2011). *The condemnation of Blackness: Race, crime, and the making of modern urban America*. Harvard University Press.

Sealey-Ruiz, Y. (2016). Why Black girls' literacies matter: New literacies for a new era. *English Education*, *48*(4), 290–298.

Singleton, G. E. (2015). *Courageous conversations about race: A field guide for achieving equity in schools*. Corwin.

Stelloh, T., & Connor, T. (2015, October 27). *Video shows cop body-slamming high school girl in S. C. classroom*. NBC News. https://www.nbcnews.com/news/us-news/video-appears-show-cop-body-slamming-student-s-c-classroom-n451896

Waite, S.R., Mentor, M., & Bristol, T. J. (2018). Growing our own: Reflections on developing a pipeline for male teachers of color. *Journal of the Center for Policy Analysis and Research*, *1*(1), 148–166.

Watson, T. N. (2018). Zero tolerance school discipline policies and Black girls: The (un)intended consequences. *Journal of the Center for Policy Analysis & Research*, *1*(1), 167–187.

Watson T. N. (2019, February 24). Response: 'Holla if you see us': Black girls in spaces we call schools. *Education Week*. http://blogs.edweek.org/teachers/classroom_qa_with_larry_ferlazzo/2019/02/response_holla_if_you_see_us_black_girls_in_spaces_we_call_schools.html

White, B. A. (2018). The invisible victims of the school-to-prison pipeline: Understanding Black girls, school push-out, and the impact of the Every Student Succeeds Act. *William & Mary Journal of Race, Gender, and Social Justice*, *24*(3), 640–663. https://scholarship.law.wm.edu/wmjowl/vol24/iss3/8

PART III. "DON'T TOUCH MY HAIR"—SOLANGE

CHAPTER 26: She Wears a Crown: Centering Black Girlhood in Schools

Campbell, A. (2012, April). *Police handcuff 6-year-old student in Georgia*. CNN. http://www.cnn.com/2012/04/17/justice/georgia-student-handcuffed/

Chavez, N., & Alonso, M. (2020, February). *Police took a 6-year-old girl to a mental health facility in Florida because she was 'out of control' at school*. CNN. https://www.cnn.com/2020/02/15/us/florida-girl-mental-health-baker-act/index.html

Crenshaw, K. W., Gotanda, N., Peller, G., & Thomas, K. (Eds.). (1995). *Critical race theory: The key writings that formed the movement*. The New Press.

CROWN Act, California SB 188 § 1–2 (2019).

CROWN Act, H.R. 5309, 116th Cong. (2019).

CROWN Act, New Jersey SB 3945 § 1–2 (2019).

CROWN Act, New York 6209 § 1–3 (2019).

CROWN Coalition. (2020). *The CROWN Act state by state*. https://www.thecrownact.com/crown-updates

Delgado, R., & Stefancic, J. (Eds.). (2001). *Critical race theory: An introduction* (2nd ed.). NYU Press.

Epstein, R., Blake, J. J, & González, T. (2017). *Girlhood interrupted: The erasure of Black girls' childhood*. Georgetown Law, Center on Poverty and Inequality. http://www.law.georgetown.edu/academics/centers-institutes/poverty-inequality/upload/girlhood-interrupted.pdf

Jacobs, J., & Levin, D. (2018). Black girl sent home from school over hair extensions. *New York Times*. https://www.nytimes.com/2018/08/21/us/black-student-extensions-louisiana.html

Klein, R. (2013, May). Kiera Wilmot, 16, arrested and expelled for explosive 'science experiment.' *Huffington Post*. https://www.huffingtonpost.com/2013/05/01/kiera-wilmot-arrested-science-experiment_n_3194768.html

Mbilishaka, A. M., & Apugo, D. (2020). Brushed aside: African American women's narratives of hair bias in school. *Race Ethnicity and Education*, *23*(5), 1–20.

Morris, M. (2012). *Race, gender, and the school-to-prison pipeline: Expanding our discussion to include Black girls*. African American Policy Forum.

Morris, M. W. (2016). *Pushout: The criminalization of Black girls in schools*. The New Press.

National Women's Law Center. (2017). *Let her learn: Stopping school pushout for girls of color*. https://nwlc.org/resources/stopping-school-pushout-for-girls-of-color/.

O'Brien-Richardson, P. (2019). Hair harassment in urban schools and how it shapes the physical activity of Black adolescent girls. *The Urban Review*, *51*(3), 523–534.

Rivera, Z. (2019, November 18). Black Michigan girl denied school picture because of her red braids gets special photo shoot. *Black Entertainment Television*. https://www.bet.com/news/national/2019/11/18/black-michigan-girl-denied-school-picture-because-of-her-red-bra.html

Watson, T. N. (2016). "Talking back": The perceptions and experiences of Black girls who attend City High School. *The Journal of Negro Education*, *85*(3), 239–249.

Watson, T. N. (2018). Black girls, White privilege, and schooling. In J. Brooks & G. Theoharis (Eds.), *Whiteucation: Privilege, power, and prejudice in school and society* (pp. 116–131). Routledge.

Yosso, T. J. (2005). Whose culture has capital? A critical race theory discussion of community cultural wealth. *Race Ethnicity and Education*, *8*(1), 69–91.

Chapter 27: I Am Not My Hair

Adams, C. (2018, August 23). Black girl removed from Louisiana Catholic school in tears over hairstyle: It's 'very upsetting.' *People*. https://people.com/human-interest/faith-fennidy-hair-removed-catholic-school/

Barris, K. (Executive Producer). (2020). *Black-ish* [Television series]. ABC Studios.

Bundles, A. (2001). *On her own ground*. Scribner.

Byrd, A. D., & Tharps, L. (2014). *Hair story: Untangling the roots of Black hair in America*. St. Martin's Press.

Capatides, C. (2016, October 13). *Mom shares teacher's note complaining about her daughter's hair*. CBS News. https://www.cbsnews.com/news/mom-shares-teachers-note-complaining-about-her-daughters-hair-post-goes-viral/

CROWN Act, H.R. 5309, 116th Cong. (2019).

Epstein, R., Blake, J. J., & González, T. (2017). *Girlhood interrupted: The erasure of Black girls' childhood*. Georgetown Law, Center on Poverty and Inequality. http://www.law.georgetown.edu/academics/centers-institutes/poverty-inequality/upload/girlhood-interrupted.pdf

Haydar, M. (2017). *Hijabi* [Video]. https://www.youtube.com/watch?v=XOX9O_kVPeo

Hill, L. (2017). Disturbing disparities: Black girls and the school-to-prison pipeline. *Fordham Urban Law Journal*, *45*, 201, 203.

Ivey, K. (2006, February 21). *Combing the history of Black hair*. Tucson.com. https://tucson.com/news/state-and-regional/history-and-culture/combing-the-history-of-black-hair/article_de82dbdc-a457-5da9-b1b2-3bbbd21e4475.html

Joy Collective. (2019). *The CROWN research study*. https://static1.squarespace.com/static/5edc69fd622c36173f56651f/t/5edeaa2fe5ddef345e087361/1591650865168/Dove_research_brochure2020_FINAL3.pdf

Kim, C. (2013, November 26). *Florida school threatens to expel student over 'natural hair.'* MSNBC. http://www.msnbc.com/the-last-word-94

Lee, S. (Director). (1988). *School daze* [Motion picture]. Columbia Pictures.

Mettler, K. (2017, May 22). Black girls at Mass. school win freedom to wear hair braid extensions. *Washington Post.* https://www.bostonglobe.com/staff/lazar?p1=Article_Byline

Nittle, N. K. (2020, February 25). How racism affects minority students in public schools. *ThoughtCo.* https://www.thoughtco.com/how-racism-affects-public-school-minorities-4025361

Press, A. (2017, June 28). *The 'adultification' of Black girls: Less protection, more discipline.* *NBC News.* https://www.nbcnews.com/news/nbcblk/adultification-black-girls-less-protection-more-discipline-n777591

Rock, C. (Director). (2006). *Everybody hates Chris.* [Television series]. Paramount Studios.

Rock, C. (Director). (2010). *Good hair* [Motion picture]. Chris Rock Productions and HBO Films.

Nicolaides, S. (Producer), & Singleton, J. C. (Director). (1991) *Boyz in the hood* [Motion picture]. Columbia Pictures.

Singleton. G. (2015). *Courageous conversations about race.* Corwin.

Singleton, J. C. (Director). (1993). *Poetic justice* [Motion picture]. Columbia Pictures.

Sue, D. W., Capodilupo, C. M., Torino, G. C., Bucceri, J. M., Holder, A. M., Nadal, K. L., & Esquilin, M. (2007). Racial microaggressions in everyday life: Implications for clinical practice. *American Psychologist, 62*(4), 271–286. https://doi.org/10.1037/0003-66X.62.4.271.

Book Review: *I Am Enough*

Brooks, W., & McNair, J. (2015). "Combing" through representations of Black girls' hair in African American children's literature. *Children's Literature in Education, 46*(3), 296–307. https://doi.org/10.1007/s10583-014-9235-x

Byers, G. (2018). *I am enough.* HarperCollins.

PART IV. "WE WANT TO TURN VICTIMS INTO SURVIVORS—AND SURVIVORS INTO THRIVERS" —TARANA BURKE

CHAPTER 28: Voice Activation and Volume Control in the Workplace

Arnautović, I. (2013). Theoretical aspects in the defining of mobbing (or bullying). *South East Europe Review (SEER), 16*(2), 193–204.

Ferris, P. (2004). A preliminary typology of organizational response to allegations of workplace bullying: See no evil, hear no evil, speak no evil. *British Journal of Guidance & Counseling, 32*(3), 389–395. http://doi.org/10.1080/03069880410001723576.

Keashly, L. (2010). Some things you need to know but may have been afraid to ask: A researcher speaks to the ombudsman about workplace bullying. *Journal of the International Ombudsman Association. 3*(2), 10–23.

Kirk, B. A., Schutte, N. S., & Hine, D. W. (2011). The effect of an expressive writing intervention for employees on emotional self-efficacy and emotional incivility. *Journal of Applied Social Psychology, 4*(1), 179–195. https://doi.org/10.1111/j.1559-1816.2010.00708.x.

Lewis, J., Coursol, D., & Wahl, K. H. (2002). Addressing issues of workplace harassment: counseling the targets. *Journal of Employment Counseling, 39*(3), 109.

Namie, G. (2003). Workplace bullying: Escalated incivility. *Ivy Business Journal, 68*(2), 1–6.

Neves, P. (2014). Taking it out on survivors: Submissive employees, downsizing, and abusive supervision. *Journal of Occupational and Organizational Psychology, 87*(3), 507–534. https://doi.org/10.1111/joop.12061

Porath, C. L., & Pearson, C. M. (2012). Emotional and behavioral responses to workplace incivility and the impact of hierarchical status. *Journal of Applied Social Psychology, 42*, E326–E357. https://doi.org/10.1111/j.1559-1896.2012

Sperry, L., & Duffy, M. (2009). Workplace mobbing: Family dynamics and therapeutic considerations. *American Journal of Family Therapy, 37*(5), 433–442. https://doi.org/10.1080/01926180902945756

Van den Brande. W., Bailen, E., Vander Elst, T., De White, H., Van den Broeck. A., & Godderis, L. (2017). Exposure to workplace bullying: The role of coping strategies in dealing with work stressors. *BioMed Research International, 2017*, 1–12. https://doi.org/10.1155/2017/1019529

PART V. "FREEDOM IS A CONSTANT STRUGGLE."—ANGELA DAVIS

CHAPTER 29: When She's The Only One: High-Achieving Black Girls in Suburban Schools

Billingham, C. M. (2019). Within-district racial segregation and the elusiveness of white student return to urban public schools. *Urban Education, 54*(2), 151–181.

Campbell, S. L. (2012). For colored girls? Factors that influence teacher recommendations into advanced courses for black girls. *The Review of Black Political Economy, 39*(4), 389–402.

Carter Andrews, D. J. (2012). Black achievers' experiences with racial spotlighting and ignoring in a predominantly white high school. *Teachers College Record, 114*(10), 1–46.

Chapman, T. K. (2014). Is integration a dream deferred? Students of color in majority white suburban schools. *The Journal of Negro Education, 83*(3), 311–326.

Diem, S., Welton, A. D., Frankenberg, E., & Jellison Holme, J. (2016). Racial diversity in the suburbs: How race-neutral responses to demographic change perpetuate inequity in suburban school districts. *Race Ethnicity and Education, 19*(4), 731–762.

Eggleston, T. A., & Miranda, A. H. (2009). Black girls' voices: Exploring their lived experiences in a predominately white high school. *Race/Ethnicity: Multidisciplinary Global Contexts*, 259–285.

Ford, D. Y. (2010). Underrepresentation of culturally different students in gifted education: Reflections about current problems and recommendations for the future. *Gifted Child Today, 33*(3), 31–35.

Fordham, S. (2016). *Downed by friendly fire: Black girls, white girls, and suburban schooling.* University of Minnesota Press.

Glass, I. (Host), & Hannah-Jones, N. (Guest). (2015a, July 31). The problem we all live with—part one. In *This American life* [Audio podcast episode]. WBEZ Chicago. https://www.thisamericanlife.org/562/the-problem-we-all-live-with-part-one

Glass, I. (Host), & Hannah-Jones, N. (Guest). (2015b, August 7). The problem we all live with—part two. *This American life* [Audio podcast episodes]. WBEZ Chicago. https://www.thisamericanlife.org/562/the-problem-we-all-live-with-part-one

Hill, K. D. (2009). Code-switching pedagogies and African American student voices: Acceptance and resistance. *Journal of Adolescent & Adult Literacy, 53*(2), 120–131.

Hyland, N. E. (2005). Being a good teacher of black students? White teachers and unintentional racism. *Curriculum Inquiry, 35*(4), 429–459.

Ispa-Landa, S. (2013). Gender, race, and justifications for group exclusion: Urban Black students bussed to affluent suburban schools. *Sociology of Education, 86*(3), 218–233.

King, J. E. (1991). Dysconscious racism: Ideology, identity, and the miseducation of teachers. *The Journal of Negro Education, 60*(2), 133–146.

King, L. J. (2019). An introduction to Black history research: The problems, advances, and a new vision. In L. King (Ed.), *Perspectives of black histories in schools* (pp. xv–xiv). Information Age.

Leath, S., Mathews, C., Harrison, A., & Chavous, T. (2019). Racial identity, racial discrimination, and classroom engagement outcomes among Black girls and boys in predominantly Black and predominantly white school districts. *American Educational Research Journal, 56*(4), 1318–1352.

Lewis-McCoy, R. L. H. (2018). Suburban Black lives matter. *Urban Education, 53*(2), 145–161.

Morris, M. W. (2016). *Pushout: The criminalization of Black girls in schools.* The New Press.

Myers-Scotton, C. (1993). Common and uncommon ground: Social and structural factors in codeswitching. *Language in Society, 22*(4), 475–503.

Russell, L. S. (2015). Negotiating identity: Black female identity construction in a predominantly-white suburban context. *Urban Education Research & Policy Annuals, 3*(1), 9–23.

Siegel-Hawley, G., & Frankenberg, E. (2012, April 23). *Spaces of inclusion? Teachers' perceptions of school communities with differing student racial & socioeconomic contexts.* The Civil Rights Project, UCLA. https://www.civilrightsproject.ucla.edu/research/k-12-education/integration-and-diversity/spaces-of-inclusion-school-communities

Vickery, A. E. (2016). 'I know what you are about to enter': Lived experiences as the curricular foundation for teaching citizenship. *Gender and Education, 28*(6), 725–741.

Welton, A. D., Diem, S., & Holme, J. J. (2015). Color conscious, cultural blindness: Suburban school districts and demographic change. *Education and Urban Society, 47*(6), 695–722.

Whiting, G. W., & Ford, D. Y. (2009). Multicultural issues: Black students and advanced placement classes: Summary, concerns, and recommendations. *Gifted Child Today, 32*(1), 23–26.

Wun, C. (2016). Against captivity: Black girls and school discipline policies in the afterlife of slavery. *Educational Policy, 30*(1), 171–196.

CHAPTER 30: Liminal and Limitless: Black Girls in Independent Schools

Anderson, M. (2016). Preventing bullying. *The Atlantic.* https://www.theatlantic.com/education/archive/2016/03/the-criminalization-of-black-girls-in-schools/473718/

Berry, J. W. (1997). Immigration, acculturation, and adaptation. *Applied Psychology, 46,* 5–34. https://doi.org/10.1111/j.1464-0597.1997.tb01087.x

Berry, J. W. (2003). Conceptual approaches to acculturation. *American Psychological Association,* 17–37. https://doi.org/10.1037/10472-004

Bourdieu, P., & Passeron, J. C. (1977, 1990). *Reproduction in education, society and culture.* Sage.

Brosnan, M. (2001). Diversity efforts in independent schools. *Fordham Urban Law Journal* *29*(2), 467–487. https://ir.lawnet.fordham.edu/ulj/vol29/iss2/1

Correll, S. J., & Ridgeway, C. L. (2003). Expectation states theory. In J. Delamater (Ed.), *Handbook of Social Psychology* (p. 29–51). Kluwer Academic/Plenum.

Cross, W. (1991). *Shades of Black: Diversity in African-American identity.* Temple University Press.

Feldman, J. (2019). *Grading for equity.* Corwin.

Gaztambide-Fernández, R. (2009). *The best of the best: Becoming elite at an American boarding school.* Harvard University Press.

Gilmore, P. (1985). Gimme room: School resistance, attitude, and access to literacy. *Journal of Education*, *167*(1), 111–128. https://doi.org/10.1177/002205748516700108

Hammond, Z. (2015). *Culturally responsive teaching and the brain: Promoting authentic engagement and rigor among culturally and linguistically diverse students.* Corwin.

Katz, J. (2009). *White culture and racism: Working for organizational change in the United States* [Whiteness Paper No. 3]. Crandall, Dostie, & Douglass Books.

Monahan, K. C., VanDerhei, S., Bechtold, J., & Cauffman, E. (2014). From the school yard to the squad car: School discipline, truancy, and arrest. *Journal of Youth and Adolescence*, *43*, 1110–1122. https://doi.org/10.1007/s10964-014-0103-1

Morris, M. W. (2016). *Pushout: The criminalization of Black girls in schools.* The New Press.

National Association of Independent Schools (NAIS). (2012, August 24). *Facts at a glance.* https://www.nais.org/statistics/pages/nais-independent-school-facts-at-a-glance/

National Association of Independent Schools (NAIS). (2019, January 2). *Facts at a glance.* https://www.nais.org/statistics/pages/nais-independent-school-facts-at-a-glance/

Shapin, S. (2012). The ivory tower: The history of a figure of speech and its cultural uses. *The British Journal for the History of Science 45*(1), 1–27.

Sims-Bishop, R. (1990). Mirrors, windows, and sliding glass doors. *Perspectives*, *1*(3), ix–xi.

Tatum, B. (1997). *Why are all the Black kids sitting together in the cafeteria? And other conversations about race.* Basic Books.

Book Review: *A Good Kind of Trouble*

Ramee, L. M. (2019). *A good kind of trouble.* Harper Collins.

PART VI "DREAMKEEPERS"—GLORIA LADSON-BILLINGS

CHAPTER 31: Mrs. Ruby Middleton Forsythe and the Power of Sankofa

Alexander, K. (Author), & Nelson, K. (Illustrator). (2019). *The undefeated.* Versify.

Baratz, S., & Baratz, J. (1969). Negro ghetto children and urban education: A cultural solution. *Social Education*, *33*(4), 148–150.

Bond, H. M. (1934). *The education of the Negro in the American social order.* Prentice Hall.

Brown v. Board of Education, 347 U.S. 483 (1954).

Bullock, H. (1967). *A history of negro education in the South from 1619 to the present.* Harvard University Press.

Byers, G. (Author), & Bobo, K. A. (Illustrator). (2018). *I am enough.* Balzer + Bray.

Cole, M. (1971). *The cultural context of thinking and learning.* Basic Books.

Crenshaw, K., Ocen, P., & Nanda, J. (2015). *Black girls matter: Pushed out, over-policed and under-protected*. https://www.atlanticphilanthropies.org/wp-content/uploads/2015/09/BlackGirlsMatter_Report.pdf

Delpit, L. (1988). The silenced dialogue: Power and pedagogy in educating other people's children. *Harvard Educational Review, 58*(3), 280–298.

Drago, E. L. (1990). *Initiative, paternalism, and race relations: Charleston's Avery Normal School*. The University of Georgia Press.

Du Bois, W. E. B. (1935). Does the Negro need separate schools? *The Journal of Negro Education 4*(3), 328–335.

Gordon, A. H. (1929). *Sketches of negro life and history in South Carolina* (2nd ed.). University of South Carolina Press.

Hale-Benson, H. (1986). *Black children: Their roots, culture, and learning styles*. (2nd ed.). New York: Harvard University Press.

Hudson, M. J., & Holmes, B. J. (1994). Missing teachers, impaired communities: The unanticipated consequences of Brown v. Board of Education on the African American teaching force at the precollegiate level. *The Journal of Negro Education, 63* (3), 388–393.

Kunjufu, J. (1990). *Countering the conspiracy to destroy Black boys*. African American Images.

Ladson-Billings, G. (1995). Toward a theory of culturally relevant pedagogy. *American Educational Research Journal, 32*(3), 465–491.

Ladson-Billings, G. J. (1999). Preparing teachers for diverse student populations: A critical race theory perspective. *Review of Research in Education, 24*(1), 211–247.

Ladson-Billings, G. (2012). Through a glass darkly: The persistence of race in education research & scholarship. *Educational Researcher, 41*(4), 115–120.

Lanker, B., & Summers, B. (Eds). (1989). *I dream a world: Portraits of Black women who changed America*. Stewart, Tabori & Chang.

Milner, R. T., & Howard, T. C. (2004). Black teachers, Black students, Black communities, and Brown: Perspectives and insights from experts. *The Journal of Negro Education, 73*(3), 285–297.

Penick, M. W. (1991, August). *Miss Ruby: An island in the sun: The educational achievements of Mrs. Ruby Middleton Forsythe*. [Unpublished dissertation]. University of Iowa.

The power of Sankofa: Know history. (n.d.) Berea College, Carter G. *Woodson Center*. https://www.berea.edu/cgwc/the-power-of-sankofa/

Shade, B. J. (1989). Culture and learning style within the Afro-American Community. In B. J. Shade (Ed.), *Culture, style and the educative process* (pp. 16–32). Charles C Thomas.

Woodson, C. G. (1919). *The education of the Negro prior to 1861: A history of the education of colored people of the United States from the beginning of slavery to the Civil War*. The Associated Press.

Woodson, C. G. (1933). *The mis-education of the Negro*. Winston-Derek.

Woodson, J. (Author), & Lewis, E. B (Illustrator). (2012). *Each kindness*. Nancy Paulsen Books.

Vignette: A Black Woman's Reflections on the Road I Made While Walking

Lubiano, W. H. (1997). *The house that race built: Original essays by Toni Morrison, Angela Y. Davis, Cornel West, and others on Black Americans and politics in America today*. Vintage Books.

Book Review: *Voice of Freedom: Fannie Lou Hamer—Spirit of the Civil Rights Movement.*

Weatherford, C.B. (Author) & Holmes, E. (Illustrator). (2015). *Voice of freedom: Fannie Lou Hamer—Spirit of the civil rights movement.* Candlewick Press.

Connecting

PART I. "SUCH AS I AM, A PRECIOUS GIFT"—ZORA NEALE HURSTON

CHAPTER 32: Black Girls Got it Goin' On, Yet Their Best Can Be Better

Abdurraqib, H. (2019, August 7). *The generosity of Toni Morrison.* BuzzFeed News. https://www.buzzfeednews.com/article/hanifabdurraqib/toni-morrison-death-ohio-midwest

Angelou, M. (1994). *The complete collected poems of Maya Angelou.* Random House.

Atwater, D. F. (2010). *African American women's rhetoric: The search for dignity, personhood, and honor.* Lexington Books.

Benberry, C. (1990). *Always there: The African American presence in American quilts.* The Kentucky Quilt Project.

Bond, B. (Ed.). (2017). *Black girls rock! Owning our magic. Rocking our truth.* Atria Books.

Borris, C. (n. d.). *The power of poetry.* https://www.scholastic.com/teachers/articles/teaching-content/power-poetry

Brown, P. L. (1996, April 4). Life threads stitched into quilts. *New York Times*, Section C, p. 1.

Brown, R. N. (2013). *Hear our truth: The creative potential of Black girlhood.* University of Illinois Press.

Burroughs, M. (1968/1992). *Homage to Black Madonnas.* https://www.poetryfoundation.org/poems/146266/homage-to-black-madonnas

Cadet, D. (2019, August 7). Toni Morrison wrote for Black women—but she gave us so much more. *Refinery29.* https://www.refinery29.com/en-us/2019/08/239940/toni-morrison-novels-gift-to-black-women

Cannie, R. L. (2018). *Daring to differ: A culturally responsive research study of self* [Doctoral dissertation]. University of Washington.

Canyon, K. (2019, March 29). *Must read poetry books by Black/African American women.* Medium. https://medium.com/poetickat/must-read-poetry-books-by-black-african-american-women-a3cab6b62bc

Carey, P. (11/7/2019). Morning open thread: African American quilt making and the art of Harriet Powers (1839–1910). *Daily Kos.* https://www.dailykos.com/stories/2019/11/7/1897283/-Morning-Open-Thread-African-American-Quilt-Making-amp-the-Art-of-Harriet-Powers-1839-1910

Carter Andrews, D. J., Brown, T., Castro, E. & Id-Deen, E. (2019). The impossibility of being "perfect and white:" Black girls' racialized and gendered schooling experiences. *American Educational Research Journal, 56*(6), 2531–2572.

Cash, F. B. (1995). Kinship and quilting: An examination of an African American tradition. *Journal of Negro Education, 80*(1), 30–41.

Coelho, P. (2013). *The alchemist.* HarperCollins.

Evans, G. (2019, August 6). *Toni Morrison remembered: Oprah Winfrey joins Barack Obama, Shonda Rhimes in praise of author*. Deadline. https://deadline.com/2019/08/toni-morrison-remembered-shonda-rhimes-vivica-fox-robin-roberts

Fokenflik, D. O. (2019, August 7). *Remembering Toni Morrison: A friend of our minds*. WBUR on Point. https://www.wbur.org/onpoint/2019/08/07/toni-morrison-beloved-literature-writing-legacy

Freeman, R. (1986). *A communion of spirits: Africa American quilters, preservers, and their stories*. Rutledge Hill Press.

Gale, T. (2006). Hair and beauty culture in the United States. *Encyclopedia of African American Culture and History*. https://www.encyclopedia.com/history/encyclopedias-almanacs-transcripts-and-maps/hair-and-beauty-culture-united-states

Giorgis, H. (6/19, 2018). How Freda DeKnight's cookbook, *A Date With a Dish, inspired generations of Black cooks*. https://www.bonappetit.com/story/freda-deknight-cookbook-a-date-with-a-dish

Greene, D. T. (2020). Black female teachers are our school parents: Academic othermothering depicted in multicultural young adult texts. *Journal of Language and Literacy Education*, *16*(1), 1–19.

Greene, M. (1984). The art of being present: Educating for aesthetic encounters. *Journal of Education*, *166*(2), 123–135.

Hamlet, J. D. (2011). Word! The African American oral tradition and its rhetorical impact on American popular culture. *Black History Bulletin*, *74*(1), 27–31.

Harris, J. (2015, October 4). *Dear Black girl: Letters from the souls of Black women*. https://www.theroot.com/dear-black-girl-letters-from-the-souls-of-black-women-1790861287

Jackson, R. L., & Richardson, E. B. (Eds.). (2003). *Understanding African American rhetoric: Classic origins to contemporary innovations*. Routledge.

Kousky, V. (n.d.). *10 points on the power of poetry*. Read Brightly. https://www.readbrightly.com/10-points-power-poetry

Lahart, S. (n.d.). *Quotes*. Goodreads. https://www.goodreads.com/quotes/tag/stephanie-lahart

Milton, D. (2014). *For my little Black girl*. https://colorismhealing.com/poetrycontest/little-black-girl/

My Black is beautiful (Poem). (n.d.). https://www.pinterest.com/pin/68539225563756815/

Obama, M. (2019, August 9). *Beloved*: Eight Black female writers and thinkers on Toni Morrison's life and legacy. *The Washington Post*. https://www.washingtonpost.com/opinions/2019/08/09/eight-black-women-including-michelle-obama-toni-morrisons-life-legacy

Popova, M. (2016). *Adrienne Rich on the political power of poetry and its role in the immigrant experience*. Brain Pickings. https://www.brainpickings.org/2016/08/23/adrienne-rich-poetry-politics/

Raman, V. K. (2011). The agony and ecstasy of being Black and female: A true voice of African American Women poets. *Theory and Practice in Language Studies*, *1*(1), 52–60.

Rigueur, L. W. (2019, August 9). *Beloved*: Eight black female writers and thinkers on Toni Morrison's life and legacy. *The Washington Post*. https://www.washingtonpost.com/opinions/2019/08/09/eight-black-women-including-michelle-obama-toni-morrisons-life-legacy

Smart-Grosvenor, V. (1982). We got a way with words. *Essence*, *13*(6), 138.

Spencer, S. J., Logel, C., & Davies, P. G. (2016). Stereotype threat. *Annual Review of Psychology*, *67*, 415–437.

theonlychase. (2017, August 26). *I am a Black girl.* https://powerpoetry.org/poems/i-am-black-girl-4

Wassiliwizky, E., Koelsch, S., Wagner, V., Jacobsen, T., & Menninghaus, W. (2017). The emotional power of poetry: Neural, circuitry, psychophysiology, and compositional principles. *Social Cognitive and Affective Neuroscience*, *12*(8), 1229–1240. https://doi.org/10.1093/scan/nsx069

Wahlman, M. S. (1993). *Signs and symbols: African images in African American quilts.* Dutton.

CHAPTER 33: Learning to Listen to Her: Psychological Verve With Black Girls

Boykin, A. W. (1979). Psychological/behavioral verve: Some theoretical explorations and empirical manifestations. In A. W. Boykin, A. J. Franklin, & J. F. Yates (Eds.) *Research directions of Black psychologists* (pp. 351–367). Russell Sage Press.

Boykin. A. W. (1982). Task variability and the performance of black and white schoolchildren. *Journal of Black Studies*, *12*(4), 469–485.

Boykin, A. W. (2001). *Culture matters in psychosocial experience and schooling of African American students* [Manuscript submitted for publication].

Carter, N. P., Hawkins, T. N., & Natesan, P. (2008). The relationship between verve and the academic achievement of African American students in reading and mathematics in an urban middle school. *Educational Foundations*, *22*(1–2), 29–46.

Carter, N. P., & Larke, P. J. (2003). Examining INTASC standards through the lens of *multicultural education: Meeting the needs of underserved students.* In N. P. Carter (Ed.), *Convergence and divergence: Alignment of standards, assessment and issues of diversity* (pp. 55–70). American Association of Colleges for Teacher Educators.

Collins, P. H. (1990). *Black feminist thought: Knowledge, consciousness, and the politics of empowerment.* Routledge.

Corneille, M. A., Ashcroft, A. M., & Belgrave, F. Z. (2005). What's culture got to do with it? Prevention programs for African American adolescent girls. *Journal of Health Care for the Poor and Underserved*, *16*(4), 38–47.

Ellison, C. M., Boykin, A. W., Towns, D. P., & Stokes, A. (2000). *Classroom cultural ecology: The dynamics of classroom life in schools serving low-income African American children.* CRESPAR Technical Report 44. https://files.eric.ed.gov/fulltext/ED442886.pdf

Ford, D. Y., Howard, T. C., Harris, J. J., III, & Tyson, C. A. (2000). Creating culturally responsive classrooms for gifted African American students. *Journal for the Education of the Gifted*, *23*(4), 397–427.

George, J. A. (2015). Stereotype and school pushout: Race, gender and discipline disparities. *Arkansas Law Review*, *68*, 101–129.

Ladson-Billings, G. (2009). *The dreamkeepers: Successful teachers of African American children* (2nd ed.). John Wiley & Sons.

Martin, R., & Murtagh, E. (2015). Preliminary findings of Active Classrooms: An intervention to increase physical activity levels of primary school children during class time. *Teaching and Teacher Education*, *52*, 113–127. https://doi.org/10.1016/j.tate.2015.09.007

Milne, B. A. (2013). *Colouring in the white spaces: Reclaiming cultural identity in whitestream schools* [Doctoral dissertation, University of Waikato]. UW Campus Repository. https://hdl.handle.net/10289/7868

Morris, M. W. (2012, January). Race, gender, and the school-to-prison pipeline: Expanding our discussion to include Black girls. *African American Policy Forum*, 1–23.

Morris, M. W. (2016). *Pushout: The criminalization of Black girls in schools*. The New Press.

Morris, M. W., Conteh, M., & Harris-Perry, M. (2018). *Pushout: the criminalization of Black girls in schools*. The New Press.

Raffaele Mendez, L. M., & Knoff, H. M. (2003). Who gets suspended from school and why? A demographic analysis of schools and disciplinary infractions in a large school district. *Education and Treatment of Children*, 26(1), 30–51.

Raffaele Mendez, L. M., Knoff, H. M., & Ferron, J. M. (2002). School demographic variables and out-of-school suspension rates: A quantitative and qualitative analysis of a large ethnically diverse school district. *Psychology in the Schools*, 39(3), 259–277.

Richardson, E. (2013). My ill literacy narrative: Growing up Black, po and a girl, in the hood. *Gender and Education 21*(6), 753–767.

Scott, D. M. (2018). The science behind psychological verve and what it means for Black students. In E. Moore, A. Michael, & M. W. Penick-Parks (Eds.), *The guide for White women who teach Black boys* (pp. 121–127). Corwin.

Skiba, R. J., Michael, R. S., Nardo, A. C., & Peterson, R. L. (2002). The color of discipline: Sources of racial and gender disproportionality in school punishment. *The Urban Review*, 34(4), 317–342.

Tyler, K. M., Dillihunt, M. L., Boykin, A. W., Coleman, S. T., Scott, D. M., Tyler, C., & Hurley, E. A. (2008). Examining cultural socialization within African American and European American households. *Cultural Diversity and Ethnic Minority Psychology*, 14(3), 201–204.

Ward, J. V. (1996). Raising resisters: The role of truth telling in the psychological development of African American girls. In B. J. R. Leadbeater & N. Way (Eds.), *Urban girls: Resisting stereotypes, creating identities* (pp. 85–99). NYU Press.

West, C. M. (1995). Mammy, Sapphire, and jezebel: Historical images of Black women and their implications for psychotherapy. *Psychotherapy*, 32(3), 458–466.

Wood, G. K. & Lemley, C. K. (2015). Mapping cultural boundaries in schools and communities: Redefining spaces through organizing. *Democracy and Education, 23(*1), 1–9.

PART II. #1000BLACKGIRLBOOKS—MARLEY DIAS

CHAPTER 34: Selecting and Using BACE (Blackcentric, Authentic, and Culturally Engaging) Books: She Looks Like Me

Aronson, K. M., Callahan, B. D., & O'Brien, A. S. (2018). Messages matter: Investigating the thematic content of picture books portraying underrepresented racial and cultural groups. *Sociological Forum*, 33(1), 165–185. https://doi.org/10.1111/socf.12404

Bishop, R. S. (1990a). Walk tall in the world: African American literature for today's children. *Journal of Negro Education*, 59(4), 556–565.

Bishop, R. S. (1990b). Windows and mirrors: Children's books and parallel cultures. In M. Atwell & A. Klein (Eds.), *Celebrating literacy: Proceedings of the Annual Reading*

Conference at California State University (pp. 3–12). California State University. https://files.eric.ed.gov/fulltext/ED337744.pdf#page=11

Bishop, R. S. (2011). African American children's literature: Researching its development, exploring its voices. In S. A. Wolf, K. Coats, P. Enciso, & C. A. Jenkins. *Handbook of research on children's and young adult literature* (pp. 225–235). Routledge.

Brooks, W. (2006). Reading representations of themselves: Urban youth use culture and African American textual features to develop literary understandings. *Reading Research Quarterly, 41*(3), 372–392.

Brooks, W., & McNair, J. (2015). "Combing" through representations of Black Girls' hair in African American children's literature. *Children's Literature in Education, 46*(3), 296–307. https://link.springer.com/article/10.1007/s10583-014-9235-x

Cherry, M. A. (2019). *Hair love*. New York: Kokila, Penguin Books.

Crippen, M. (2012). *The value of children's literature*. Oneota Reading Journal. http://oneotareadingjournal.com/2012/value-of-childrens-literature/

Cueto, D., & Brooks, W. M. (2019). Drawing humanity: How picturebook illustrations counter antiblackness. In H. Johnson, J. Mathis, & K. G. Short (Eds.), *Critical content analysis of visual images in books for young people* (pp. 41–58). Routledge.

Derman-Sparks, L. (2016, April 14). *Guide for selecting anti-bias children's books*. Teaching for Change. http://www.teachingforchange.org/selecting-anti-bias-books

Dior, C. (2018). *13 books every young Black girl should read*. From Caterpillars to Butterflies. http://fromcaterpillarstobutterflies.com/inspiration/13-books-every-young-black-girl-should-read/

Foxx, A. (2013). Brown girl bookshelf: 10 books to read to our daughters. *Essence*. https://www.essence.com/lifestyle/parenting/brown-girl-bookshelf-10-books-read-our-daughters/

Frank, P. (2016, December). *Black women artists tackle the dangerous stereotypes that have never defined them—Let's look beyond the Mammy, the Jezebel and the Sapphire*. Huffington Post. https://www.huffpost.com/entry/black-woman-artists-stereotypes_n_58471907e4b016eb81d8868b

Gordon, C. (2017). *Black girl magic: 33 picture books featuring Black female protagonists*. Read Brightly. https://www.readbrightly.com/picture-books-featuring-black-female-protagonists/

GrassROOTS Community Foundation. (2019). *1000 Black girl books resource guide*. https://grassrootscommunityfoundation.org/1000-black-girl-books-resourceguide/#1458673364920-b547bb2d-5238

Griffin-EL, N. (2018). *20 books that inspire Black girls to strive toward greatness*. Carnegie Library of Pittsburgh. https://www.carnegielibrary.org/20-books-that-inspire-black-girls-to-strive-toward-greatness/

Harris, V. J. (1990). African American children's literature: The first one hundred years. *Journal of Negro Education, 59*(4), 540–555.

Haynes, C., Stewart, S., & Allen, E. (2016). Three paths, one struggle: Black women and girls battling invisibility in U.S. classrooms. *Journal of Negro Education, 85*(3), 380–391.

Horning, K. T., Lindgren, M. V., Schliesman, M., & Tyner, M. (2019). *A few observations: Literature in 2018*. https://ccbc.education.wisc.edu/books/choiceintro19.asp

Jacobs, C. E. (2016). Developing the "oppositional gaze": Using critical media pedagogy and Black feminist thought to promote Black girls' identity development. *Journal of Negro Education, 85*(3), 225–238. https://www.jstor.org/stable/10.7709/jnegroeducation.85.3.0225?seq=1

Johnson, N. J., Koss, M. D., & Martinez, M. (2018). Through the sliding glass door: #EmpowerTheReader. *Reading Teacher, 71*(5), 569–577. https://ila.onlinelibrary.wiley.com/doi/abs/10.1002/trtr.1659

Katherine. (2020, May 30). Broadening the story: 60 picture books starring Black mighty girls. *A Mighty Girl.* https://www.amightygirl.com/blog?p=11056

Knott-Dawson, S. (2020, February 21). *We're teaching Black history month all wrong.* Education Post. https://educationpost.org/were-teaching-black-history-month-all-wrong/

McGrath, M. (2017, June 13). From activist to author: How 12-year-old Marley Dias is changing the face of children's literature. *Forbes.* https://www.forbes.com/sites/maggiemcgrath/2017/06/13/from-activist-to-author-how-12-year-old-marley-dias-is-changing-the-face-of-childrens-literature/#7c93b3f24ce0

McNair, J. C. (2008). A comparative analysis of The Brownies' Book and contemporary African American children's literature written by Patricia C. McKissack. In W. M. Brooks & J. C. McNair (Eds.), *Embracing, evaluating, and examining African American children's and young adult literature* (pp. 3–29). Scarecrow Press.

McNair, J. C. (2010). Classic African American children's literature. *Reading Teacher, 64*(2), 96–105. https://ila.onlinelibrary.wiley.com/doi/abs/10.1598/RT.64.2.2

Morrison, T. (n.d.). *Quotes.* https://www.goodreads.com/quotes/9866511-i-stood-at-the-border-stood-at-the-edge-and

Morrison, T., & Cirillo, C. (2019, July 16). *Sisters read bedtime stories on Facebook Live so kids can fall asleep to a story each night.* Good Morning America. https://www.goodmorningamerica.com/family/story/sisters-read-bedtime-stories-facebook-live-kids-fall-64300308

Myers, C., & Bersani, H. (2008). Ten quick ways to analyze children's books for ableism. *Rethinking Schools, 23*(2), 1–5.

Nunn, N. M. (2018). Super-girl: Strength and sadness in Black girlhood. *Gender and Education, 30*(2), 239–258.

Rogers, R. E. (2015). *Slavery on their minds: Representing the institution in children's picture books* [Doctoral dissertation.] Doctoral Dissertations, 396. https://scholarworks.umass.edu/cgi/viewcontent.cgi?article=1412&context=dissertations_2]]

Rogers, R. E. (2018). *Representations of slavery in children's picture books: Teaching and learning about slavery in K–12 classrooms* (Vol. 21). Routledge.

Smith-D'Arezzo, W., & Musgrove, M. (2011). Two professors critique the representations of Africans and African Americans in picture books. *Equity & Excellence in Education, 44*(2), 188–202. https://doi.org/10.1080/10665684.2011.559863

25empowering books for little Black girls. (2013). *For Harriet.* http://www.forharriet.com/2013/10/25-empowering-books-for-little-black.html

CHAPTER 35: Hair Representation Matters: Selecting Children's Books for Black Girls

Annamma, S. A., Jackson, D. D., & Morrison, D. (2017). Conceptualizing color-evasiveness: Using dis/ability critical race theory to expand a color-blind racial ideology in education and society. *Race Ethnicity and Education, 20*(2), 147–162.

Banks, I. (2000). *Hair matters: Beauty, power, and Black women's consciousness.* NYU Press.

Bishop, R. S. (1990). Mirrors, windows, and sliding glass doors. *Perspectives: Choosing and Using Books for the Classroom, 6*(3), ix–xi.

Brooks, W. M., & McNair, J. C. (2014). "Combing" through representations of black girls' hair in African American children's literature. *Children's Literature in Education*, *46*(3), 296–307.

Byrd, A., & Tharps, L. (2014). *Hair story: Untangling the roots of Black hair in America*. St. Martin's Griffin.

Capodilupo, C. M. (2015). One size does not fit all: Using variables other than the thin ideal to understand Black women's body image. *Cultural Diversity and Ethnic Minority Psychology*, *21*(2), 268–278.

Cherry, M. A. and Harrison, V. (2019). *Hair love*. Kokila.

Cooperative Children's Book Center. (2020, June 18). *The numbers are in: 2019 CCBC diversity statistics*. Cooperative Children's Book Center, School of Education, University of Wisconsin–Madison. Retrieved Jan 1, 2021, from http://ccblogc.blogspot.com/2020/06/the-numbers-are-in-2019-ccbc-diversity.html

Cueva, M., Dignan, M., & Kuhnley, R. (2012). Readers' theatre: A communication tool for colorectal cancer screening. *Journal of Cancer Education*, *27*(2), 281–286.

Derman-Sparks, L. (2013). Guide for selecting anti-bias children's books. *Teaching for Change Books*. https://www.teachingforchange.org/selecting-anti-bias-books

Derman-Sparks, L., & Edwards, J. O. (2010). *Anti bias education for young children and ourselves 2012*. National Association for the Education of Young Children.

Derman-Sparks, L., & Edwards, J. O. (2019). Understanding anti-bias education: Bringing the four core goals to every facet of your curriculum. *YC Young Children*, *74*(5), 6–12.

Hamilton, V. (1987). The known, the remembered, and the imagined: Celebrating AfroAmerican folktales. *Children's Literature in Education*, *18*(2), 67–75.

hooks, b. (1999). *Happy to be nappy*. Little, Brown Books for Young Readers.

Jeffries, R., & Jeffries, D. (2014). Cultural signification through reader's theatre: An analysis of African American girls and their hair. *Multicultural Learning and Teaching*, *9*(2), 203–218.

Jones-DeWeever, A. (2009). *Black girls in New York City: Untold strength & resilience*. Institute for Women's Policy Research.

Ladson-Billings, G. (2000). Fighting for our lives: Preparing teachers to teach African American students. *Journal of Teacher Education*, *51*(3), 206–214.

Miller, S. (2018). *Don't touch my hair!* Little, Brown Books for Young Readers.

Rooks, N. (1996). *Hair raising: Beauty, culture, and African American women*. Rutgers University Press.

Tarpley, N. (1998). *I love my hair!* Little, Brown.

Tatum, B. D. (1997). *Why are all the Black kids sitting together in the cafeteria? And other conversations about race*. Basic Books.

Toliver, S. R. (2018). Imagining new hopescapes: Expanding Black girls' windows and mirrors. *Research on Diversity in Youth Literature*, *1*(1), 3.

Book Review: *The Night Is Yours*

Burch, A. D. S. (2018, December 4). On the front porch, black life in full view. *New York Times*. https://www.nytimes.com/2018/12/04/us/porch-detroit-black-life.html

Zachariah, A. (2019). *The night is yours*. Penguin Random House.

Butler-Barnes, S. T., & Inniss-Thompson, M. N. (2020). "My teacher doesn't like me": Perceptions of teacher discrimination and school disciplinary infractions among African-American and Caribbean Black adolescent girls. *Education Sciences, 10*(2), 44.

Crenshaw, K. W., Ocen, P., & Nanda, J. (2015). *Black girls matter: Pushed out, overpoliced and underprotected.* Center for Intersectionality and Social Policy Studies, Columbia University. https://www.atlanticphilanthropies.org/wp-content/uploads/2015/09/BlackGirlsMatter_Report.pdf

Educational Video Group (Producer). (2014). *Malcolm X: "Who Taught You to Hate?"* May 5, 1962 speech excerpt [Video file]. American History in Video database. https://www.youtube.com/watch?v=kboP3AWCTkA

Garcia, S. B., & Ortiz, A. A. (1988). Preventing inappropriate referrals of language minority students to special education. The National Clearinghouse for Bilingual Education (NCBE), *Occasional Papers in Bilingual Education, 5*, 1–12.

Geiger, A. (2018, August 27). *America's public school teachers are far less racially and ethnically diverse than their students.* Pew Research Center. https://www.pewresearch.org/fact-tank/2018/08/27/americas-public-school-teachers-are-far-less-racially-and-ethnically-diverse-than-their-students/

Hansen, M., & Quintero, D. (2019. March 7). The diversity gap for public school teachers is actually growing across generations. *Brookings Brown Center Chalkboard.* https://www.brookings.edu/blog/brown-center-chalkboard/2019/03/07/the-diversity-gap-for-public-school-teachers-is-actually-growing-across-generations/

Hilliard, A. G. (1980). Cultural diversity and special education. *Exceptional Children, 46*(8), 584–588.

Hughes-Hassell, S, Bracy P. B., & Rawson, C. H. (2017). *Libraries, literacy, and African American youth: Research and practice.* Libraries Unlimited.

Jimenez, L. M., & Beckert, B. (2020, January 28). Where is the diversity in publishing? The 2019 diversity baseline survey results. *Lee and Low Books.* https://blog.leeandlow.com/2020/01/28/2019diversitybaselinesurvey/

Ladson-Billings, G. (1995). Toward a theory of culturally relevant pedagogy. *American Educational Research Journal, 32*(3), 465–491.

Ladson-Billings, G. (2009). Just what is critical race theory and what's it doing in a nice field like education? In E. Taylor, D. Gillborn, & G. Ladson-Billings (Eds.), *Foundations of critical race theory in education* (pp. 17–36). Routledge.

Love, B. L. (2019). *We want to do more than survive: Abolitionist teaching and the pursuit of educational freedom.* Beacon Press.

Miller, D. B., & MacIntosh, R. (1999). Promoting resilience in urban African American adolescents: Racial socialization and identity as protective factors. *Social Work Research, 23*(3), 159–169.

Morris, E. W. (2007). "Ladies" or "loudies"? Perceptions and experiences of Black girls in classrooms. *Youth & Society, 38*(4), 490–515.

Morris, M. W. (2016). *Pushout: The criminalization of Black girls in schools.* [Kindle edition]. The New Press. https://www.amazon.com

Nel, P. (2017). *Was the cat in the hat Black? The hidden racism of children's literature, and the need for diverse books.* Oxford University Press.

Rabinowitz, K., Emamdjomeh, A., & Meckler, L. (2019). How the nation's growing racial diversity is changing our schools. *Washington Post*. https://www.washingtonpost.com/graphics/2019/local/school-diversity-data

Smith, J. P. (2019, March 1). *Jordyn Woods shares the truth* (00:11:32). Red Table Talk [Video file]. https://www.facebook.com/redtabletalk/videos/416230735613094/

Tatum, B. D. (2017). *Why are all the black kids sitting together in the cafeteria? And other conversations about race*. Basic Books.

Text graffiti. (n.d.). Teaching strategy at Teaching Tolerance website. Retrieved November 30, 2020, from https://www.tolerance.org/classroom-resources/teaching-strategies/close-and-critical-reading/text-graffiti

Book Review: *Children of Blood and Bone*

Adeyemi, T. (2018). *Children of blood and bone*. Henry Holt.

PART III. "I AM DELIBERATE AND AFRAID OF NOTHING."—AUDRE LORDE

Chapter 37: Black Girl Sisterhood as Resilience and Resistance

Crenshaw, K. (1990). Mapping the margins: Intersectionality, identity politics, and violence against women of color. *Stanford Law Review*, *43*, 1241–1299.

Dixon, T. L., & Maddox, K. B. (2005). Skin tone, crime news, and social reality judgments: Priming the stereotype of the dark and dangerous Black criminal. *Journal of Applied Social Psychology*, *35*(8), 1555–1570. https://doi.org/10.1111/j.1559-1816.2005.tb02184.x

Epstein, R., Blake, J., & Gonzalez, T. (2017). *Girlhood interrupted: The erasure of Black girls' childhood*. SSRN Electronic Journal. https://doi.org/10.2139/ssrn.3000695

Mendelberg, T. (2008). Racial priming revived. *Perspectives on Politics*, *6*(01), 109–123. https://doi.org/10.1017/s1537592708080092

Rambo, S. S. (2015). *Paying attention to ourselves: An exploration of Black girlhood in Toni Morrison's The Bluest Eye and Sapphire's Push*. [Doctoral dissertation]. University of Louisiana at Lafayette.

Rosenberg, R. (1987). Seeds in hard ground: Black girlhood in The Bluest Eye. *Black American Literature Forum*, *21*(4), 435–445. https://doi.org/10.2307/2904114

Rudman, L. A., & Phelan, J. E. (2010). The effect of priming gender roles on women's implicit gender beliefs and career aspirations. *Social Psychology*, *41*(3), 192–202. https://doi.org/10.1027/1864-9335/a000027

Steele, J. R., & Ambady, N. (2006). "Math is hard!" The effect of gender priming on women's attitudes. *Journal of Experimental Social Psychology*, *42*(4), 428–436. https://doi.org/10.1016/j.jesp.2005.06.003

Wilderson, F. B. (2010). *Red, white & Black: Cinema and the structure of U.S. antagonisms*. Duke University Press.

CHAPTER 38: Respect Black Girls: Prioritize, Embrace, and Value

Abagond. (2008, March 7). The Sapphire stereotype. *Abagond*. http://abagond.wordpress.com/2008/03/07/the-sapphire-stereotype

Cooper, B. C. (2018). *Eloquent rage: A Black feminist discovers her superpower*. St. Martin's Press.

DeGruy, J. (2005). *Post traumatic slave syndrome: America's legacy of enduring injury and healing.* Joy Degruy Publications.

Feldman, R. S. (1985). Nonverbal behavior, race, and the classroom teacher. *Theory Into Practice, 24*(1), 45–49. https://doi.org/10.1080/00405848509543145

Fordham, S. (1993). "Those loud Black girls": (Black) women, silence, and gender "passing" in the academy. *Anthropology & Education Quarterly, 24*(1), 3–32.

Hoose, P. (2009). *Claudette Colvin: Twice Toward Justice.* Farrar Straus Giroux.

Morton, J. M. (2014). Vulture code-switching: Straddling the achievement gap. *The Journal of Political Philosophy, 22*(3), 259–281.

Pilgrim, D. (2012). *The Sapphire caricature.* Jim Crow Museum, Ferris State University. https://www.ferris.edu/HTMLS/news/jimcrow/antiblack/sapphire.htm (Original work published 2008)

Shetterly, M. L. (Author), & Freeman, L. (Illustrator). (2018). *Hidden figures: The true history of four Black women and the space race.* Harper Collins.

Shetterly, M. L. (2016). *Hidden figures: The American dream and the untold story of the Black women mathematicians who helped win the space race.* William Morrow.

Stevenson, H. C. (2014). *Promoting racial literacy in schools: Differences That Make a Difference.* Teachers College Press.

Weatherford, C. B. (Author), & Nelson, K. (Illustrator). (2006). *Moses: When Harriet Tubman led her people to freedom.* Hyperion Books.

Yonan, N. (2020). *Challenging the traditional narrative: A discussion on Ntozake Shange's for Colored Girls Who Have Considered Suicide/When the Rainbow is Enuf and Beyoncé's Lemonade.* Santa Clara University Scholar Commons. https://scholarcommons.scu.edu/cgi/viewcontent.cgi?article=1010&context=canterbury

CHAPTER 39: Understanding the Intersecting Identities of Black Girls

Alrubail, R. (2020, April 24). *Educator voice: Supporting students online during Ramadan.* PBS NewsHour Extra. https://www.pbs.org/newshour/extra/2020/04/educator-voice-how-teachers-can-support-students-online-during-ramadan/

Arki, S. J. (2016). Teachers as activists: Using a Black, feminist pedagogy to prevent classroom bullying. In A. Osanloo, C. Reed, & J. Schwartz (Eds), *Creating and negotiating collaborative spaces for socially-just anti-bullying interventions for K–12 schools* (pp. 241–256). Information Age.

Berry, T. R. (2010). Engaged pedagogy and critical race feminism. *Educational Foundations, 24*(3-4), 19–26.

Blake, J. J., Butler, B. R., Lewis, C. W., & Darensbourg, A. (2011). Unmasking the inequitable discipline experiences of urban Black girls: Implications for urban educational stakeholders. *The Urban Review, 43*(1), 90–106.

Cho, S., Crenshaw, K. W., & McCall, L. (2013). Toward a field of intersectionality studies: Theory, applications, and praxis. *Signs: Journal of Women in Culture and Society, 38*(4), 785–810.

Collins, P. H. (1990). *Black feminist thought: Knowledge, consciousness, and the politics of empowerment.* Routledge.

Collins, P. H., & Bilge, S. (2016). *Intersectionality.* John Wiley & Sons.

Crenshaw, K. (1991). Mapping the margins: Intersectionality, identity politics, and violence against women of color. *Stanford Law Review, 43*(6), 1241–1299.

Epstein, R., Blake, J., & González, T. (2017). *Girlhood interrupted: The erasure of Black girls' childhood*. https://www.blendedandblack.com/wp-content/uploads/2017/08/girlhood-interrupted.pdf.

Goldbach, J. (2019, May 7). Activity 1: Introduction Identity. *The MSW@USC diversity tool kit: A guide to discussing identity, power and privilege*. University of Southern California. https://msw.usc.edu/mswusc-blog/diversity-workshop-guide-to-discussing-identity-power-and-privilege/#unpack

hooks, b. (1994). *Teaching to transgress: Education as the practice of freedom*. Routledge.

Ladson-Billings, G. (2009). *The dreamkeepers: Successful teachers of African American children* (2nd ed.). John Wiley & Sons.

Roy, A. (2004, November 3). *Peace and the new corporate liberation theology*. The 2004 Sydney Peace Prize Lecture. University of Sydney, Australia.

Sankofa Community Empowerment. (2001). *The SCRR model*. http://www.sankofaempowerment.org/

Shorter-Gooden, K., & Washington, N. C. (1996). Young, Black, and female: The challenge of weaving an identity. *Journal of Adolescence, 19*(5), 465–475.

Terrell, F., & Barrett, R. K. (1979). Interpersonal trust among college students as a function of race, sex, and socioeconomic class. *Perceptual and Motor Skills, 48*, 1194–1197.

Thomas, D. E., Townsend, T. G., & Belgrave, F. Z. (2003). The influence of cultural and racial identification on the psychosocial adjustment of inner-city African American children in school. *American Journal of Community Psychology, 32*(3–4), 217–228.

Williams, W., Karlin, T., & Wallace, D. (2012). Project SisterCircle: Risk, intersectionality, and intervening in urban schools. *Journal of School Counseling, 10*(17), 1–28.

CHAPTER 40: #StudentAsSignMaker: Curating Classrooms For Identity Development

Arki, S. J. (2016). Teachers as activists: Using a Black, feminist pedagogy to prevent classroom bullying. In A. Osanloo, C. Reed, & J. Schwartz (Eds.), *Creating and negotiating collaborative spaces for socially-just anti-bullying interventions for K–12 schools* (pp. 241–256). Information Age.

Banks, J. A. (1974). *Multicultural education: In search of definitions and goals*. http://files.eric.ed.gov/fulltext/ED100792.pdf

Crenshaw, K. W. (1995). Mapping the margins: Intersectionality, identity politics and violence against women of color. In K. Crenshaw, N. Gotanda, G. Peller, & K. Thomas (Eds.), *Critical race theory: The key writings that formed the movement.* (pp. 357–383). The New Press.

Daniel, B. J. (2009). Conversations on race in teacher education cohorts. *Teaching Education, 20*(2), 175–188.

Delgado, R., Stefancic, J., & Liendo, E. (2012). *Critical race theory: An introduction* (2nd ed.). https://ebookcentral.proquest.com

Evans-Winters, V., & Bethune, M. C. (2014). *(Re)Teaching Trayvon: Education for racial justice and human freedom*. Sense.

Freire, P. (2000). *Pedagogy of the oppressed* (30th anniversary edition). Bloomsbury. (Original work published 1970)

Gallagher, S. (1992). *Hermeneutics and education*. SUNY Press.

Harris-Perry, M. V. (2012). *Sister citizen: Shame, stereotypes and Black women in America*. Yale University Press.

Hill, A. (2015). *I realized that one shouldn't combat ignorance with hate, but with information*. http://www.maltzmuseum.org/wp- content/uploads/2015/05/15StoptheHate .pdf#page=8

Karenga, M. (2008). *Kwanzaa: A celebration of family, community and culture*. University of Sankore Press.

Kumashiro, K. (2000). Towards a theory of anti-oppressive education. *Review of Educational Research, 70*(1), 25–53. https://doi.org/10.3102/00346543070001025

Ladson-Billings, G. (1999). Just what is critical race theory, and what's it doing in a nice field like education? In L. Parker, D. Deyhle, & S. Villenas (Eds.), *Race is . . . race isn't: Critical race theory and qualitative studies in education* (pp. 7–30). Westview Press.

Ladson-Billings, G. (2013). Critical race theory—what it is not! In M. Lynn & A. D. Dixson (Eds.), *Handbook of critical race theory in education* (pp. 34–47). Routledge.

Lorde, A. (2007). Age, race, class, and sex: Women redefining difference. In *Sister Outsider*. (pp. 114–123). Crossing Press. (Original work published 1984)

Love, B. (2019). *We want to do more than survive: Abolitionist teaching and the pursuit of educational freedom*. Beacon Press.

Morris, M. W. (2016). *Pushout: The criminalization of Black girls in schools*. The New Press.

Rogers, R. (2011a). Critical approaches to discourse analysis in educational research. In R. Rogers (Ed.), *An introduction to critical discourse analysis in education* (pp. 1–20). Routledge.

Rogers, R. (2011b). Preface. In R. Rogers (Ed), *An Introduction to critical discourse analysis in education* (pp. xv–xxviii). Routledge.

Schwandt, T. A. (2000). Three epistemological stances for qualitative inquiry: Interpretivism, hermeneutics, and social constructionism. In N. Denzin & Y. Lincoln (Eds.), *The SAGE handbook of qualitative research* (2nd. ed., pp. 189–213).

Vignette: Beautiful, Brilliant, Black and Deaf

Lundqvist, A., Liljander, V., Gummerus, J., & van Riel, A. (2012). The impact of storytelling on the consumer brand experience: The case of a firm-originated story. *Journal of Brand Management, 20*(4), 283–297. https://link.springer.com/article/10.1057/bm.2012.15

CHAPTER 41: Black Men Teaching Beautiful and Brilliant Black Girls: Resisting Patriarchal and Sexist Socializations

Cooper, B. C. (2017). *Beyond respectability: The intellectual thought of race women*. University of Illinois Press.

Nicolaides, S. (Producer), & Singleton, J. (Director). (1991). *Boyz n the hood* [Motion picture]. Columbia Pictures.

Shetterly, M. L. (2016). *Hidden figures*. HarperCollins.

Smith, B. (Ed.). (1983). *Home girls: A black feminist anthology*. Rutgers University Press.

Taylor, K. Y. (Ed.). (2017). *How we get free: Black feminism and the Combahee River Collective*. Haymarket Books.

Woods, J. (2009). The black male privileges checklist. *Privilege: A reader* (2nd ed., pp. 27–37). Westview Press.

Chapter 42: Black Girl Magic: Beauty, Brilliance, and Coming to Voice in the Classroom

Angelou, M. (1978). *Phenomenal woman*. https://www.poetryfoundation.org/poems/ 48985/phenomenal-woman

Brown, R. N. (2009). *Black girlhood celebration: Toward a hip hop feminist pedagogy*. Peter Lang.

Brown, R. N. (2013). *Hear our truths: The creative potential of Black girlhood*. University of Illinois Press.

Ford, A. (2016). There is nothing wrong with Black girl magic. *Elle*. www.elle.com/life-love/a33251/there-is-nothing-wrong-with-black-girl-magic/

Hope, C. (2017). Who gets to own "Black girl magic"? *Jezebel*. www.jezebel.com/who-gets-to-own-black-girl-magic-1793924053

Imani, B. (2018). *Modern herstory: Stories of women and nonbinary people rewriting history*. Penguin Random House.

Johnson, D. (2015). Disrupting invisibility: Education scholarship meeting the needs of African American elementary and secondary school girls. In D. Johnson & A. Ginsberg (Eds.), *Difficult dialogues about twenty-first century girls* (pp. 19–55). SUNY.

Kincaid, J. (1978). Girl. *New Yorker*. https://www.newyorker.com/magazine/1978/06/26/girl

Lorde, A. (1978). A litany for survival. *Poetry Foundation*. https://www.poetryfoundation.org/poems/147275/a-litany-for-survival

Morris, M. (2015). *Pushout: The criminalization of Black girls in schools*. The New Press.

Thomas, D. (2015). Why everyone's saying "Black girls are magic." *Los Angeles Times*. http://www.latimes.com/nation/nationnow/la-na-nn-everyones-saying-black-girls-are-magic-20150909-htmlstory.html

The Visionary. (n.d.). *SOLHOT: Saving our lives, hear our truths*. Retrieved December 14, 2020, from https://www.solhot.com/the-visionary

PART IV. "PERSEVERANCE IS MY MOTTO."—MADAM C. J. WALKER

CHAPTER 43: Listen to Her! Black Girls Constructing Activist Identities in a School-Based Leadership Program

Archer-Banks, D. A. M., & Behar-Horenstein, L. S. (2012). Ogbu revisited: Unpacking high-achieving African American girls' high school experiences. *Urban Education*, *47*(1), 198–223.

Berry, T. R. (2010). Engaged pedagogy and critical race feminism. *Educational Foundations*, *24*(3-4), 19–26.

Carr, K. (2020). *Listen to her!: Perspectives on identity, leadership, social justice and service from adolescent girls of color* [Doctoral dissertation]. Saint Mary's College of California.

Clonan-Roy, K., Jacobs, C. E., & Nakkula, M. J. (2016). Towards a positive model of youth development specific to girls of color: Perspectives on development, resilience, and empowerment. *Gender Issues*, *33*, 96–121. https://doi.org/10.1007/s12147-016-9156-7

Collins, P. H. (2000). *Black feminist thought: Knowledge, consciousness, and the politics of empowerment* (2nd ed.). Routledge.

Crenshaw, K. W., Ocen, P., & Nanda, J. (2015). *Black girls matter: Pushed out, over-policed, and underprotected*. African American Policy Forum and the Center for Intersectionality and Social Policy Studies. http://static1.squarespace.com/static/53f20d90e4b0b80451158d8c/t/54dcc1ece4b001c03e323448/1423753708557/AAPF_BlackGirlsMatterReport.pdf

Evans, G. (1988). Those loud black girls. In D. Spender & E. Sarah (Eds.), *Learning to lose: Sexism and education* (Vol. 2, pp. 183–190). Women's Press.

Evans-Winters, V. E. (2011). *Teaching Black girls: Resiliency in urban classrooms* (2nd ed.). Peter Lang.

Evans-Winters, V. E., & Esposito, J. (2010). Other people's daughters: Critical race feminism and Black girls' education. *Educational Foundations, 24*(1–2), 11–24.

Freire, P. (2002). *Pedagogy of the oppressed* (30th anniversary ed., rev.). Continuum Press. (Original work published 1970).

Grant, L. (1984). Black females' "place" in desegregated classrooms. *Sociology of Education, 57*(2), 98–111.

Harris, B. G., Hayes, C., & Smith, D. T. (2020). Not a "who done it" mystery: On how whiteness sabotages equity aims in teacher preparation programs. *The Urban Review, 52*(1), 198–213.

Juárez Harris, B. G., Smith, D. T., & Hayes, C. (2016). Just do what we tell you: White rules for well-behaved minorities. In N. Hartlep & C. Hayes (Eds.), *Unhooking from Whiteness: Resisting the Esprit de Corps* (pp. 107–120). Sense Publishers.

Ladson-Billings, G. (1995). But that's just good teaching! The case for culturally relevant pedagogy. *Theory Into Practice, 34*(3), 159–165. DOI:10.1080/00405849509543675

Lane, M. (2017). Reclaiming our queendom: Black feminist pedagogy and the identity formation of African American girls. *Equity & Excellence in Education, 50*(1), 13–24.

Lane, M. (in press). *Engendering #BlackGirlJoy: How to cultivate empowered identities and educational persistence in struggling schools.* Peter Lang.

Levine-Rasky, C. (2000). Framing whiteness: Working through the tensions in introducing whiteness to educators. *Race Ethnicity and Education, 3*(3), 271–292.

Love, B. (2017). A ratchet lens: Black queer youth, agency, hip hop, and the Black ratchet imagination. *Educational Researcher, 46*(9), 539–547.

McArthur, S., & Lane, M. (2018). Schoolin' Black girls: Politicized caring and healing as pedagogical love. *The Urban Review, 51*(3), 535–536.

Mitchell, T. D. (2010). Challenges and possibilities: Linking social justice and service-learning. *Michigan Journal of Community Service Learning, 17*(1), 94–98.

Morris, E. W. (2007). "Ladies" or "loudies"? Perceptions and experiences of Black girls in classrooms. *Youth and Society, 38*(4), 490–515.

Morris, M. W. (2016). *Pushout: The criminalization of Black girls in schools.* The New Press.

The NAACP Legal Defense and Educational Fund & The National Women's Law Center. (2014). *Unlocking opportunity for African American girls: A call to action for educational equity.* Author.

Sealey-Ruiz, Y. (2007). Rising above reality: The voices of reentry Black mothers and their daughters. *Journal of Negro Education, 76*(2), 141–153.

Social identity wheel. (n.d.). LSA Inclusive Teaching Initiative, University of Michigan. https://sites.lsa.umich.edu/inclusive-teaching/wp-content/uploads/sites/732/2020/07/Social-Identity-WheelDefinitions.pdf

U.S. Department of Education, National Center for Education Statistics. (2019). *Digest of Education Statistics, 2017* (NCES 2018-070). Author.

Yosso, T. J. (2005). Whose culture has capital? A critical race theory discussion of community cultural wealth. *Race Ethnicity and Education, 8*(1), 69–91. https://doi.org/10.1080/1361332052000341006

CHAPTER 44: When You Imagine a Scientist, Technologist, Engineer, Artist, or Mathematician, Imagine a Black Girl

Ashby, E. (2012). *Doc McStuffins*. Common Sense Media. TV review. https://www.commonsensemedia.org/tv-reviews/doc-mcstuffins.

Barbie + Tynker: Robotics engineer. (n.d.). Retrieved July 31, 2018, from https://barbie.mattel.com/en-us/about/barbie-tynker.html?icid=home_body-1_aspot_coty-learn-more_p3

Barnes, B. (2012). Disney finds a cure for the common stereotype with "Doc McStuffins." *New York Times* (section C, p. 1). https://www.nytimes.com/2012/07/31/arts/television/disneys-doc-mcstuffins-connects-with-Black-viewers.html.

Berman, E. (2017, December 25). Hollywood's once and future classic. *Time Magazine*. http://time.com/wrinkle-in-time

Bodies . . . the Exhibition Atlanta. (2019). *Educators resources*. https://bodiesatlanta.com/educators

Boyle. A. (2017, February 28). From "Hidden Figures" to minifigures: Lego toys immortalize the women of NASA. *Geekwire*. https://www.geekwire.com/2017/hidden-figures-minifigures-women-nasa-lego

Boyle, A. (2018, March 6). "Hidden Figures" no more: New barbie dolls honor NASA's Katherine Johnson and 1 other woman. *Geekwire*. https://www.geekwire.com/2018/hidden-figures-no-barbie-dolls-honor-nasas-katherine-johnson-16-women

Brickhouse, N., Lowery, P., & Schultz, K. (2000). What kind of girl does science? The construction of school science identities. *Journal of Research in Science Teaching* 3(5), 441–458. https://doi.org/10.1002/(SICI)1098-2736(200005)37:5<441::AID-TEA4>3.0.CO;2-3

Burke, P., & Stets, J. (2009). *Identity theory*. Oxford University Press.

Hom, E. (2014, February 11). What is STEAM education? *Live Science*. https://www.livescience.com/43296-what-is-STEAM-education.html.

Lee, J. (1998). Which kids can "become" scientists? Effects of gender, self-concepts, and perceptions of scientists. *Social Psychology Quarterly 61*(3), 199–219.

Maggs, S. (2016). *Wonder women: 25 innovators, inventors, and trailblazers who changed history*. Quirk Books.

Merolla, D. M., & Serpe, R. T. (2013). STEAM enrichment programs and graduate school matriculation: The role of science identity salience. *Social Psychology of Education 16*(4), 575–597.

Merolla, D. M., Serpe, R. T., Stryker, S., & Schultz, P. W. (2012). Structural precursors to identity processes: The role of proximate social structures. *Social Psychology Quarterly*, 75(2), 149–172.

National 4-H Council. (n.d.). *STEM and agriculture*. Retrieved December 14, 2020, from https://4-h.org/parents/stem-agriculture

National Science Foundation, National Center for Science and Engineering Statistics. (2017). *Women, minorities, and persons with disabilities in science and engineering: 2017*. Special Report NSF 17-310. https://www.nsf.gov/statistics/2017/nsf17310/static/downloads/nsf17310-digest.pdf

Rock Holdings. (n.d.). *Dictionary.com*. Retrieved December 27, 2020, from https://www.dictionary.com/browse/vision-board

Rosenthal, L., London, B., Levy, S. R., & Lobel, M. (2011). The roles of perceived identity compatibility and social support for women in a single-sex STEM program at a co-educational university. *Sex Roles, 65*(9–10), 725–736. https://doi.org/10.1007/s11199-011-9945-0

Settles, I. (2014). Women in STEAM: Challenges and determinants of success and well-being. *Psychological Science Agenda*. American Psychological Association. http://www.apa.org/science/about/psa/2014/10/women-STEAM.aspx

Shuri. (n.d.). In *Marvel cinematic universe wiki*. Retrieved July 31, 2018, from http://marvelcinematicuniverse.wikia.com/wiki/Shuri.

Steinke, J. (2017). Adolescent girls' STEAM identity formation and media images of STEAM professionals: Considering the influence of contextual cues. *Frontiers in Psychology, 8*, 716. https://www.frontiersin.org/article/10.3389/fpsyg.2017.00716

U.S. Department of Education. (n.d.). *Science, technology, engineering and math: Education for global leadership*. https://www.ed.gov/STEAM.

Chapter 45: Developing an Ethic of Engaging Black Girls in Digital Spaces

Bailey, M. (2015). #transform (ing) DH writing and research: An autoethnography of digital humanities and feminist ethics. *Digital Humanities Quarterly, 9*(2), 1.

Brown, R. N. (2012). *Hear our truths: The creative potential of black girlhood*. University of Illinois Press.

Crenshaw, K. W., Ocen, P., & Nanda, J. (2014). *Black girls matter: Pushed out, overpoliced, and underprotected*. African American Policy Forum. https://static1.squarespace.com/static/53f20d90e4b0b80451158d8c/t/54dcc1ece4b001c03e323448/1423753708557/AAPF_BlackGirlsMatterReport.pdf

Simpson, A. (2014). *Mohawk interruptus: Political life across the borders of settler states*. Duke University Press.

CHAPTER 46: A Matter of Media: Cultural Appropriation and Expectations of Black Girls

Adams-Bass, V. N., & Bentley-Edwards, K. L. (2020). The trouble with Black girl magic for Black girls. In D. Apugo, L. Mawhinney, & A. Mbilishaka (Eds.), *Strong Black Girls* (pp. 99–117). Teachers College Press.

Adams-Bass, V. N., Bentley-Edwards, K. L., & Stevenson, H. (2014). That's not me I see on TV: African American youth interpret images of Black females. *Women, Gender and Families of Color, 2*(1), 79–100.

Adam-Bass, V. N., & Henrici, E. (2019). Hardly ever . . . I don't see it: Black youth speak about positive media images of Black men. In O. Banjo (Ed.), *African diasporic media, content, consumers, and global influence* (pp. 148–162). Routledge.

Adams, V. N., & Stevenson H. C., Jr. (2012). Media socialization, Black media images and Black adolescent identity. In D. Slaughter-Defoe (Ed.), *Racial stereotyping and child development contributions to human development* (Vol. 25, pp. 28–46). Karger.

Alvermann, D., & Hagood, M. (2000). Fandom and critical media literacy. *Journal of Adolescent & Adult Literacy, 43*(5), 436–446. www.jstor.org/stable/40017080

Aufderheide, P. (1992). Cable television and the public interest. *Journal of Communication, 42*(1), 52–65. https://doi.org/10.1111/j.1460-2466.1992.tb00768.x

Balaji, M. (2009). Why do good girls have to be bad? The cultural industry's production of the other and the complexities of agency. *Popular Communication: The International Journal of Media and Culture, 7*(4), 225–236.

Bentley-Edwards, K. L., & Adams-Bass, V. N. (in press). The whole picture: Examining Black women through the life span. In H. O. Jackson Lowman (Ed.), *Afrikan American women: Living at the crossroads of race, gender, class, and culture* (2nd ed., pp. 189–201). Cognella Press.

Bogle, D. (2016). *Toms, coons, mulattoes, mammies & bucks: An interpretive history of Blacks in American films* (5th ed.). Continuum International Publishing Group.

Buckley, T. R., & Carter, R. T. (2005). Black adolescent girls: Do gender role and racial identity impact their self-esteem? *Sex Roles, 53*(9), 647–661.

Hall, H. R., & Smith. E. L. (2012). This is not reality . . . it's only TV: African American girls respond to media (mis)representations. *The New Educator, 8*(3), 222–242.

Hesse-Biber, S. N., Howling, S., A., Leavy, P., & Lovejoy, M. (2004). Racial identity and the development of body image issues among African American adolescent girls. *The Qualitative Report, 9*(1), 49–79.

Hill, S. A. (2001). Class, race and gender dimensions of child rearing in African American families. *Journal of Black Studies, 31*(4), 494–508.

Hill, S. A. (2002). Teaching and doing gender in African American families. *Sex Roles, 47*(11–12), 493–506.

Jackson, R. L. (2006). *Scripting the black masculine body: Identity, discourse, and racial politics in popular media.* SUNY Press.

Kellner, D., & Share, J. (2007a). Critical media literacy, democracy, and the reconstruction of education. In D. Macedo & S. R. Steinberg (Eds.), *Media literacy: A reader* (pp. 3–23). Peter Lang.

Kellner, D., & Share, J. (2007b). Critical media literacy is not an option. *Learning Inquiry, 1*(1), 59–69.

King, J. (2011, March 2). *For girls who love themselves enough to talk back to Lil Wayne.* Colorlines. https://www.colorlines.com/articles/girls-who-love-themselves-enough -talk-back-lil-wayne

National Association for Media Literacy Education (NAMLE). (2007). *Core principles of media literacy education in the United States.* https://namle.net/wp-content/ uploads/2020/09/Namle-Core-Principles-of-MLE-in-the-United-States.pdf

Neal-Jackson, A. (2018). A meta-ethnographic review of the experiences of African American girls and young women in K–12 education. *Review of Educational Research, 88*(4), 508–546.

Orlowski, P. (2006). Educating in an era of Orwellian spin: Critical media literacy in the classroom. *Canadian Journal of Education/Revue canadienne de l'éducation, 29*(1), 176–198.

Sanders, J. L., & Bradley, C. (2005). Multiple-lens paradigm: Evaluating African American girls and their development. *Journal of Counseling and Development, 83*(3), 299–304.

Sims, Y. (2020, August 20). *Blaxploitation movies.* https://www.britannica.com/art/ blaxploitation-movie

Spencer, M. B. (1995). Old issues and new theorizing about African American youth: A phenomenological variant of ecological systems theory. In R. L. Taylor (Ed.), *Black youth: Perspectives on their status in the United States* (pp. 37–69). Praeger.

Spencer, M. B., Dupree, D., & Swanson, D. P. (1996). Parental monitoring and adolescents' sense of responsibility for their own learning: An examination of sex differences. *Journal of Negro Education, 65*(1), 30–43.

Stephens, D. P., & Phillips, L. (2005). Integrating Black feminist thought into conceptual frameworks of African American adolescent women's sexual scripting processes *Sexualities, Evolution & Gender, 7*(1), 37–55.

Swanson, D., & Cunningham, M., Youngblood, J., & Spencer, M. (2009). *Racial identity development during childhood.* GSE Publications.

Yasui, M., Dorham, C. L., & Dishion, T. J. (2004). Ethnic identity and psychological adjustment: A validity analysis for European American and African American adolescents. *Journal of Adolescent Research, 19*(6), 807–825.

CHAPTER 47: "Catch This Magic": How Schools Get in the Way of Gifted Black Girls

Anderson, B. N., & Martin, J. A. (2018). The survival of the gifted Black girls: What K–12 educators need to know about teaching gifted Black girls battling perfectionism and stereotype threat. *Gifted Child Today, 41*(3), 117–124.

Besnoy, K. D., Dantzler, J., Besnoy, L. R., & Byrne, C. (2016). Using exploratory and confirmatory factor analysis to measure construct validity of the Traits, Aptitudes, and Behaviors Scale (TABS). *Journal for the Education of the Gifted, 39*(1), 3–22.

Civil Rights Data Collection. (2013). *Educational equity report.* https://ocrdata.ed.gov/DataAnalysisTools/DataSetBuilder?Report=7

Crenshaw, K. (1991). Mapping the margins: Intersectionality, identity politics, and violence against women of color. *Stanford Law Review, 43*(6), 1241–1299. https://doi.org/10.2307/1229039

Evans-Winters, V. E. (2014). Are Black girls not gifted? Race, gender, and resilience. *Interdisciplinary Journal of Teaching and Learning, 4*(1), 22–30.

Evans, E. A. (2015). *Young, gifted, Black, and blocked: A critical inquiry of barriers that hinder Black students' participation in gifted and advanced placement programs* [Doctoral dissertation, Georgia Southern University]. Electronic Theses & Dissertations Paper No. 1355. http://digitalcommons.georgiasouthern.edu/etd/1355

Ford, D. Y. (1998). The underrepresentation of minority students in gifted education: Problems and promises in recruitment and retention. *The Journal of Special Education, 32*(1), 4–14.

Ford, D. Y. (2011). *Multicultural gifted education: Rationale, models, strategies, & resources* (2nd ed.). Prufrock Press.

Ford, D. Y. (2013). *Recruiting and retaining culturally different students in gifted education.* Prufrock Press.

Ford, D. Y., Grantham, T. C., & Whiting, G. W. (2008). Another look at the achievement gap: Learning from the experiences of gifted Black students. *Urban Education, 43*(2), 216–239.

Frasier, M. M. (1991). Disadvantaged and culturally diverse gifted students. *Journal for the Education of the Gifted, 14*(3), 234–245.

Frasier, M. M. (1997). Multiple criteria: The mandate and the challenge. *Roeper Review, 20*(2), A4–A6.

Frasier, M. M., Martin, D., García, J. H., Finley, V. S., Frank, E., Krisel, S., & King, L. L. (1995). *A new window for looking at gifted children* [RM95222]. The National Research Center on the Gifted and Talented, University of Connecticut.

Frasier, M. M., & Passow, A. H. (1994). *Towards a new paradigm for identifying talent potential* [Research monograph 94112]. National Research Center on the Gifted and Talented, University of Connecticut.

Gholson, M., & Martin, D. B. (2014). Smart girls, Black girls, mean girls, and bullies: At the intersection of identities and the mediating role of young girls' social network in mathematical communities of practice. *Journal of Education, 194*(1), 19–33.

Grantham, T. C., & Ford, D. Y. (2003). Beyond self-concept and self-esteem: Racial identity and gifted African American students. *The High School Journal, 87*(1), 18–29.

Greene, D. T. (2016). "We need more 'US' in schools!!" Centering Black adolescent girls' literacy and language practices in online school spaces. *The Journal of Negro Education, 85*(3), 274–289.

Grissom, J. A., & Redding, C. (2016). Discretion and disproportionality: Explaining the underrepresentation of high-achieving students of color in gifted programs. *AERA Online, 2*(1), 1–15.

Harper, F. K., & Anderson, B. N. (2020). "I just get all stressed out": Coping with perfectionism as a Black gifted girl in mathematics. In N. Joseph, *Understanding the intersections of race, gender, and gifted education: An anthology by and about talented Black girls and women in STEM* (pp. 27–52). Information Age.

Henry, A. (1998). "Invisible" and "womanish": Black girls negotiating their lives in an African-centered school in the USA. *Race Ethnicity and Education, 1*(2), 151–170.

Hines, M. E., Anderson, B. N., & Grantham, T. C. (2016). Promoting opportunity, rigor, and achievement for underrepresented students. In R. D. Eckert & J. H. Robins (Eds.), *Designing services and programs for high-ability learners: A guidebook for gifted education* (2nd ed., pp. 151–168). Corwin.

Maxwell, M. (2007). Career counseling is personal counseling: A constructivist approach to nurturing the development of gifted female adolescents. *The Career Development Quarterly, 55*, 206–224.

McBee, M. T. (2006). A descriptive analysis of referral sources for gifted identification screening by race and socioeconomic status. *Journal of Secondary Gifted Education, 17*(2), 103–111.

O'Connor, C. (1997). Dispositions toward (collective) struggle and educational resilience in the inner city: A case analysis of six African-American high school students. *American Educational Research Journal, 34*(4), 593–629.

Trotman Scott, M., & Moss-Bouldin, S. (2014). We need more drama: A comparison of Ford, Hurston, and Boykin's African American characteristics and instructional strategies for the culturally different classroom. *Interdisciplinary Journal of Teaching and Learning, 4*(2), 68–80.

Wright, B. L. (2011). Valuing the "everyday" practices of African American students K–12 and their engagement in STEM learning: A position. *The Journal of Negro Education, 80*(1), 5–11.

PART V. "BE THANKFUL THAT YOU'VE BEEN GIVEN THAT GIFT, BECAUSE [BLACK] GIRLS ARE AMAZING."—KOBE BRYANT

Book Review: *Juneteenth for Mazie*

Cooper, F. (2015). *Juneteenth for Mazie*. Capstone.

Robbins L. (2020). *These states now recognize Juneteenth, but what are their other holidays?* WUSA9. https://www.wusa9.com/article/news/nation-world/juneteenth-us-states-official-holidays/507-aa8e98a6-8e01-4f39-b3b5-632d3bf8c83b

Vignette: Love Letter

Roy, A. (2004, November 3). *Peace and the new corporate liberation theology*. The 2004 Sydney Peace Prize Lecture. University of Sydney, Australia.

PART VI "WE WILL FIGHT TILL THE LAST OF US FALLS IN THE BATTLEFIELD."—NANA YAA ASANTEWAA, QUEEN MOTHER OF EJISU IN THE ASHANTI EMPIRE, GHANA

Dewan, S., & Oppel, R. A., Jr. (2015, January 22). In Tamir Rice case, many errors by Cleveland police, then a fatal one. *New York Times*. https://www.nytimes.com/2015/01/23/us/in-tamir-rice-shooting-in-cleveland-many-errors-by-police-then-a-fatal-one.html

CHAPTER 48: Motherwork as Pedagogy

Arki, S. J. (2016). Teachers as activists: Using a black, feminist pedagogy to prevent classroom bullying. In A. Osanloo, C. Reed, & J. Schwartz, (Eds.), *Creating and negotiating collaborative spaces for socially-just anti-bullying interventions for K–12 schools* (pp. 241–256). Information Age.

Arki, S. J. (2018). Ruminations from a #BlackMommyActivist. In E. Moore Jr., A. Michael, & M. W. Penick-Parks (Eds.), *The guide for white women who teach Black boys* (pp. 270–274). Corwin.

Cha-Jua, S. (2013). Organic intellectual: Robert Chrisman and the construction of a black radical scholar's activist legacy. *Black Scholar, 43*(3), 10–16.

Collins, P. H. (1990). *Black feminist thought: Knowledge, consciousness, and the politics of empowerment*. Unwin Hyman.

Collins, P. H. (1994). Shifting the center: Race, class and feminist theorizing about motherhood. In E. N. Glenn, G. Chang, & L. R. Forcey (Eds.), *Mothering: Ideology, experience and agency* (pp. 45–65). Routledge.

DuBois, W. E. B. (1991). The souls of black folks. *Society, 28*(5), 74–80. https://doi.org/10.1007/BF02695692

Emdin, C. (2016). *For white folks who teach in the hood . . . and the rest of y'all too: Reality pedagogy and urban education*. Beacon Press.

Freire, P. (2000). *Pedagogy of the oppressed* (30th anniversary edition). Bloomsbury. (Original work published 1970)

Guy-Sheftall, B. (1995). The Combahee River Collective. In B. Guy-Sheftall (Ed.), *Words of fire: An anthology of African American feminist thought* (p. 231). The New Press.

Hilliard, D. (2013). *Educating for struggle . . . in the academy* [Video file]. http://youtu.be/HdrD5nU5Tt4

hooks, b. (1994). *Teaching to transgress: Education as the practice of freedom.* Routledge.

Kaplan, E. (2000). We are what we collect, we collect what we are: Archives and the construction of identity. *The American Archivist, 63*(1), 126–151. www.jstor.org/stable/40283823

King, D. K. (1995). Multiple jeopardy, multiple consciousness: The context of Black feminist ideology. In B. Guy-Sheftall (Ed.), *Words of fire: An anthology of African American feminist thought* (pp. 291–317). The New Press.

Ladson-Billings, G. (1998). Just what is critical race theory and what's it doing in a nice field like education? *International Journal of Qualitative Studies in Education, 11*(1), 7–24. https://doi.org/10.1080/095183998236863

Lorde, A. (2003). The master's tools will never dismantle the master's house. In R. Lewis & S. Mills (Eds.), *Feminist postcolonial theory: A reader* (pp. 25–28). Edinburgh University Press. https://doi.org/10.3366/j.ctvxcr9q0.5

Love, B. (2016). Anti-Black state violence, classroom edition: The spirit murdering of Black children. *Journal of Curriculum and Pedagogy, 13*(1), 22–25. https://doi.org/10.1080/15505170.2016.1138258

Love, B. (2019). *We want to do more than survive: Abolitionist teaching and the pursuit of educational freedom.* Beacon Press.

Morgan, J. (1999). *When chickenheads come home to roost: My life as a hip-hop feminist.* Simon & Schuster.

Rabaka, R. (2009). *Africana critical theory: Reconstructing the black radical tradition from W. E. B. DuBois and C. L. R. James to Frantz Fanon and Amilcar Cabral.* Lexington Books.

Sankofa Waters, B. (2015). *We can speak for ourselves: Parent involvement and ideologies of Black mothers in Chicago.* Sense.

Wallace, M. (2015). *Black macho and the myth of the superwoman.* Verso.

Washington, T. N. (2013). "The sea never dies." Yemoja: The infinitely flowing mother force of Africana literature and cinema. In S. Otero & T. Falola (Eds.), *Yemoja: Gender, sexuality, and creativity in the Latino/a and Afro-Atlantic diasporas* (pp. 215–266). SUNY Press.

Index

Bishop, R. S., 338, 344

Black, authentic, and culturally engaging (BACE), 16, 336–339, 339–341 (table), 342

Black, Indigenous, or People of Color (BIPOC), 238, 391

Black adults, 70

Black American immigrant girls, 216–217

Black children, 437

Black culture, 71

Black Deaf Girls, 393–395

Black Girl Excellence

Black feminist movement, 208, 463

Black Feminist's Search for Sisterhood, A (Wallace), 208

Black feminist thought (BFT), 204, 463, 464

Black Genius and Black Excellence, 291

Black Girl Fears Motherhood (Prescod), 469–471

Black Girl Got Magic (Pugh), 33–34

Black Girlhood, 26, 39, 139, 248, 256, 257, 280–282, 303, 365, 407, 431, 442

#BlackGirlJoy, 417

#BlackGirlMagic, 371, 405–406

Black Girl Priming, 364–365
   for Chico, 366

Black Girls, White Privilege, and Schooling (Watson), 256

#BlackGirlsAreMagic, 3, 76, 101, 371, 405

Black Girls Are Precious Gifts: Educators, Don't Be Kryptonite (Pugh), 316–318

Black Girls as Leaders (Tucker, Williams and Keaton), 419–420

Black Girls Break Bread organization, 45

Black Girls Own their Futures! (Salaam), 453

Black Girls Say #MeToo (Ragland), 270–271

Black Girls Trapped in our Foster Care System (Stiller), 122–123

Black history, 295–296

Black humanity, 364

Black identities, 370

Black immigrant diversity, 215–216

Black Indigenous Person of Color (BIPOC), 125

Black Lives Matter, 2, 5, 41, 58, 222, 372, 380, 394

#BlackLivesMatter (#BLM), 376, 385–387, 391, 394, 465, 467

Black Muslim Girls, 381–383

Blackness, 2, 7–9, 29, 70, 94, 96, 103, 104, 157, 160, 166, 173, 177, 207, 239, 274, 276, 278, 286, 305, 306, 313, 320, 321, 328, 333, 335, 354, 363–365, 370, 375, 456

Black Panther, 425

Black Power movement, 207–208

Black skin, 70

Black Student, White Teacher (Sgwentu), 102–104

Black Super Girls, 42, 46

Black transwomen, 222

Black Woman's Reflections on the Road I Made While Walking, A: Remarks From My Retirement Ceremony (Mobley), 298–299

Black Woman Who Attended a Predominantly White School Returns to Teach Black Girls in Predominantly White Schools, A (Paige), 286–287

Blake, J. J., 76

Blay, Y., 409–411

Blindness. *See* Color-blindness

Bloodmother, 464

Bloom, S., 116

Bobo, K. A., 264

Bolden, T., 210–211

Bond, B., 305

Bond, B. (Ed.), 311

Bond, H. M., 292

Borris, C., 312

Bourdieu, P., 280

Bowden, S., 265–266

Boykin, A. W., 324

Boyz n the Hood, 397

Bracy P. B., 353

Brandon-Felder, T., 471–472

"Brilliance," 25–26

Brooks, W., 344

Brown, K. L., 200–201

Brown, P. L., 309

Brown, R. N., 407

Brownies' Book, The (Du Bois), 338

Brown v. Board of Education, 293

Bryant, K., 15, 17, 451

Buck, C., 238

Burke, T., 12, 14, 132, 265, 269, 406

Burroughs, M., 313

Butler, C. N., 119

Byers, G., 264

Cadet, D., 306–307

Cain, S., 85

Calig, L., 186–187

Cannie, R., 23, 24, 28, 29, 32, 303, 311

Cara, C., 39

Carr, K., 417–418

Carter, N. P., 325

Carter G. Woodson Center for Interracial Education, 292

Center on Poverty and Inequality, 109

Chapman, S., 218–220

Character, 121

Child-rearing approach, 138

A SAGE Publishing Company

CORWIN HAS ONE MISSION: to enhance education through intentional professional learning.

We build long-term relationships with our authors, educators, clients, and associations who partner with us to develop and continuously improve the best evidence-based practices that establish and support lifelong learning.